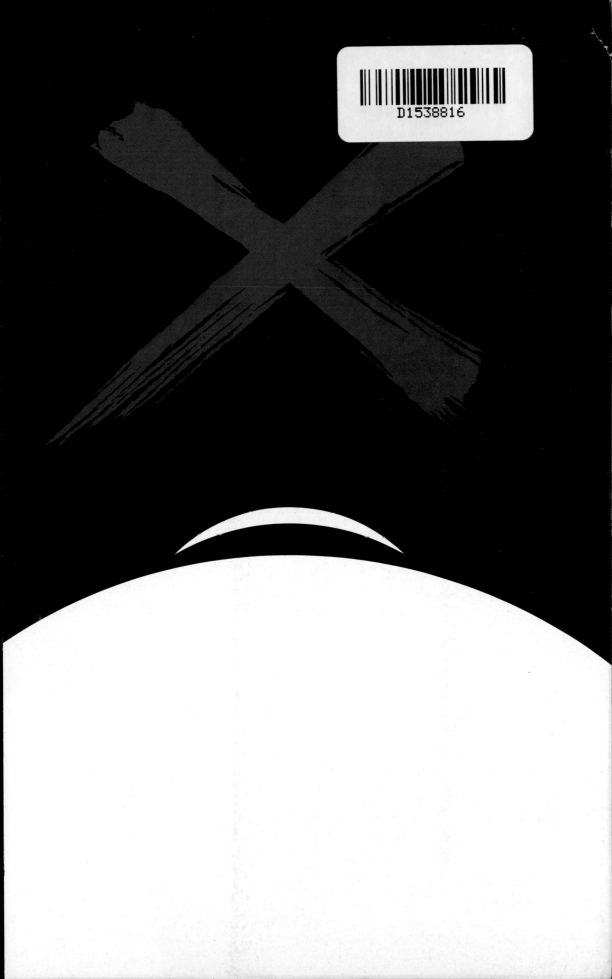

UNIVERSE X

Collecting Universe X issues 0, 1-7, Cap. 4 & Spidey

ALEX ROSS
COVER/CONCEPT/CHARACTER DESIGNS

JIM KRUEGER
STORY/SCRIPT

DOUG BRAITHWAITE WITH THOMAS YEATS,
JACKSON GUICE (LAYOUTS ON SPIDEY) AND BRENT ANDERSON
PENCILS

BILL REINHOLD WITH AL WILLIAMSON,
ROBIN RIGGS, GARRY LEACH, JOHN TOTLEBEN, RON RANDAL, JOHN ROMITA SR.,
AL MILGROM, JOHN STANISCI AND WILL BLYBERG
INKS

LAURA DEPUY WITH PETE PANTAZIS AND NICK BELL
COLORS

TODD KLEIN
LETTERS

MIKE MARTS
ORIGINAL SERIES EDITOR

JG & COMICRAFT'S ERIC ENG WONG
BOOK DESIGN

JOE QUESADA   DAN BUCKLEY
EDITOR IN CHIEF   PRESIDENT

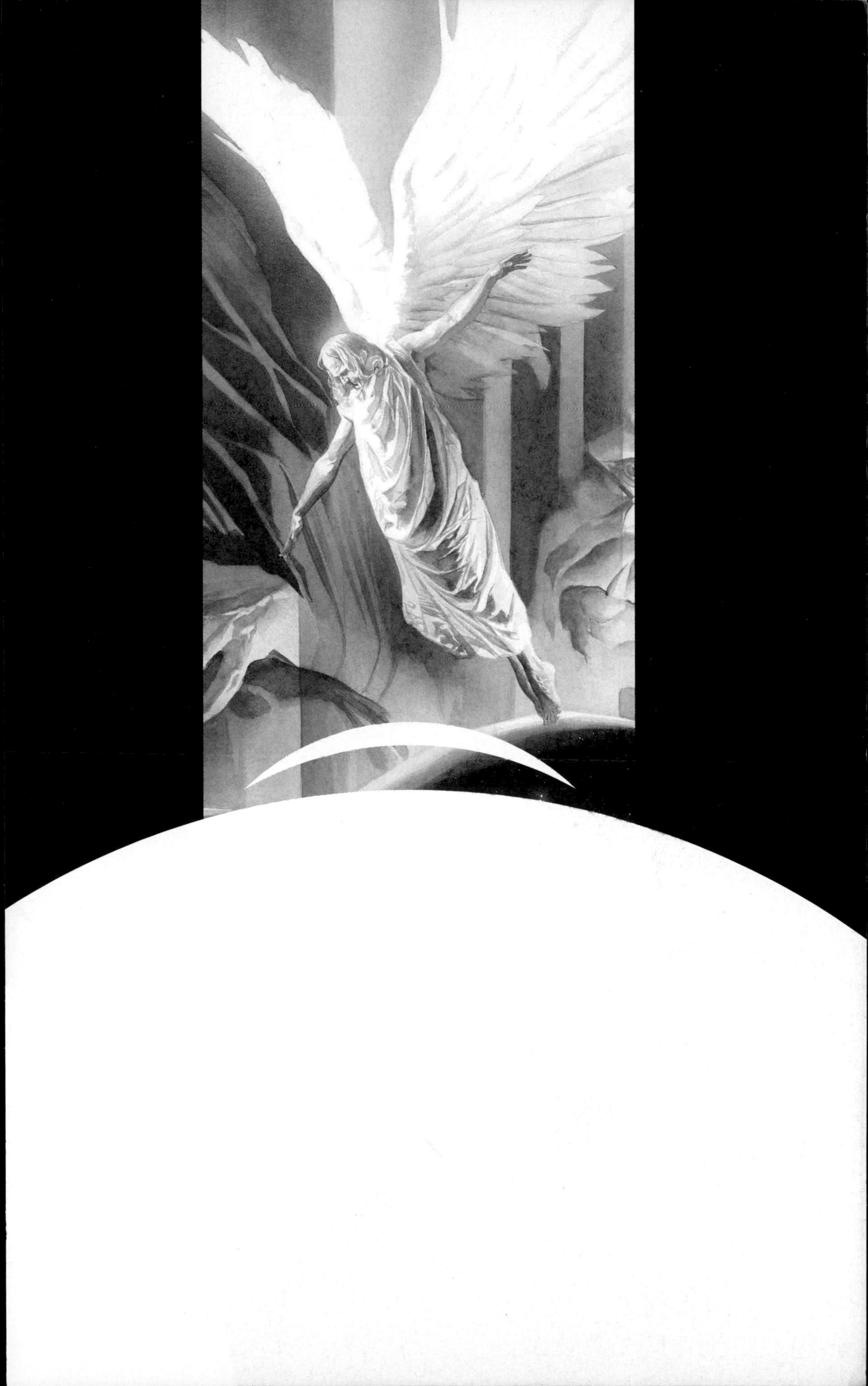

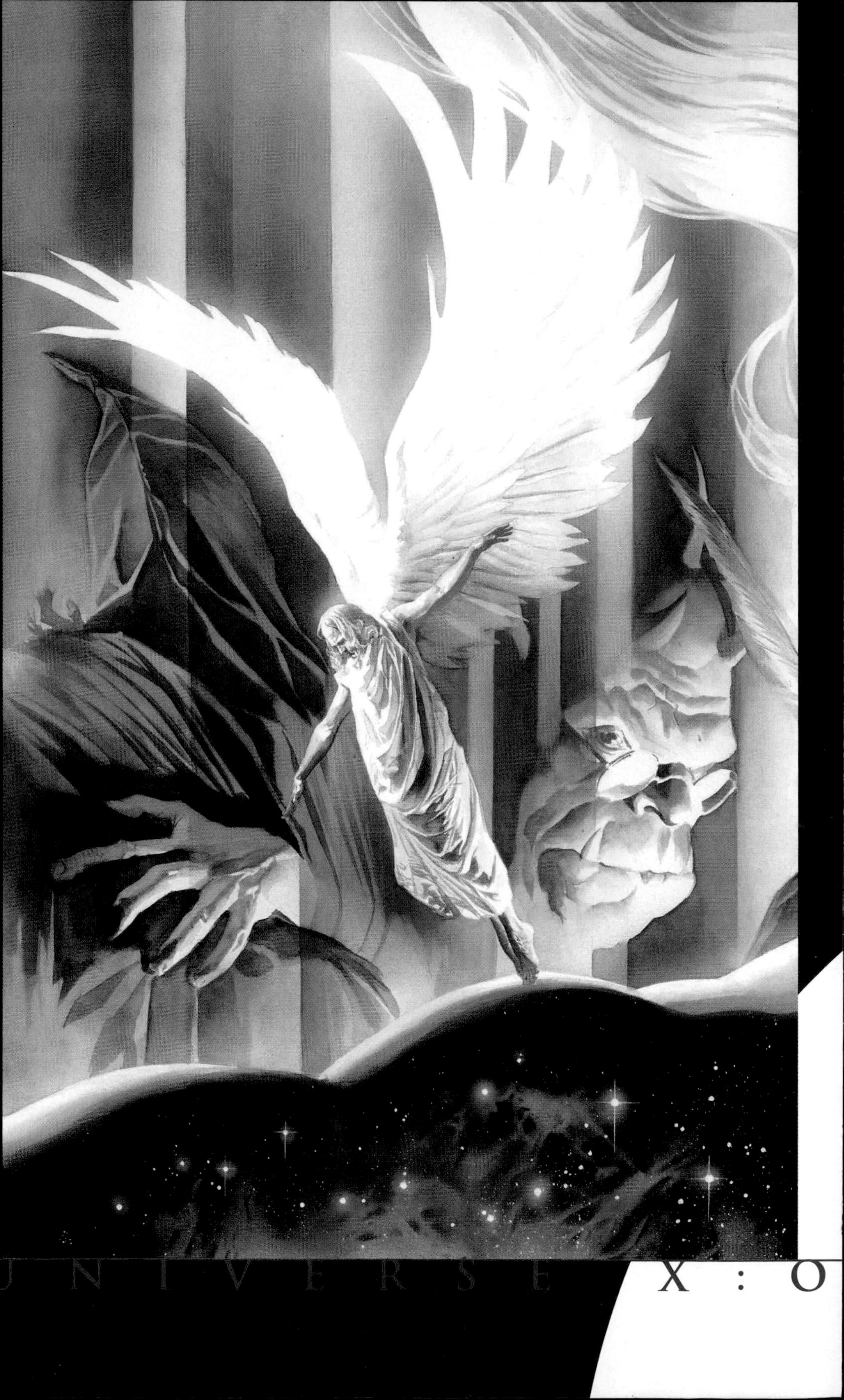
UNIVERSE X : O

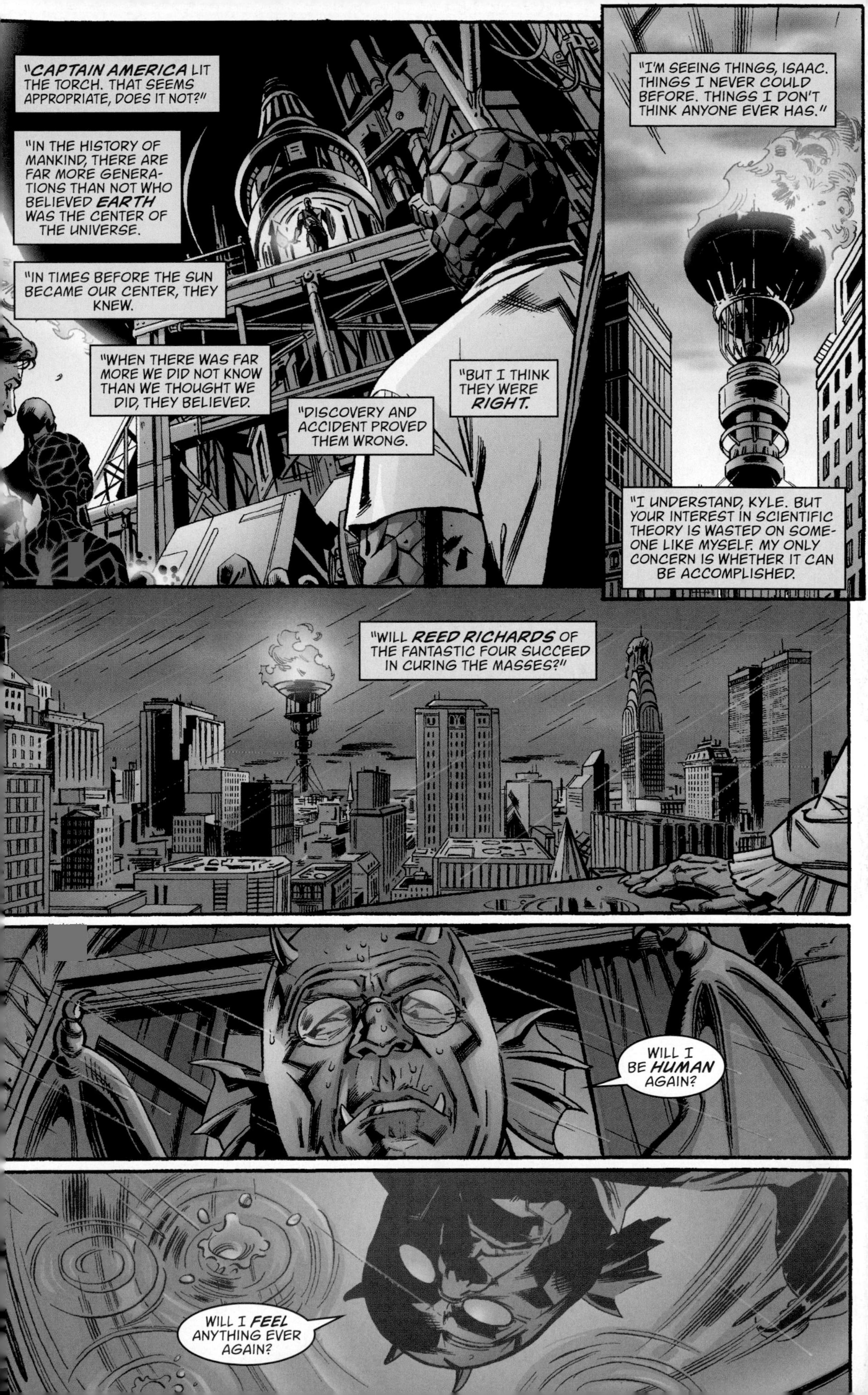
"CAPTAIN AMERICA LIT THE TORCH. THAT SEEMS APPROPRIATE, DOES IT NOT?"
"IN THE HISTORY OF MANKIND, THERE ARE FAR MORE GENERATIONS THAN NOT WHO BELIEVED EARTH WAS THE CENTER OF THE UNIVERSE.
"IN TIMES BEFORE THE SUN BECAME OUR CENTER, THEY KNEW.
"WHEN THERE WAS FAR MORE WE DID NOT KNOW THAN WE THOUGHT WE DID, THEY BELIEVED.
"DISCOVERY AND ACCIDENT PROVED THEM WRONG.
"BUT I THINK THEY WERE RIGHT.
"I'M SEEING THINGS, ISAAC. THINGS I NEVER COULD BEFORE. THINGS I DON'T THINK ANYONE EVER HAS."
"I UNDERSTAND, KYLE. BUT YOUR INTEREST IN SCIENTIFIC THEORY IS WASTED ON SOMEONE LIKE MYSELF. MY ONLY CONCERN IS WHETHER IT CAN BE ACCOMPLISHED.
"WILL REED RICHARDS OF THE FANTASTIC FOUR SUCCEED IN CURING THE MASSES?"
WILL I BE HUMAN AGAIN?
WILL I FEEL ANYTHING EVER AGAIN?

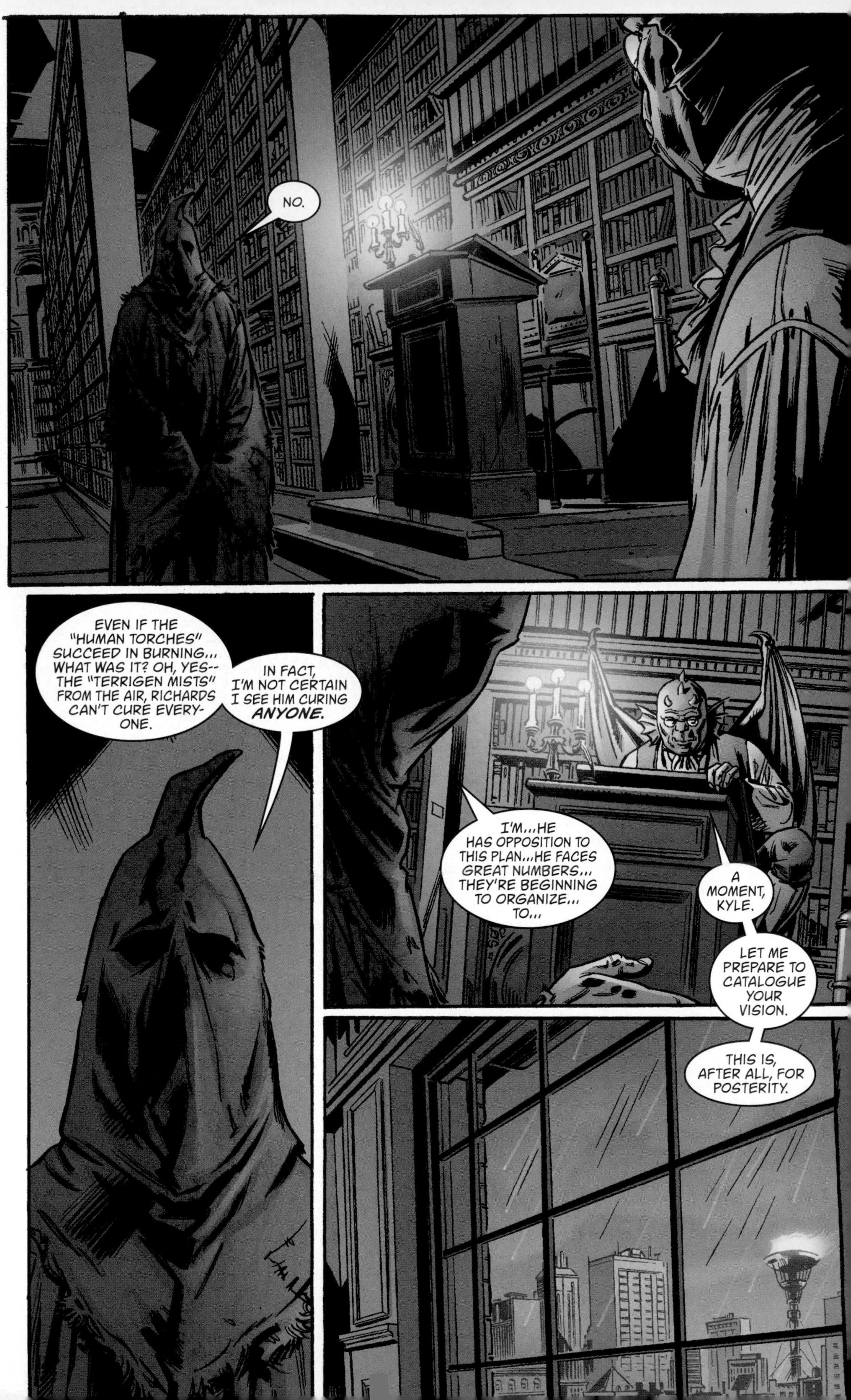
NO.
EVEN IF THE "HUMAN TORCHES" SUCCEED IN BURNING... WHAT WAS IT? OH, YES-- THE "TERRIGEN MISTS" FROM THE AIR, RICHARDS CAN'T CURE EVERY-ONE.
IN FACT, I'M NOT CERTAIN I SEE HIM CURING ***ANYONE.***
I'M...HE HAS OPPOSITION TO THIS PLAN...HE FACES GREAT NUMBERS... THEY'RE BEGINNING TO ORGANIZE... TO...
A MOMENT, KYLE.
LET ME PREPARE TO CATALOGUE YOUR VISION.
THIS IS, AFTER ALL, FOR POSTERITY.

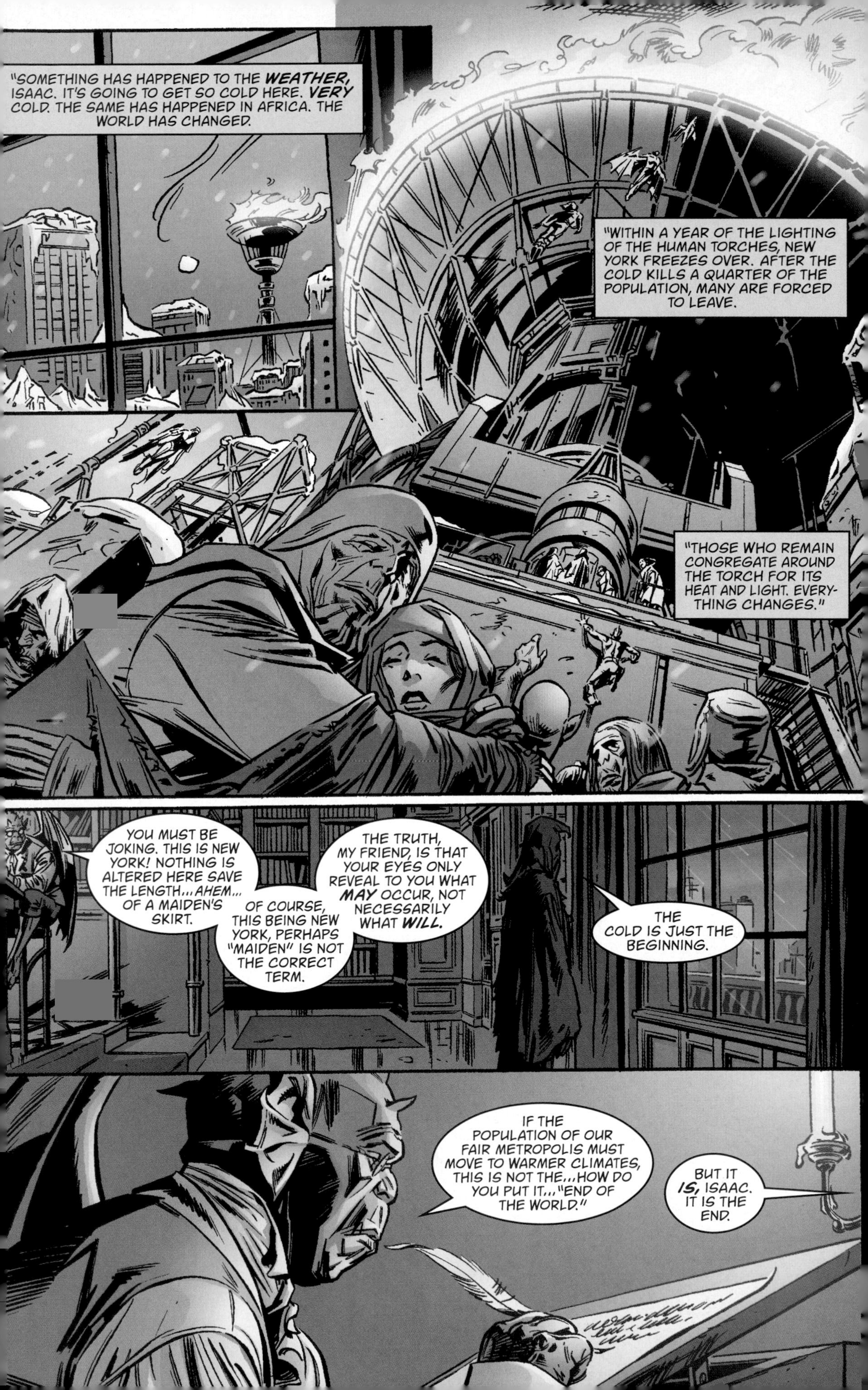
"SOMETHING HAS HAPPENED TO THE WEATHER, ISAAC. IT'S GOING TO GET SO COLD HERE. VERY COLD. THE SAME HAS HAPPENED IN AFRICA. THE WORLD HAS CHANGED.
"WITHIN A YEAR OF THE LIGHTING OF THE HUMAN TORCHES, NEW YORK FREEZES OVER. AFTER THE COLD KILLS A QUARTER OF THE POPULATION, MANY ARE FORCED TO LEAVE.
"THOSE WHO REMAIN CONGREGATE AROUND THE TORCH FOR ITS HEAT AND LIGHT. EVERYTHING CHANGES."
YOU MUST BE JOKING. THIS IS NEW YORK! NOTHING IS ALTERED HERE SAVE THE LENGTH... AHEM... OF A MAIDEN'S SKIRT.
OF COURSE, THIS BEING NEW YORK, PERHAPS "MAIDEN" IS NOT THE CORRECT TERM.
THE TRUTH, MY FRIEND, IS THAT YOUR EYES ONLY REVEAL TO YOU WHAT MAY OCCUR, NOT NECESSARILY WHAT WILL.
THE COLD IS JUST THE BEGINNING.
IF THE POPULATION OF OUR FAIR METROPOLIS MUST MOVE TO WARMER CLIMATES, THIS IS NOT THE... HOW DO YOU PUT IT... "END OF THE WORLD."
BUT IT IS, ISAAC. IT IS THE END.

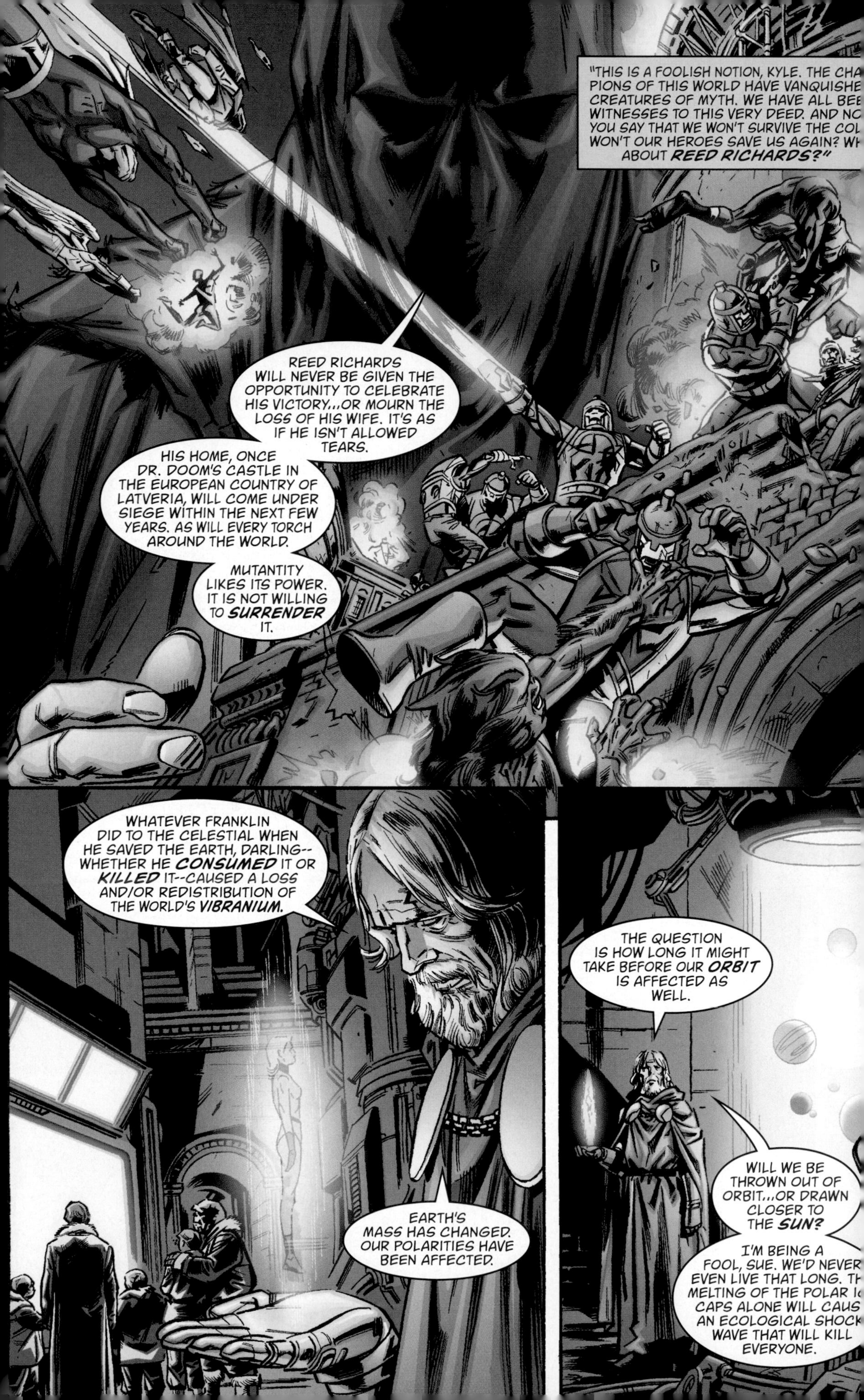
"THIS IS A FOOLISH NOTION, KYLE. THE CHA PIONS OF THIS WORLD HAVE VANQUISHE CREATURES OF MYTH. WE HAVE ALL BEE WITNESSES TO THIS VERY DEED. AND NO YOU SAY THAT WE WON'T SURVIVE THE COL WON'T OUR HEROES SAVE US AGAIN? WH ABOUT REED RICHARDS?"
REED RICHARDS WILL NEVER BE GIVEN THE OPPORTUNITY TO CELEBRATE HIS VICTORY...OR MOURN THE LOSS OF HIS WIFE. IT'S AS IF HE ISN'T ALLOWED TEARS.
HIS HOME, ONCE DR. DOOM'S CASTLE IN THE EUROPEAN COUNTRY OF LATVERIA, WILL COME UNDER SIEGE WITHIN THE NEXT FEW YEARS. AS WILL EVERY TORCH AROUND THE WORLD.
MUTANTITY LIKES ITS POWER. IT IS NOT WILLING TO SURRENDER IT.
WHATEVER FRANKLIN DID TO THE CELESTIAL WHEN HE SAVED THE EARTH, DARLING-- WHETHER HE CONSUMED IT OR KILLED IT--CAUSED A LOSS AND/OR REDISTRIBUTION OF THE WORLD'S VIBRANIUM.
EARTH'S MASS HAS CHANGED. OUR POLARITIES HAVE BEEN AFFECTED.
THE QUESTION IS HOW LONG IT MIGHT TAKE BEFORE OUR ORBIT IS AFFECTED AS WELL.
WILL WE BE THROWN OUT OF ORBIT...OR DRAWN CLOSER TO THE SUN?
I'M BEING A FOOL, SUE. WE'D NEVER EVEN LIVE THAT LONG. TH MELTING OF THE POLAR I CAPS ALONE WILL CAUS AN ECOLOGICAL SHOCK WAVE THAT WILL KILL EVERYONE.

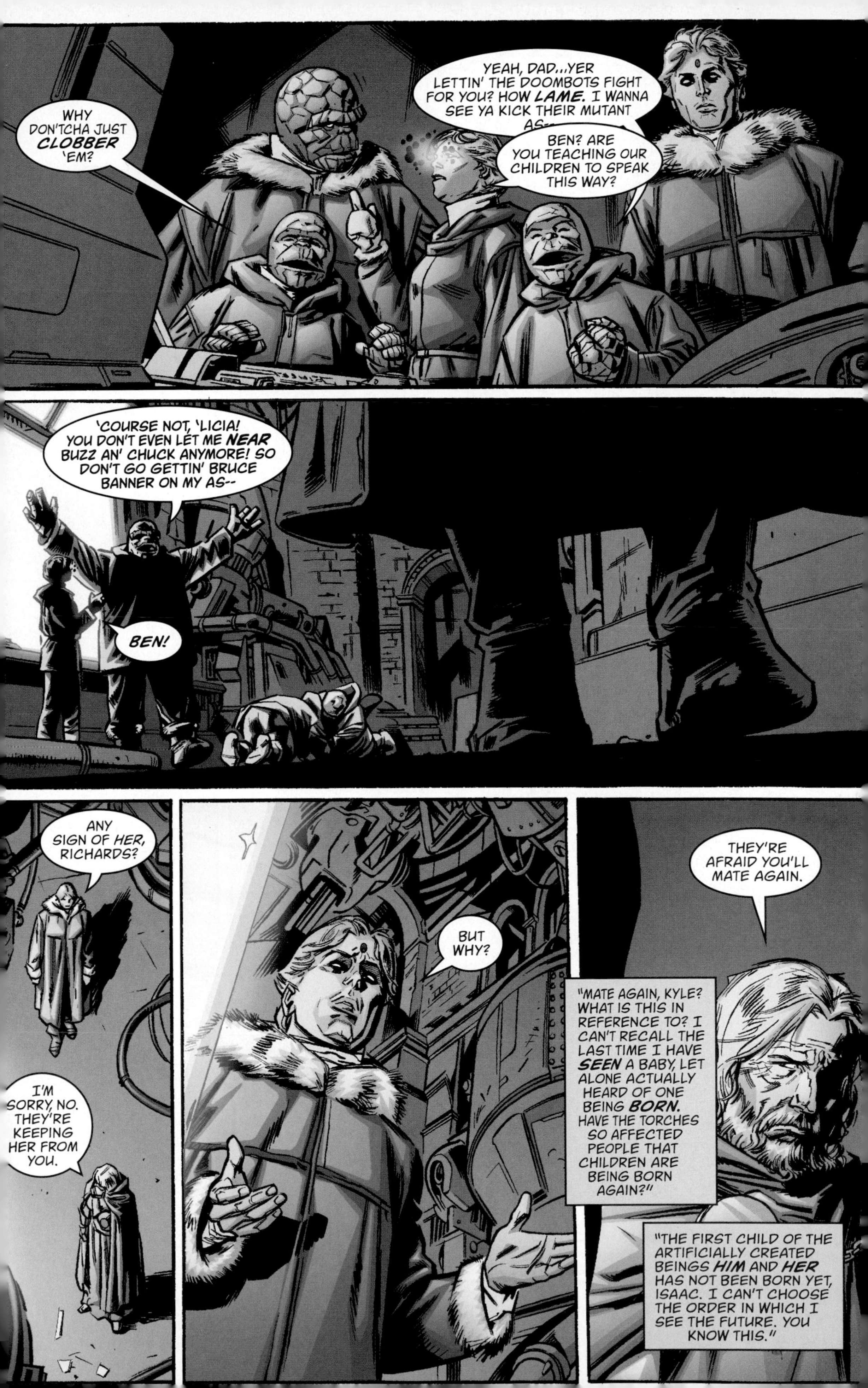
WHY DON'TCHA JUST CLOBBER 'EM?
YEAH, DAD...YER LETTIN' THE DOOMBOTS FIGHT FOR YOU? HOW LAME. I WANNA SEE YA KICK THEIR MUTANT AS--
BEN? ARE YOU TEACHING OUR CHILDREN TO SPEAK THIS WAY?
'COURSE NOT, 'LICIA! YOU DON'T EVEN LET ME NEAR BUZZ AN' CHUCK ANYMORE! SO DON'T GO GETTIN' BRUCE BANNER ON MY AS--
BEN!
ANY SIGN OF HER, RICHARDS?
I'M SORRY, NO. THEY'RE KEEPING HER FROM YOU.
BUT WHY?
THEY'RE AFRAID YOU'LL MATE AGAIN.
"MATE AGAIN, KYLE? WHAT IS THIS IN REFERENCE TO? I CAN'T RECALL THE LAST TIME I HAVE SEEN A BABY, LET ALONE ACTUALLY HEARD OF ONE BEING BORN. HAVE THE TORCHES SO AFFECTED PEOPLE THAT CHILDREN ARE BEING BORN AGAIN?"
"THE FIRST CHILD OF THE ARTIFICIALLY CREATED BEINGS HIM AND HER HAS NOT BEEN BORN YET, ISAAC. I CAN'T CHOOSE THE ORDER IN WHICH I SEE THE FUTURE. YOU KNOW THIS."

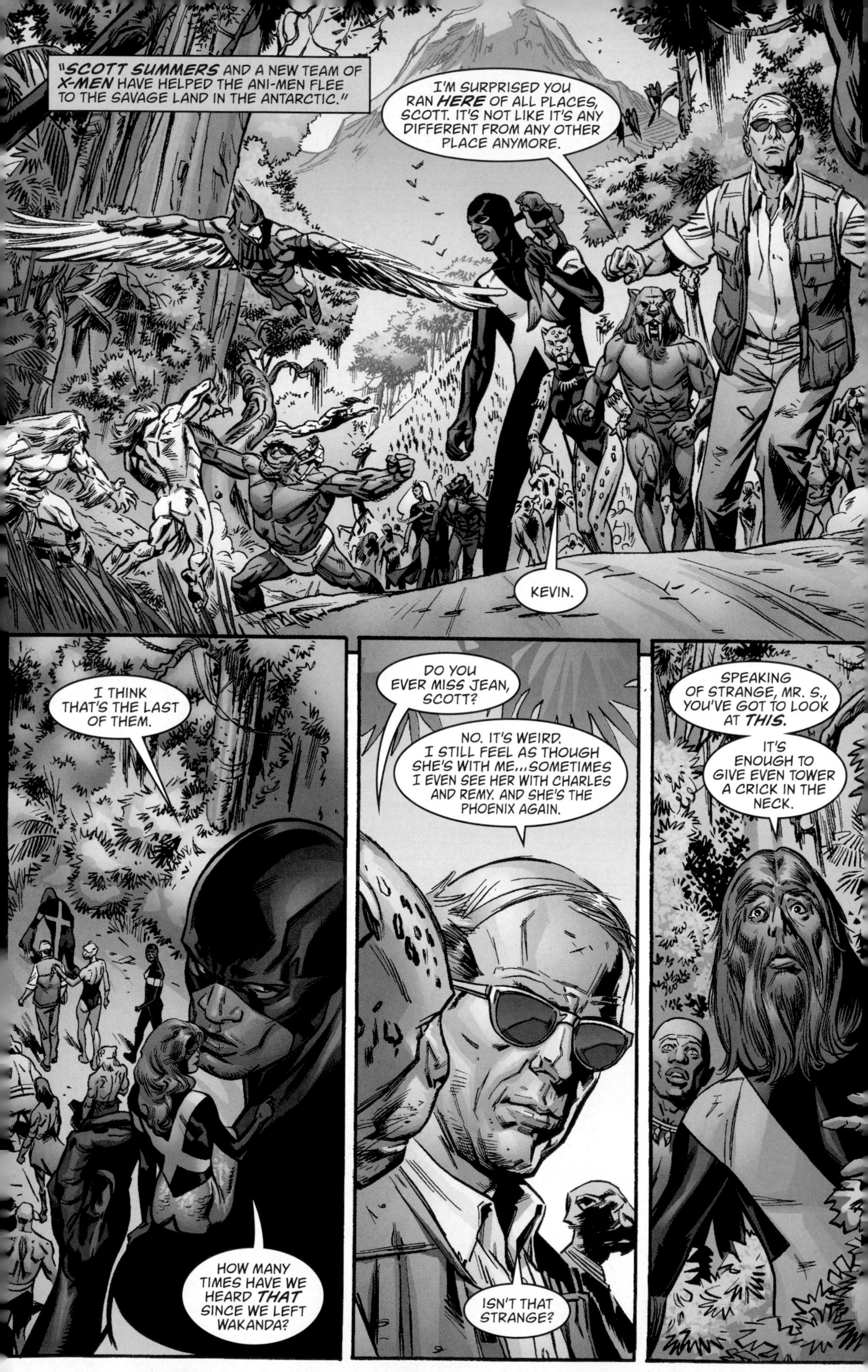
"SCOTT SUMMERS AND A NEW TEAM OF X-MEN HAVE HELPED THE ANI-MEN FLEE TO THE SAVAGE LAND IN THE ANTARCTIC."
I'M SURPRISED YOU RAN HERE OF ALL PLACES, SCOTT. IT'S NOT LIKE IT'S ANY DIFFERENT FROM ANY OTHER PLACE ANYMORE.
KEVIN.
I THINK THAT'S THE LAST OF THEM.
HOW MANY TIMES HAVE WE HEARD THAT SINCE WE LEFT WAKANDA?
DO YOU EVER MISS JEAN, SCOTT?
NO. IT'S WEIRD. I STILL FEEL AS THOUGH SHE'S WITH ME...SOMETIMES I EVEN SEE HER WITH CHARLES AND REMY. AND SHE'S THE PHOENIX AGAIN.
ISN'T THAT STRANGE?
SPEAKING OF STRANGE, MR. S., YOU'VE GOT TO LOOK AT THIS.
IT'S ENOUGH TO GIVE EVEN TOWER A CRICK IN THE NECK.

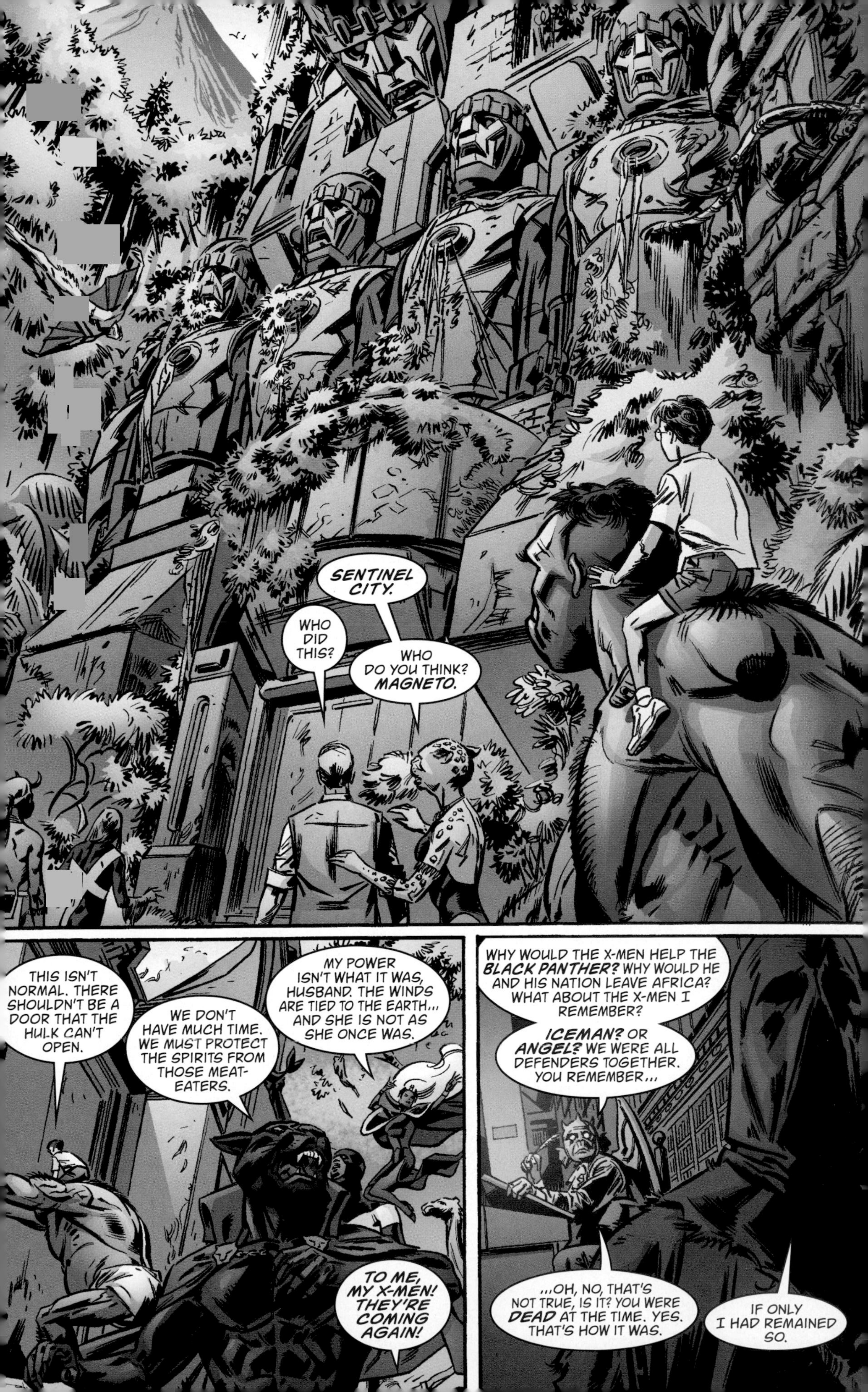
SENTINEL CITY.
WHO DID THIS?
WHO DO YOU THINK? MAGNETO.
THIS ISN'T NORMAL. THERE SHOULDN'T BE A DOOR THAT THE HULK CAN'T OPEN.
WE DON'T HAVE MUCH TIME. WE MUST PROTECT THE SPIRITS FROM THOSE MEAT-EATERS.
MY POWER ISN'T WHAT IT WAS, HUSBAND. THE WINDS ARE TIED TO THE EARTH... AND SHE IS NOT AS SHE ONCE WAS.
TO ME, MY X-MEN! THEY'RE COMING AGAIN!
WHY WOULD THE X-MEN HELP THE BLACK PANTHER? WHY WOULD HE AND HIS NATION LEAVE AFRICA? WHAT ABOUT THE X-MEN I REMEMBER?
ICEMAN? OR ANGEL? WE WERE ALL DEFENDERS TOGETHER. YOU REMEMBER...
...OH, NO, THAT'S NOT TRUE, IS IT? YOU WERE DEAD AT THE TIME. YES. THAT'S HOW IT WAS.
IF ONLY I HAD REMAINED SO.

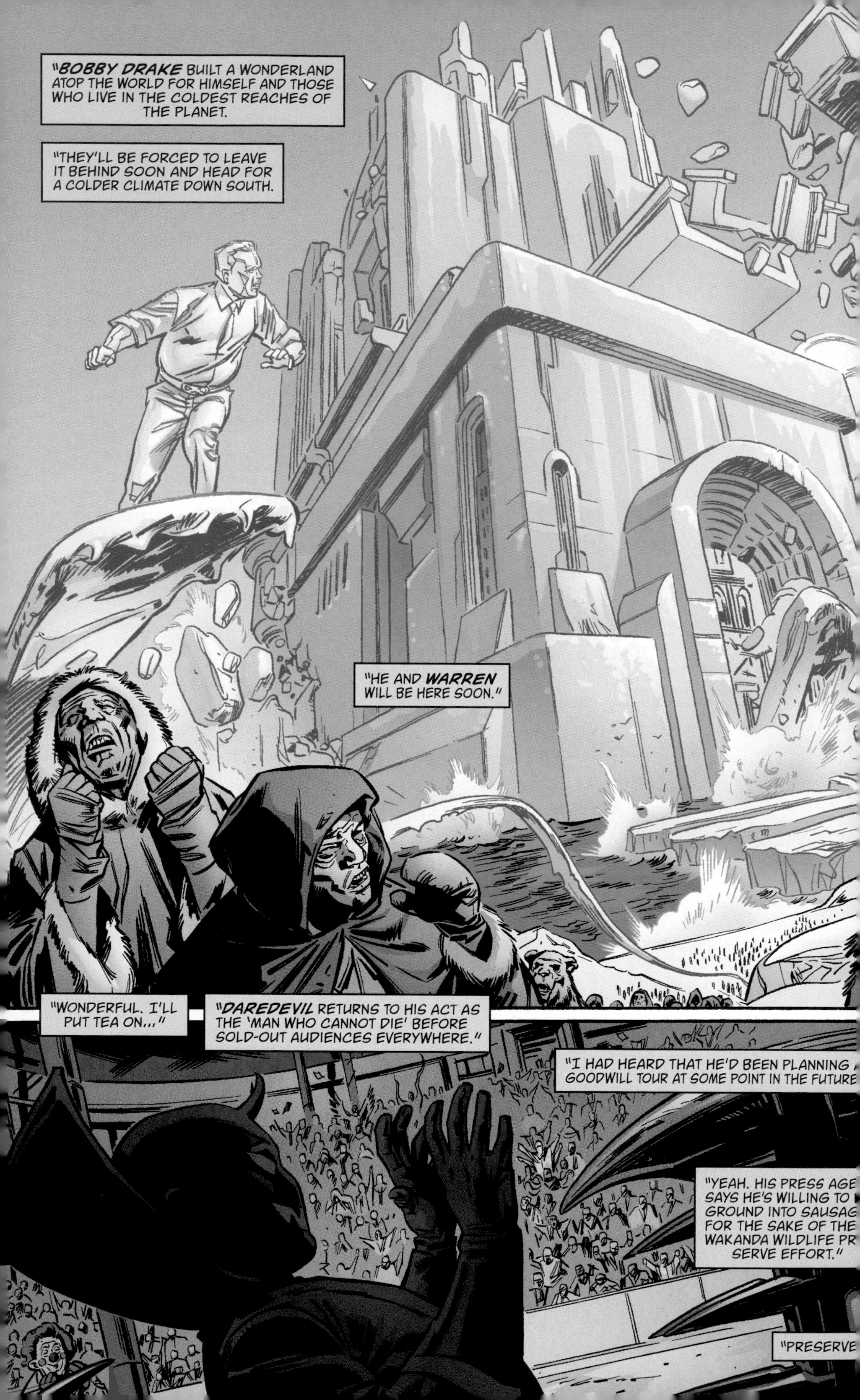
"BOBBY DRAKE BUILT A WONDERLAND ATOP THE WORLD FOR HIMSELF AND THOSE WHO LIVE IN THE COLDEST REACHES OF THE PLANET.
"THEY'LL BE FORCED TO LEAVE IT BEHIND SOON AND HEAD FOR A COLDER CLIMATE DOWN SOUTH.
"HE AND WARREN WILL BE HERE SOON."
"WONDERFUL. I'LL PUT TEA ON..."
"DAREDEVIL RETURNS TO HIS ACT AS THE 'MAN WHO CANNOT DIE' BEFORE SOLD-OUT AUDIENCES EVERYWHERE."
"I HAD HEARD THAT HE'D BEEN PLANNING GOODWILL TOUR AT SOME POINT IN THE FUTURE
"YEAH. HIS PRESS AGE SAYS HE'S WILLING TO GROUND INTO SAUSAG FOR THE SAKE OF THE WAKANDA WILDLIFE PR SERVE EFFORT."
"PRESERVE

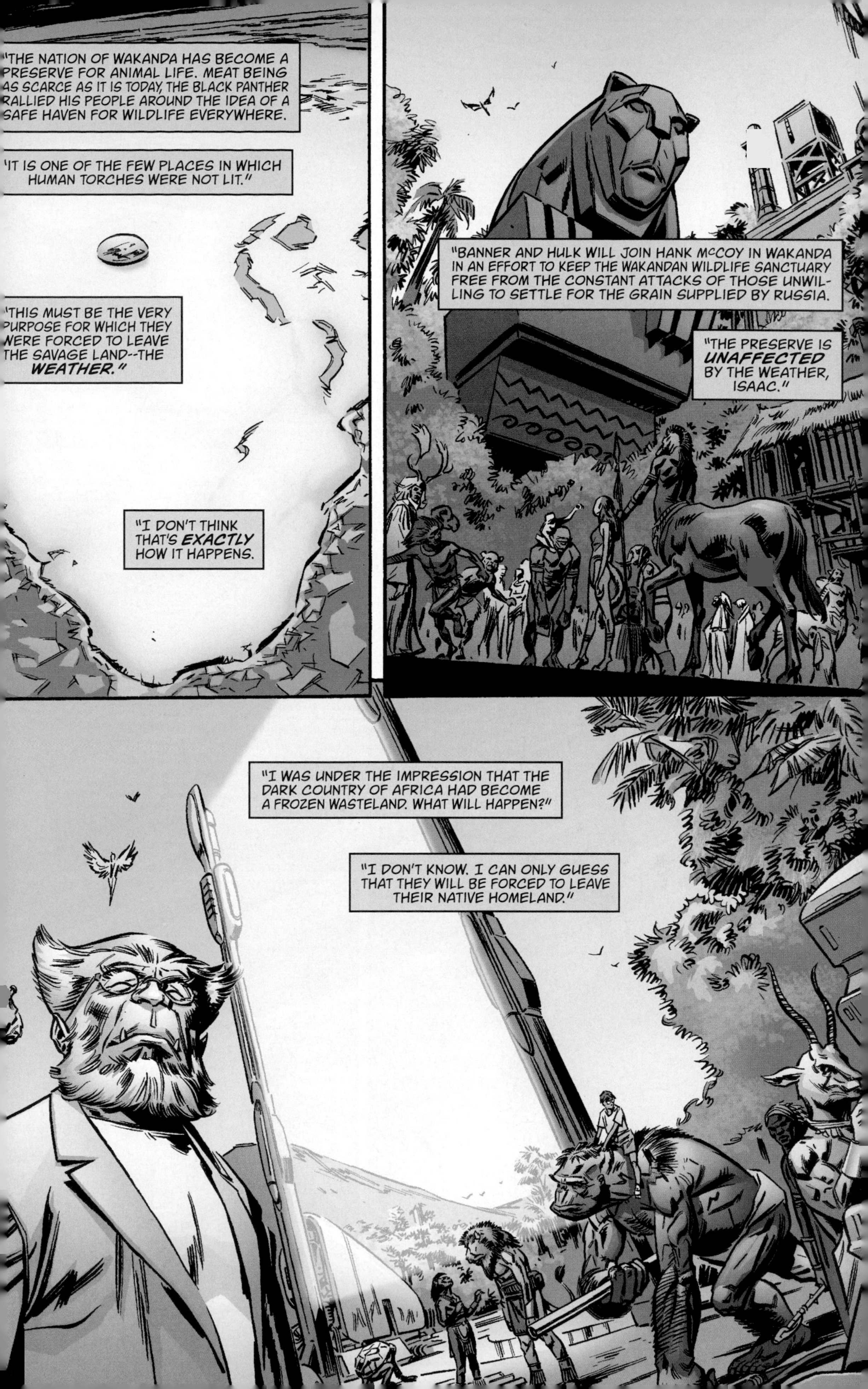
"THE NATION OF WAKANDA HAS BECOME A PRESERVE FOR ANIMAL LIFE. MEAT BEING AS SCARCE AS IT IS TODAY, THE BLACK PANTHER RALLIED HIS PEOPLE AROUND THE IDEA OF A SAFE HAVEN FOR WILDLIFE EVERYWHERE.
"IT IS ONE OF THE FEW PLACES IN WHICH HUMAN TORCHES WERE NOT LIT."
"THIS MUST BE THE VERY PURPOSE FOR WHICH THEY WERE FORCED TO LEAVE THE SAVAGE LAND--THE *WEATHER.*"
"I DON'T THINK THAT'S *EXACTLY* HOW IT HAPPENS.
"BANNER AND HULK WILL JOIN HANK McCOY IN WAKANDA IN AN EFFORT TO KEEP THE WAKANDAN WILDLIFE SANCTUARY FREE FROM THE CONSTANT ATTACKS OF THOSE UNWILLING TO SETTLE FOR THE GRAIN SUPPLIED BY RUSSIA.
"THE PRESERVE IS *UNAFFECTED* BY THE WEATHER, ISAAC."
"I WAS UNDER THE IMPRESSION THAT THE DARK COUNTRY OF AFRICA HAD BECOME A FROZEN WASTELAND. WHAT WILL HAPPEN?"
"I DON'T KNOW. I CAN ONLY GUESS THAT THEY WILL BE FORCED TO LEAVE THEIR NATIVE HOMELAND."

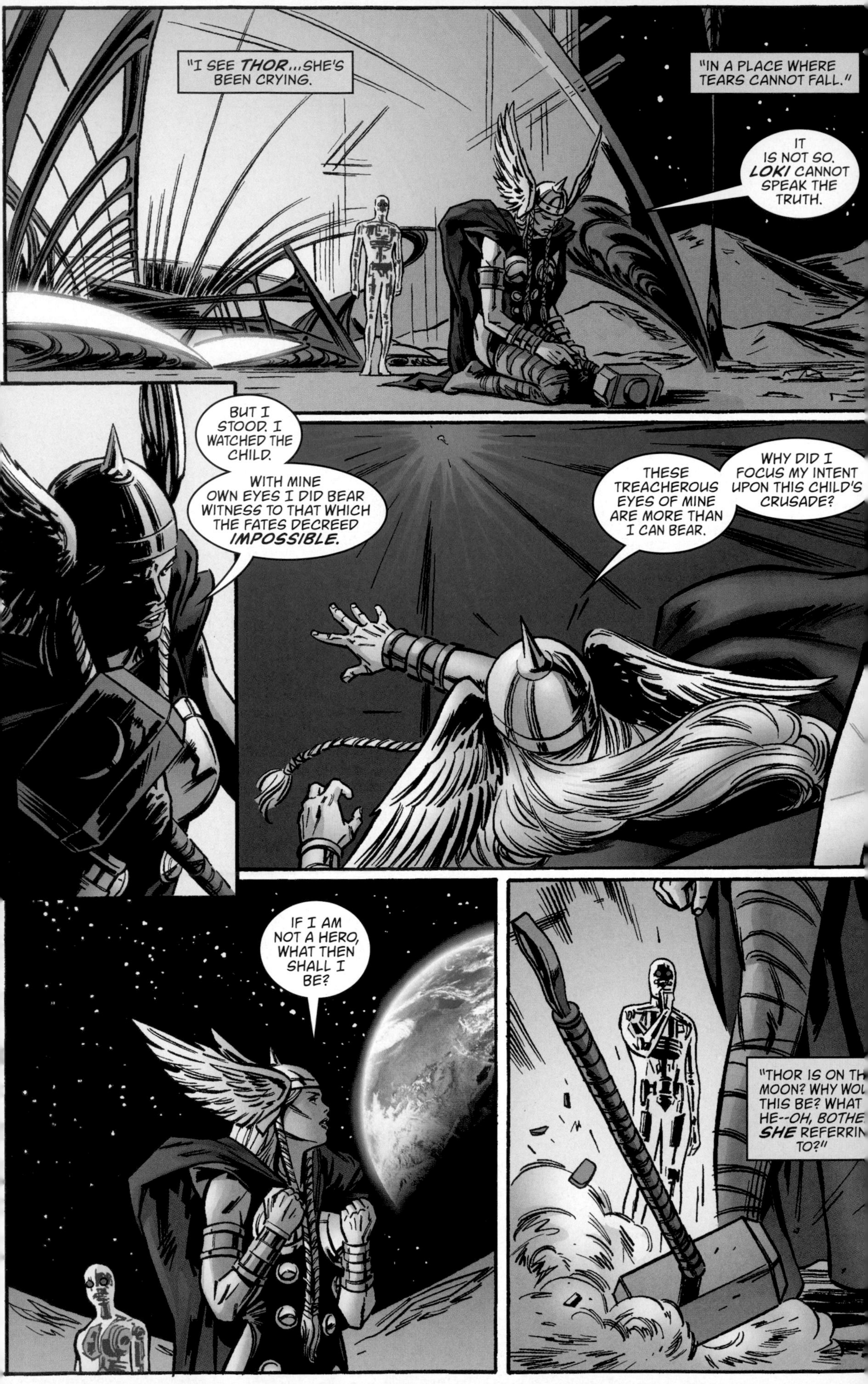
"I SEE THOR...SHE'S BEEN CRYING.
"IN A PLACE WHERE TEARS CANNOT FALL."
IT IS NOT SO. LOKI CANNOT SPEAK THE TRUTH.
BUT I STOOD. I WATCHED THE CHILD.
WITH MINE OWN EYES I DID BEAR WITNESS TO THAT WHICH THE FATES DECREED IMPOSSIBLE.
THESE TREACHEROUS EYES OF MINE ARE MORE THAN I CAN BEAR.
WHY DID I FOCUS MY INTENT UPON THIS CHILD'S CRUSADE?
IF I AM NOT A HERO, WHAT THEN SHALL I BE?
"THOR IS ON TH MOON? WHY WOU THIS BE? WHAT HE--OH, BOTHE SHE REFERRIN TO?"

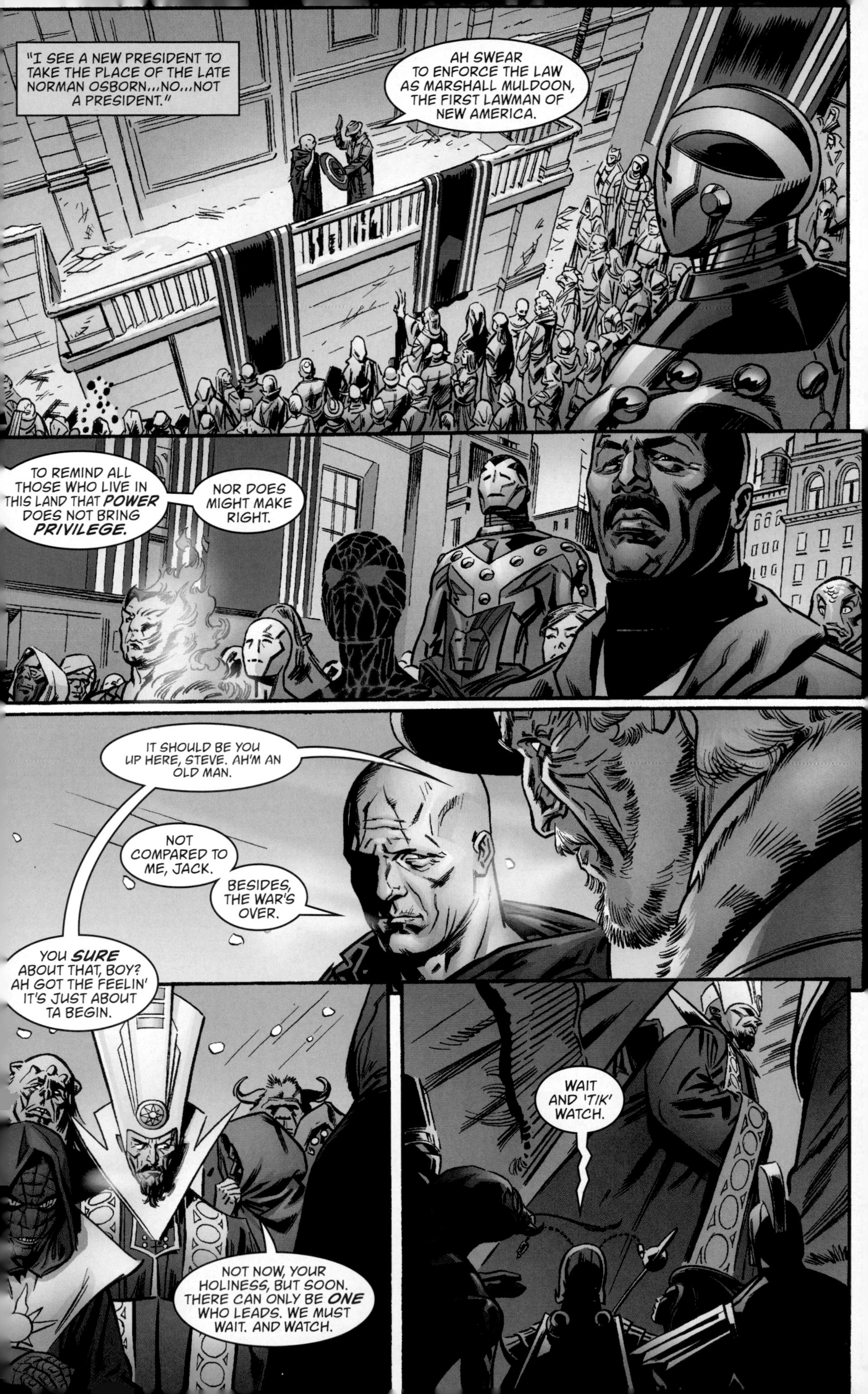
"I SEE A NEW PRESIDENT TO TAKE THE PLACE OF THE LATE NORMAN OSBORN...NO...NOT A PRESIDENT."
AH SWEAR TO ENFORCE THE LAW AS MARSHALL MULDOON, THE FIRST LAWMAN OF NEW AMERICA.
TO REMIND ALL THOSE WHO LIVE IN THIS LAND THAT POWER DOES NOT BRING PRIVILEGE.
NOR DOES MIGHT MAKE RIGHT.
IT SHOULD BE YOU UP HERE, STEVE. AH'M AN OLD MAN.
NOT COMPARED TO ME, JACK.
BESIDES, THE WAR'S OVER.
YOU SURE ABOUT THAT, BOY? AH GOT THE FEELIN' IT'S JUST ABOUT TA BEGIN.
NOT NOW, YOUR HOLINESS, BUT SOON. THERE CAN ONLY BE ONE WHO LEADS. WE MUST WAIT. AND WATCH.
WAIT AND 'TIK' WATCH.

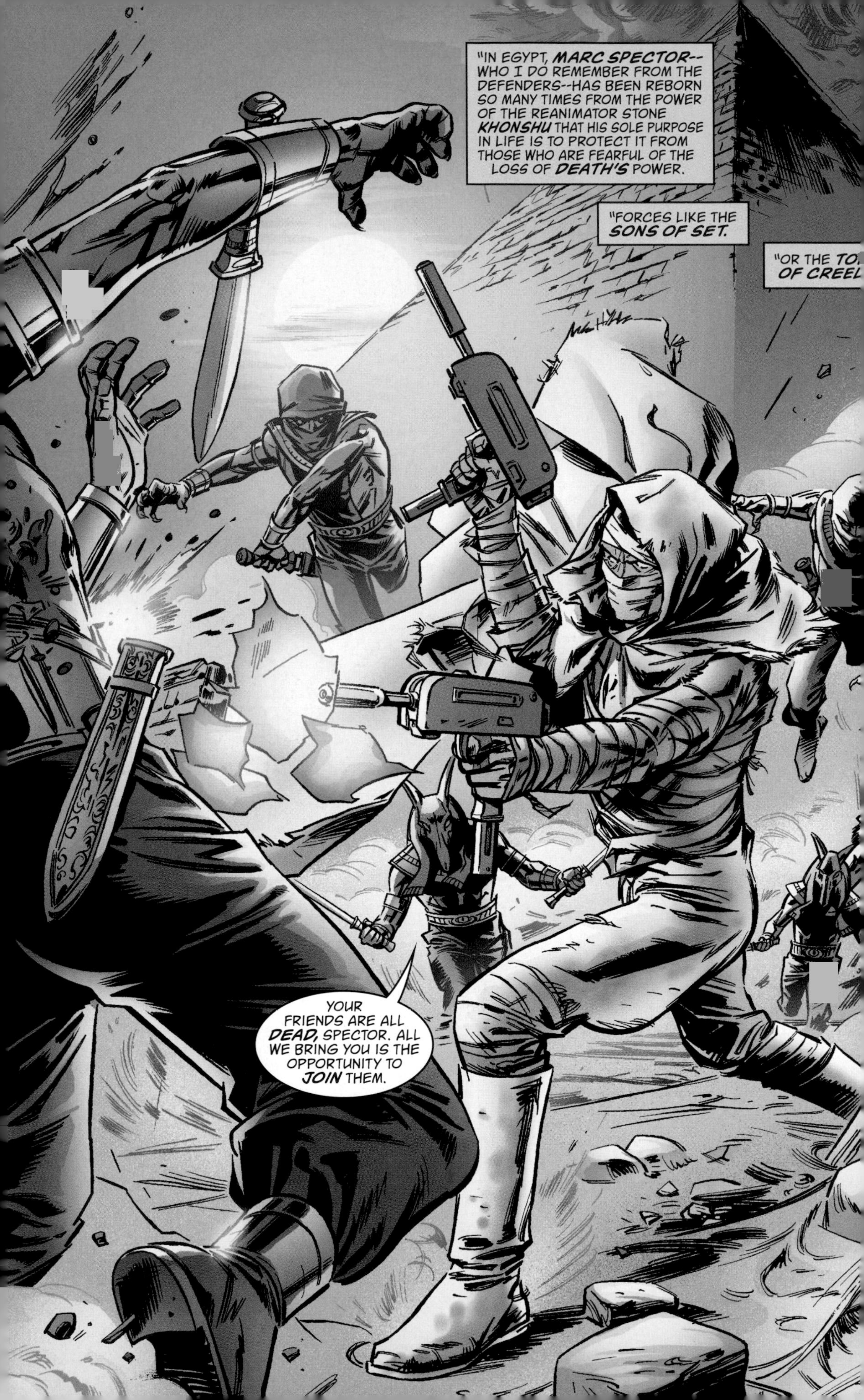
"IN EGYPT, MARC SPECTOR--WHO I DO REMEMBER FROM THE DEFENDERS--HAS BEEN REBORN SO MANY TIMES FROM THE POWER OF THE REANIMATOR STONE KHONSHU THAT HIS SOLE PURPOSE IN LIFE IS TO PROTECT IT FROM THOSE WHO ARE FEARFUL OF THE LOSS OF DEATH'S POWER.
"FORCES LIKE THE SONS OF SET.
"OR THE TO
OF CREEL
YOUR FRIENDS ARE ALL DEAD, SPECTOR. ALL WE BRING YOU IS THE OPPORTUNITY TO JOIN THEM.

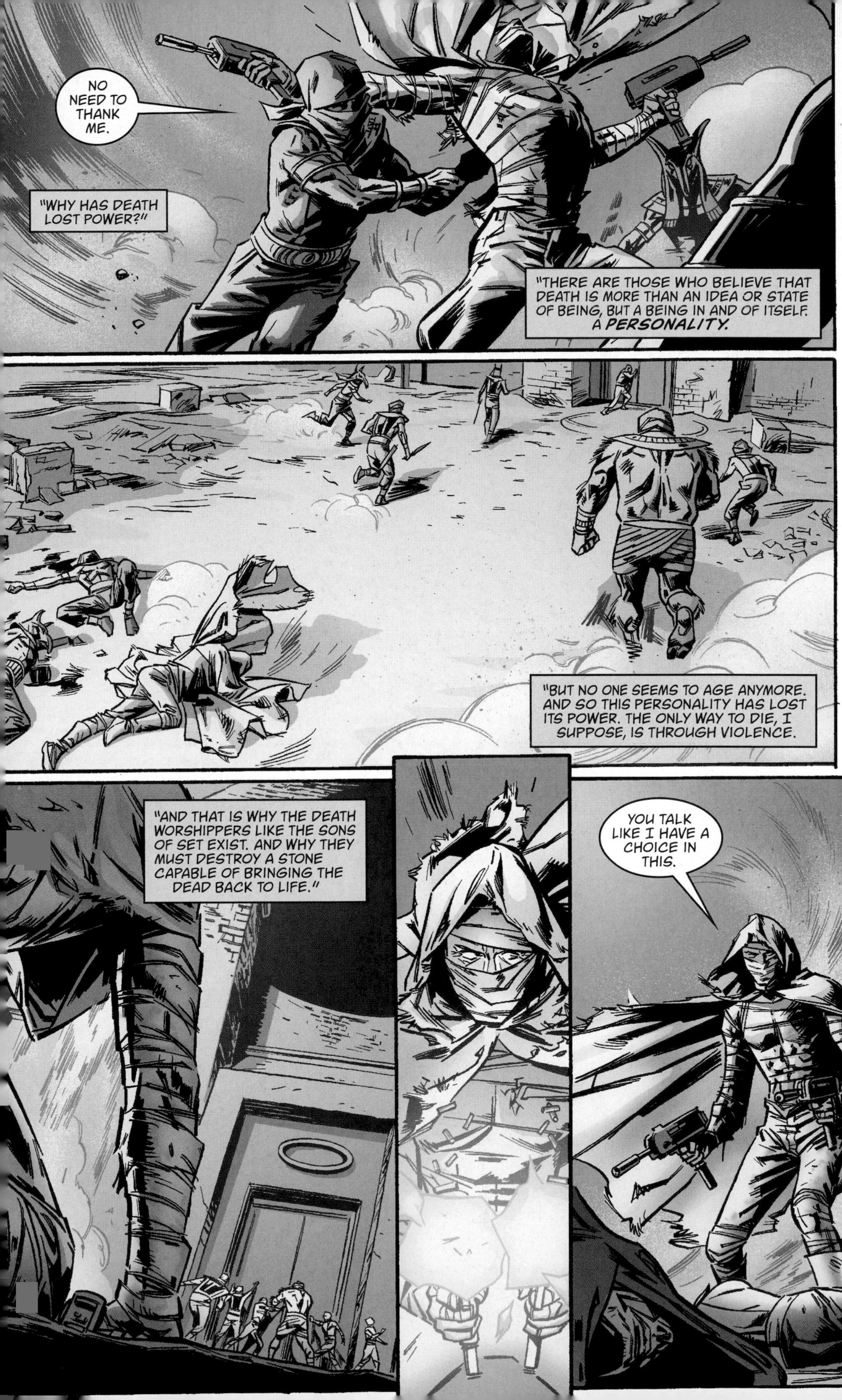
NO NEED TO THANK ME.
"WHY HAS DEATH LOST POWER?"
"THERE ARE THOSE WHO BELIEVE THAT DEATH IS MORE THAN AN IDEA OR STATE OF BEING, BUT A BEING IN AND OF ITSELF. A PERSONALITY.
"BUT NO ONE SEEMS TO AGE ANYMORE. AND SO THIS PERSONALITY HAS LOST ITS POWER. THE ONLY WAY TO DIE, I SUPPOSE, IS THROUGH VIOLENCE.
"AND THAT IS WHY THE DEATH WORSHIPPERS LIKE THE SONS OF SET EXIST. AND WHY THEY MUST DESTROY A STONE CAPABLE OF BRINGING THE DEAD BACK TO LIFE."
YOU TALK LIKE I HAVE A CHOICE IN THIS.

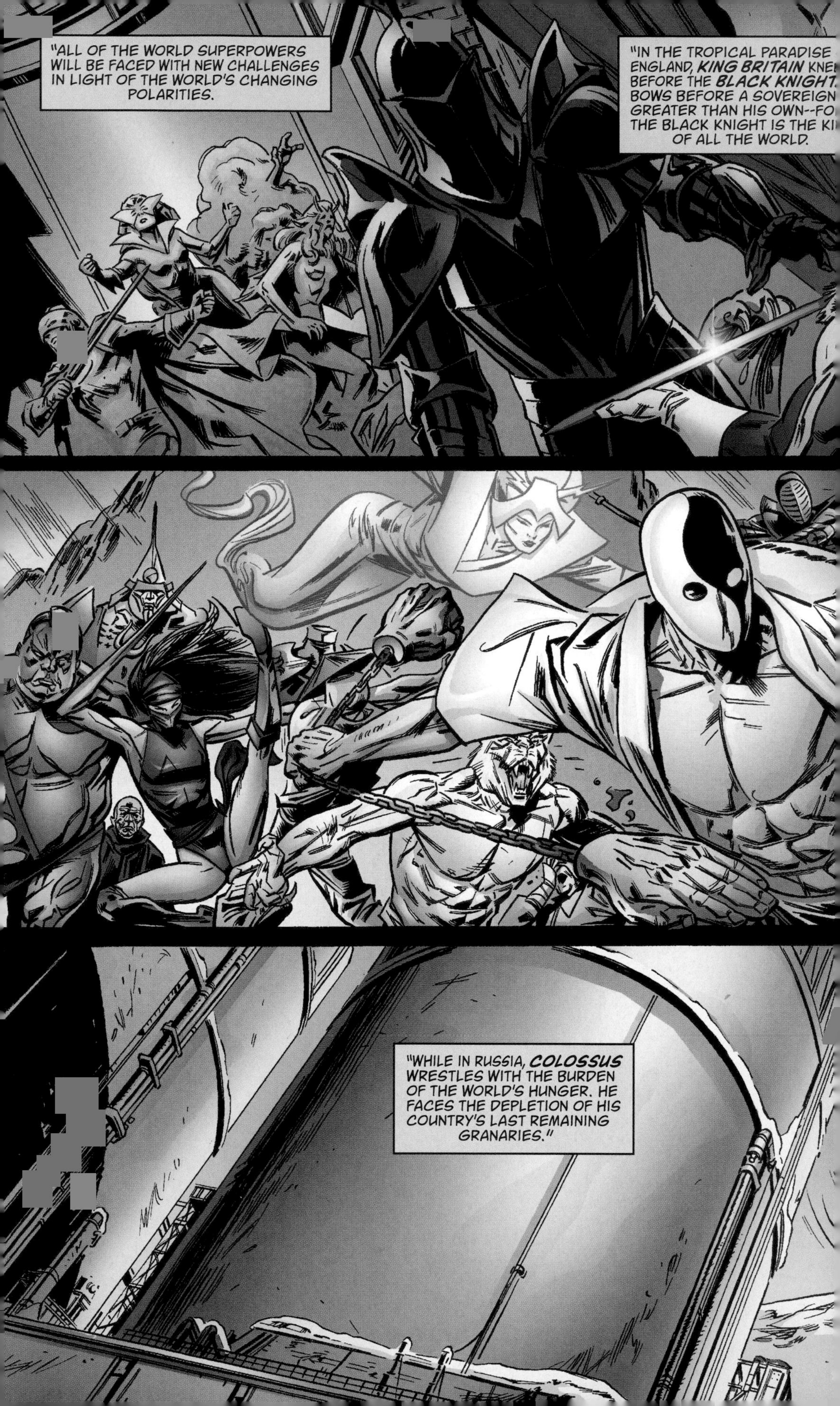
"ALL OF THE WORLD SUPERPOWERS WILL BE FACED WITH NEW CHALLENGES IN LIGHT OF THE WORLD'S CHANGING POLARITIES.
"IN THE TROPICAL PARADISE ENGLAND, KING BRITAIN KNE BEFORE THE BLACK KNIGHT. BOWS BEFORE A SOVEREIGN GREATER THAN HIS OWN--FO THE BLACK KNIGHT IS THE KI OF ALL THE WORLD.
"WHILE IN RUSSIA, COLOSSUS WRESTLES WITH THE BURDEN OF THE WORLD'S HUNGER. HE FACES THE DEPLETION OF HIS COUNTRY'S LAST REMAINING GRANARIES."

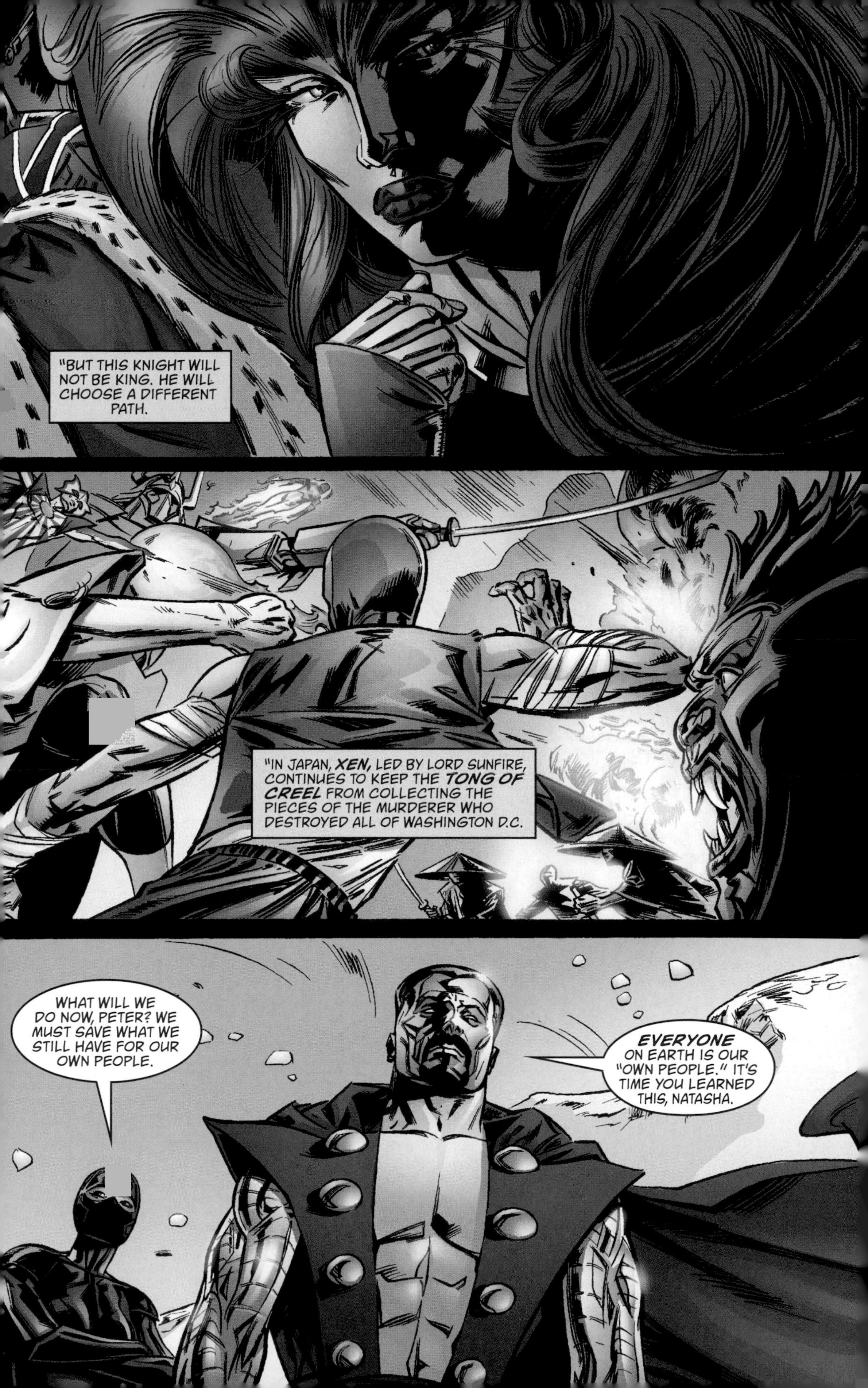
"BUT THIS KNIGHT WILL NOT BE KING. HE WILL CHOOSE A DIFFERENT PATH.
"IN JAPAN, XEN, LED BY LORD SUNFIRE, CONTINUES TO KEEP THE TONG OF CREEL FROM COLLECTING THE PIECES OF THE MURDERER WHO DESTROYED ALL OF WASHINGTON D.C.
WHAT WILL WE DO NOW, PETER? WE MUST SAVE WHAT WE STILL HAVE FOR OUR OWN PEOPLE.
EVERYONE ON EARTH IS OUR "OWN PEOPLE." IT'S TIME YOU LEARNED THIS, NATASHA.

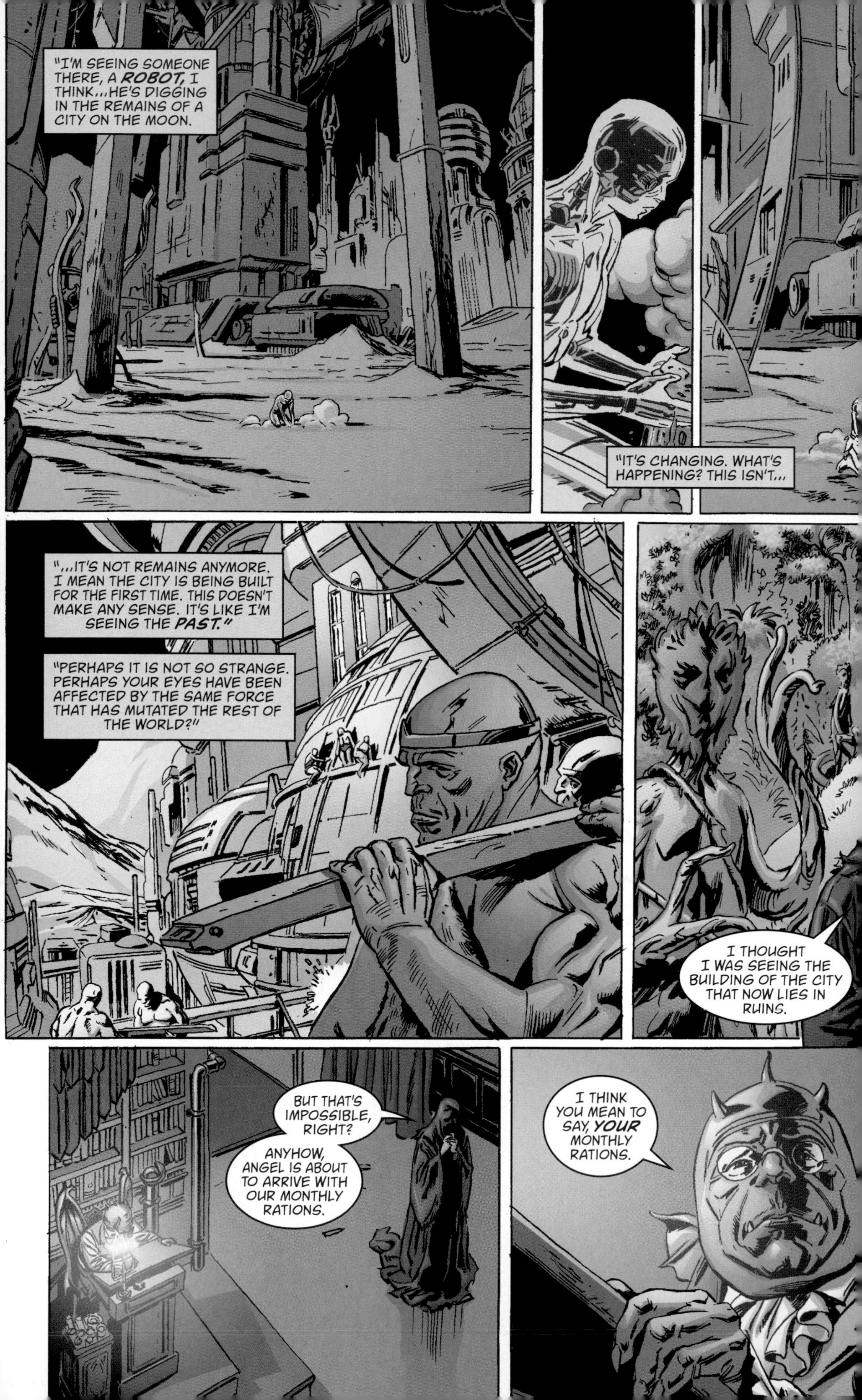
"I'M SEEING SOMEONE THERE, A ROBOT, I THINK...HE'S DIGGING IN THE REMAINS OF A CITY ON THE MOON.
"IT'S CHANGING. WHAT'S HAPPENING? THIS ISN'T...
"...IT'S NOT REMAINS ANYMORE. I MEAN THE CITY IS BEING BUILT FOR THE FIRST TIME. THIS DOESN'T MAKE ANY SENSE. IT'S LIKE I'M SEEING THE PAST."
"PERHAPS IT IS NOT SO STRANGE. PERHAPS YOUR EYES HAVE BEEN AFFECTED BY THE SAME FORCE THAT HAS MUTATED THE REST OF THE WORLD?"
I THOUGHT I WAS SEEING THE BUILDING OF THE CITY THAT NOW LIES IN RUINS.
BUT THAT'S IMPOSSIBLE, RIGHT?
ANYHOW, ANGEL IS ABOUT TO ARRIVE WITH OUR MONTHLY RATIONS.
I THINK YOU MEAN TO SAY, YOUR MONTHLY RATIONS.

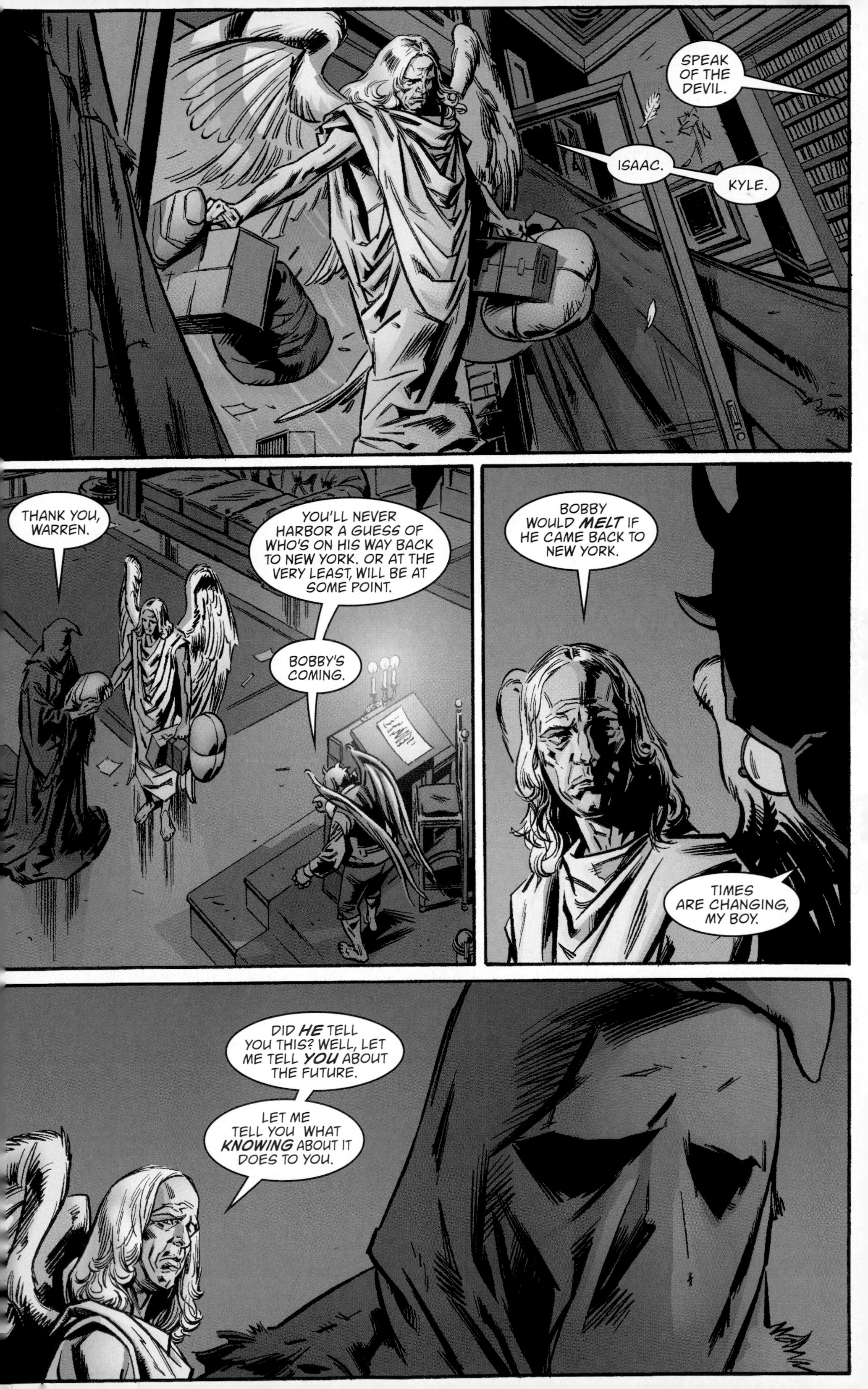
SPEAK OF THE DEVIL.
ISAAC.
KYLE.
THANK YOU, WARREN.
YOU'LL NEVER HARBOR A GUESS OF WHO'S ON HIS WAY BACK TO NEW YORK. OR AT THE VERY LEAST, WILL BE AT SOME POINT.
BOBBY'S COMING.
BOBBY WOULD MELT IF HE CAME BACK TO NEW YORK.
TIMES ARE CHANGING, MY BOY.
DID HE TELL YOU THIS? WELL, LET ME TELL YOU ABOUT THE FUTURE.
LET ME TELL YOU WHAT KNOWING ABOUT IT DOES TO YOU.

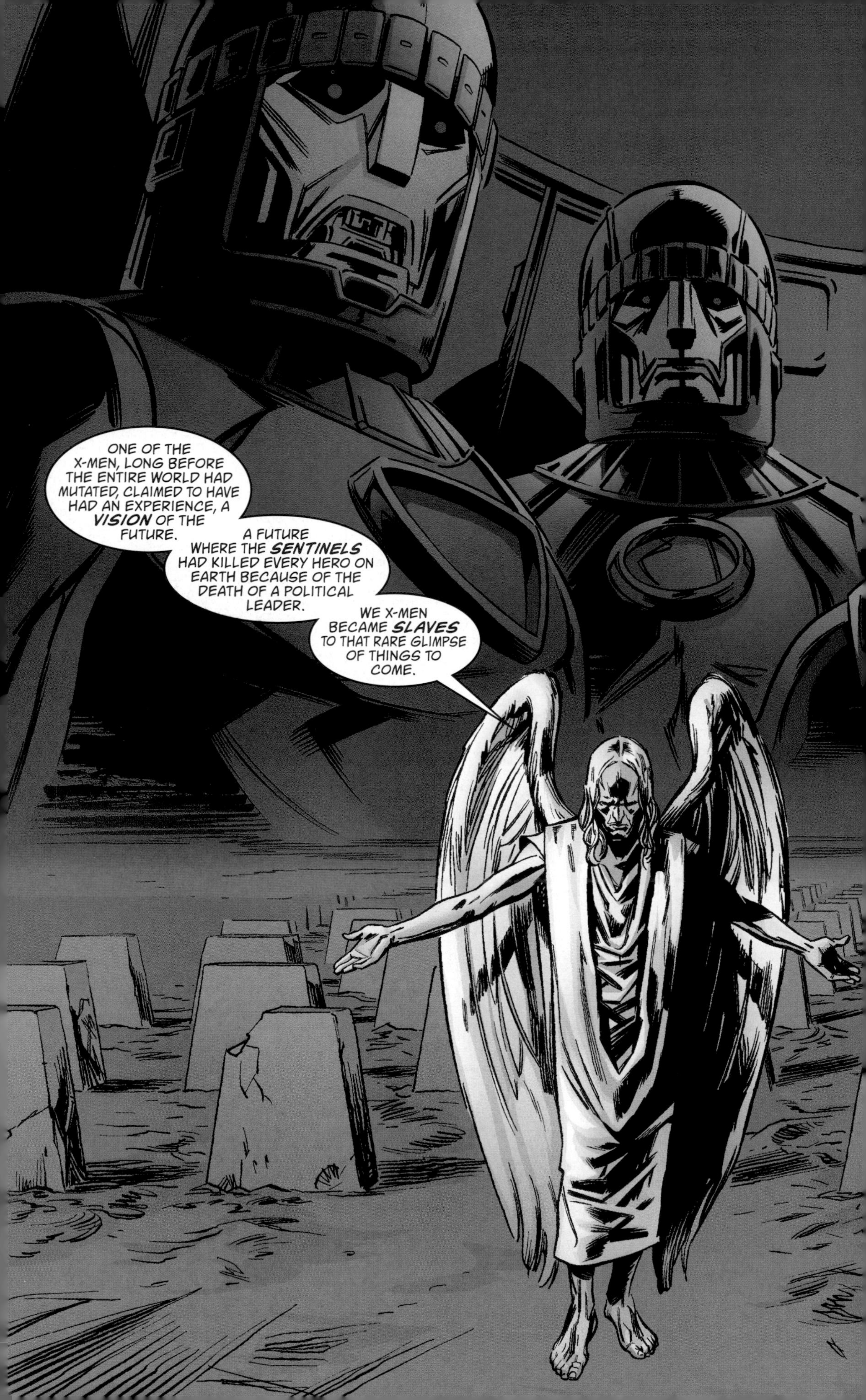
ONE OF THE X-MEN, LONG BEFORE THE ENTIRE WORLD HAD MUTATED, CLAIMED TO HAVE HAD AN EXPERIENCE, A VISION OF THE FUTURE.
A FUTURE WHERE THE SENTINELS HAD KILLED EVERY HERO ON EARTH BECAUSE OF THE DEATH OF A POLITICAL LEADER.
WE X-MEN BECAME SLAVES TO THAT RARE GLIMPSE OF THINGS TO COME.

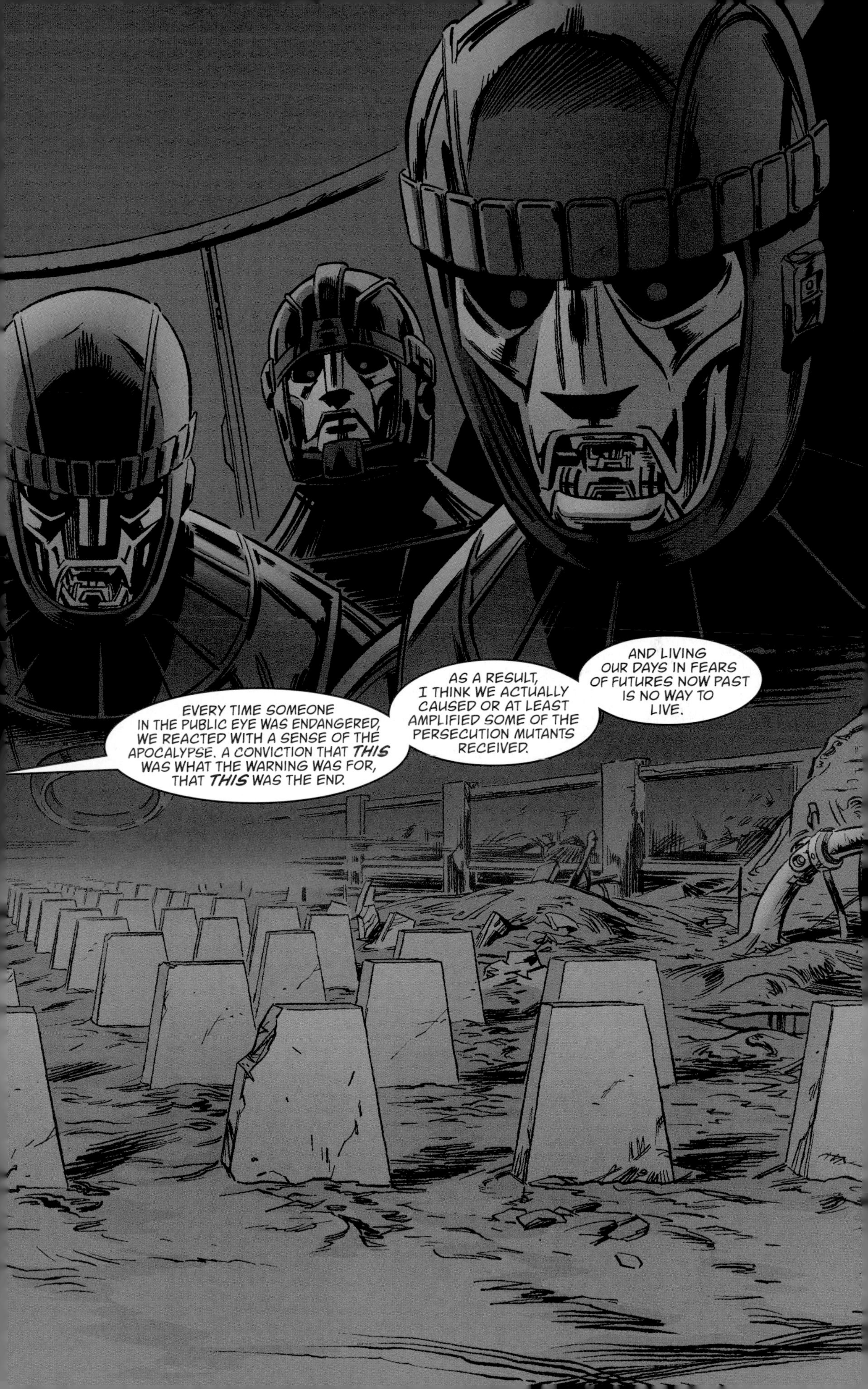
EVERY TIME SOMEONE IN THE PUBLIC EYE WAS ENDANGERED, WE REACTED WITH A SENSE OF THE APOCALYPSE. A CONVICTION THAT *THIS* WAS WHAT THE WARNING WAS FOR, THAT *THIS* WAS THE END.
AS A RESULT, I THINK WE ACTUALLY CAUSED OR AT LEAST AMPLIFIED SOME OF THE PERSECUTION MUTANTS RECEIVED.
AND LIVING OUR DAYS IN FEARS OF FUTURES NOW PAST IS NO WAY TO LIVE.

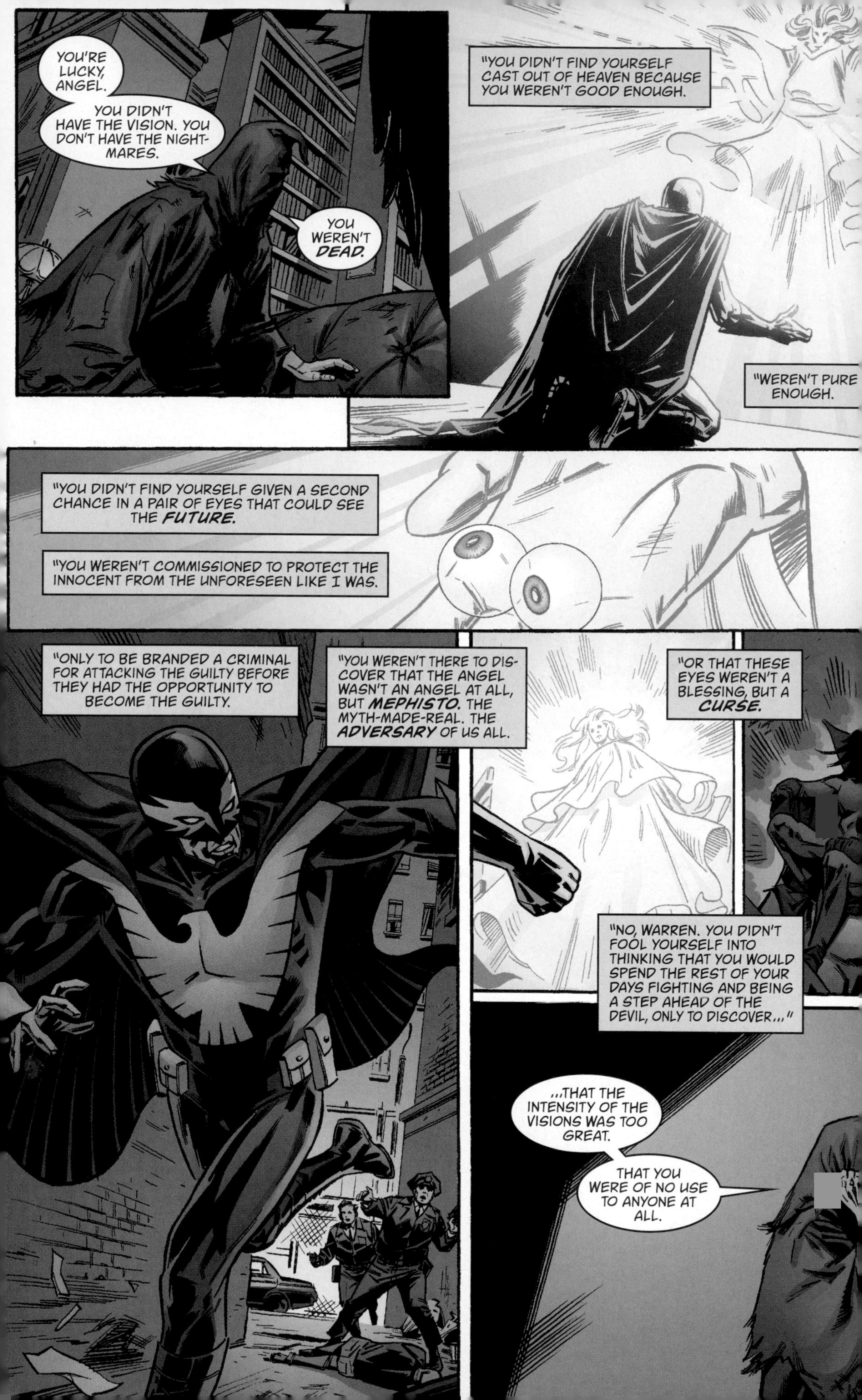
YOU'RE LUCKY, ANGEL.
YOU DIDN'T HAVE THE VISION. YOU DON'T HAVE THE NIGHT-MARES.
YOU WEREN'T DEAD.
"YOU DIDN'T FIND YOURSELF CAST OUT OF HEAVEN BECAUSE YOU WEREN'T GOOD ENOUGH.
"WEREN'T PURE ENOUGH.
"YOU DIDN'T FIND YOURSELF GIVEN A SECOND CHANCE IN A PAIR OF EYES THAT COULD SEE THE FUTURE.
"YOU WEREN'T COMMISSIONED TO PROTECT THE INNOCENT FROM THE UNFORESEEN LIKE I WAS.
"ONLY TO BE BRANDED A CRIMINAL FOR ATTACKING THE GUILTY BEFORE THEY HAD THE OPPORTUNITY TO BECOME THE GUILTY.
"YOU WEREN'T THERE TO DIS-COVER THAT THE ANGEL WASN'T AN ANGEL AT ALL, BUT MEPHISTO. THE MYTH-MADE-REAL. THE ADVERSARY OF US ALL.
"OR THAT THESE EYES WEREN'T A BLESSING, BUT A CURSE.
"NO, WARREN. YOU DIDN'T FOOL YOURSELF INTO THINKING THAT YOU WOULD SPEND THE REST OF YOUR DAYS FIGHTING AND BEING A STEP AHEAD OF THE DEVIL, ONLY TO DISCOVER..."
...THAT THE INTENSITY OF THE VISIONS WAS TOO GREAT.
THAT YOU WERE OF NO USE TO ANYONE AT ALL.

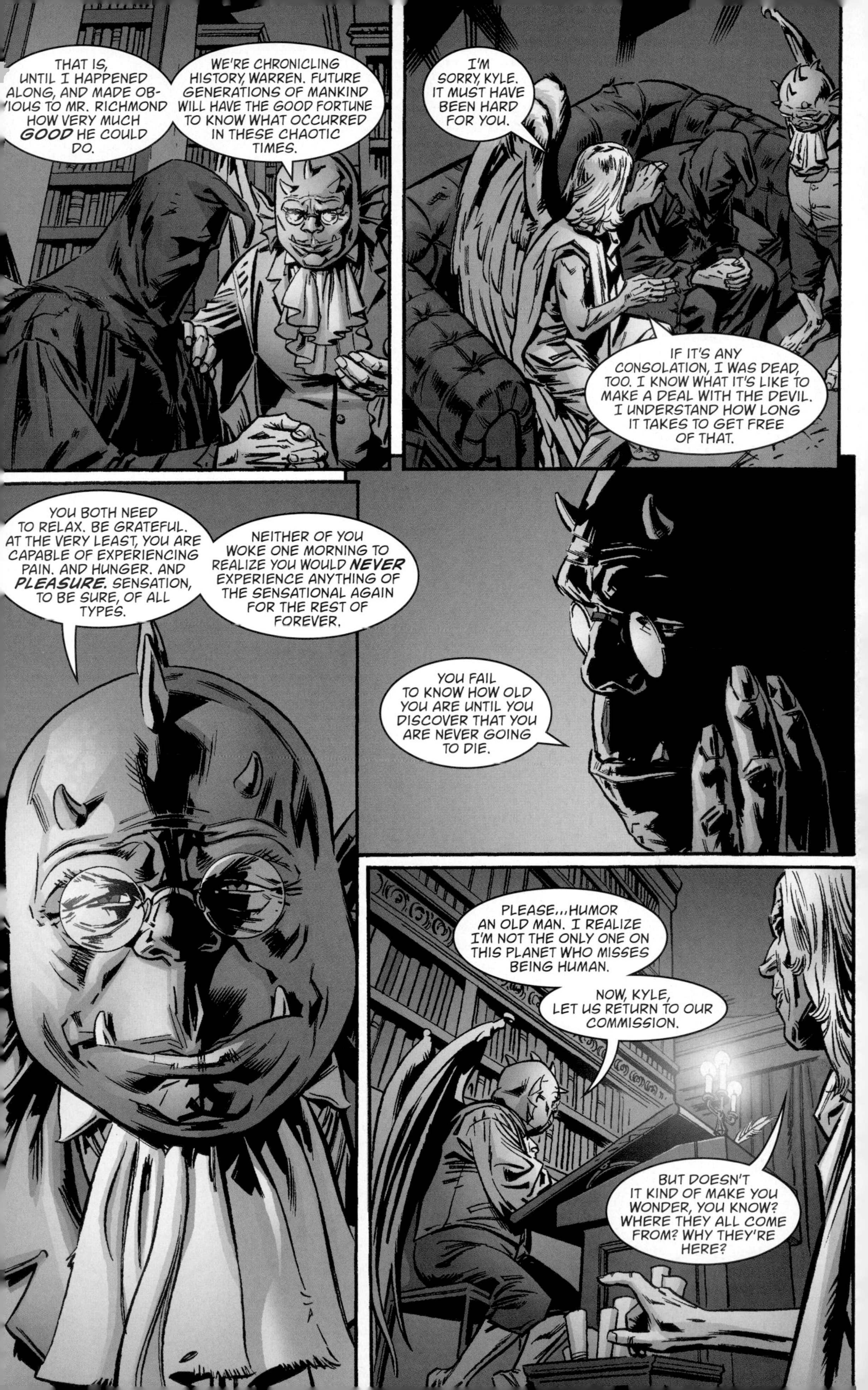
THAT IS, UNTIL I HAPPENED ALONG, AND MADE OB-VIOUS TO MR. RICHMOND HOW VERY MUCH GOOD HE COULD DO.
WE'RE CHRONICLING HISTORY, WARREN. FUTURE GENERATIONS OF MANKIND WILL HAVE THE GOOD FORTUNE TO KNOW WHAT OCCURRED IN THESE CHAOTIC TIMES.
I'M SORRY, KYLE. IT MUST HAVE BEEN HARD FOR YOU.
IF IT'S ANY CONSOLATION, I WAS DEAD, TOO. I KNOW WHAT IT'S LIKE TO MAKE A DEAL WITH THE DEVIL. I UNDERSTAND HOW LONG IT TAKES TO GET FREE OF THAT.
YOU BOTH NEED TO RELAX. BE GRATEFUL. AT THE VERY LEAST, YOU ARE CAPABLE OF EXPERIENCING PAIN. AND HUNGER. AND PLEASURE. SENSATION, TO BE SURE, OF ALL TYPES.
NEITHER OF YOU WOKE ONE MORNING TO REALIZE YOU WOULD NEVER EXPERIENCE ANYTHING OF THE SENSATIONAL AGAIN FOR THE REST OF FOREVER.
YOU FAIL TO KNOW HOW OLD YOU ARE UNTIL YOU DISCOVER THAT YOU ARE NEVER GOING TO DIE.
PLEASE...HUMOR AN OLD MAN. I REALIZE I'M NOT THE ONLY ONE ON THIS PLANET WHO MISSES BEING HUMAN.
NOW, KYLE, LET US RETURN TO OUR COMMISSION.
BUT DOESN'T IT KIND OF MAKE YOU WONDER, YOU KNOW? WHERE THEY ALL COME FROM? WHY THEY'RE HERE?

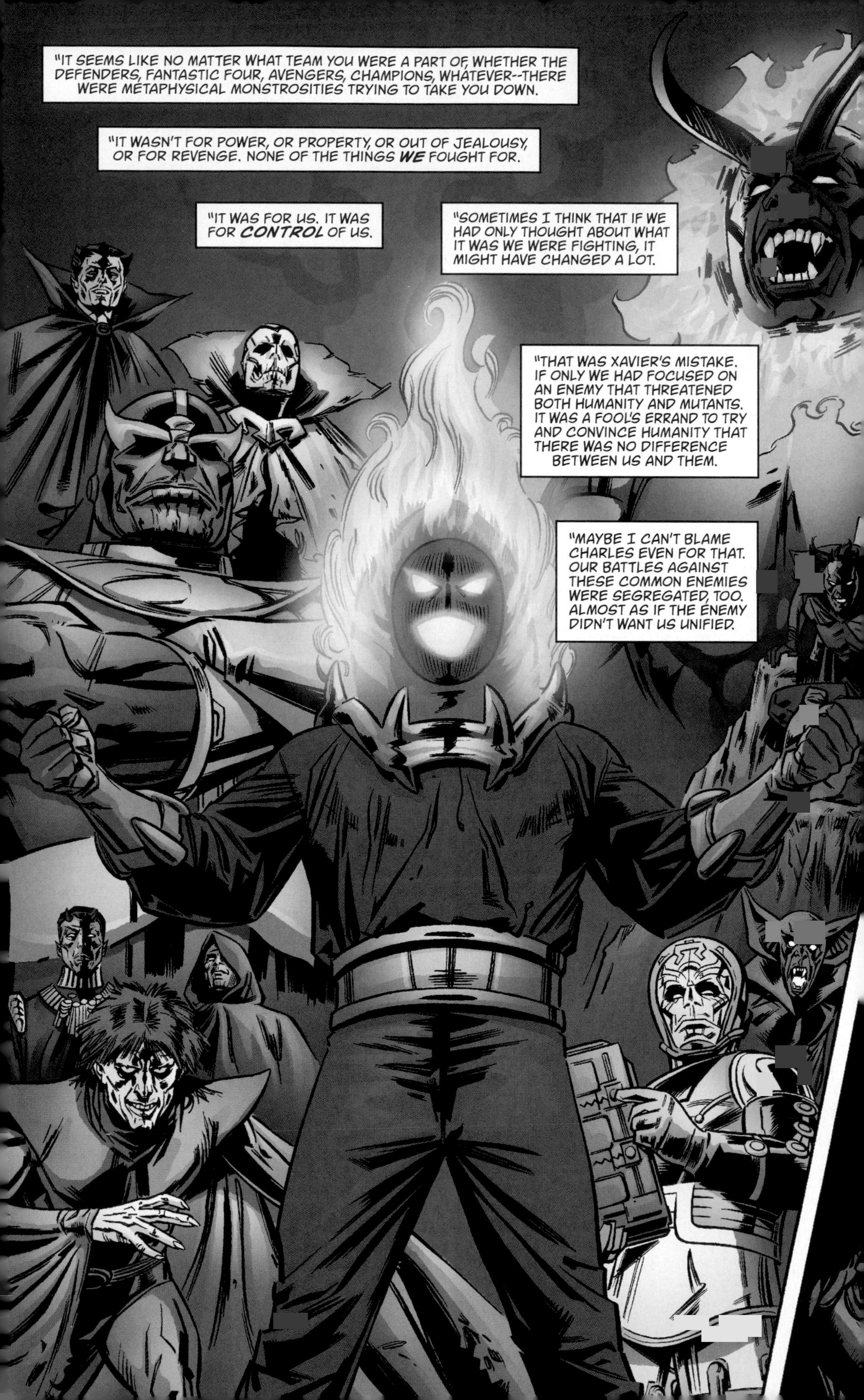
"IT SEEMS LIKE NO MATTER WHAT TEAM YOU WERE A PART OF, WHETHER THE DEFENDERS, FANTASTIC FOUR, AVENGERS, CHAMPIONS, WHATEVER--THERE WERE METAPHYSICAL MONSTROSITIES TRYING TO TAKE YOU DOWN.
"IT WASN'T FOR POWER, OR PROPERTY, OR OUT OF JEALOUSY, OR FOR REVENGE. NONE OF THE THINGS *WE* FOUGHT FOR.
"IT WAS FOR US. IT WAS FOR *CONTROL* OF US.
"SOMETIMES I THINK THAT IF WE HAD ONLY THOUGHT ABOUT WHAT IT WAS WE WERE FIGHTING, IT MIGHT HAVE CHANGED A LOT.
"THAT WAS XAVIER'S MISTAKE. IF ONLY WE HAD FOCUSED ON AN ENEMY THAT THREATENED BOTH HUMANITY AND MUTANTS. IT WAS A FOOL'S ERRAND TO TRY AND CONVINCE HUMANITY THAT THERE WAS NO DIFFERENCE BETWEEN US AND THEM.
"MAYBE I CAN'T BLAME CHARLES EVEN FOR THAT. OUR BATTLES AGAINST THESE COMMON ENEMIES WERE SEGREGATED, TOO. ALMOST AS IF THE ENEMY DIDN'T WANT US UNIFIED.

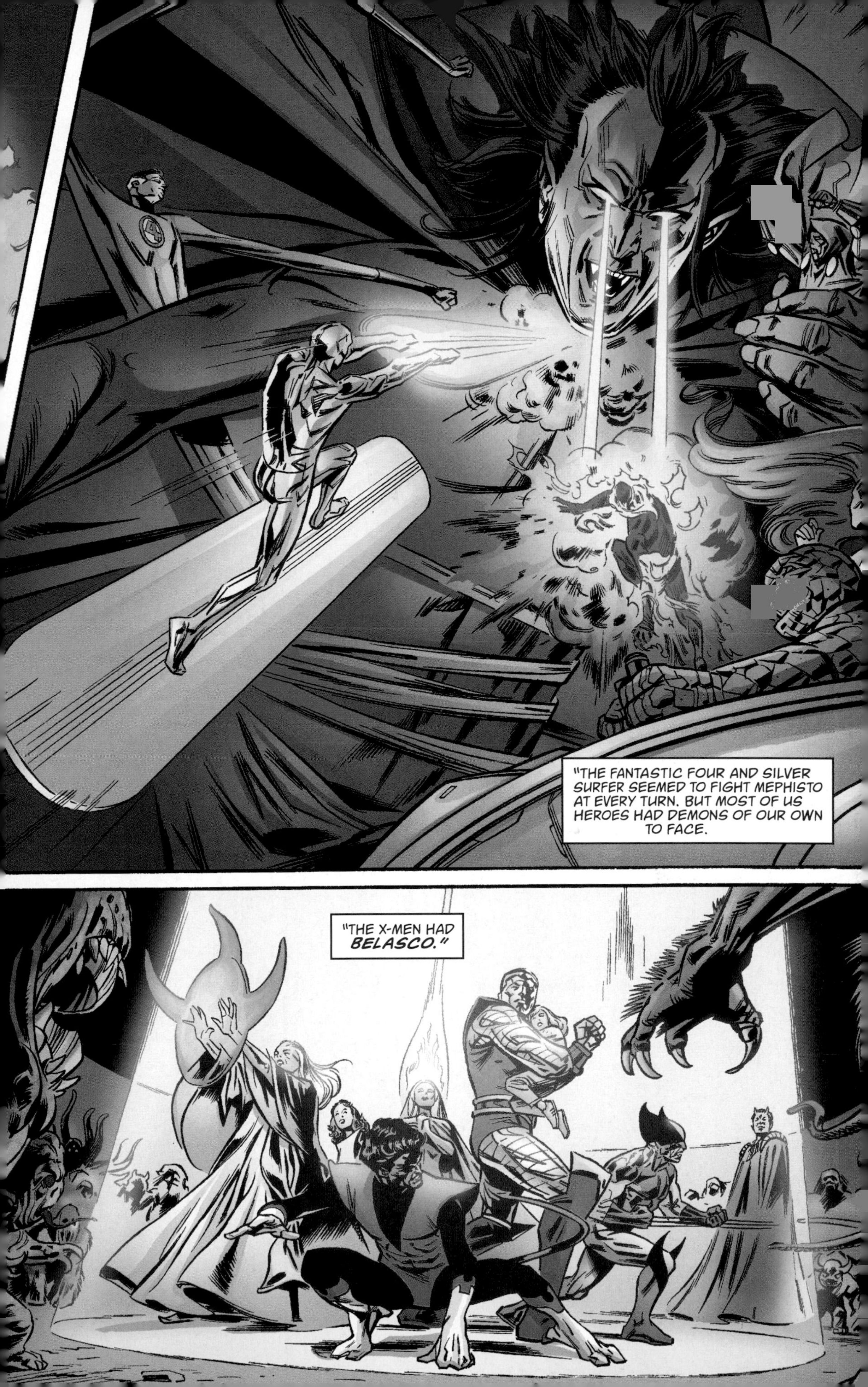
"THE FANTASTIC FOUR AND SILVER SURFER SEEMED TO FIGHT MEPHISTO AT EVERY TURN. BUT MOST OF US HEROES HAD DEMONS OF OUR OWN TO FACE.
"THE X-MEN HAD *BELASCO*."

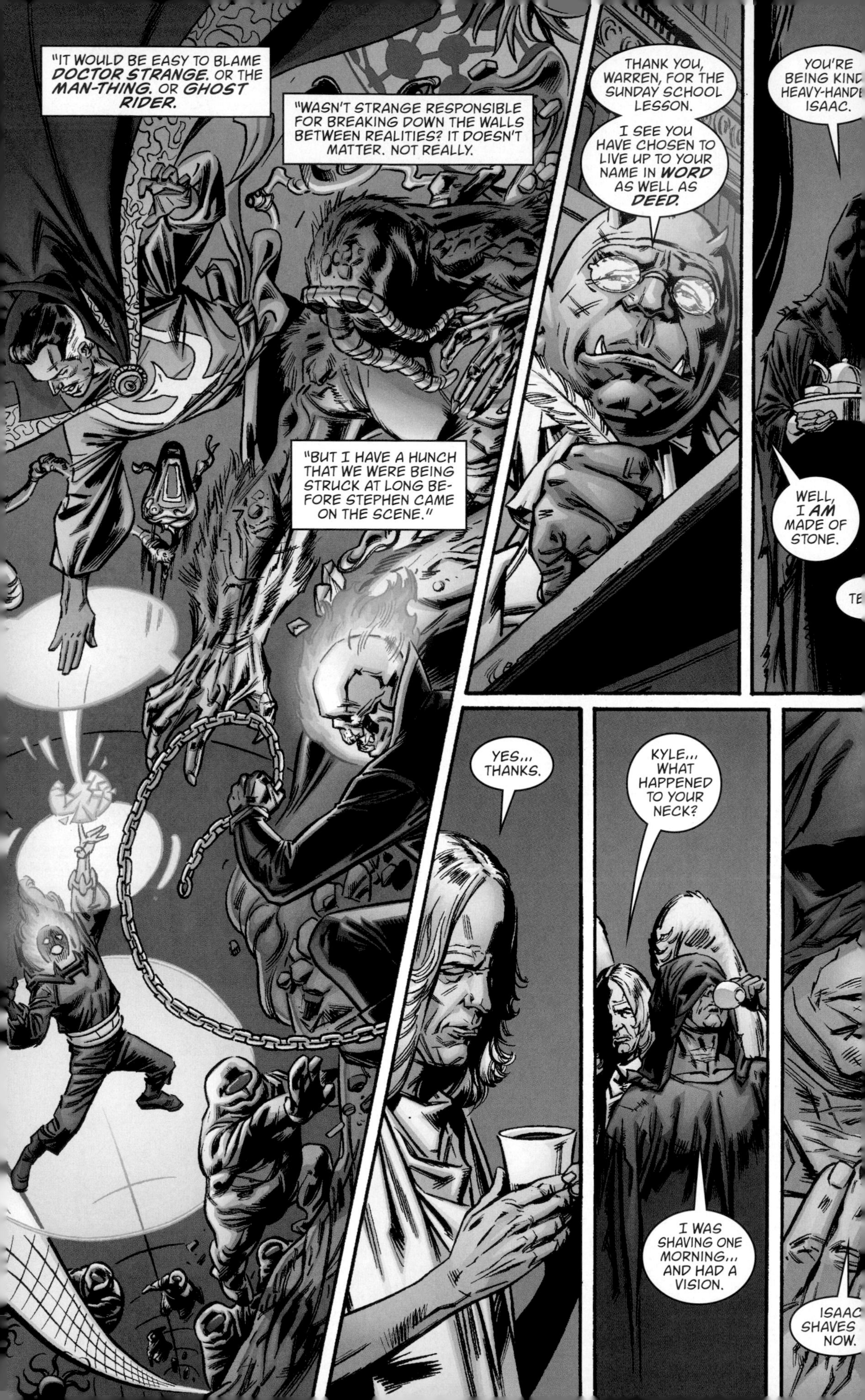
"IT WOULD BE EASY TO BLAME DOCTOR STRANGE. OR THE MAN-THING. OR GHOST RIDER.
"WASN'T STRANGE RESPONSIBLE FOR BREAKING DOWN THE WALLS BETWEEN REALITIES? IT DOESN'T MATTER. NOT REALLY.
"BUT I HAVE A HUNCH THAT WE WERE BEING STRUCK AT LONG BEFORE STEPHEN CAME ON THE SCENE."
THANK YOU, WARREN, FOR THE SUNDAY SCHOOL LESSON.
I SEE YOU HAVE CHOSEN TO LIVE UP TO YOUR NAME IN WORD AS WELL AS DEED.
YOU'RE BEING KIND HEAVY-HANDE ISAAC.
WELL, I AM MADE OF STONE.
YES... THANKS.
KYLE... WHAT HAPPENED TO YOUR NECK?
I WAS SHAVING ONE MORNING... AND HAD A VISION.
ISAAC SHAVES NOW.

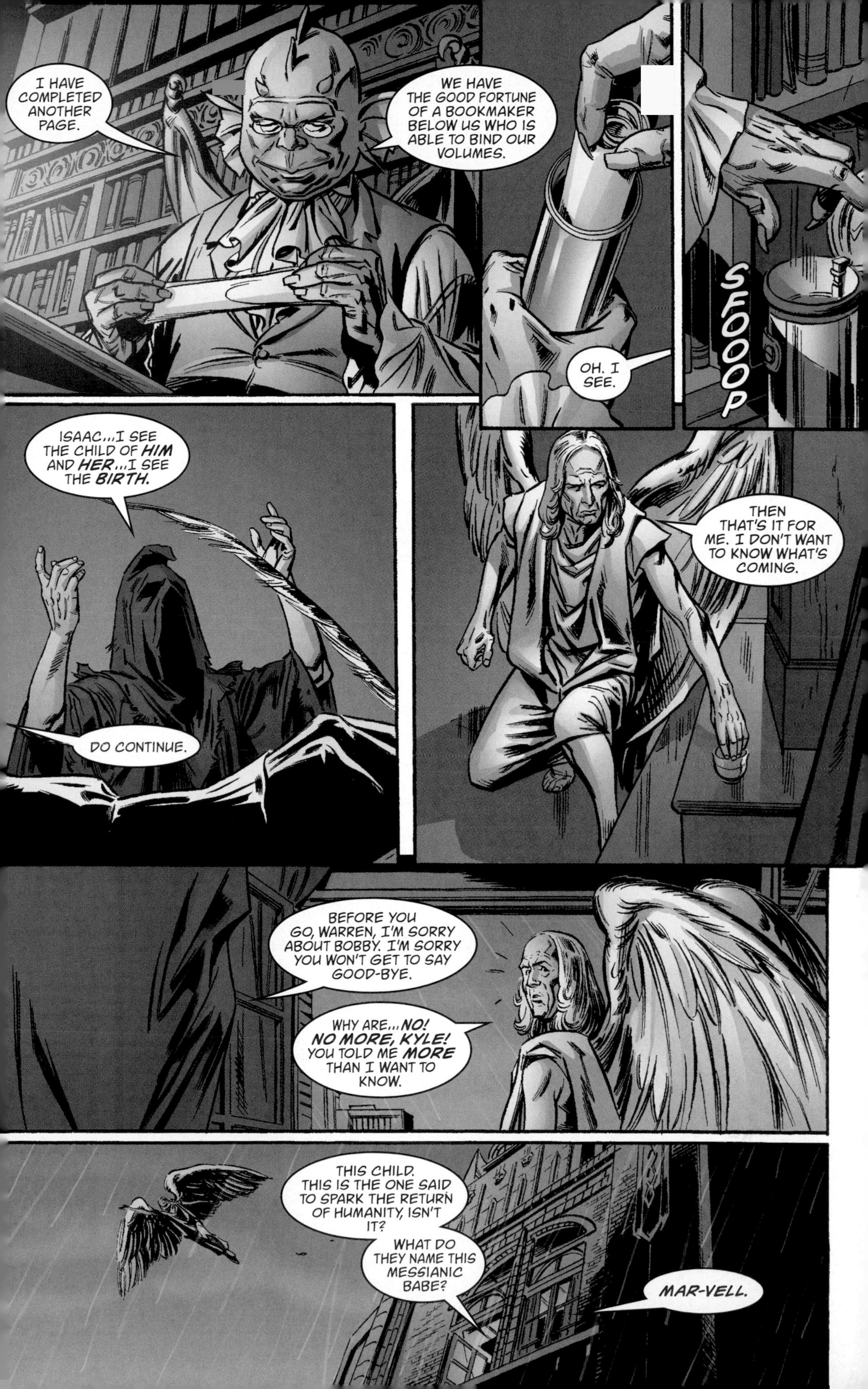
I HAVE COMPLETED ANOTHER PAGE.
WE HAVE THE GOOD FORTUNE OF A BOOKMAKER BELOW US WHO IS ABLE TO BIND OUR VOLUMES.
OH. I SEE.
SFOOOP
ISAAC...I SEE THE CHILD OF *HIM* AND *HER*...I SEE THE *BIRTH.*
DO CONTINUE.
THEN THAT'S IT FOR ME. I DON'T WANT TO KNOW WHAT'S COMING.
BEFORE YOU GO, WARREN, I'M SORRY ABOUT BOBBY. I'M SORRY YOU WON'T GET TO SAY GOOD-BYE.
WHY ARE... *NO! NO MORE, KYLE!* YOU TOLD ME *MORE* THAN I WANT TO KNOW.
THIS CHILD. THIS IS THE ONE SAID TO SPARK THE RETURN OF HUMANITY, ISN'T IT?
WHAT DO THEY NAME THIS MESSIANIC BABE?
MAR-VELL.

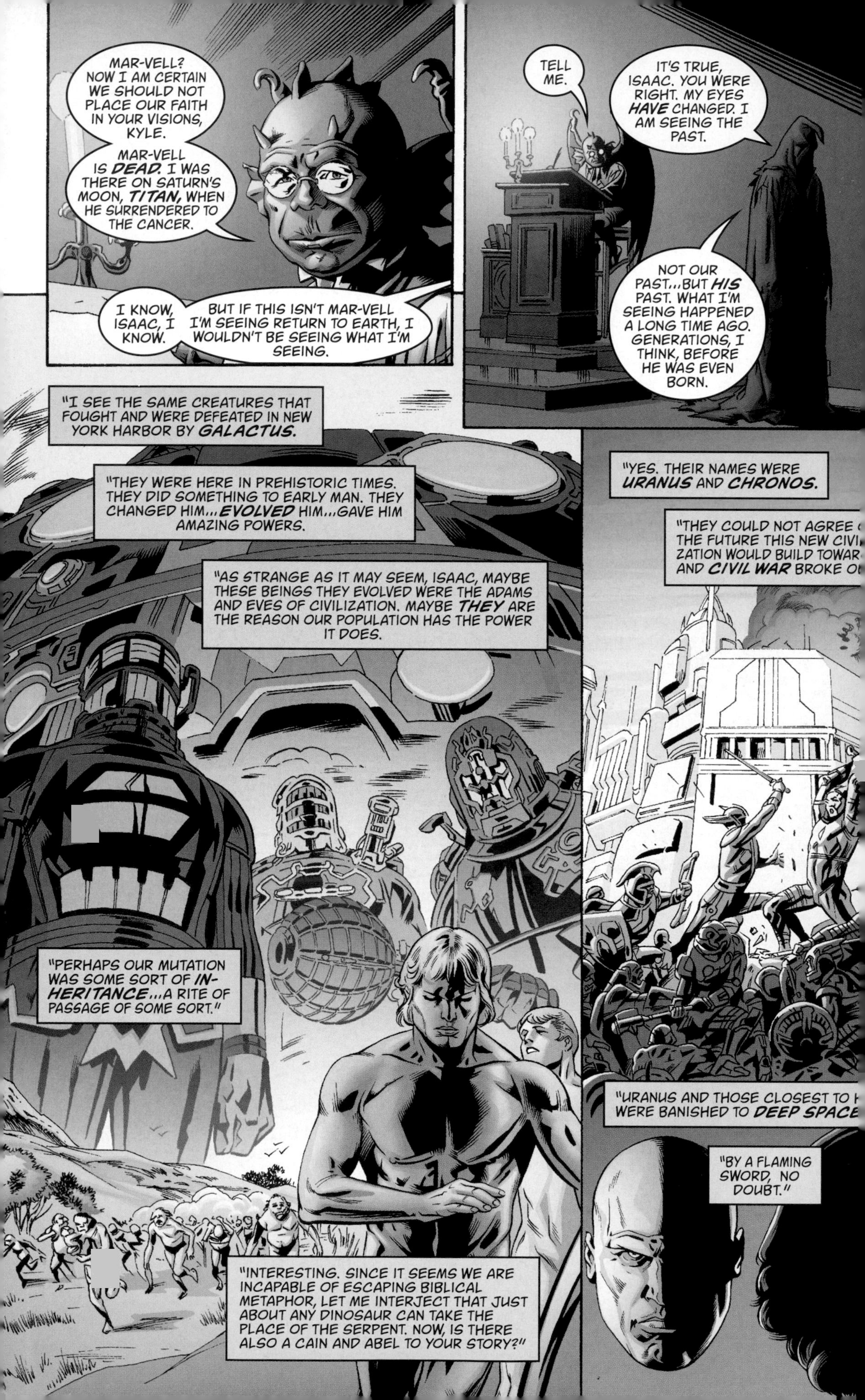
MAR-VELL? NOW I AM CERTAIN WE SHOULD NOT PLACE OUR FAITH IN YOUR VISIONS, KYLE.
MAR-VELL IS DEAD. I WAS THERE ON SATURN'S MOON, TITAN, WHEN HE SURRENDERED TO THE CANCER.
I KNOW, ISAAC, I KNOW.
BUT IF THIS ISN'T MAR-VELL I'M SEEING RETURN TO EARTH, I WOULDN'T BE SEEING WHAT I'M SEEING.
TELL ME.
IT'S TRUE, ISAAC. YOU WERE RIGHT. MY EYES HAVE CHANGED. I AM SEEING THE PAST.
NOT OUR PAST...BUT HIS PAST. WHAT I'M SEEING HAPPENED A LONG TIME AGO. GENERATIONS, I THINK, BEFORE HE WAS EVEN BORN.
"I SEE THE SAME CREATURES THAT FOUGHT AND WERE DEFEATED IN NEW YORK HARBOR BY GALACTUS.
"THEY WERE HERE IN PREHISTORIC TIMES. THEY DID SOMETHING TO EARLY MAN. THEY CHANGED HIM...EVOLVED HIM...GAVE HIM AMAZING POWERS.
"AS STRANGE AS IT MAY SEEM, ISAAC, MAYBE THESE BEINGS THEY EVOLVED WERE THE ADAMS AND EVES OF CIVILIZATION. MAYBE THEY ARE THE REASON OUR POPULATION HAS THE POWER IT DOES.
"PERHAPS OUR MUTATION WAS SOME SORT OF INHERITANCE...A RITE OF PASSAGE OF SOME SORT."
"INTERESTING. SINCE IT SEEMS WE ARE INCAPABLE OF ESCAPING BIBLICAL METAPHOR, LET ME INTERJECT THAT JUST ABOUT ANY DINOSAUR CAN TAKE THE PLACE OF THE SERPENT. NOW, IS THERE ALSO A CAIN AND ABEL TO YOUR STORY?"
"YES. THEIR NAMES WERE URANUS AND CHRONOS.
"THEY COULD NOT AGREE
THE FUTURE THIS NEW CIVI
ZATION WOULD BUILD TOWAR
AND CIVIL WAR BROKE O
"URANUS AND THOSE CLOSEST TO
WERE BANISHED TO DEEP SPACE
"BY A FLAMING SWORD, NO DOUBT."

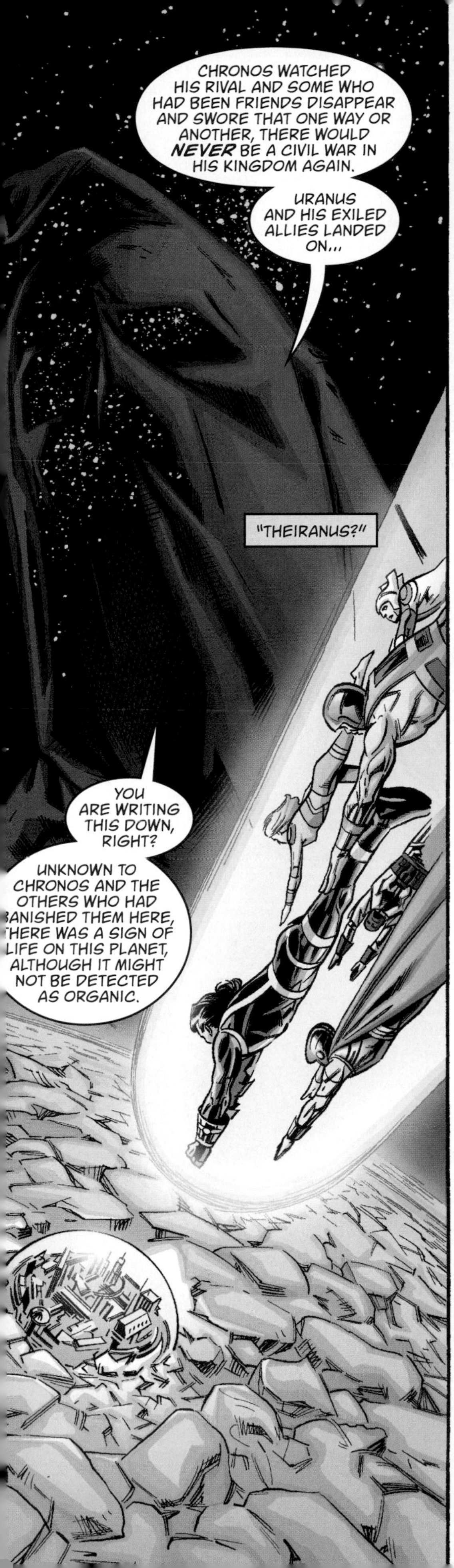
CHRONOS WATCHED HIS RIVAL AND SOME WHO HAD BEEN FRIENDS DISAPPEAR AND SWORE THAT ONE WAY OR ANOTHER, THERE WOULD **NEVER** BE A CIVIL WAR IN HIS KINGDOM AGAIN.
URANUS AND HIS EXILED ALLIES LANDED ON...
"THEIRANUS?"
YOU ARE WRITING THIS DOWN, RIGHT?
UNKNOWN TO CHRONOS AND THE OTHERS WHO HAD BANISHED THEM HERE, THERE WAS A SIGN OF LIFE ON THIS PLANET, ALTHOUGH IT MIGHT NOT BE DETECTED AS ORGANIC.

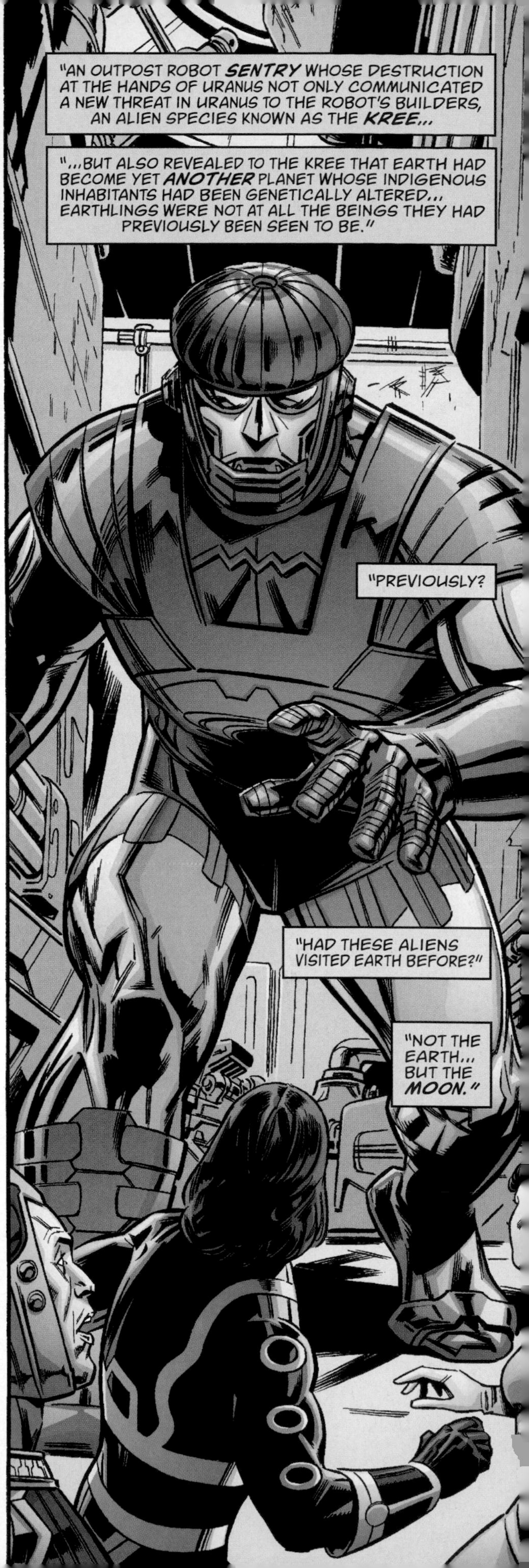
"AN OUTPOST ROBOT **SENTRY** WHOSE DESTRUCTION AT THE HANDS OF URANUS NOT ONLY COMMUNICATED A NEW THREAT IN URANUS TO THE ROBOT'S BUILDERS, AN ALIEN SPECIES KNOWN AS THE **KREE**...
"...BUT ALSO REVEALED TO THE KREE THAT EARTH HAD BECOME YET **ANOTHER** PLANET WHOSE INDIGENOUS INHABITANTS HAD BEEN GENETICALLY ALTERED... EARTHLINGS WERE NOT AT ALL THE BEINGS THEY HAD PREVIOUSLY BEEN SEEN TO BE."
"PREVIOUSLY?
"HAD THESE ALIENS VISITED EARTH BEFORE?"
"NOT THE EARTH... BUT THE **MOON**."

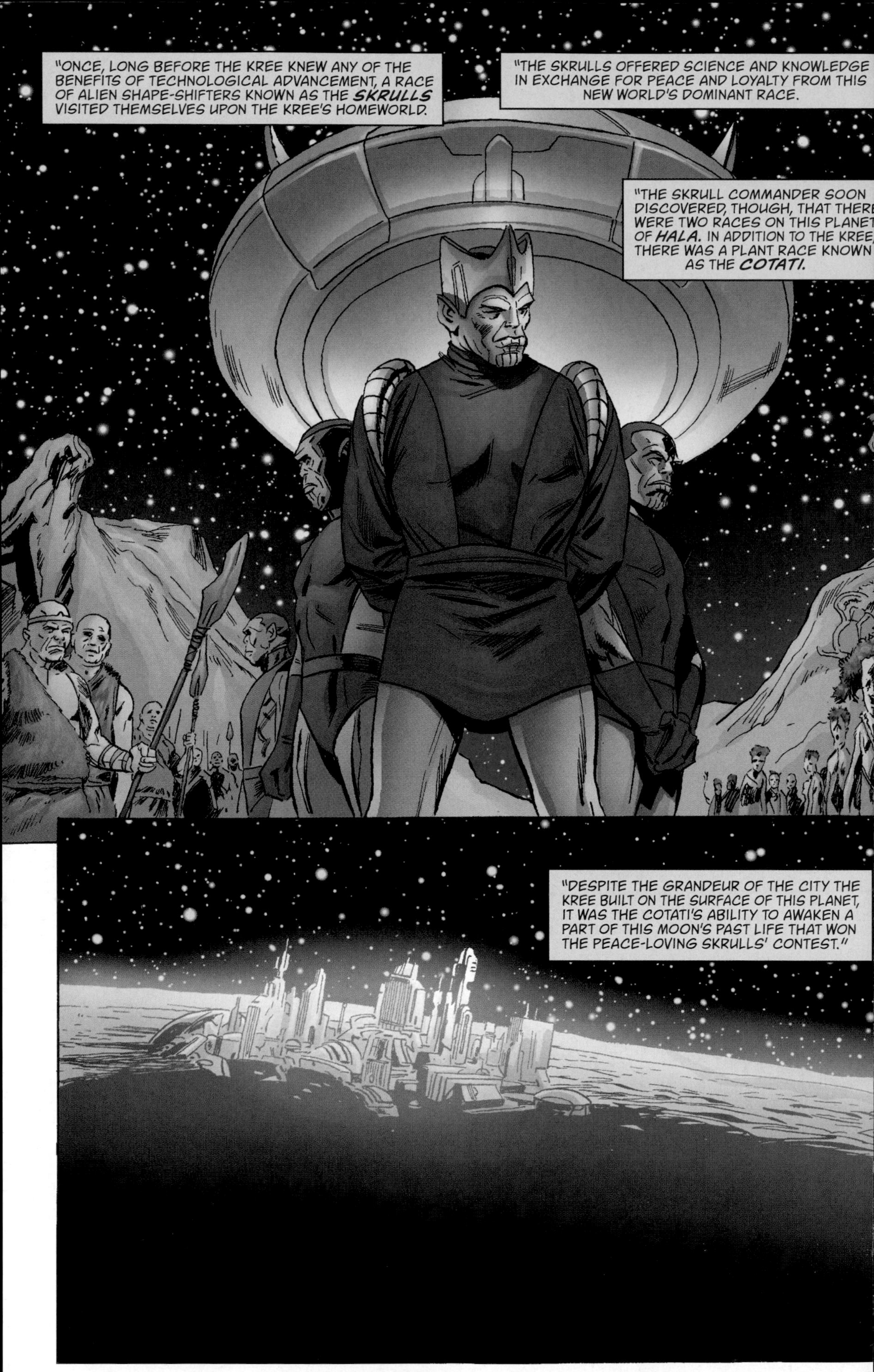
"ONCE, LONG BEFORE THE KREE KNEW ANY OF THE BENEFITS OF TECHNOLOGICAL ADVANCEMENT, A RACE OF ALIEN SHAPE-SHIFTERS KNOWN AS THE SKRULLS VISITED THEMSELVES UPON THE KREE'S HOMEWORLD.
"THE SKRULLS OFFERED SCIENCE AND KNOWLEDGE IN EXCHANGE FOR PEACE AND LOYALTY FROM THIS NEW WORLD'S DOMINANT RACE.
"THE SKRULL COMMANDER SOON DISCOVERED, THOUGH, THAT THERE WERE TWO RACES ON THIS PLANET OF HALA. IN ADDITION TO THE KREE, THERE WAS A PLANT RACE KNOWN AS THE COTATI.
"DESPITE THE GRANDEUR OF THE CITY THE KREE BUILT ON THE SURFACE OF THIS PLANET, IT WAS THE COTATI'S ABILITY TO AWAKEN A PART OF THIS MOON'S PAST LIFE THAT WON THE PEACE-LOVING SKRULLS' CONTEST."

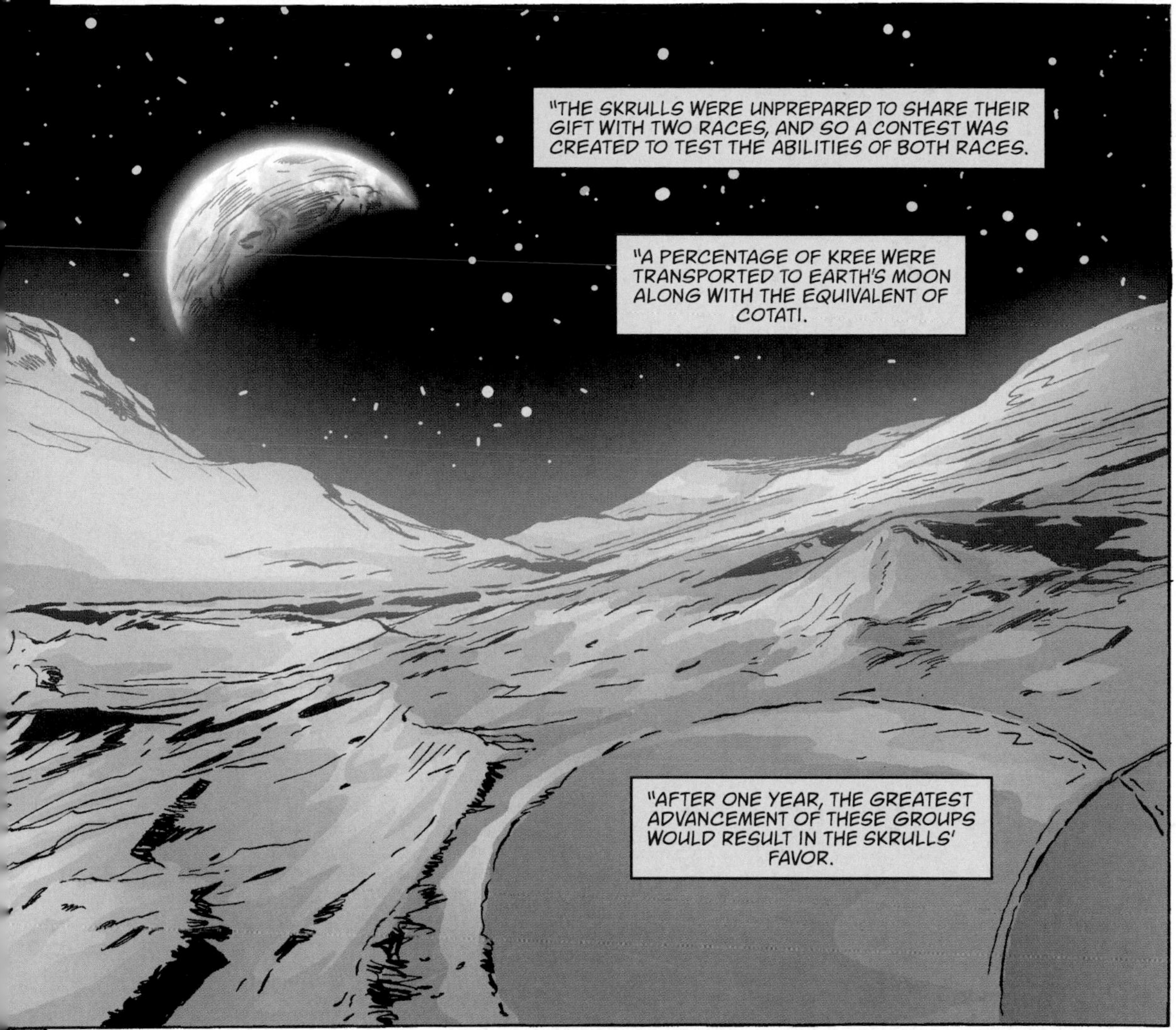
"THE SKRULLS WERE UNPREPARED TO SHARE THEIR GIFT WITH TWO RACES, AND SO A CONTEST WAS CREATED TO TEST THE ABILITIES OF BOTH RACES.
"A PERCENTAGE OF KREE WERE TRANSPORTED TO EARTH'S MOON ALONG WITH THE EQUIVALENT OF COTATI.
"AFTER ONE YEAR, THE GREATEST ADVANCEMENT OF THESE GROUPS WOULD RESULT IN THE SKRULLS' FAVOR.

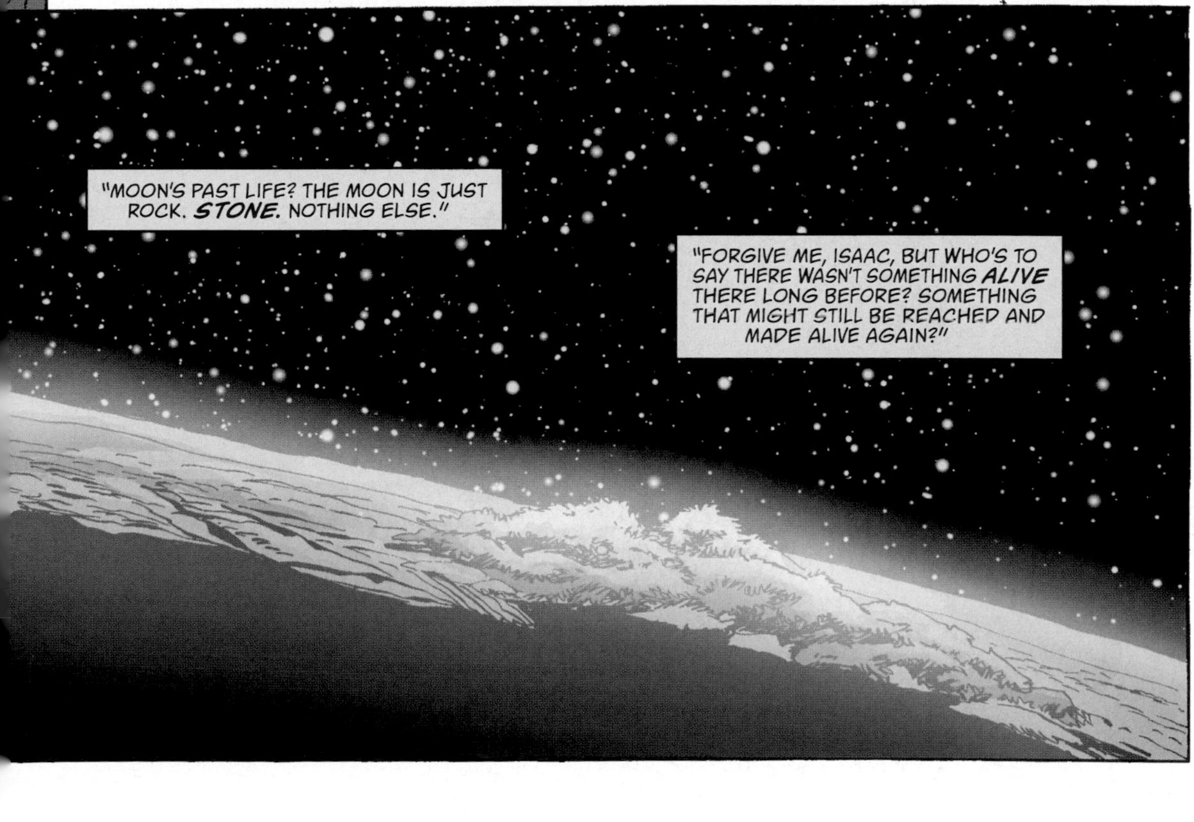
"MOON'S PAST LIFE? THE MOON IS JUST ROCK. STONE. NOTHING ELSE."
"FORGIVE ME, ISAAC, BUT WHO'S TO SAY THERE WASN'T SOMETHING ALIVE THERE LONG BEFORE? SOMETHING THAT MIGHT STILL BE REACHED AND MADE ALIVE AGAIN?"

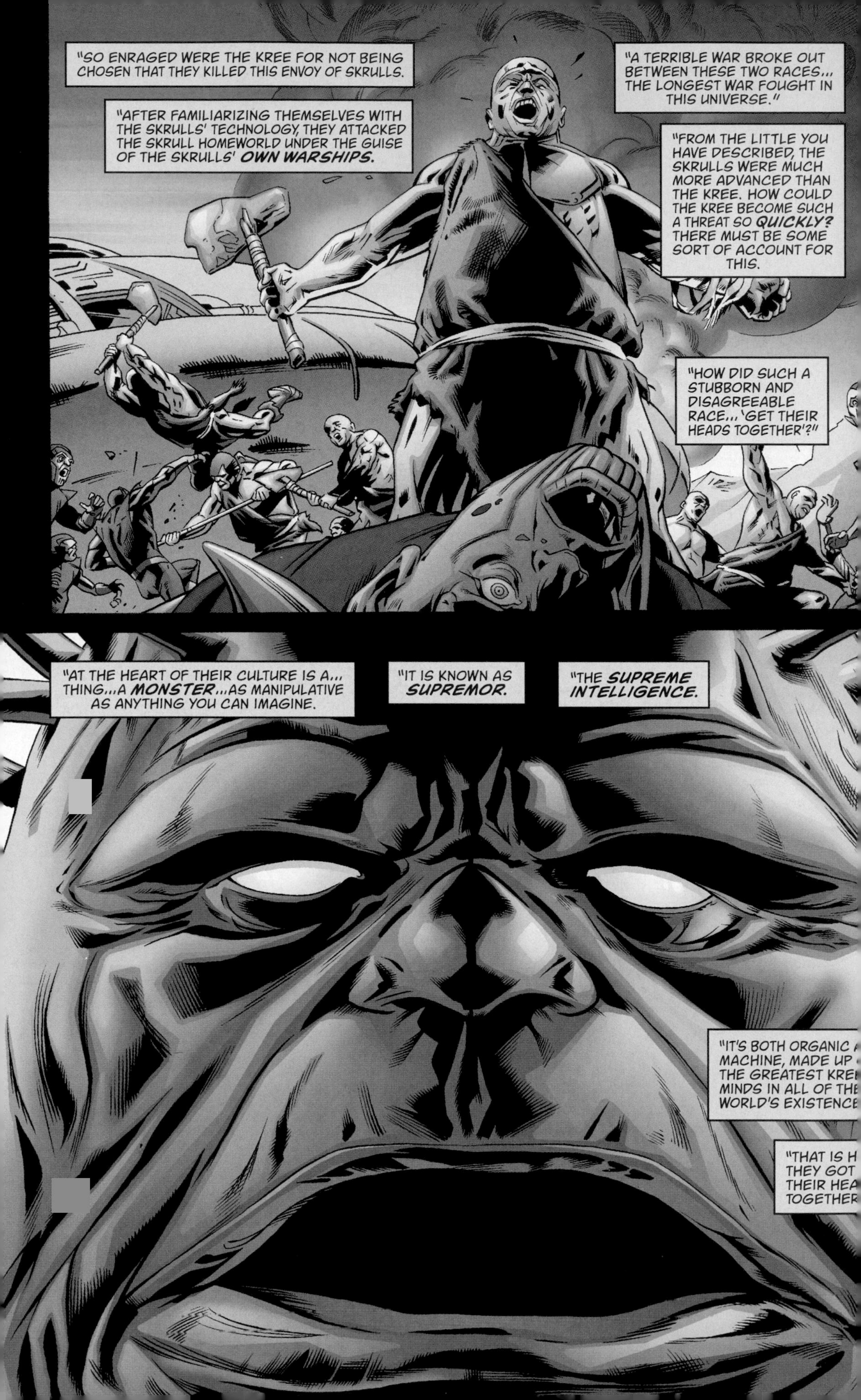
"SO ENRAGED WERE THE KREE FOR NOT BEING CHOSEN THAT THEY KILLED THIS ENVOY OF SKRULLS.
"AFTER FAMILIARIZING THEMSELVES WITH THE SKRULLS' TECHNOLOGY, THEY ATTACKED THE SKRULL HOMEWORLD UNDER THE GUISE OF THE SKRULLS' OWN WARSHIPS.
"A TERRIBLE WAR BROKE OUT BETWEEN THESE TWO RACES... THE LONGEST WAR FOUGHT IN THIS UNIVERSE."
"FROM THE LITTLE YOU HAVE DESCRIBED, THE SKRULLS WERE MUCH MORE ADVANCED THAN THE KREE. HOW COULD THE KREE BECOME SUCH A THREAT SO QUICKLY? THERE MUST BE SOME SORT OF ACCOUNT FOR THIS.
"HOW DID SUCH A STUBBORN AND DISAGREEABLE RACE... 'GET THEIR HEADS TOGETHER'?"
"AT THE HEART OF THEIR CULTURE IS A... THING... A MONSTER... AS MANIPULATIVE AS ANYTHING YOU CAN IMAGINE.
"IT IS KNOWN AS SUPREMOR.
"THE SUPREME INTELLIGENCE.
"IT'S BOTH ORGANIC MACHINE, MADE UP THE GREATEST KRE MINDS IN ALL OF THE WORLD'S EXISTENCE
"THAT IS H THEY GOT THEIR HEA TOGETHER

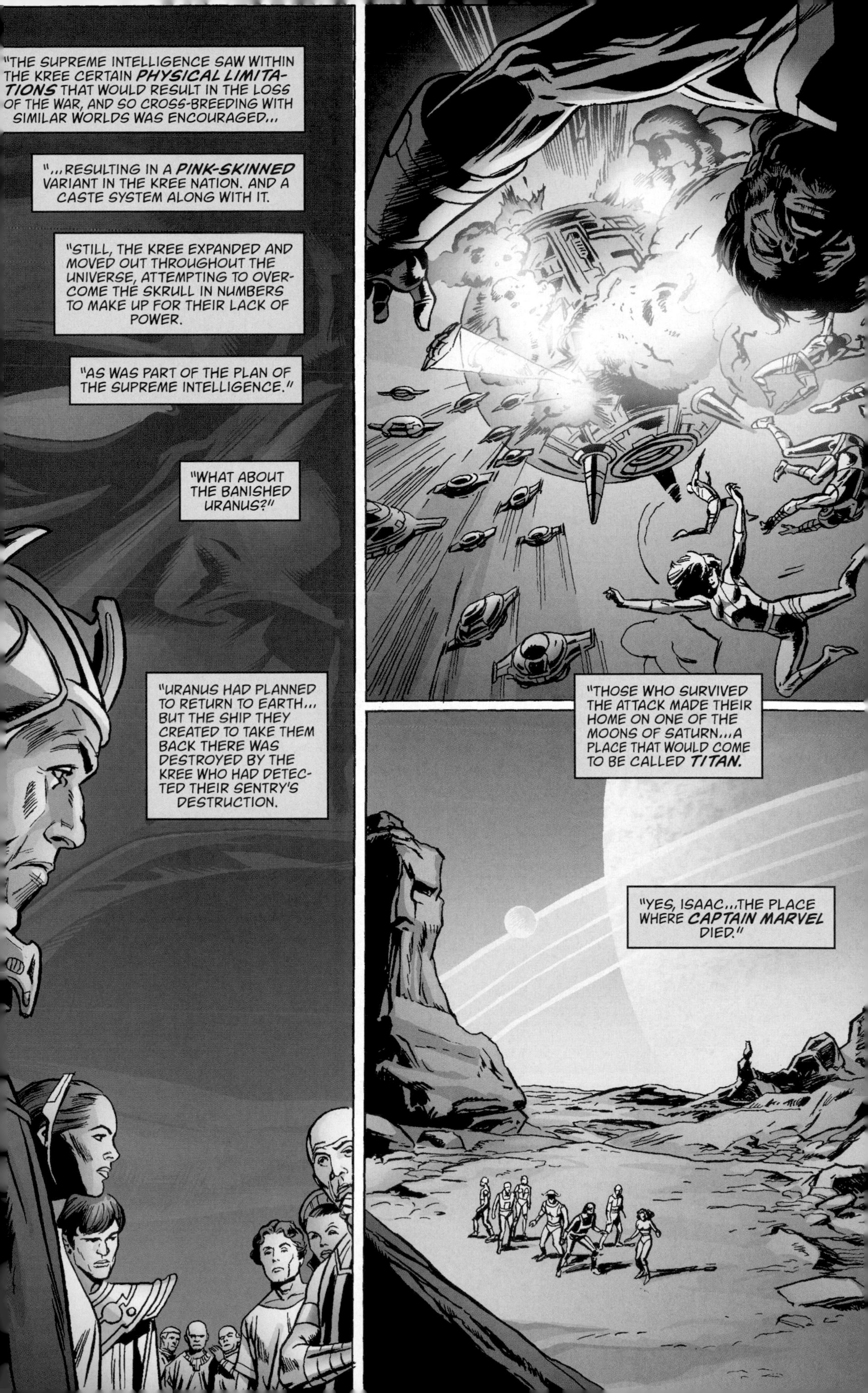

"THE SUPREME INTELLIGENCE SAW WITHIN THE KREE CERTAIN PHYSICAL LIMITATIONS THAT WOULD RESULT IN THE LOSS OF THE WAR, AND SO CROSS-BREEDING WITH SIMILAR WORLDS WAS ENCOURAGED...
"...RESULTING IN A PINK-SKINNED VARIANT IN THE KREE NATION. AND A CASTE SYSTEM ALONG WITH IT.
"STILL, THE KREE EXPANDED AND MOVED OUT THROUGHOUT THE UNIVERSE, ATTEMPTING TO OVERCOME THE SKRULL IN NUMBERS TO MAKE UP FOR THEIR LACK OF POWER.
"AS WAS PART OF THE PLAN OF THE SUPREME INTELLIGENCE."
"WHAT ABOUT THE BANISHED URANUS?"
"URANUS HAD PLANNED TO RETURN TO EARTH... BUT THE SHIP THEY CREATED TO TAKE THEM BACK THERE WAS DESTROYED BY THE KREE WHO HAD DETECTED THEIR SENTRY'S DESTRUCTION.
"THOSE WHO SURVIVED THE ATTACK MADE THEIR HOME ON ONE OF THE MOONS OF SATURN...A PLACE THAT WOULD COME TO BE CALLED TITAN.
"YES, ISAAC...THE PLACE WHERE CAPTAIN MARVEL DIED."

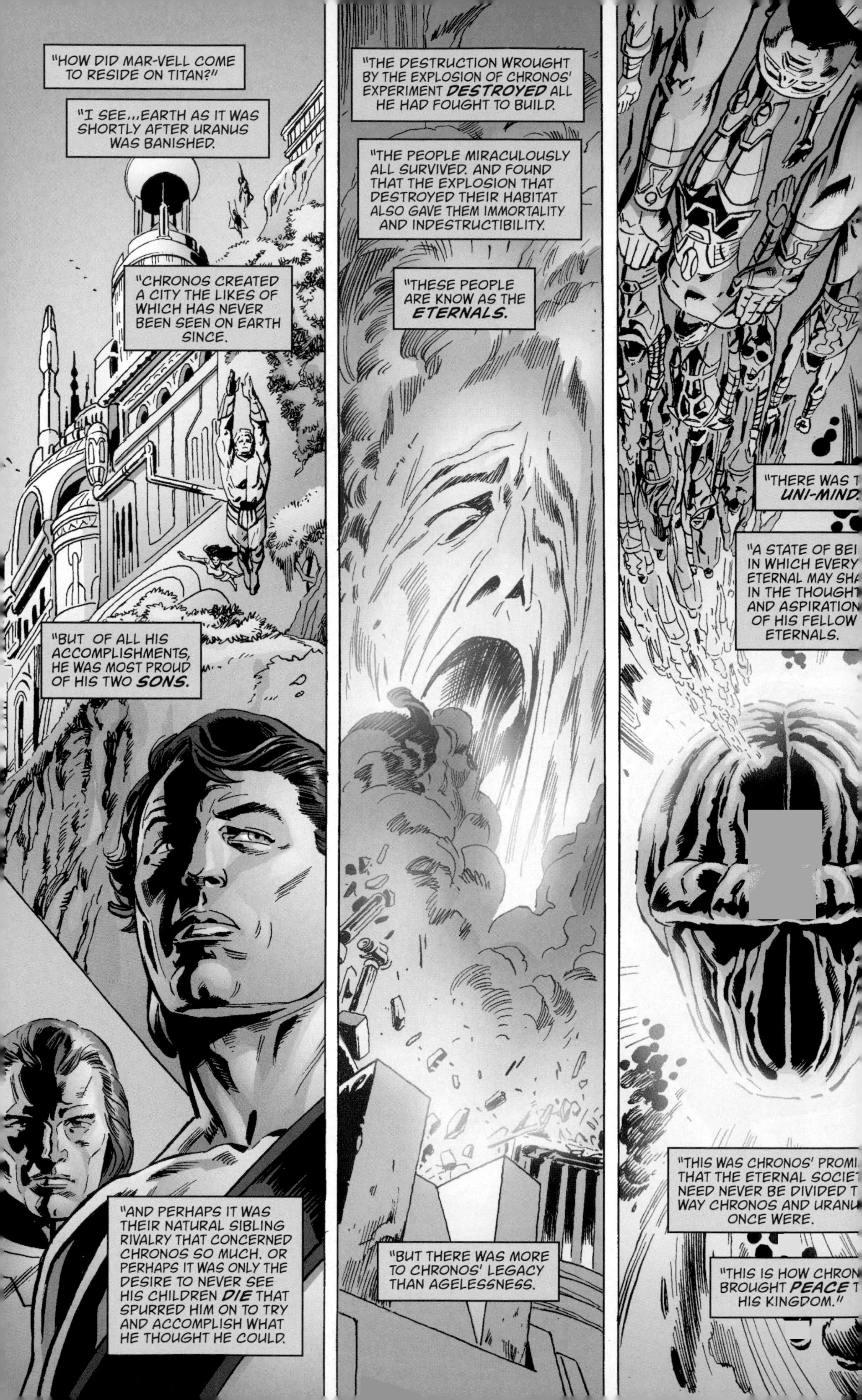
"HOW DID MAR-VELL COME TO RESIDE ON TITAN?"
"I SEE...EARTH AS IT WAS SHORTLY AFTER URANUS WAS BANISHED.
"CHRONOS CREATED A CITY THE LIKES OF WHICH HAS NEVER BEEN SEEN ON EARTH SINCE.
"BUT OF ALL HIS ACCOMPLISHMENTS, HE WAS MOST PROUD OF HIS TWO SONS.
"AND PERHAPS IT WAS THEIR NATURAL SIBLING RIVALRY THAT CONCERNED CHRONOS SO MUCH. OR PERHAPS IT WAS ONLY THE DESIRE TO NEVER SEE HIS CHILDREN DIE THAT SPURRED HIM ON TO TRY AND ACCOMPLISH WHAT HE THOUGHT HE COULD.
"THE DESTRUCTION WROUGHT BY THE EXPLOSION OF CHRONOS' EXPERIMENT DESTROYED ALL HE HAD FOUGHT TO BUILD.
"THE PEOPLE MIRACULOUSLY ALL SURVIVED. AND FOUND THAT THE EXPLOSION THAT DESTROYED THEIR HABITAT ALSO GAVE THEM IMMORTALITY AND INDESTRUCTIBILITY.
"THESE PEOPLE ARE KNOW AS THE ETERNALS.
"BUT THERE WAS MORE TO CHRONOS' LEGACY THAN AGELESSNESS.
"THERE WAS T UNI-MIND.
"A STATE OF BEI IN WHICH EVERY ETERNAL MAY SHA IN THE THOUGHT AND ASPIRATION OF HIS FELLOW ETERNALS.
"THIS WAS CHRONOS' PROMI THAT THE ETERNAL SOCIE NEED NEVER BE DIVIDED T WAY CHRONOS AND URANU ONCE WERE.
"THIS IS HOW CHRON BROUGHT PEACE T HIS KINGDOM."

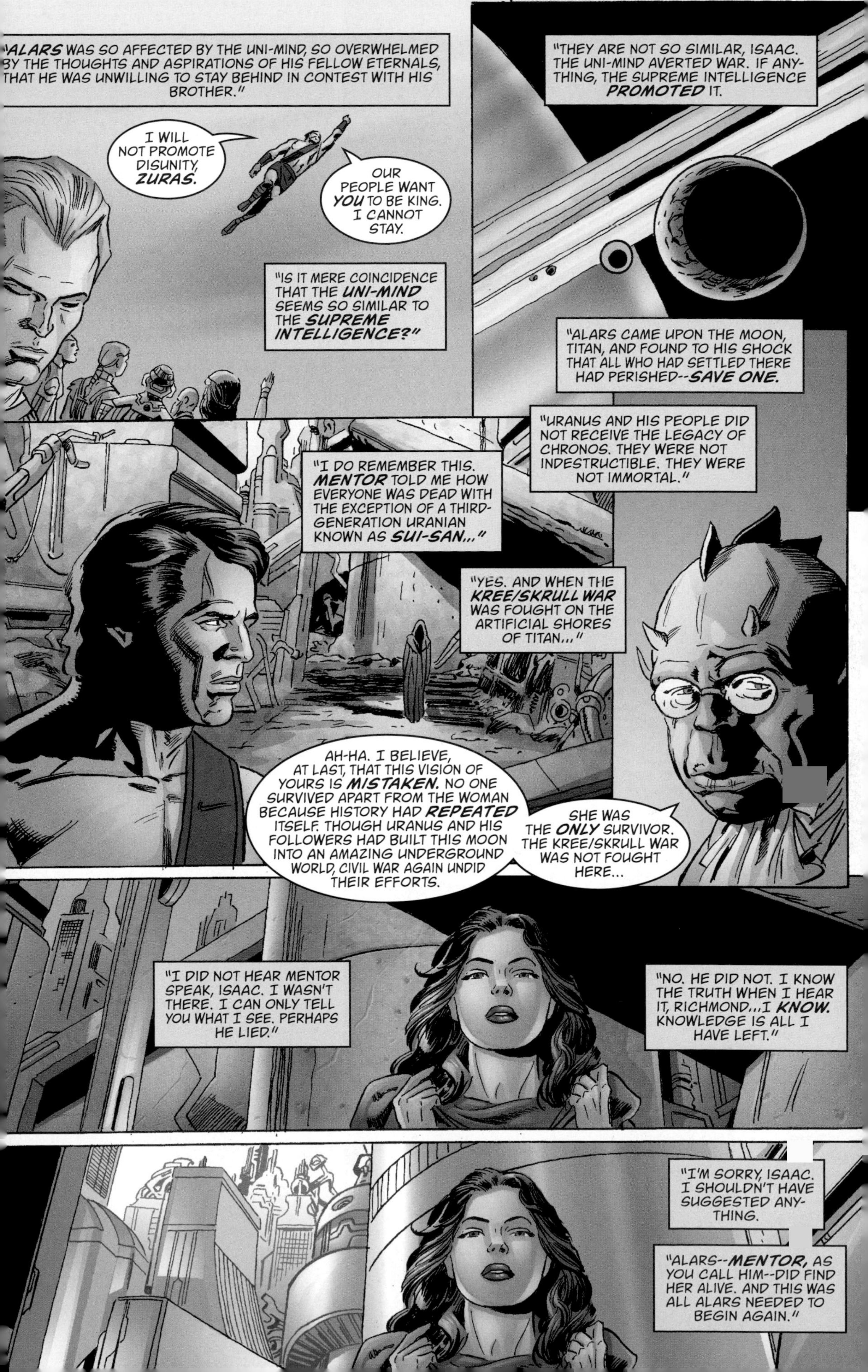
"ALARS WAS SO AFFECTED BY THE UNI-MIND, SO OVERWHELMED BY THE THOUGHTS AND ASPIRATIONS OF HIS FELLOW ETERNALS, THAT HE WAS UNWILLING TO STAY BEHIND IN CONTEST WITH HIS BROTHER."
I WILL NOT PROMOTE DISUNITY, ZURAS.
OUR PEOPLE WANT YOU TO BE KING. I CANNOT STAY.
"IS IT MERE COINCIDENCE THAT THE UNI-MIND SEEMS SO SIMILAR TO THE SUPREME INTELLIGENCE?"
"THEY ARE NOT SO SIMILAR, ISAAC. THE UNI-MIND AVERTED WAR. IF ANYTHING, THE SUPREME INTELLIGENCE PROMOTED IT.
"ALARS CAME UPON THE MOON, TITAN, AND FOUND TO HIS SHOCK THAT ALL WHO HAD SETTLED THERE HAD PERISHED--SAVE ONE.
"URANUS AND HIS PEOPLE DID NOT RECEIVE THE LEGACY OF CHRONOS. THEY WERE NOT INDESTRUCTIBLE. THEY WERE NOT IMMORTAL."
"I DO REMEMBER THIS. MENTOR TOLD ME HOW EVERYONE WAS DEAD WITH THE EXCEPTION OF A THIRD-GENERATION URANIAN KNOWN AS SUI-SAN..."
"YES. AND WHEN THE KREE/SKRULL WAR WAS FOUGHT ON THE ARTIFICIAL SHORES OF TITAN..."
AH-HA. I BELIEVE, AT LAST, THAT THIS VISION OF YOURS IS MISTAKEN. NO ONE SURVIVED APART FROM THE WOMAN BECAUSE HISTORY HAD REPEATED ITSELF. THOUGH URANUS AND HIS FOLLOWERS HAD BUILT THIS MOON INTO AN AMAZING UNDERGROUND WORLD, CIVIL WAR AGAIN UNDID THEIR EFFORTS.
SHE WAS THE ONLY SURVIVOR. THE KREE/SKRULL WAR WAS NOT FOUGHT HERE...
"I DID NOT HEAR MENTOR SPEAK, ISAAC. I WASN'T THERE. I CAN ONLY TELL YOU WHAT I SEE. PERHAPS HE LIED."
"NO. HE DID NOT. I KNOW THE TRUTH WHEN I HEAR IT, RICHMOND...I KNOW. KNOWLEDGE IS ALL I HAVE LEFT."
"I'M SORRY, ISAAC. I SHOULDN'T HAVE SUGGESTED ANYTHING.
"ALARS--MENTOR, AS YOU CALL HIM--DID FIND HER ALIVE. AND THIS WAS ALL ALARS NEEDED TO BEGIN AGAIN."

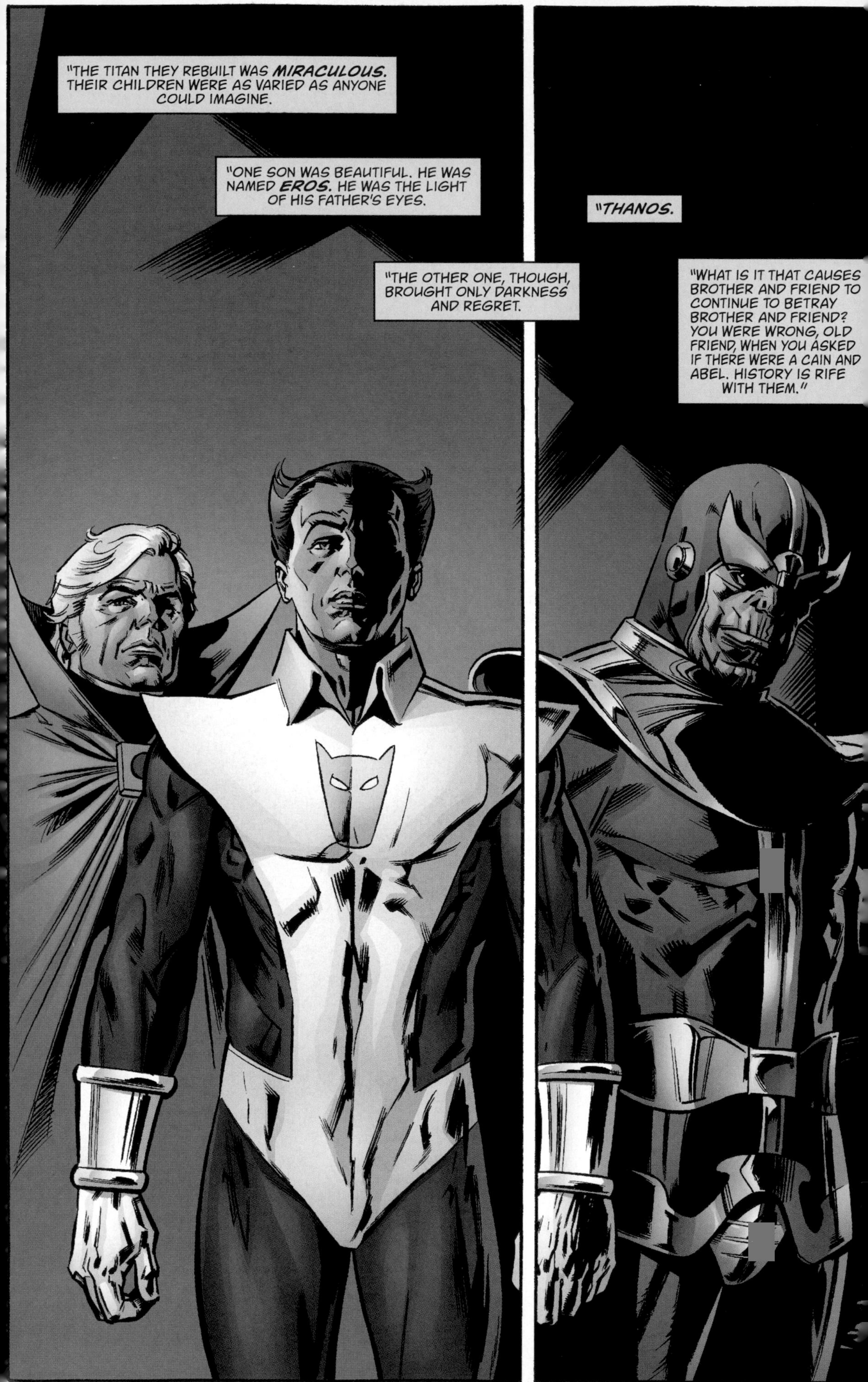
"THE TITAN THEY REBUILT WAS MIRACULOUS. THEIR CHILDREN WERE AS VARIED AS ANYONE COULD IMAGINE.
"ONE SON WAS BEAUTIFUL. HE WAS NAMED EROS. HE WAS THE LIGHT OF HIS FATHER'S EYES.
"THE OTHER ONE, THOUGH, BROUGHT ONLY DARKNESS AND REGRET.
"THANOS.
"WHAT IS IT THAT CAUSES BROTHER AND FRIEND TO CONTINUE TO BETRAY BROTHER AND FRIEND? YOU WERE WRONG, OLD FRIEND, WHEN YOU ASKED IF THERE WERE A CAIN AND ABEL. HISTORY IS RIFE WITH THEM."

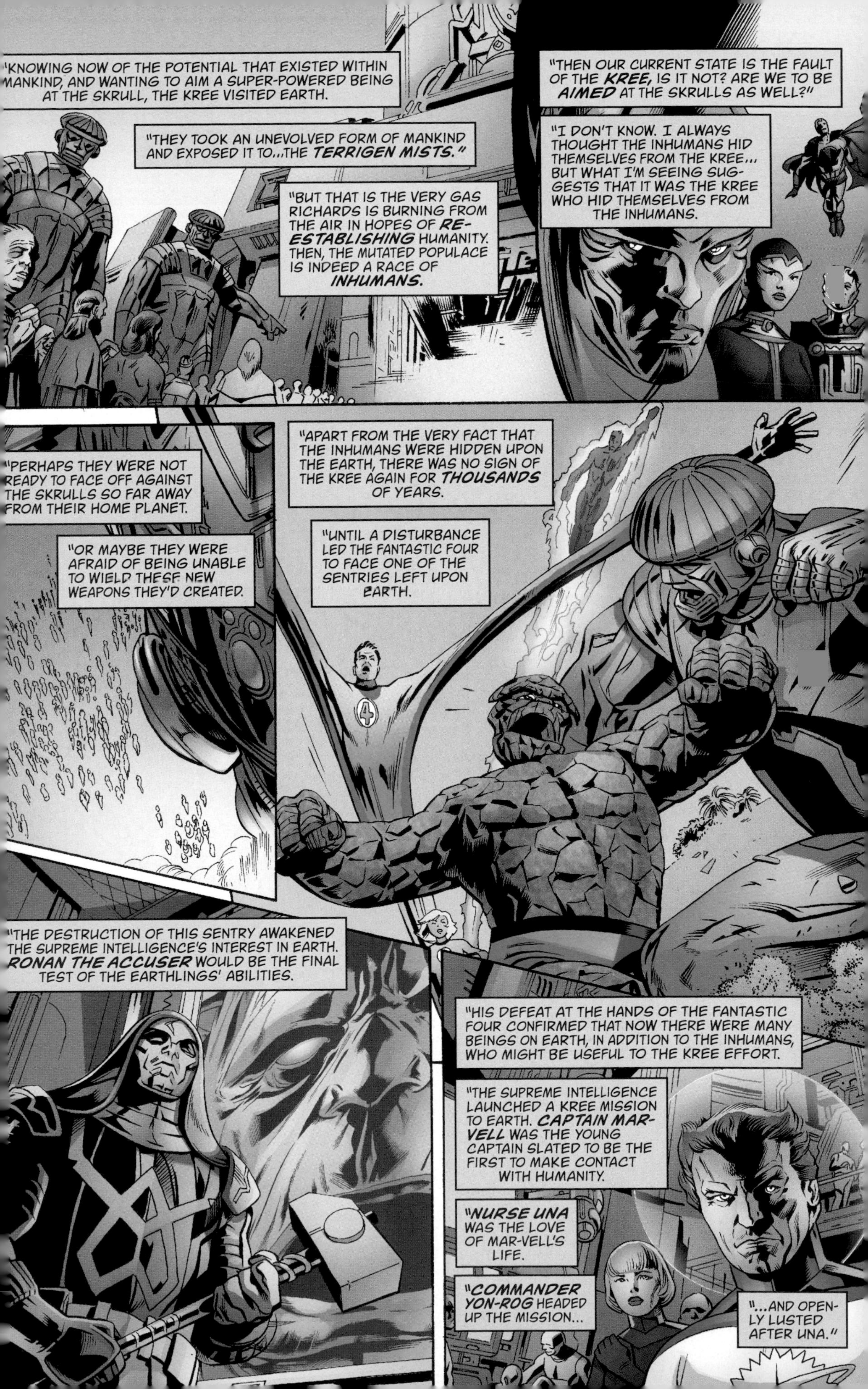
"KNOWING NOW OF THE POTENTIAL THAT EXISTED WITHIN MANKIND, AND WANTING TO AIM A SUPER-POWERED BEING AT THE SKRULL, THE KREE VISITED EARTH.
"THEY TOOK AN UNEVOLVED FORM OF MANKIND AND EXPOSED IT TO...THE TERRIGEN MISTS."
"BUT THAT IS THE VERY GAS RICHARDS IS BURNING FROM THE AIR IN HOPES OF RE-ESTABLISHING HUMANITY. THEN, THE MUTATED POPULACE IS INDEED A RACE OF INHUMANS.
"THEN OUR CURRENT STATE IS THE FAULT OF THE KREE, IS IT NOT? ARE WE TO BE AIMED AT THE SKRULLS AS WELL?"
"I DON'T KNOW. I ALWAYS THOUGHT THE INHUMANS HID THEMSELVES FROM THE KREE... BUT WHAT I'M SEEING SUGGESTS THAT IT WAS THE KREE WHO HID THEMSELVES FROM THE INHUMANS.
"PERHAPS THEY WERE NOT READY TO FACE OFF AGAINST THE SKRULLS SO FAR AWAY FROM THEIR HOME PLANET.
"OR MAYBE THEY WERE AFRAID OF BEING UNABLE TO WIELD THESE NEW WEAPONS THEY'D CREATED.
"APART FROM THE VERY FACT THAT THE INHUMANS WERE HIDDEN UPON THE EARTH, THERE WAS NO SIGN OF THE KREE AGAIN FOR THOUSANDS OF YEARS.
"UNTIL A DISTURBANCE LED THE FANTASTIC FOUR TO FACE ONE OF THE SENTRIES LEFT UPON EARTH.
"THE DESTRUCTION OF THIS SENTRY AWAKENED THE SUPREME INTELLIGENCE'S INTEREST IN EARTH. RONAN THE ACCUSER WOULD BE THE FINAL TEST OF THE EARTHLINGS' ABILITIES.
"HIS DEFEAT AT THE HANDS OF THE FANTASTIC FOUR CONFIRMED THAT NOW THERE WERE MANY BEINGS ON EARTH, IN ADDITION TO THE INHUMANS, WHO MIGHT BE USEFUL TO THE KREE EFFORT.
"THE SUPREME INTELLIGENCE LAUNCHED A KREE MISSION TO EARTH. CAPTAIN MAR-VELL WAS THE YOUNG CAPTAIN SLATED TO BE THE FIRST TO MAKE CONTACT WITH HUMANITY.
"NURSE UNA WAS THE LOVE OF MAR-VELL'S LIFE.
"COMMANDER YON-ROG HEADED UP THE MISSION...
"...AND OPENLY LUSTED AFTER UNA."

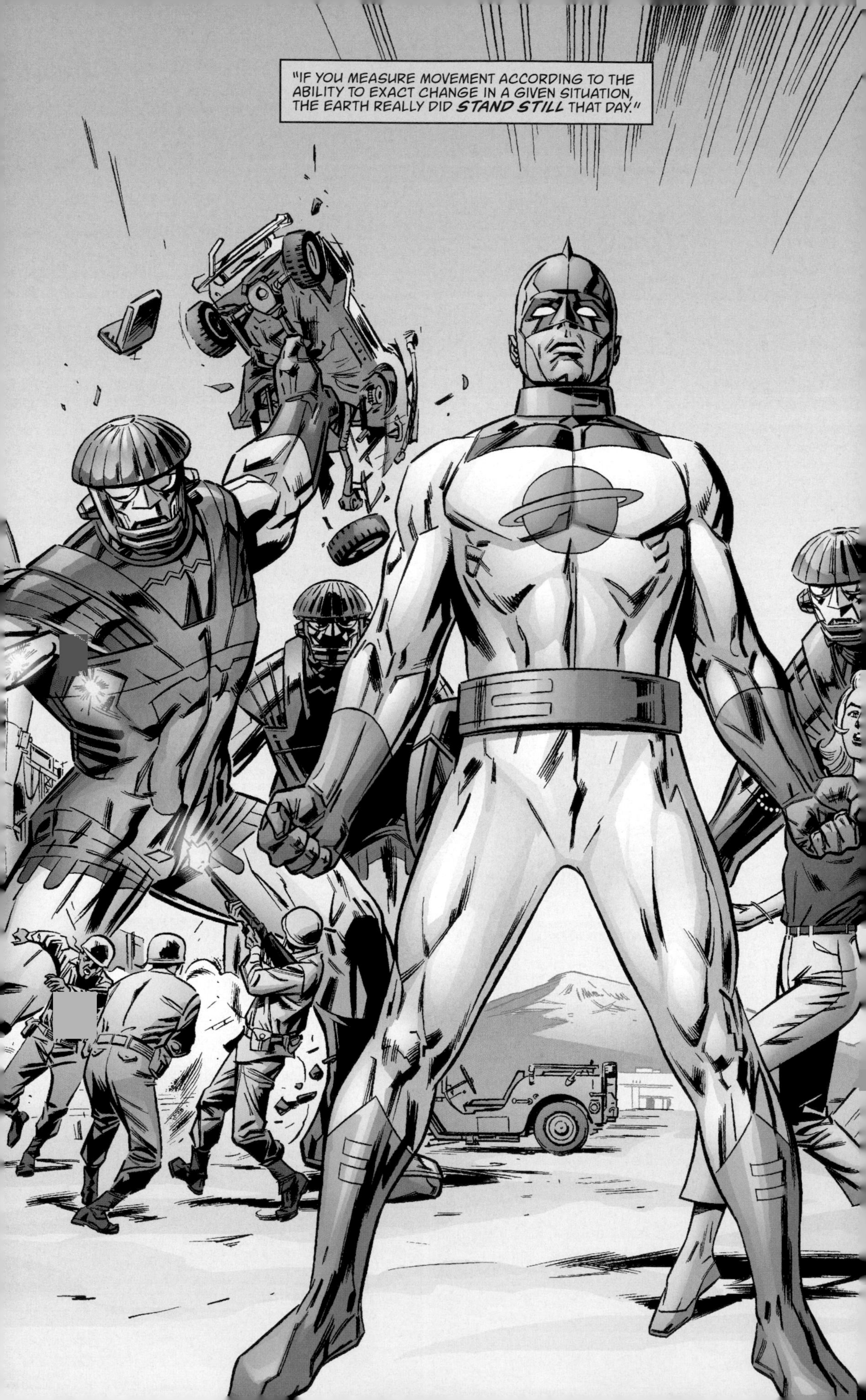
"IF YOU MEASURE MOVEMENT ACCORDING TO THE ABILITY TO EXACT CHANGE IN A GIVEN SITUATION, THE EARTH REALLY DID STAND STILL THAT DAY."

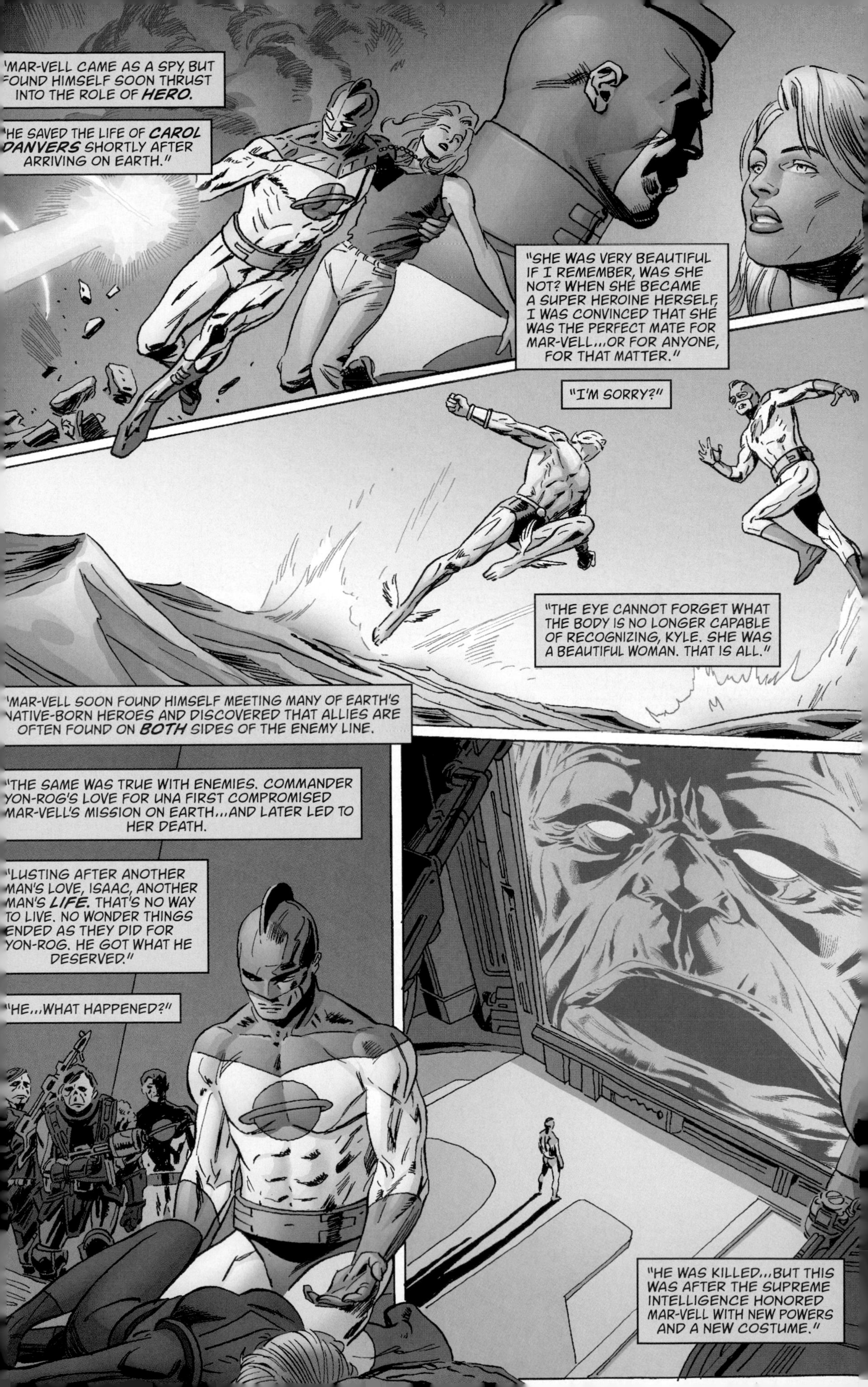
"MAR-VELL CAME AS A SPY, BUT FOUND HIMSELF SOON THRUST INTO THE ROLE OF HERO.
"HE SAVED THE LIFE OF CAROL DANVERS SHORTLY AFTER ARRIVING ON EARTH."
"SHE WAS VERY BEAUTIFUL IF I REMEMBER, WAS SHE NOT? WHEN SHE BECAME A SUPER HEROINE HERSELF, I WAS CONVINCED THAT SHE WAS THE PERFECT MATE FOR MAR-VELL...OR FOR ANYONE, FOR THAT MATTER."
"I'M SORRY?"
"THE EYE CANNOT FORGET WHAT THE BODY IS NO LONGER CAPABLE OF RECOGNIZING, KYLE. SHE WAS A BEAUTIFUL WOMAN. THAT IS ALL."
"MAR-VELL SOON FOUND HIMSELF MEETING MANY OF EARTH'S NATIVE-BORN HEROES AND DISCOVERED THAT ALLIES ARE OFTEN FOUND ON BOTH SIDES OF THE ENEMY LINE.
"THE SAME WAS TRUE WITH ENEMIES. COMMANDER YON-ROG'S LOVE FOR UNA FIRST COMPROMISED MAR-VELL'S MISSION ON EARTH...AND LATER LED TO HER DEATH.
"LUSTING AFTER ANOTHER MAN'S LOVE, ISAAC, ANOTHER MAN'S LIFE. THAT'S NO WAY TO LIVE. NO WONDER THINGS ENDED AS THEY DID FOR YON-ROG. HE GOT WHAT HE DESERVED."
"HE...WHAT HAPPENED?"
"HE WAS KILLED...BUT THIS WAS AFTER THE SUPREME INTELLIGENCE HONORED MAR-VELL WITH NEW POWERS AND A NEW COSTUME."

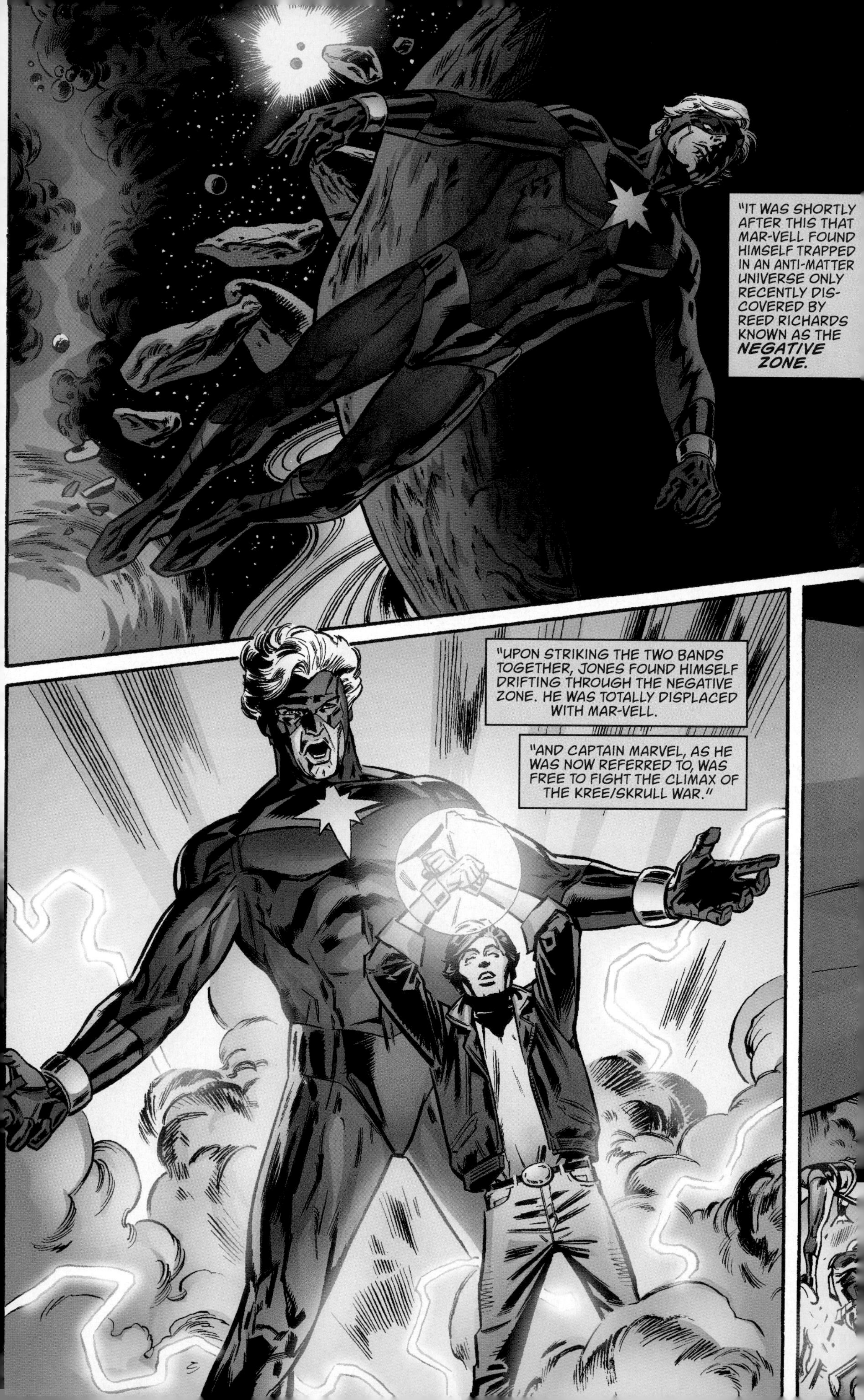
"IT WAS SHORTLY AFTER THIS THAT MAR-VELL FOUND HIMSELF TRAPPED IN AN ANTI-MATTER UNIVERSE ONLY RECENTLY DISCOVERED BY REED RICHARDS KNOWN AS THE NEGATIVE ZONE.
"UPON STRIKING THE TWO BANDS TOGETHER, JONES FOUND HIMSELF DRIFTING THROUGH THE NEGATIVE ZONE. HE WAS TOTALLY DISPLACED WITH MAR-VELL.
"AND CAPTAIN MARVEL, AS HE WAS NOW REFERRED TO, WAS FREE TO FIGHT THE CLIMAX OF THE KREE/SKRULL WAR."

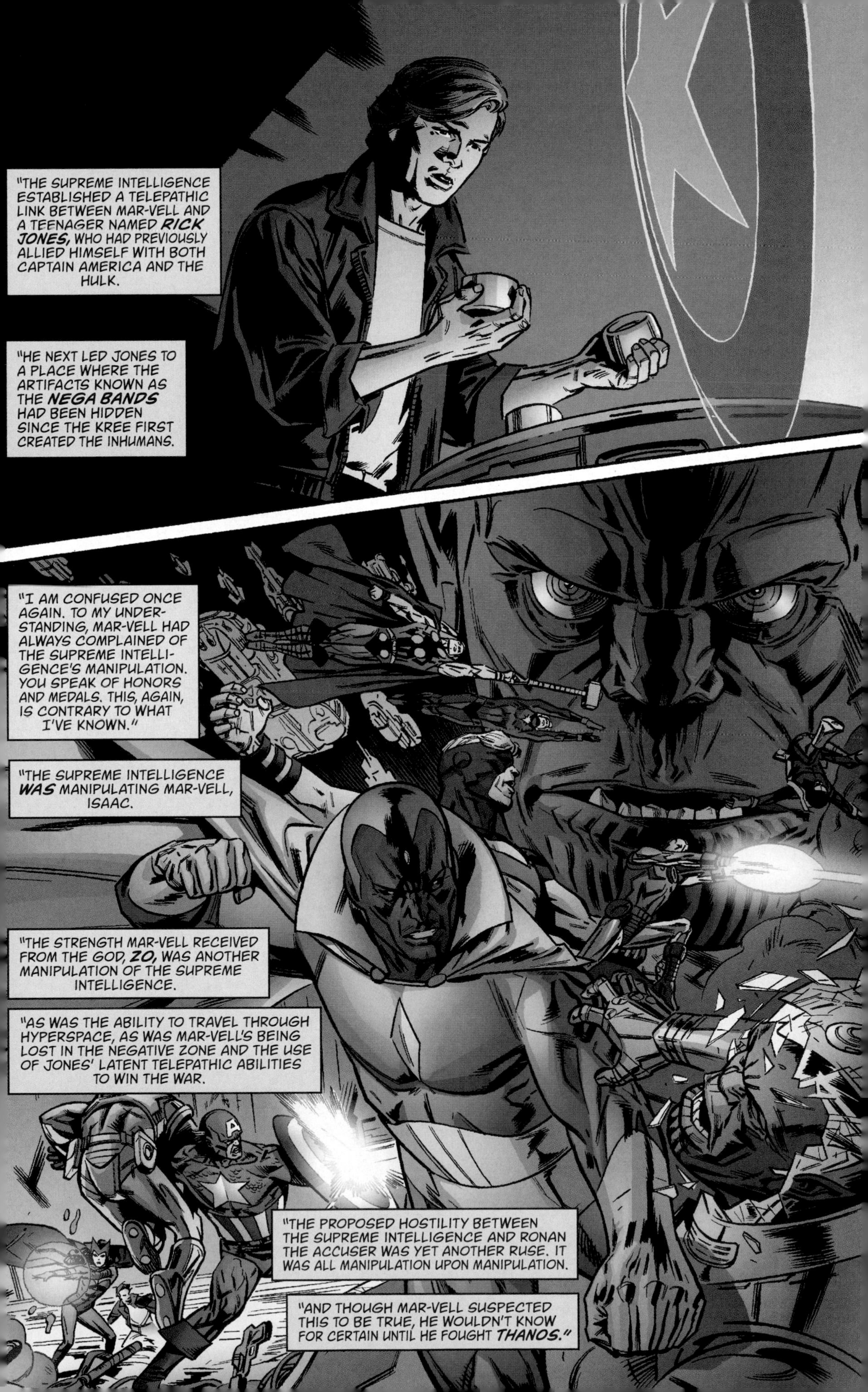
"THE SUPREME INTELLIGENCE ESTABLISHED A TELEPATHIC LINK BETWEEN MAR-VELL AND A TEENAGER NAMED RICK JONES, WHO HAD PREVIOUSLY ALLIED HIMSELF WITH BOTH CAPTAIN AMERICA AND THE HULK.
"HE NEXT LED JONES TO A PLACE WHERE THE ARTIFACTS KNOWN AS THE NEGA BANDS HAD BEEN HIDDEN SINCE THE KREE FIRST CREATED THE INHUMANS.
"I AM CONFUSED ONCE AGAIN. TO MY UNDERSTANDING, MAR-VELL HAD ALWAYS COMPLAINED OF THE SUPREME INTELLIGENCE'S MANIPULATION. YOU SPEAK OF HONORS AND MEDALS. THIS, AGAIN, IS CONTRARY TO WHAT I'VE KNOWN."
"THE SUPREME INTELLIGENCE WAS MANIPULATING MAR-VELL, ISAAC.
"THE STRENGTH MAR-VELL RECEIVED FROM THE GOD, ZO, WAS ANOTHER MANIPULATION OF THE SUPREME INTELLIGENCE.
"AS WAS THE ABILITY TO TRAVEL THROUGH HYPERSPACE, AS WAS MAR-VELL'S BEING LOST IN THE NEGATIVE ZONE AND THE USE OF JONES' LATENT TELEPATHIC ABILITIES TO WIN THE WAR.
"THE PROPOSED HOSTILITY BETWEEN THE SUPREME INTELLIGENCE AND RONAN THE ACCUSER WAS YET ANOTHER RUSE. IT WAS ALL MANIPULATION UPON MANIPULATION.
"AND THOUGH MAR-VELL SUSPECTED THIS TO BE TRUE, HE WOULDN'T KNOW FOR CERTAIN UNTIL HE FOUGHT THANOS."

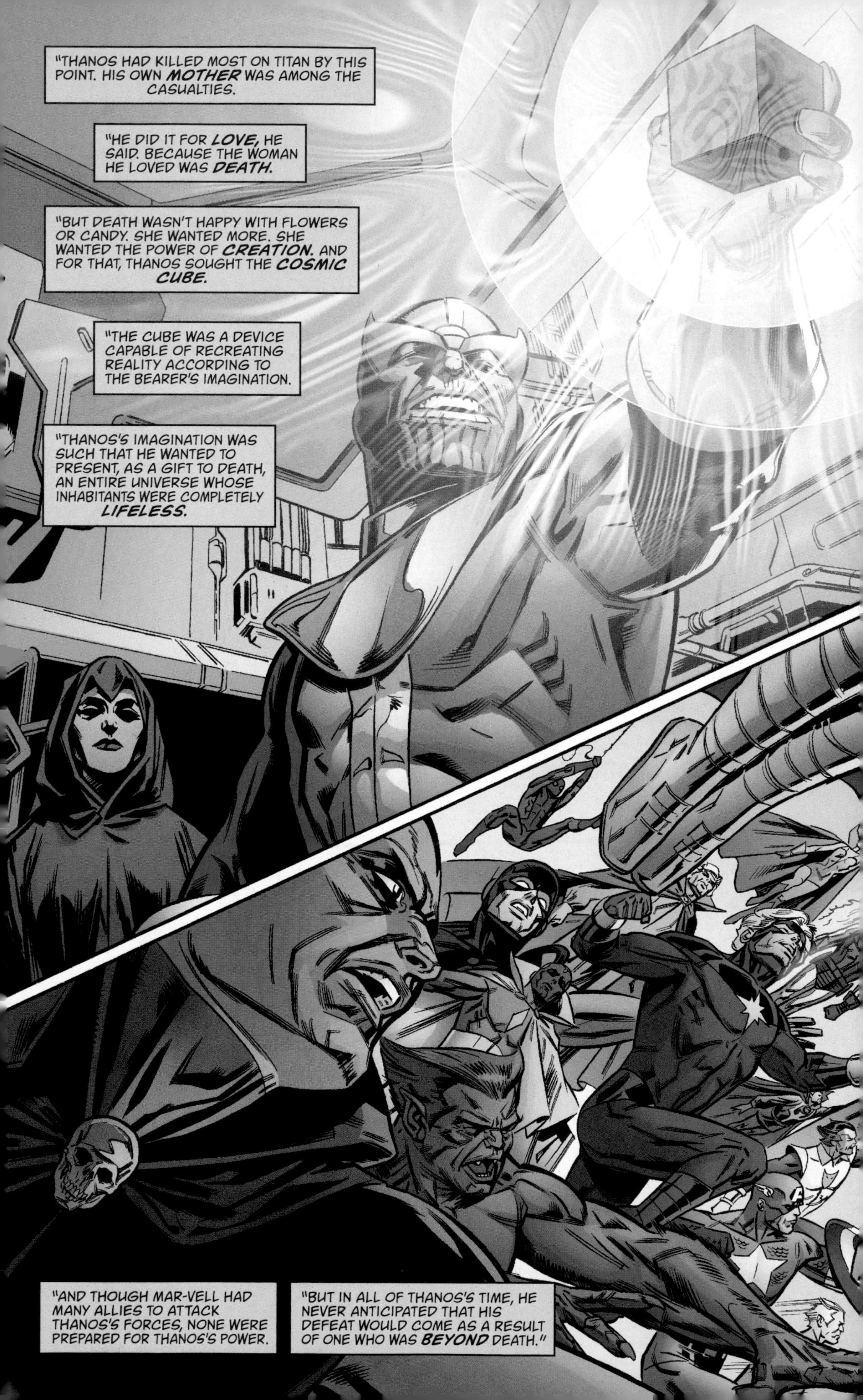
"THANOS HAD KILLED MOST ON TITAN BY THIS POINT. HIS OWN MOTHER WAS AMONG THE CASUALTIES.
"HE DID IT FOR LOVE, HE SAID. BECAUSE THE WOMAN HE LOVED WAS DEATH.
"BUT DEATH WASN'T HAPPY WITH FLOWERS OR CANDY. SHE WANTED MORE. SHE WANTED THE POWER OF CREATION. AND FOR THAT, THANOS SOUGHT THE COSMIC CUBE.
"THE CUBE WAS A DEVICE CAPABLE OF RECREATING REALITY ACCORDING TO THE BEARER'S IMAGINATION.
"THANOS'S IMAGINATION WAS SUCH THAT HE WANTED TO PRESENT, AS A GIFT TO DEATH, AN ENTIRE UNIVERSE WHOSE INHABITANTS WERE COMPLETELY LIFELESS.
"AND THOUGH MAR-VELL HAD MANY ALLIES TO ATTACK THANOS'S FORCES, NONE WERE PREPARED FOR THANOS'S POWER.
"BUT IN ALL OF THANOS'S TIME, HE NEVER ANTICIPATED THAT HIS DEFEAT WOULD COME AS A RESULT OF ONE WHO WAS BEYOND DEATH."

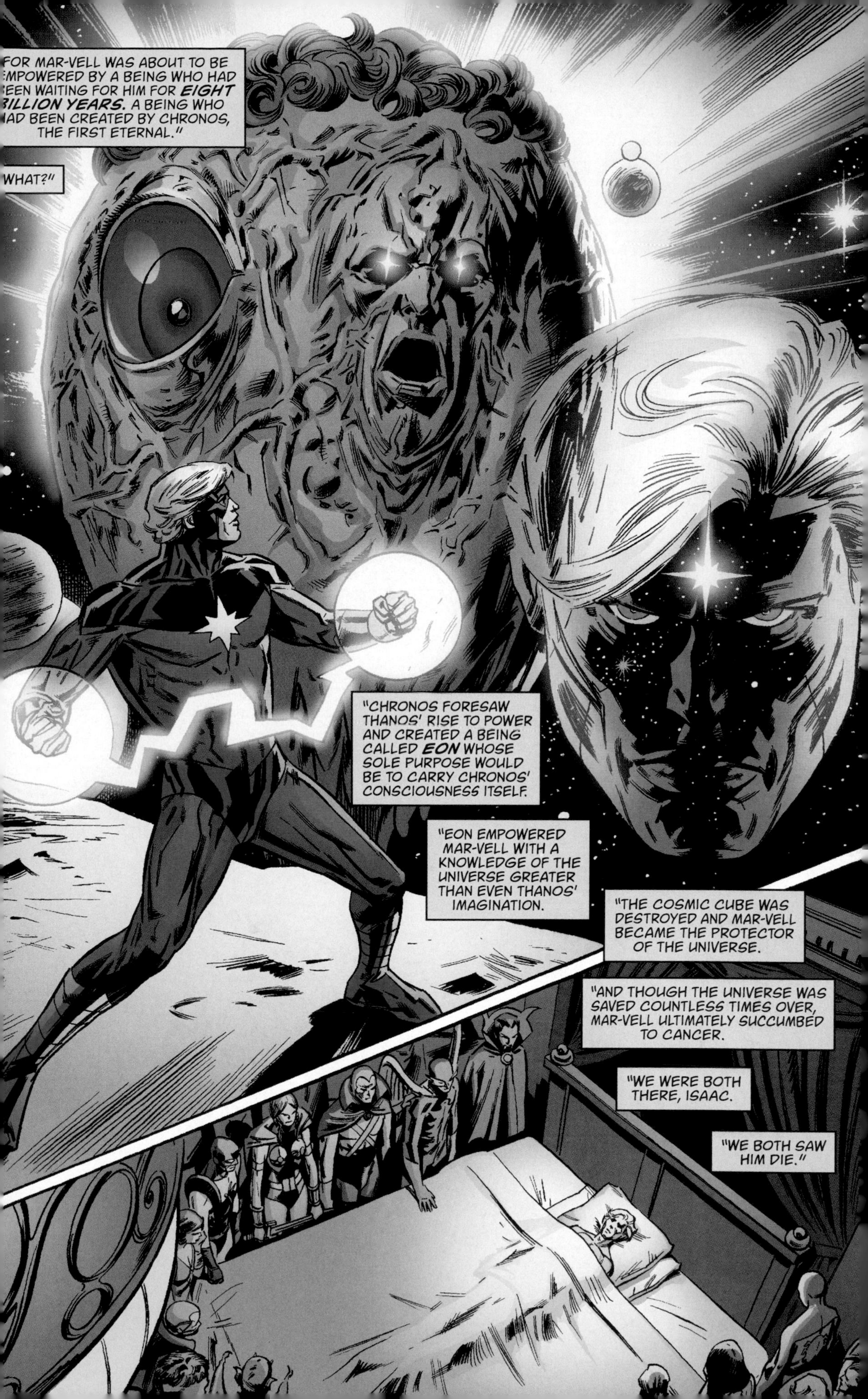
FOR MAR-VELL WAS ABOUT TO BE EMPOWERED BY A BEING WHO HAD BEEN WAITING FOR HIM FOR EIGHT BILLION YEARS. A BEING WHO HAD BEEN CREATED BY CHRONOS, THE FIRST ETERNAL."
WHAT?"
"CHRONOS FORESAW THANOS' RISE TO POWER AND CREATED A BEING CALLED EON WHOSE SOLE PURPOSE WOULD BE TO CARRY CHRONOS' CONSCIOUSNESS ITSELF.
"EON EMPOWERED MAR-VELL WITH A KNOWLEDGE OF THE UNIVERSE GREATER THAN EVEN THANOS' IMAGINATION.
"THE COSMIC CUBE WAS DESTROYED AND MAR-VELL BECAME THE PROTECTOR OF THE UNIVERSE.
"AND THOUGH THE UNIVERSE WAS SAVED COUNTLESS TIMES OVER, MAR-VELL ULTIMATELY SUCCUMBED TO CANCER.
"WE WERE BOTH THERE, ISAAC.
"WE BOTH SAW HIM DIE."

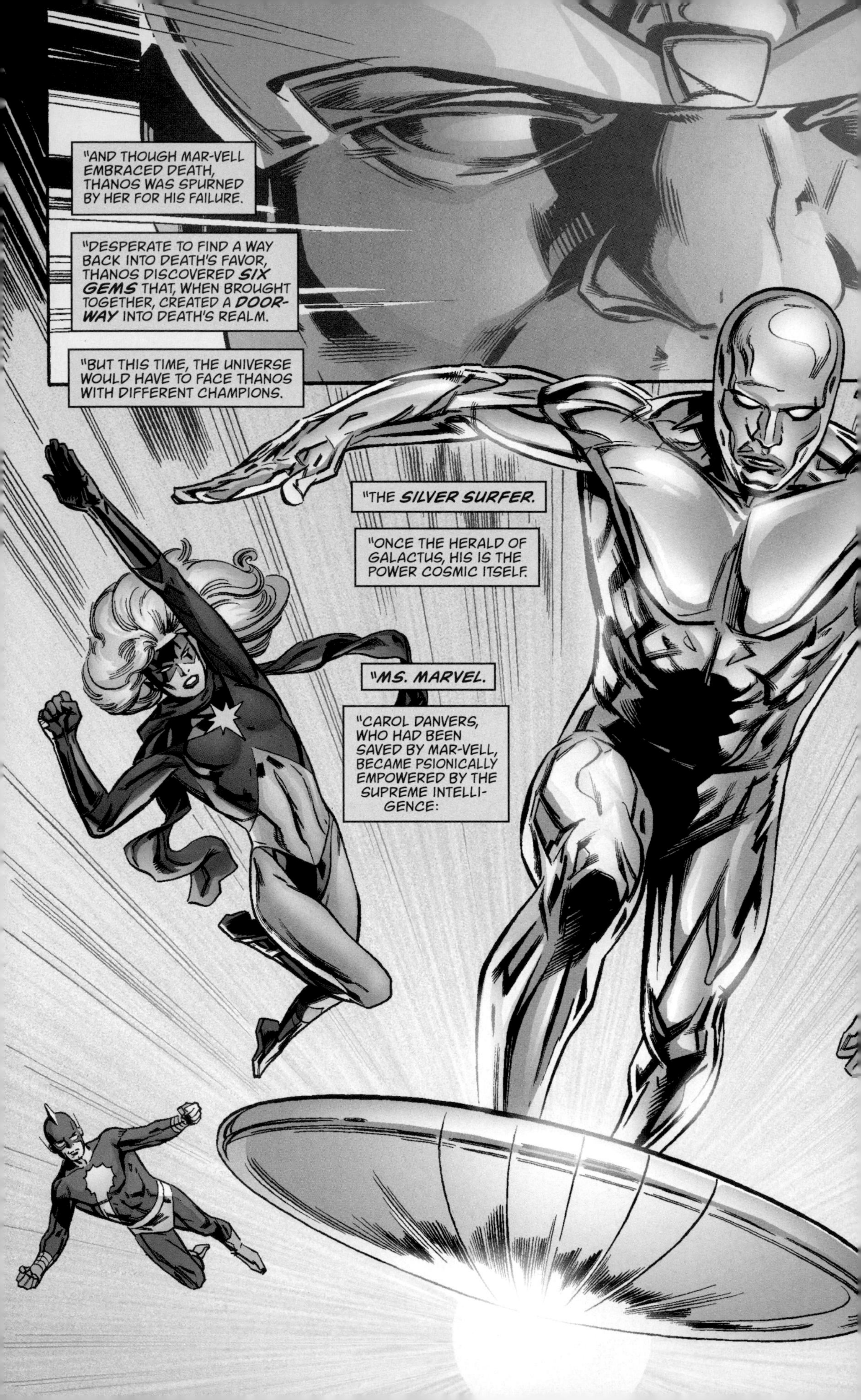
"AND THOUGH MAR-VELL EMBRACED DEATH, THANOS WAS SPURNED BY HER FOR HIS FAILURE.
"DESPERATE TO FIND A WAY BACK INTO DEATH'S FAVOR, THANOS DISCOVERED *SIX GEMS* THAT, WHEN BROUGHT TOGETHER, CREATED A *DOORWAY* INTO DEATH'S REALM.
"BUT THIS TIME, THE UNIVERSE WOULD HAVE TO FACE THANOS WITH DIFFERENT CHAMPIONS.
"THE *SILVER SURFER.*
"ONCE THE HERALD OF GALACTUS, HIS IS THE POWER COSMIC ITSELF.
"*MS. MARVEL.*
"CAROL DANVERS, WHO HAD BEEN SAVED BY MAR-VELL, BECAME PSIONICALLY EMPOWERED BY THE SUPREME INTELLIGENCE:

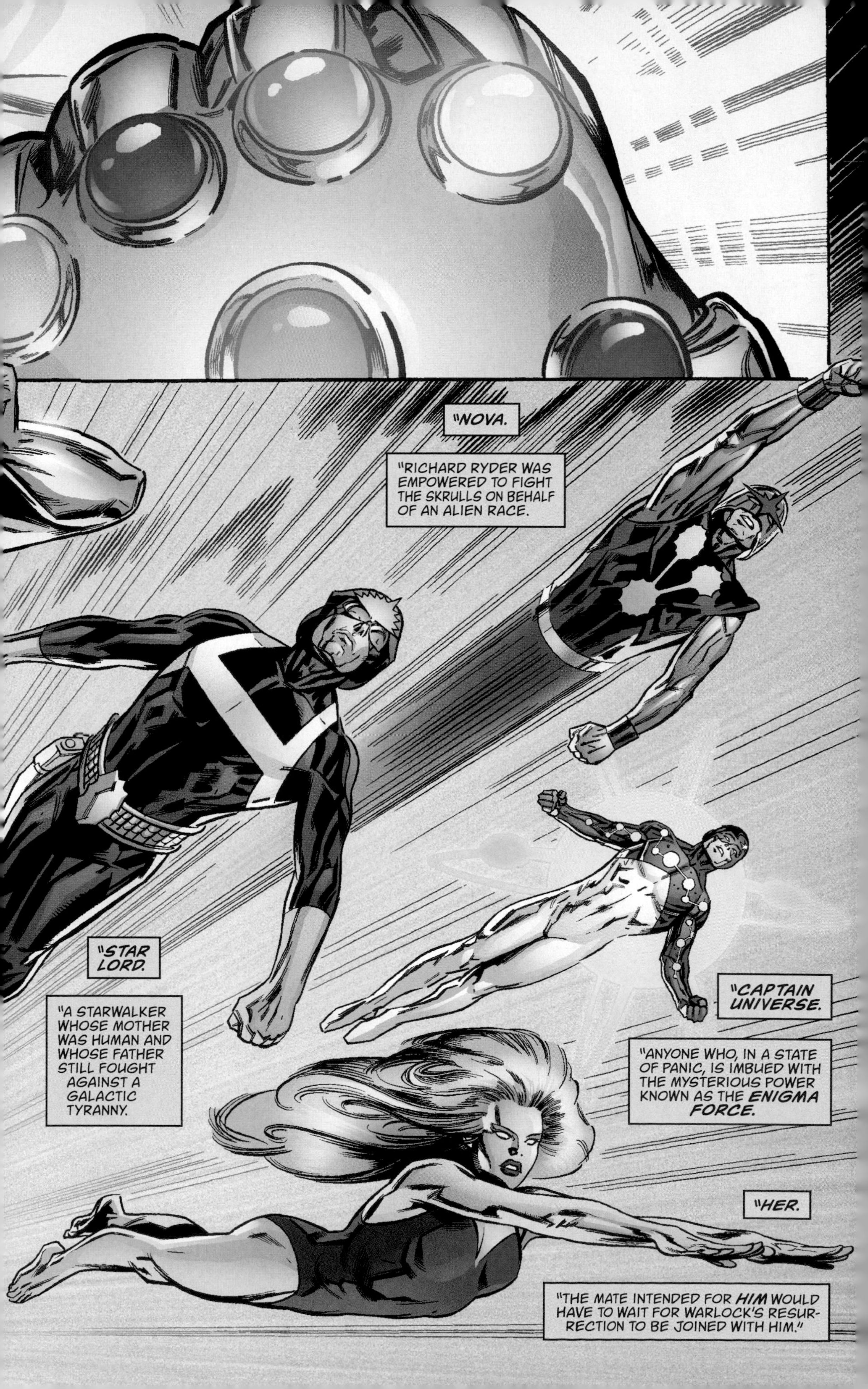
"NOVA.
"RICHARD RYDER WAS EMPOWERED TO FIGHT THE SKRULLS ON BEHALF OF AN ALIEN RACE.
"STAR LORD.
"A STARWALKER WHOSE MOTHER WAS HUMAN AND WHOSE FATHER STILL FOUGHT AGAINST A GALACTIC TYRANNY.
"CAPTAIN UNIVERSE.
"ANYONE WHO, IN A STATE OF PANIC, IS IMBUED WITH THE MYSTERIOUS POWER KNOWN AS THE ENIGMA FORCE.
"HER.
"THE MATE INTENDED FOR HIM WOULD HAVE TO WAIT FOR WARLOCK'S RESUR-RECTION TO BE JOINED WITH HIM."

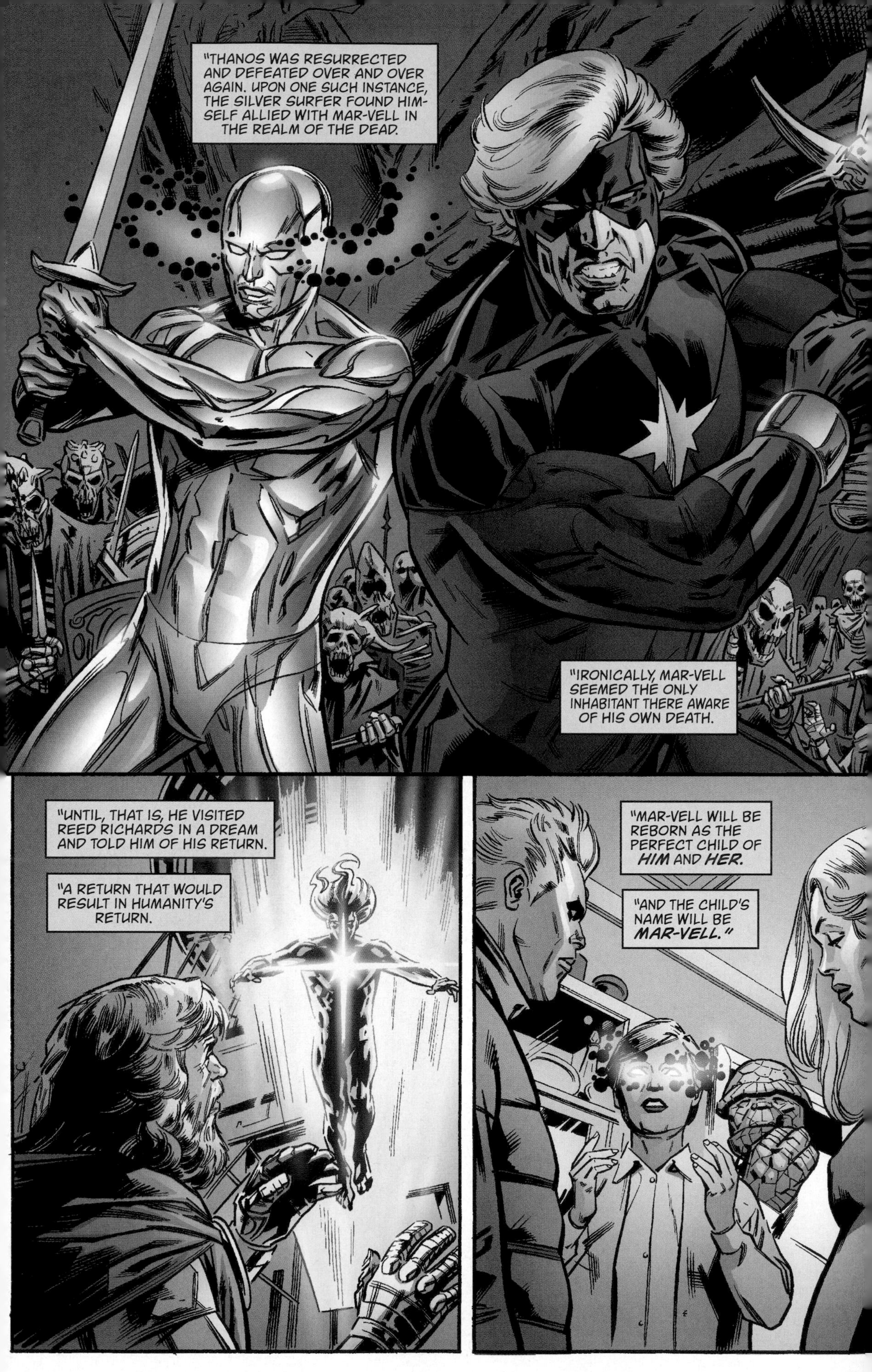
"THANOS WAS RESURRECTED AND DEFEATED OVER AND OVER AGAIN. UPON ONE SUCH INSTANCE, THE SILVER SURFER FOUND HIMSELF ALLIED WITH MAR-VELL IN THE REALM OF THE DEAD.
"IRONICALLY, MAR-VELL SEEMED THE ONLY INHABITANT THERE AWARE OF HIS OWN DEATH.
"UNTIL, THAT IS, HE VISITED REED RICHARDS IN A DREAM AND TOLD HIM OF HIS RETURN.
"A RETURN THAT WOULD RESULT IN HUMANITY'S RETURN.
"MAR-VELL WILL BE REBORN AS THE PERFECT CHILD OF ***HIM*** AND ***HER***.
"AND THE CHILD'S NAME WILL BE ***MAR-VELL.***"

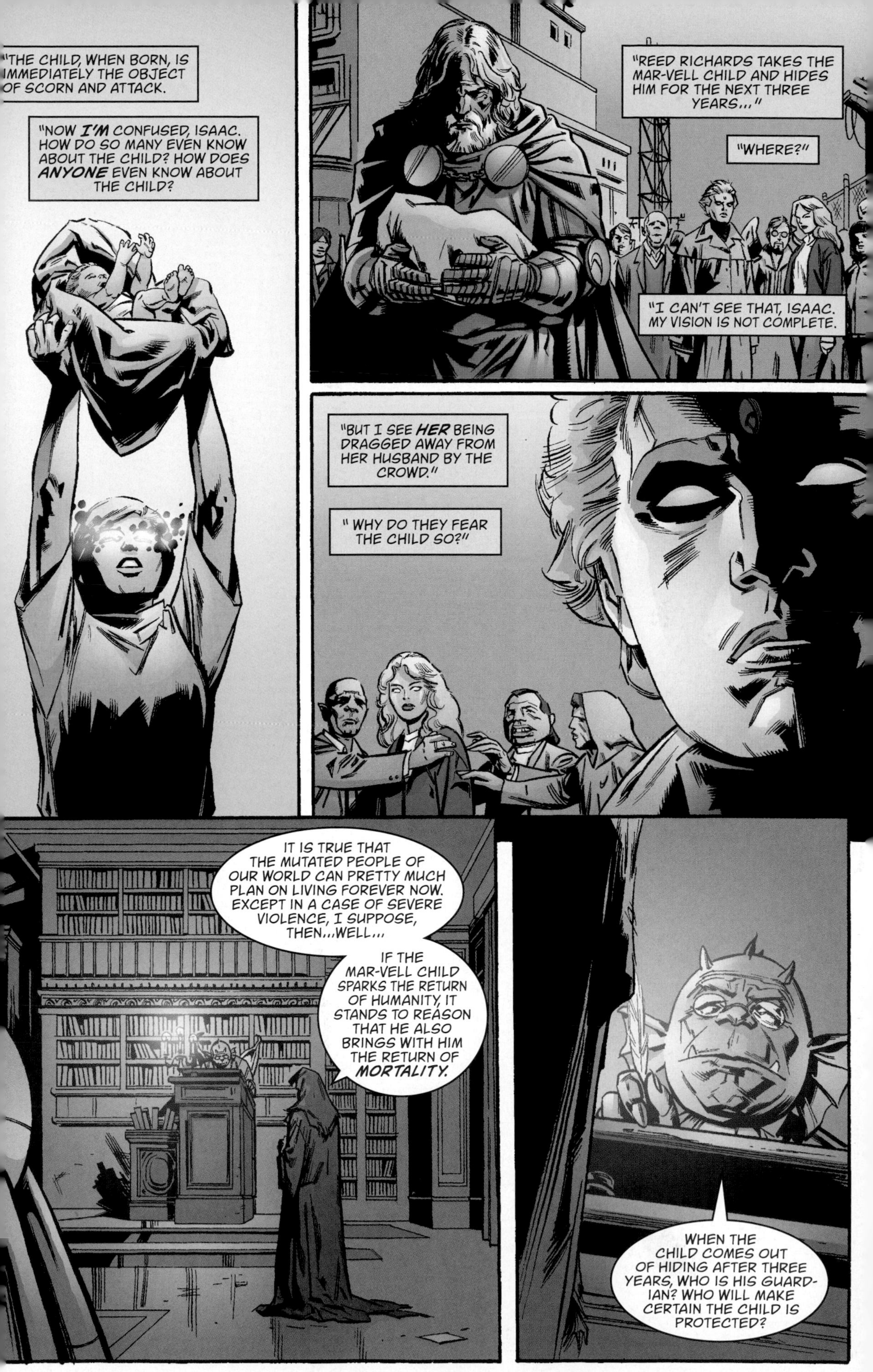
"THE CHILD, WHEN BORN, IS IMMEDIATELY THE OBJECT OF SCORN AND ATTACK.
"NOW I'M CONFUSED, ISAAC. HOW DO SO MANY EVEN KNOW ABOUT THE CHILD? HOW DOES ANYONE EVEN KNOW ABOUT THE CHILD?
"REED RICHARDS TAKES THE MAR-VELL CHILD AND HIDES HIM FOR THE NEXT THREE YEARS..."
"WHERE?"
"I CAN'T SEE THAT, ISAAC. MY VISION IS NOT COMPLETE.
"BUT I SEE HER BEING DRAGGED AWAY FROM HER HUSBAND BY THE CROWD."
" WHY DO THEY FEAR THE CHILD SO?"
IT IS TRUE THAT THE MUTATED PEOPLE OF OUR WORLD CAN PRETTY MUCH PLAN ON LIVING FOREVER NOW. EXCEPT IN A CASE OF SEVERE VIOLENCE, I SUPPOSE, THEN...WELL...
IF THE MAR-VELL CHILD SPARKS THE RETURN OF HUMANITY, IT STANDS TO REASON THAT HE ALSO BRINGS WITH HIM THE RETURN OF MORTALITY.
WHEN THE CHILD COMES OUT OF HIDING AFTER THREE YEARS, WHO IS HIS GUARDIAN? WHO WILL MAKE CERTAIN THE CHILD IS PROTECTED?

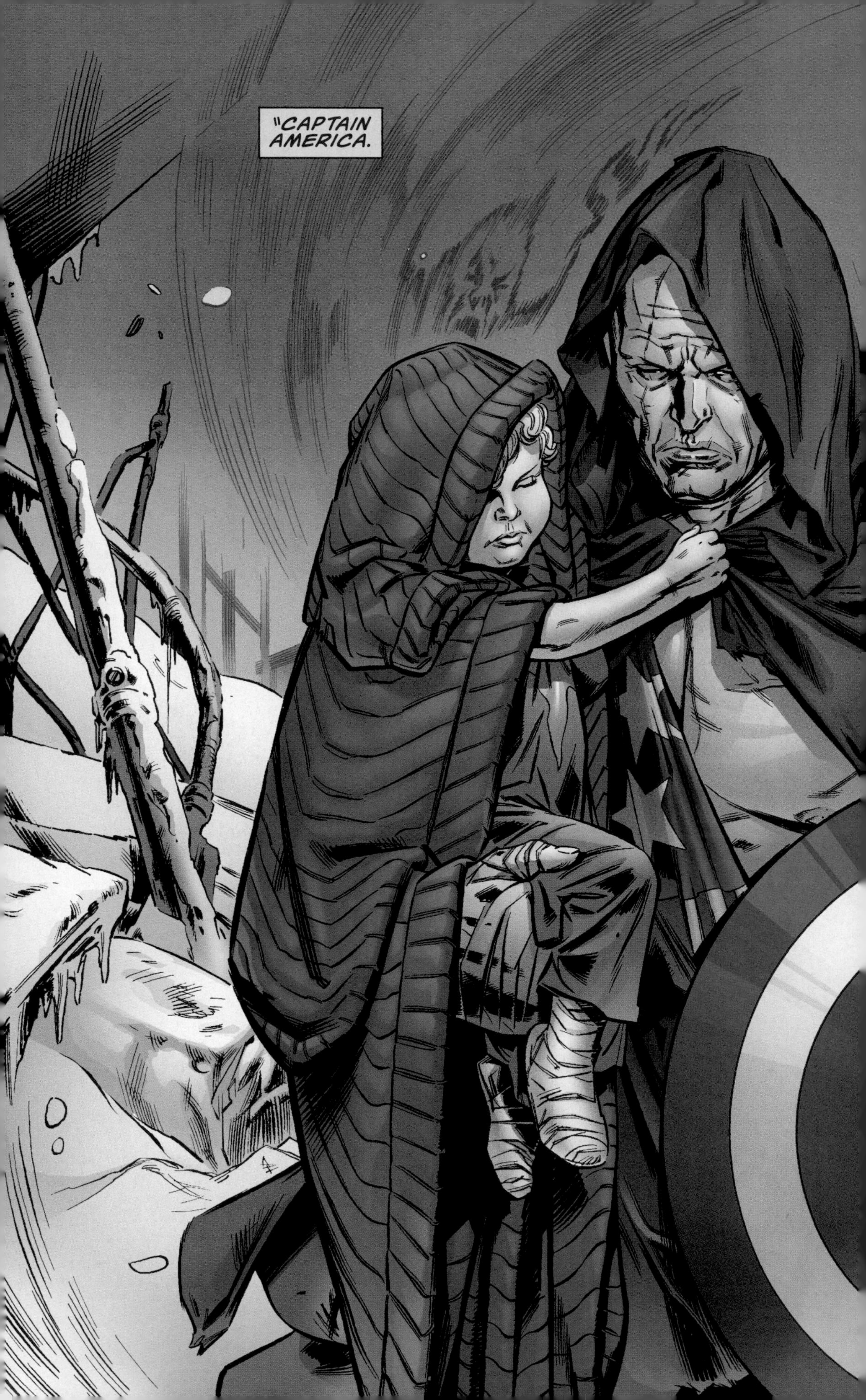
"CAPTAIN AMERICA.

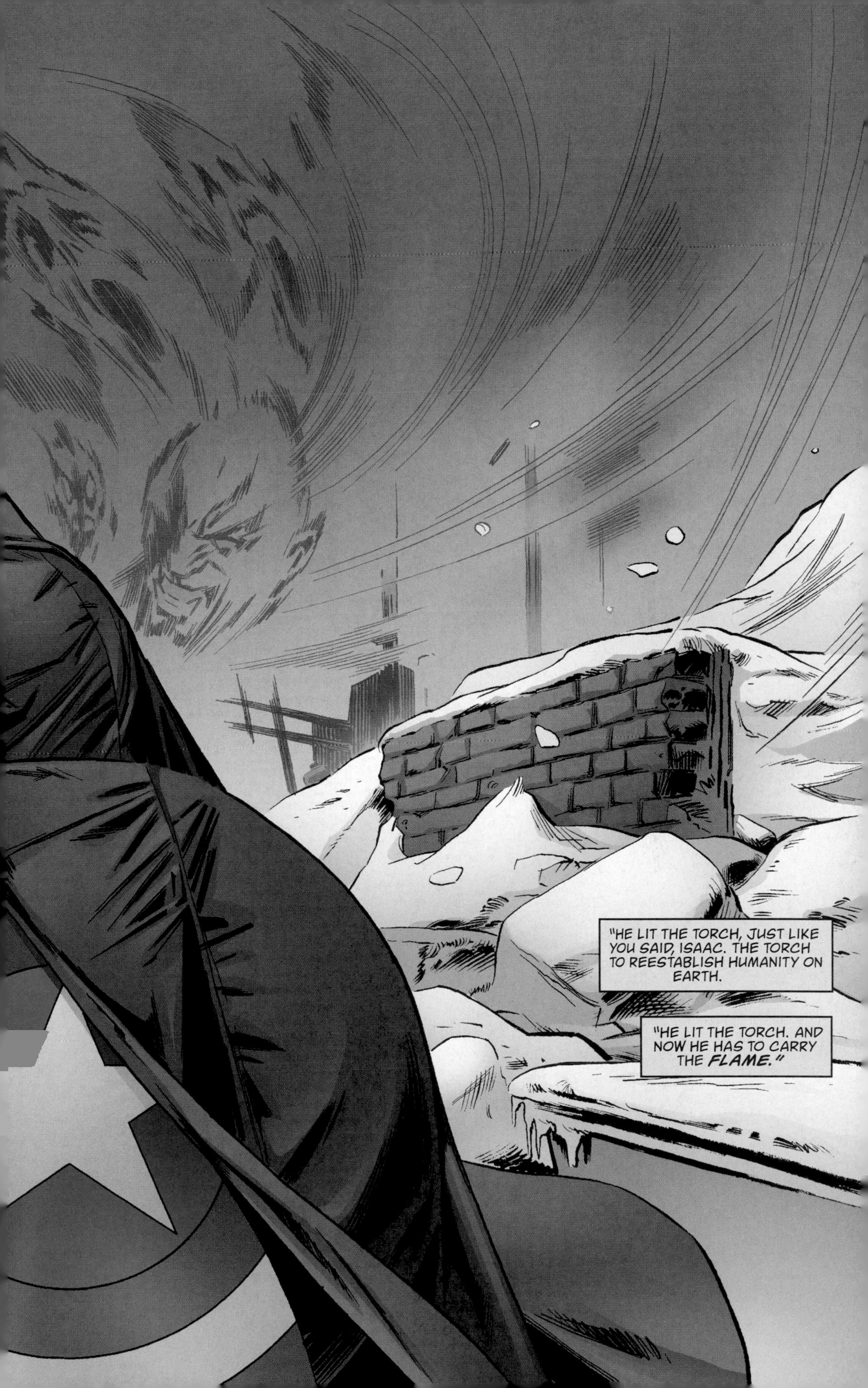
"HE LIT THE TORCH, JUST LIKE YOU SAID, ISAAC. THE TORCH TO REESTABLISH HUMANITY ON EARTH.
"HE LIT THE TORCH. AND NOW HE HAS TO CARRY THE *FLAME.*"

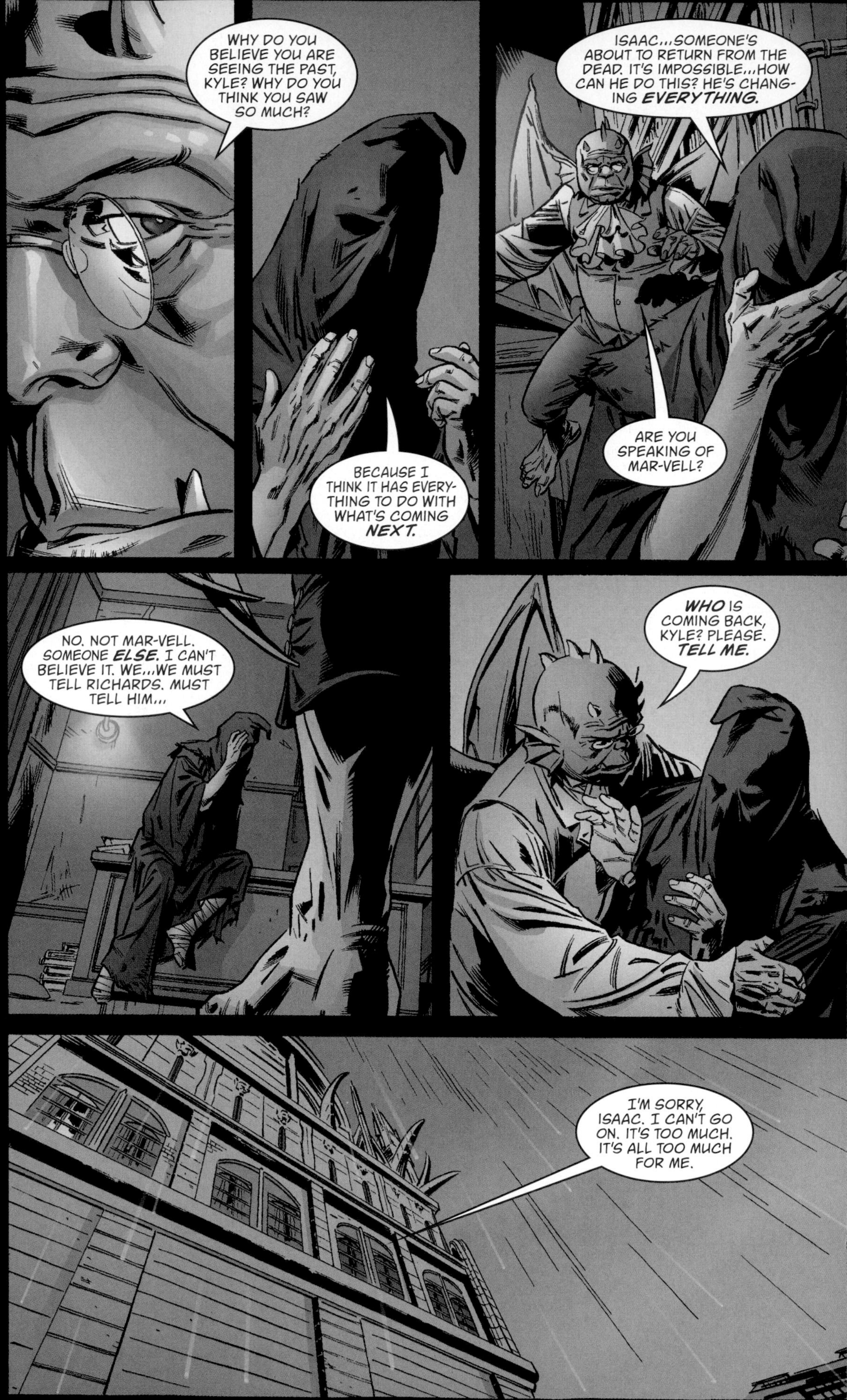
WHY DO YOU BELIEVE YOU ARE SEEING THE PAST, KYLE? WHY DO YOU THINK YOU SAW SO MUCH?
BECAUSE I THINK IT HAS EVERYTHING TO DO WITH WHAT'S COMING NEXT.
ISAAC...SOMEONE'S ABOUT TO RETURN FROM THE DEAD. IT'S IMPOSSIBLE...HOW CAN HE DO THIS? HE'S CHANGING EVERYTHING.
ARE YOU SPEAKING OF MAR-VELL?
NO. NOT MAR-VELL. SOMEONE ELSE. I CAN'T BELIEVE IT. WE...WE MUST TELL RICHARDS. MUST TELL HIM...
WHO IS COMING BACK, KYLE? PLEASE. TELL ME.
I'M SORRY, ISAAC. I CAN'T GO ON. IT'S TOO MUCH. IT'S ALL TOO MUCH FOR ME.

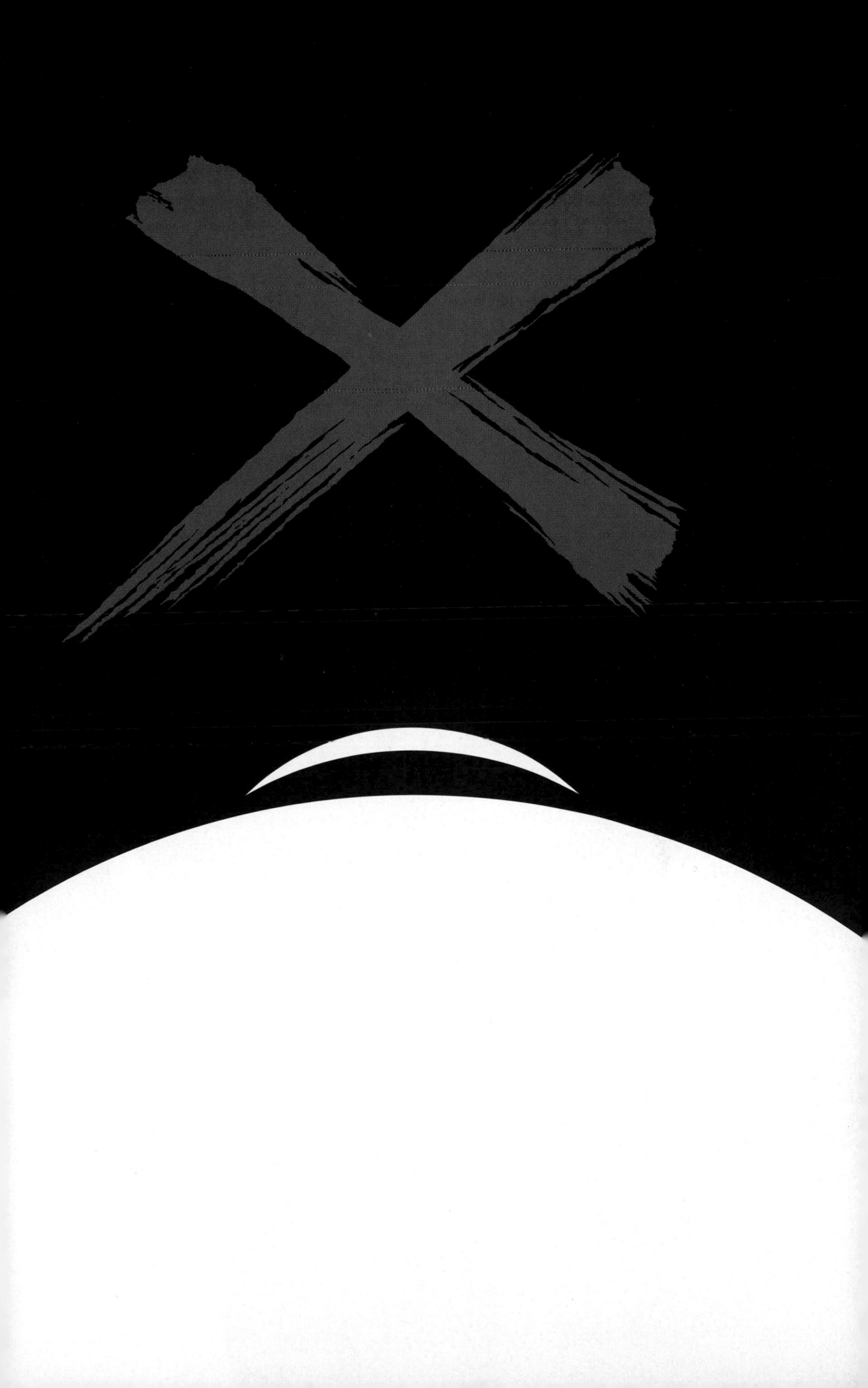

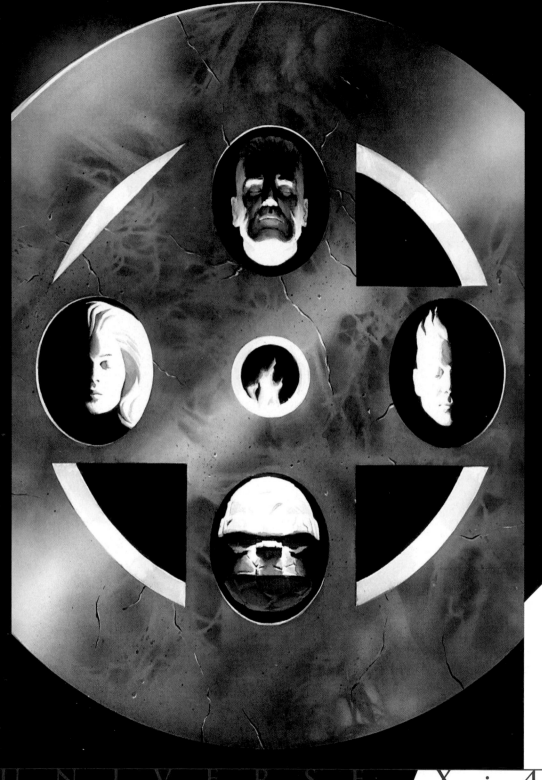

UNIVERSE X : 4

I ALWAYS BELIEVED THE MOST DIFFICULT THING IN LIFE WAS TO BE A *SON.*

TO LIVE IN SUCH A WAY THAT THE MAN WHO BUILT ME, GAVE *BIRTH* TO ME, WOULD BE PROUD. WOULD THINK THAT HE HAD ACCOMPLISHED OR JUSTIFIED HIS EXISTENCE IN ME.

AND THEN I MET *REED RICHARDS* AND DISCOVERED THAT BEING A FATHER IS FAR, FAR MORE DIFFICULT.

I'M SURPRISED TO SEE YOU HERE. I THOUGHT YOU'D GONE FOR GOOD.

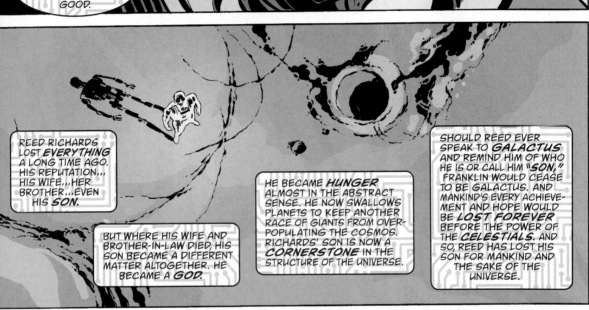

REED RICHARDS LOST *EVERYTHING* A LONG TIME AGO. HIS REPUTATION... HIS WIFE... HER BROTHER... EVEN HIS *SON.*

BUT WHERE HIS WIFE AND BROTHER-IN-LAW DIED, HIS SON BECAME A DIFFERENT MATTER ALTOGETHER. HE BECAME A *GOD.*

HE BECAME *HUNGER* ALMOST IN THE ABSTRACT SENSE. HE NOW SWALLOWS PLANETS TO KEEP ANOTHER RACE OF GIANTS FROM OVERPOPULATING THE COSMOS. RICHARDS' SON IS NOW A *CORNERSTONE* IN THE STRUCTURE OF THE UNIVERSE.

SHOULD REED EVER SPEAK TO *GALACTUS* AND REMIND HIM OF WHO HE IS OR CALL HIM *"SON,"* FRANKLIN WOULD CEASE TO BE GALACTUS. AND MANKIND'S EVERY ACHIEVEMENT AND HOPE WOULD BE *LOST FOREVER* BEFORE THE POWER OF THE *CELESTIALS.* AND SO, REED HAS LOST HIS SON FOR MANKIND AND THE SAKE OF THE UNIVERSE.

THE DECISION WAS REED'S. IT WAS A DECISION ONLY A *FATHER* COULD MAKE.

WHY ARE YOU HERE?

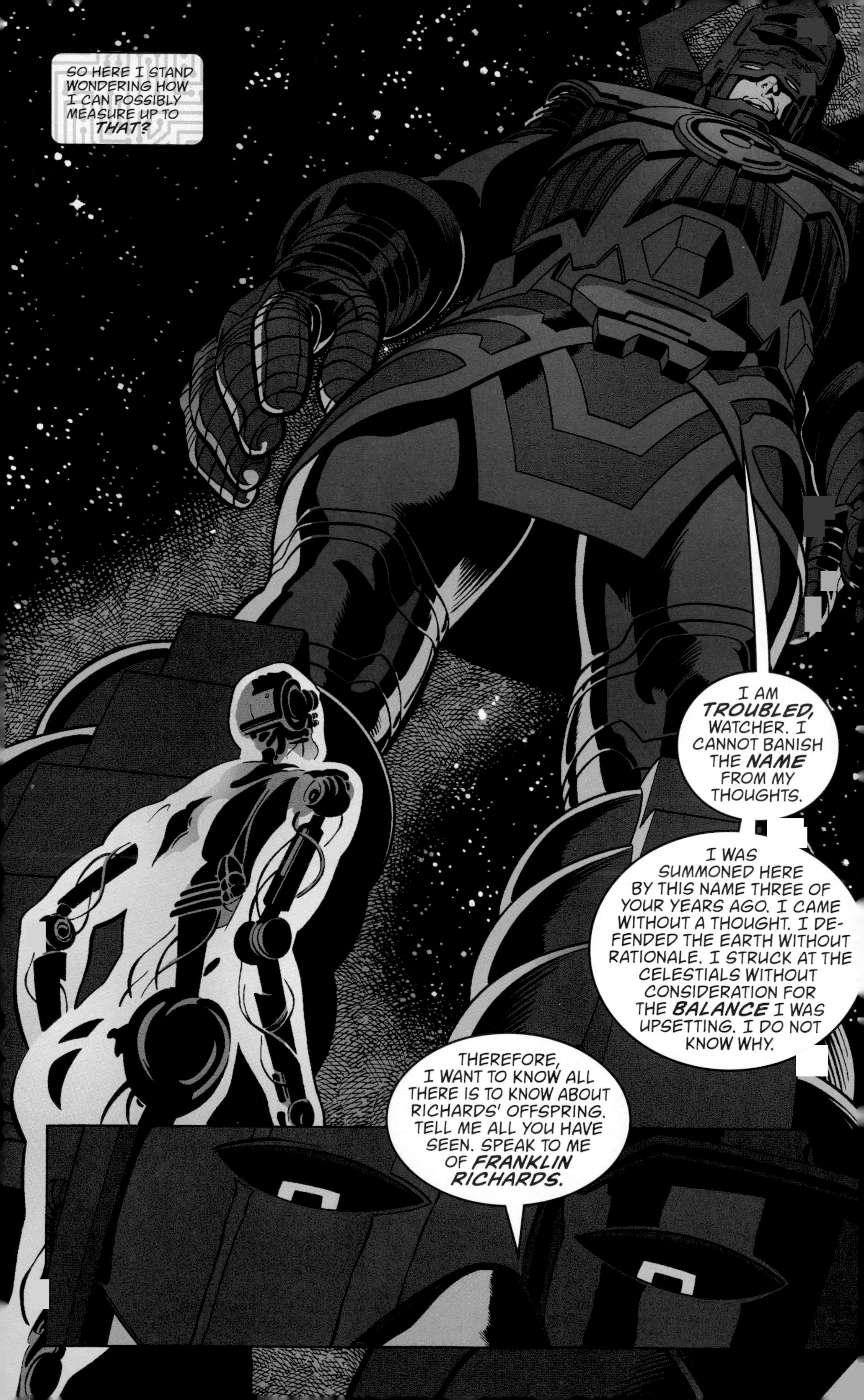
SO HERE I STAND WONDERING HOW I CAN POSSIBLY MEASURE UP TO *THAT?*
I AM *TROUBLED,* WATCHER. I CANNOT BANISH THE *NAME* FROM MY THOUGHTS.
I WAS SUMMONED HERE BY THIS NAME THREE OF YOUR YEARS AGO. I CAME WITHOUT A THOUGHT. I DEFENDED THE EARTH WITHOUT RATIONALE. I STRUCK AT THE CELESTIALS WITHOUT CONSIDERATION FOR THE *BALANCE* I WAS UPSETTING. I DO NOT KNOW WHY.
THEREFORE, I WANT TO KNOW ALL THERE IS TO KNOW ABOUT RICHARDS' OFFSPRING. TELL ME ALL YOU HAVE SEEN. SPEAK TO ME OF *FRANKLIN RICHARDS.*

I...YES, GALACTUS.

BEFORE YOU WERE BORN--BEFORE YOU CAME TO EARTH AND BEFORE FRANKLIN RICHARDS WAS BORN, A NON-APPROVED *SPACE FLIGHT* WAS LAUNCHED.

THE FLIGHT CREW CONSISTED OF *REED RICHARDS, SUSAN STORM, JOHNNY STORM* AND *BENJAMIN GRIMM.*

THIS FLIGHT WOULD END WITH THE *MUTATION* OF ALL ABOARD, THOUGH NONE, SAVE GRIMM, SUSPECTED THE DANGERS OF *COSMIC RAYS.*

MY PREDECESSOR SUGGESTED THAT RICHARDS *KNEW* OF THE DANGERS AND LIKELIHOOD OF MUTATION AND CONTINUED THE MISSION, NOT IN SPITE OF THE POSSIBILITY, BUT *BECAUSE* OF IT.

I LIKE TO BELIEVE, THOUGH, THAT REED HAD *OTHER THINGS* ON HIS MIND."

MR. RICHARDS, I'M TAKING THIS RING WE'RE FLYING AROUND THE WORLD AS A SURROGATE ENGAGEMENT RING UNTIL YOU CAN AFFORD A *REAL* ONE. YOU AND I *BETTER* BE SPENDING THE REST OF OUR LIVES TOGETHER.

TILL *DEATH* DO US PART, SUSAN..., AND THEN SOME.

HEY, IT'S IN BOTH A' YER BEST INTERESTS NOT TA MAKE ME BARF. WE'RE ABOUT TA LOSE GRAVITY.

"THE FRANKLIN CHILD IS A *MUTANT* THEN, THE SPAWN OF THEIR MATING?"

"YES. BUT IT WOULD BE SOME TIME AFTER THIS FLIGHT AND CRASH LANDING ON EARTH BEFORE FRANKLIN CAME ALONG."

"FIRST IT WAS THE *FANTASTIC FOUR* THAT WOULD NEED TO BE BORN."

WE'RE *ALIVE.*

OF COURSE WE ARE, DARLING. IT'S MY RIGHT, DON'T YOU KNOW? I GET TO SEE YOU *GROW OLD.*

I can *CURE* the world's mutations, Susan. I know this now. I know how.

I just wish *YOU* could be here to see it.

I just wish you were here.

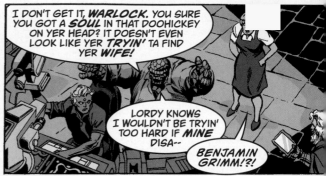

I don't get it, *WARLOCK*. You sure you got a *SOUL* in that doohickey on yer head? It doesn't even look like yer *TRYIN'* ta find yer *WIFE!*

Lordy knows I wouldn't be tryin' too hard if *MINE* disa--

BENJAMIN GRIMM!?!

Easy, 'Licia. This is *GUY TALK* between me an'...uh....*HIM.* You know I wouldn't trade ya fer nuthin', baby. I jus' have ta talk tougher'n I really am.

I ain't no fruity pie. So sometimes, I gotta talk this way ta cover up the good lovin' I give you and the boys. You know all that. It's a show. I *LOVE YA.* Really.

Marriage is the trap *NOBODY* c'n escape. Even an *ARTIFICIAL* guy like you knows that. Sometimes I won'er if it weren't ol' *DOC DOOM* hisself that invented it.

Sorry, Stretch. Wasn't thinking.

How *COULD* you, Ben? You were there when *SUSAN DIED.* For all we know, it was Doom's fault.

Well, if nobody's supposed ta even *MENTION* ol' Rusty, what're we doin' livin' in his *CASTLE*, huh?

Ben's right.

We can't undo what's been done. We're all here for a *REASON*. Sue would want us to go on.

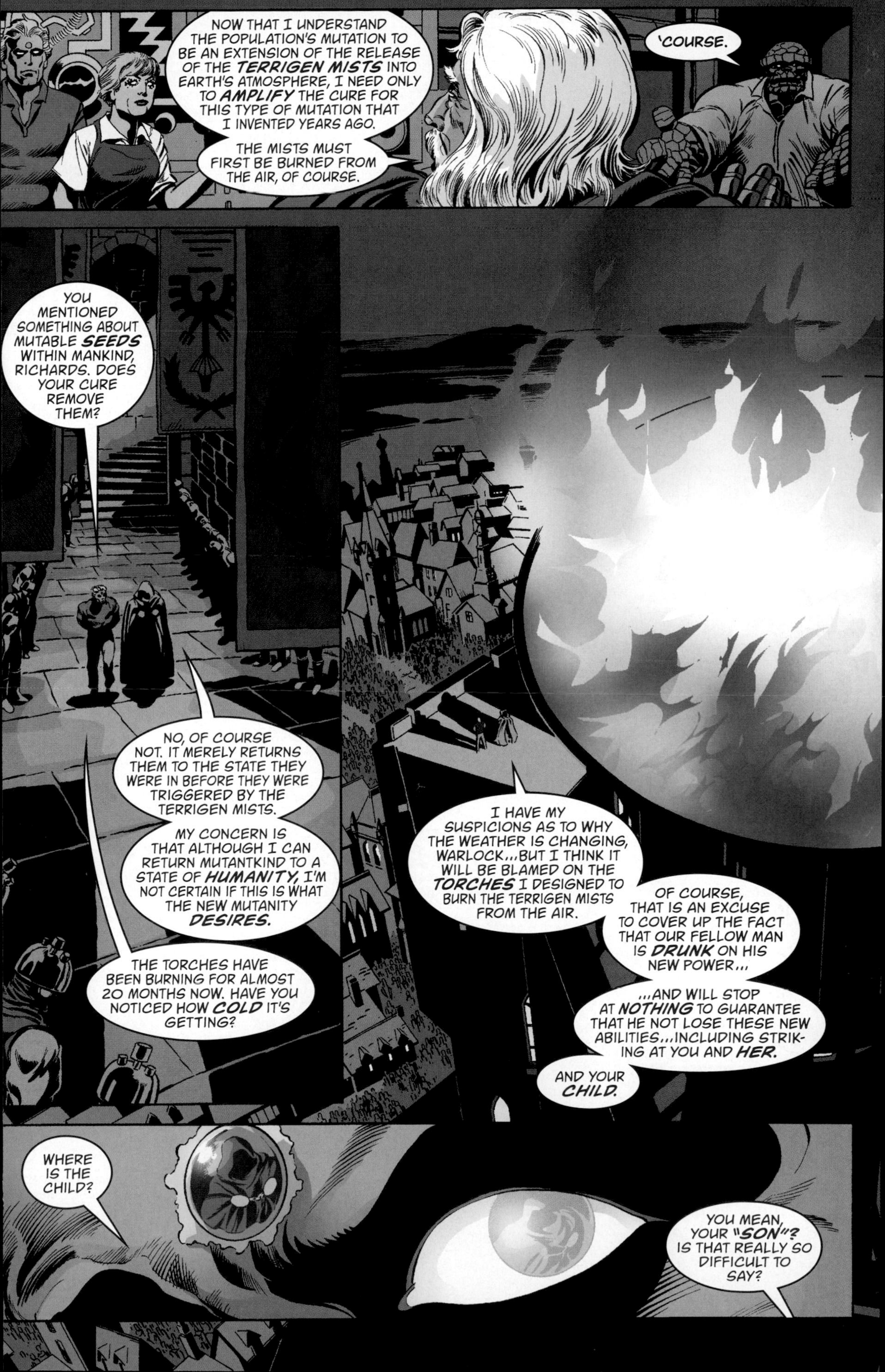
NOW THAT I UNDERSTAND THE POPULATION'S MUTATION TO BE AN EXTENSION OF THE RELEASE OF THE TERRIGEN MISTS INTO EARTH'S ATMOSPHERE, I NEED ONLY TO AMPLIFY THE CURE FOR THIS TYPE OF MUTATION THAT I INVENTED YEARS AGO.
THE MISTS MUST FIRST BE BURNED FROM THE AIR, OF COURSE.
'COURSE.
YOU MENTIONED SOMETHING ABOUT MUTABLE SEEDS WITHIN MANKIND, RICHARDS. DOES YOUR CURE REMOVE THEM?
NO, OF COURSE NOT. IT MERELY RETURNS THEM TO THE STATE THEY WERE IN BEFORE THEY WERE TRIGGERED BY THE TERRIGEN MISTS.
MY CONCERN IS THAT ALTHOUGH I CAN RETURN MUTANTKIND TO A STATE OF HUMANITY, I'M NOT CERTAIN IF THIS IS WHAT THE NEW MUTANITY DESIRES.
THE TORCHES HAVE BEEN BURNING FOR ALMOST 20 MONTHS NOW. HAVE YOU NOTICED HOW COLD IT'S GETTING?
I HAVE MY SUSPICIONS AS TO WHY THE WEATHER IS CHANGING, WARLOCK...BUT I THINK IT WILL BE BLAMED ON THE TORCHES I DESIGNED TO BURN THE TERRIGEN MISTS FROM THE AIR.
OF COURSE, THAT IS AN EXCUSE TO COVER UP THE FACT THAT OUR FELLOW MAN IS DRUNK ON HIS NEW POWER...
...AND WILL STOP AT NOTHING TO GUARANTEE THAT HE NOT LOSE THESE NEW ABILITIES...INCLUDING STRIKING AT YOU AND HER.
AND YOUR CHILD.
WHERE IS THE CHILD?
YOU MEAN, YOUR "SON"? IS THAT REALLY SO DIFFICULT TO SAY?

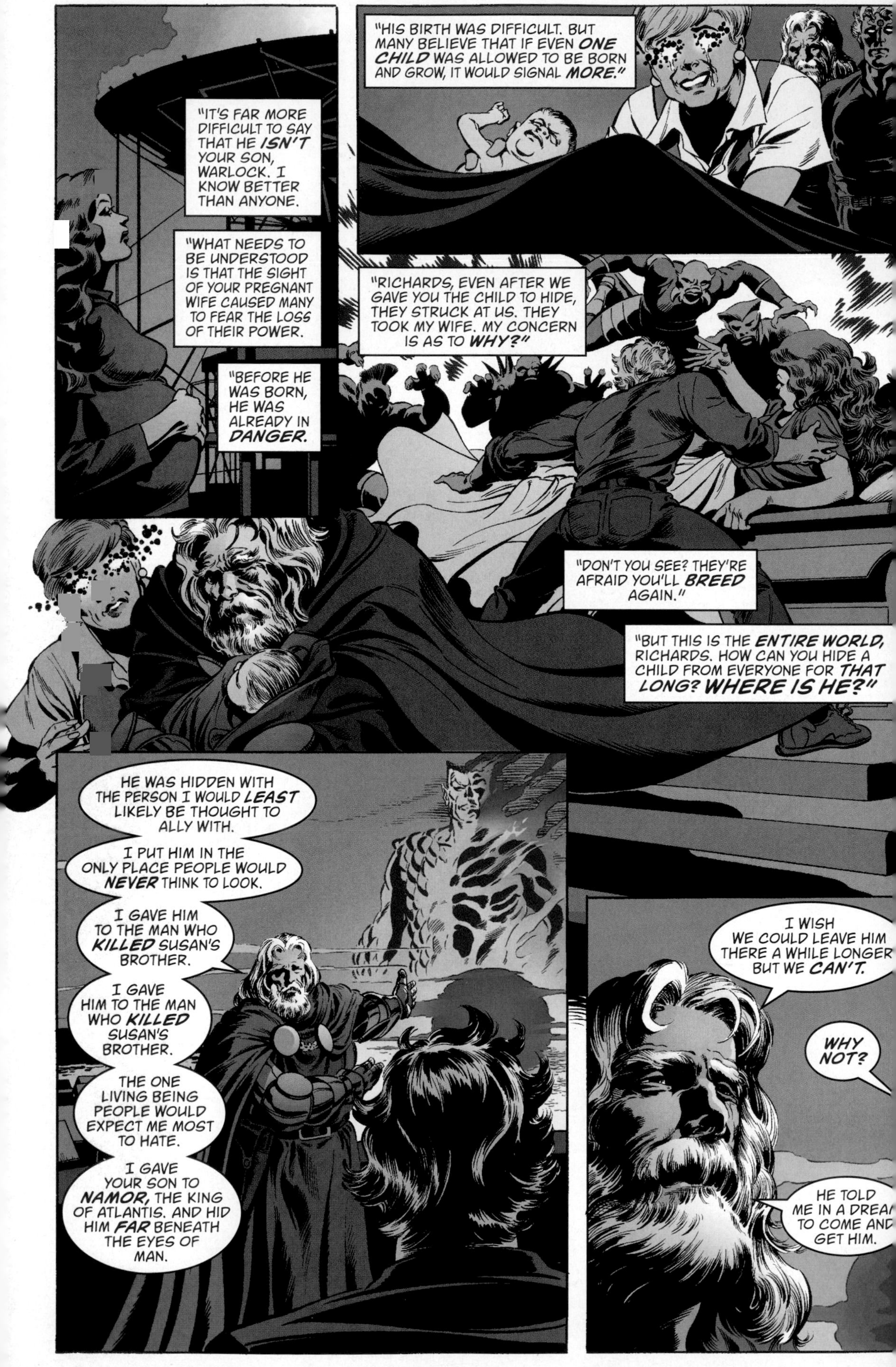
"IT'S FAR MORE DIFFICULT TO SAY THAT HE ISN'T YOUR SON, WARLOCK. I KNOW BETTER THAN ANYONE.
"WHAT NEEDS TO BE UNDERSTOOD IS THAT THE SIGHT OF YOUR PREGNANT WIFE CAUSED MANY TO FEAR THE LOSS OF THEIR POWER.
"BEFORE HE WAS BORN, HE WAS ALREADY IN DANGER.
"HIS BIRTH WAS DIFFICULT. BUT MANY BELIEVE THAT IF EVEN ONE CHILD WAS ALLOWED TO BE BORN AND GROW, IT WOULD SIGNAL MORE."
"RICHARDS, EVEN AFTER WE GAVE YOU THE CHILD TO HIDE, THEY STRUCK AT US. THEY TOOK MY WIFE. MY CONCERN IS AS TO WHY?"
"DON'T YOU SEE? THEY'RE AFRAID YOU'LL BREED AGAIN."
"BUT THIS IS THE ENTIRE WORLD, RICHARDS. HOW CAN YOU HIDE A CHILD FROM EVERYONE FOR THAT LONG? WHERE IS HE?"
HE WAS HIDDEN WITH THE PERSON I WOULD LEAST LIKELY BE THOUGHT TO ALLY WITH.
I PUT HIM IN THE ONLY PLACE PEOPLE WOULD NEVER THINK TO LOOK.
I GAVE HIM TO THE MAN WHO KILLED SUSAN'S BROTHER.
I GAVE HIM TO THE MAN WHO KILLED SUSAN'S BROTHER.
THE ONE LIVING BEING PEOPLE WOULD EXPECT ME MOST TO HATE.
I GAVE YOUR SON TO NAMOR, THE KING OF ATLANTIS. AND HID HIM FAR BENEATH THE EYES OF MAN.
I WISH WE COULD LEAVE HIM THERE A WHILE LONGER BUT WE CAN'T.
WHY NOT?
HE TOLD ME IN A DREA TO COME AND GET HIM.

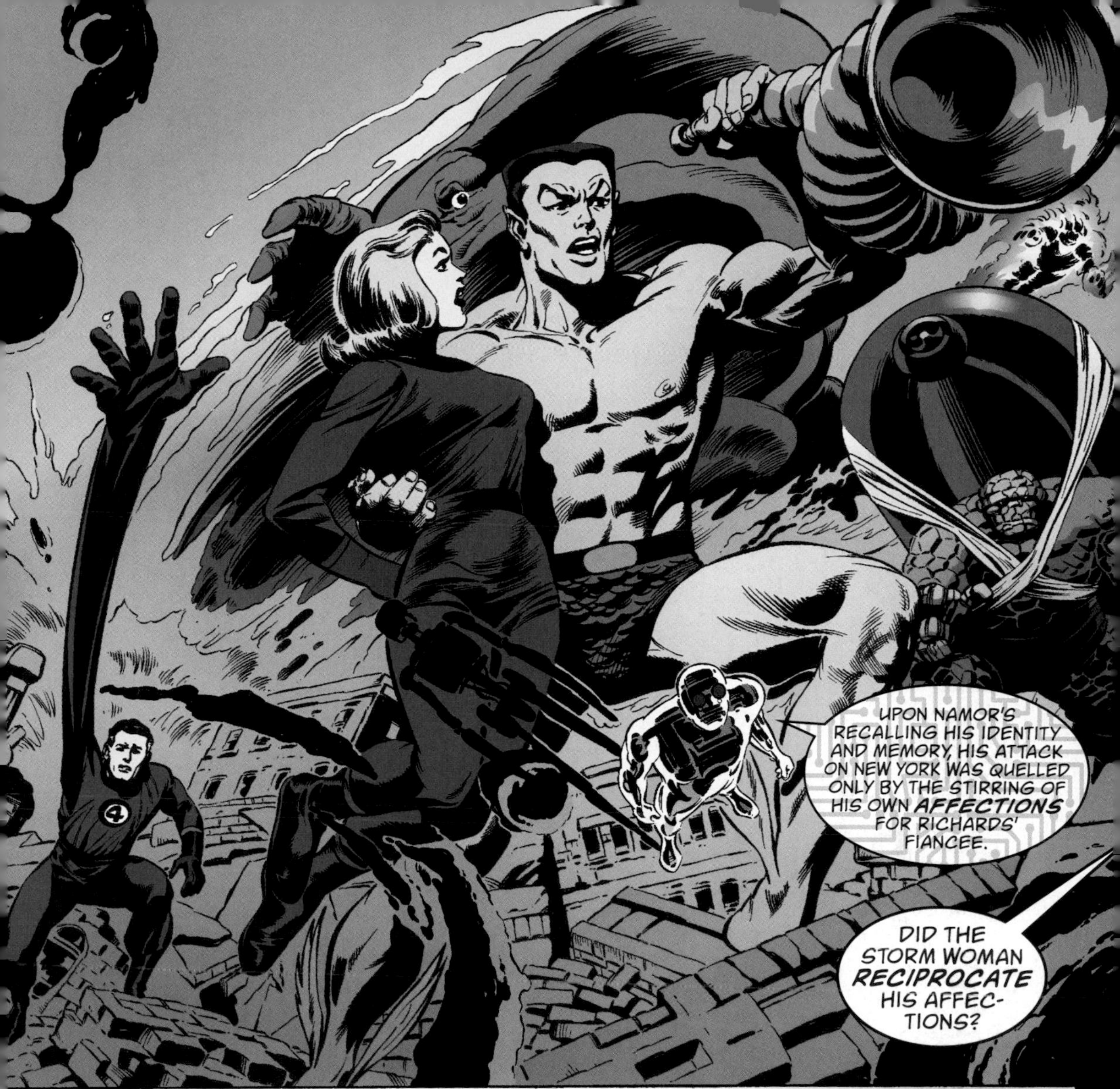
UPON NAMOR'S RECALLING HIS IDENTITY AND MEMORY, HIS ATTACK ON NEW YORK WAS QUELLED ONLY BY THE STIRRING OF HIS OWN AFFECTIONS FOR RICHARDS' FIANCEE.
DID THE STORM WOMAN RECIPROCATE HIS AFFECTIONS?

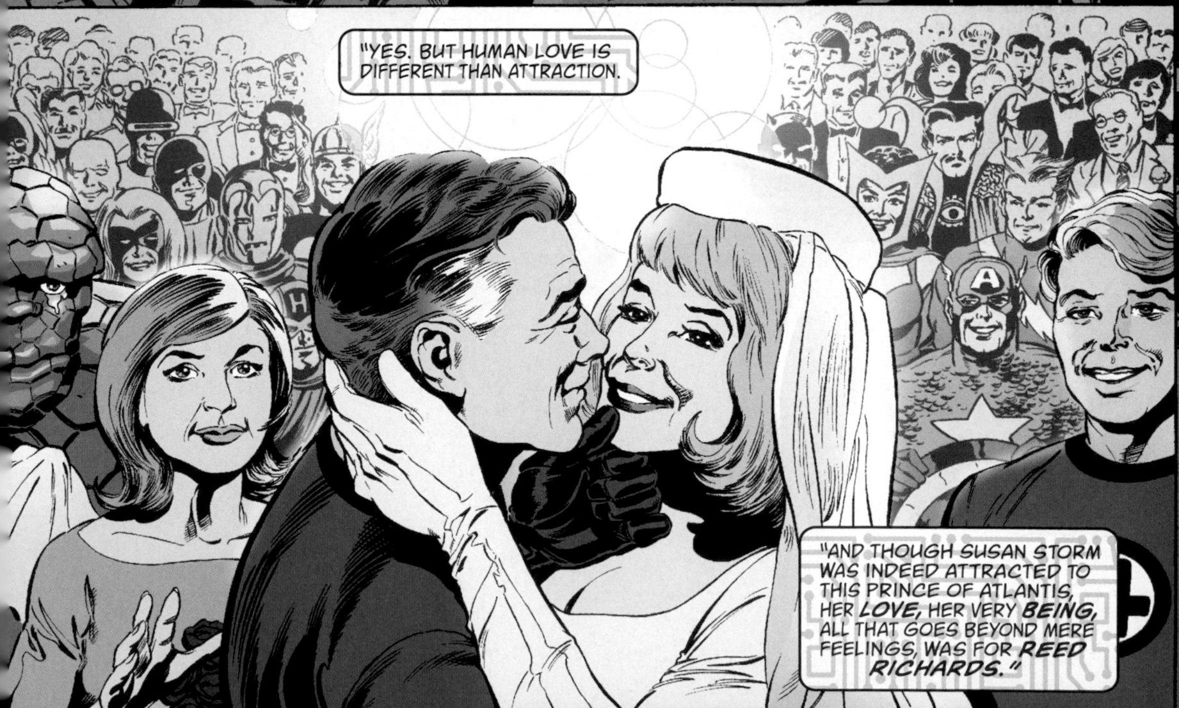
"YES. BUT HUMAN LOVE IS DIFFERENT THAN ATTRACTION.
"AND THOUGH SUSAN STORM WAS INDEED ATTRACTED TO THIS PRINCE OF ATLANTIS, HER LOVE, HER VERY BEING, ALL THAT GOES BEYOND MERE FEELINGS, WAS FOR REED RICHARDS."

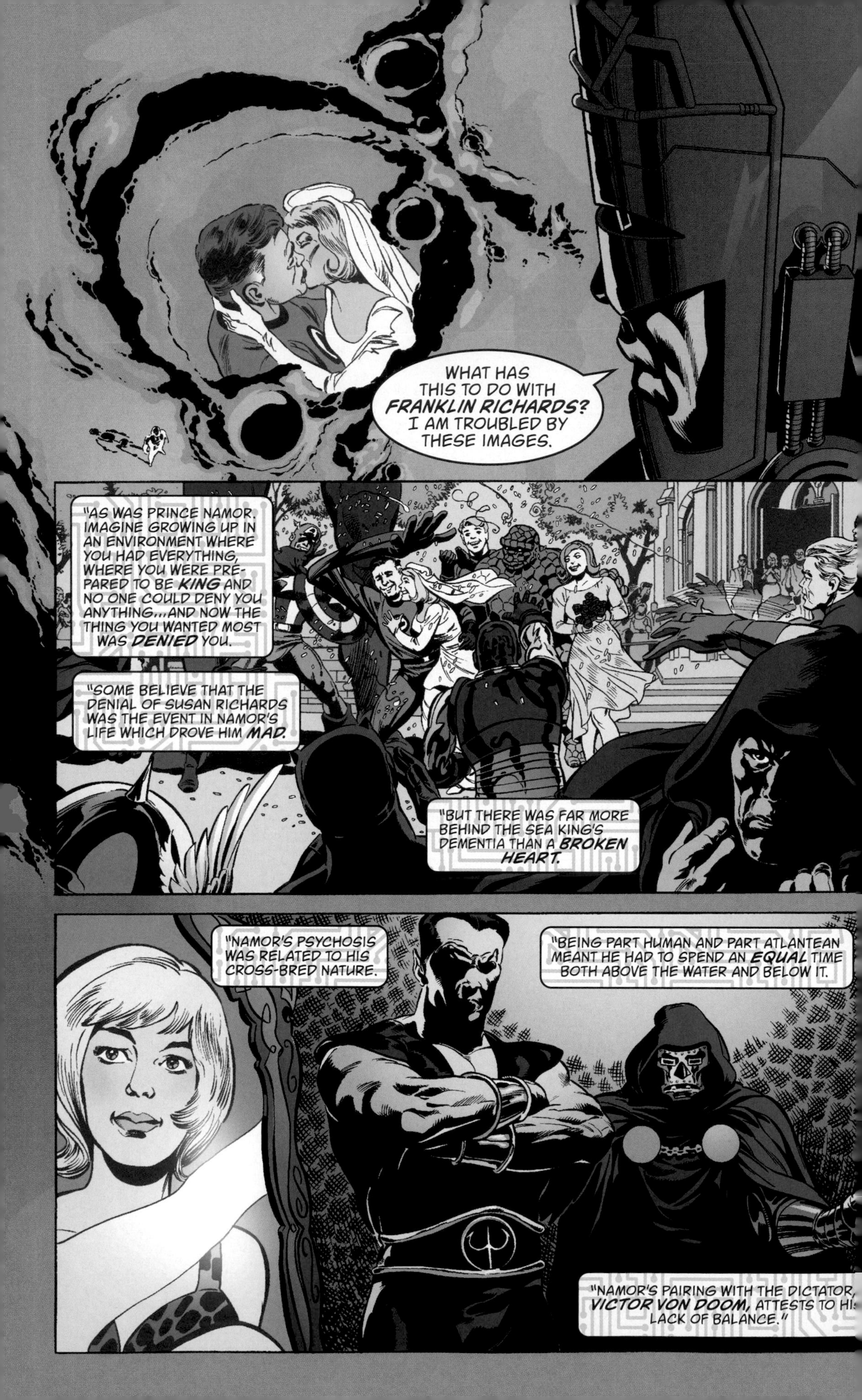
WHAT HAS THIS TO DO WITH FRANKLIN RICHARDS? I AM TROUBLED BY THESE IMAGES.
"AS WAS PRINCE NAMOR. IMAGINE GROWING UP IN AN ENVIRONMENT WHERE YOU HAD EVERYTHING, WHERE YOU WERE PREPARED TO BE KING AND NO ONE COULD DENY YOU ANYTHING...AND NOW THE THING YOU WANTED MOST WAS DENIED YOU.
"SOME BELIEVE THAT THE DENIAL OF SUSAN RICHARDS WAS THE EVENT IN NAMOR'S LIFE WHICH DROVE HIM MAD.
"BUT THERE WAS FAR MORE BEHIND THE SEA KING'S DEMENTIA THAN A BROKEN HEART.
"NAMOR'S PSYCHOSIS WAS RELATED TO HIS CROSS-BRED NATURE.
"BEING PART HUMAN AND PART ATLANTEAN MEANT HE HAD TO SPEND AN EQUAL TIME BOTH ABOVE THE WATER AND BELOW IT.
"NAMOR'S PAIRING WITH THE DICTATOR, VICTOR VON DOOM, ATTESTS TO HI LACK OF BALANCE."

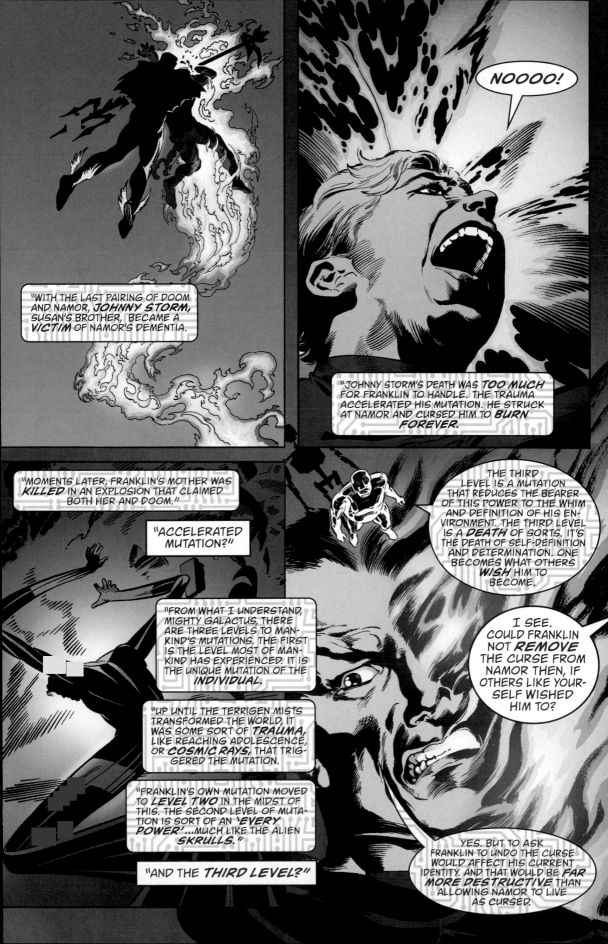

"WITH THE LAST PAIRING OF DOOM AND NAMOR, **JOHNNY STORM**, SUSAN'S BROTHER, BECAME A **VICTIM** OF NAMOR'S DEMENTIA."

NOOOO!

"JOHNNY STORM'S DEATH WAS **TOO MUCH** FOR FRANKLIN TO HANDLE. THE TRAUMA ACCELERATED HIS MUTATION. HE STRUCK AT NAMOR AND CURSED HIM TO **BURN FOREVER**."

"MOMENTS LATER, FRANKLIN'S MOTHER WAS **KILLED** IN AN EXPLOSION THAT CLAIMED BOTH HER AND DOOM."

"ACCELERATED MUTATION?"

"FROM WHAT I UNDERSTAND, MIGHTY GALACTUS, THERE ARE THREE LEVELS TO MAN-KIND'S MUTATIONS. THE FIRST IS THE LEVEL MOST OF MAN-KIND HAS EXPERIENCED. IT IS THE UNIQUE MUTATION OF THE **INDIVIDUAL**."

"UP UNTIL THE TERRIGEN MISTS TRANSFORMED THE WORLD, IT WAS SOME SORT OF **TRAUMA**, LIKE REACHING ADOLESCENCE, OR **COSMIC RAYS**, THAT TRIG-GERED THE MUTATION."

"FRANKLIN'S OWN MUTATION MOVED TO **LEVEL TWO** IN THE MIDST OF THIS. THE SECOND LEVEL OF MUTA-TION IS SORT OF AN **'EVERY POWER'**...MUCH LIKE THE ALIEN **SKRULLS**."

"AND THE **THIRD LEVEL?**"

THE THIRD LEVEL IS A MUTATION THAT REDUCES THE BEARER OF THIS POWER TO THE WHIM AND DEFINITION OF HIS EN-VIRONMENT. THE THIRD LEVEL IS A **DEATH** OF SORTS. IT'S THE DEATH OF SELF-DEFINITION AND DETERMINATION. ONE BECOMES WHAT OTHERS **WISH** HIM TO BECOME.

I SEE. COULD FRANKLIN NOT **REMOVE** THE CURSE FROM NAMOR THEN, IF OTHERS LIKE YOUR-SELF WISHED HIM TO?

YES. BUT TO ASK FRANKLIN TO UNDO THE CURSE WOULD AFFECT HIS CURRENT IDENTITY. AND THAT WOULD BE **FAR MORE DESTRUCTIVE** THAN ALLOWING NAMOR TO LIVE AS CURSED.

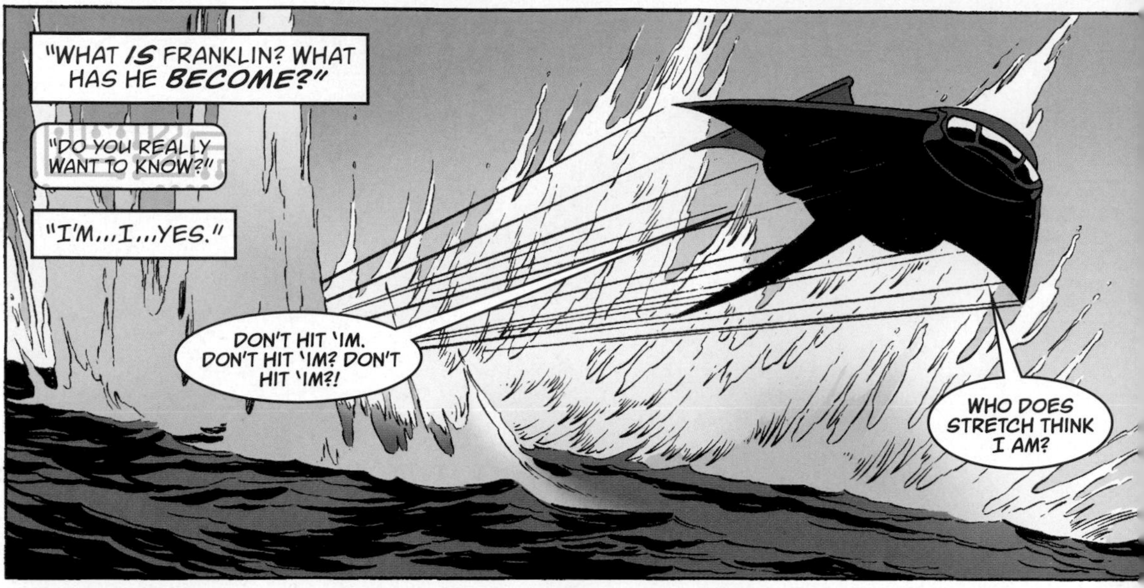
"WHAT IS FRANKLIN? WHAT HAS HE BECOME?"
"DO YOU REALLY WANT TO KNOW?"
"I'M...I...YES."
DON'T HIT 'IM. DON'T HIT 'IM? DON'T HIT 'IM?!
WHO DOES STRETCH THINK I AM?

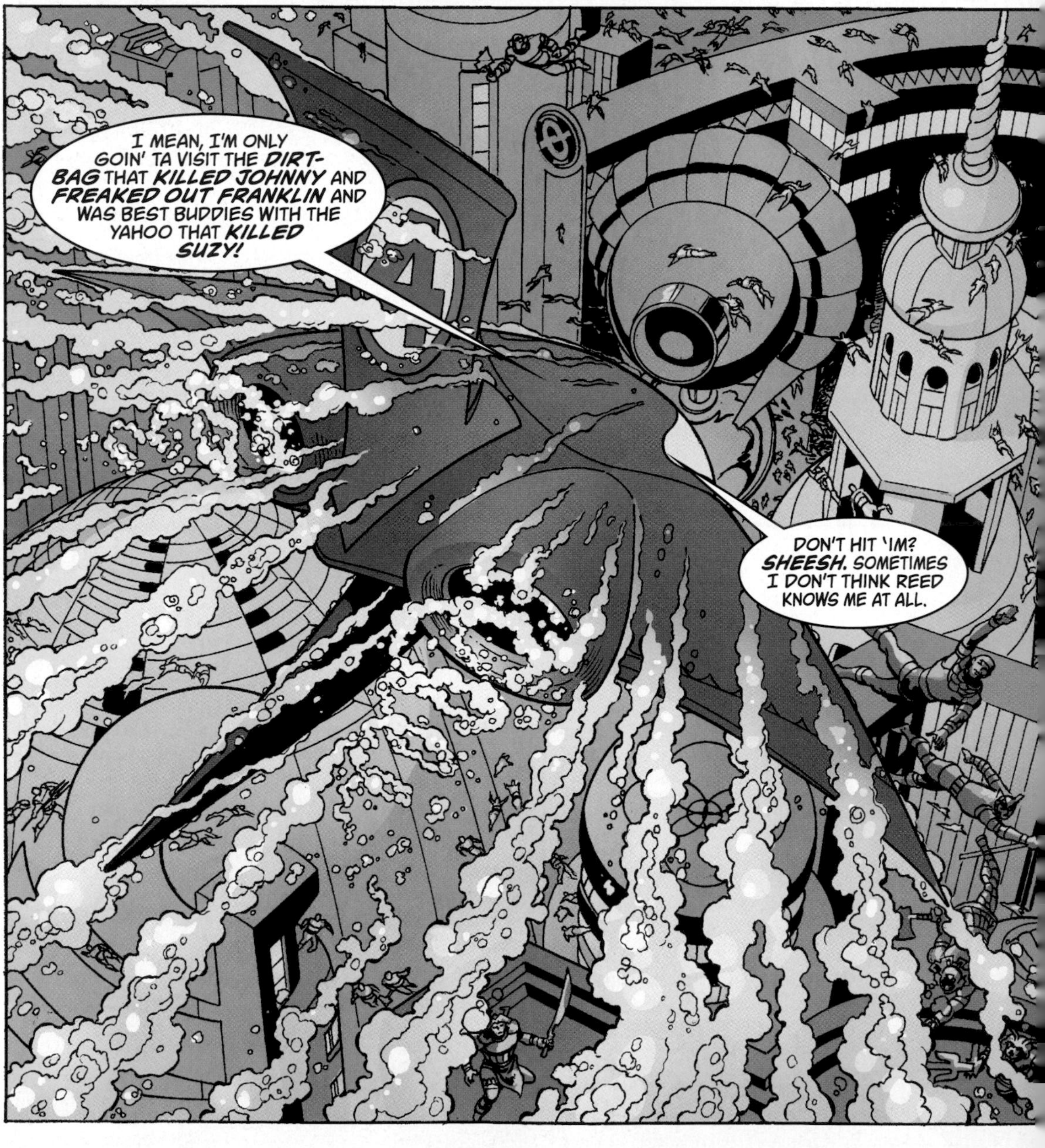
I MEAN, I'M ONLY GOIN' TA VISIT THE DIRT-BAG THAT KILLED JOHNNY AND FREAKED OUT FRANKLIN AND WAS BEST BUDDIES WITH THE YAHOO THAT KILLED SUZY!
DON'T HIT 'IM? SHEESH. SOMETIMES I DON'T THINK REED KNOWS ME AT ALL.

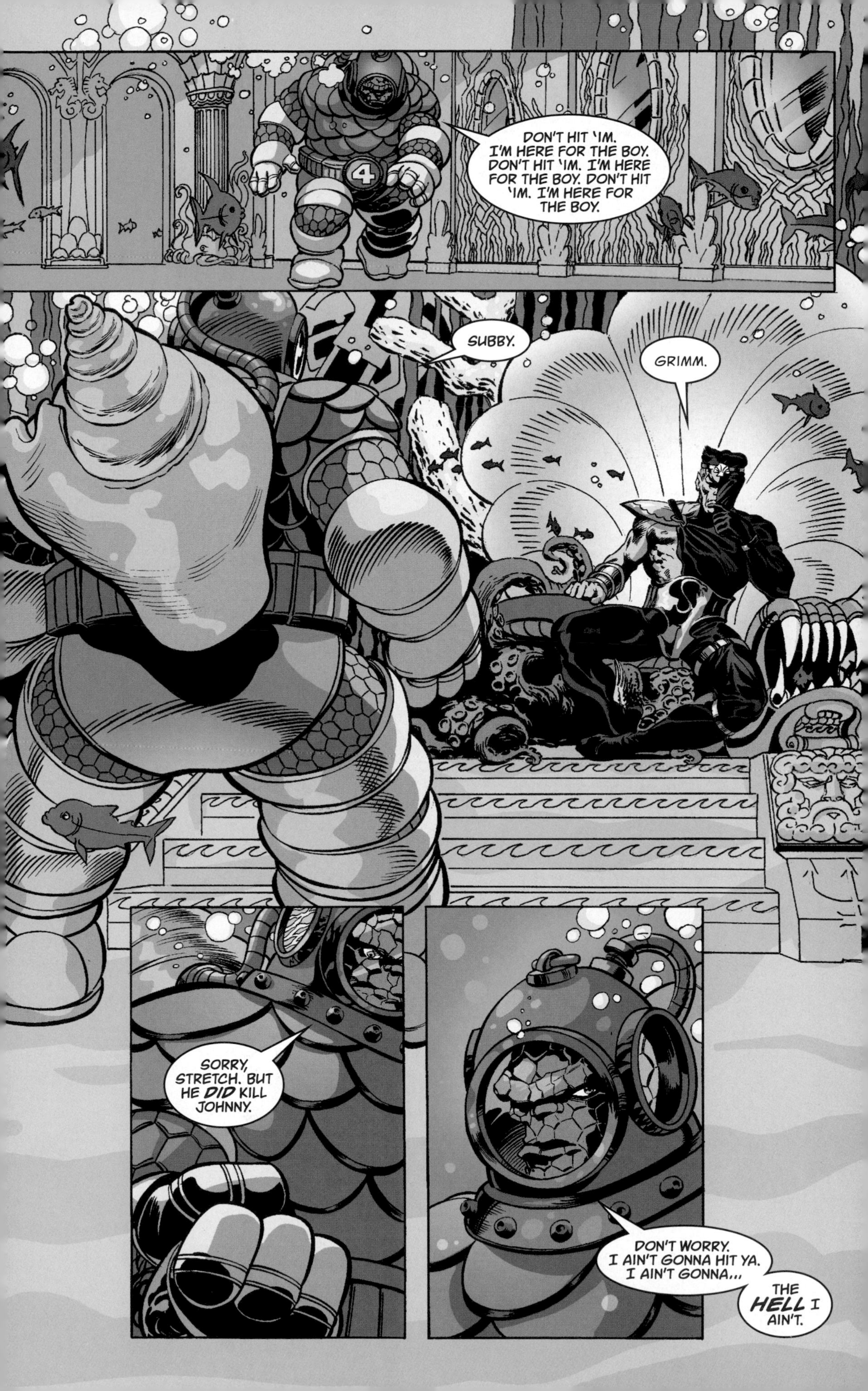
DON'T HIT 'IM. I'M HERE FOR THE BOY. DON'T HIT 'IM. I'M HERE FOR THE BOY. DON'T HIT 'IM. I'M HERE FOR THE BOY.
SUBBY.
GRIMM.
SORRY, STRETCH. BUT HE *DID* KILL JOHNNY.
DON'T WORRY. I AIN'T GONNA HIT YA. I AIN'T GONNA...
THE *HELL* I AIN'T.

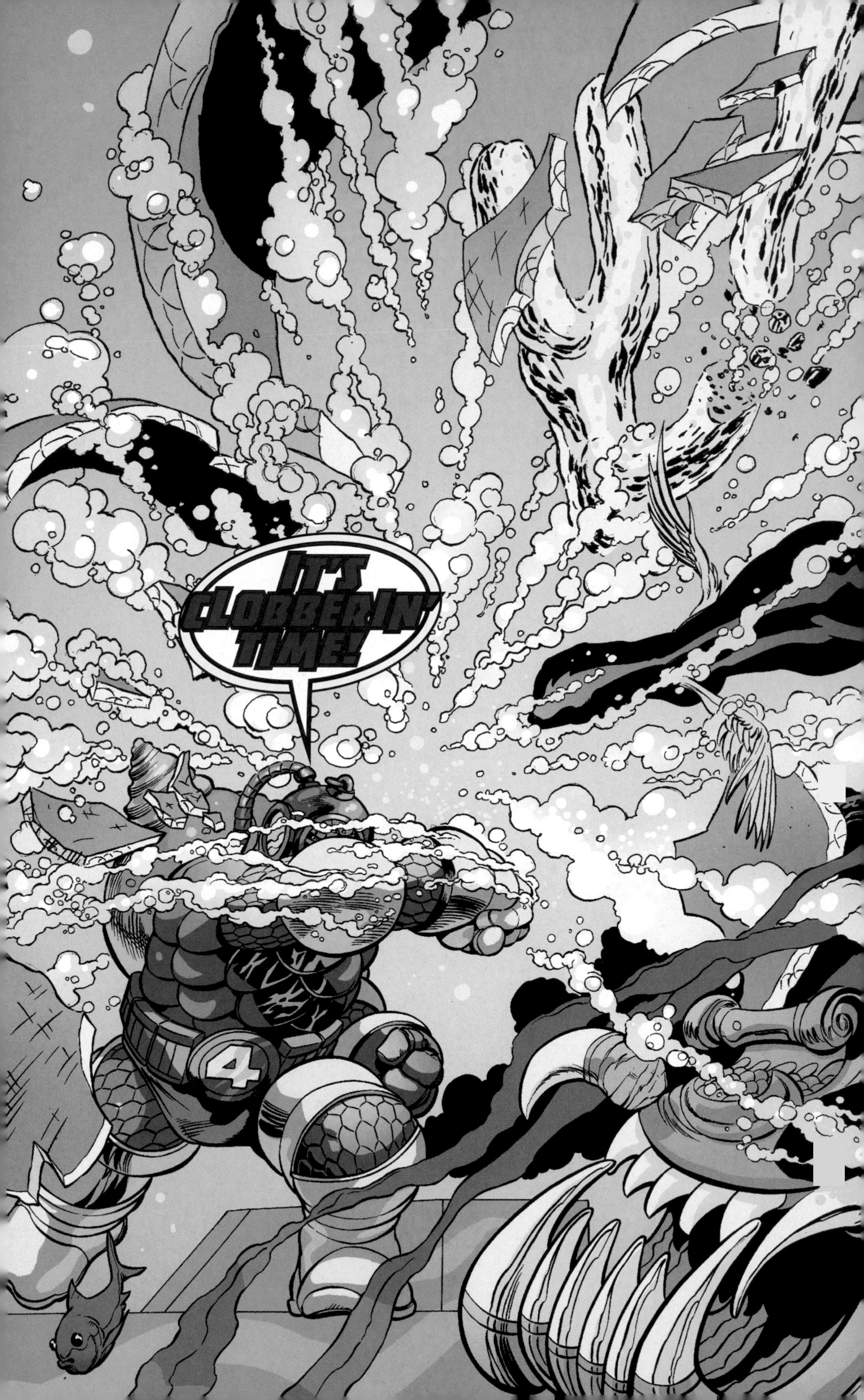
IT'S CLOBBERIN' TIME!

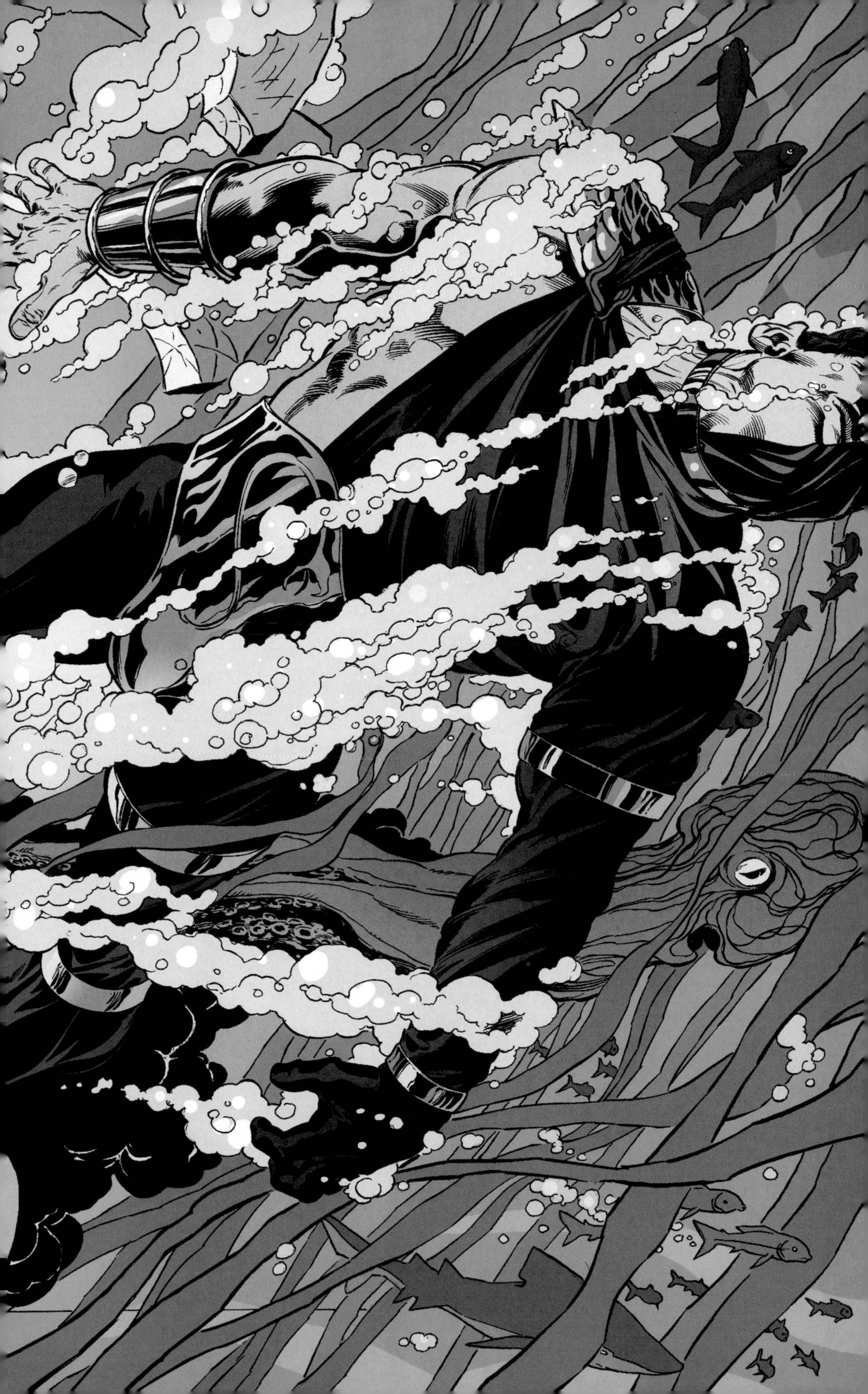

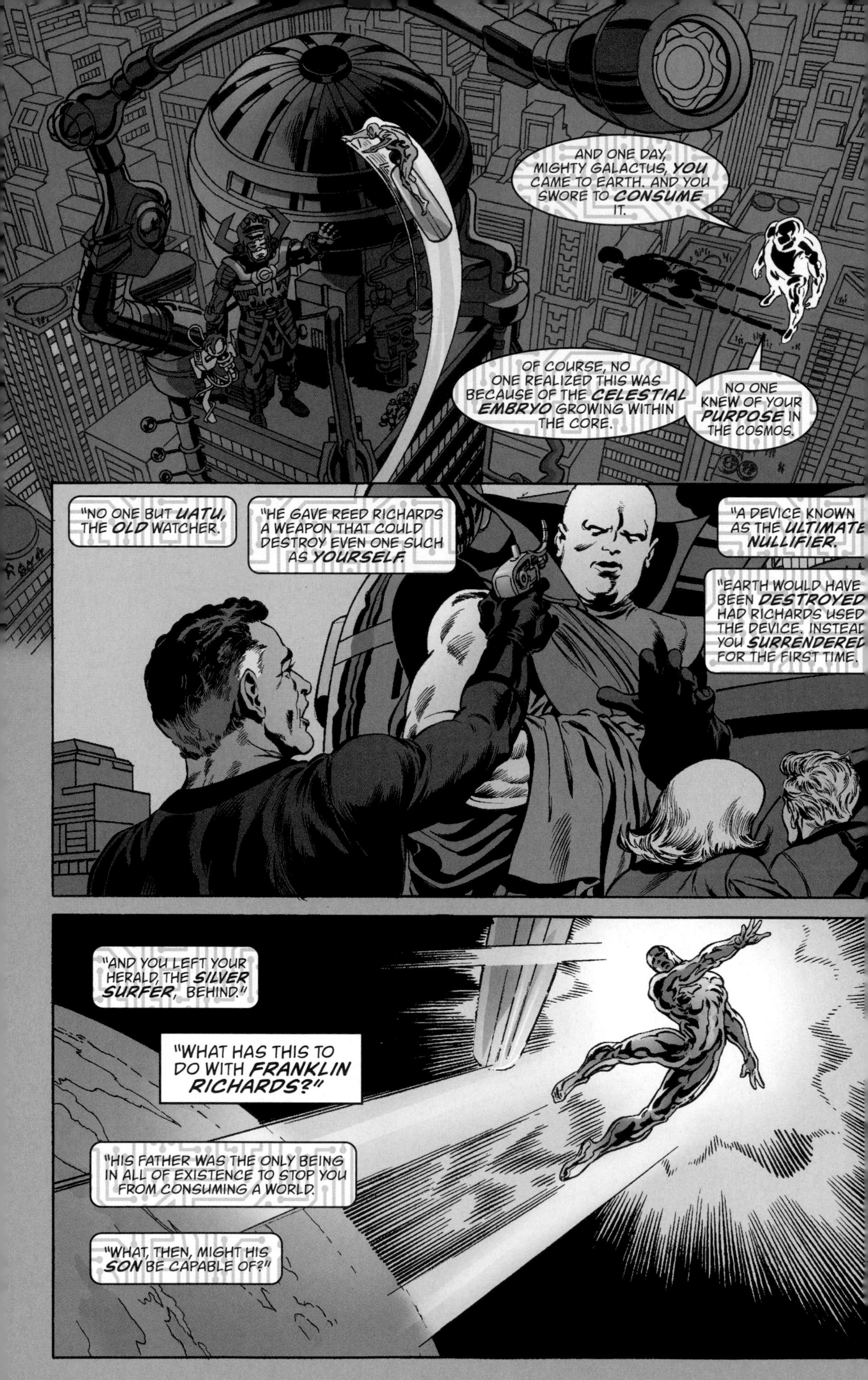
AND ONE DAY, MIGHTY GALACTUS, YOU CAME TO EARTH. AND YOU SWORE TO CONSUME IT.
OF COURSE, NO ONE REALIZED THIS WAS BECAUSE OF THE CELESTIAL EMBRYO GROWING WITHIN THE CORE.
NO ONE KNEW OF YOUR PURPOSE IN THE COSMOS.
"NO ONE BUT UATU, THE OLD WATCHER.
"HE GAVE REED RICHARDS A WEAPON THAT COULD DESTROY EVEN ONE SUCH AS YOURSELF.
"A DEVICE KNOWN AS THE ULTIMATE NULLIFIER.
"EARTH WOULD HAVE BEEN DESTROYED HAD RICHARDS USED THE DEVICE. INSTEAD YOU SURRENDERED FOR THE FIRST TIME.
"AND YOU LEFT YOUR HERALD, THE SILVER SURFER, BEHIND."
"WHAT HAS THIS TO DO WITH FRANKLIN RICHARDS?"
"HIS FATHER WAS THE ONLY BEING IN ALL OF EXISTENCE TO STOP YOU FROM CONSUMING A WORLD.
"WHAT, THEN, MIGHT HIS SON BE CAPABLE OF?"

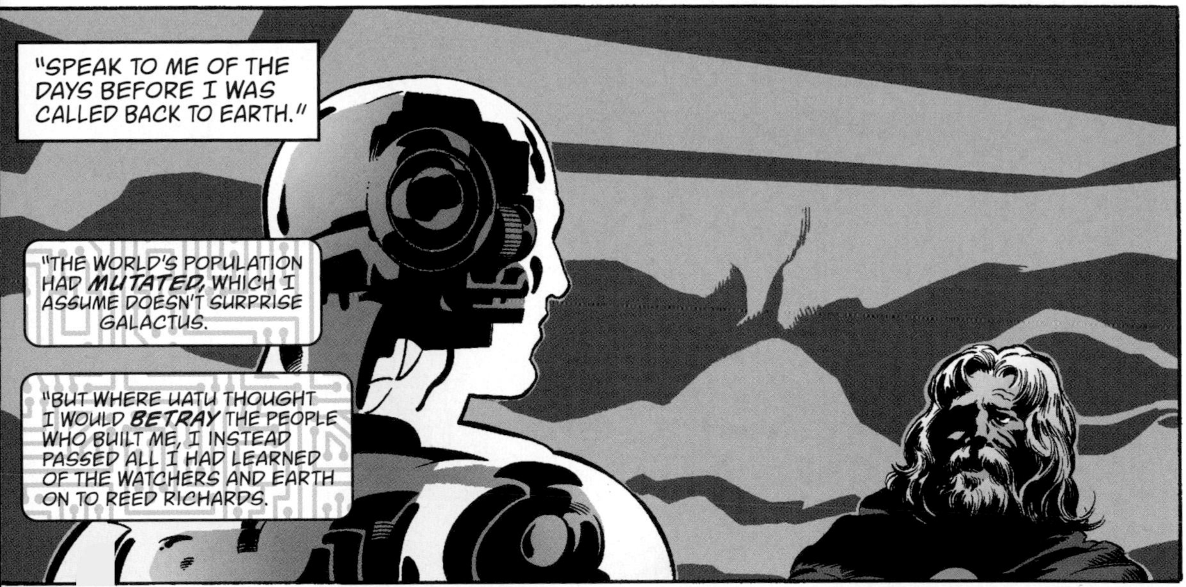
"SPEAK TO ME OF THE DAYS BEFORE I WAS CALLED BACK TO EARTH."
"THE WORLD'S POPULATION HAD *MUTATED*, WHICH I ASSUME DOESN'T SURPRISE GALACTUS.
"BUT WHERE UATU THOUGHT I WOULD *BETRAY* THE PEOPLE WHO BUILT ME, I INSTEAD PASSED ALL I HAD LEARNED OF THE WATCHERS AND EARTH ON TO REED RICHARDS.

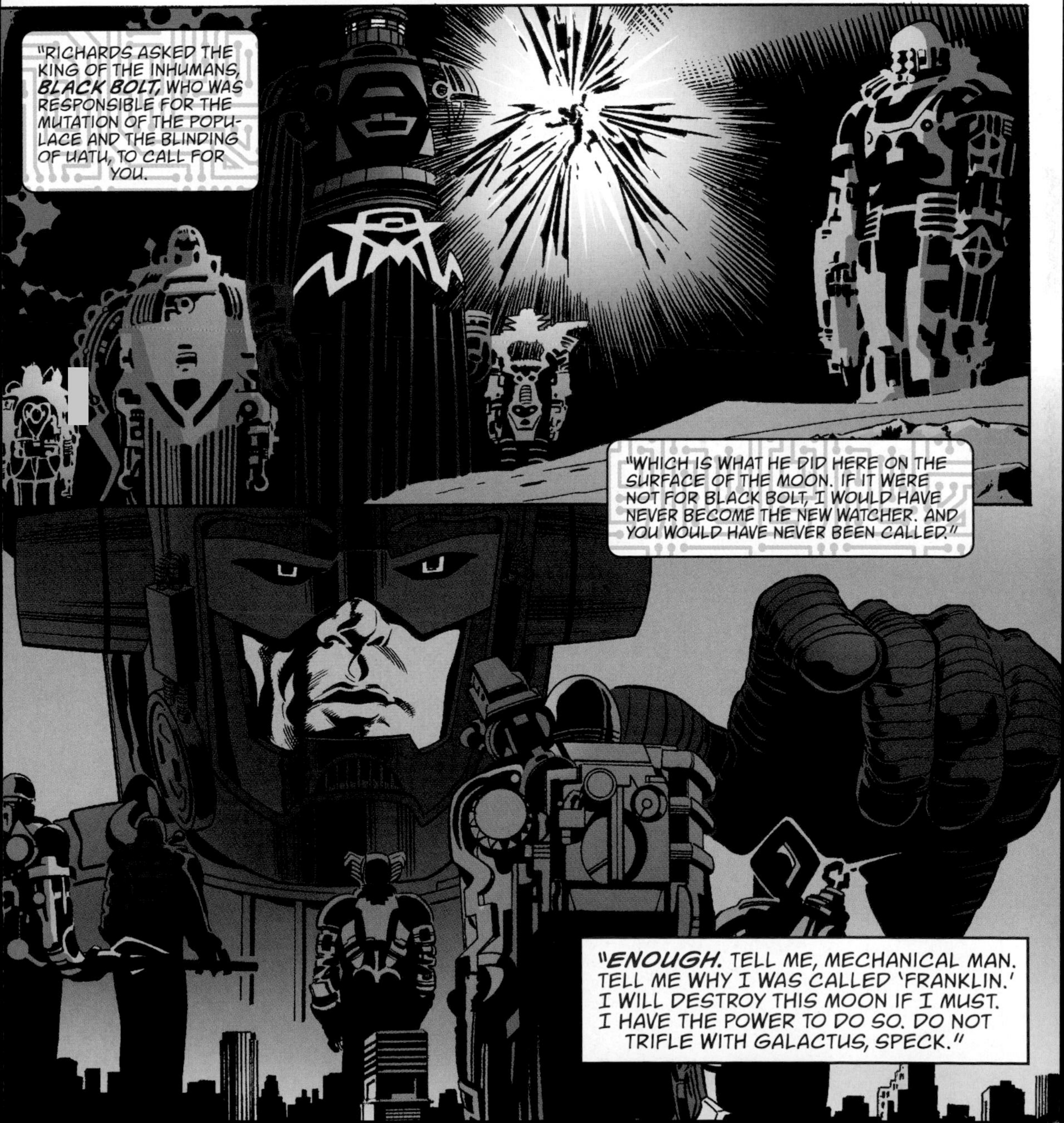
"RICHARDS ASKED THE KING OF THE INHUMANS, *BLACK BOLT*, WHO WAS RESPONSIBLE FOR THE MUTATION OF THE POPULACE AND THE BLINDING OF UATU, TO CALL FOR YOU.
"WHICH IS WHAT HE DID HERE ON THE SURFACE OF THE MOON. IF IT WERE NOT FOR BLACK BOLT, I WOULD HAVE NEVER BECOME THE NEW WATCHER. AND YOU WOULD HAVE NEVER BEEN CALLED."
"*ENOUGH.* TELL ME, MECHANICAL MAN. TELL ME WHY I WAS CALLED 'FRANKLIN.' I WILL DESTROY THIS MOON IF I MUST. I HAVE THE POWER TO DO SO. DO NOT TRIFLE WITH GALACTUS, SPECK."

THIS'S FER *JOHNNY,* YA TWO-FACED FIN-FOOTED GALOOT!

NO, GRIMM! *DON'T!*

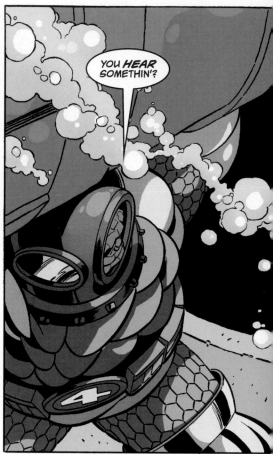

YOU *HEAR* SOMETHIN'?

CRIPES.

YOU'RE A *FOOL,* GRIMM. I WILL *NOT* BE RESPONSIBLE FOR ANOTHER OF YOUR FAMILY'S DEATHS.

YEAH? WELL, I GOTTA TELL YA, SUBBY, I'VE YET TA FIND A PAIR A TEETH THAT CAN CAUSE MY HIDE ANY HARM.

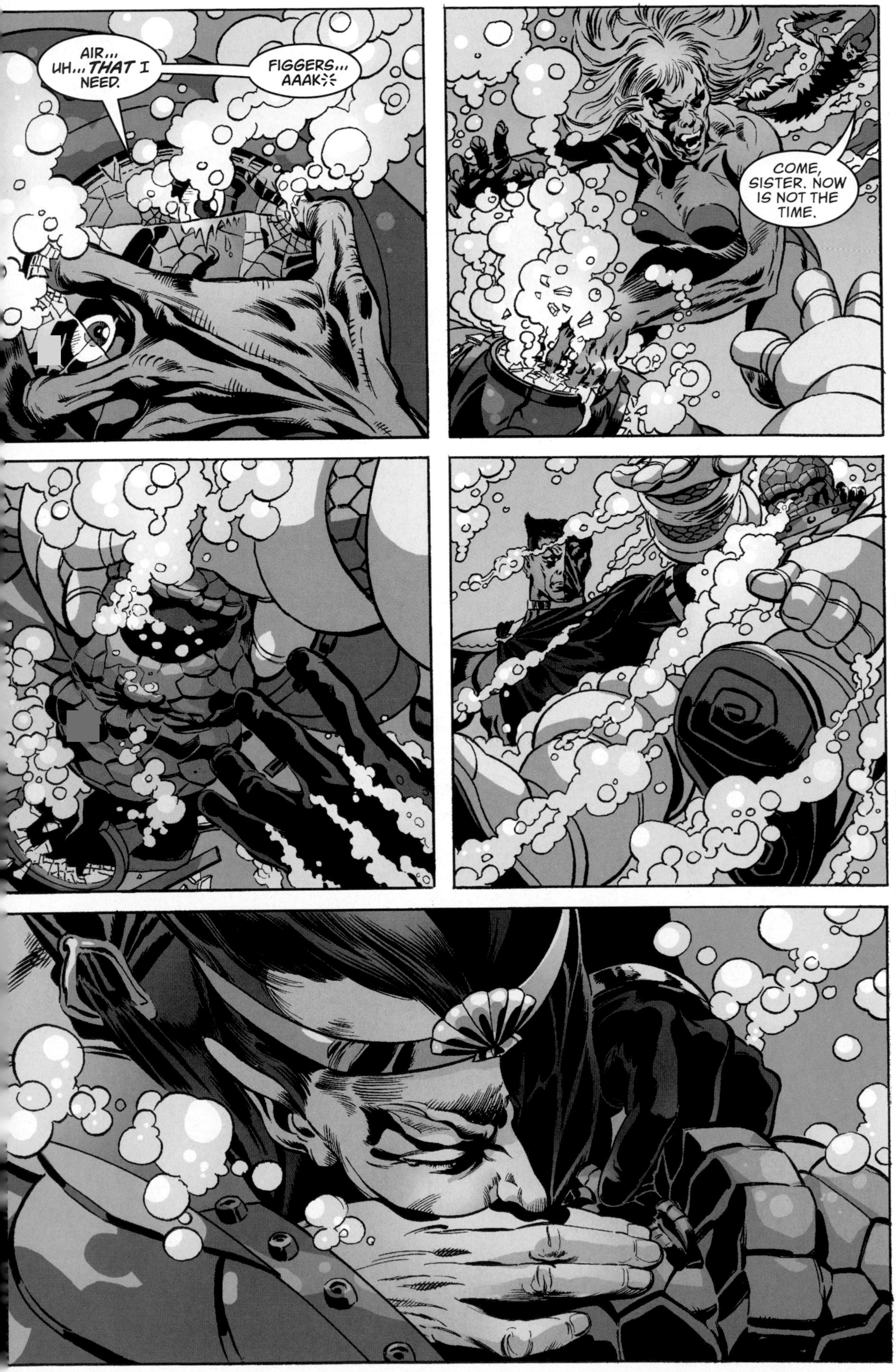
AIR... UH... THAT I NEED.
FIGGERS... AAAK!
COME, SISTER. NOW IS NOT THE TIME.

THERE, GRIMM. THIS CONSTRUCTION SHOULD AID YOUR RECOVERY.

≥KAFF≤... ≥COFF≤

MOUTH-TA-MOUTH? TALK ABOUT YER *REVOLTIN' DEVELOPMENTS!* I C'N NEVER SHOW MY PUSS ON *YANCY STREET* AGAIN.

I WAS ONLY GONNA BEAT THE LIVIN' SPIT OUTTA YA BEFORE...NOW I GOTTA *KILL* YA.

BEN?

MARV? YER YAPPIN' ALREADY?

NAMOR HAS BEEN A GREAT HELP TO ME.

THERE IS NO NEED TO FIGHT HIM.

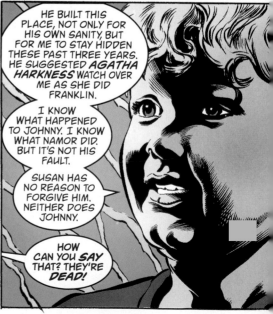

HE BUILT THIS PLACE, NOT ONLY FOR HIS OWN SANITY, BUT FOR ME TO STAY HIDDEN THESE PAST THREE YEARS. HE SUGGESTED *AGATHA HARKNESS* WATCH OVER ME AS SHE DID FRANKLIN.

I KNOW WHAT HAPPENED TO JOHNNY. I KNOW WHAT NAMOR DID. BUT IT'S NOT HIS FAULT.

SUSAN HAS NO REASON TO FORGIVE HIM. NEITHER DOES JOHNNY.

HOW CAN YOU *SAY* THAT? THEY'RE *DEAD!*

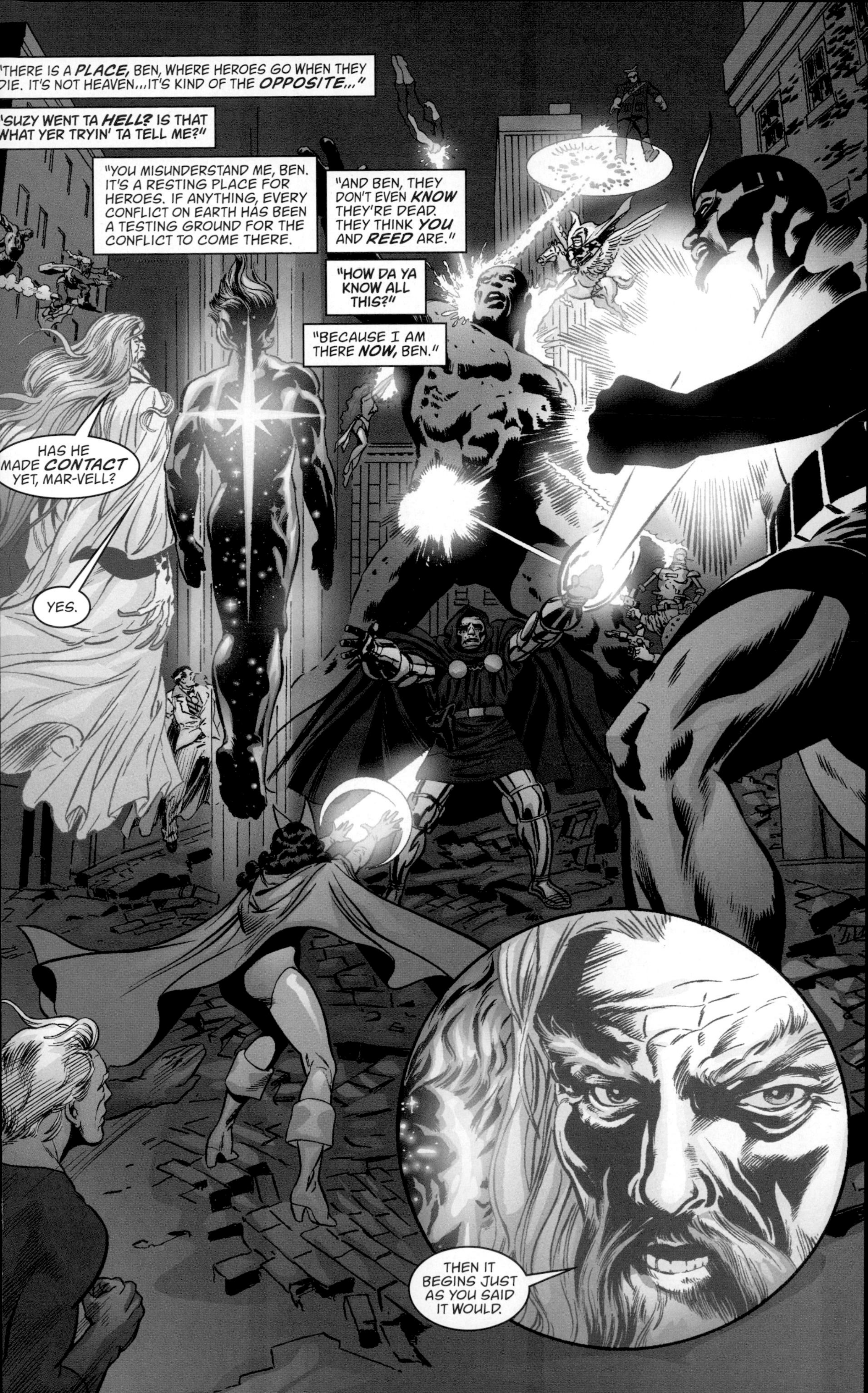
"THERE IS A PLACE, BEN, WHERE HEROES GO WHEN THEY DIE. IT'S NOT HEAVEN...IT'S KIND OF THE OPPOSITE..."
"SUZY WENT TA HELL? IS THAT WHAT YER TRYIN' TA TELL ME?"
"YOU MISUNDERSTAND ME, BEN. IT'S A RESTING PLACE FOR HEROES. IF ANYTHING, EVERY CONFLICT ON EARTH HAS BEEN A TESTING GROUND FOR THE CONFLICT TO COME THERE.
"AND BEN, THEY DON'T EVEN KNOW THEY'RE DEAD. THEY THINK YOU AND REED ARE."
"HOW DA YA KNOW ALL THIS?"
"BECAUSE I AM THERE NOW, BEN."
HAS HE MADE CONTACT YET, MAR-VELL?
YES.
THEN IT BEGINS JUST AS YOU SAID IT WOULD.

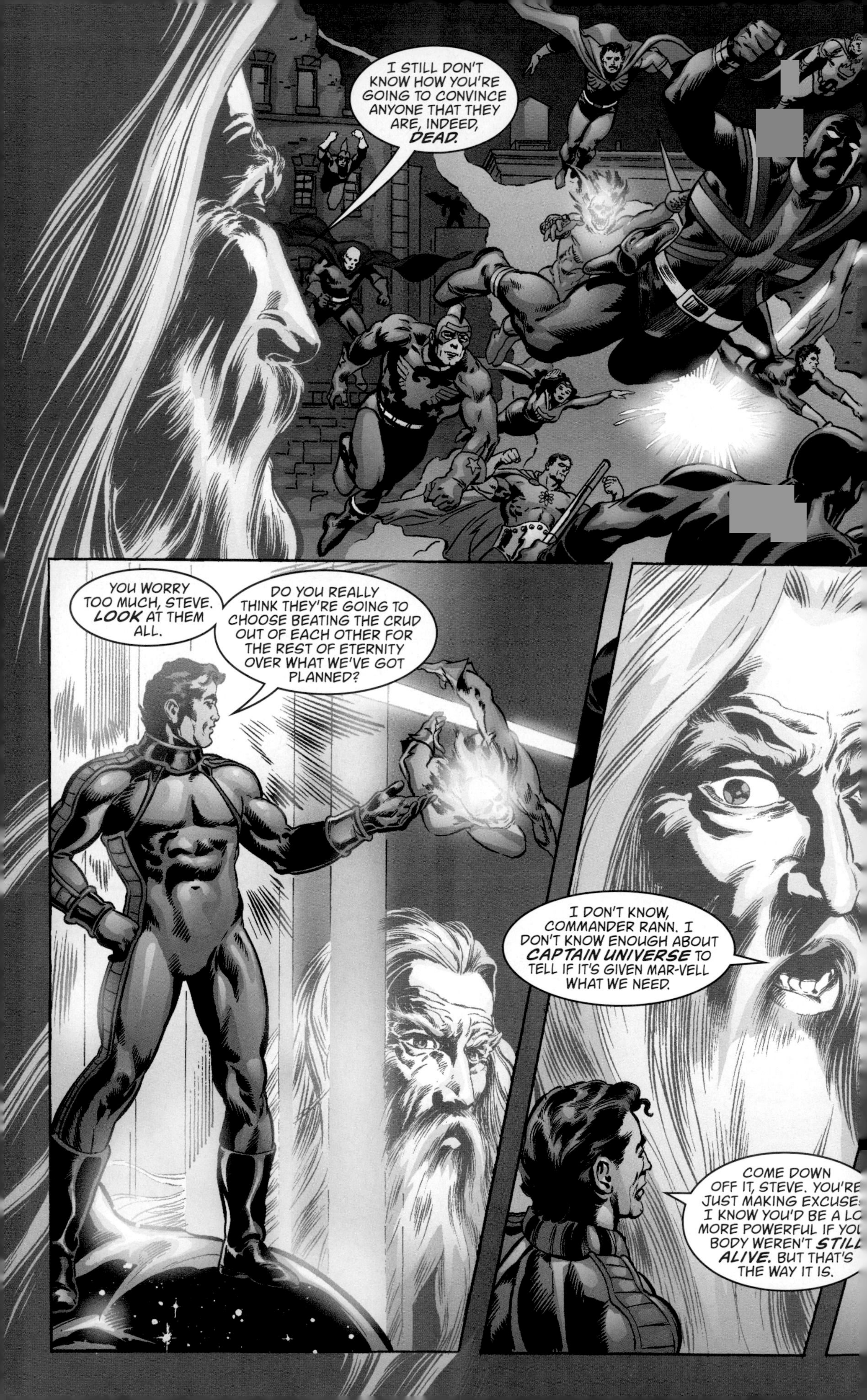
I STILL DON'T KNOW HOW YOU'RE GOING TO CONVINCE ANYONE THAT THEY ARE, INDEED, *DEAD.*
YOU WORRY TOO MUCH, STEVE. *LOOK* AT THEM ALL.
DO YOU REALLY THINK THEY'RE GOING TO CHOOSE BEATING THE CRUD OUT OF EACH OTHER FOR THE REST OF ETERNITY OVER WHAT WE'VE GOT PLANNED?
I DON'T KNOW, COMMANDER RANN. I DON'T KNOW ENOUGH ABOUT *CAPTAIN UNIVERSE* TO TELL IF IT'S GIVEN MAR-VELL WHAT WE NEED.
COME DOWN OFF IT, STEVE. YOU'RE JUST MAKING EXCUSE I KNOW YOU'D BE A LO MORE POWERFUL IF YOU BODY WEREN'T *STILL ALIVE.* BUT THAT'S THE WAY IT IS.

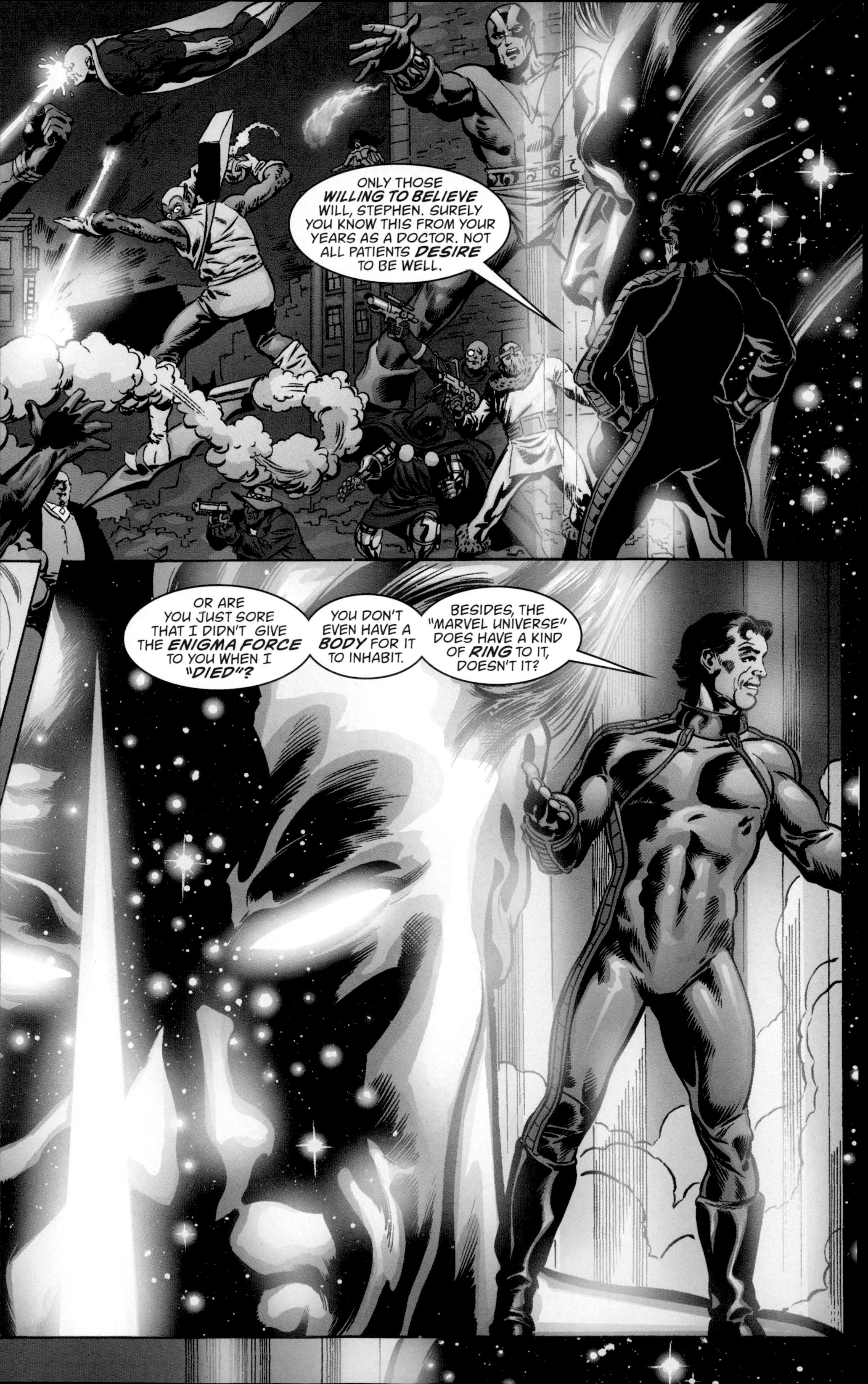
ONLY THOSE WILLING TO BELIEVE WILL, STEPHEN. SURELY YOU KNOW THIS FROM YOUR YEARS AS A DOCTOR. NOT ALL PATIENTS DESIRE TO BE WELL.
OR ARE YOU JUST SORE THAT I DIDN'T GIVE THE ENIGMA FORCE TO YOU WHEN I "DIED"?
YOU DON'T EVEN HAVE A BODY FOR IT TO INHABIT.
BESIDES, THE "MARVEL UNIVERSE" DOES HAVE A KIND OF RING TO IT, DOESN'T IT?

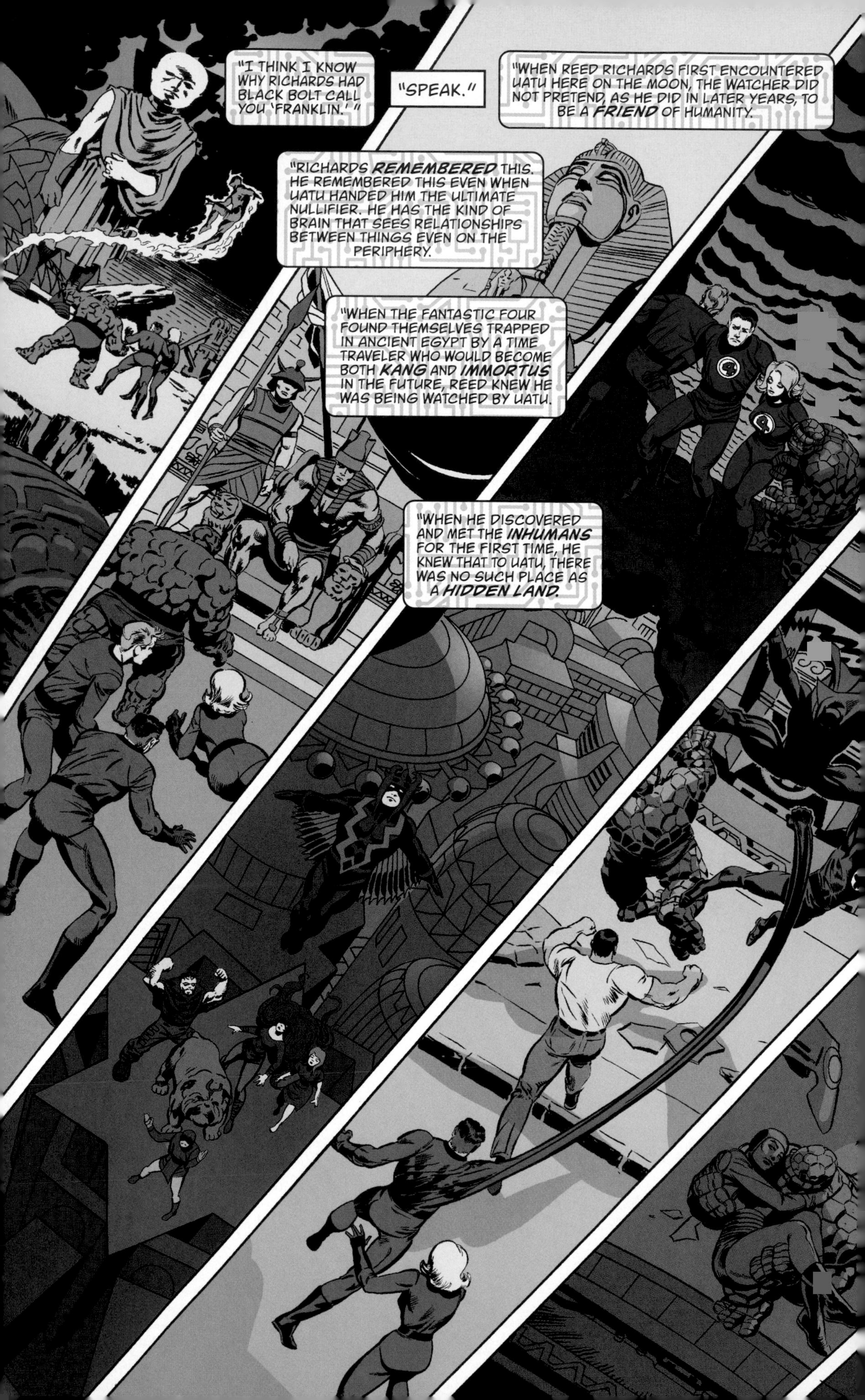
"I THINK I KNOW WHY RICHARDS HAD BLACK BOLT CALL YOU 'FRANKLIN.' "
"SPEAK."
"WHEN REED RICHARDS FIRST ENCOUNTERED UATU HERE ON THE MOON, THE WATCHER DID NOT PRETEND, AS HE DID IN LATER YEARS, TO BE A FRIEND OF HUMANITY.
"RICHARDS REMEMBERED THIS. HE REMEMBERED THIS EVEN WHEN UATU HANDED HIM THE ULTIMATE NULLIFIER. HE HAS THE KIND OF BRAIN THAT SEES RELATIONSHIPS BETWEEN THINGS EVEN ON THE PERIPHERY.
"WHEN THE FANTASTIC FOUR FOUND THEMSELVES TRAPPED IN ANCIENT EGYPT BY A TIME TRAVELER WHO WOULD BECOME BOTH KANG AND IMMORTUS IN THE FUTURE, REED KNEW HE WAS BEING WATCHED BY UATU.
"WHEN HE DISCOVERED AND MET THE INHUMANS FOR THE FIRST TIME, HE KNEW THAT TO UATU, THERE WAS NO SUCH PLACE AS A HIDDEN LAND.

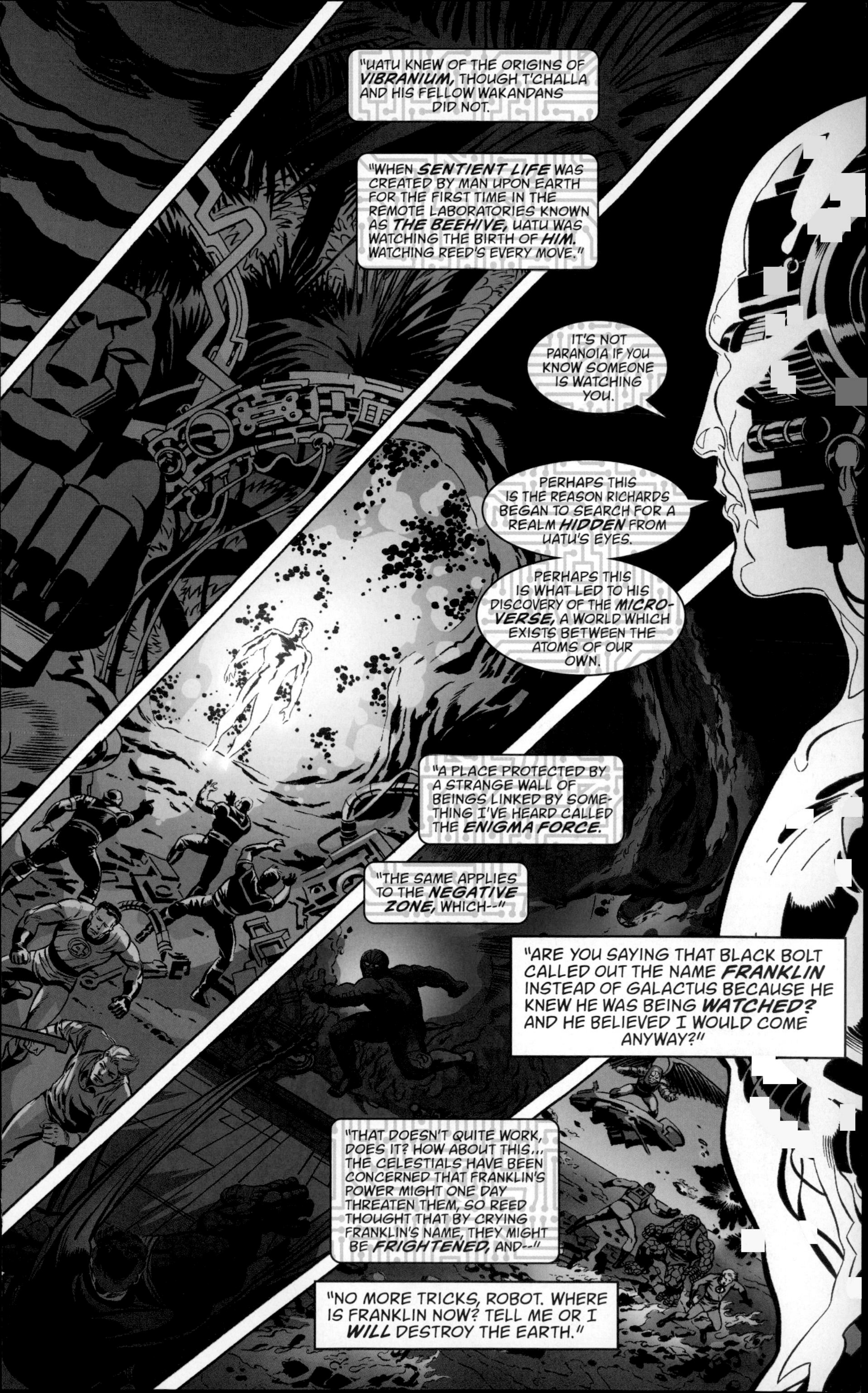
"UATU KNEW OF THE ORIGINS OF VIBRANIUM, THOUGH T'CHALLA AND HIS FELLOW WAKANDANS DID NOT.
"WHEN SENTIENT LIFE WAS CREATED BY MAN UPON EARTH FOR THE FIRST TIME IN THE REMOTE LABORATORIES KNOWN AS THE BEEHIVE, UATU WAS WATCHING THE BIRTH OF HIM. WATCHING REED'S EVERY MOVE."
IT'S NOT PARANOIA IF YOU KNOW SOMEONE IS WATCHING YOU.
PERHAPS THIS IS THE REASON RICHARDS BEGAN TO SEARCH FOR A REALM HIDDEN FROM UATU'S EYES.
PERHAPS THIS IS WHAT LED TO HIS DISCOVERY OF THE MICRO-VERSE, A WORLD WHICH EXISTS BETWEEN THE ATOMS OF OUR OWN.
"A PLACE PROTECTED BY A STRANGE WALL OF BEINGS LINKED BY SOME-THING I'VE HEARD CALLED THE ENIGMA FORCE.
"THE SAME APPLIES TO THE NEGATIVE ZONE, WHICH--"
"ARE YOU SAYING THAT BLACK BOLT CALLED OUT THE NAME FRANKLIN INSTEAD OF GALACTUS BECAUSE HE KNEW HE WAS BEING WATCHED? AND HE BELIEVED I WOULD COME ANYWAY?"
"THAT DOESN'T QUITE WORK, DOES IT? HOW ABOUT THIS... THE CELESTIALS HAVE BEEN CONCERNED THAT FRANKLIN'S POWER MIGHT ONE DAY THREATEN THEM, SO REED THOUGHT THAT BY CRYING FRANKLIN'S NAME, THEY MIGHT BE FRIGHTENED, AND--"
"NO MORE TRICKS, ROBOT. WHERE IS FRANKLIN NOW? TELL ME OR I WILL DESTROY THE EARTH."

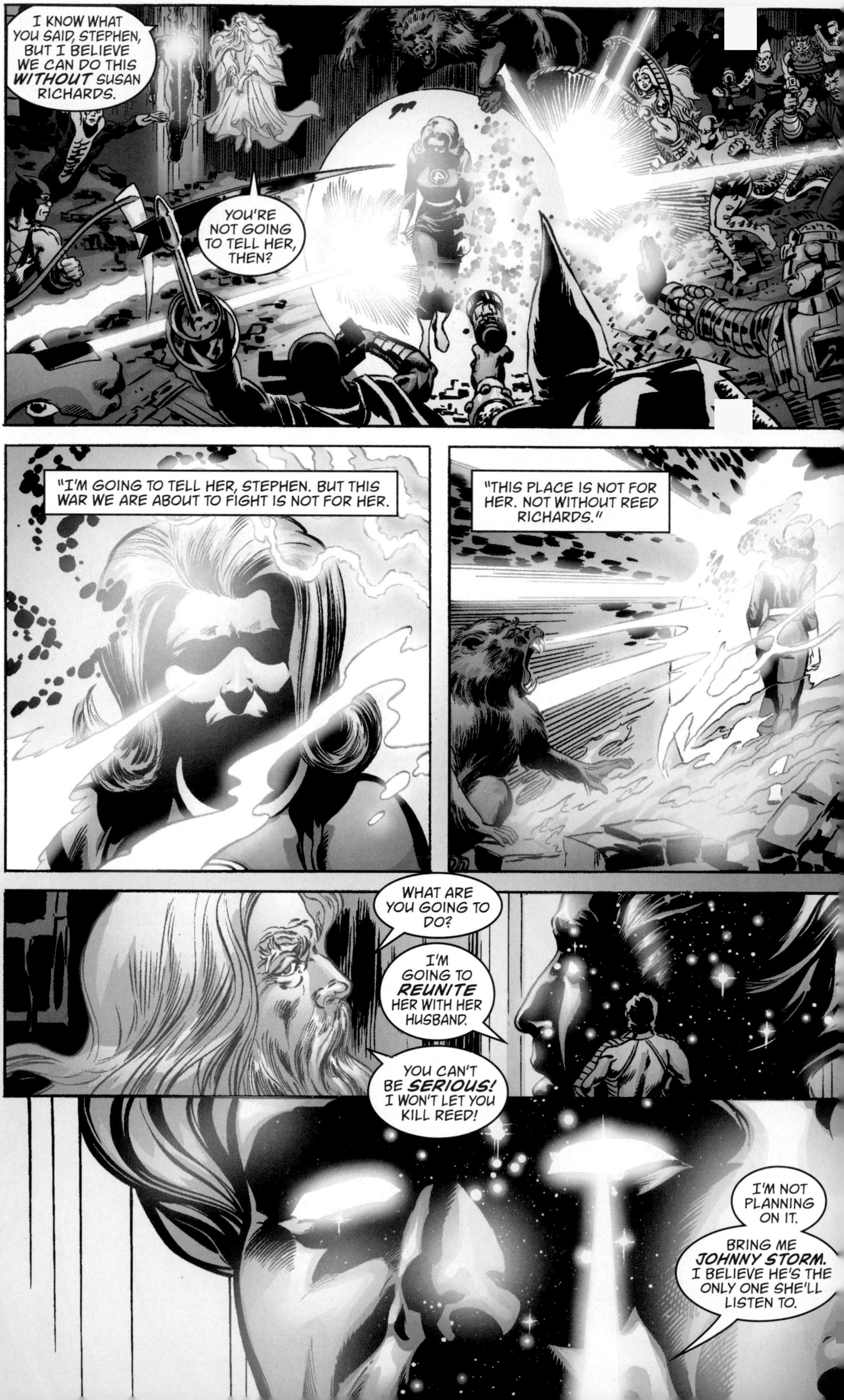
I KNOW WHAT YOU SAID, STEPHEN, BUT I BELIEVE WE CAN DO THIS WITHOUT SUSAN RICHARDS.
YOU'RE NOT GOING TO TELL HER, THEN?
"I'M GOING TO TELL HER, STEPHEN. BUT THIS WAR WE ARE ABOUT TO FIGHT IS NOT FOR HER.
"THIS PLACE IS NOT FOR HER. NOT WITHOUT REED RICHARDS."
WHAT ARE YOU GOING TO DO?
I'M GOING TO REUNITE HER WITH HER HUSBAND.
YOU CAN'T BE SERIOUS! I WON'T LET YOU KILL REED!
I'M NOT PLANNING ON IT.
BRING ME JOHNNY STORM. I BELIEVE HE'S THE ONLY ONE SHE'LL LISTEN TO.

SIS? MAR-VELL MEANS IT. I THINK HE CAN DO IT. IF HE CAN CONVINCE ME THAT I'M *DEAD*, SURELY HE CAN...

BUT JOHNNY, YOU'RE *NOT DEAD*. REED AND FRANKLIN AND BEN ARE. I UNDERSTAND WHAT YOU'RE TRYING TO DO, BUT I CAN'T STOP FEELING THE WAY I DO.

THAT'S JUST IT. YOU CAN'T STOP LOVING REED BECAUSE YOU *KNOW* HE'S NOT DEAD. MAR-VELL SAW YOUR LOVE SO EASILY. WE *ALL* DO. YOU CAN'T MAKE THAT INVISIBLE.

DON'T YOU THINK I *WANT* THAT TO BE THE CASE? DON'T YOU THINK I WISH THAT IT WAS *ME* AND *NOT THEM* WHO DIED THAT DAY?

THIS ISN'T FUNNY, JOHNNY.

IS THERE ANYTHING THAT WOULD CONVINCE YOU?

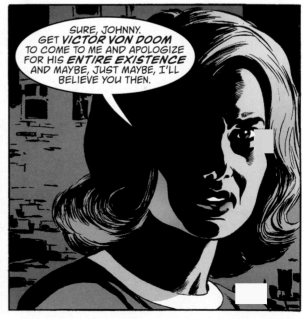

SURE, JOHNNY. GET *VICTOR VON DOOM* TO COME TO ME AND APOLOGIZE FOR HIS *ENTIRE EXISTENCE* AND MAYBE, JUST MAYBE, I'LL BELIEVE YOU THEN.

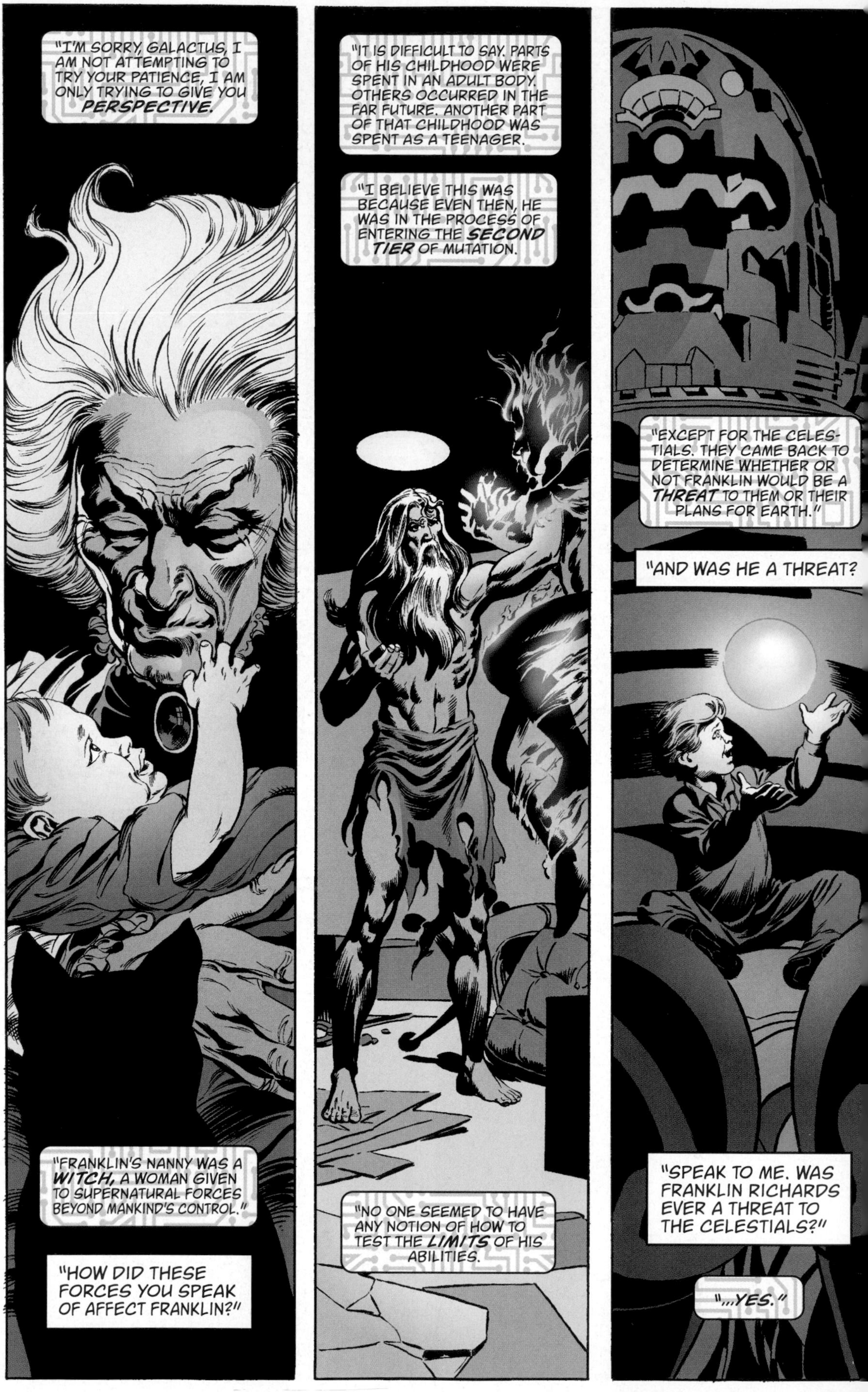
"I'M SORRY, GALACTUS, I AM NOT ATTEMPTING TO TRY YOUR PATIENCE, I AM ONLY TRYING TO GIVE YOU PERSPECTIVE.
"FRANKLIN'S NANNY WAS A WITCH, A WOMAN GIVEN TO SUPERNATURAL FORCES BEYOND MANKIND'S CONTROL."
"HOW DID THESE FORCES YOU SPEAK OF AFFECT FRANKLIN?"
"IT IS DIFFICULT TO SAY. PARTS OF HIS CHILDHOOD WERE SPENT IN AN ADULT BODY. OTHERS OCCURRED IN THE FAR FUTURE. ANOTHER PART OF THAT CHILDHOOD WAS SPENT AS A TEENAGER.
"I BELIEVE THIS WAS BECAUSE EVEN THEN, HE WAS IN THE PROCESS OF ENTERING THE SECOND TIER OF MUTATION.
"NO ONE SEEMED TO HAVE ANY NOTION OF HOW TO TEST THE LIMITS OF HIS ABILITIES.
"EXCEPT FOR THE CELESTIALS. THEY CAME BACK TO DETERMINE WHETHER OR NOT FRANKLIN WOULD BE A THREAT TO THEM OR THEIR PLANS FOR EARTH."
"AND WAS HE A THREAT?
"SPEAK TO ME. WAS FRANKLIN RICHARDS EVER A THREAT TO THE CELESTIALS?"
"...YES."

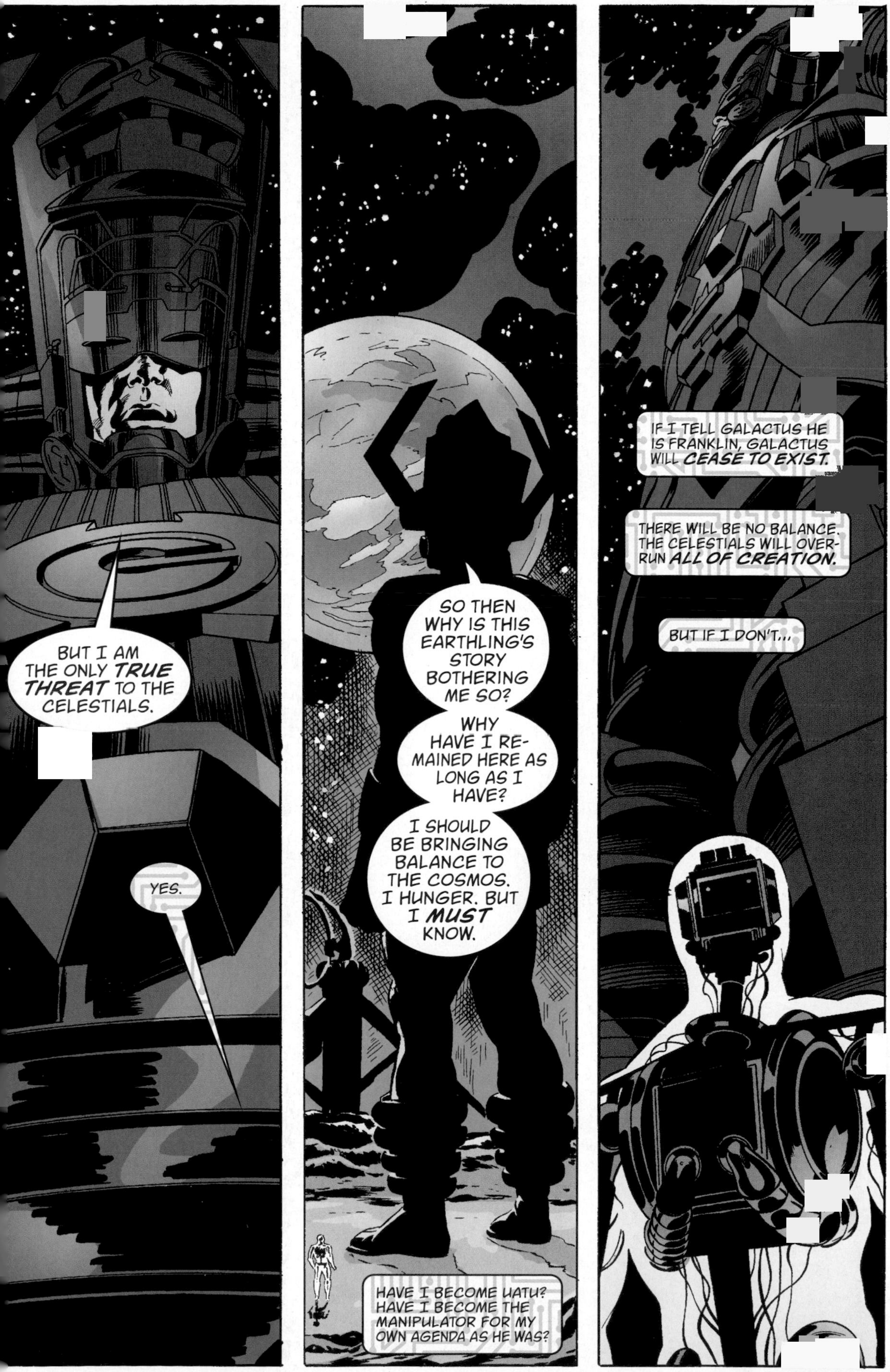
BUT I AM THE ONLY TRUE THREAT TO THE CELESTIALS.
YES.
SO THEN WHY IS THIS EARTHLING'S STORY BOTHERING ME SO?
WHY HAVE I REMAINED HERE AS LONG AS I HAVE?
I SHOULD BE BRINGING BALANCE TO THE COSMOS. I HUNGER. BUT I MUST KNOW.
HAVE I BECOME UATU? HAVE I BECOME THE MANIPULATOR FOR MY OWN AGENDA AS HE WAS?
IF I TELL GALACTUS HE IS FRANKLIN, GALACTUS WILL CEASE TO EXIST.
THERE WILL BE NO BALANCE. THE CELESTIALS WILL OVERRUN ALL OF CREATION.
BUT IF I DON'T...

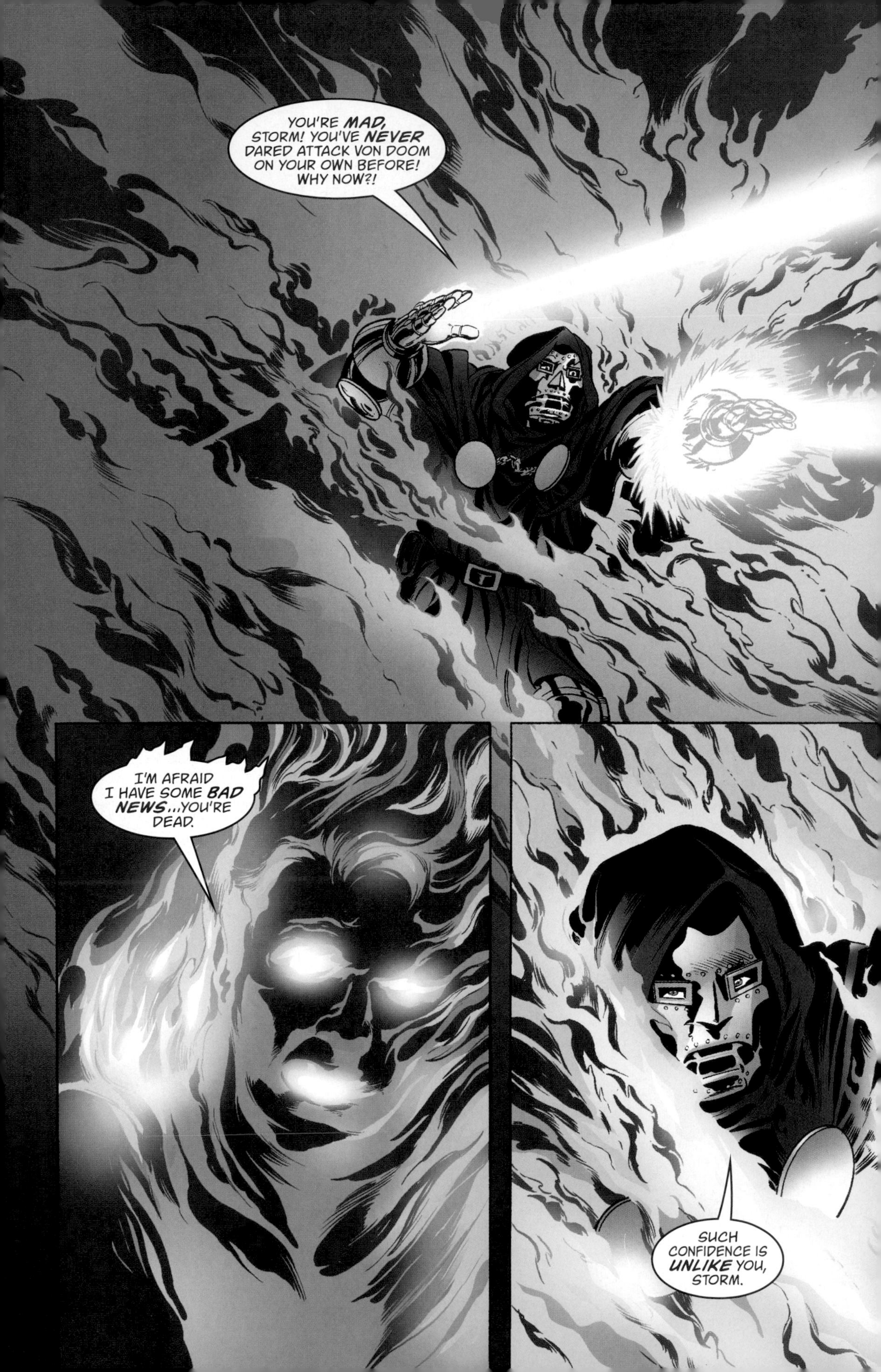

YOU'RE MAD, STORM! YOU'VE NEVER DARED ATTACK VON DOOM ON YOUR OWN BEFORE! WHY NOW?!
I'M AFRAID I HAVE SOME BAD NEWS...YOU'RE DEAD.
SUCH CONFIDENCE IS UNLIKE YOU, STORM.

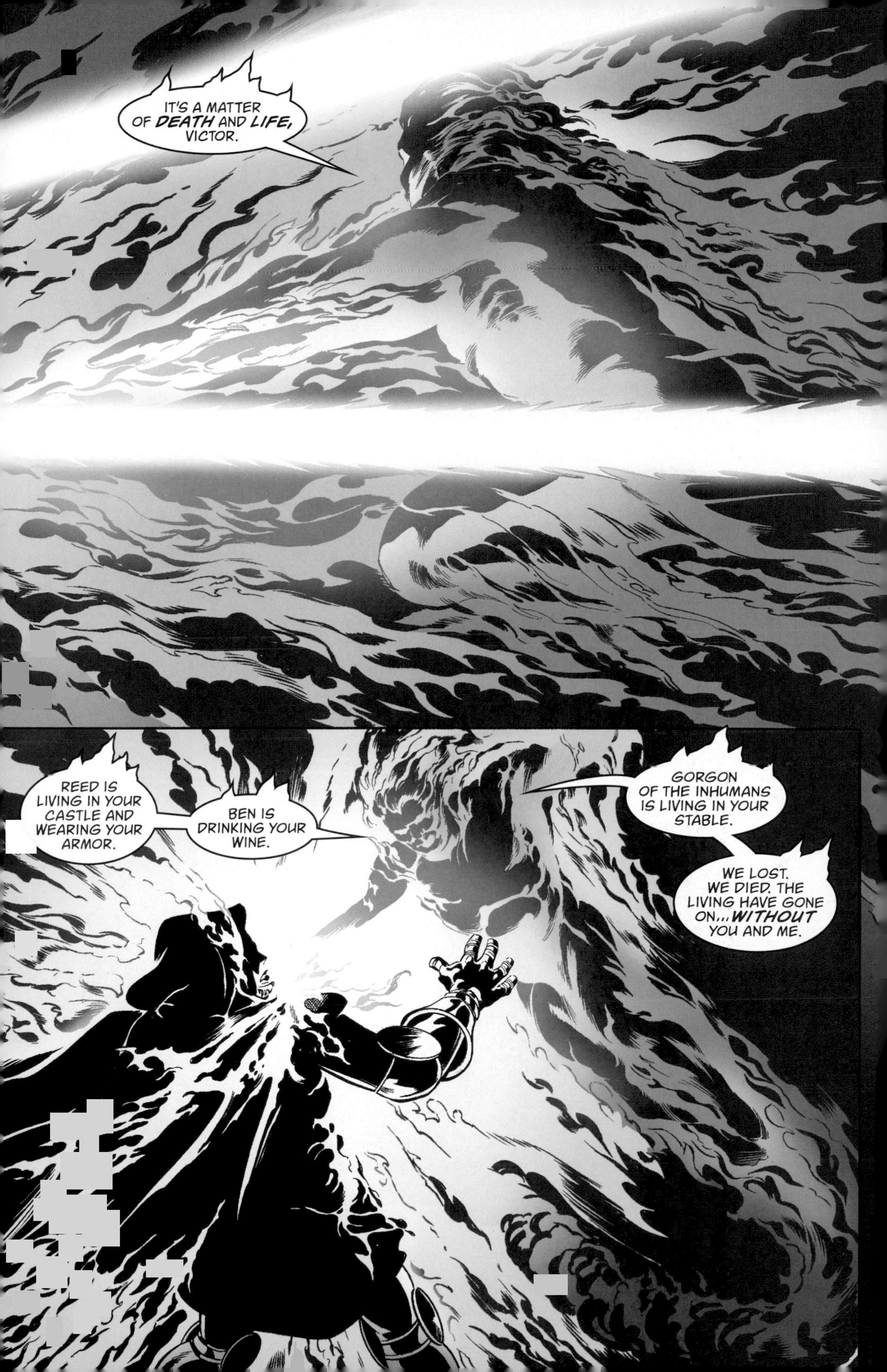
IT'S A MATTER OF DEATH AND LIFE, VICTOR.
REED IS LIVING IN YOUR CASTLE AND WEARING YOUR ARMOR.
BEN IS DRINKING YOUR WINE.
GORGON OF THE INHUMANS IS LIVING IN YOUR STABLE.
WE LOST. WE DIED. THE LIVING HAVE GONE ON...WITHOUT YOU AND ME.

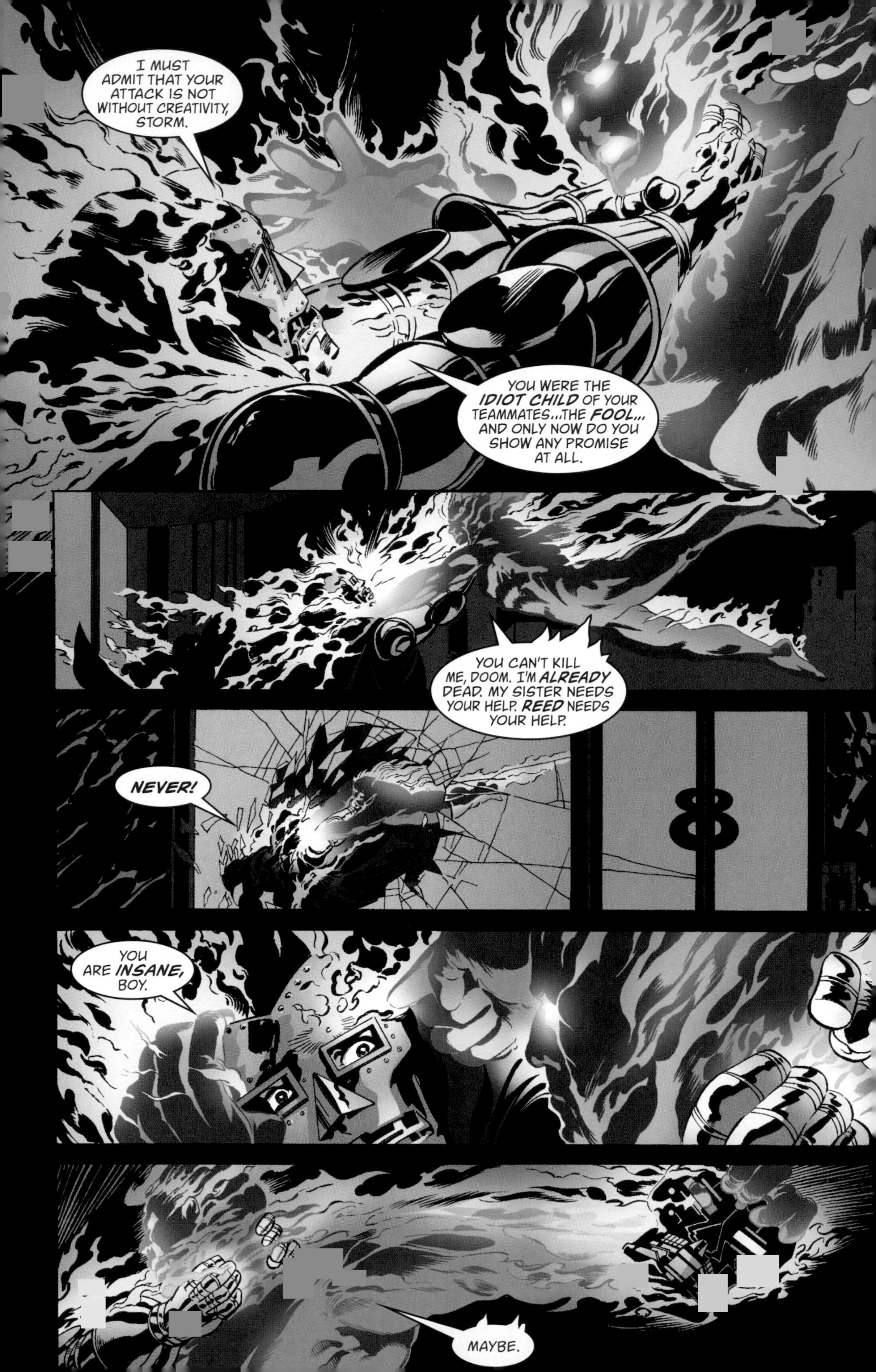
I MUST ADMIT THAT YOUR ATTACK IS NOT WITHOUT CREATIVITY, STORM.
YOU WERE THE IDIOT CHILD OF YOUR TEAMMATES...THE FOOL... AND ONLY NOW DO YOU SHOW ANY PROMISE AT ALL.
YOU CAN'T KILL ME, DOOM. I'M ALREADY DEAD. MY SISTER NEEDS YOUR HELP. REED NEEDS YOUR HELP.
NEVER!
YOU ARE INSANE, BOY.
MAYBE.

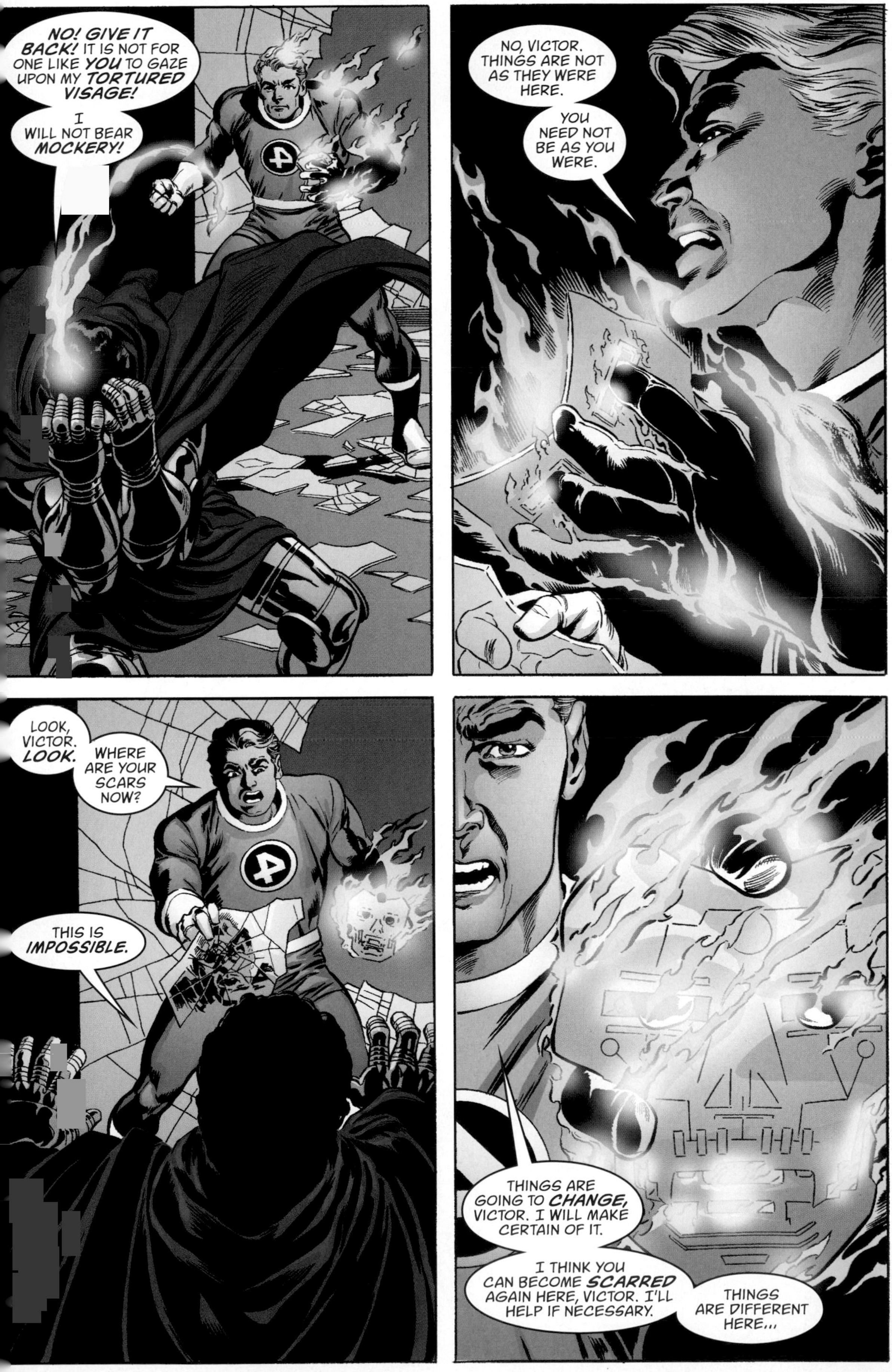
NO! GIVE IT BACK! IT IS NOT FOR ONE LIKE YOU TO GAZE UPON MY TORTURED VISAGE!
I WILL NOT BEAR MOCKERY!
NO, VICTOR. THINGS ARE NOT AS THEY WERE HERE.
YOU NEED NOT BE AS YOU WERE.
LOOK, VICTOR. LOOK.
WHERE ARE YOUR SCARS NOW?
THIS IS IMPOSSIBLE.
THINGS ARE GOING TO CHANGE, VICTOR. I WILL MAKE CERTAIN OF IT.
I THINK YOU CAN BECOME SCARRED AGAIN HERE, VICTOR. I'LL HELP IF NECESSARY.
THINGS ARE DIFFERENT HERE...

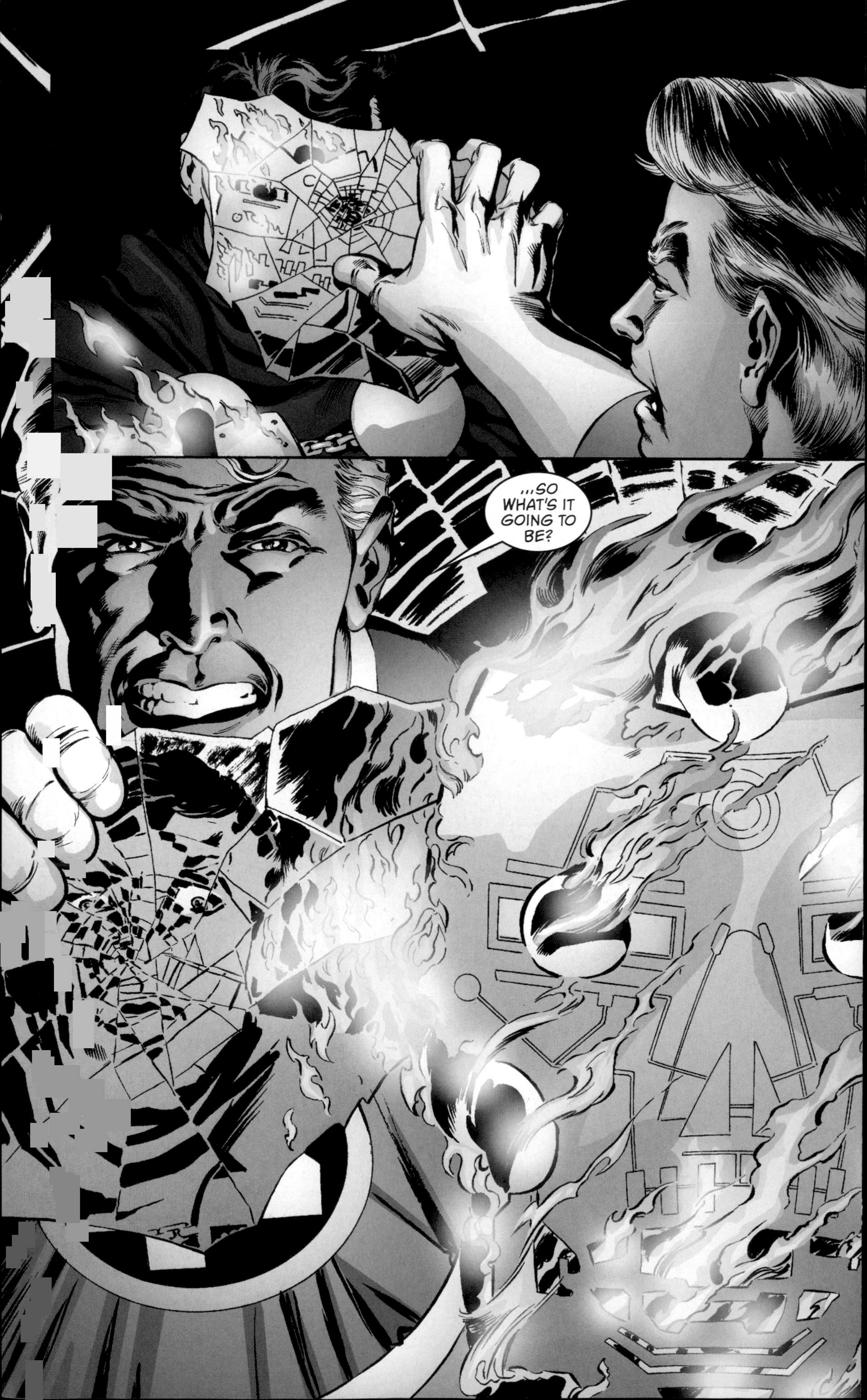
...SO WHAT'S IT GOING TO BE?

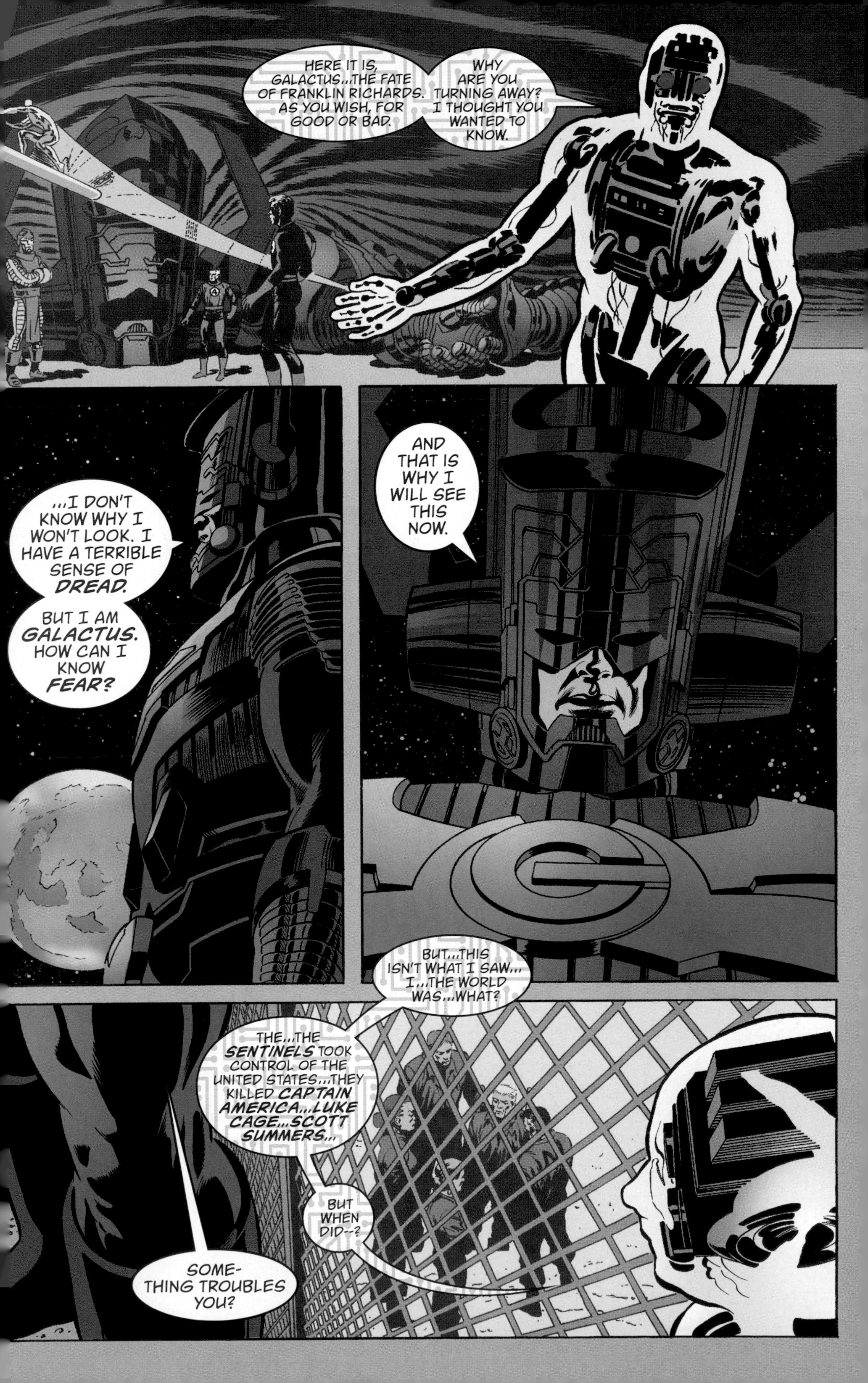
HERE IT IS, GALACTUS...THE FATE OF FRANKLIN RICHARDS. AS YOU WISH, FOR GOOD OR BAD.
WHY ARE YOU TURNING AWAY? I THOUGHT YOU WANTED TO KNOW.
...I DON'T KNOW WHY I WON'T LOOK. I HAVE A TERRIBLE SENSE OF DREAD.
BUT I AM GALACTUS. HOW CAN I KNOW FEAR?
AND THAT IS WHY I WILL SEE THIS NOW.
BUT...THIS ISN'T WHAT I SAW... I...THE WORLD WAS...WHAT?
THE...THE SENTINELS TOOK CONTROL OF THE UNITED STATES...THEY KILLED CAPTAIN AMERICA...LUKE CAGE...SCOTT SUMMERS...
BUT WHEN DID--?
SOME-THING TROUBLES YOU?

"AN *UNDERGROUND STRIKE-FORCE* WAS CREATED TO ATTACK THE MUTANT-HUNTING SENTINELS. FRANKLIN WAS A MEMBER OF THIS MILITIA.

"LED BY *WOLVERINE,* THEIR MISSION WAS TO ATTACK THE SENTINELS' COMMAND CENTER...

"...A MANHATTAN HIGH-RISE KNOWN AS THE *BAXTER BUILDING.*"

"THE *HOME* OF THE *FANTAS-TIC FOUR?*"

"YES. THE SENTINELS LEARNED OF THE ATTACK, AND *COUNTERED.*

"THIS...WAS HOW FRANKLIN RICHARDS... DIED."

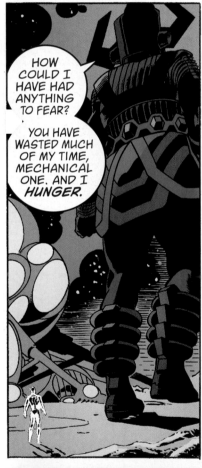

HOW COULD I HAVE HAD ANYTHING TO FEAR?

YOU HAVE WASTED MUCH OF MY TIME, MECHANICAL ONE. AND I *HUNGER.*

BUT THAT'S NOT HOW IT HAPPENED AT ALL.

WHAT'S GOING ON? WHY AM I SEEING SOMETHING LIKE THIS?

THE LAST THING I EVER WANTED TO DO WAS TO HAVE TO TALK TO *UATU* AGAIN.

SUSAN RICHARDS

REED RICHARDS

JOHNNY STORM

BEN GRIMM

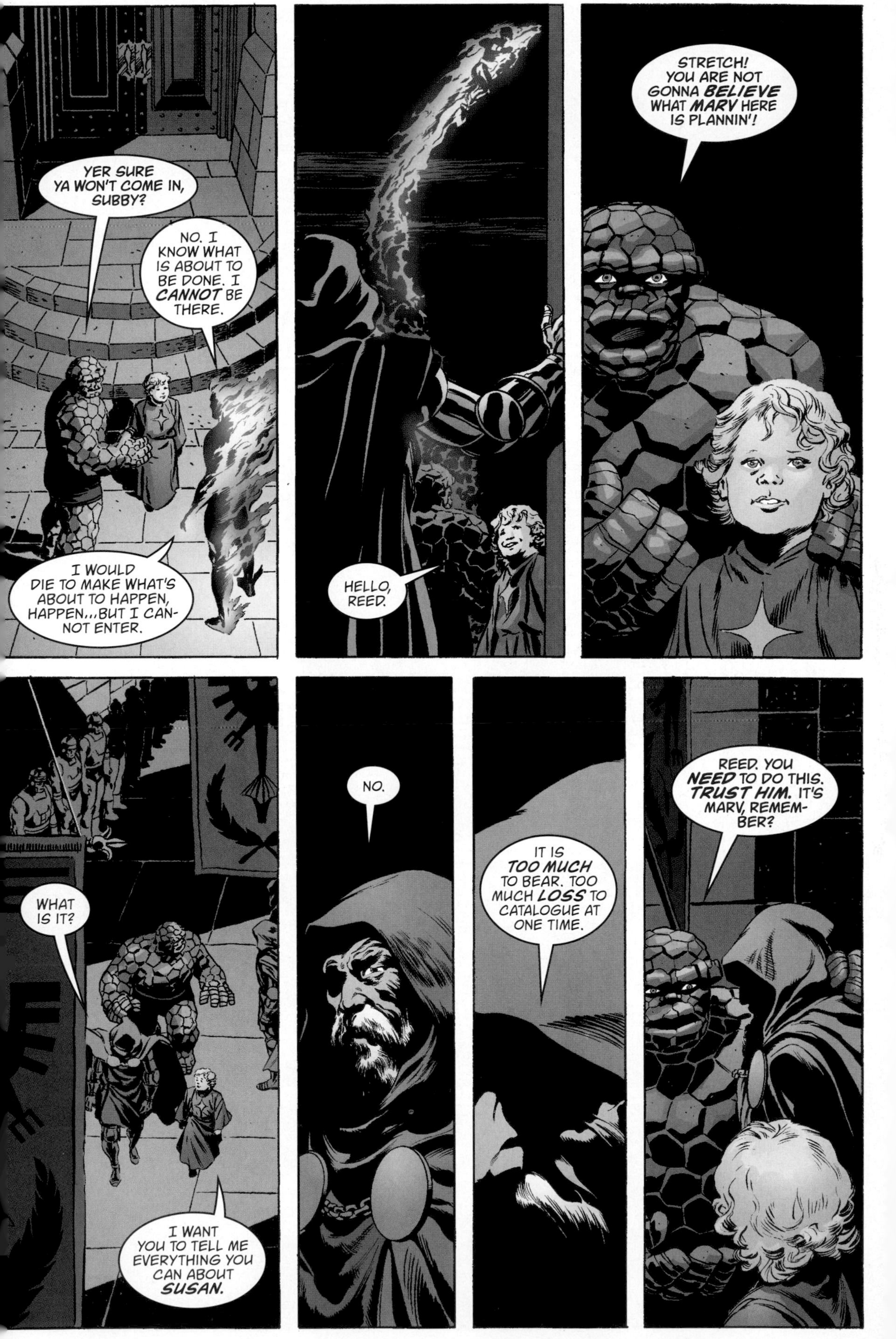
YER SURE YA WON'T COME IN, SUBBY?
NO. I KNOW WHAT IS ABOUT TO BE DONE. I *CANNOT* BE THERE.
I WOULD DIE TO MAKE WHAT'S ABOUT TO HAPPEN, HAPPEN...BUT I CAN-NOT ENTER.
HELLO, REED.
STRETCH! YOU ARE NOT GONNA *BELIEVE* WHAT *MARV* HERE IS PLANNIN'!
WHAT IS IT?
I WANT YOU TO TELL ME EVERYTHING YOU CAN ABOUT *SUSAN.*
NO.
IT IS *TOO MUCH* TO BEAR. TOO MUCH *LOSS* TO CATALOGUE AT ONE TIME.
REED. YOU *NEED* TO DO THIS. *TRUST HIM.* IT'S MARV, REMEM-BER?

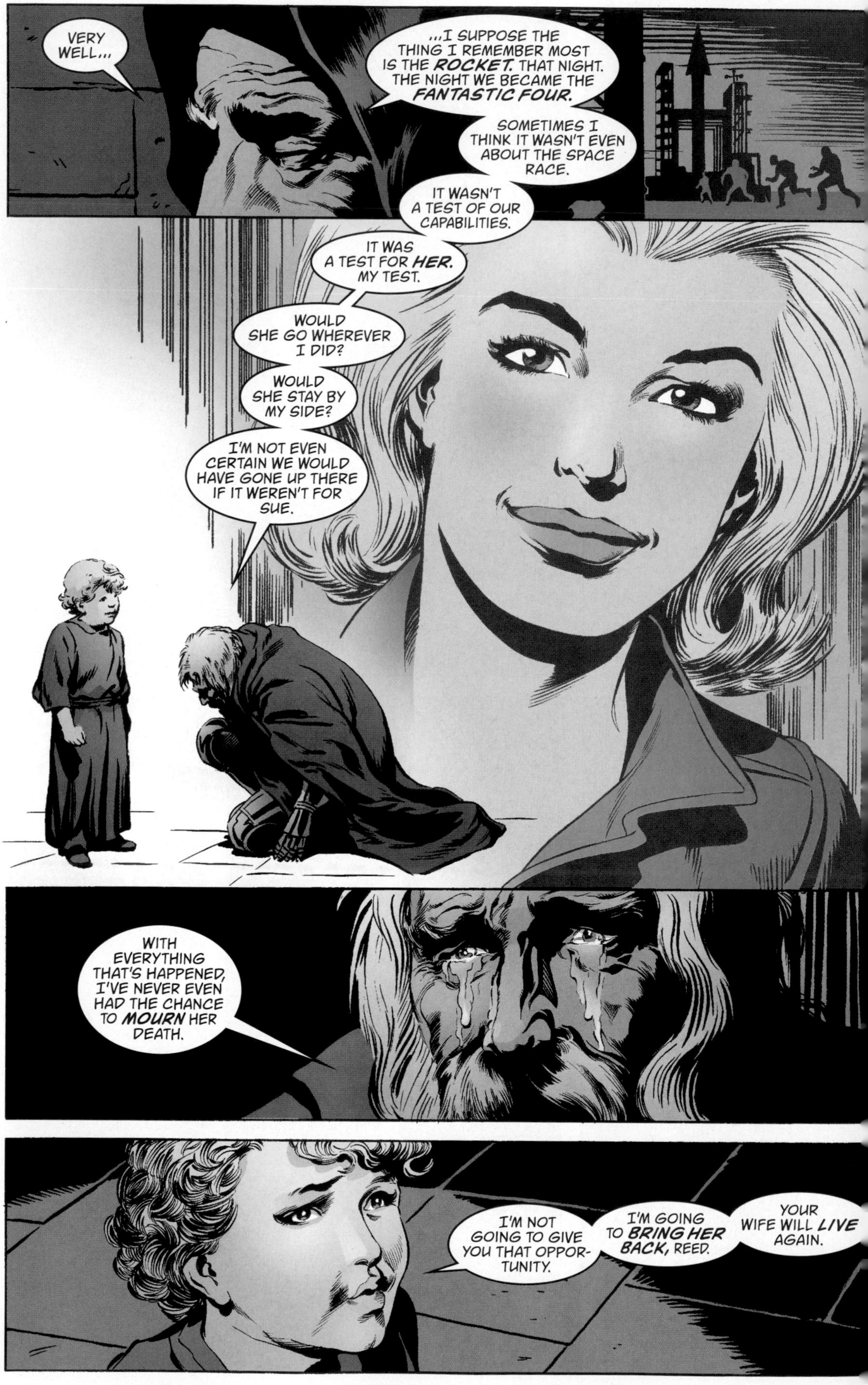
VERY WELL...
...I SUPPOSE THE THING I REMEMBER MOST IS THE ROCKET. THAT NIGHT. THE NIGHT WE BECAME THE FANTASTIC FOUR.
SOMETIMES I THINK IT WASN'T EVEN ABOUT THE SPACE RACE.
IT WASN'T A TEST OF OUR CAPABILITIES.
IT WAS A TEST FOR HER. MY TEST.
WOULD SHE GO WHEREVER I DID?
WOULD SHE STAY BY MY SIDE?
I'M NOT EVEN CERTAIN WE WOULD HAVE GONE UP THERE IF IT WEREN'T FOR SUE.
WITH EVERYTHING THAT'S HAPPENED, I'VE NEVER EVEN HAD THE CHANCE TO MOURN HER DEATH.
I'M NOT GOING TO GIVE YOU THAT OPPOR-TUNITY.
I'M GOING TO BRING HER BACK, REED.
YOUR WIFE WILL LIVE AGAIN.

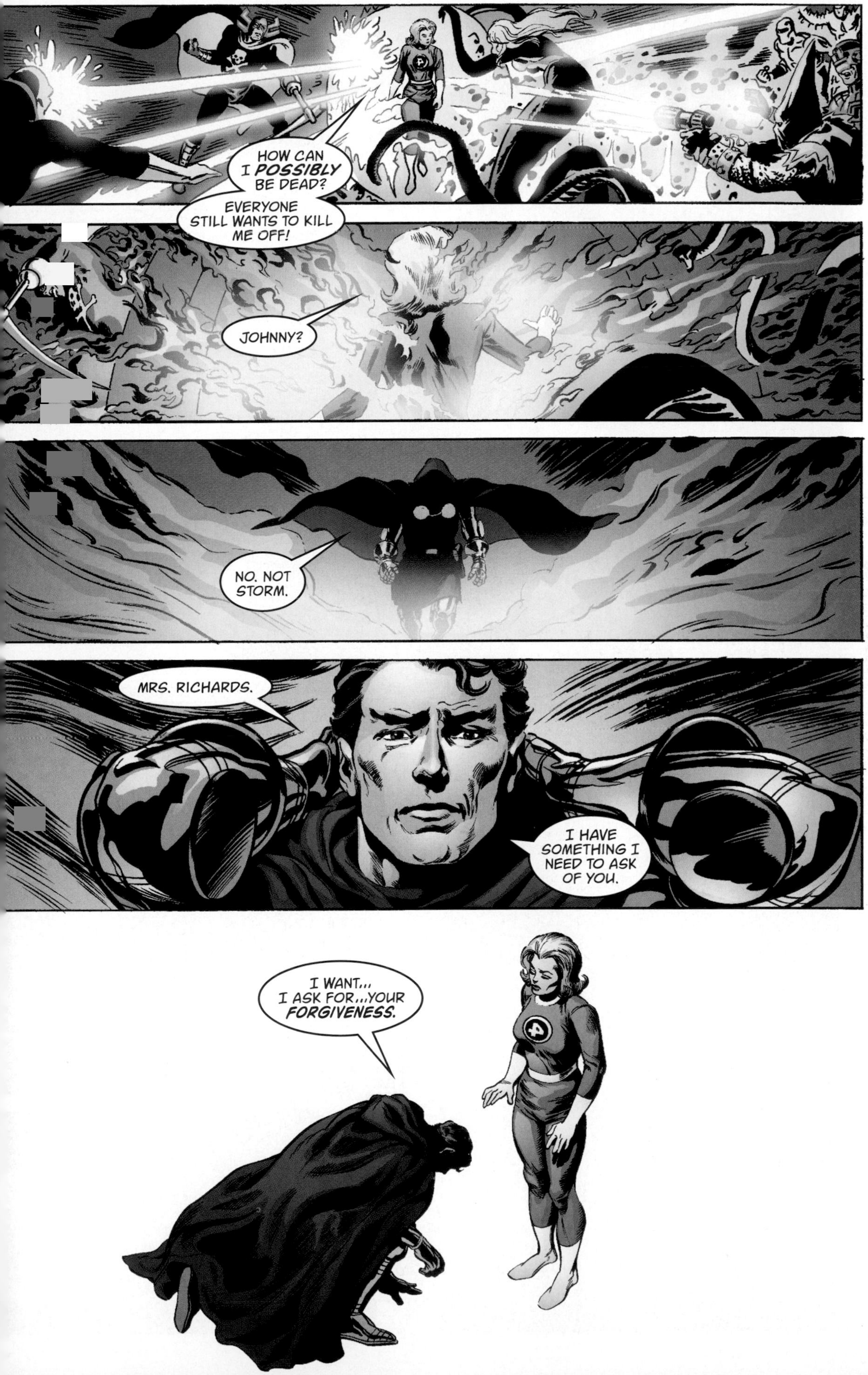
HOW CAN I *POSSIBLY* BE DEAD?
EVERYONE STILL WANTS TO KILL ME OFF!
JOHNNY?
NO. NOT STORM.
MRS. RICHARDS.
I HAVE SOMETHING I NEED TO ASK OF YOU.
I WANT... I ASK FOR...YOUR *FORGIVENESS.*

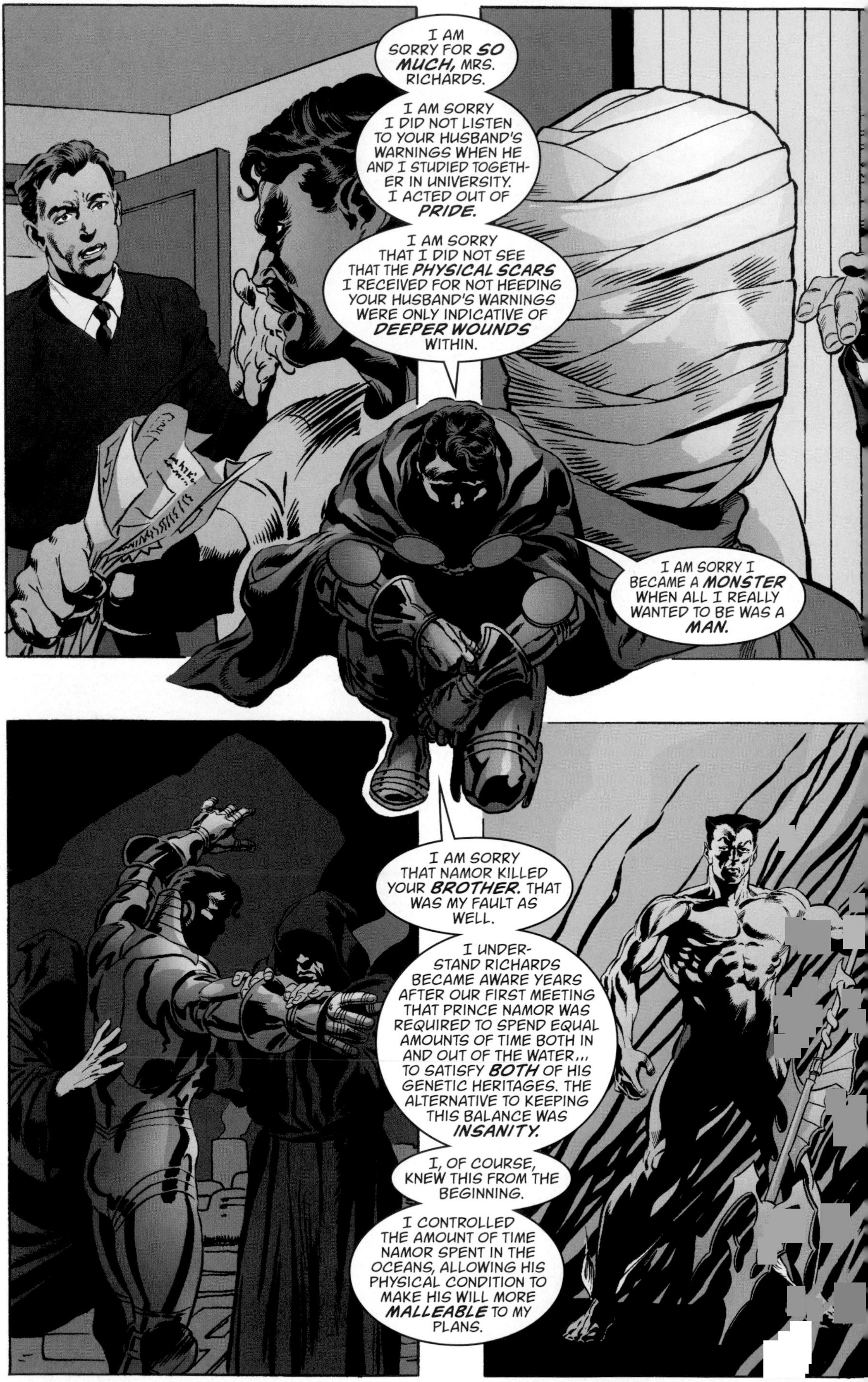
I AM SORRY FOR SO MUCH, MRS. RICHARDS.
I AM SORRY I DID NOT LISTEN TO YOUR HUSBAND'S WARNINGS WHEN HE AND I STUDIED TOGETH-ER IN UNIVERSITY. I ACTED OUT OF PRIDE.
I AM SORRY THAT I DID NOT SEE THAT THE PHYSICAL SCARS I RECEIVED FOR NOT HEEDING YOUR HUSBAND'S WARNINGS WERE ONLY INDICATIVE OF DEEPER WOUNDS WITHIN.
I AM SORRY I BECAME A MONSTER WHEN ALL I REALLY WANTED TO BE WAS A MAN.
I AM SORRY THAT NAMOR KILLED YOUR BROTHER. THAT WAS MY FAULT AS WELL.
I UNDER-STAND RICHARDS BECAME AWARE YEARS AFTER OUR FIRST MEETING THAT PRINCE NAMOR WAS REQUIRED TO SPEND EQUAL AMOUNTS OF TIME BOTH IN AND OUT OF THE WATER... TO SATISFY BOTH OF HIS GENETIC HERITAGES. THE ALTERNATIVE TO KEEPING THIS BALANCE WAS INSANITY.
I, OF COURSE, KNEW THIS FROM THE BEGINNING.
I CONTROLLED THE AMOUNT OF TIME NAMOR SPENT IN THE OCEANS, ALLOWING HIS PHYSICAL CONDITION TO MAKE HIS WILL MORE MALLEABLE TO MY PLANS.

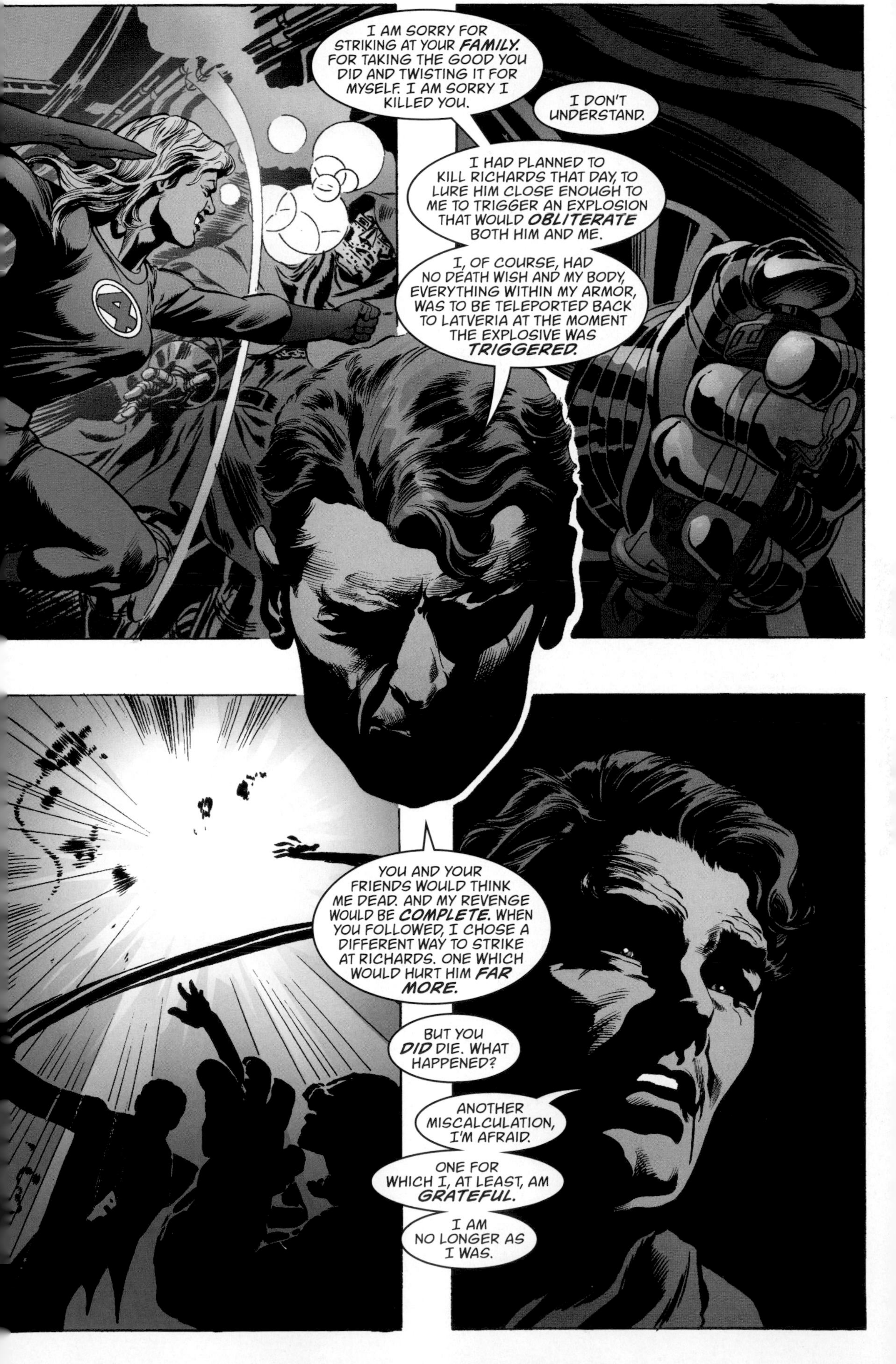
I AM SORRY FOR STRIKING AT YOUR FAMILY. FOR TAKING THE GOOD YOU DID AND TWISTING IT FOR MYSELF. I AM SORRY I KILLED YOU.
I DON'T UNDERSTAND.
I HAD PLANNED TO KILL RICHARDS THAT DAY, TO LURE HIM CLOSE ENOUGH TO ME TO TRIGGER AN EXPLOSION THAT WOULD OBLITERATE BOTH HIM AND ME.
I, OF COURSE, HAD NO DEATH WISH AND MY BODY, EVERYTHING WITHIN MY ARMOR, WAS TO BE TELEPORTED BACK TO LATVERIA AT THE MOMENT THE EXPLOSIVE WAS TRIGGERED.
YOU AND YOUR FRIENDS WOULD THINK ME DEAD. AND MY REVENGE WOULD BE COMPLETE. WHEN YOU FOLLOWED, I CHOSE A DIFFERENT WAY TO STRIKE AT RICHARDS. ONE WHICH WOULD HURT HIM FAR MORE.
BUT YOU DID DIE. WHAT HAPPENED?
ANOTHER MISCALCULATION, I'M AFRAID.
ONE FOR WHICH I, AT LEAST, AM GRATEFUL.
I AM NO LONGER AS I WAS.

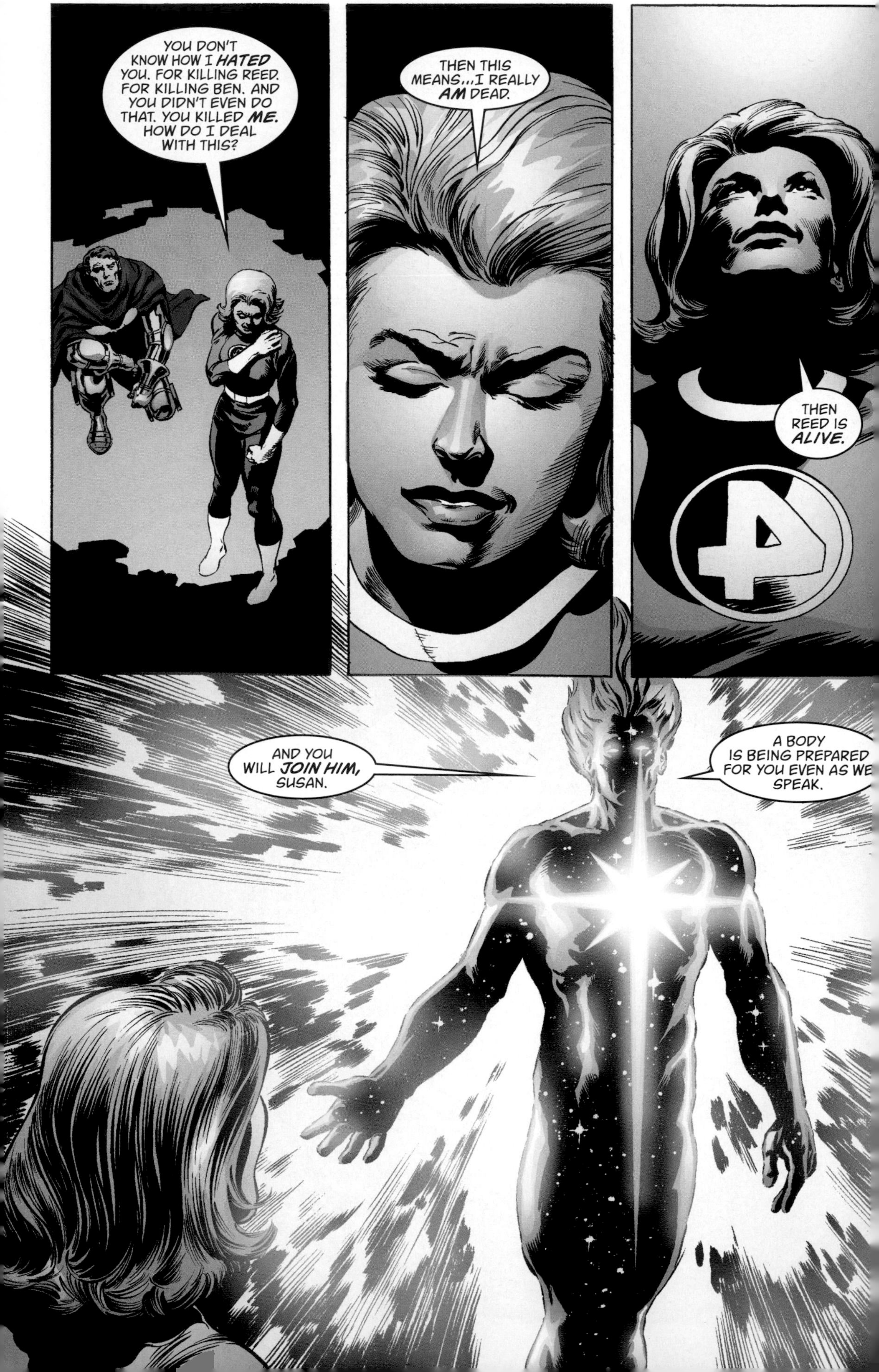
YOU DON'T KNOW HOW I HATED YOU. FOR KILLING REED. FOR KILLING BEN. AND YOU DIDN'T EVEN DO THAT. YOU KILLED ME. HOW DO I DEAL WITH THIS?
THEN THIS MEANS...I REALLY AM DEAD.
THEN REED IS ALIVE.
AND YOU WILL JOIN HIM, SUSAN.
A BODY IS BEING PREPARED FOR YOU EVEN AS WE SPEAK.

YOU CAN BRING HER *BACK?* I'D GIVE MY *RIGHT ARM* TO SEE HER AGAIN.

GOOD. BECAUSE THAT IS WHAT I REQUIRE.

ALICIA?

JUST TRY TO *RELAX,* REED.

I KNOW IT HURTS TO STRETCH.

I CAN CREATE *LIFE,* REED.

IT'S MY MUTATION. MY *GIFT.*

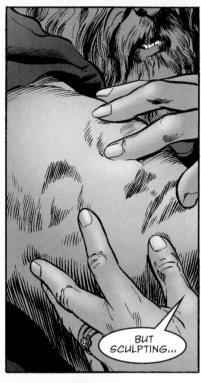

BUT SCULPTING...

...THIS WAS MY *FATHER'S* GIFT...

...WHICH I GIVE TO YOU.

SHE HAS TO BE PERFECT, REED.

SHE'S YOUR WIFE.

FLESH OF YOUR FLESH.

BONE OF YOUR BONE.

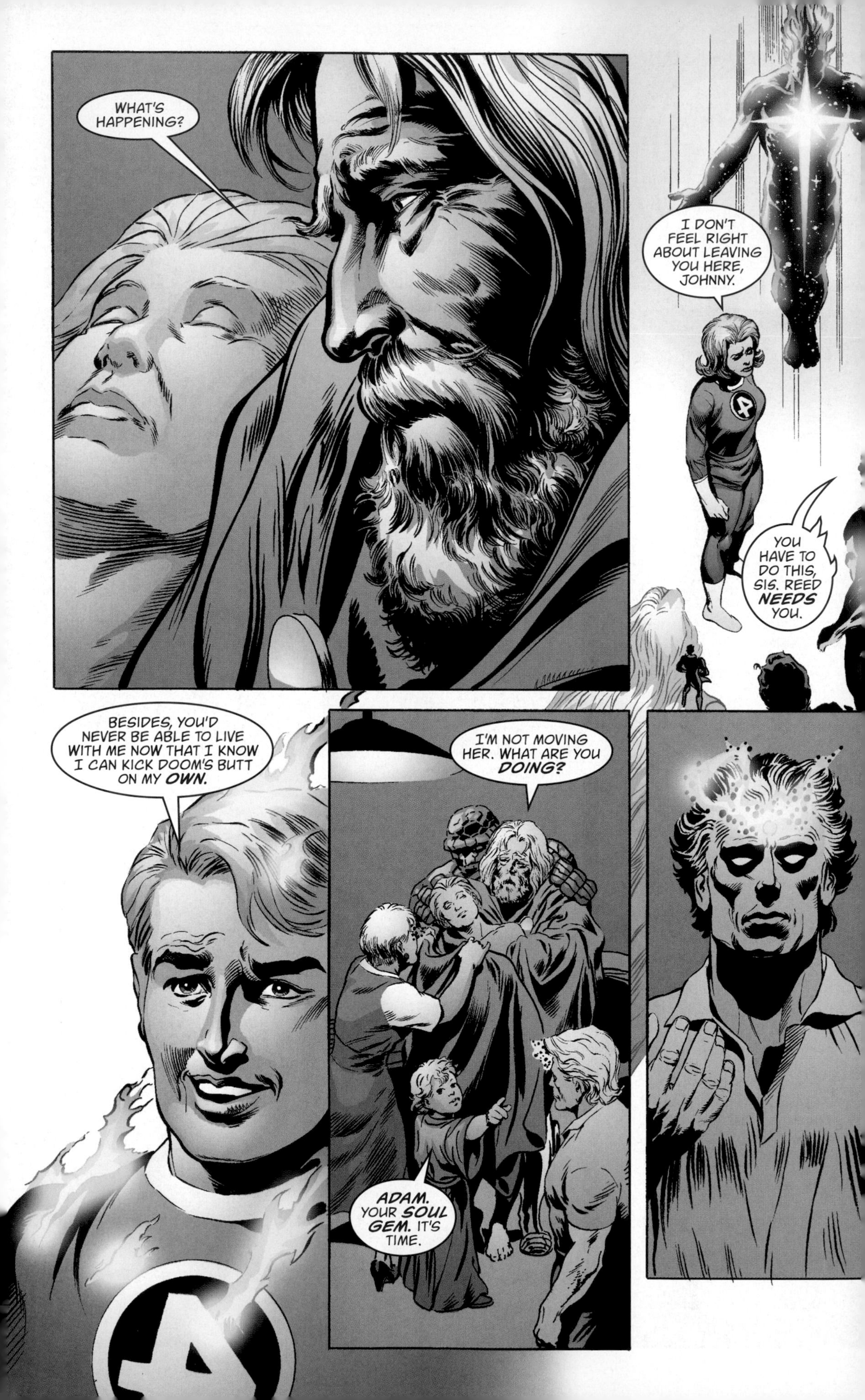
WHAT'S HAPPENING?
I DON'T FEEL RIGHT ABOUT LEAVING YOU HERE, JOHNNY.
YOU HAVE TO DO THIS, SIS. REED **NEEDS** YOU.
BESIDES, YOU'D NEVER BE ABLE TO LIVE WITH ME NOW THAT I KNOW I CAN KICK DOOM'S BUTT ON MY **OWN.**
I'M NOT MOVING HER. WHAT ARE YOU **DOING?**
ADAM. YOUR **SOUL GEM.** IT'S TIME.

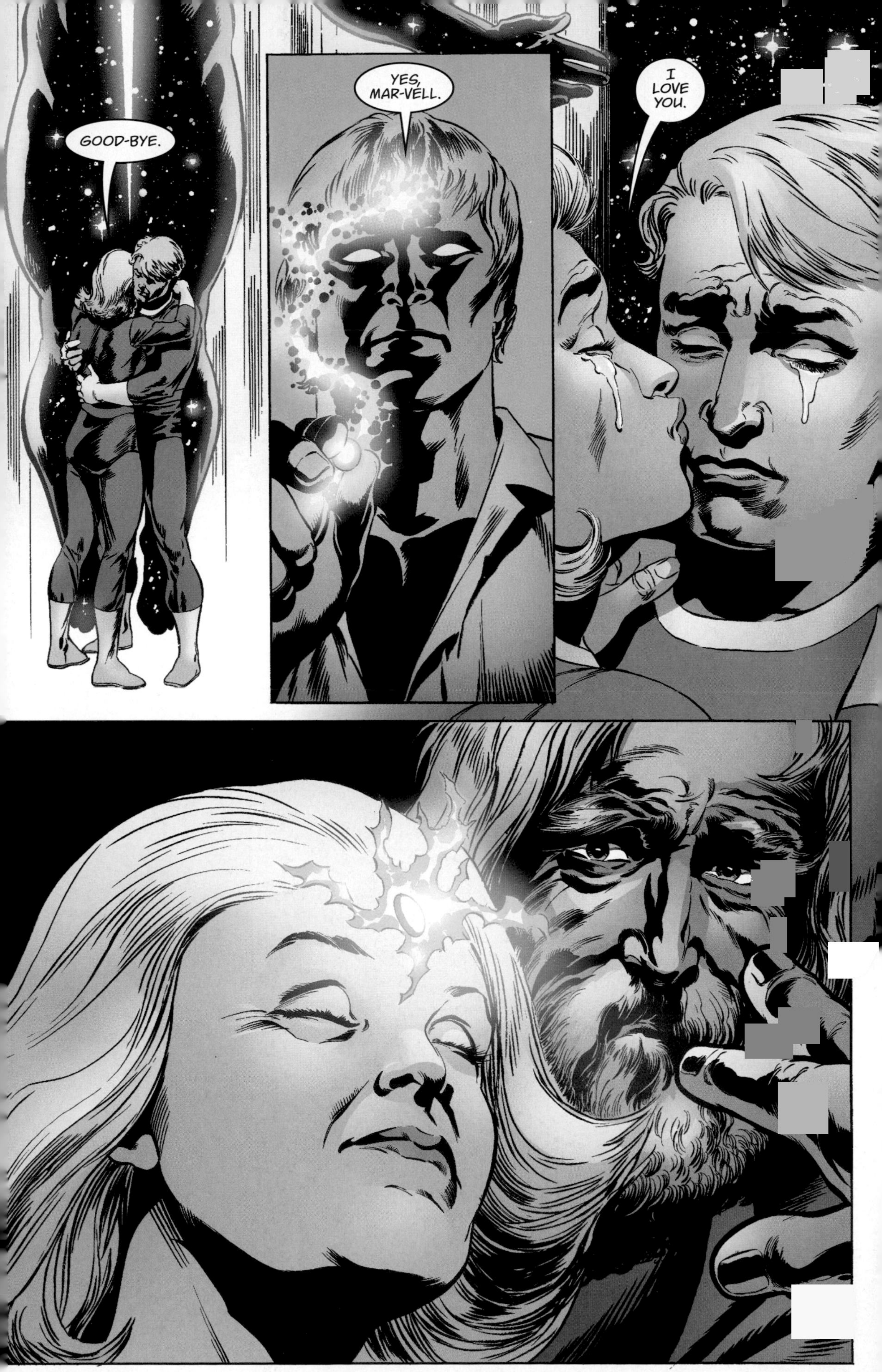
GOOD-BYE.
YES, MAR-VELL.
I LOVE YOU.

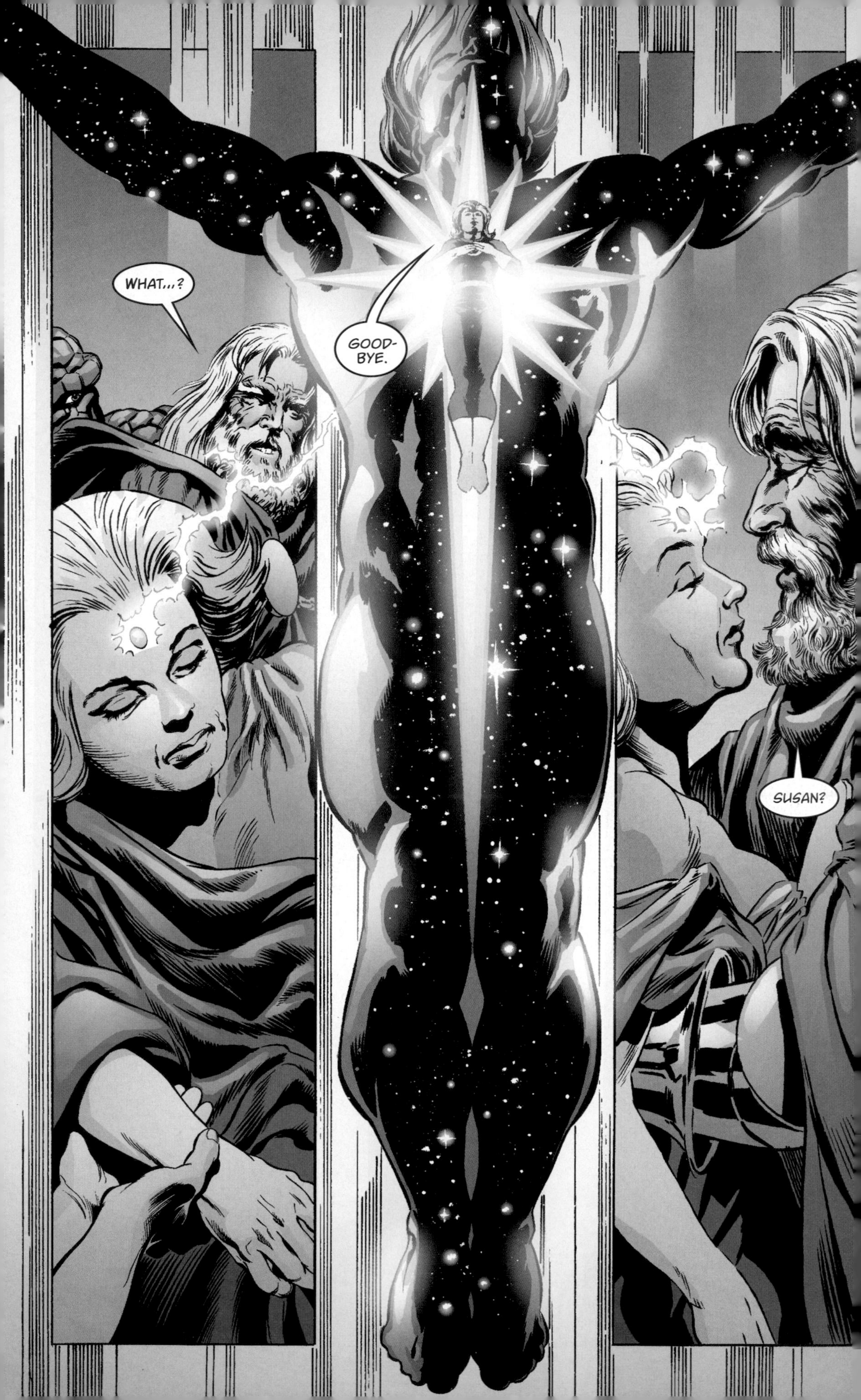
WHAT...?
GOOD-BYE.
SUSAN?

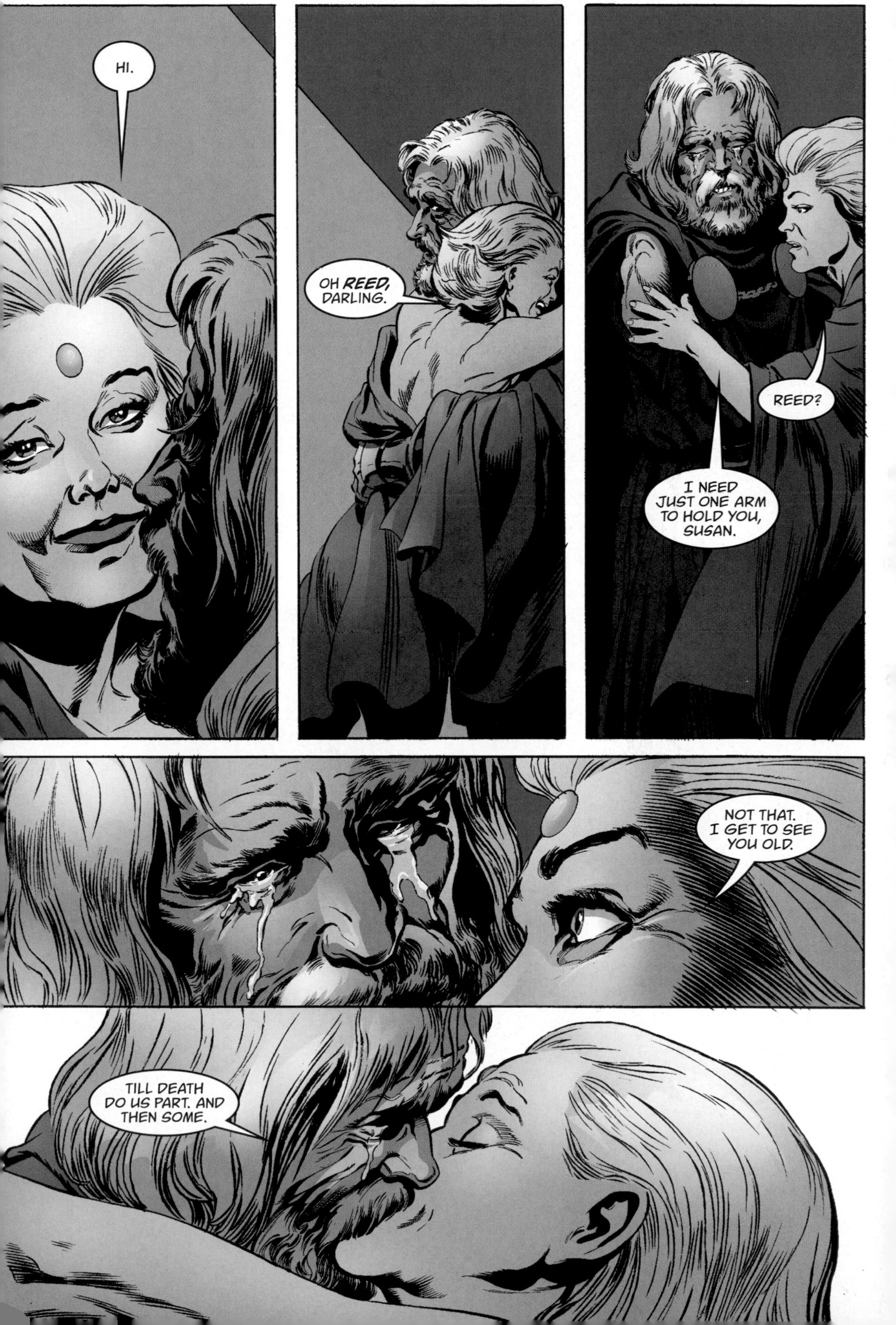
HI.
OH **REED,** DARLING.
REED?
I NEED JUST ONE ARM TO HOLD YOU, SUSAN.
NOT THAT. I GET TO SEE YOU OLD.
TILL DEATH DO US PART. AND THEN SOME.

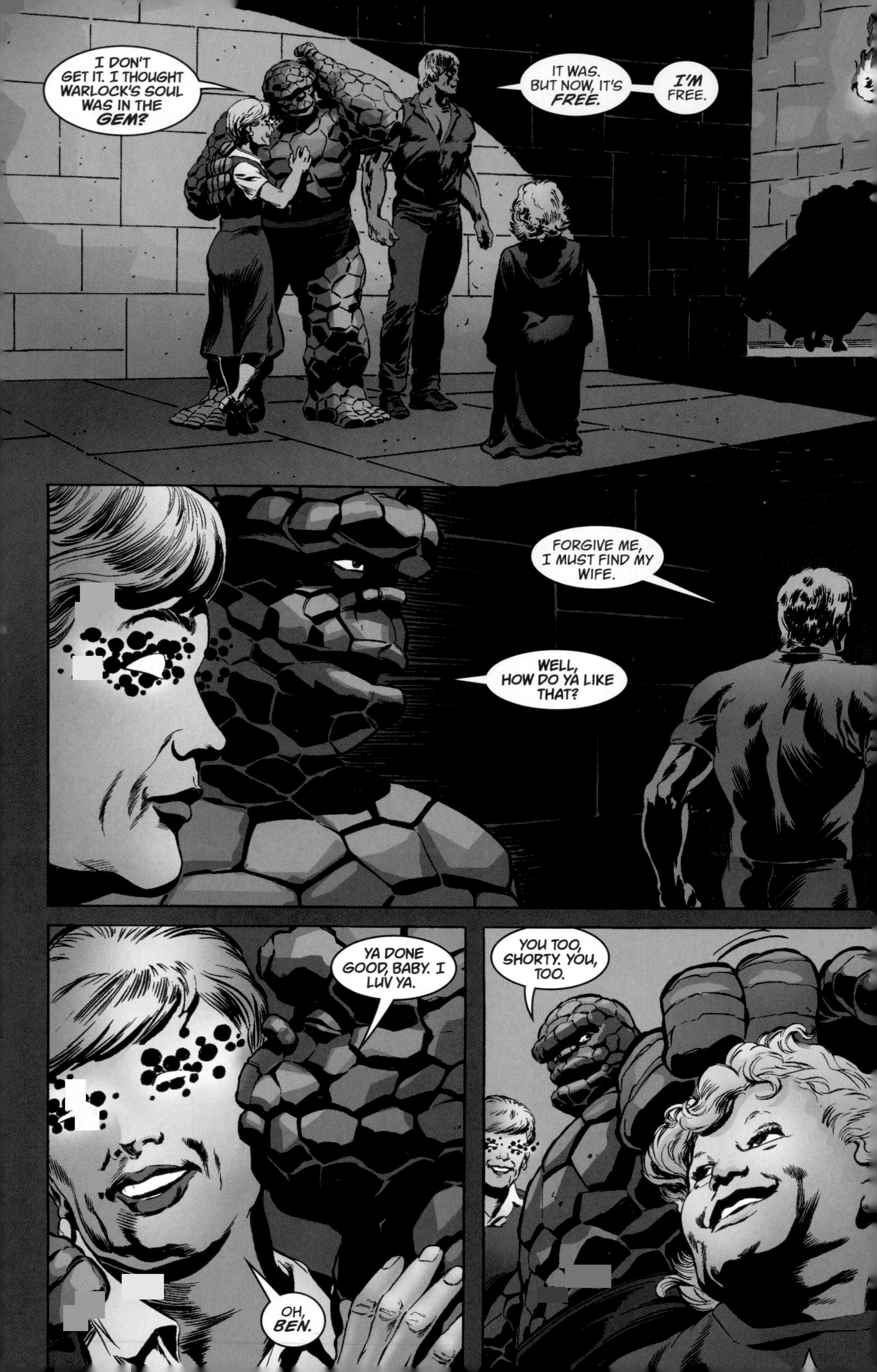
I DON'T GET IT. I THOUGHT WARLOCK'S SOUL WAS IN THE GEM?
IT WAS. BUT NOW, IT'S FREE.
I'M FREE.
FORGIVE ME, I MUST FIND MY WIFE.
WELL, HOW DO YA LIKE THAT?
YA DONE GOOD, BABY. I LUV YA.
OH, BEN.
YOU TOO, SHORTY. YOU, TOO.

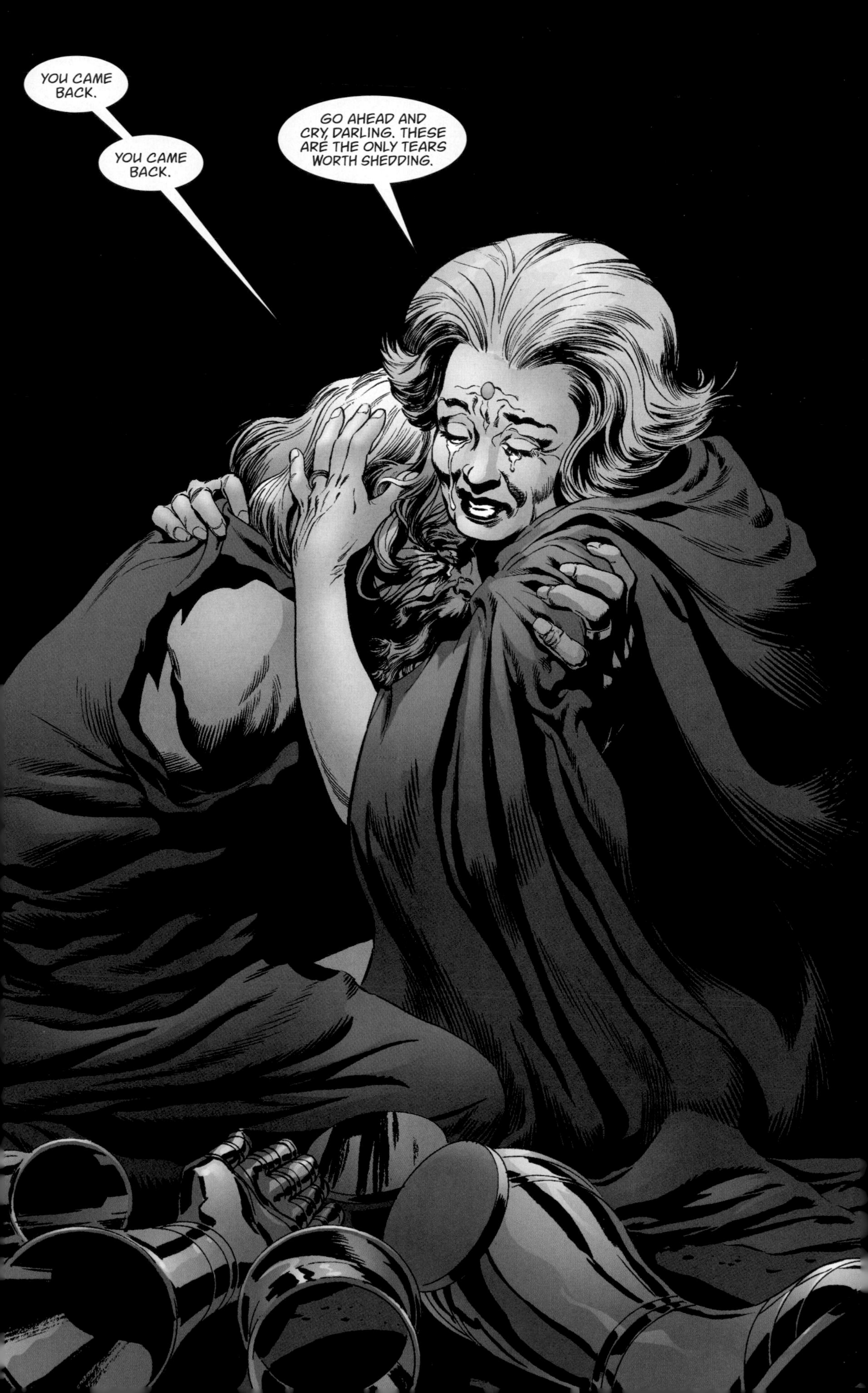
YOU CAME BACK.
YOU CAME BACK.
GO AHEAD AND CRY, DARLING. THESE ARE THE ONLY TEARS WORTH SHEDDING.

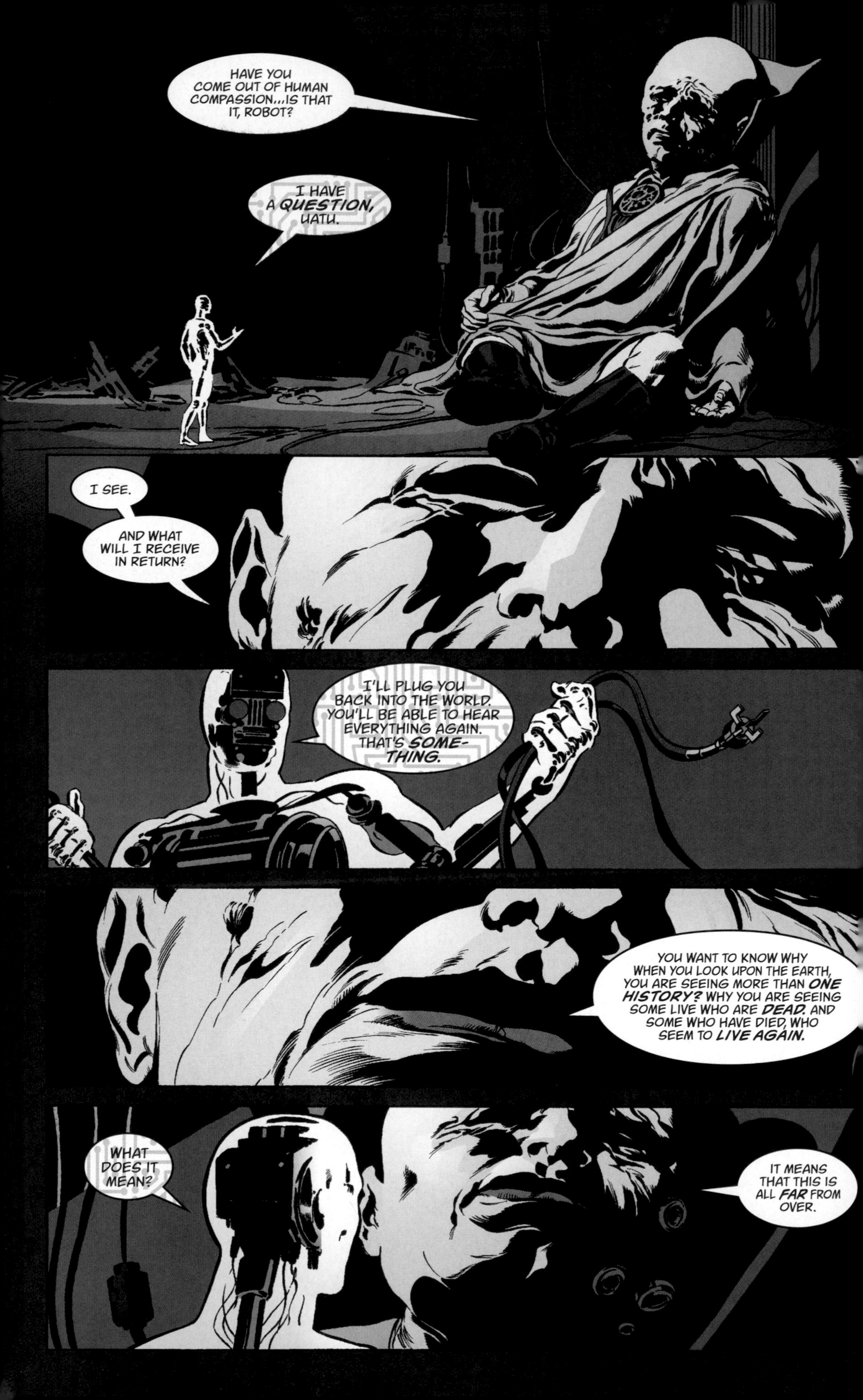
HAVE YOU COME OUT OF HUMAN COMPASSION...IS THAT IT, ROBOT?
I HAVE A QUESTION, UATU.
I SEE.
AND WHAT WILL I RECEIVE IN RETURN?
I'LL PLUG YOU BACK INTO THE WORLD. YOU'LL BE ABLE TO HEAR EVERYTHING AGAIN. THAT'S SOME-THING.
YOU WANT TO KNOW WHY WHEN YOU LOOK UPON THE EARTH, YOU ARE SEEING MORE THAN ONE HISTORY? WHY YOU ARE SEEING SOME LIVE WHO ARE DEAD. AND SOME WHO HAVE DIED, WHO SEEM TO LIVE AGAIN.
WHAT DOES IT MEAN?
IT MEANS THAT THIS IS ALL FAR FROM OVER.

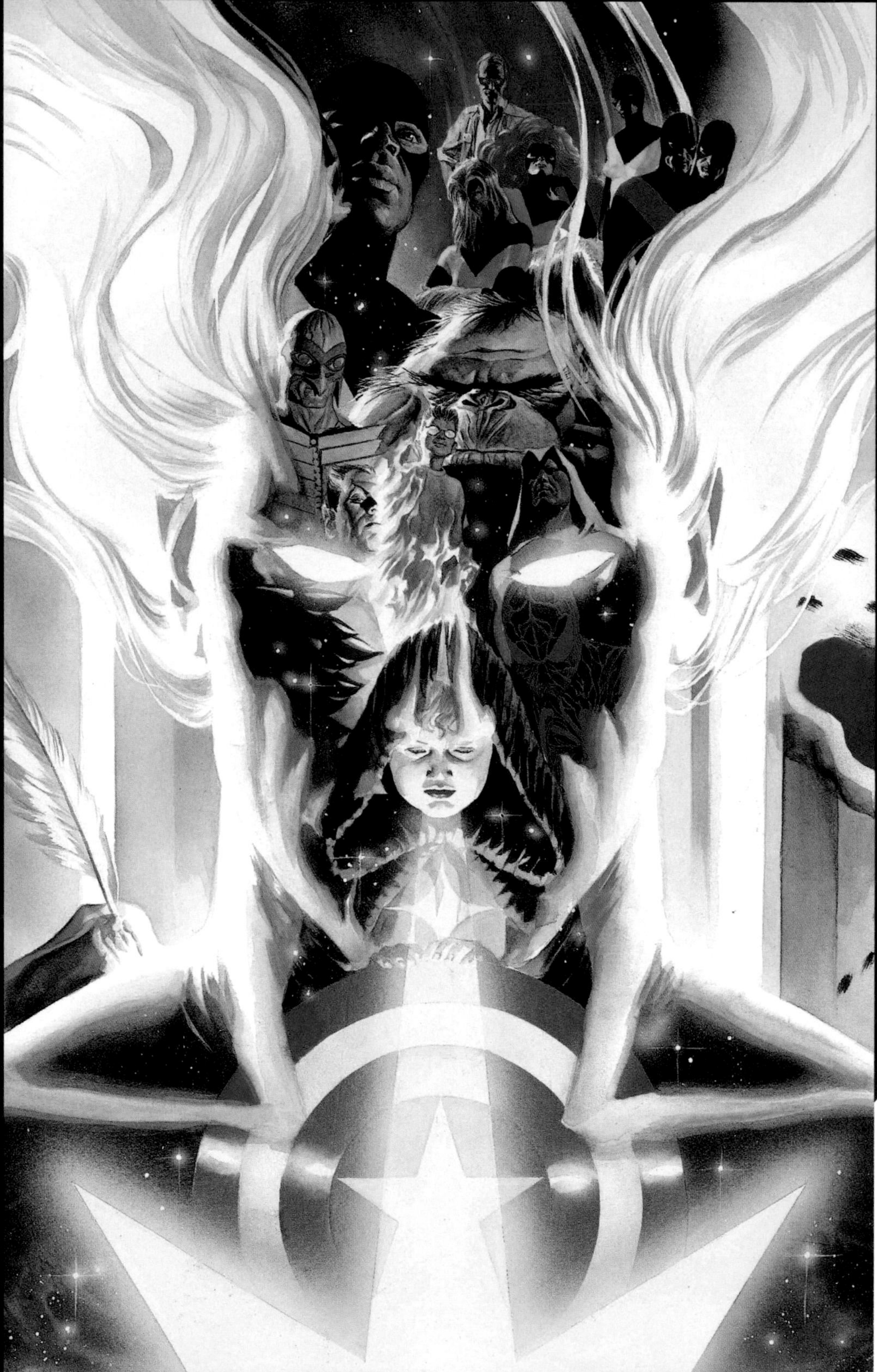

CHAPTER ONE

It doesn't matter whether mutanity reverts back to humanity or if they remain as they are."

"Why not, old friend? Please speak without fearing my reaction. For I am stone and will outlive you all."

"It's not that. I'm not trying to protect you again. The reason New York is freezing over while the Arctic is beginning to thaw is because the elements themselves cannot support what has happened to our world. Something has changed the planet. Soon, Earth won't be capable of sustaining life regardless of what humanity becomes."

"Then all life upon the Earth is going to cease? So, after all that mankind has been through, after all the enemies we've vanquished, we come to an end – and it is not the fault of a single soul upon the planet?"

"I didn't say that."

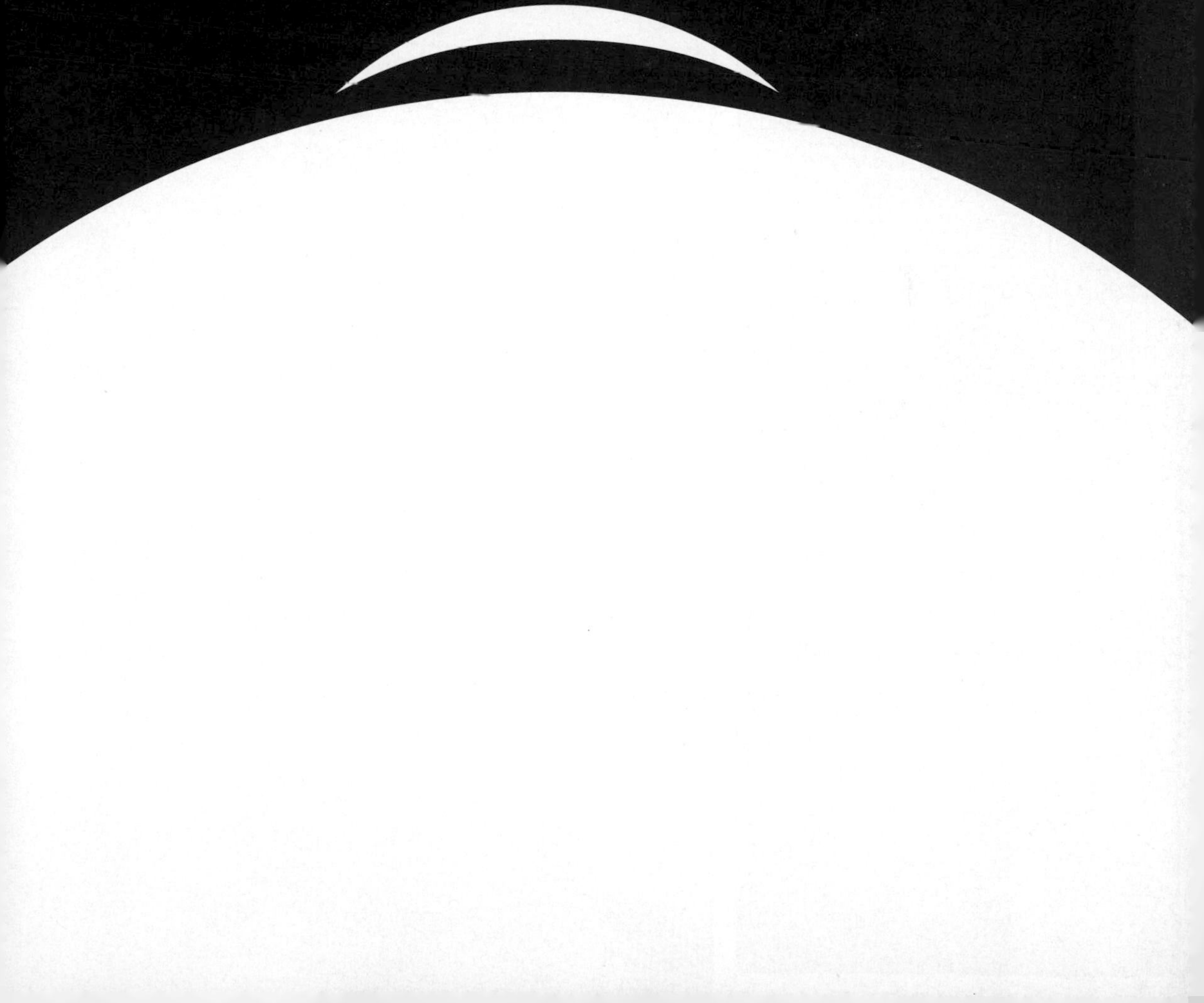

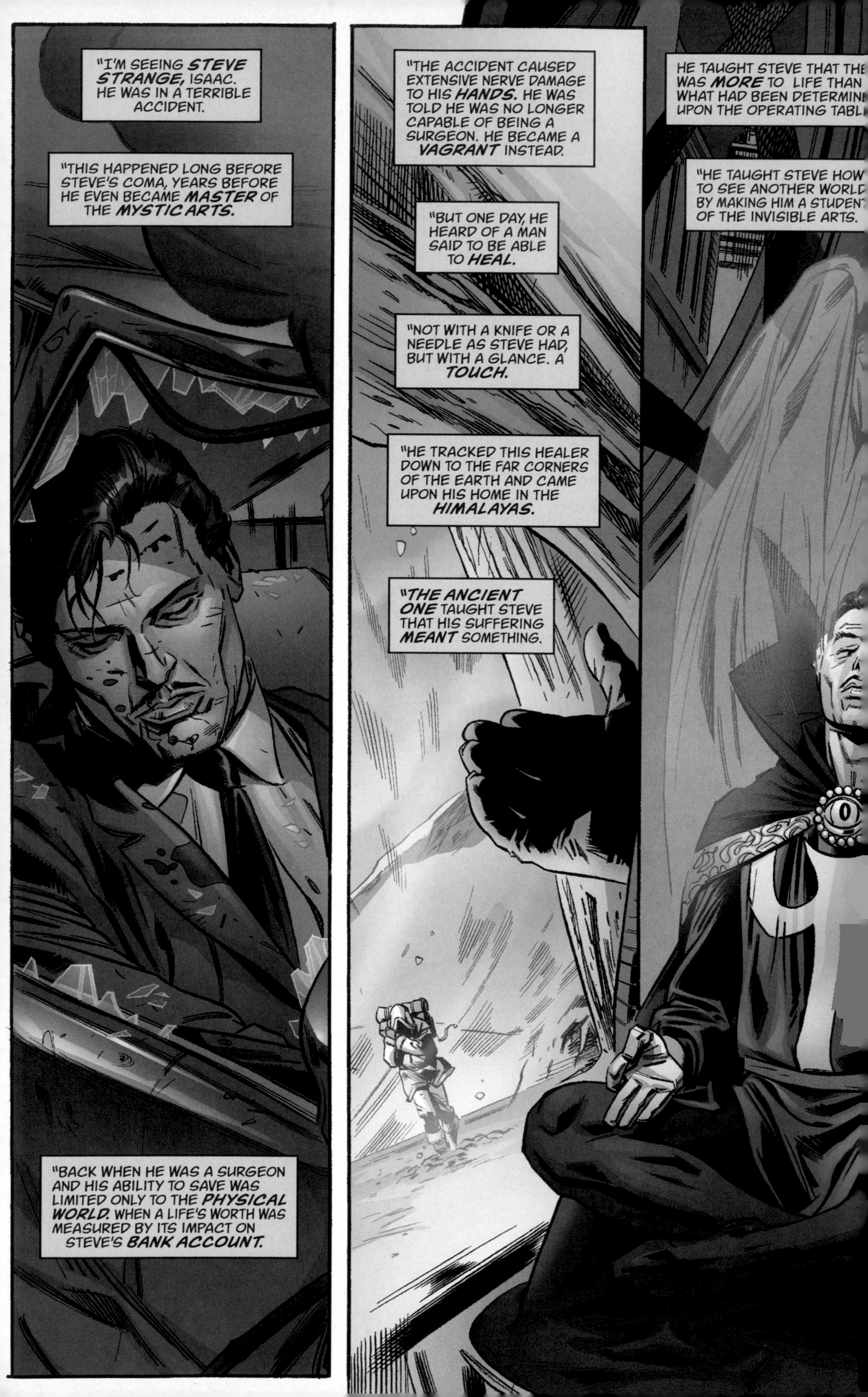
"I'M SEEING STEVE STRANGE, ISAAC. HE WAS IN A TERRIBLE ACCIDENT.
"THIS HAPPENED LONG BEFORE STEVE'S COMA, YEARS BEFORE HE EVEN BECAME MASTER OF THE MYSTIC ARTS.
"BACK WHEN HE WAS A SURGEON AND HIS ABILITY TO SAVE WAS LIMITED ONLY TO THE PHYSICAL WORLD. WHEN A LIFE'S WORTH WAS MEASURED BY ITS IMPACT ON STEVE'S BANK ACCOUNT.
"THE ACCIDENT CAUSED EXTENSIVE NERVE DAMAGE TO HIS HANDS. HE WAS TOLD HE WAS NO LONGER CAPABLE OF BEING A SURGEON. HE BECAME A VAGRANT INSTEAD.
"BUT ONE DAY, HE HEARD OF A MAN SAID TO BE ABLE TO HEAL.
"NOT WITH A KNIFE OR A NEEDLE AS STEVE HAD, BUT WITH A GLANCE. A TOUCH.
"HE TRACKED THIS HEALER DOWN TO THE FAR CORNERS OF THE EARTH AND CAME UPON HIS HOME IN THE HIMALAYAS.
"THE ANCIENT ONE TAUGHT STEVE THAT HIS SUFFERING MEANT SOMETHING.
HE TAUGHT STEVE THAT THE WAS MORE TO LIFE THAN WHAT HAD BEEN DETERMIN UPON THE OPERATING TABL
"HE TAUGHT STEVE HOW TO SEE ANOTHER WORLD BY MAKING HIM A STUDENT OF THE INVISIBLE ARTS.

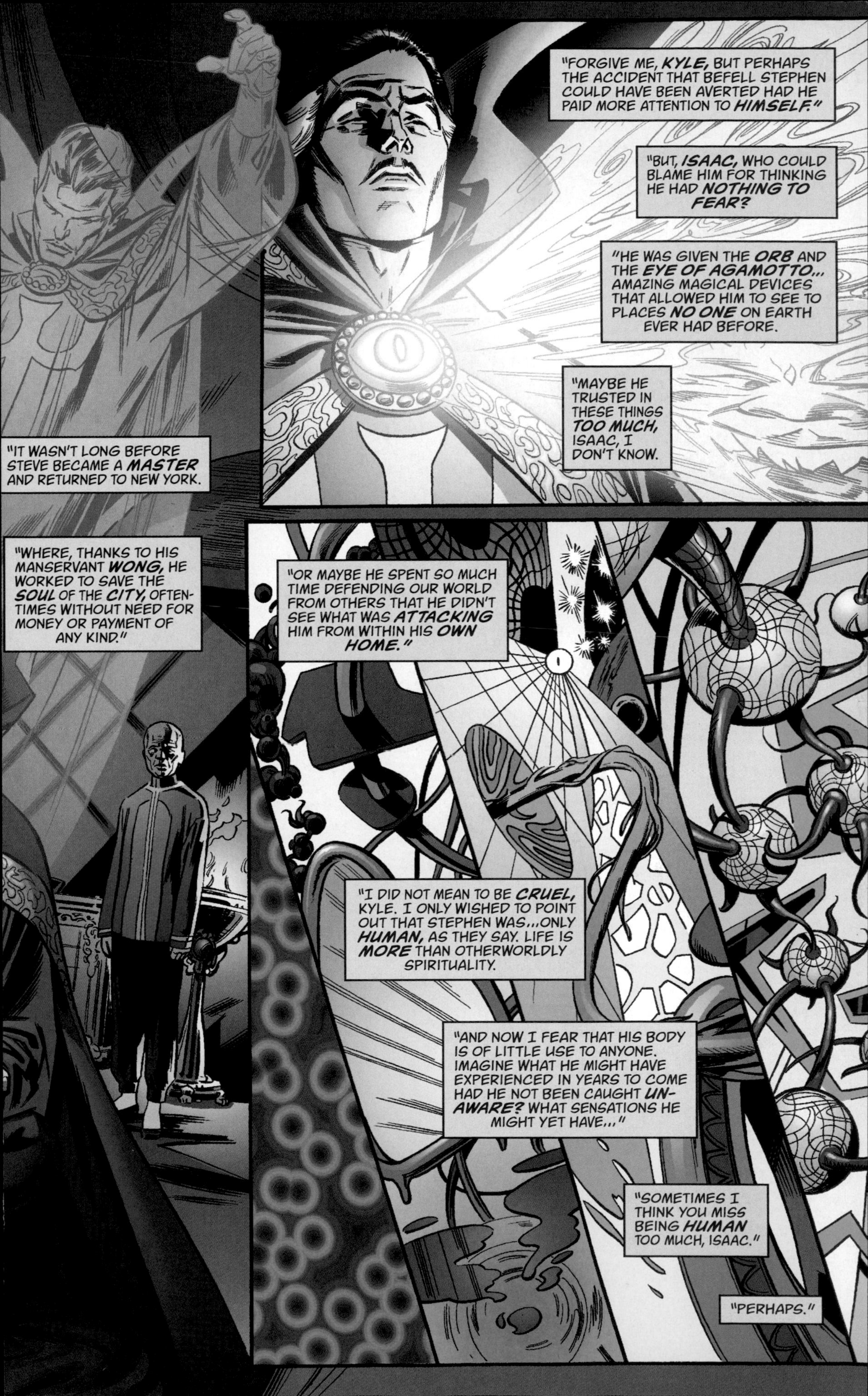
"FORGIVE ME, KYLE, BUT PERHAPS THE ACCIDENT THAT BEFELL STEPHEN COULD HAVE BEEN AVERTED HAD HE PAID MORE ATTENTION TO HIMSELF."
"BUT, ISAAC, WHO COULD BLAME HIM FOR THINKING HE HAD NOTHING TO FEAR?
"HE WAS GIVEN THE ORB AND THE EYE OF AGAMOTTO... AMAZING MAGICAL DEVICES THAT ALLOWED HIM TO SEE TO PLACES NO ONE ON EARTH EVER HAD BEFORE.
"MAYBE HE TRUSTED IN THESE THINGS TOO MUCH, ISAAC, I DON'T KNOW.
"IT WASN'T LONG BEFORE STEVE BECAME A MASTER AND RETURNED TO NEW YORK.
"WHERE, THANKS TO HIS MANSERVANT WONG, HE WORKED TO SAVE THE SOUL OF THE CITY, OFTEN-TIMES WITHOUT NEED FOR MONEY OR PAYMENT OF ANY KIND."
"OR MAYBE HE SPENT SO MUCH TIME DEFENDING OUR WORLD FROM OTHERS THAT HE DIDN'T SEE WHAT WAS ATTACKING HIM FROM WITHIN HIS OWN HOME."
"I DID NOT MEAN TO BE CRUEL, KYLE. I ONLY WISHED TO POINT OUT THAT STEPHEN WAS...ONLY HUMAN, AS THEY SAY. LIFE IS MORE THAN OTHERWORLDLY SPIRITUALITY.
"AND NOW I FEAR THAT HIS BODY IS OF LITTLE USE TO ANYONE. IMAGINE WHAT HE MIGHT HAVE EXPERIENCED IN YEARS TO COME HAD HE NOT BEEN CAUGHT UN-AWARE? WHAT SENSATIONS HE MIGHT YET HAVE..."
"SOMETIMES I THINK YOU MISS BEING HUMAN TOO MUCH, ISAAC."
"PERHAPS."

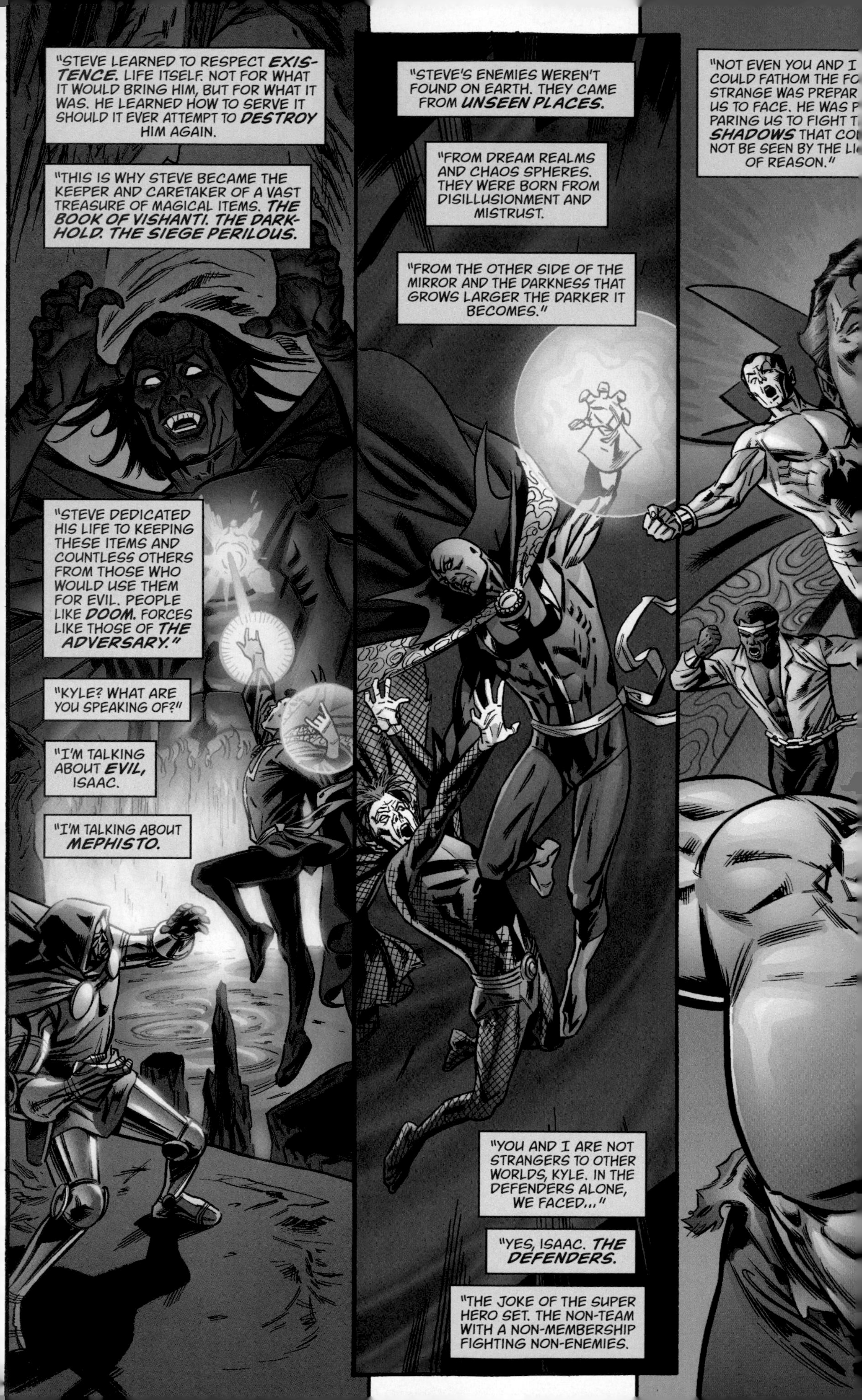
"STEVE LEARNED TO RESPECT EXISTENCE. LIFE ITSELF. NOT FOR WHAT IT WOULD BRING HIM, BUT FOR WHAT IT WAS. HE LEARNED HOW TO SERVE IT SHOULD IT EVER ATTEMPT TO DESTROY HIM AGAIN.
"THIS IS WHY STEVE BECAME THE KEEPER AND CARETAKER OF A VAST TREASURE OF MAGICAL ITEMS. THE BOOK OF VISHANTI. THE DARKHOLD. THE SIEGE PERILOUS.
"STEVE DEDICATED HIS LIFE TO KEEPING THESE ITEMS AND COUNTLESS OTHERS FROM THOSE WHO WOULD USE THEM FOR EVIL. PEOPLE LIKE DOOM. FORCES LIKE THOSE OF THE ADVERSARY."
"KYLE? WHAT ARE YOU SPEAKING OF?"
"I'M TALKING ABOUT EVIL, ISAAC.
"I'M TALKING ABOUT MEPHISTO.
"STEVE'S ENEMIES WEREN'T FOUND ON EARTH. THEY CAME FROM UNSEEN PLACES.
"FROM DREAM REALMS AND CHAOS SPHERES. THEY WERE BORN FROM DISILLUSIONMENT AND MISTRUST.
"FROM THE OTHER SIDE OF THE MIRROR AND THE DARKNESS THAT GROWS LARGER THE DARKER IT BECOMES."
"YOU AND I ARE NOT STRANGERS TO OTHER WORLDS, KYLE. IN THE DEFENDERS ALONE, WE FACED..."
"YES, ISAAC. THE DEFENDERS.
"THE JOKE OF THE SUPER HERO SET. THE NON-TEAM WITH A NON-MEMBERSHIP FIGHTING NON-ENEMIES.
"NOT EVEN YOU AND I COULD FATHOM THE FO STRANGE WAS PREPAR US TO FACE. HE WAS P PARING US TO FIGHT T SHADOWS THAT CO NOT BE SEEN BY THE LI OF REASON."

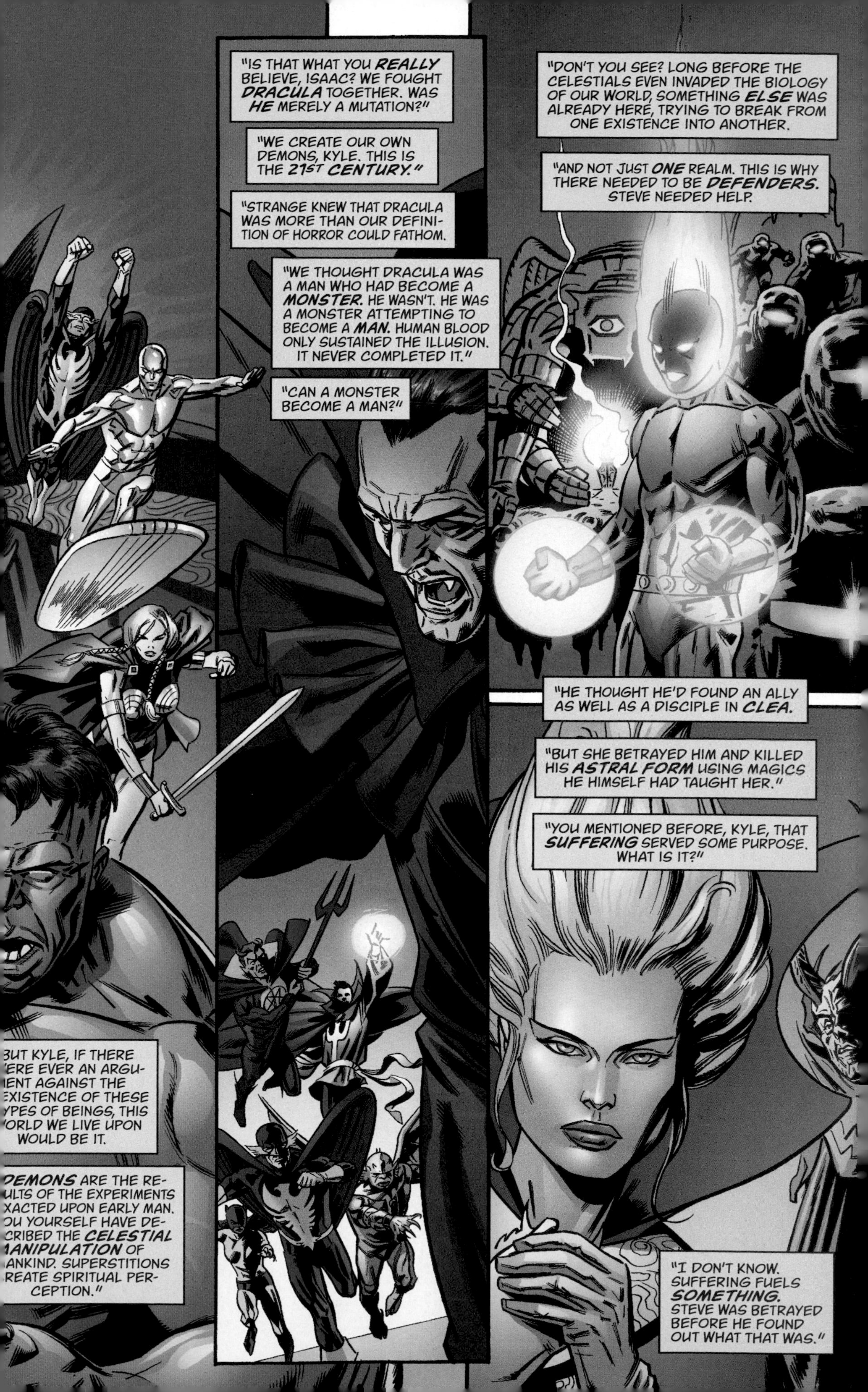

BUT KYLE, IF THERE ERE EVER AN ARGU- IENT AGAINST THE EXISTENCE OF THESE YPES OF BEINGS, THIS ORLD WE LIVE UPON WOULD BE IT.
DEMONS ARE THE RE- ULTS OF THE EXPERIMENTS XACTED UPON EARLY MAN. OU YOURSELF HAVE DE- CRIBED THE CELESTIAL ANIPULATION OF ANKIND. SUPERSTITIONS REATE SPIRITUAL PER- CEPTION."
"IS THAT WHAT YOU REALLY BELIEVE, ISAAC? WE FOUGHT DRACULA TOGETHER. WAS HE MERELY A MUTATION?"
"WE CREATE OUR OWN DEMONS, KYLE. THIS IS THE 21ST CENTURY."
"STRANGE KNEW THAT DRACULA WAS MORE THAN OUR DEFINI- TION OF HORROR COULD FATHOM.
"WE THOUGHT DRACULA WAS A MAN WHO HAD BECOME A MONSTER. HE WASN'T. HE WAS A MONSTER ATTEMPTING TO BECOME A MAN. HUMAN BLOOD ONLY SUSTAINED THE ILLUSION. IT NEVER COMPLETED IT."
"CAN A MONSTER BECOME A MAN?"
"DON'T YOU SEE? LONG BEFORE THE CELESTIALS EVEN INVADED THE BIOLOGY OF OUR WORLD, SOMETHING ELSE WAS ALREADY HERE, TRYING TO BREAK FROM ONE EXISTENCE INTO ANOTHER.
"AND NOT JUST ONE REALM. THIS IS WHY THERE NEEDED TO BE DEFENDERS. STEVE NEEDED HELP.
"HE THOUGHT HE'D FOUND AN ALLY AS WELL AS A DISCIPLE IN CLEA.
"BUT SHE BETRAYED HIM AND KILLED HIS ASTRAL FORM USING MAGICS HE HIMSELF HAD TAUGHT HER."
"YOU MENTIONED BEFORE, KYLE, THAT SUFFERING SERVED SOME PURPOSE. WHAT IS IT?"
"I DON'T KNOW. SUFFERING FUELS SOMETHING. STEVE WAS BETRAYED BEFORE HE FOUND OUT WHAT THAT WAS."

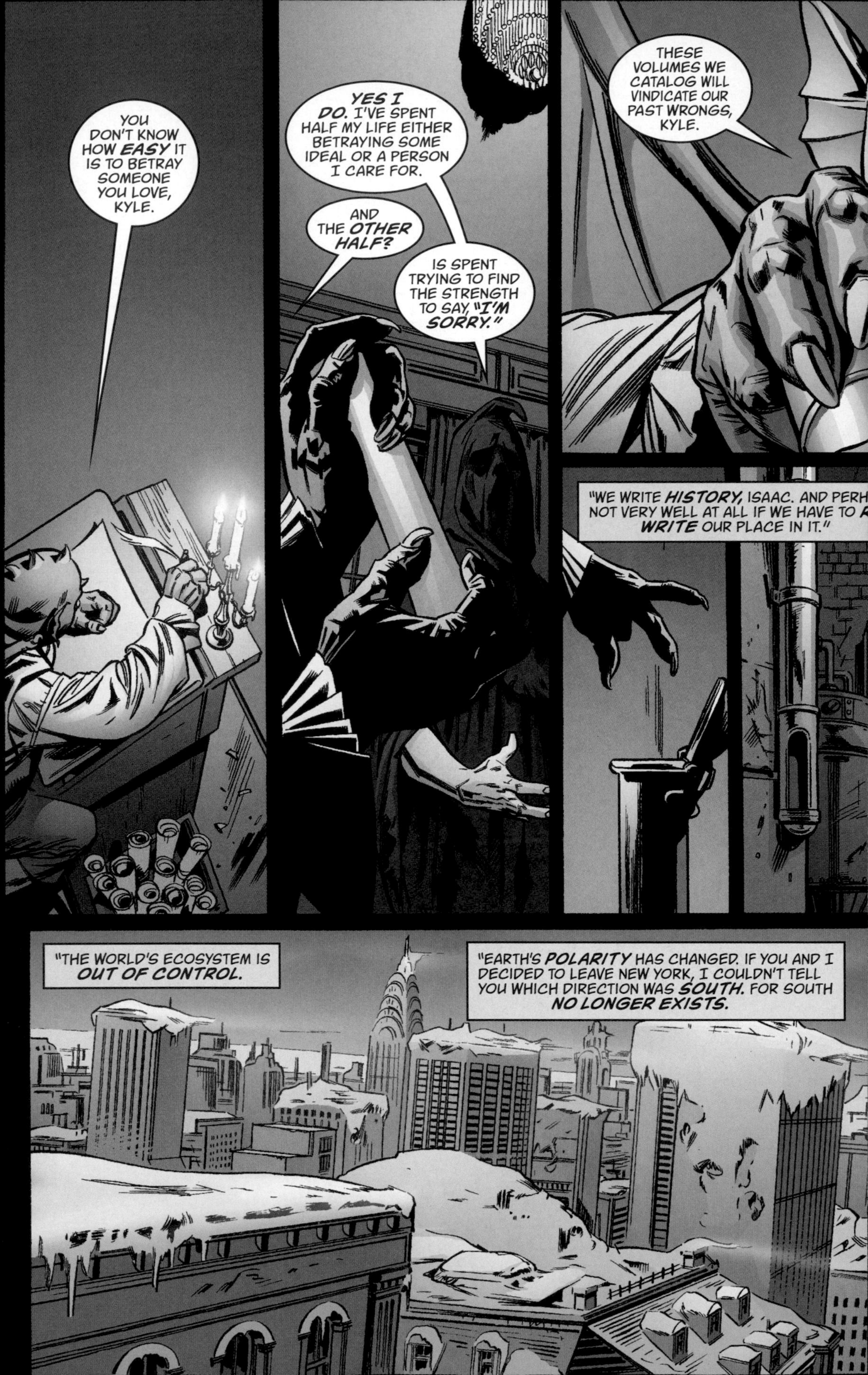
YOU DON'T KNOW HOW EASY IT IS TO BETRAY SOMEONE YOU LOVE, KYLE.
YES I DO. I'VE SPENT HALF MY LIFE EITHER BETRAYING SOME IDEAL OR A PERSON I CARE FOR.
AND THE OTHER HALF?
IS SPENT TRYING TO FIND THE STRENGTH TO SAY, "I'M SORRY."
THESE VOLUMES WE CATALOG WILL VINDICATE OUR PAST WRONGS, KYLE.
"WE WRITE HISTORY, ISAAC. AND PERH
NOT VERY WELL AT ALL IF WE HAVE TO R
WRITE OUR PLACE IN IT."
"THE WORLD'S ECOSYSTEM IS OUT OF CONTROL.
"EARTH'S POLARITY HAS CHANGED. IF YOU AND I DECIDED TO LEAVE NEW YORK, I COULDN'T TELL YOU WHICH DIRECTION WAS SOUTH. FOR SOUTH NO LONGER EXISTS.

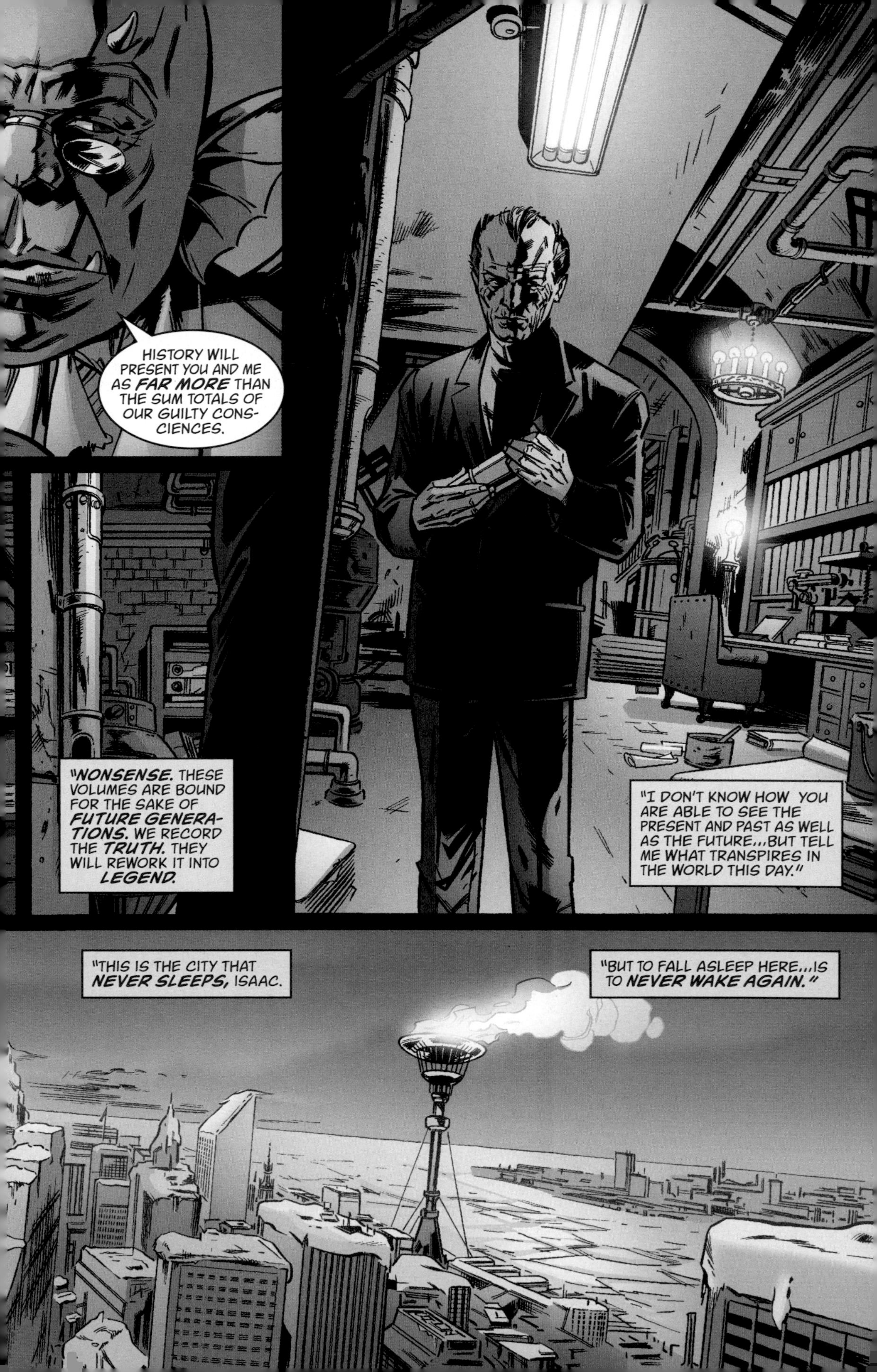
HISTORY WILL PRESENT YOU AND ME AS FAR MORE THAN THE SUM TOTALS OF OUR GUILTY CONSCIENCES.
"NONSENSE. THESE VOLUMES ARE BOUND FOR THE SAKE OF FUTURE GENERATIONS. WE RECORD THE TRUTH. THEY WILL REWORK IT INTO LEGEND.
"I DON'T KNOW HOW YOU ARE ABLE TO SEE THE PRESENT AND PAST AS WELL AS THE FUTURE...BUT TELL ME WHAT TRANSPIRES IN THE WORLD THIS DAY."
"THIS IS THE CITY THAT NEVER SLEEPS, ISAAC.
"BUT TO FALL ASLEEP HERE...IS TO NEVER WAKE AGAIN."

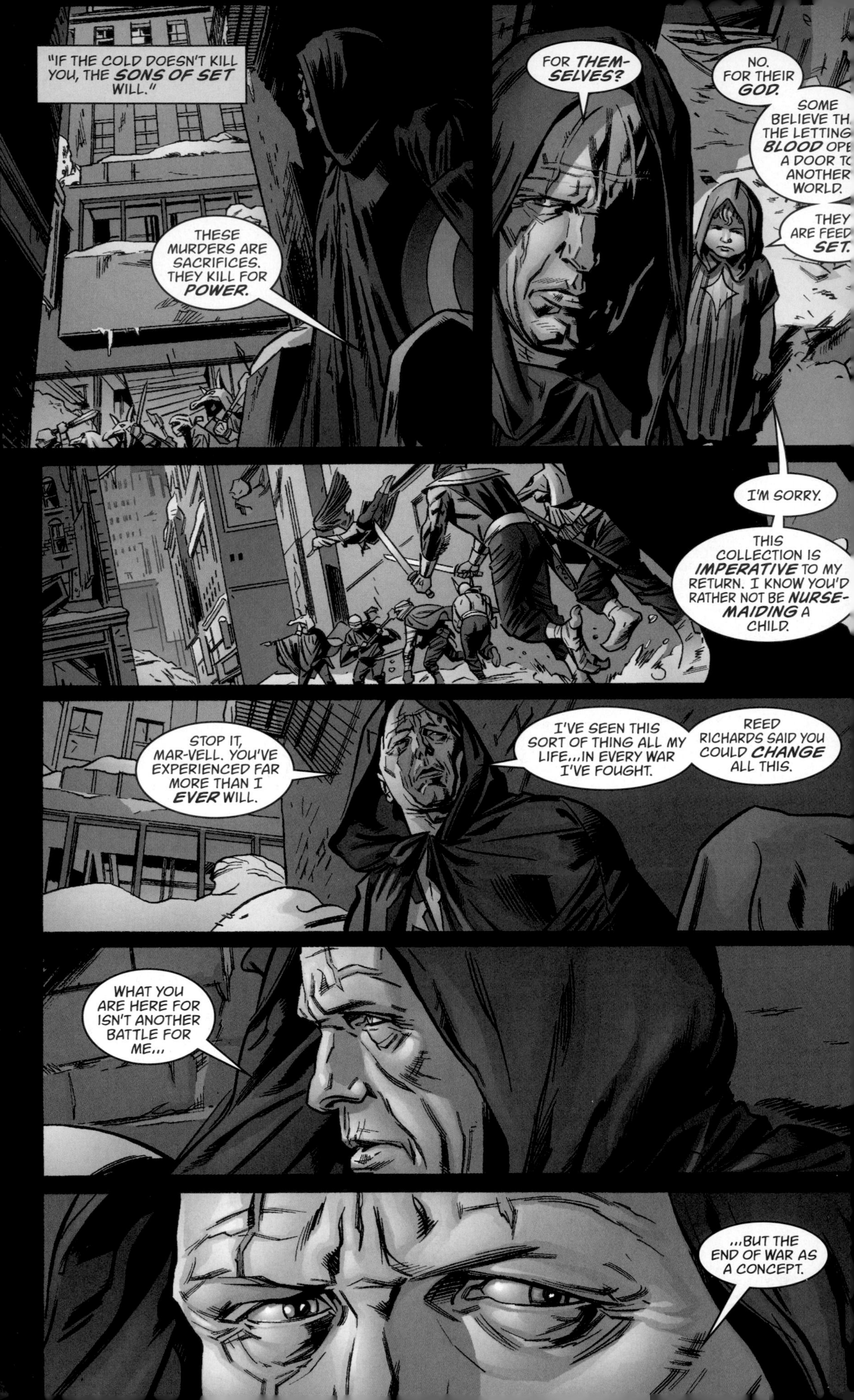
"IF THE COLD DOESN'T KILL YOU, THE SONS OF SET WILL."
THESE MURDERS ARE SACRIFICES. THEY KILL FOR POWER.
FOR THEMSELVES?
NO. FOR THEIR GOD.
SOME BELIEVE TH THE LETTING BLOOD OPE A DOOR TO ANOTHER WORLD.
THEY ARE FEED SET.
I'M SORRY.
THIS COLLECTION IS IMPERATIVE TO MY RETURN. I KNOW YOU'D RATHER NOT BE NURSE-MAIDING A CHILD.
STOP IT, MAR-VELL. YOU'VE EXPERIENCED FAR MORE THAN I EVER WILL.
I'VE SEEN THIS SORT OF THING ALL MY LIFE...IN EVERY WAR I'VE FOUGHT.
REED RICHARDS SAID YOU COULD CHANGE ALL THIS.
WHAT YOU ARE HERE FOR ISN'T ANOTHER BATTLE FOR ME...
...BUT THE END OF WAR AS A CONCEPT.

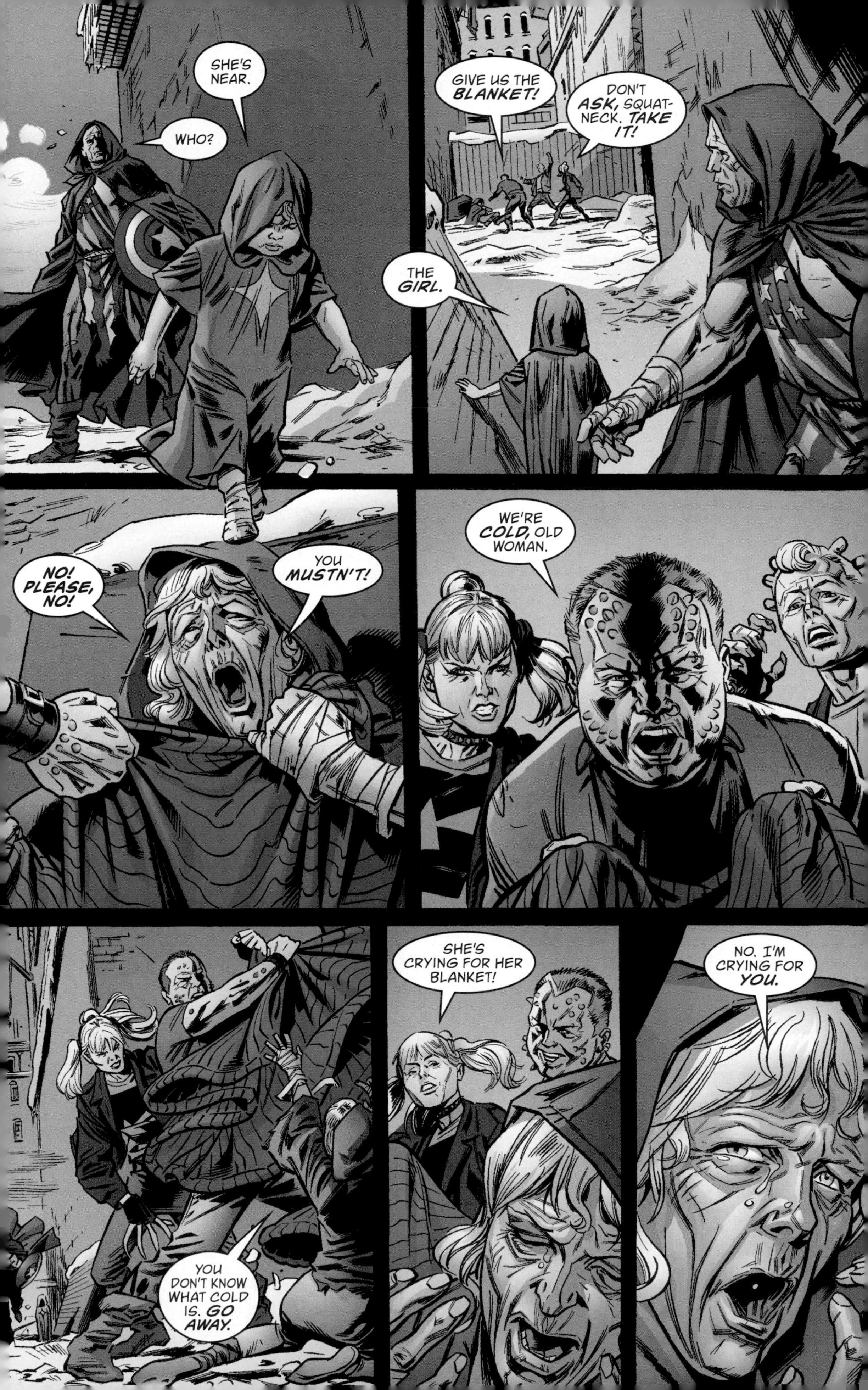
SHE'S NEAR.
WHO?
GIVE US THE BLANKET!
DON'T ASK, SQUAT-NECK. TAKE IT!
THE GIRL.
NO! PLEASE, NO!
YOU MUSTN'T!
WE'RE COLD, OLD WOMAN.
YOU DON'T KNOW WHAT COLD IS. GO AWAY.
SHE'S CRYING FOR HER BLANKET!
NO. I'M CRYING FOR YOU.

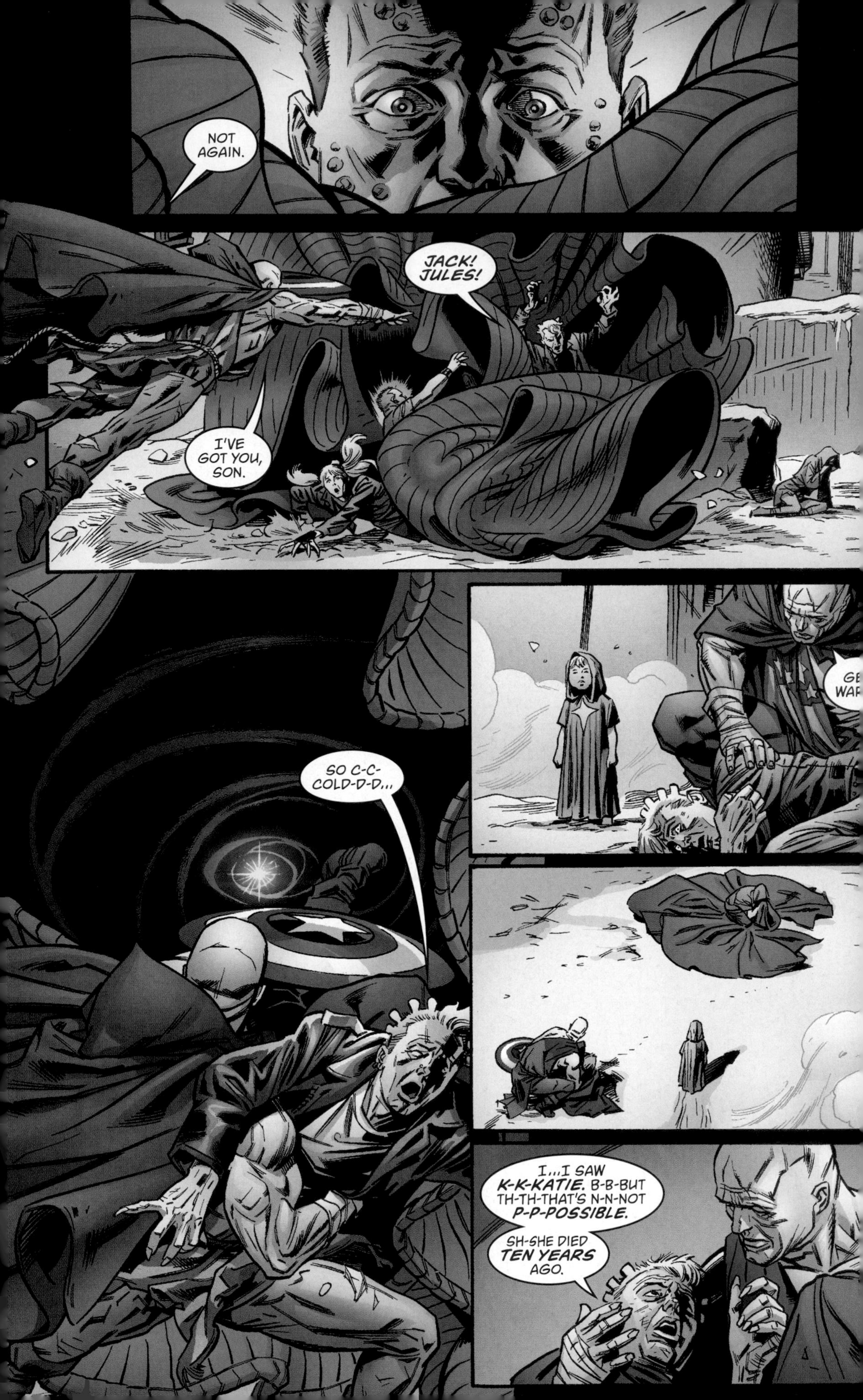
NOT AGAIN.
JACK! JULES!
I'VE GOT YOU, SON.
SO C-C-COLD-D-D...
I...I SAW K-K-KATIE. B-B-BUT TH-TH-THAT'S N-N-NOT P-P-POSSIBLE.
SH-SHE DIED TEN YEARS AGO.

I LET MORE BE *CLAIMED*, TY. IT TOOK MORE PEOPLE. I FAILED *AGAIN*.

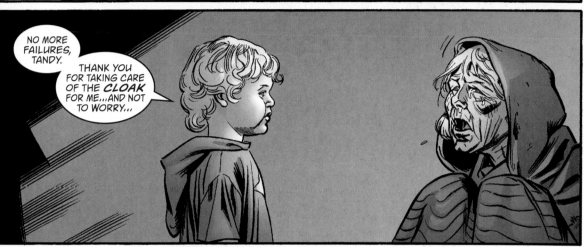

NO MORE FAILURES, TANDY.

THANK YOU FOR TAKING CARE OF THE *CLOAK* FOR ME...AND NOT TO WORRY...

...TY IS *FINE*. HE'S GONE TO THE *OTHER SIDE*.

BUT...

YOU *COULDN'T* BRING HIM BACK, EVEN WITH ALL YOUR *LIGHT*.

HE TELLS OF YOUR BEAUTY TO ANY WHO WILL LISTEN.

HE DOES?

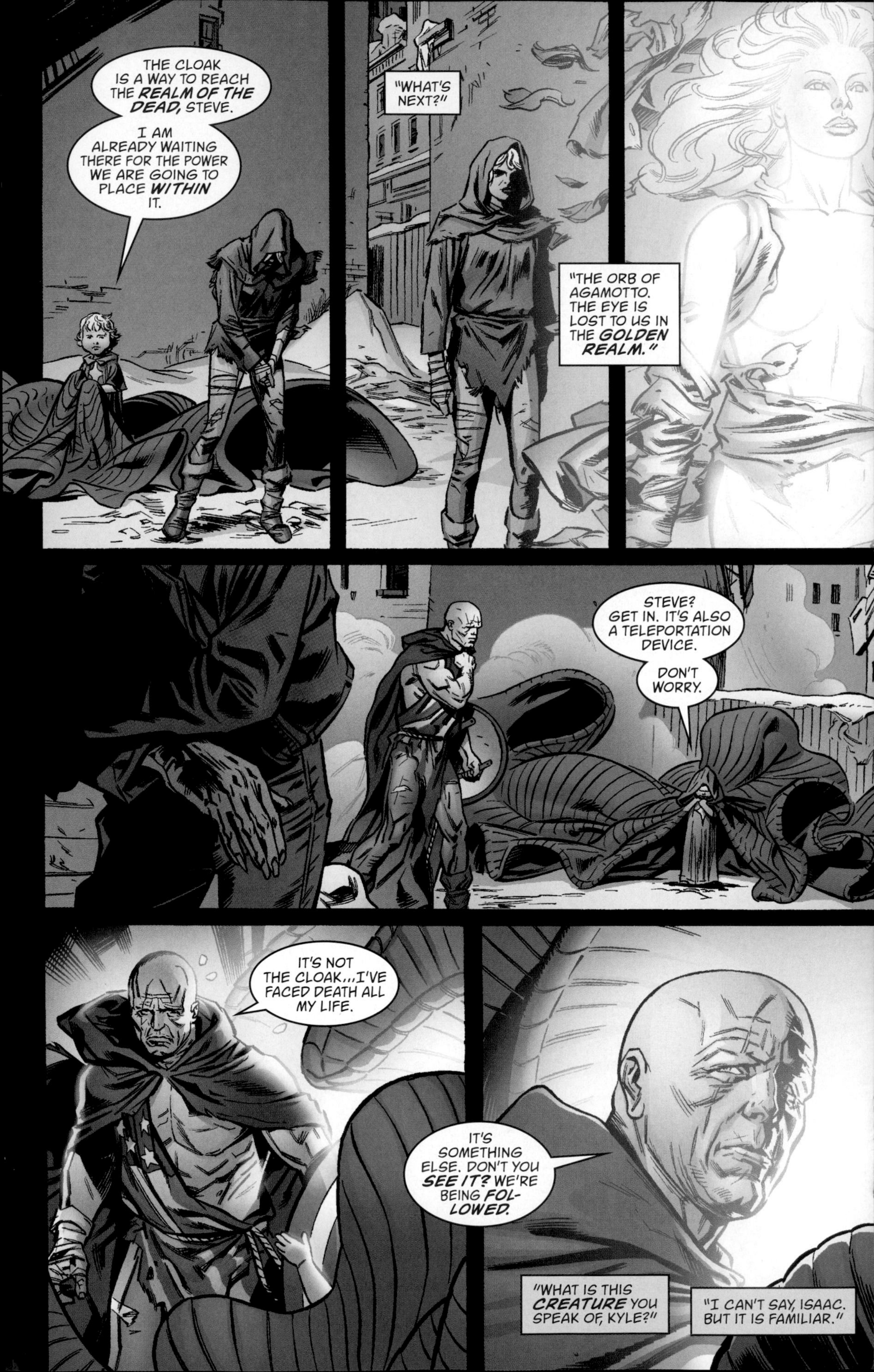
THE CLOAK IS A WAY TO REACH THE REALM OF THE DEAD, STEVE.
I AM ALREADY WAITING THERE FOR THE POWER WE ARE GOING TO PLACE WITHIN IT.
"WHAT'S NEXT?"
"THE ORB OF AGAMOTTO. THE EYE IS LOST TO US IN THE GOLDEN REALM."
STEVE? GET IN. IT'S ALSO A TELEPORTATION DEVICE.
DON'T WORRY.
IT'S NOT THE CLOAK...I'VE FACED DEATH ALL MY LIFE.
IT'S SOMETHING ELSE. DON'T YOU SEE IT? WE'RE BEING FOL-LOWED.
"WHAT IS THIS CREATURE YOU SPEAK OF, KYLE?"
"I CAN'T SAY, ISAAC. BUT IT IS FAMILIAR."

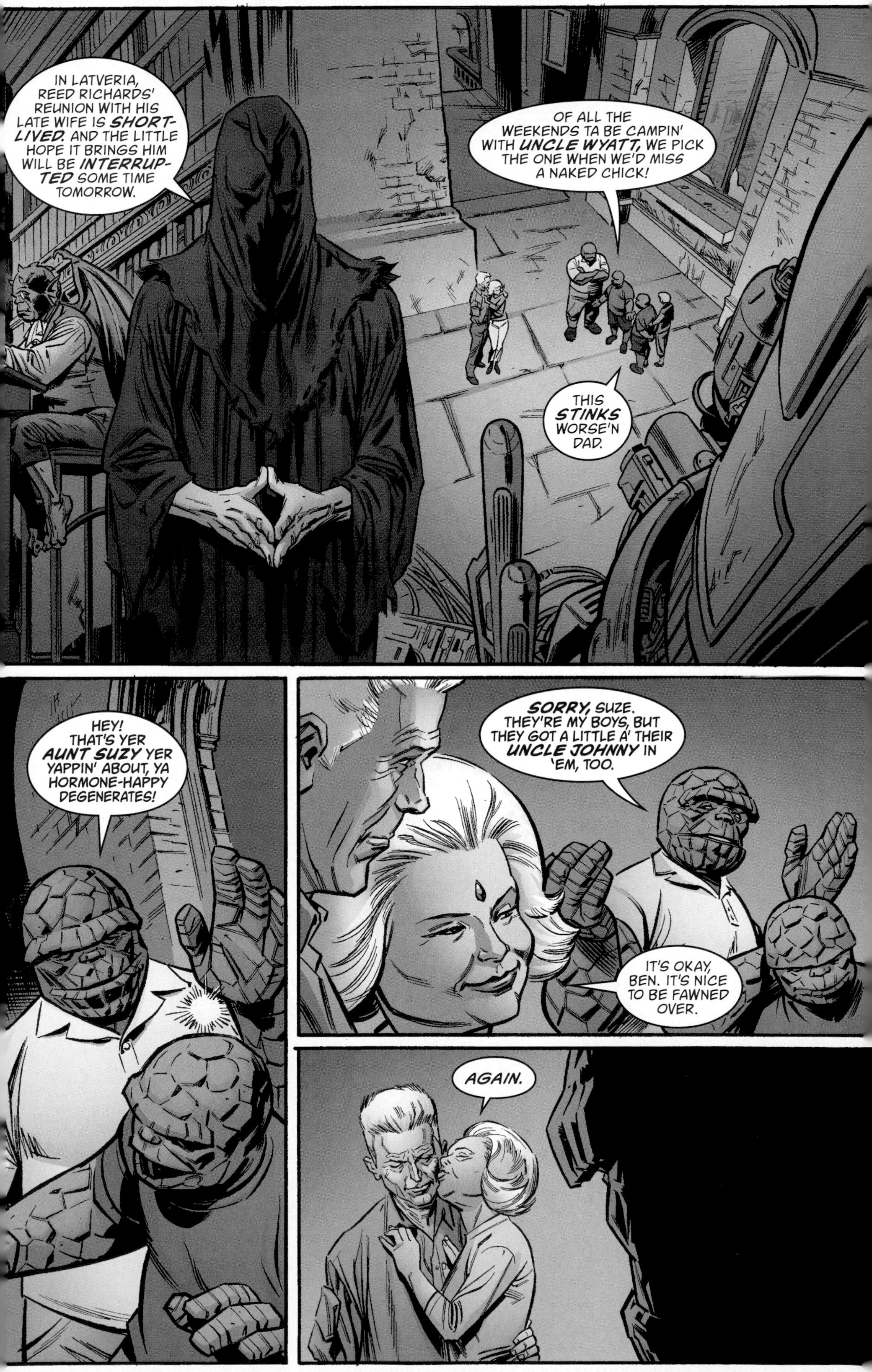
IN LATVERIA, REED RICHARDS' REUNION WITH HIS LATE WIFE IS SHORT-LIVED, AND THE LITTLE HOPE IT BRINGS HIM WILL BE INTERRUP-TED SOME TIME TOMORROW.
OF ALL THE WEEKENDS TA BE CAMPIN' WITH UNCLE WYATT, WE PICK THE ONE WHEN WE'D MISS A NAKED CHICK!
THIS STINKS WORSE'N DAD.
HEY! THAT'S YER AUNT SUZY YER YAPPIN' ABOUT, YA HORMONE-HAPPY DEGENERATES!
SORRY, SUZE. THEY'RE MY BOYS, BUT THEY GOT A LITTLE A' THEIR UNCLE JOHNNY IN 'EM, TOO.
IT'S OKAY, BEN. IT'S NICE TO BE FAWNED OVER.
AGAIN.

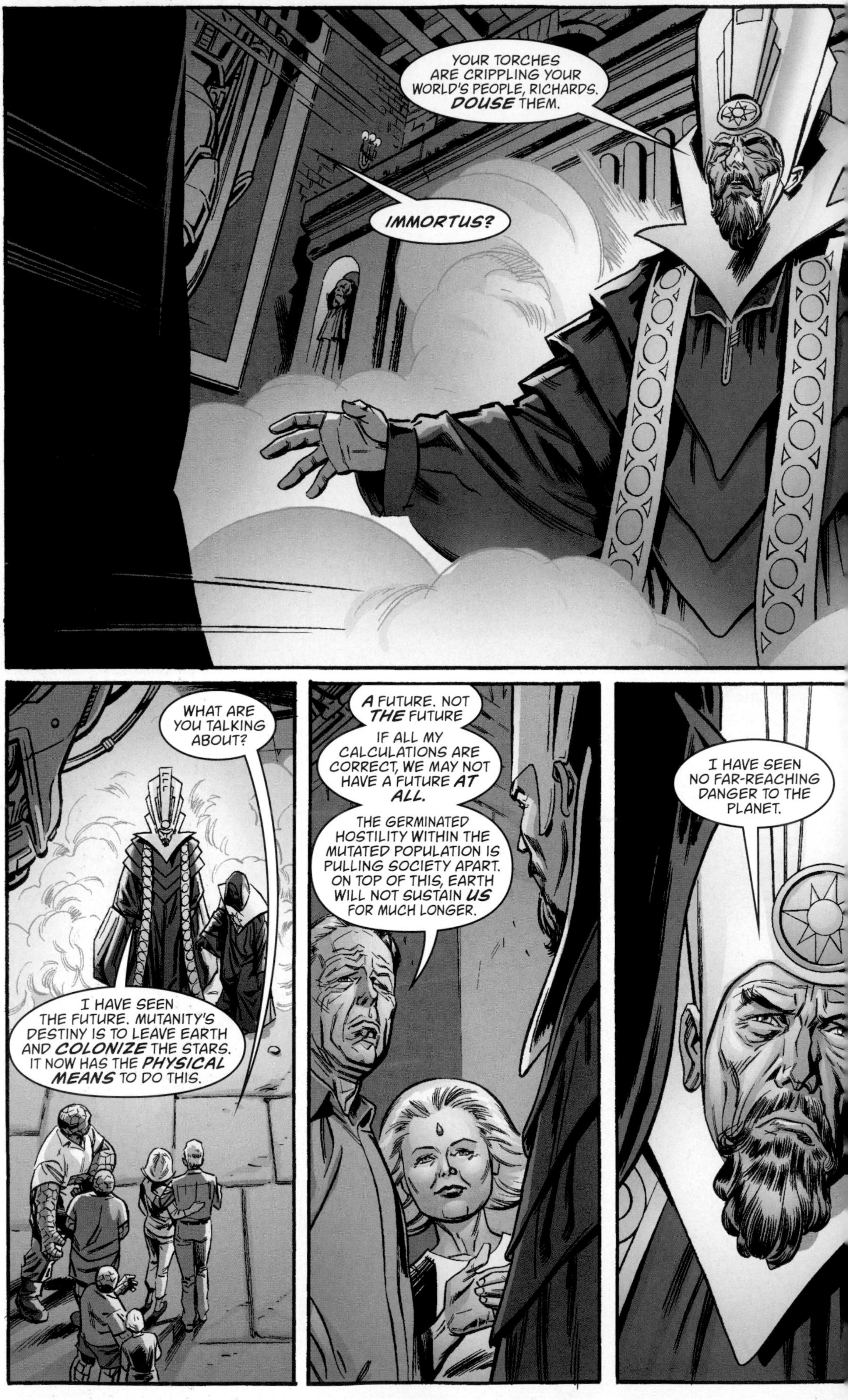
YOUR TORCHES ARE CRIPPLING YOUR WORLD'S PEOPLE, RICHARDS. DOUSE THEM.
IMMORTUS?
WHAT ARE YOU TALKING ABOUT?
I HAVE SEEN THE FUTURE. MUTANITY'S DESTINY IS TO LEAVE EARTH AND COLONIZE THE STARS. IT NOW HAS THE PHYSICAL MEANS TO DO THIS.
A FUTURE. NOT THE FUTURE
IF ALL MY CALCULATIONS ARE CORRECT, WE MAY NOT HAVE A FUTURE AT ALL.
THE GERMINATED HOSTILITY WITHIN THE MUTATED POPULATION IS PULLING SOCIETY APART. ON TOP OF THIS, EARTH WILL NOT SUSTAIN US FOR MUCH LONGER.
I HAVE SEEN NO FAR-REACHING DANGER TO THE PLANET.

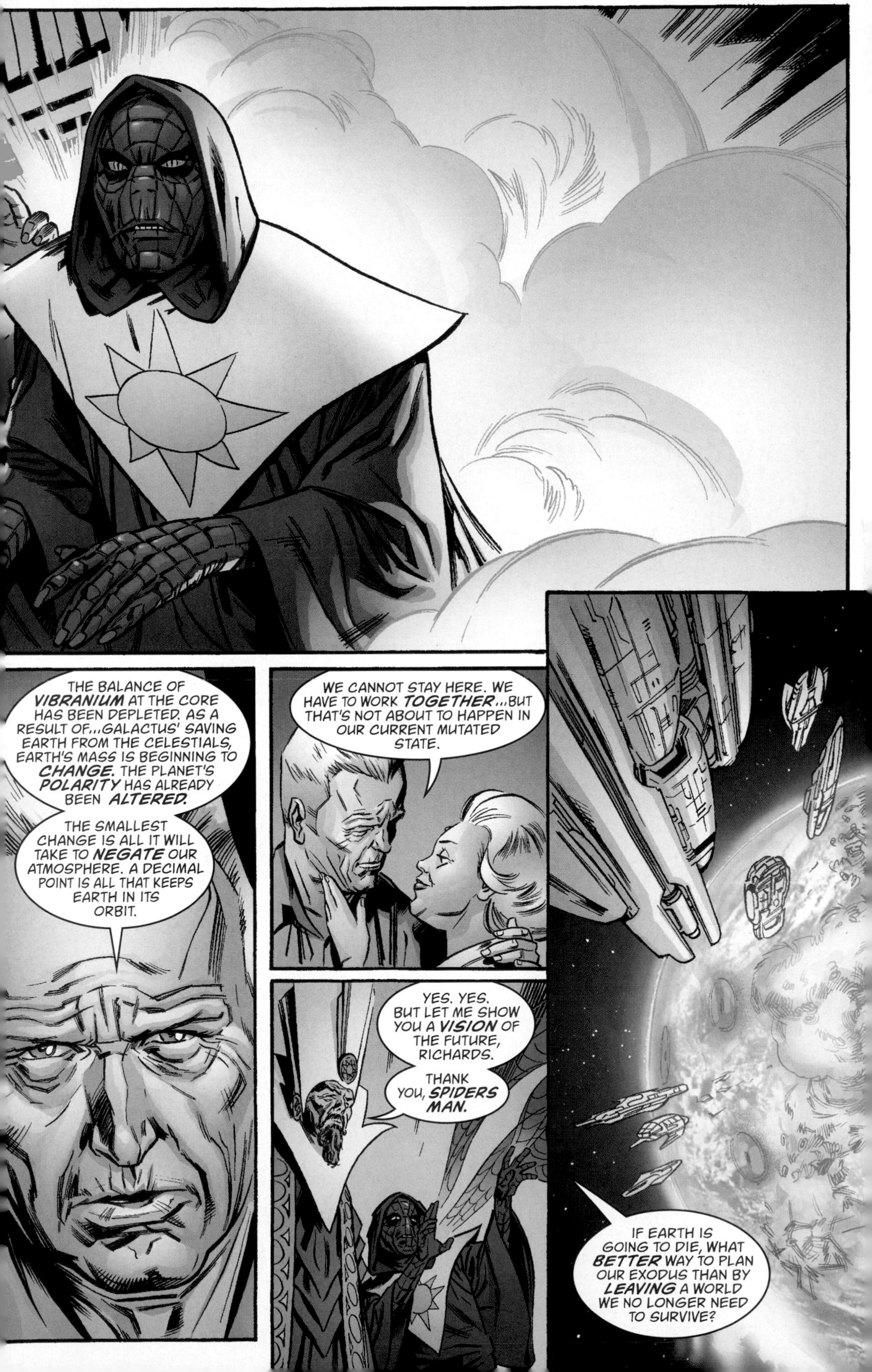

THE BALANCE OF **VIBRANIUM** AT THE CORE HAS BEEN DEPLETED. AS A RESULT OF...GALACTUS' SAVING EARTH FROM THE CELESTIALS, EARTH'S MASS IS BEGINNING TO **CHANGE.** THE PLANET'S **POLARITY** HAS ALREADY BEEN **ALTERED.**
THE SMALLEST CHANGE IS ALL IT WILL TAKE TO **NEGATE** OUR ATMOSPHERE. A DECIMAL POINT IS ALL THAT KEEPS EARTH IN ITS ORBIT.
WE CANNOT STAY HERE. WE HAVE TO WORK **TOGETHER...**BUT THAT'S NOT ABOUT TO HAPPEN IN OUR CURRENT MUTATED STATE.
YES. YES. BUT LET ME SHOW YOU A **VISION** OF THE FUTURE, RICHARDS.
THANK YOU, **SPIDERS MAN.**
IF EARTH IS GOING TO DIE, WHAT **BETTER** WAY TO PLAN OUR EXODUS THAN BY **LEAVING** A WORLD WE NO LONGER NEED TO SURVIVE?

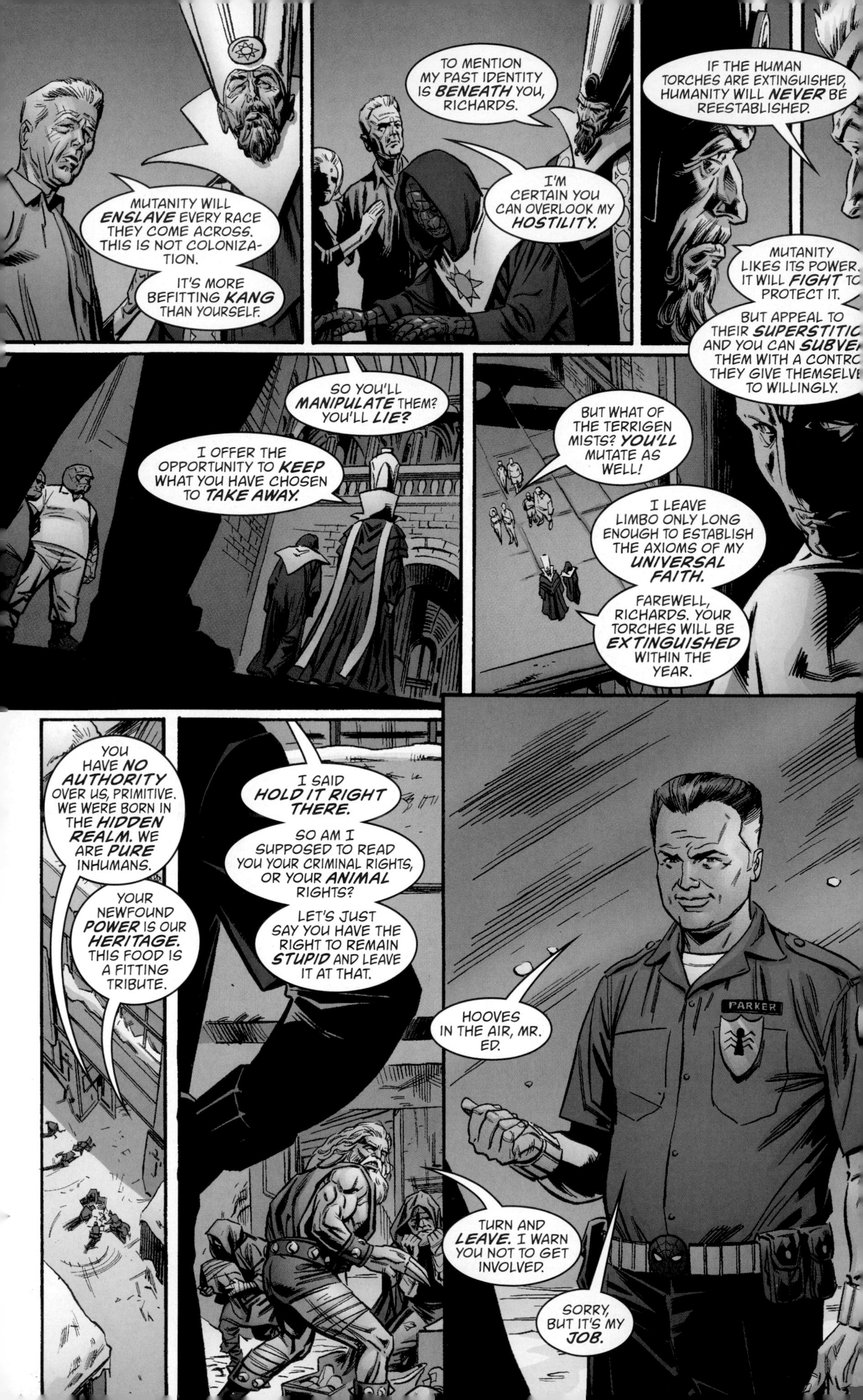
MUTANITY WILL ENSLAVE EVERY RACE THEY COME ACROSS. THIS IS NOT COLONIZATION.
IT'S MORE BEFITTING KANG THAN YOURSELF.
TO MENTION MY PAST IDENTITY IS BENEATH YOU, RICHARDS.
I'M CERTAIN YOU CAN OVERLOOK MY HOSTILITY.
IF THE HUMAN TORCHES ARE EXTINGUISHED, HUMANITY WILL NEVER BE REESTABLISHED.
MUTANITY LIKES ITS POWER. IT WILL FIGHT TO PROTECT IT.
BUT APPEAL TO THEIR SUPERSTITIC AND YOU CAN SUBVE THEM WITH A CONTRO THEY GIVE THEMSELVE TO WILLINGLY.
SO YOU'LL MANIPULATE THEM? YOU'LL LIE?
I OFFER THE OPPORTUNITY TO KEEP WHAT YOU HAVE CHOSEN TO TAKE AWAY.
BUT WHAT OF THE TERRIGEN MISTS? YOU'LL MUTATE AS WELL!
I LEAVE LIMBO ONLY LONG ENOUGH TO ESTABLISH THE AXIOMS OF MY UNIVERSAL FAITH.
FAREWELL, RICHARDS. YOUR TORCHES WILL BE EXTINGUISHED WITHIN THE YEAR.
YOU HAVE NO AUTHORITY OVER US, PRIMITIVE. WE WERE BORN IN THE HIDDEN REALM. WE ARE PURE INHUMANS.
YOUR NEWFOUND POWER IS OUR HERITAGE. THIS FOOD IS A FITTING TRIBUTE.
I SAID HOLD IT RIGHT THERE.
SO AM I SUPPOSED TO READ YOU YOUR CRIMINAL RIGHTS, OR YOUR ANIMAL RIGHTS?
LET'S JUST SAY YOU HAVE THE RIGHT TO REMAIN STUPID AND LEAVE IT AT THAT.
HOOVES IN THE AIR, MR. ED.
PARKER
TURN AND LEAVE. I WARN YOU NOT TO GET INVOLVED.
SORRY, BUT IT'S MY JOB.

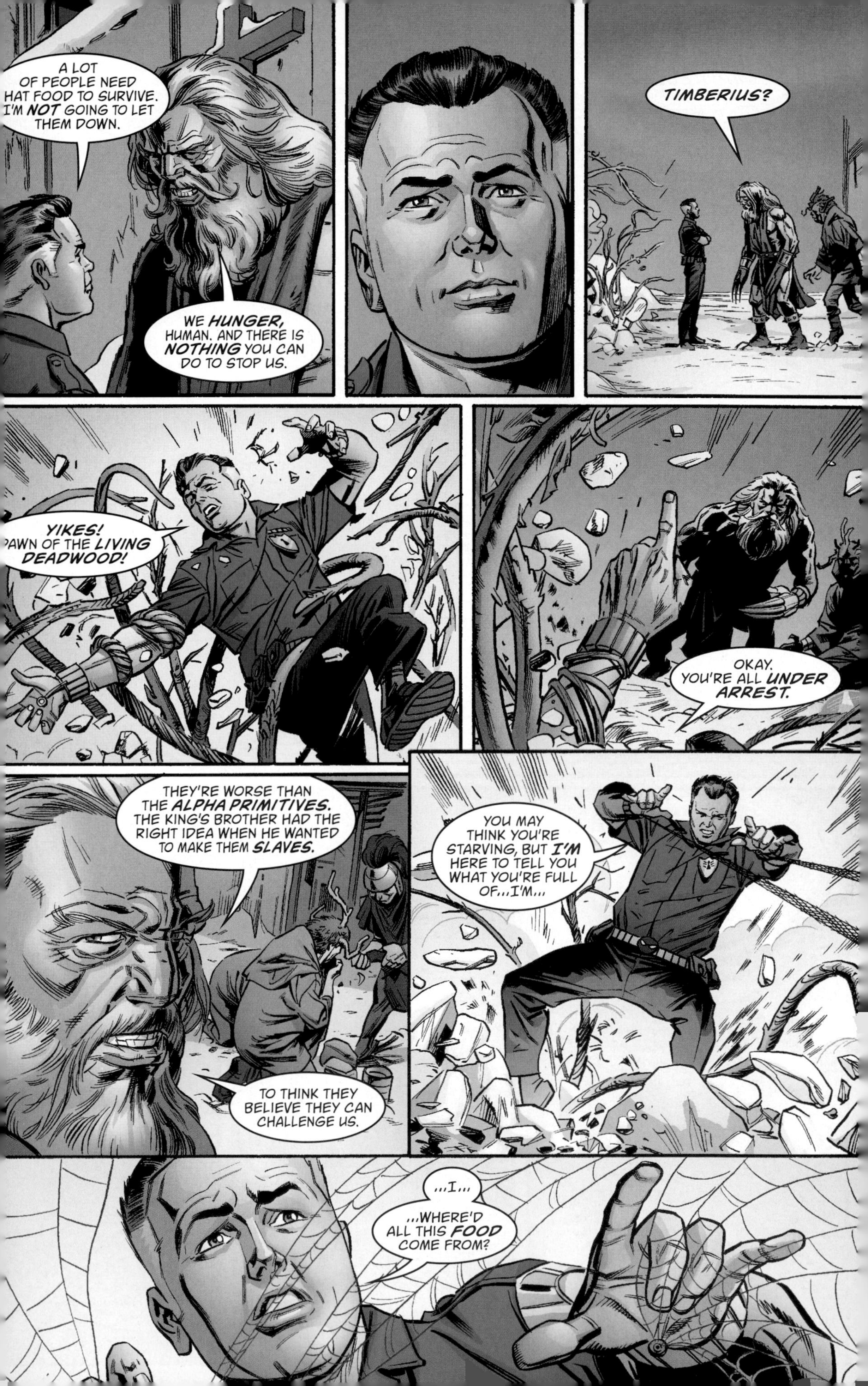
A LOT OF PEOPLE NEED HAT FOOD TO SURVIVE. I'M NOT GOING TO LET THEM DOWN.
WE HUNGER, HUMAN. AND THERE IS NOTHING YOU CAN DO TO STOP US.
TIMBERIUS?
YIKES! AWN OF THE LIVING DEADWOOD!
OKAY. YOU'RE ALL UNDER ARREST.
THEY'RE WORSE THAN THE ALPHA PRIMITIVES. THE KING'S BROTHER HAD THE RIGHT IDEA WHEN HE WANTED TO MAKE THEM SLAVES.
TO THINK THEY BELIEVE THEY CAN CHALLENGE US.
YOU MAY THINK YOU'RE STARVING, BUT I'M HERE TO TELL YOU WHAT YOU'RE FULL OF...I'M...
...I...
...WHERE'D ALL THIS FOOD COME FROM?

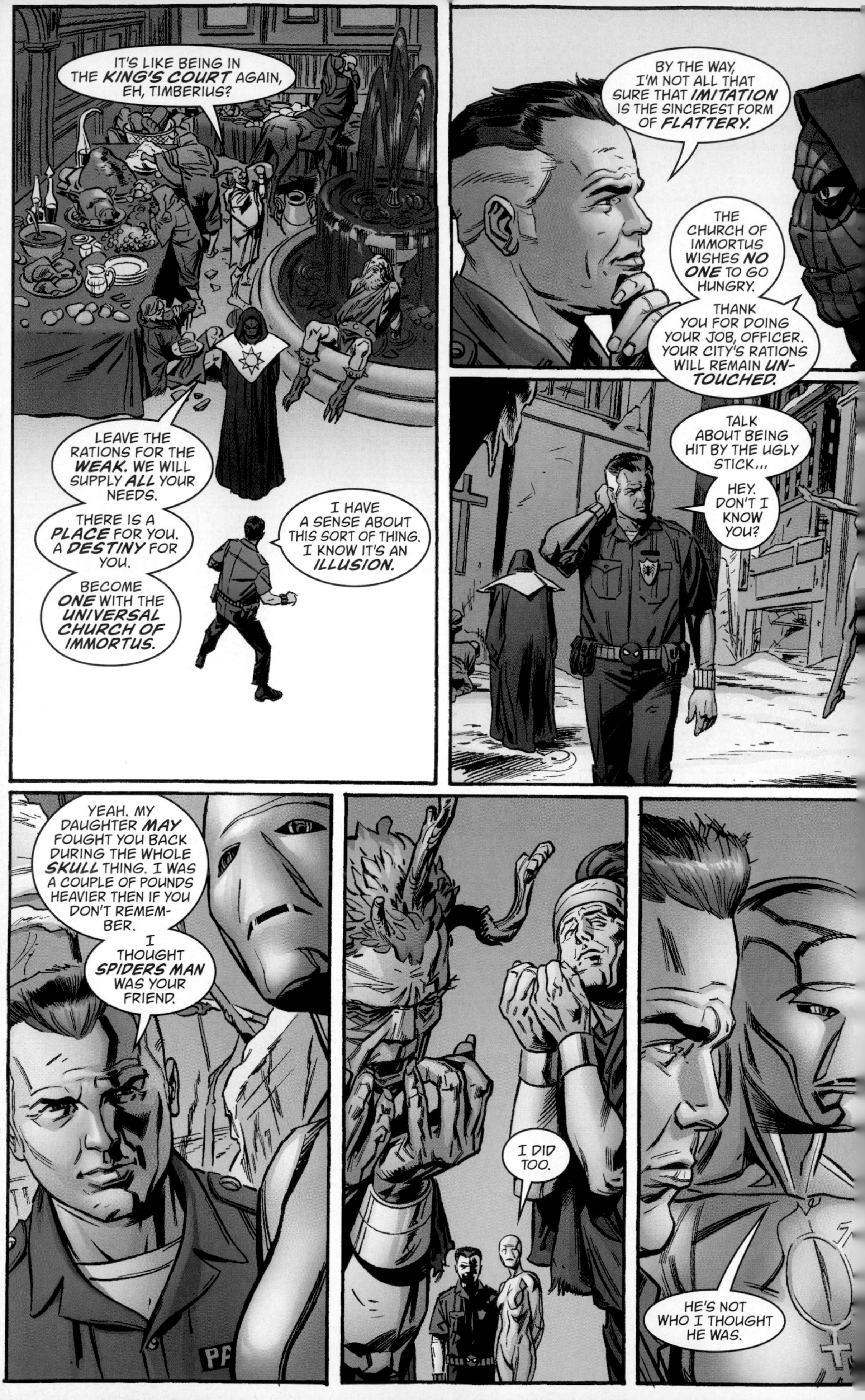

IT'S LIKE BEING IN THE KING'S COURT AGAIN, EH, TIMBERIUS?
LEAVE THE RATIONS FOR THE WEAK. WE WILL SUPPLY ALL YOUR NEEDS.
THERE IS A PLACE FOR YOU. A DESTINY FOR YOU.
BECOME ONE WITH THE UNIVERSAL CHURCH OF IMMORTUS.
I HAVE A SENSE ABOUT THIS SORT OF THING. I KNOW IT'S AN ILLUSION.
BY THE WAY, I'M NOT ALL THAT SURE THAT IMITATION IS THE SINCEREST FORM OF FLATTERY.
THE CHURCH OF IMMORTUS WISHES NO ONE TO GO HUNGRY.
THANK YOU FOR DOING YOUR JOB, OFFICER. YOUR CITY'S RATIONS WILL REMAIN UN-TOUCHED.
TALK ABOUT BEING HIT BY THE UGLY STICK...
HEY. DON'T I KNOW YOU?
YEAH. MY DAUGHTER MAY FOUGHT YOU BACK DURING THE WHOLE SKULL THING. I WAS A COUPLE OF POUNDS HEAVIER THEN IF YOU DON'T REMEM-BER.
I THOUGHT SPIDERS MAN WAS YOUR FRIEND.
I DID TOO.
HE'S NOT WHO I THOUGHT HE WAS.

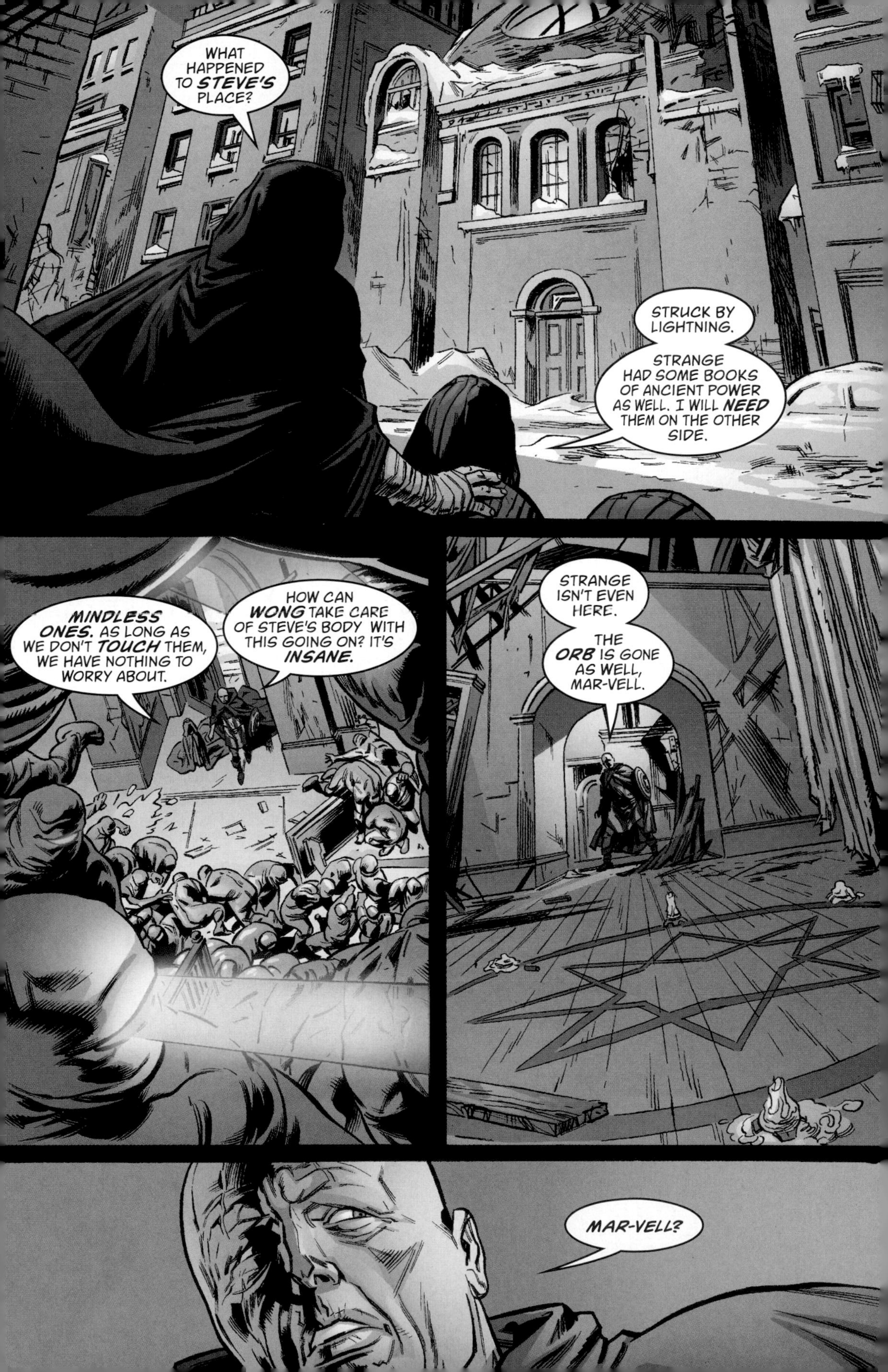
WHAT HAPPENED TO STEVE'S PLACE?
STRUCK BY LIGHTNING.
STRANGE HAD SOME BOOKS OF ANCIENT POWER AS WELL. I WILL NEED THEM ON THE OTHER SIDE.
MINDLESS ONES. AS LONG AS WE DON'T TOUCH THEM, WE HAVE NOTHING TO WORRY ABOUT.
HOW CAN WONG TAKE CARE OF STEVE'S BODY WITH THIS GOING ON? IT'S INSANE.
STRANGE ISN'T EVEN HERE.
THE ORB IS GONE AS WELL, MAR-VELL.
MAR-VELL?

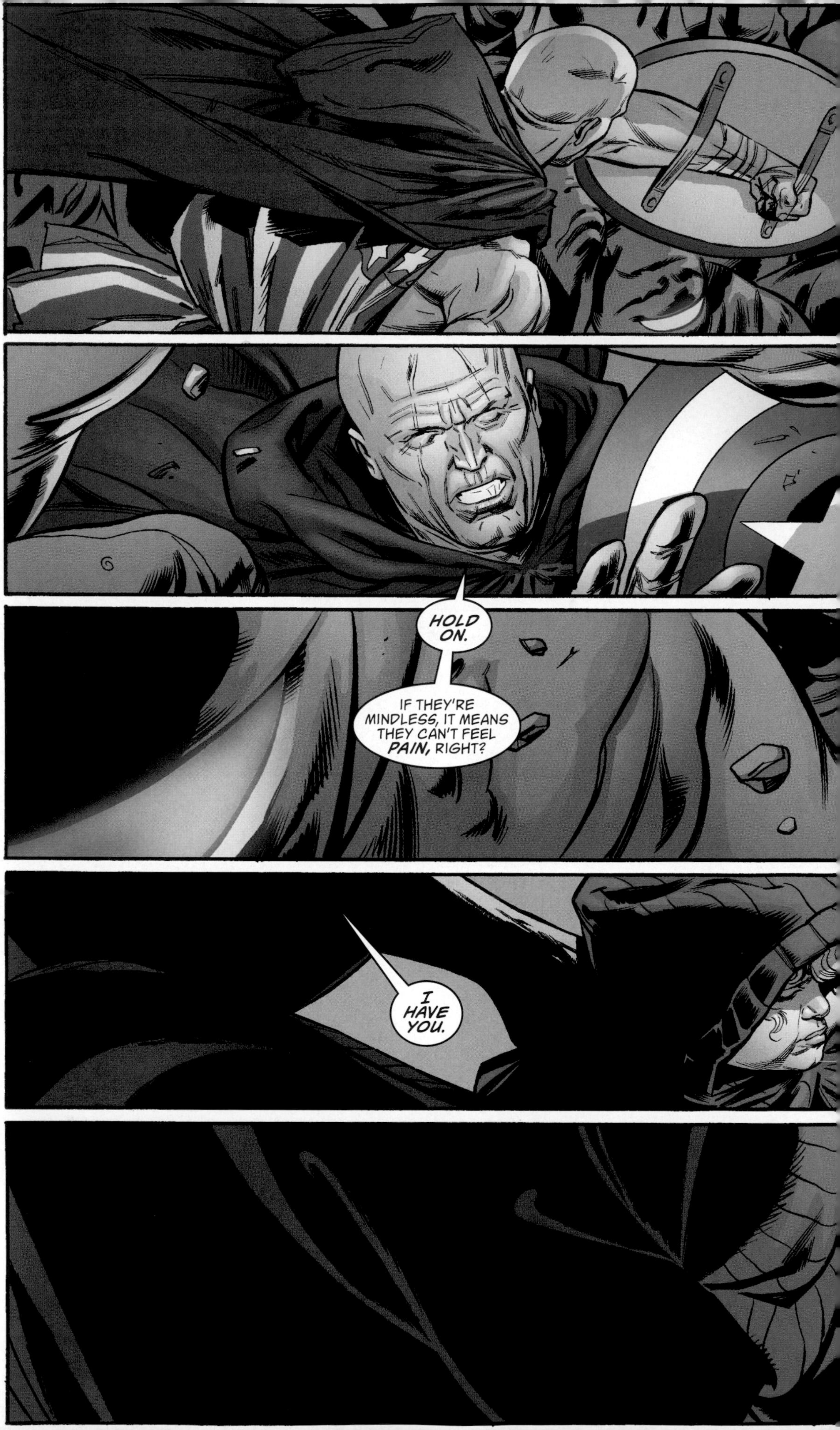
HOLD ON.
IF THEY'RE MINDLESS, IT MEANS THEY CAN'T FEEL PAIN, RIGHT?
I HAVE YOU.

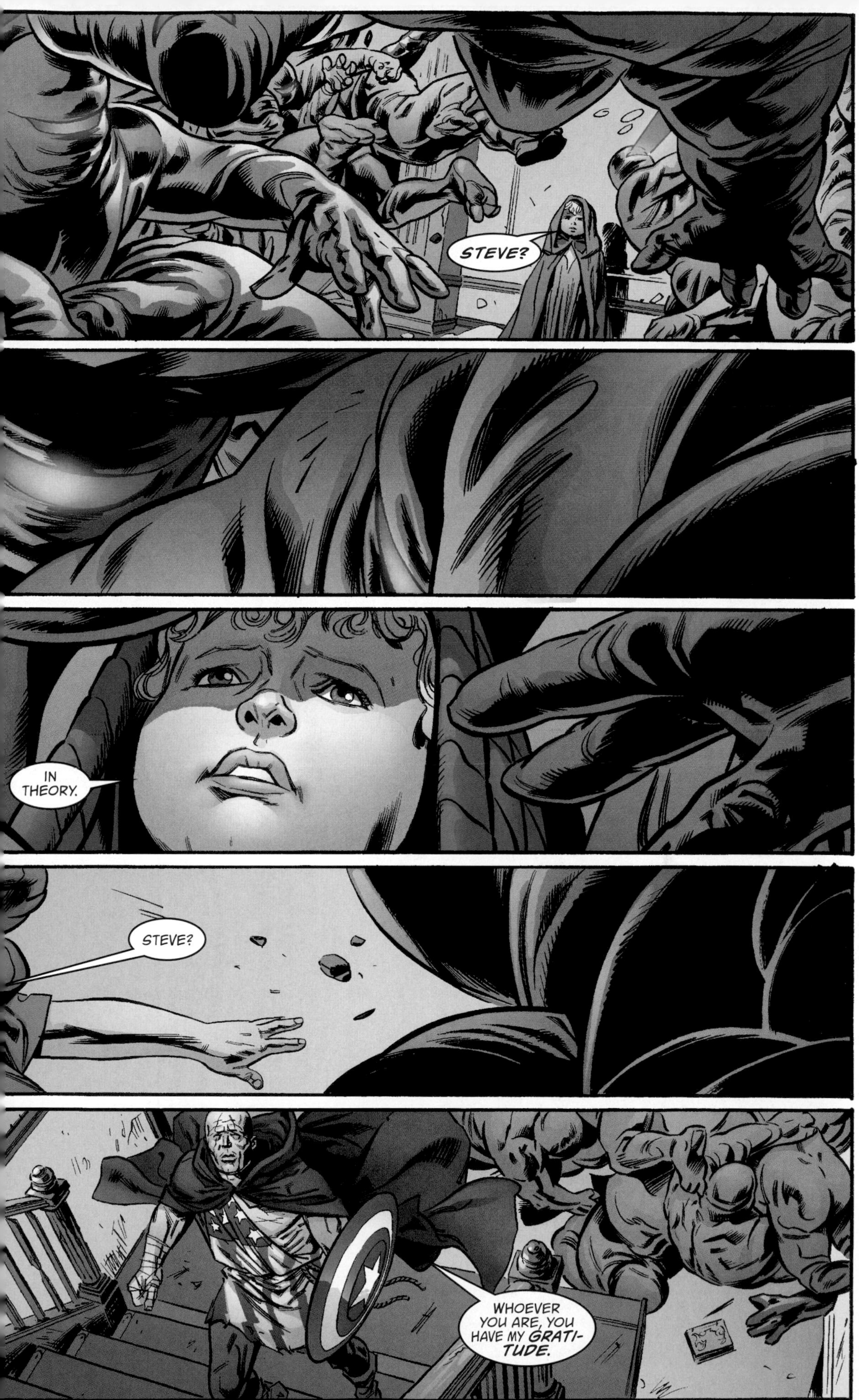
STEVE?
IN THEORY.
STEVE?
WHOEVER YOU ARE, YOU HAVE MY GRATI-TUDE.

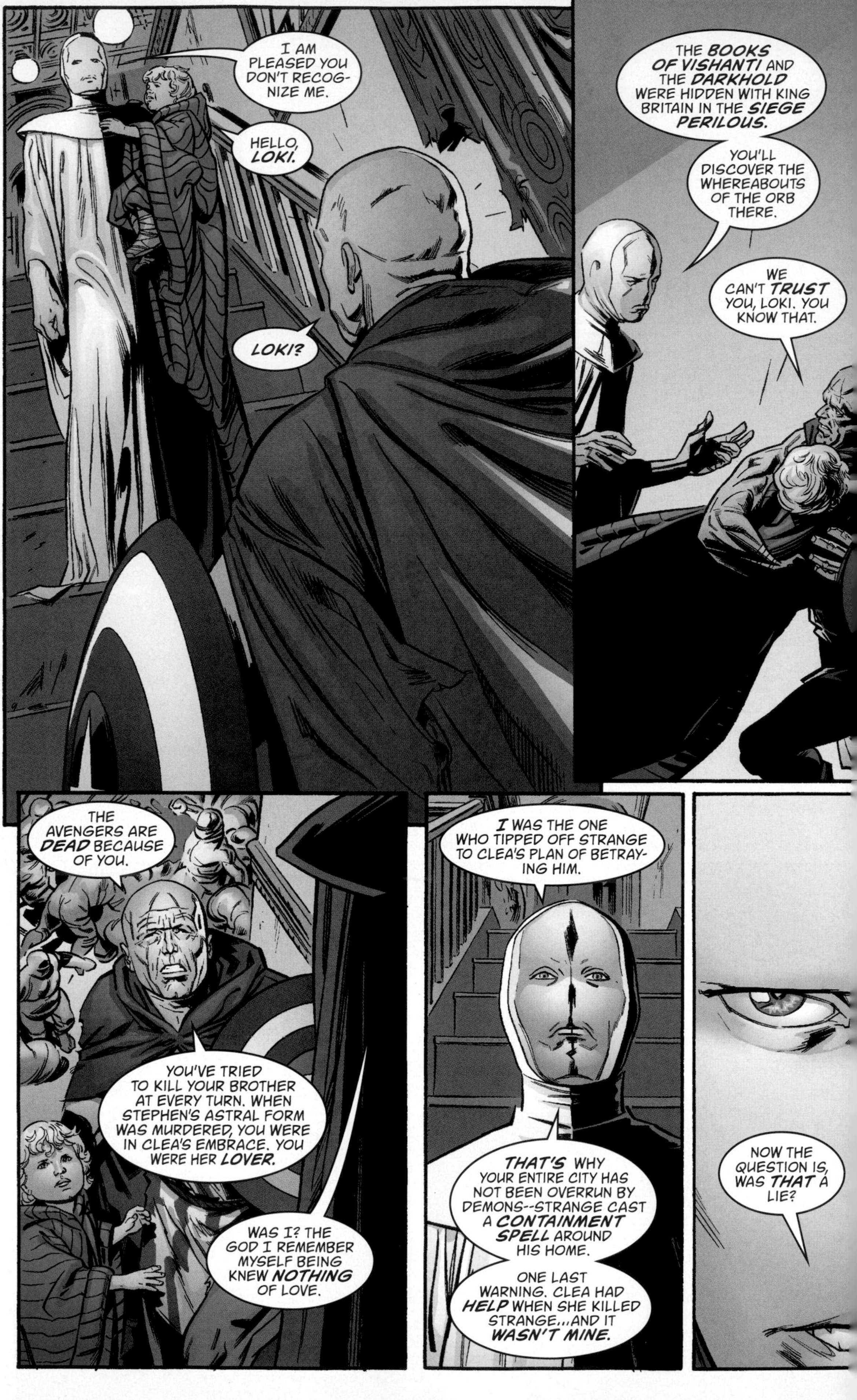
I AM PLEASED YOU DON'T RECOGNIZE ME.
HELLO, LOKI.
LOKI?
THE BOOKS OF VISHANTI AND THE DARKHOLD WERE HIDDEN WITH KING BRITAIN IN THE SIEGE PERILOUS.
YOU'LL DISCOVER THE WHEREABOUTS OF THE ORB THERE.
WE CAN'T TRUST YOU, LOKI. YOU KNOW THAT.
THE AVENGERS ARE DEAD BECAUSE OF YOU.
YOU'VE TRIED TO KILL YOUR BROTHER AT EVERY TURN. WHEN STEPHEN'S ASTRAL FORM WAS MURDERED, YOU WERE IN CLEA'S EMBRACE. YOU WERE HER LOVER.
WAS I? THE GOD I REMEMBER MYSELF BEING KNEW NOTHING OF LOVE.
I WAS THE ONE WHO TIPPED OFF STRANGE TO CLEA'S PLAN OF BETRAYING HIM.
THAT'S WHY YOUR ENTIRE CITY HAS NOT BEEN OVERRUN BY DEMONS--STRANGE CAST A CONTAINMENT SPELL AROUND HIS HOME.
ONE LAST WARNING. CLEA HAD HELP WHEN SHE KILLED STRANGE...AND IT WASN'T MINE.
NOW THE QUESTION IS, WAS THAT A LIE?

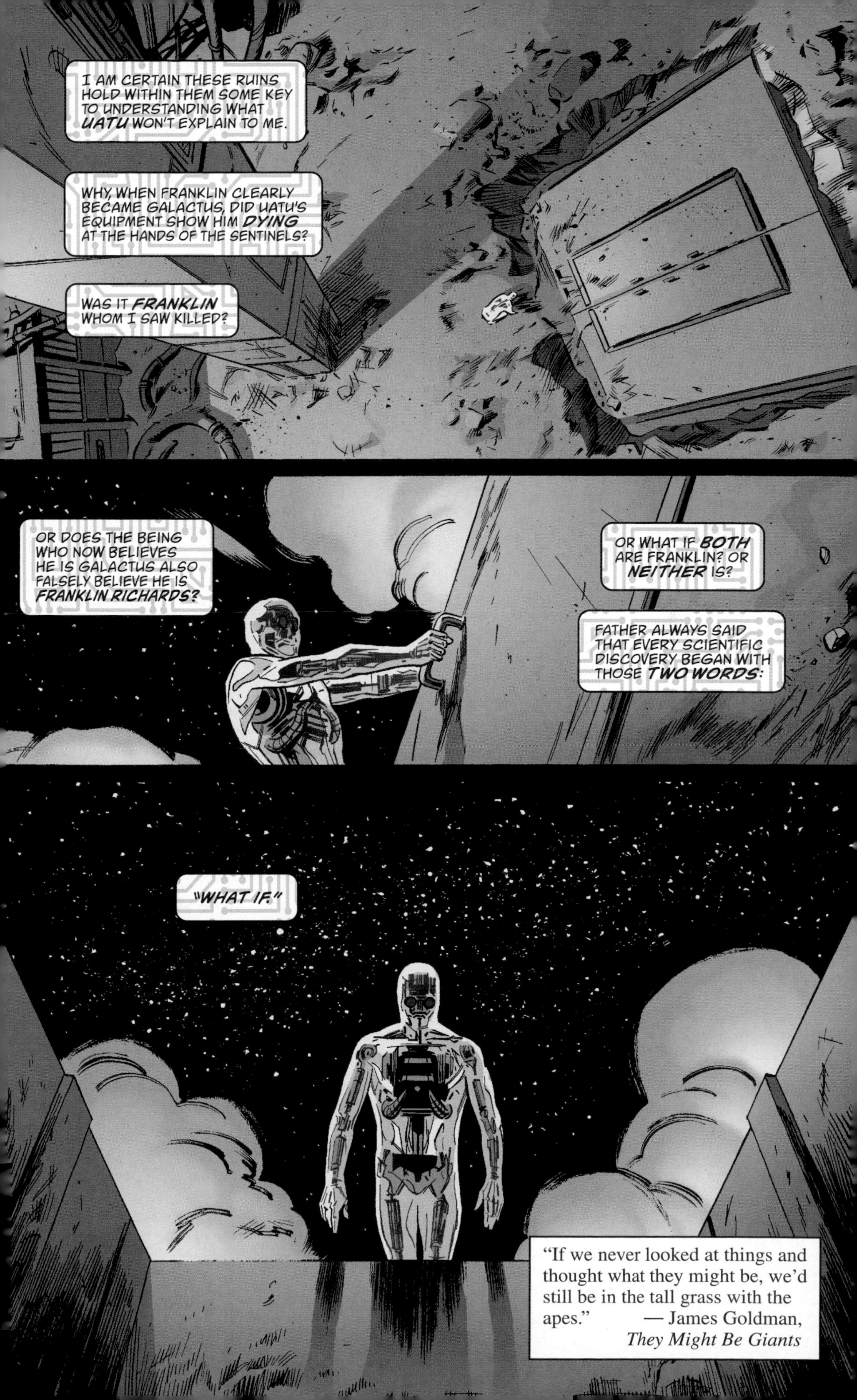
I AM CERTAIN THESE RUINS HOLD WITHIN THEM SOME KEY TO UNDERSTANDING WHAT UATU WON'T EXPLAIN TO ME.
WHY, WHEN FRANKLIN CLEARLY BECAME GALACTUS, DID UATU'S EQUIPMENT SHOW HIM DYING AT THE HANDS OF THE SENTINELS?
WAS IT FRANKLIN WHOM I SAW KILLED?
OR DOES THE BEING WHO NOW BELIEVES HE IS GALACTUS ALSO FALSELY BELIEVE HE IS FRANKLIN RICHARDS?
OR WHAT IF BOTH ARE FRANKLIN? OR NEITHER IS?
FATHER ALWAYS SAID THAT EVERY SCIENTIFIC DISCOVERY BEGAN WITH THOSE TWO WORDS:
"WHAT IF."
"If we never looked at things and thought what they might be, we'd still be in the tall grass with the apes." — James Goldman, *They Might Be Giants*

UNIVERSE X

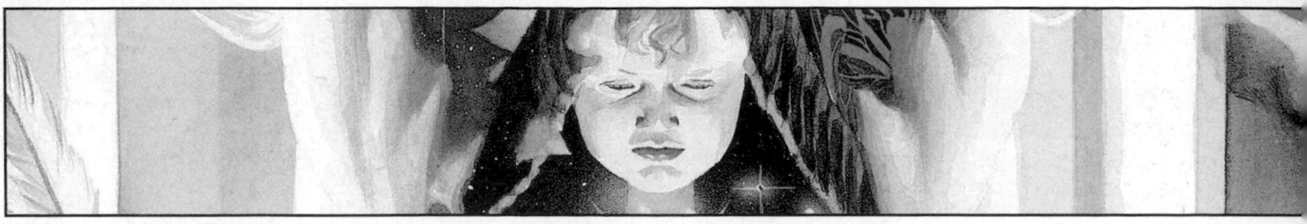

APPENDIX TO CHAPTER ONE

WRITTEN BY JIM KRUEGE

"X-51?"

"Yes, Uatu?"

"You have kept your word and reconnected me to the world. Much has changed. I can hear your planet's eco-structure shifting. I can hear the slow cracks forming in the polar ice caps. Your people are becoming scared. They are hungry. And for those used to the cold, they fear the beads of sweat forming on their brow. For those accustomed to the tropics, they cannot stop the chattering of their bones."

"Yes, Uatu. I know. New York will soon become a frozen wasteland."

"How do you know this?"

"Kyle Richmond has eyes that allow him to peer into the future. He and Isaac Christians..."

"The Gargoyle."

"Yeah. Christians is writing down Richmond's visions of the future to act as sort of a history for generations to learn from. And while the chronology of what Richmond sees is not perfectly ordered, the intent is easily understood. The polarity of the planet has shifted due to the death of the Celestial within."

"I warned you of this, X-51. I told you that there was no way to save your world."

"But there was a way. Reed Richards found it. His son had the power to both defend the world from your masters, the Celestials, and destroy the Celestial that grew within the impregnated planet Earth. He saved everyone."

"For how long?"

"Every moment counts, Uatu."

"Does it?"

"What?"

"I speak of time and history, X-51. Does every moment, every measurable fraction when added upon itself, truly "count"? I have shown you whole races that have risen and fallen. I have shown you birth and death – and what has it amounted to?"

"I don't know, Uatu. Perhaps it only counts in the present. Perhaps history itself is as cruel as your masters and yourself. Maybe history makes one cruel. But in this moment right now, wouldn't humanity choose life over death?

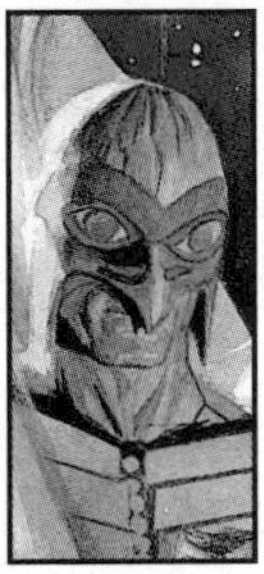

"If the choice were theirs to make, X-51, but it is not. Your victory does nothing to suggest that your people's purpose is anything greater than biological. The lifespan of your race has not increased, only perhaps the span of a finitude of individuals."

"Remind me again why I needed to speak with you? Why I bothered to let you back into the world?"

"You have begun to see visions of alternate history, X-51."

"Call me Aaron."

"As I was saying, X-51, you have need of answers. Are these answers less important than the label by which I refer to you?"

"I was afraid. Franklin Richards came to me believing himself to be the world devourer. He came wanting to know who Franklin Richards really was. When I showed him his history, his destiny was different. He did not become Galactus and forget who he was. Instead, he was slain by the mutant-hunting Sentinels in a present very different than this one. How could that be?"

"The answer is simple, X-51. This reality you cling to and hold so dear to for your very meaning and purpose is but a glimmer of all that is. It is a wink in the cosmic order of being. A fraction of history that hardly 'counts' at all."

"I've heard of alternate realities... but why would your equipment choose to show that specific fate for Franklin? "

"It did not. You did."

"No, I didn't."

"Come now, X-51. Must you always give life to inanimate machines?"

"Runs in the family."

"Of course it does. All the secrets of this citadel are yours to use as you will. It is your will that is flawed. It is a mix of machine and your accursed programmed humanity."

"I don't understand."

"I assume Galactus came wanting to know more about his true identity – Franklin Richards. I also assume that this quest of the Devourer placed you in a position of... how would those you are programmed to mock put it... oh yes, a moral dilemma."

"We've been through this before, Uatu. There is no good. There is no evil. There is only change. I know that is what you believe. Get on with it."

"Yes. I can see that patience is one of the human virtues that you have not been programmed with. So you were placed in the dilemma. Do you reveal what you know of Franklin? Do you undo all the heroics and self-denial of Reed Richards for the sake of the entire universe? Or do you become myself? A manipulator of history according to your own agenda?"

"That's not fair, Uatu."

"Fairness? Do you know me so little? How amazing that your species continues to justify itself while failing to uphold even its own flawed law."

"What do you mean?"
"You killed the Celestial, X-51. Your species killed for the sake of its own survival. You made a decision that one life was more important than another."
"It was self-defense. One life against billions."
"So you did the "right" thing, is that it, X-51?"
"Yes. Of course. How can you...?"
"I can because I have watched you for years. You claim to be in touch with something higher than your animalistic survival-of-the-fittest mentality, but you are not. You force your higher hopes into positions of justifiable servitude to the needs of the moment. Right and wrong are situational justifications, X-51. Galactus is a murderer on the cosmic scale."
"But there has to be a balance."
"There does? Are you the authority on the matter of what ought to be amongst the universe?"
"But?"
"Your laws of morality, while sounding noble in times of peace and prosperity, are little more than children's brawls at recess. They are 'Says Who' arguments with no substantiation. Attempts to control each other with the hope that you are something greater than you are. And when the Celestials made that fallow hope a reality, you struck at them. I told you long ago that mankind's nature is to strike at its own gods. This is the reason your "heroes" were the objects of scorn and hatred. This is the reason that in one reality, the robot enforcers known as the Sentinels exterminated every hero on Earth. It was Franklin's death in this reality that served your need for a solution to the Galactus problem."
"My solution?"
"Your programmed fear triggered the citadel's equipment in such a way that it switched from the reality where Franklin becomes Galactus and it focussed upon one of the alternative realities – one that featured the death of Franklin Richards instead of his subsequent transformation. Now, if I have given you enough to satisfy your imagined curiosity, I have some questions of my own."
"Okay, Uatu. What do you want to know?"
"I am concerned regarding these eyes you speak of."
"They were given to Kyle Richmond by Mephisto."
"Then it is true."
"What?"
"I have been separated from my brethren and am damned."
"What do you mean? How can someone without a moral structure as yourself be damned?"
"This means nothing to you or to your fool's errand of protecting the masses who live upon your world. The consequence is mine alone. And that is how it will remain."
"These alternatives you speak of?"
"Yes?"
"They have Watchers of their own?"
"Yes."
"Earths of their own?"
"Yes."
"Are these Earth's also... Impregnated?"
"Tell me of what has happened these last three years. What has occurred since you cut me off from the world?"
"You didn't answer my question, Uatu."
"Again, you do not require an answer. I, on the other hand, must know what is going on upon the Earth."
"I can see this is going to be a problem, Uatu. I need answers you're not willing to give. And you need to hear of what's going on Earth. I didn't ask you to change me or make me your replacement after you were blinded by the King of the Inhumans. It was your decision. Your mistake. In the meantime, I need you, too."

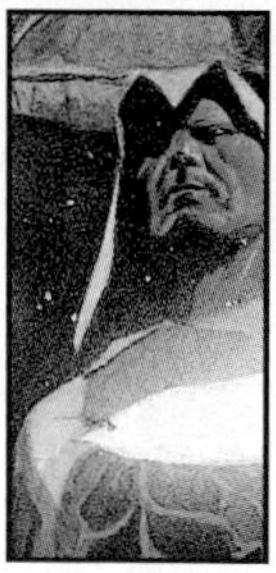

"Very well, Machine Man. In exchange for the knowledge I require, I will give you a larger understanding of the nature of reality. This will begin with the knowledge I require.
"Tell me now what has happened. And tell of Richmond's visions and what is about to happen."
"Okay, Uatu. Reed Richards, in cooperation with the other nations and heroes of the Earth, created a device known as the Human Torch. The purpose of this devise is to burn the Terrigen Mists from the air so that Reed's cure for the world's mutations can be administered."
"But the world's mutated population is unwilling to give up its power, is it not, X-51?"
"Yes. How did you know?"
"I have watched your kind since its beginnings, X-51. I know your inclinations. The death of the Celestial within the Earth is destroying your planet. Had you listened to me, perhaps your race might have survived."
"What are you saying, Uatu?"
"I am saying that your race might have evolved to the point at which it was no longer dependent upon this planet for its continued life. I'm saying the coming birth might have been your liberation. Instead, the death of the Celestial fetus has doomed your race."
"I don't believe you, Uatu."
"Why, because I don't fit within your Good vs. Evil grid? Because my purpose for watching your race was biological and not moral, you believe my purpose can only ever be that of the destruction of life? The role of Watcher is to see what is actually happening."
"I did, Uatu. And now I need to know why you still want to watch. I don't think it's out of boredom. I want to know why I'm going to be digging in the ruins of the Kree City here on the moon."
"How should I know?"
"I want to know why Kyle Richmond is having visions of me digging there. What might I find?"
"Ah. You will find that your belief in the good of the universe is far out-rated. And you will find that the deaths you are so eager to prevent are part of the very fabric of the natural order. You see yourself as a hero because you have cheated death. But this is not heroic literature that is being written down by Isaac Christians, X-51. It is tragedy. Now tell me, who has risen up to lead the masses against the controls set upon them by Richards and his antiquated alliances?"
"Immortus. He says he has seen a future where the mutated mankind leaves Earth to colonize the universe. He speaks of a glorious destiny."
"A destiny, as I have shown, that will now be denied mankind because of the death of the Celestial at the heart of the Earth."

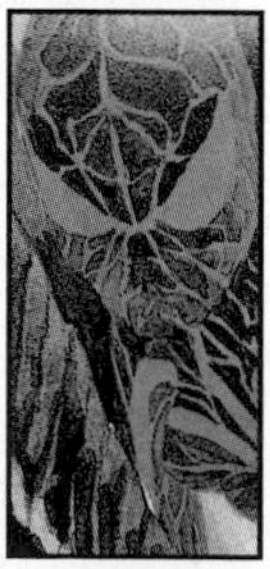

"So the vision is wrong. What will happen, Uatu?"
"Look to Richmond, X-51. What does he say?"
"He says it's a waste to write everything down. Because there isn't going to be anyone around to read these histories anyhow."
"That is very doubtful, X-51. I expect that they are being read even while we speak."

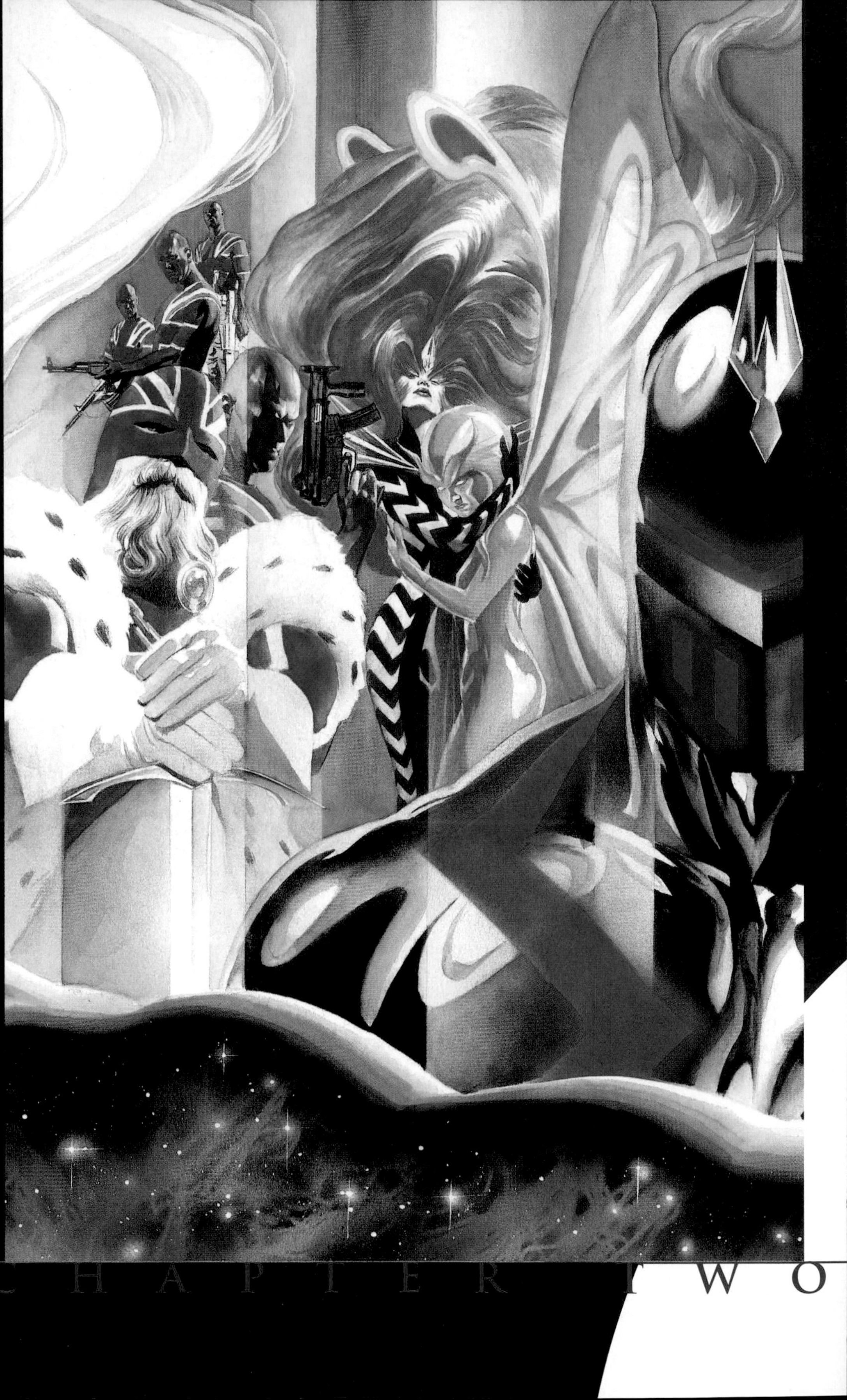

CHAPTER TWO

The mute spoke that day. The dead fought without knowledge that they were dead. And myth became reality while reality walked in the realm of myth."

"Hold your vision, Kyle. While my fingers never tire of chronicling what you speak of, my hand is incapable of the speeds at which you ofttimes demand."

"Sorry. Ready? Okay. After this, Richards knew that there was no hope of saving Earth. And so, he began to plan an exodus from the planet for all those willing to join him. It was a sad day when..."

"Kyle?"

"Yes, Isaac?"

"You're speaking in the past tense...as if these events have already happened."

"To me, Isaac, they already have. That's the problem. How can someone like me offer you hope when I know what's coming?"

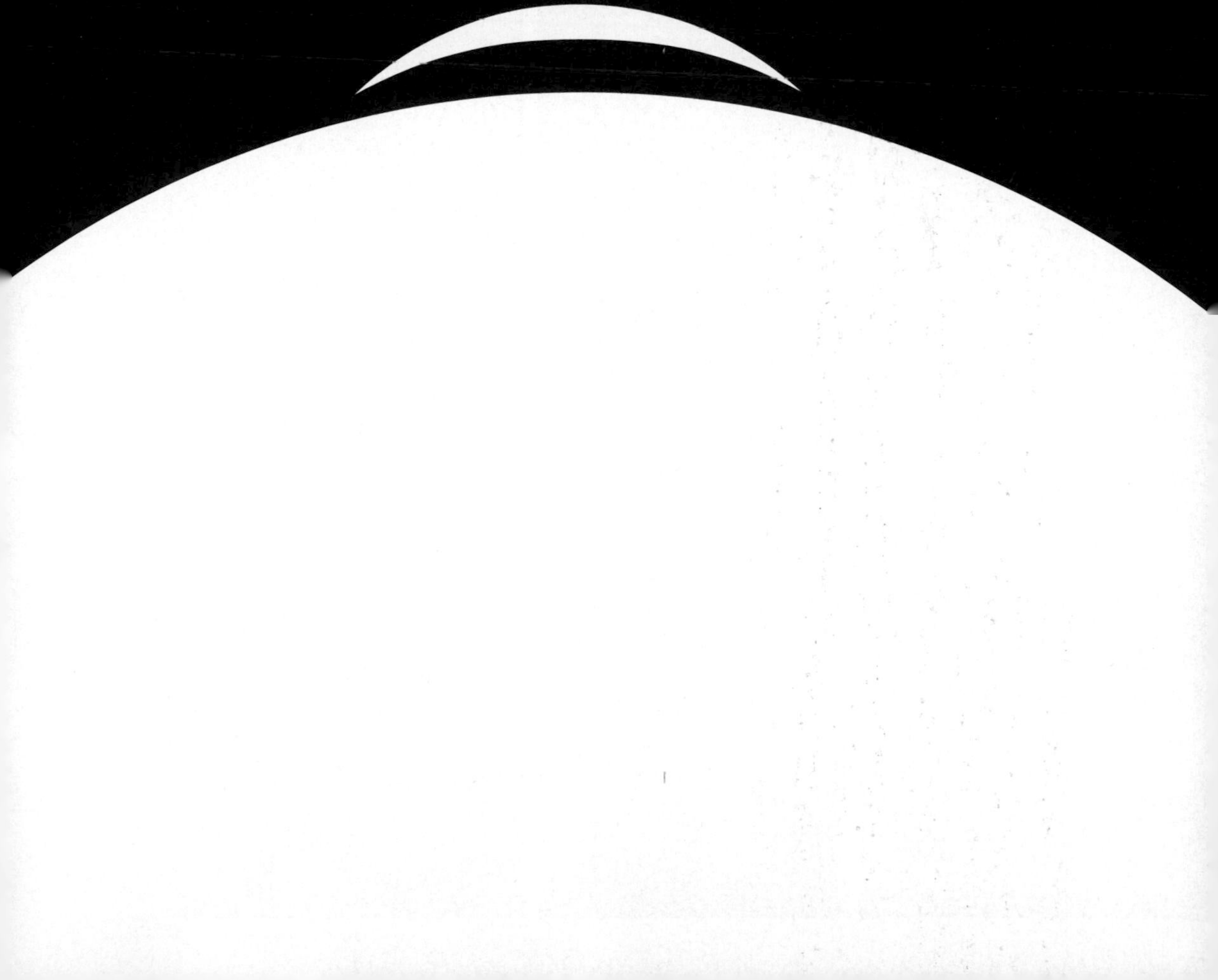

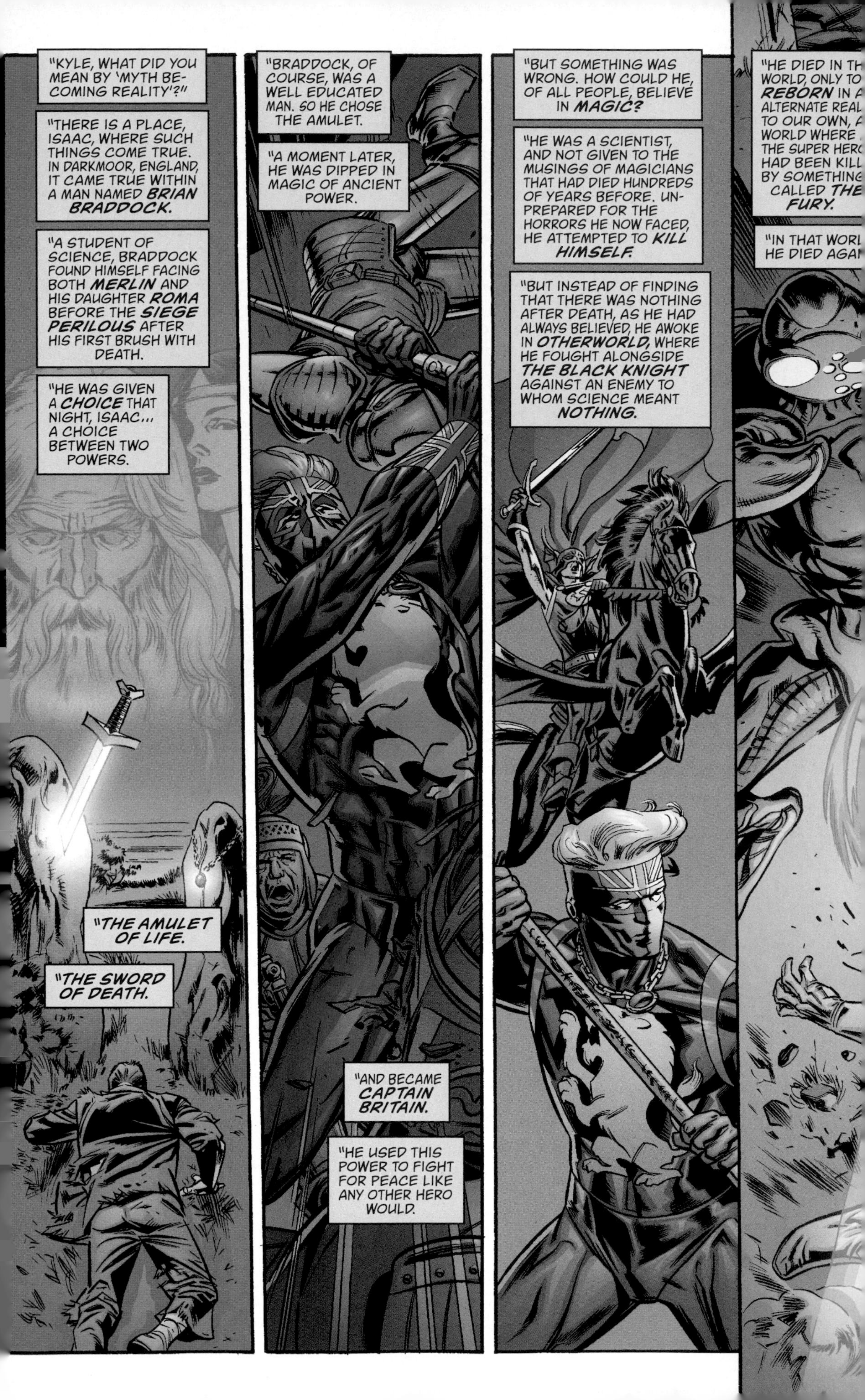
"KYLE, WHAT DID YOU MEAN BY 'MYTH BE-COMING REALITY'?"
"THERE IS A PLACE, ISAAC, WHERE SUCH THINGS COME TRUE. IN DARKMOOR, ENGLAND, IT CAME TRUE WITHIN A MAN NAMED BRIAN BRADDOCK.
"A STUDENT OF SCIENCE, BRADDOCK FOUND HIMSELF FACING BOTH MERLIN AND HIS DAUGHTER ROMA BEFORE THE SIEGE PERILOUS AFTER HIS FIRST BRUSH WITH DEATH.
"HE WAS GIVEN A CHOICE THAT NIGHT, ISAAC... A CHOICE BETWEEN TWO POWERS.
"THE AMULET OF LIFE.
"THE SWORD OF DEATH.
"BRADDOCK, OF COURSE, WAS A WELL EDUCATED MAN. SO HE CHOSE THE AMULET.
"A MOMENT LATER, HE WAS DIPPED IN MAGIC OF ANCIENT POWER.
"AND BECAME CAPTAIN BRITAIN.
"HE USED THIS POWER TO FIGHT FOR PEACE LIKE ANY OTHER HERO WOULD.
"BUT SOMETHING WAS WRONG. HOW COULD HE, OF ALL PEOPLE, BELIEVE IN MAGIC?
"HE WAS A SCIENTIST, AND NOT GIVEN TO THE MUSINGS OF MAGICIANS THAT HAD DIED HUNDREDS OF YEARS BEFORE. UN-PREPARED FOR THE HORRORS HE NOW FACED, HE ATTEMPTED TO KILL HIMSELF.
"BUT INSTEAD OF FINDING THAT THERE WAS NOTHING AFTER DEATH, AS HE HAD ALWAYS BELIEVED, HE AWOKE IN OTHERWORLD, WHERE HE FOUGHT ALONGSIDE THE BLACK KNIGHT AGAINST AN ENEMY TO WHOM SCIENCE MEANT NOTHING.
"HE DIED IN TH WORLD, ONLY TO REBORN IN A ALTERNATE REAL TO OUR OWN, A WORLD WHERE THE SUPER HERO HAD BEEN KILL BY SOMETHING CALLED THE FURY.
"IN THAT WORL HE DIED AGAI

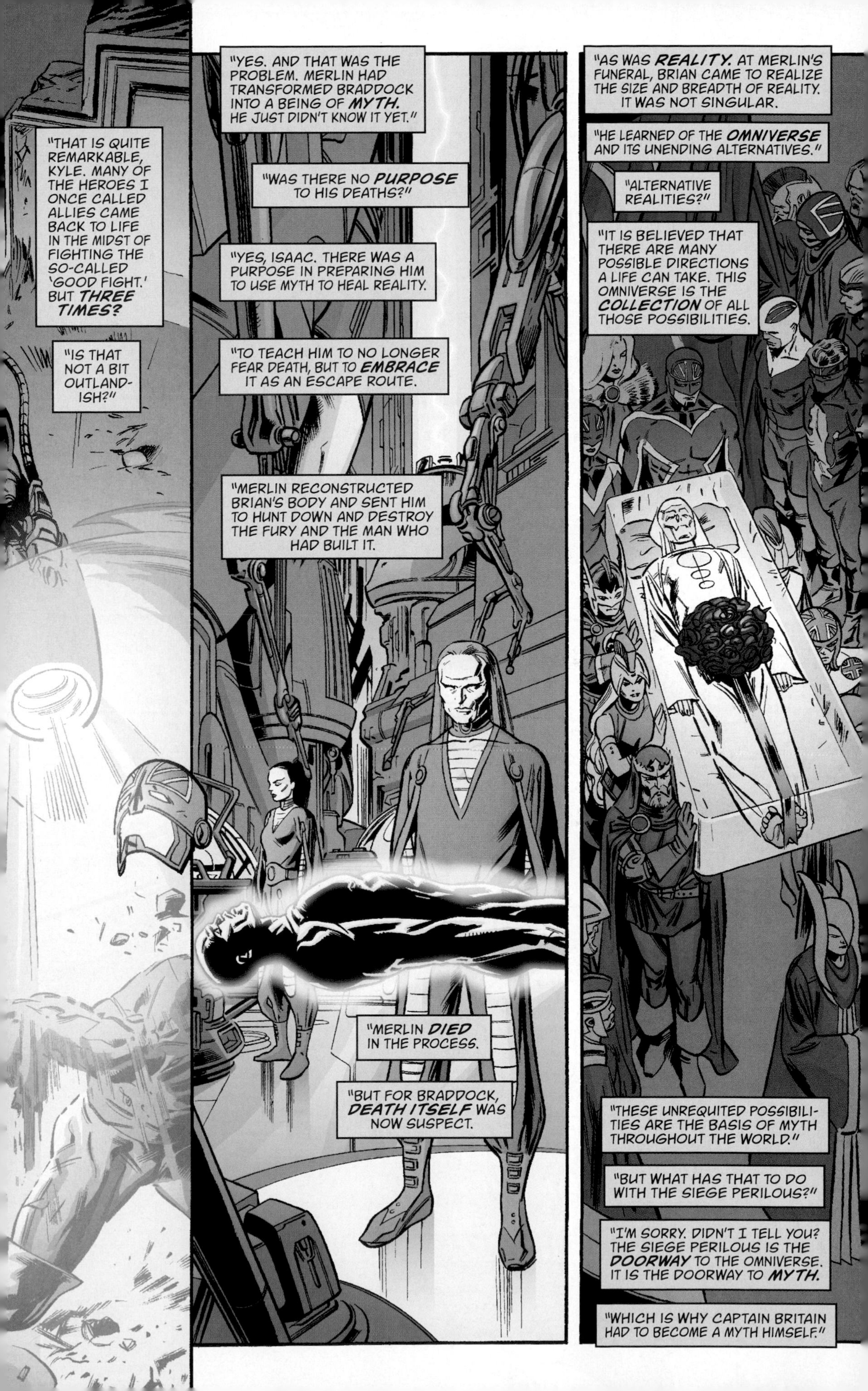

"THAT IS QUITE REMARKABLE, KYLE. MANY OF THE HEROES I ONCE CALLED ALLIES CAME BACK TO LIFE IN THE MIDST OF FIGHTING THE SO-CALLED 'GOOD FIGHT.' BUT THREE TIMES?
"IS THAT NOT A BIT OUTLANDISH?"
"YES. AND THAT WAS THE PROBLEM. MERLIN HAD TRANSFORMED BRADDOCK INTO A BEING OF MYTH. HE JUST DIDN'T KNOW IT YET."
"WAS THERE NO PURPOSE TO HIS DEATHS?"
"YES, ISAAC. THERE WAS A PURPOSE IN PREPARING HIM TO USE MYTH TO HEAL REALITY.
"TO TEACH HIM TO NO LONGER FEAR DEATH, BUT TO EMBRACE IT AS AN ESCAPE ROUTE.
"MERLIN RECONSTRUCTED BRIAN'S BODY AND SENT HIM TO HUNT DOWN AND DESTROY THE FURY AND THE MAN WHO HAD BUILT IT.
"MERLIN DIED IN THE PROCESS.
"BUT FOR BRADDOCK, DEATH ITSELF WAS NOW SUSPECT.
"AS WAS REALITY. AT MERLIN'S FUNERAL, BRIAN CAME TO REALIZE THE SIZE AND BREADTH OF REALITY. IT WAS NOT SINGULAR.
"HE LEARNED OF THE OMNIVERSE AND ITS UNENDING ALTERNATIVES."
"ALTERNATIVE REALITIES?"
"IT IS BELIEVED THAT THERE ARE MANY POSSIBLE DIRECTIONS A LIFE CAN TAKE. THIS OMNIVERSE IS THE COLLECTION OF ALL THOSE POSSIBILITIES.
"THESE UNREQUITED POSSIBILITIES ARE THE BASIS OF MYTH THROUGHOUT THE WORLD."
"BUT WHAT HAS THAT TO DO WITH THE SIEGE PERILOUS?"
"I'M SORRY. DIDN'T I TELL YOU? THE SIEGE PERILOUS IS THE DOORWAY TO THE OMNIVERSE. IT IS THE DOORWAY TO MYTH.
"WHICH IS WHY CAPTAIN BRITAIN HAD TO BECOME A MYTH HIMSELF."

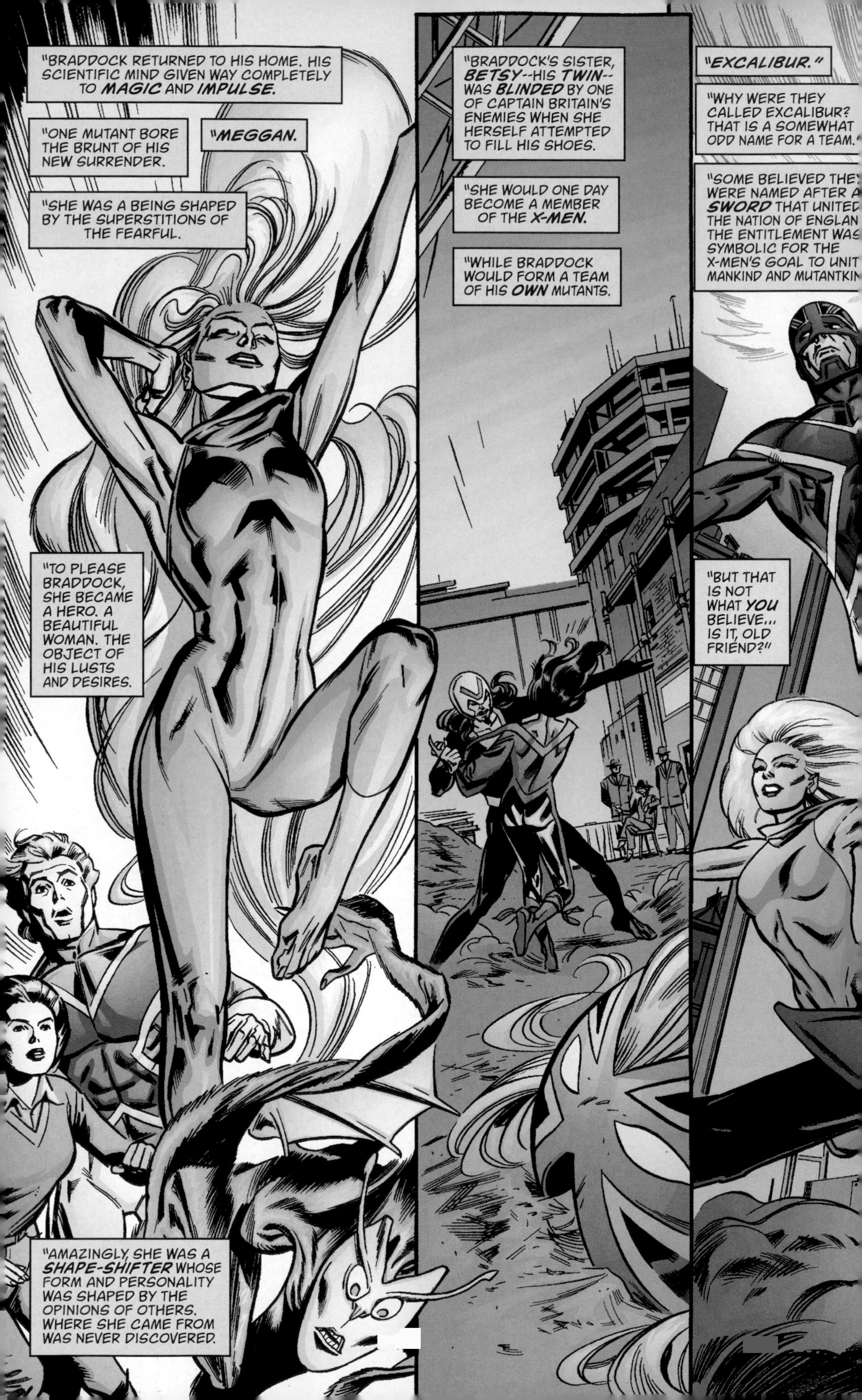
"BRADDOCK RETURNED TO HIS HOME. HIS SCIENTIFIC MIND GIVEN WAY COMPLETELY TO MAGIC AND IMPULSE.
"ONE MUTANT BORE THE BRUNT OF HIS NEW SURRENDER.
"MEGGAN.
"SHE WAS A BEING SHAPED BY THE SUPERSTITIONS OF THE FEARFUL.
"TO PLEASE BRADDOCK, SHE BECAME A HERO. A BEAUTIFUL WOMAN. THE OBJECT OF HIS LUSTS AND DESIRES.
"AMAZINGLY, SHE WAS A SHAPE-SHIFTER WHOSE FORM AND PERSONALITY WAS SHAPED BY THE OPINIONS OF OTHERS. WHERE SHE CAME FROM WAS NEVER DISCOVERED.
"BRADDOCK'S SISTER, BETSY--HIS TWIN--WAS BLINDED BY ONE OF CAPTAIN BRITAIN'S ENEMIES WHEN SHE HERSELF ATTEMPTED TO FILL HIS SHOES.
"SHE WOULD ONE DAY BECOME A MEMBER OF THE X-MEN.
"WHILE BRADDOCK WOULD FORM A TEAM OF HIS OWN MUTANTS.
"EXCALIBUR."
"WHY WERE THEY CALLED EXCALIBUR? THAT IS A SOMEWHAT ODD NAME FOR A TEAM."
"SOME BELIEVED THE WERE NAMED AFTER A SWORD THAT UNITED THE NATION OF ENGLAN THE ENTITLEMENT WAS SYMBOLIC FOR THE X-MEN'S GOAL TO UNIT MANKIND AND MUTANTKIN
"BUT THAT IS NOT WHAT YOU BELIEVE... IS IT, OLD FRIEND?"

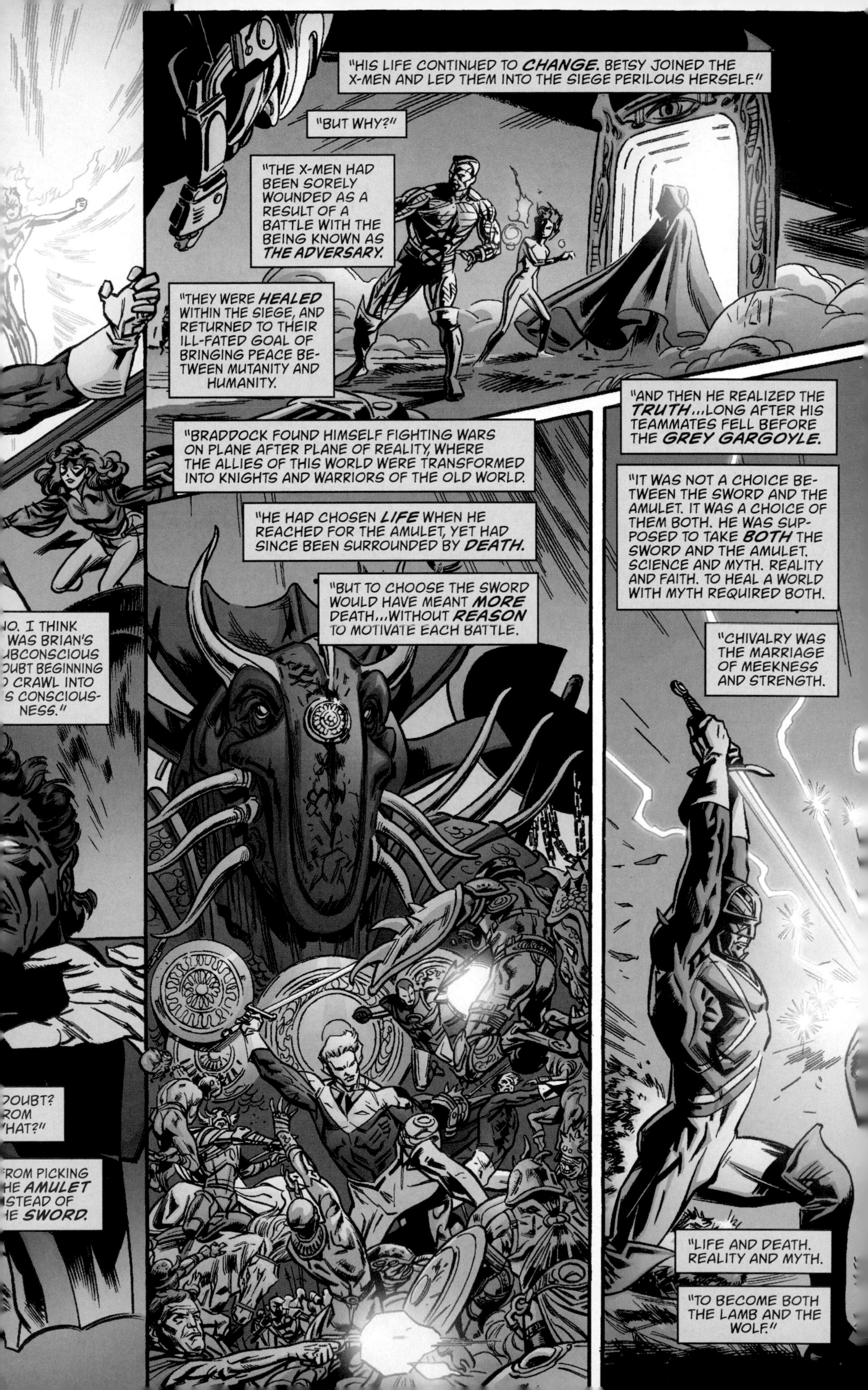

"HIS LIFE CONTINUED TO CHANGE. BETSY JOINED THE X-MEN AND LED THEM INTO THE SIEGE PERILOUS HERSELF."
"BUT WHY?"
"THE X-MEN HAD BEEN SORELY WOUNDED AS A RESULT OF A BATTLE WITH THE BEING KNOWN AS THE ADVERSARY.
"THEY WERE HEALED WITHIN THE SIEGE, AND RETURNED TO THEIR ILL-FATED GOAL OF BRINGING PEACE BETWEEN MUTANITY AND HUMANITY.
NO. I THINK WAS BRIAN'S UBCONSCIOUS OUBT BEGINNING CRAWL INTO S CONSCIOUSNESS."
OUBT? ROM HAT?"
FROM PICKING HE AMULET STEAD OF HE SWORD.
"BRADDOCK FOUND HIMSELF FIGHTING WARS ON PLANE AFTER PLANE OF REALITY, WHERE THE ALLIES OF THIS WORLD WERE TRANSFORMED INTO KNIGHTS AND WARRIORS OF THE OLD WORLD.
"HE HAD CHOSEN LIFE WHEN HE REACHED FOR THE AMULET, YET HAD SINCE BEEN SURROUNDED BY DEATH.
"BUT TO CHOOSE THE SWORD WOULD HAVE MEANT MORE DEATH...WITHOUT REASON TO MOTIVATE EACH BATTLE.
"AND THEN HE REALIZED THE TRUTH...LONG AFTER HIS TEAMMATES FELL BEFORE THE GREY GARGOYLE.
"IT WAS NOT A CHOICE BETWEEN THE SWORD AND THE AMULET. IT WAS A CHOICE OF THEM BOTH. HE WAS SUPPOSED TO TAKE BOTH THE SWORD AND THE AMULET. SCIENCE AND MYTH. REALITY AND FAITH. TO HEAL A WORLD WITH MYTH REQUIRED BOTH.
"CHIVALRY WAS THE MARRIAGE OF MEEKNESS AND STRENGTH.
"LIFE AND DEATH. REALITY AND MYTH.
"TO BECOME BOTH THE LAMB AND THE WOLF."

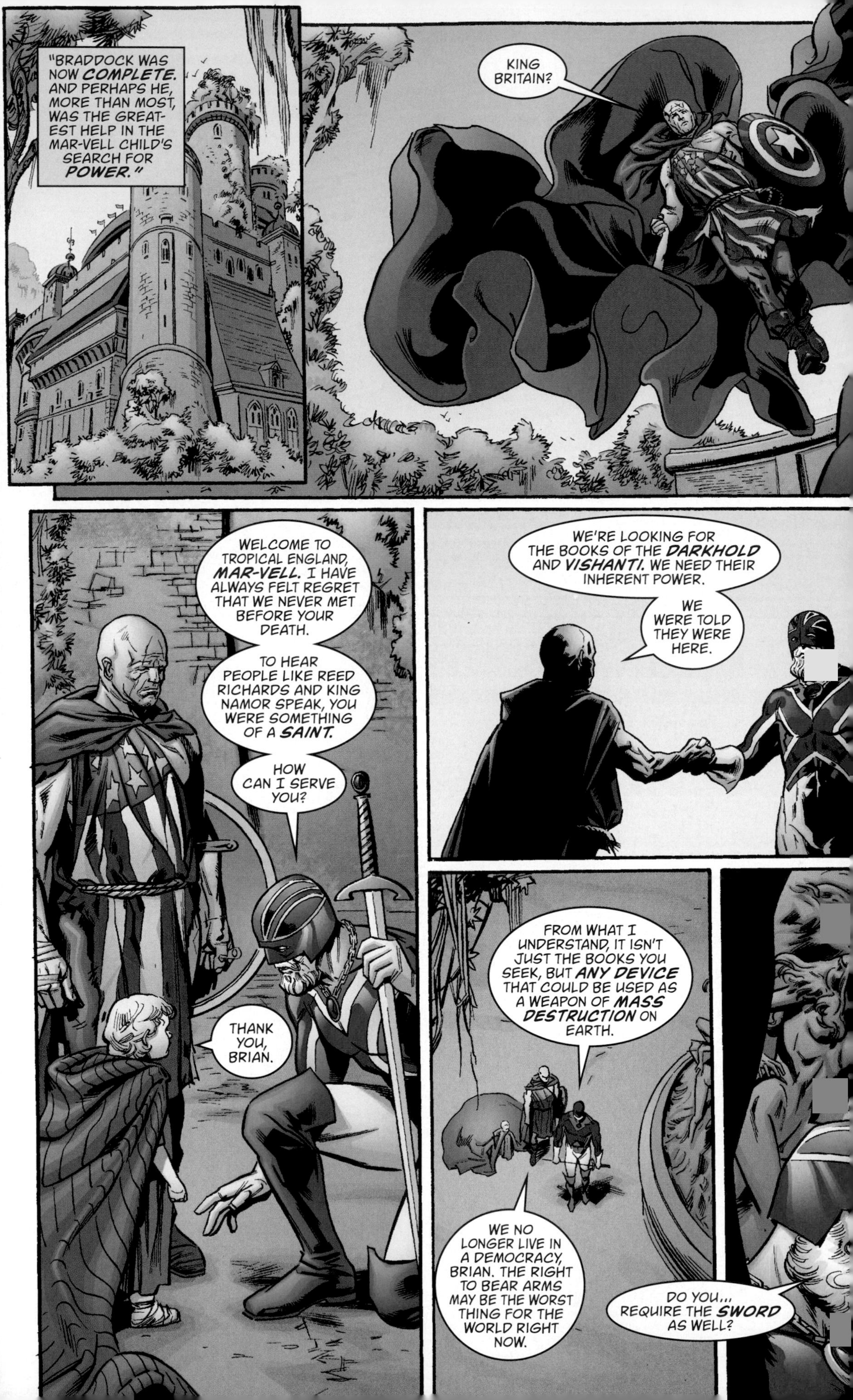
"BRADDOCK WAS NOW COMPLETE. AND PERHAPS HE, MORE THAN MOST, WAS THE GREATEST HELP IN THE MAR-VELL CHILD'S SEARCH FOR POWER."
KING BRITAIN?
WELCOME TO TROPICAL ENGLAND, MAR-VELL. I HAVE ALWAYS FELT REGRET THAT WE NEVER MET BEFORE YOUR DEATH.
TO HEAR PEOPLE LIKE REED RICHARDS AND KING NAMOR SPEAK, YOU WERE SOMETHING OF A SAINT.
HOW CAN I SERVE YOU?
THANK YOU, BRIAN.
WE'RE LOOKING FOR THE BOOKS OF THE DARKHOLD AND VISHANTI. WE NEED THEIR INHERENT POWER.
WE WERE TOLD THEY WERE HERE.
FROM WHAT I UNDERSTAND, IT ISN'T JUST THE BOOKS YOU SEEK, BUT ANY DEVICE THAT COULD BE USED AS A WEAPON OF MASS DESTRUCTION ON EARTH.
WE NO LONGER LIVE IN A DEMOCRACY, BRIAN. THE RIGHT TO BEAR ARMS MAY BE THE WORST THING FOR THE WORLD RIGHT NOW.
DO YOU... REQUIRE THE SWORD AS WELL?

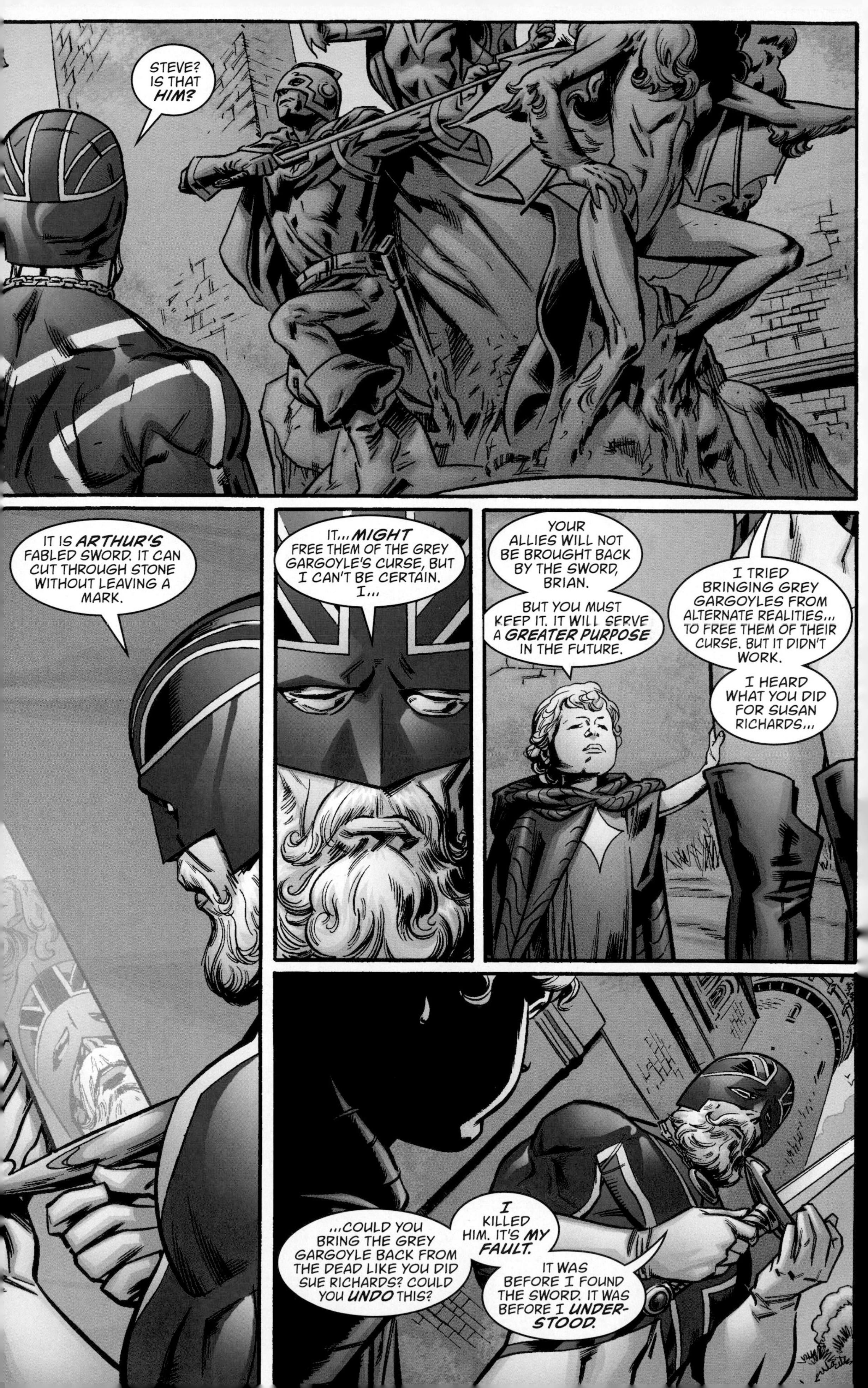

STEVE? IS THAT *HIM?*
IT IS ***ARTHUR'S*** FABLED SWORD. IT CAN CUT THROUGH STONE WITHOUT LEAVING A MARK.
IT... ***MIGHT*** FREE THEM OF THE GREY GARGOYLE'S CURSE, BUT I CAN'T BE CERTAIN. I...
YOUR ALLIES WILL NOT BE BROUGHT BACK BY THE SWORD, BRIAN.
BUT YOU MUST KEEP IT. IT WILL SERVE A ***GREATER PURPOSE*** IN THE FUTURE.
I TRIED BRINGING GREY GARGOYLES FROM ALTERNATE REALITIES... TO FREE THEM OF THEIR CURSE. BUT IT DIDN'T WORK.
I HEARD WHAT YOU DID FOR SUSAN RICHARDS...
...COULD YOU BRING THE GREY GARGOYLE BACK FROM THE DEAD LIKE YOU DID SUE RICHARDS? COULD YOU ***UNDO*** THIS?
I KILLED HIM. IT'S ***MY FAULT.***
IT WAS BEFORE I FOUND THE SWORD. IT WAS BEFORE I ***UNDER-STOOD.***

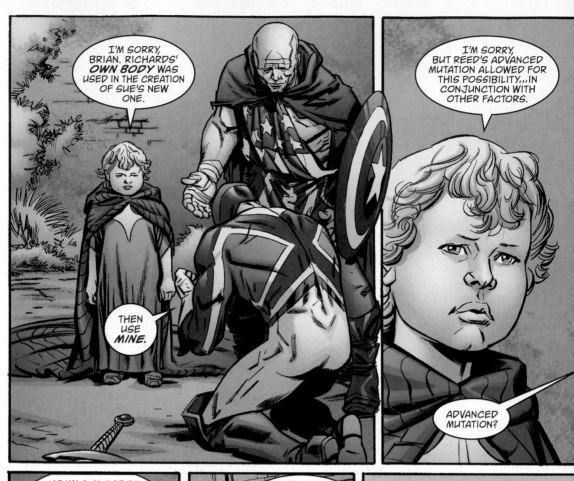

I'M SORRY, BRIAN. RICHARDS' **OWN BODY** WAS USED IN THE CREATION OF SUE'S NEW ONE.

THEN USE **MINE**.

I'M SORRY, BUT REED'S ADVANCED MUTATION ALLOWED FOR THIS POSSIBILITY...IN CONJUNCTION WITH OTHER FACTORS.

ADVANCED MUTATION?

HE WAS CLOSE TO THE **FINAL STAGE** OF MANKIND'S MUTATION. THE THIRD LEVEL IS TO BECOME SO POWERFUL THAT YOUR SHAPE AND BEING TAKE ON THE FORM OF THE NEEDS OF THOSE AROUND YOU.

I'M SO SORRY, MEGAN. I DIDN'T KNOW.

I MADE YOU SO SMALL.

I WAS SO...

DID **KURT** ESCAPE?

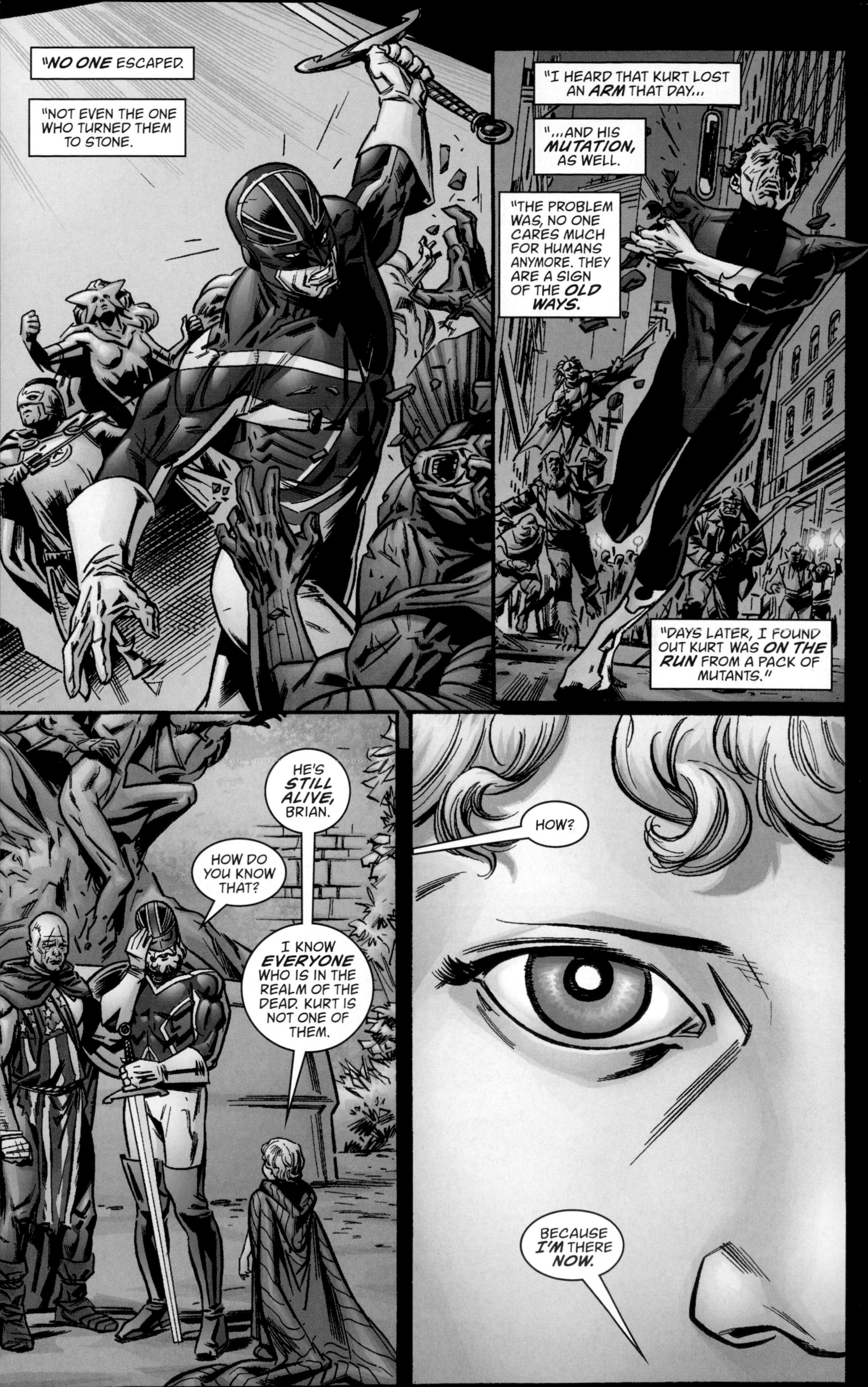
"NO ONE ESCAPED.
"NOT EVEN THE ONE WHO TURNED THEM TO STONE.
"I HEARD THAT KURT LOST AN ARM THAT DAY...
"...AND HIS MUTATION, AS WELL.
"THE PROBLEM WAS, NO ONE CARES MUCH FOR HUMANS ANYMORE. THEY ARE A SIGN OF THE OLD WAYS.
"DAYS LATER, I FOUND OUT KURT WAS ON THE RUN FROM A PACK OF MUTANTS."
HE'S STILL ALIVE, BRIAN.
HOW DO YOU KNOW THAT?
I KNOW EVERYONE WHO IS IN THE REALM OF THE DEAD. KURT IS NOT ONE OF THEM.
HOW?
BECAUSE I'M THERE NOW.

"WHAT DO YOU SEE, KYLE?"

"I SAW *STEVE STRANGE.* AND *JOHNNY STORM.* AND *PHOENIX.* THEY WERE NOT ALONE."

"THAT IS HIGHLY IMPROBABLE, KYLE. THEY'RE ALL *DEAD.*"

"I KNOW, ISAAC. BUT I SAW THE PLACE HEROES GO WHEN THEY DIE."

HAVE YOU FOUND HIM YET?

NO, STEPHEN. BUT HE AND I NEVER REALLY MET. MAYBE RICH WOULD BE MORE APT TO FIND HIM.

IT'S OKA BOB. YOU DOING FI WE'LL FI HIM.

ANOTHER CITY.

ARE YOU CERTAIN SHE CAN'T SEE THEM?

WE SHOULDN'T SPEAK OF THIS. SHE CAN'T SEE THEM...BUT SHE CAN *HEAR* US.

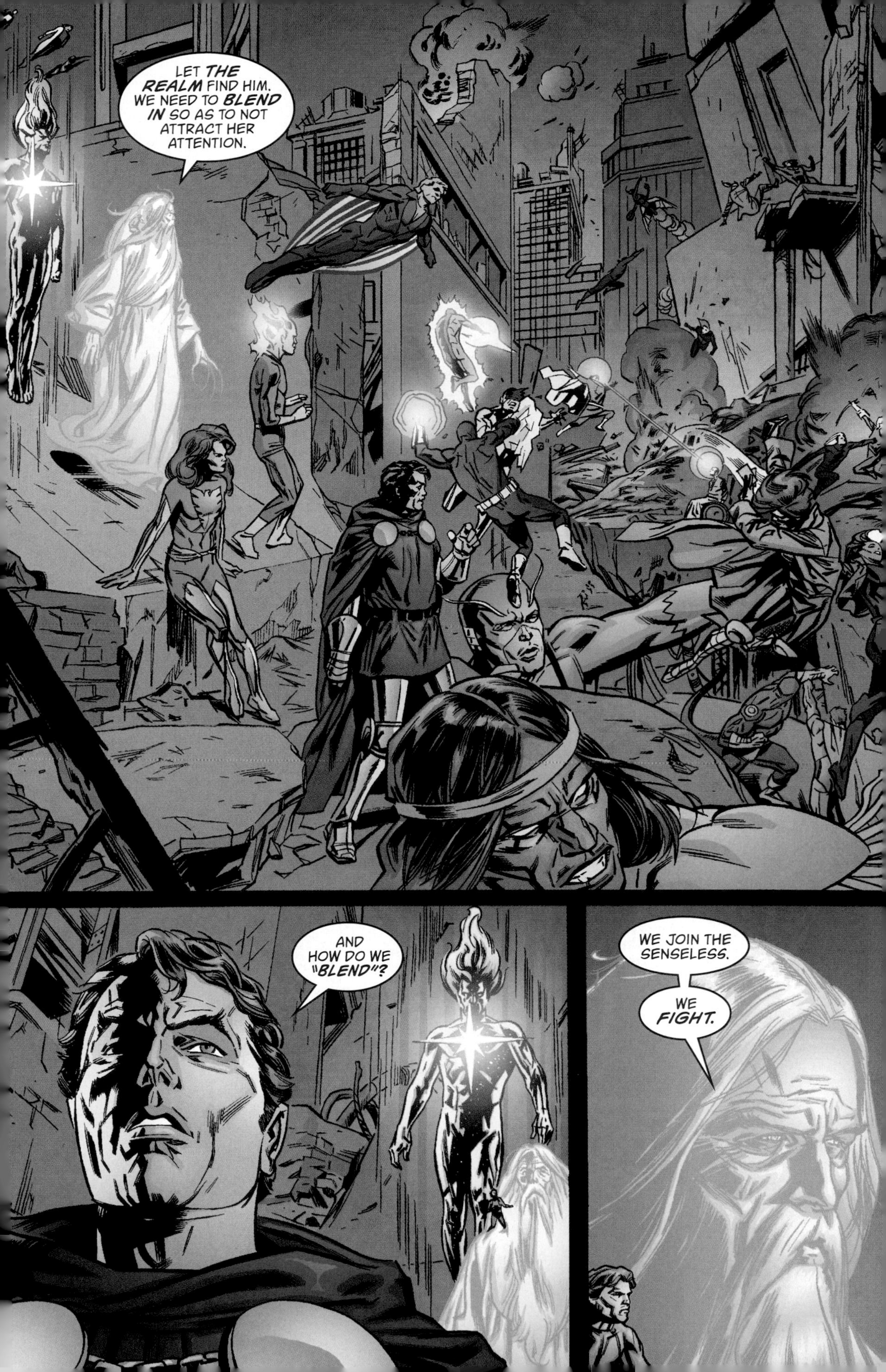
LET THE REALM FIND HIM. WE NEED TO BLEND IN SO AS TO NOT ATTRACT HER ATTENTION.
AND HOW DO WE "BLEND"?
WE JOIN THE SENSELESS.
WE FIGHT.

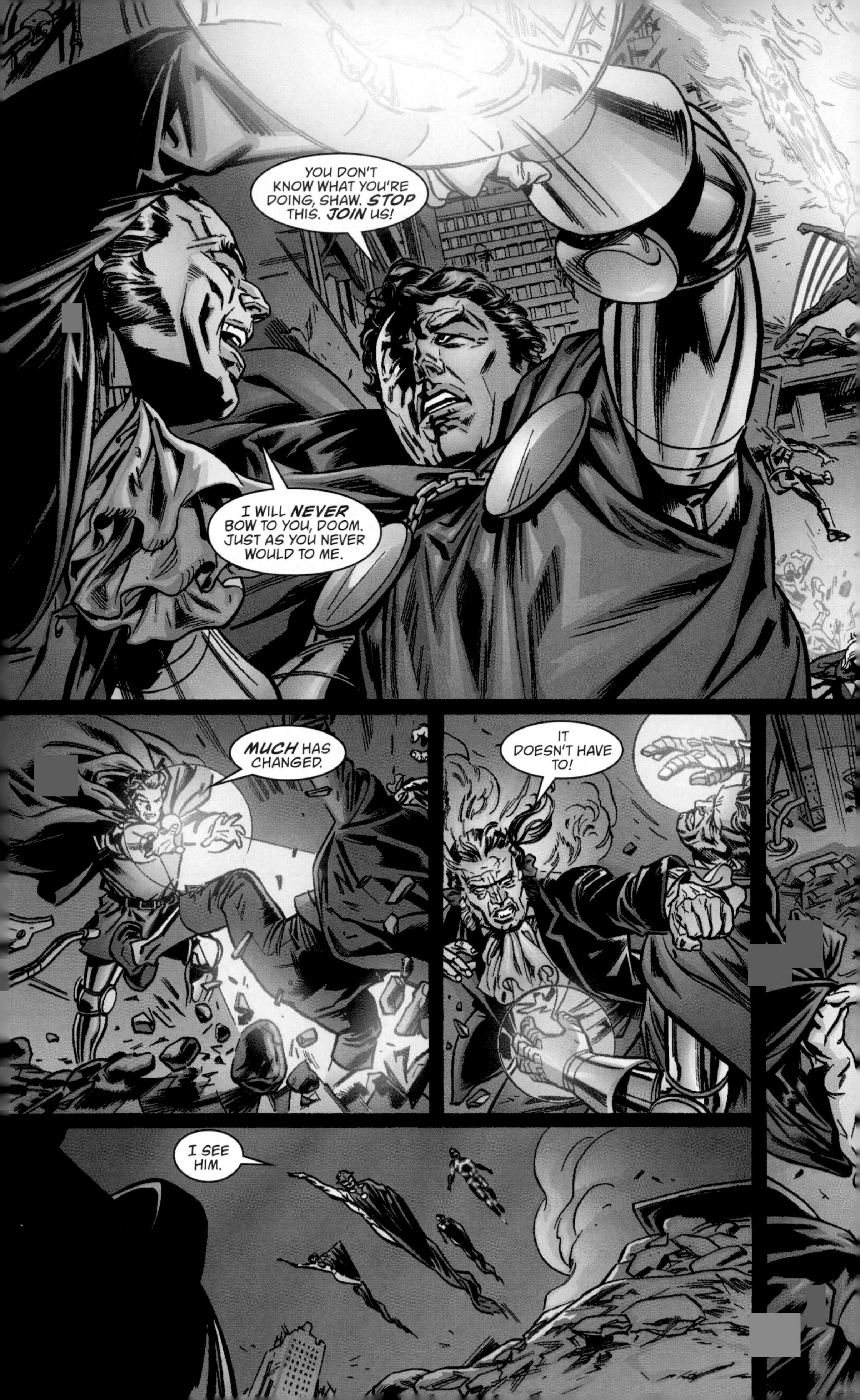
YOU DON'T KNOW WHAT YOU'RE DOING, SHAW. STOP THIS. JOIN US!
I WILL NEVER BOW TO YOU, DOOM. JUST AS YOU NEVER WOULD TO ME.
MUCH HAS CHANGED.
IT DOESN'T HAVE TO!
I SEE HIM.

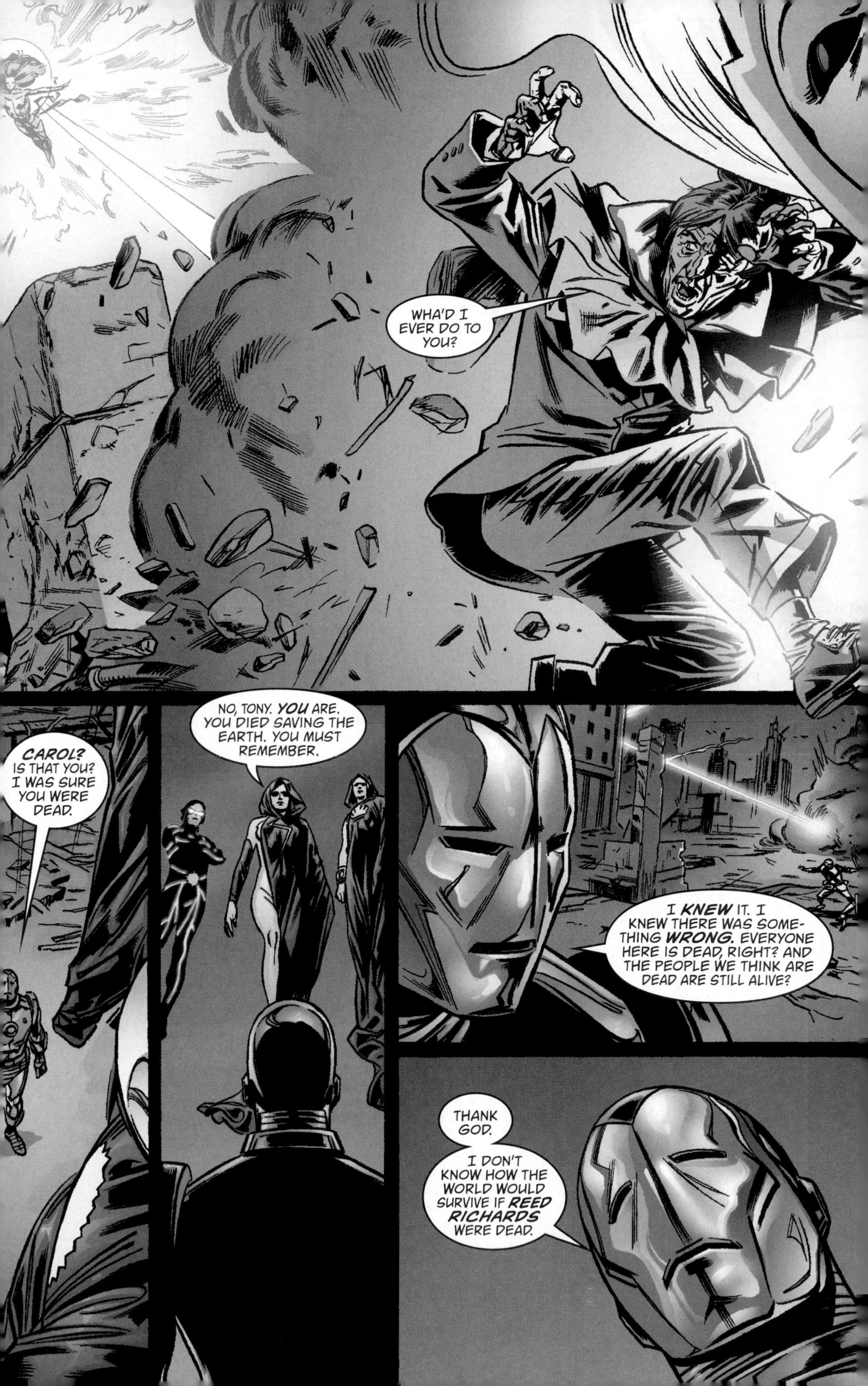
WHA'D I EVER DO TO YOU?
CAROL? IS THAT YOU? I WAS SURE YOU WERE DEAD.
NO, TONY. YOU ARE. YOU DIED SAVING THE EARTH. YOU MUST REMEMBER.
I KNEW IT. I KNEW THERE WAS SOMETHING WRONG. EVERYONE HERE IS DEAD, RIGHT? AND THE PEOPLE WE THINK ARE DEAD ARE STILL ALIVE?
THANK GOD.
I DON'T KNOW HOW THE WORLD WOULD SURVIVE IF REED RICHARDS WERE DEAD.

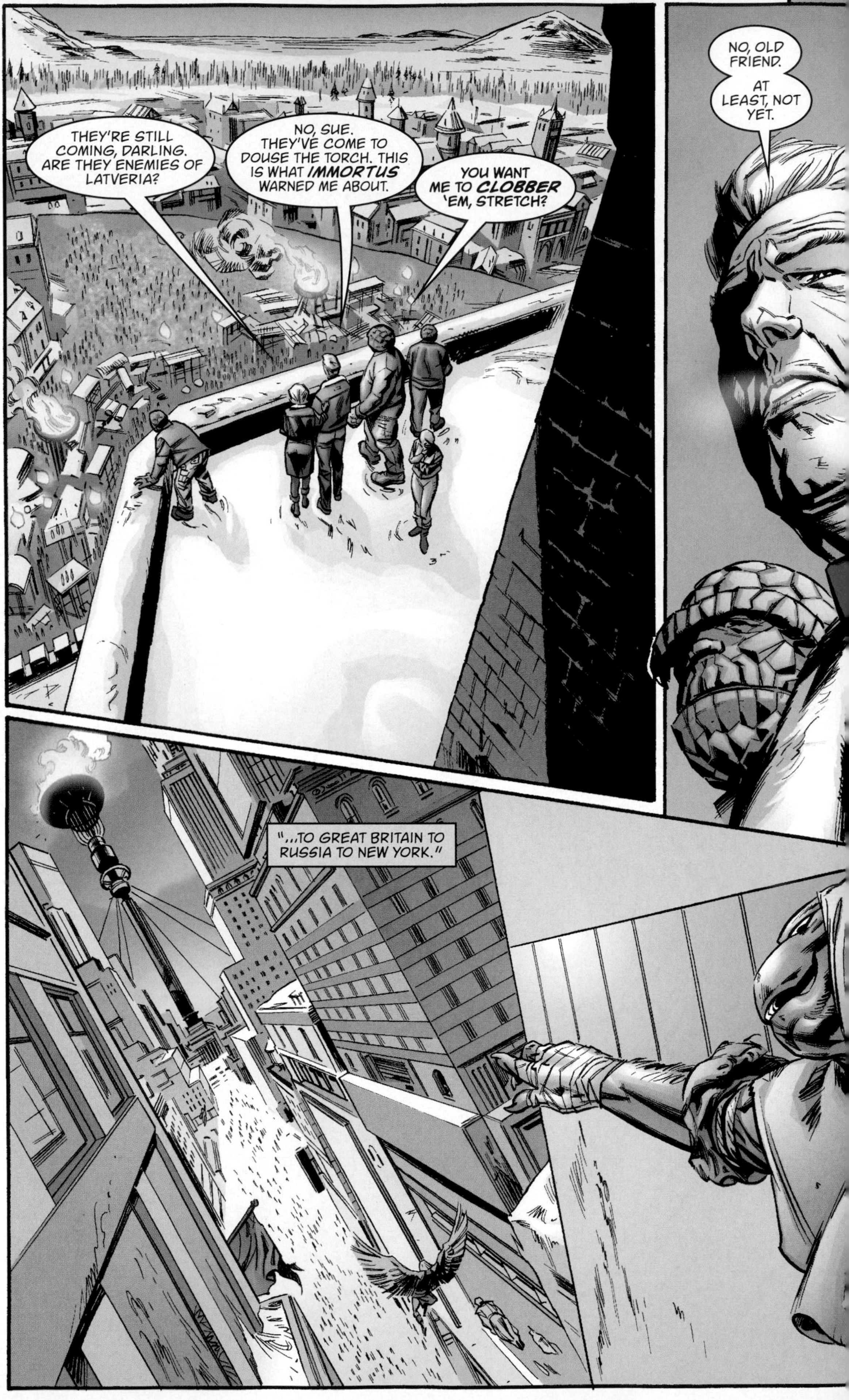
THEY'RE STILL COMING, DARLING. ARE THEY ENEMIES OF LATVERIA?
NO, SUE. THEY'VE COME TO DOUSE THE TORCH. THIS IS WHAT IMMORTUS WARNED ME ABOUT.
YOU WANT ME TO CLOBBER 'EM, STRETCH?
NO, OLD FRIEND.
AT LEAST, NOT YET.
"...TO GREAT BRITAIN TO RUSSIA TO NEW YORK."

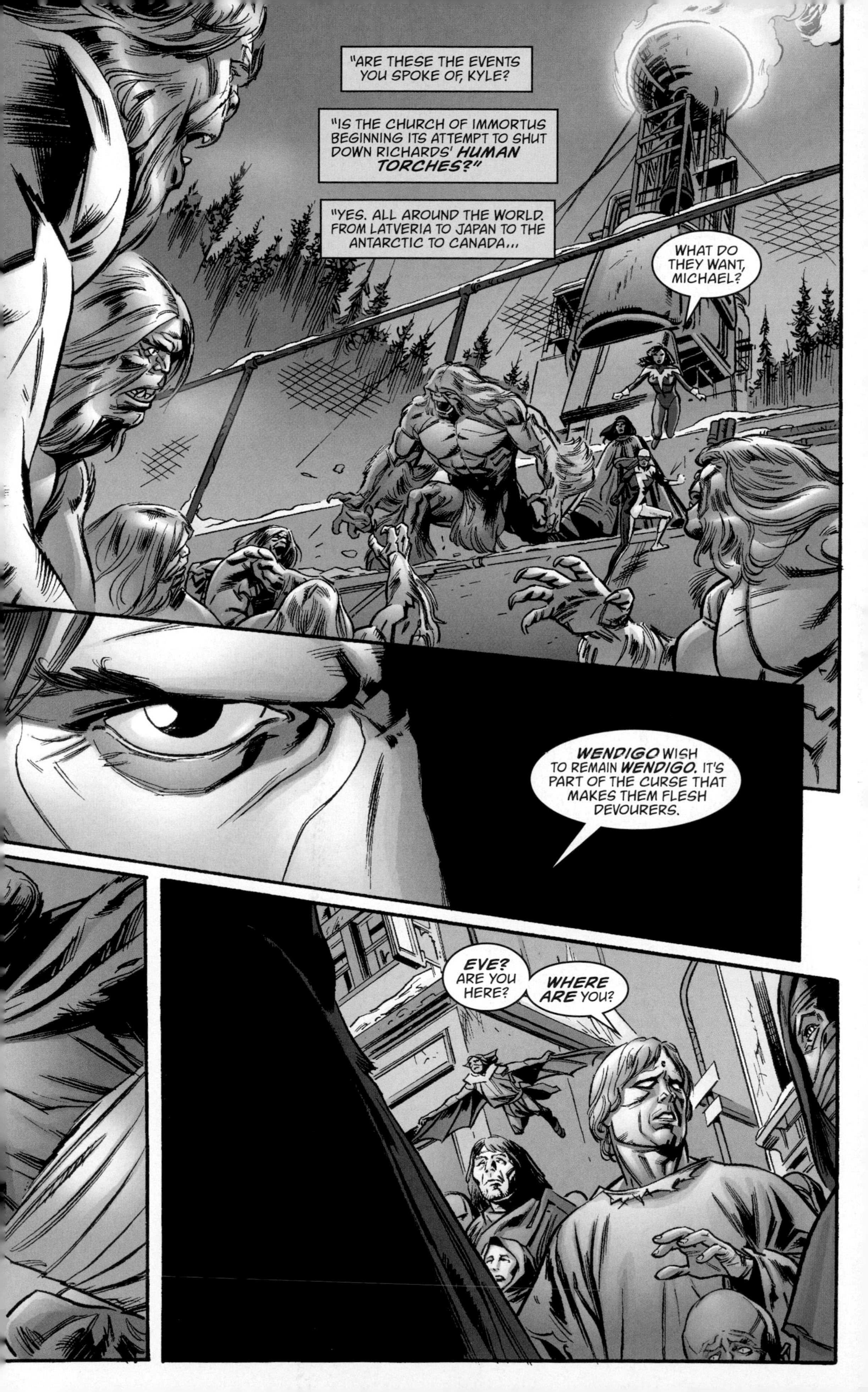
"ARE THESE THE EVENTS YOU SPOKE OF, KYLE?
"IS THE CHURCH OF IMMORTUS BEGINNING ITS ATTEMPT TO SHUT DOWN RICHARDS' HUMAN TORCHES?"
"YES. ALL AROUND THE WORLD. FROM LATVERIA TO JAPAN TO THE ANTARCTIC TO CANADA...
WHAT DO THEY WANT, MICHAEL?
WENDIGO WISH TO REMAIN WENDIGO. IT'S PART OF THE CURSE THAT MAKES THEM FLESH DEVOURERS.
EVE? ARE YOU HERE?
WHERE ARE YOU?

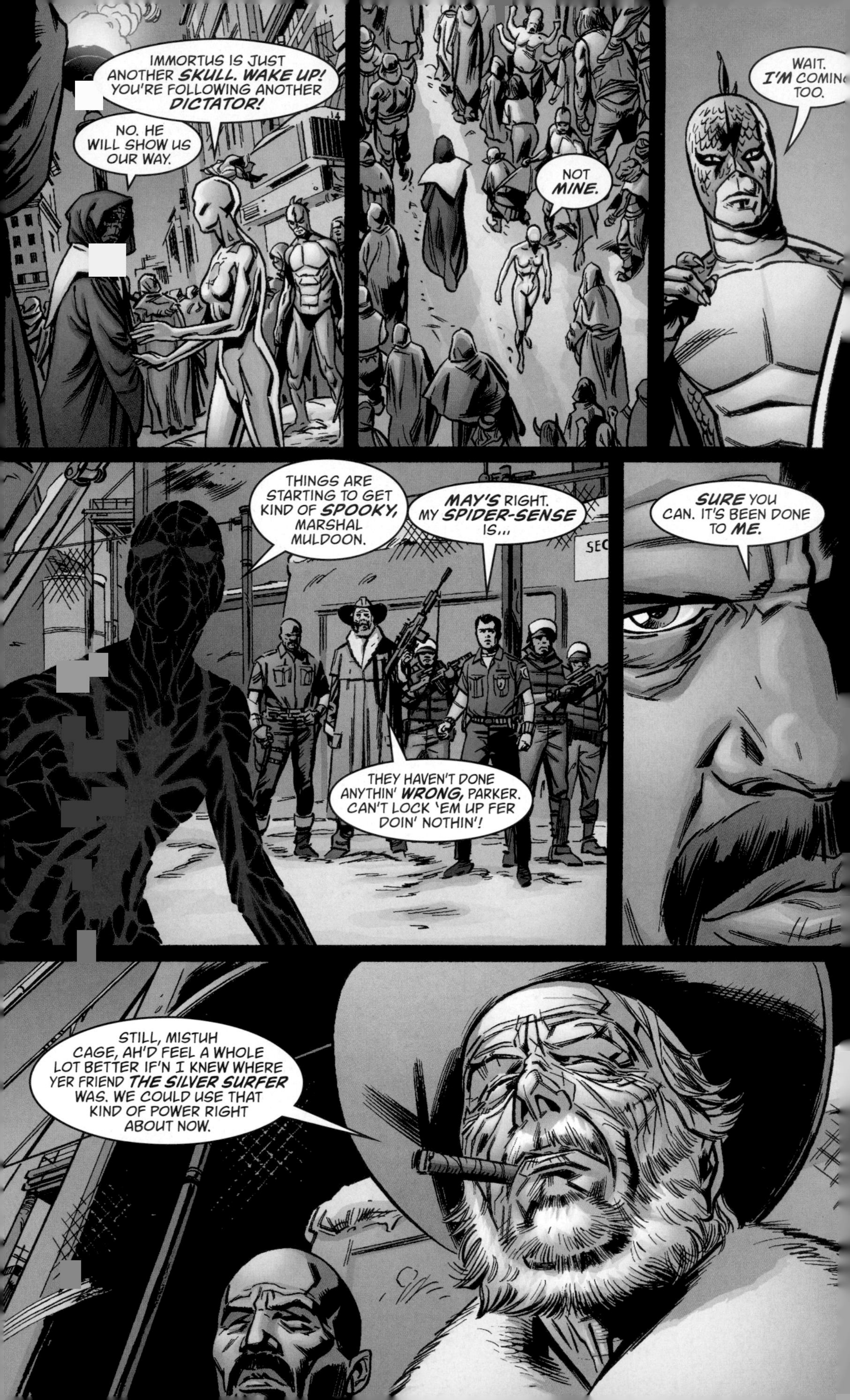

IMMORTUS IS JUST ANOTHER SKULL. WAKE UP! YOU'RE FOLLOWING ANOTHER DICTATOR!
NO. HE WILL SHOW US OUR WAY.
NOT MINE.
WAIT. I'M COMIN TOO.
THINGS ARE STARTING TO GET KIND OF SPOOKY, MARSHAL MULDOON.
MAY'S RIGHT. MY SPIDER-SENSE IS...
SEC
THEY HAVEN'T DONE ANYTHIN' WRONG, PARKER. CAN'T LOCK 'EM UP FER DOIN' NOTHIN'!
SURE YOU CAN. IT'S BEEN DONE TO ME.
STILL, MISTUH CAGE, AH'D FEEL A WHOLE LOT BETTER IF'N I KNEW WHERE YER FRIEND THE SILVER SURFER WAS. WE COULD USE THAT KIND OF POWER RIGHT ABOUT NOW.

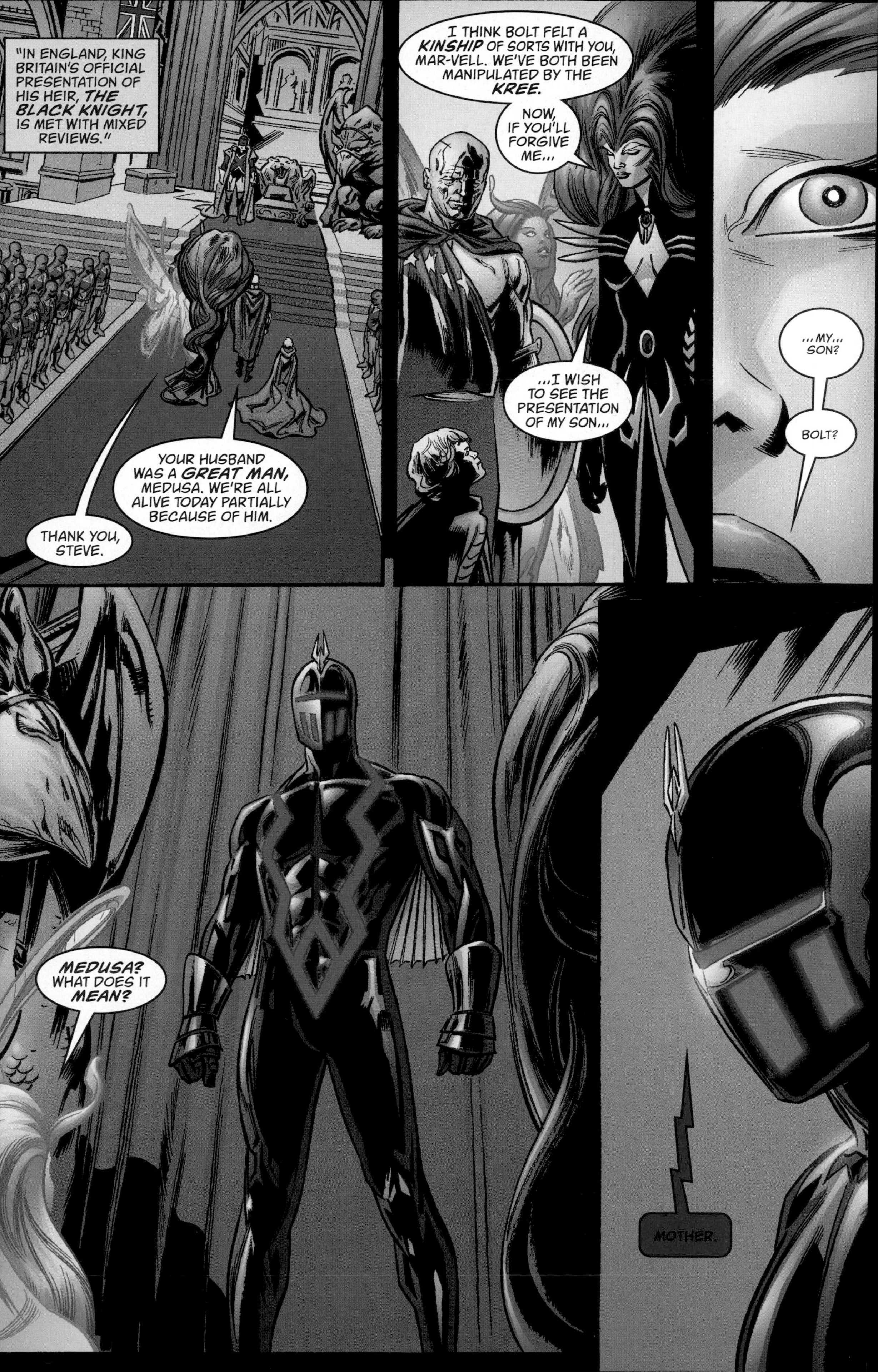
"IN ENGLAND, KING BRITAIN'S OFFICIAL PRESENTATION OF HIS HEIR, THE BLACK KNIGHT, IS MET WITH MIXED REVIEWS."
YOUR HUSBAND WAS A GREAT MAN, MEDUSA. WE'RE ALL ALIVE TODAY PARTIALLY BECAUSE OF HIM.
THANK YOU, STEVE.
I THINK BOLT FELT A KINSHIP OF SORTS WITH YOU, MAR-VELL. WE'VE BOTH BEEN MANIPULATED BY THE KREE.
NOW, IF YOU'LL FORGIVE ME...
...I WISH TO SEE THE PRESENTATION OF MY SON...
...MY... SON?
BOLT?
MEDUSA? WHAT DOES IT MEAN?
MOTHER.

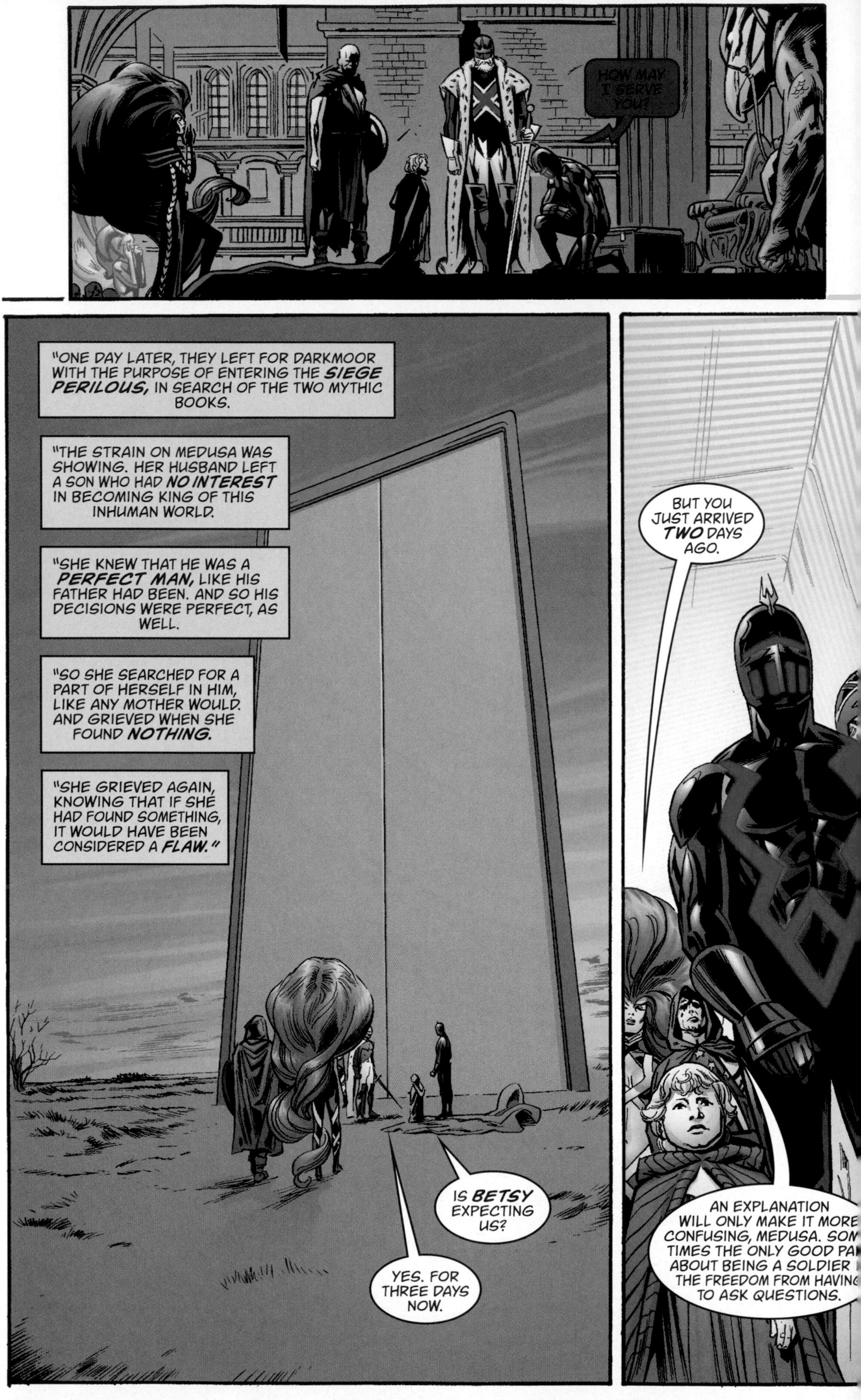
HOW MAY I SERVE YOU?
"ONE DAY LATER, THEY LEFT FOR DARKMOOR WITH THE PURPOSE OF ENTERING THE SIEGE PERILOUS, IN SEARCH OF THE TWO MYTHIC BOOKS.
"THE STRAIN ON MEDUSA WAS SHOWING. HER HUSBAND LEFT A SON WHO HAD NO INTEREST IN BECOMING KING OF THIS INHUMAN WORLD.
"SHE KNEW THAT HE WAS A PERFECT MAN, LIKE HIS FATHER HAD BEEN. AND SO HIS DECISIONS WERE PERFECT, AS WELL.
"SO SHE SEARCHED FOR A PART OF HERSELF IN HIM, LIKE ANY MOTHER WOULD. AND GRIEVED WHEN SHE FOUND NOTHING.
"SHE GRIEVED AGAIN, KNOWING THAT IF SHE HAD FOUND SOMETHING, IT WOULD HAVE BEEN CONSIDERED A FLAW."
IS BETSY EXPECTING US?
YES. FOR THREE DAYS NOW.
BUT YOU JUST ARRIVED TWO DAYS AGO.
AN EXPLANATION WILL ONLY MAKE IT MORE CONFUSING, MEDUSA. SOM TIMES THE ONLY GOOD PA ABOUT BEING A SOLDIER I THE FREEDOM FROM HAVING TO ASK QUESTIONS.

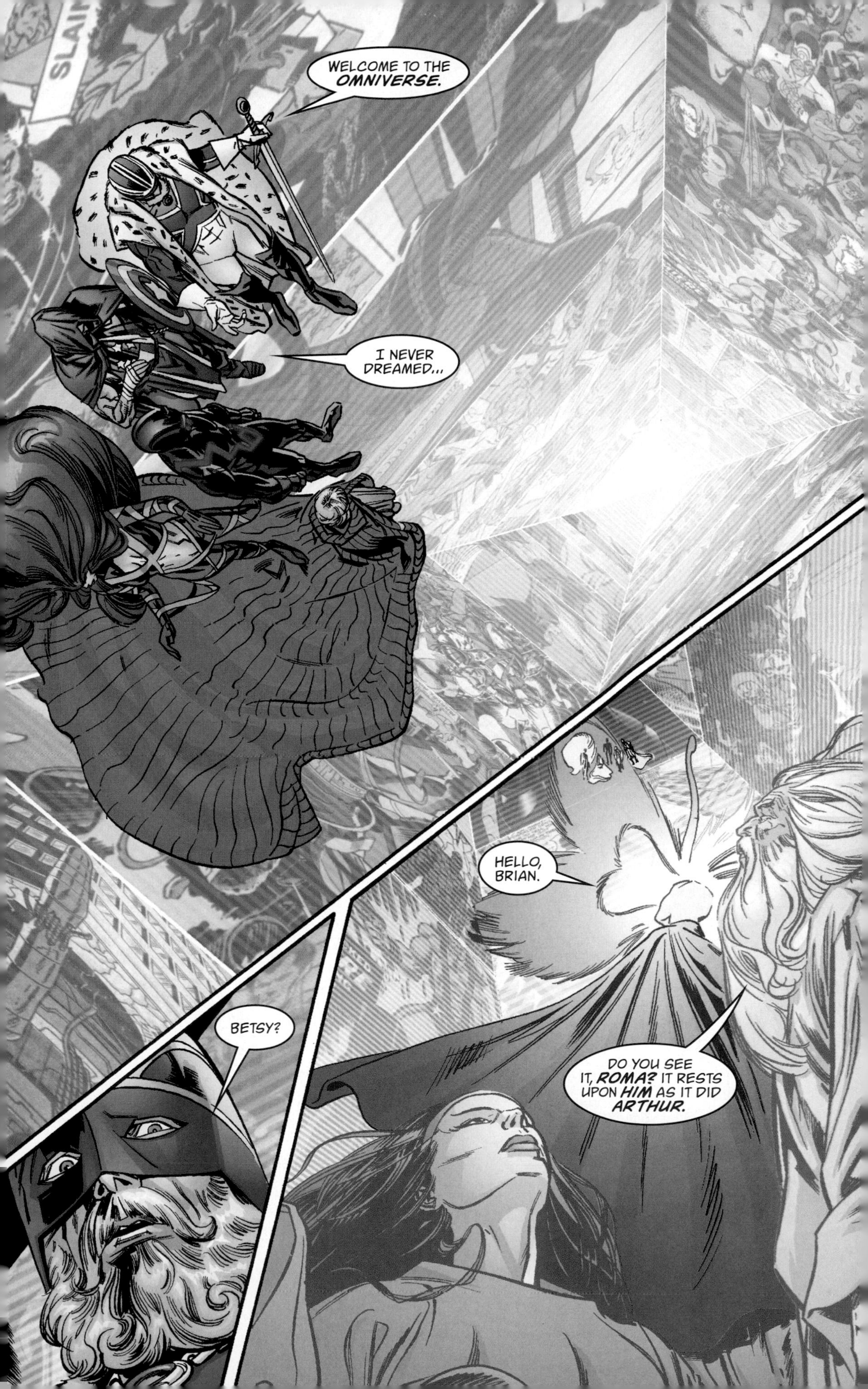
WELCOME TO THE OMNIVERSE.
I NEVER DREAMED...
HELLO, BRIAN.
BETSY?
DO YOU SEE IT, ROMA? IT RESTS UPON HIM AS IT DID ARTHUR.

I MEAN "ARTHUR"...WHAT DOES HE MEAN BY THAT?

WHAT'S HE TALKING ABOUT?

THE *COSMIC CONSCIOUS-NESS.*

THIS LAD WAS NOT THE *FIRST* TO RECEIVE A PIECE OF OMNISCIENCE, KNIGHT.

A *PIECE?* I HAD THE *FULL* COSMIC CONSCIOUS-NESS.

"COSMIC CONSCIOUSNESS"? WHAT DID YOU THINK IT *WAS,* YOUNG SQUIRE?

WE HAVE THE *BOOKS* YOU REQUIRE. THAT IS, UNTIL YOU YOURSELF HAVE BEEN MADE *COMPLETE.*

BUT BE WARNED, CHILD, IF YOU TRULY HA[D] THIS OMNISCIENC[E] YOU SPEAK OF, YO[U] WOULD HAVE KNO[WN] HOW TO CURE TH[E] *CANCER* THAT STO[LE] YOUR LIFE THE *FIRST TIME.*

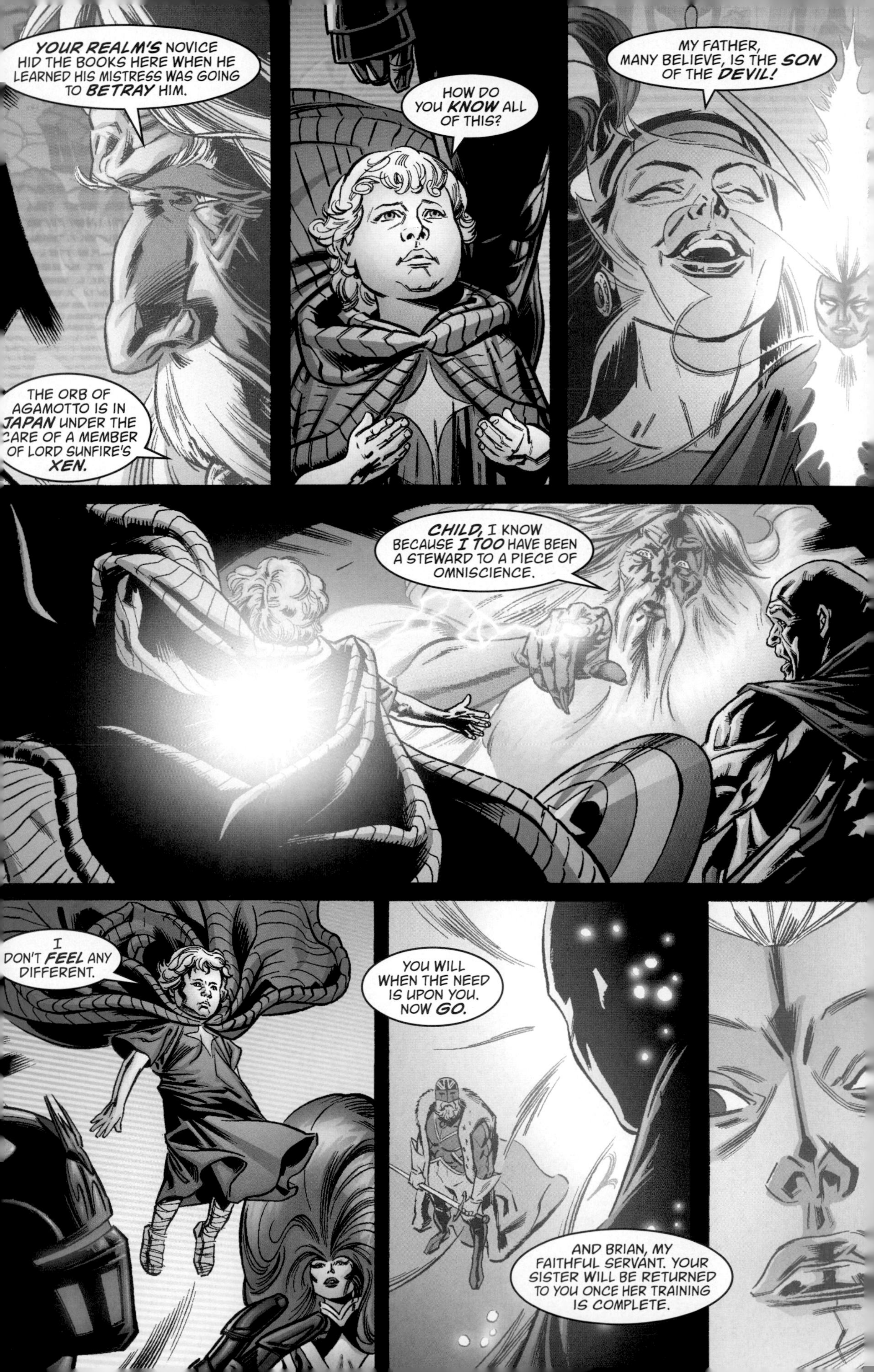
YOUR REALM'S NOVICE HID THE BOOKS HERE WHEN HE LEARNED HIS MISTRESS WAS GOING TO BETRAY HIM.
THE ORB OF AGAMOTTO IS IN JAPAN UNDER THE CARE OF A MEMBER OF LORD SUNFIRE'S XEN.
HOW DO YOU KNOW ALL OF THIS?
MY FATHER, MANY BELIEVE, IS THE SON OF THE DEVIL!
CHILD, I KNOW BECAUSE I TOO HAVE BEEN A STEWARD TO A PIECE OF OMNISCIENCE.
I DON'T FEEL ANY DIFFERENT.
YOU WILL WHEN THE NEED IS UPON YOU. NOW GO.
AND BRIAN, MY FAITHFUL SERVANT. YOUR SISTER WILL BE RETURNED TO YOU ONCE HER TRAINING IS COMPLETE.

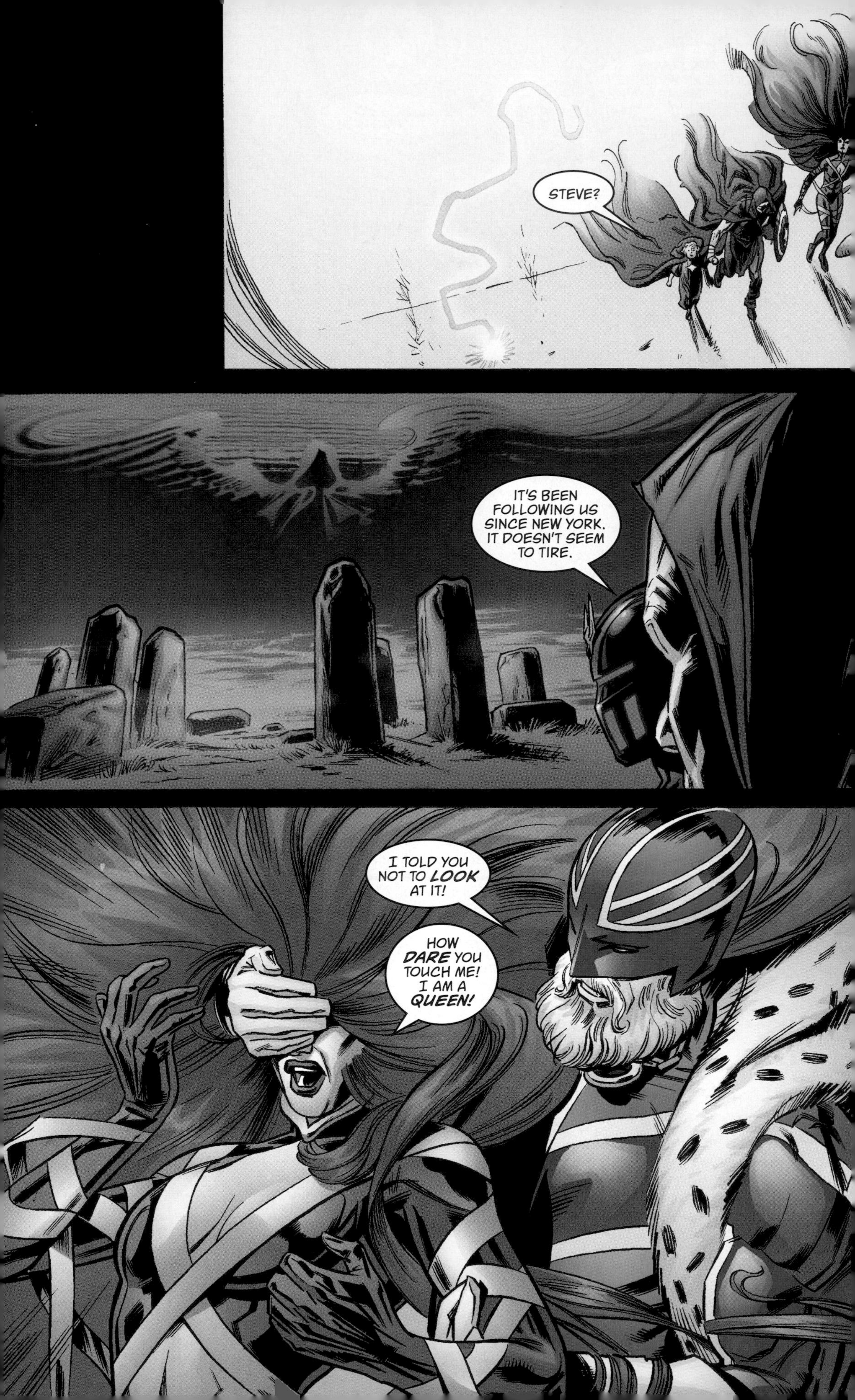
STEVE?
IT'S BEEN FOLLOWING US SINCE NEW YORK. IT DOESN'T SEEM TO TIRE.
I TOLD YOU NOT TO LOOK AT IT!
HOW DARE YOU TOUCH ME! I AM A QUEEN!

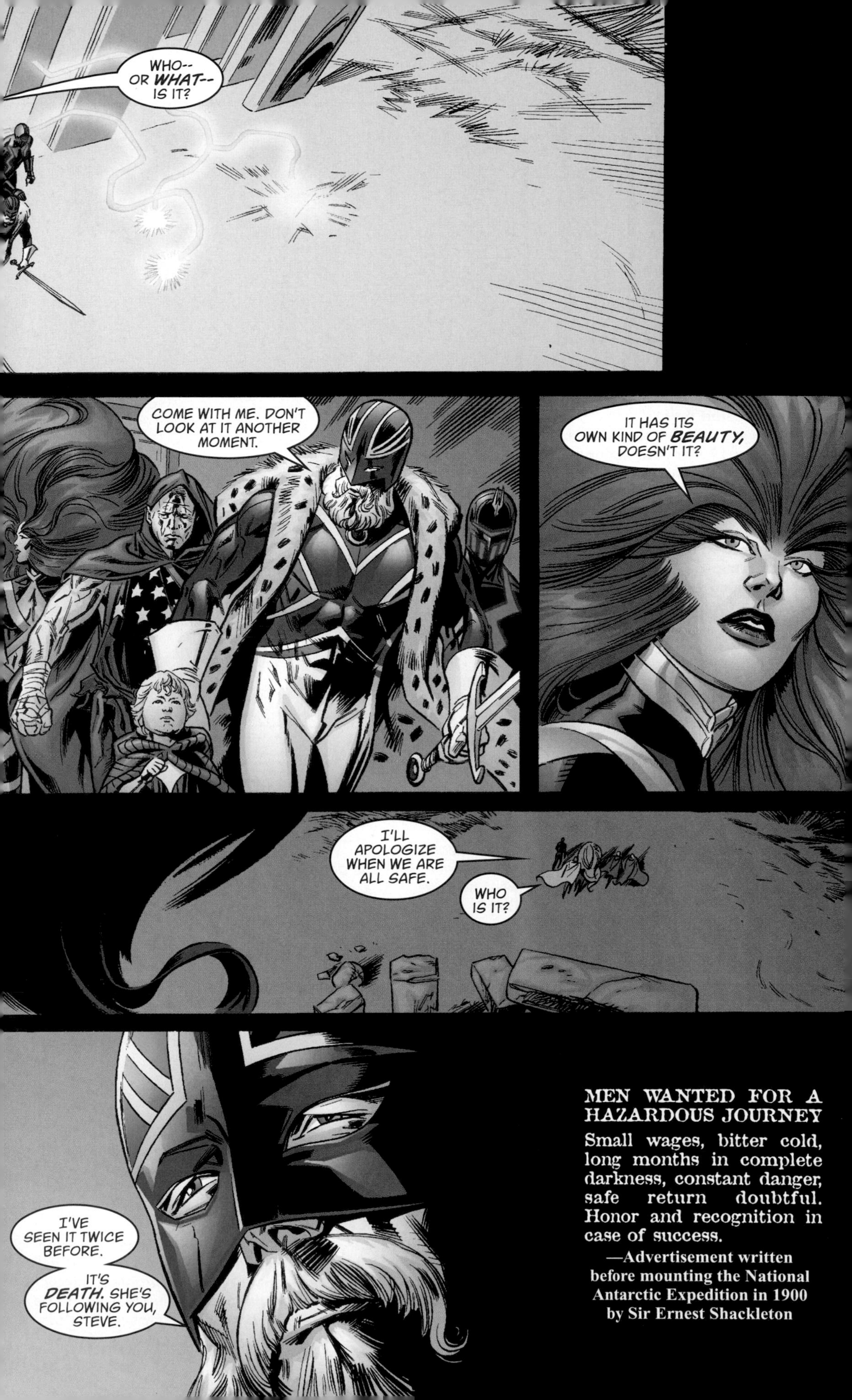
WHO-- OR WHAT-- IS IT?
COME WITH ME. DON'T LOOK AT IT ANOTHER MOMENT.
IT HAS ITS OWN KIND OF BEAUTY, DOESN'T IT?
I'LL APOLOGIZE WHEN WE ARE ALL SAFE.
WHO IS IT?
I'VE SEEN IT TWICE BEFORE.
IT'S DEATH. SHE'S FOLLOWING YOU, STEVE.

MEN WANTED FOR A HAZARDOUS JOURNEY

Small wages, bitter cold, long months in complete darkness, constant danger, safe return doubtful. Honor and recognition in case of success.

—Advertisement written before mounting the National Antarctic Expedition in 1900 by Sir Ernest Shackleton

APPENDIX TO
CHAPTER TWO

W R I T T E N   B Y
J I M   K R U E G E R

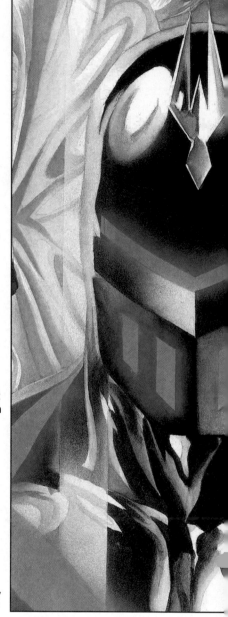

"Uatu?"

"Yes, robot?"

"What's in the Kree ruins?"

"Why do you ask?"

"There's someone on Earth who is capable of seeing the future. His visions include my digging through the Kree ruins. What will I find there?"

"Ah, yes. Kyle Richmond. Are his visions now governing your actions? Are your actions now assured because one Earthman has seen you dig in the ruins? Are your actions truly so easily controlled?"

"Stop it, Uatu. Stop it. What's there? Or must I dig to find out?"

"You must not do this thing, robot. You must not dig."

"You forget, Uatu, that though I look it, I am no robot. Your commands are as meaningless to me as your opinions."

"Did your father include 'self-righteous, moralistic ass' to your programmed personality, robot? Listening to you is like being forced to endure a vinyl recording of country music with a skip in it."

"Fine, Uatu. Make your judgements. What I learned from Kyle Richmond's visions was this. There is not one reality, as I'd believed, but many. And somehow these multiple realities fit together. There is a place known as the Siege Perilous in which these realities join. Something known as the Captain Britain Corps is the sole protectors of these realities."

"Anything else?"

"Yes. There is a realm that your machinery is incapable of seeing within, Uatu. It's the place where heroes go when they die -- the realm of the dead."

"Have you seen Black Bolt yet? Have you seen...?"

"I don't know. I can't actually see into the realm. All I can do is hear what Richmond says. Tell you what he sees."

"Well, I don't see because of Black Bolt."

"And he would never have received the power to hurt anyone if it weren't for the mutations your masters caused. So do you really want to complain to me?"

"No, robot. I simply wish that the pompous ranting of victory that you have tortured me with would end. You have won nothing."

"I am afraid, Uatu, that you may be right. Something is wrong with the world. And I can't quite put my finger on it."

"You don't have fingers."

"Why, Uatu? Why must you continually attack my humanity?"

"Because it does not exist. And my defeat has been as a result of that lie you embrace and nurture like a "human" mother."

"Defeat?"

"The absence of victory does not mean there is no presence of defeat."

"What is in the ruins?"

"The Supreme Intelligence."

"All I know is the little I heard Captain Mar-Vell speak of it while he lived on Earth the first time... and the brief history Richmond exposed. The Supreme Intelligence... who is he?"

"He... robot... is an it, not a he. It is a collective depository of the brightest minds in the Kree empire. It was the Supreme Intelligence's manipulations that led Mar-Vell to be joined to Rick Jones. It was the Supreme Intelligence who orchestrated the murder of

Mar-Vell's intended mate. The Supreme Intelligence is the strategist behind the Kree's attacks on the Skrull empire. It is responsible for..."

"It's a lot like you, isn't it, Uatu?"

"No, X-51. My role was to catalogue history, not to manipulate it. Not to change it."

"Then tell me about the Supreme Intelligence. What is it? Where does it come from?"

"The Supreme Intelligence is a hybrid construction composed of both organic and cybernetic material. It is, for lack of a better term, a living computer."

"A living computer? Like me?"

"No, X-51. Not like you. It lives. You do not. It is composed of a matter that has not been subjugated to another's will as you have been. You are "alive" only because you were programmed to believe that you had any worth apart from your composite parts."

"It is a 5000 cubic foot computer. It is a composite collection of the disembodied brains of the greatest members of the alien Kree race, the greatest brains who ever... died. It is a collective consciousness."

"A collective? Then does it have a personality?"

"Of course. But it is a collective personality. A democracy of sorts."

"Isn't that a problem?"

"How so, robot?"

"Well, it's the same problem Captain America faces right now on Earth. What happens to a collective body when their choice is one of destruction? Whether it is their own destruction or that of another people... or race or civilization for that matter? Steve Rogers, even now, is fighting against one of the axioms of his nation's being – the right to bear arms. Yet he and Mar-Vell encircle the globe, trying to disarm the mutated mankind of the weapons that have the potential to destroy it."

"Again you assert a morality upon a power struggle, robot."

"Would you please stop calling me that? I almost prefer X-51."

"No. I will not stop referring to you as robot."

"Why not?"

"Because that is what you are – a robot. Your thoughts are not your own. Your actions are not, even to the smallest degree, your actions. Your 'programmed humanity' is all that you are. You are obedient to it – even to the point, I believe, of your own disassembly. You are a robot because you lack the ability to choose any action apart from your programmer's background and genetic heritage. You speak of freedom, as does your Captain America. But the painful truth is that there is no freedom. It is as mythic as the notions of good and evil you cling to. Freedom, by definition, precludes and denies all of the factors that mold any decision you might make. There is no freedom. There is no choice."

"I don't believe that."

"Of course not. You are not free to believe it. Your every choice was determined long before the man who built you was born. The choice was decided with his parents' nationality before their immigration. It was decided by their inability to educate themselves. It was determined by their own culture's superstitions."

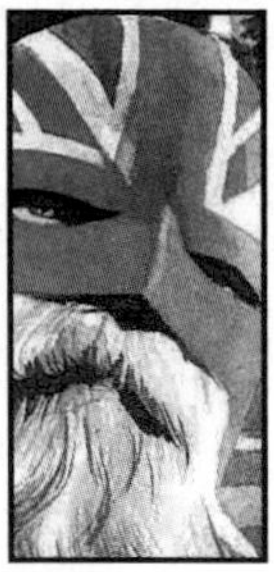

"But that's not true, Uatu. How can you claim, of all people, that all there is, is what can be seen. What does something like that say for the blind, Uatu?"

"Very well, robot. Your argument has some merit though it does not change the hypocrisy of your being. The Supreme Intelligence was originally built... created by the Science Council of the Kree. It was created for the purpose of creating the Cosmic Cube, a weapon the Kree hoped to use against the Skrulls."

"But according to what Richmond said, the Kree wouldn't have even have had a science council if it weren't for the technology they stole from the Skrulls."

"Yes."

"What happened?"

"The Supreme Intelligence decided that the Cosmic Cube was too powerful for the Kree. It refused to create the weapon for them. It ultimately rose to take control of the Kree race."

"How?"

"By affecting the minds of the nation – through mental suggestion and manipulation. And through growth."

"Growth?"

"Every five sun-cycles in the Kree empire, one of the Kree is given what is a considered the ultimate honor, the opportunity to join the Supreme Intelligence. As a result, the Supreme Intelligence, or Supremor as he has come to be called, has grown. Its influence has grown more and more powerful. The Kree people, though, had no power of their own. Unlike their enemy, the Skrulls, they were not given the key to genetic mutation and adaptation by the Celestials."

"How noble you make them, Uatu."

"Supremor knew that the Kree would never advance beyond their physical being, so it began to suggest both mentally and overtly the inbreeding of the Kree with other races. This resulted in a number of different races within the Kree nation. And all the time, Supremor continued to grow more and more powerful, until..."

"Until he was separated from the Kree and left here on the moon."

"Yes. In truth , the Skrull/Kree war has all but burned itself out. Yet still, Supremor has become more powerful."

"How?"

"I don't know."

"What will happen if I search the ruins?"

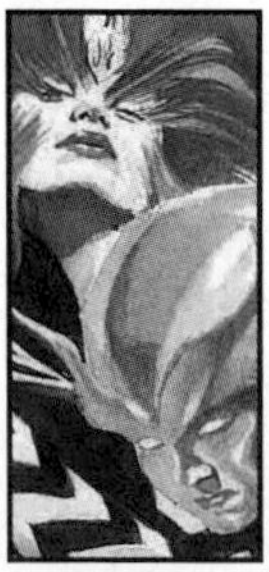

"You will free it."

"Could it save the Earth?"

"Yes."

"Would it?"

"Perhaps."

"Will you help me?"

"You would like me to help you save the Earth?"

"Yes."

"Now who's blind, robot?"

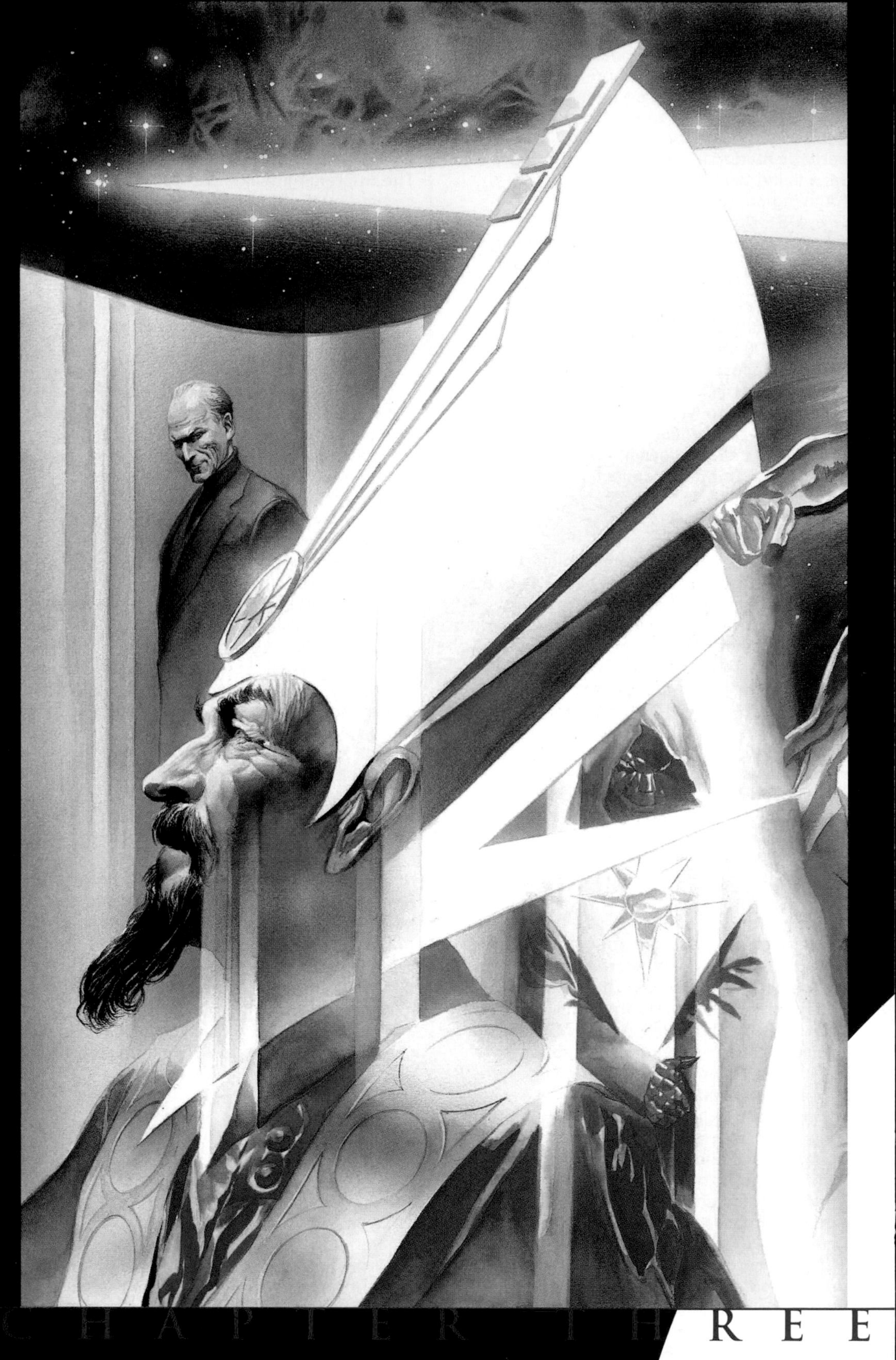

CHAPTER THREE

I have had enough talk about mutants, Kyle."

"But theirs is the seed through which the devil will come."

"...or devils for that matter. Now that these miraculous eyes of yours can see the past as well as the future, speak to me of the past, of the things which made one feel human."

"You don't understand, Isaac. The devil is coming out of the mutant race."

"Hardly. Classic myth shows the devil existing before mutants even appeared on the planet. The devil came out of God."

"Perhaps the devil you know. But the devil is timeless. And what is the past or future to someone that is not measured by time? Who's to say that the state of timelessness which myth speaks about hasn't happened yet?"

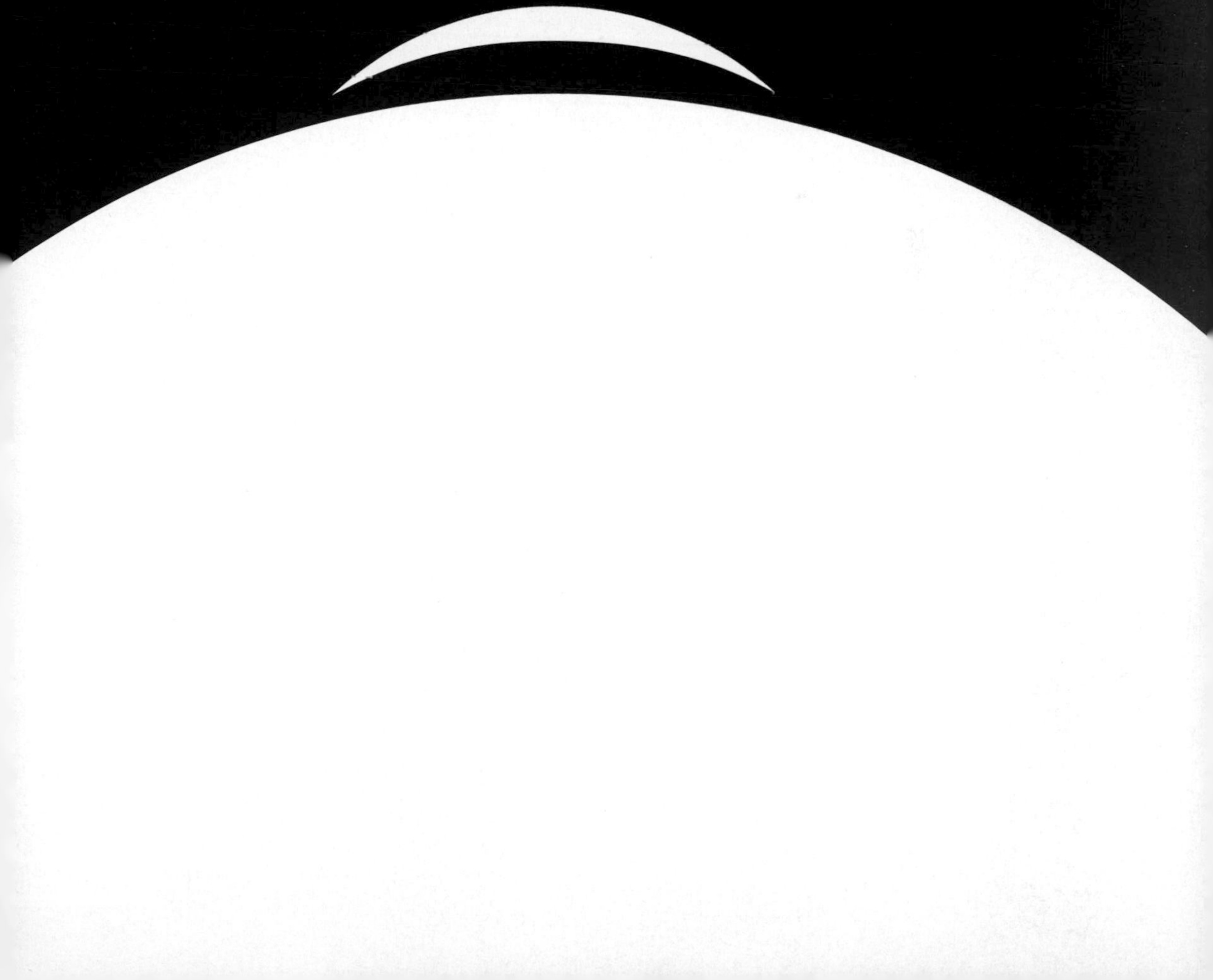

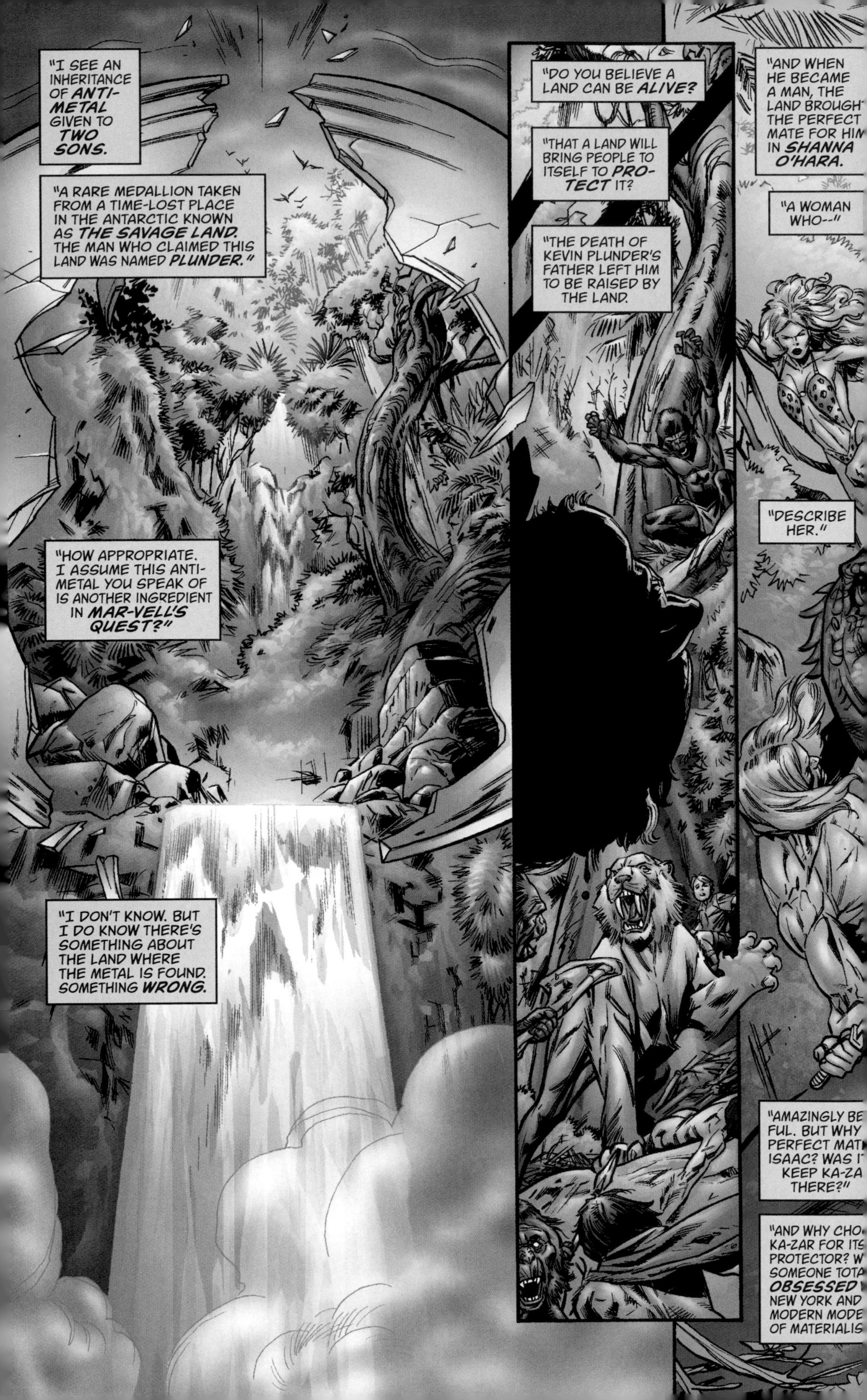
"I SEE AN INHERITANCE OF ANTI-METAL GIVEN TO TWO SONS.
"A RARE MEDALLION TAKEN FROM A TIME-LOST PLACE IN THE ANTARCTIC KNOWN AS THE SAVAGE LAND. THE MAN WHO CLAIMED THIS LAND WAS NAMED PLUNDER."
"HOW APPROPRIATE. I ASSUME THIS ANTI-METAL YOU SPEAK OF IS ANOTHER INGREDIENT IN MAR-VELL'S QUEST?"
"I DON'T KNOW. BUT I DO KNOW THERE'S SOMETHING ABOUT THE LAND WHERE THE METAL IS FOUND. SOMETHING WRONG.
"DO YOU BELIEVE A LAND CAN BE ALIVE?
"THAT A LAND WILL BRING PEOPLE TO ITSELF TO PROTECT IT?
"THE DEATH OF KEVIN PLUNDER'S FATHER LEFT HIM TO BE RAISED BY THE LAND.
"AND WHEN HE BECAME A MAN, THE LAND BROUGH THE PERFECT MATE FOR HIM IN SHANNA O'HARA.
"A WOMAN WHO--"
"DESCRIBE HER."
"AMAZINGLY BE FUL. BUT WHY PERFECT MAT ISAAC? WAS I KEEP KA-ZA THERE?"
"AND WHY CHO KA-ZAR FOR ITS PROTECTOR? W SOMEONE TOTA OBSESSED NEW YORK AND MODERN MODE OF MATERIALIS

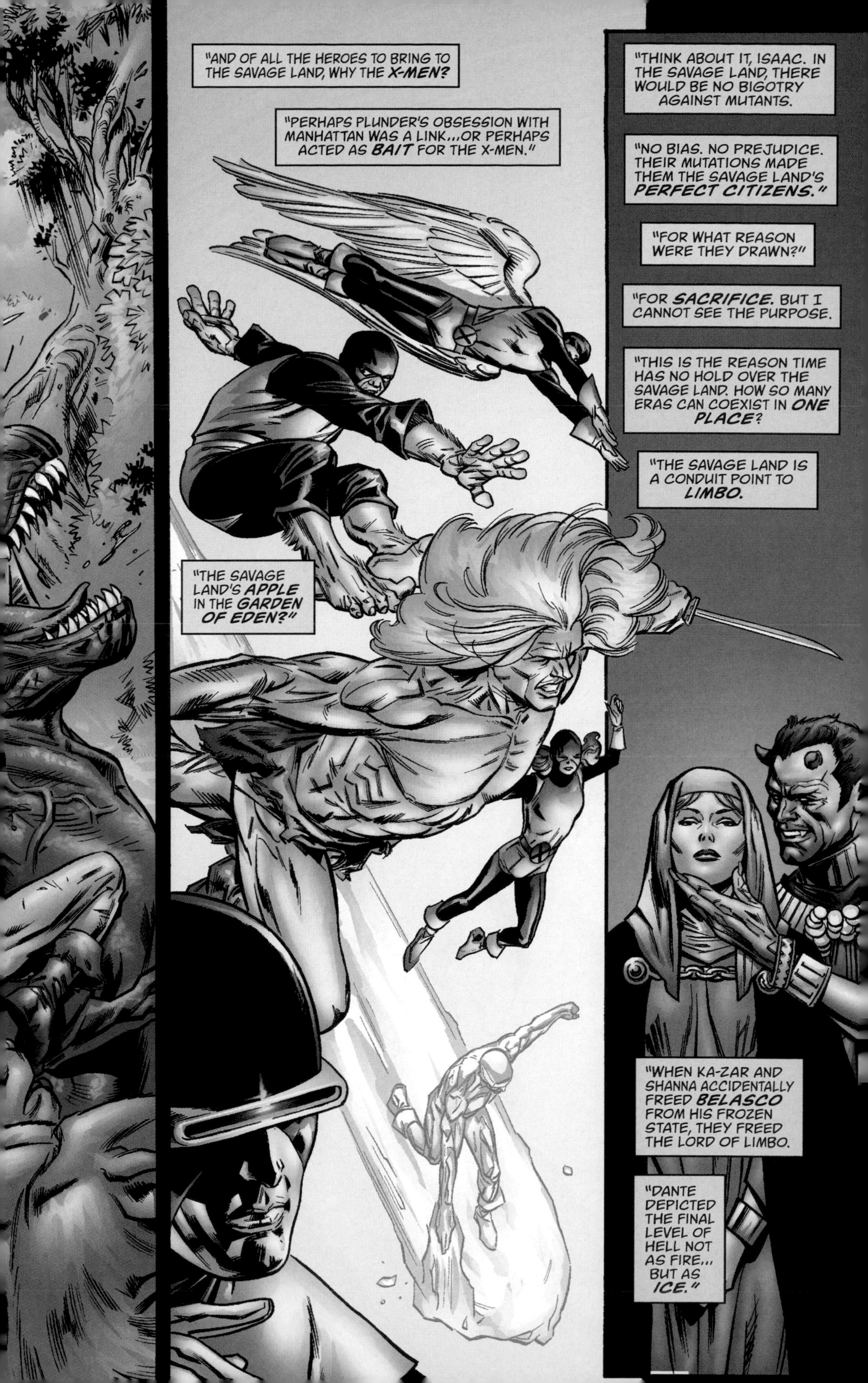
"AND OF ALL THE HEROES TO BRING TO THE SAVAGE LAND, WHY THE X-MEN?
"PERHAPS PLUNDER'S OBSESSION WITH MANHATTAN WAS A LINK...OR PERHAPS ACTED AS BAIT FOR THE X-MEN."
"THE SAVAGE LAND'S APPLE IN THE GARDEN OF EDEN?"
"THINK ABOUT IT, ISAAC. IN THE SAVAGE LAND, THERE WOULD BE NO BIGOTRY AGAINST MUTANTS.
"NO BIAS. NO PREJUDICE. THEIR MUTATIONS MADE THEM THE SAVAGE LAND'S PERFECT CITIZENS."
"FOR WHAT REASON WERE THEY DRAWN?"
"FOR SACRIFICE. BUT I CANNOT SEE THE PURPOSE.
"THIS IS THE REASON TIME HAS NO HOLD OVER THE SAVAGE LAND. HOW SO MANY ERAS CAN COEXIST IN ONE PLACE?
"THE SAVAGE LAND IS A CONDUIT POINT TO LIMBO.
"WHEN KA-ZAR AND SHANNA ACCIDENTALLY FREED BELASCO FROM HIS FROZEN STATE, THEY FREED THE LORD OF LIMBO.
"DANTE DEPICTED THE FINAL LEVEL OF HELL NOT AS FIRE... BUT AS ICE."

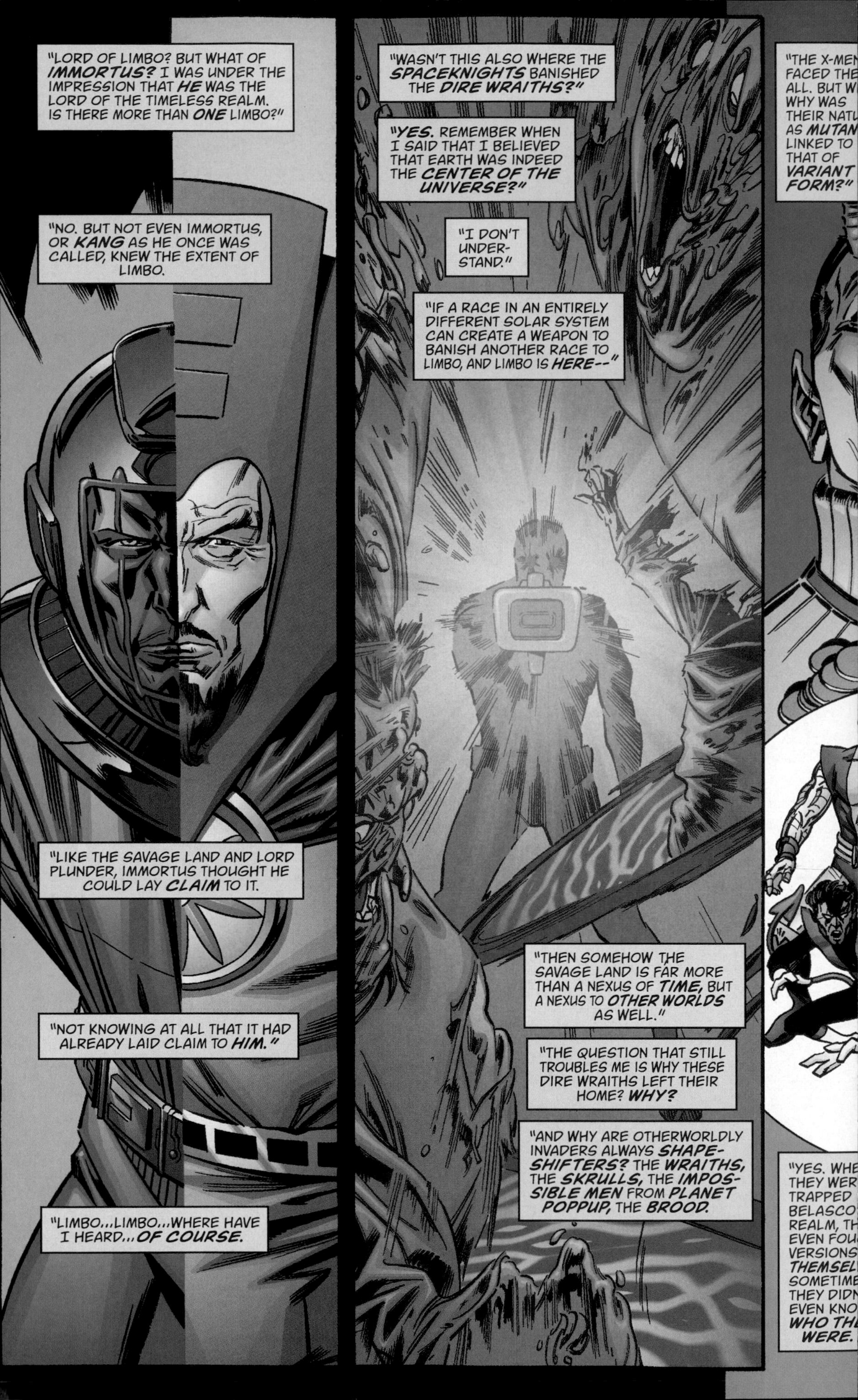
"LORD OF LIMBO? BUT WHAT OF IMMORTUS? I WAS UNDER THE IMPRESSION THAT HE WAS THE LORD OF THE TIMELESS REALM. IS THERE MORE THAN ONE LIMBO?"
"NO. BUT NOT EVEN IMMORTUS, OR KANG AS HE ONCE WAS CALLED, KNEW THE EXTENT OF LIMBO.
"LIKE THE SAVAGE LAND AND LORD PLUNDER, IMMORTUS THOUGHT HE COULD LAY CLAIM TO IT.
"NOT KNOWING AT ALL THAT IT HAD ALREADY LAID CLAIM TO HIM."
"LIMBO...LIMBO...WHERE HAVE I HEARD...OF COURSE.
"WASN'T THIS ALSO WHERE THE SPACEKNIGHTS BANISHED THE DIRE WRAITHS?"
"YES. REMEMBER WHEN I SAID THAT I BELIEVED THAT EARTH WAS INDEED THE CENTER OF THE UNIVERSE?"
"I DON'T UNDER-STAND."
"IF A RACE IN AN ENTIRELY DIFFERENT SOLAR SYSTEM CAN CREATE A WEAPON TO BANISH ANOTHER RACE TO LIMBO, AND LIMBO IS HERE--"
"THEN SOMEHOW THE SAVAGE LAND IS FAR MORE THAN A NEXUS OF TIME, BUT A NEXUS TO OTHER WORLDS AS WELL."
"THE QUESTION THAT STILL TROUBLES ME IS WHY THESE DIRE WRAITHS LEFT THEIR HOME? WHY?
"AND WHY ARE OTHERWORLDLY INVADERS ALWAYS SHAPE-SHIFTERS? THE WRAITHS, THE SKRULLS, THE IMPOS-SIBLE MEN FROM PLANET POPPUP, THE BROOD.
"THE X-MEN FACED THE ALL. BUT W WHY WAS THEIR NAT AS MUTAN LINKED TO THAT OF VARIANT FORM?"
"YES. WHE THEY WER TRAPPED BELASCO REALM, TH EVEN FOU VERSIONS THEMSEL SOMETIME THEY DIDN EVEN KNO WHO THE WERE.

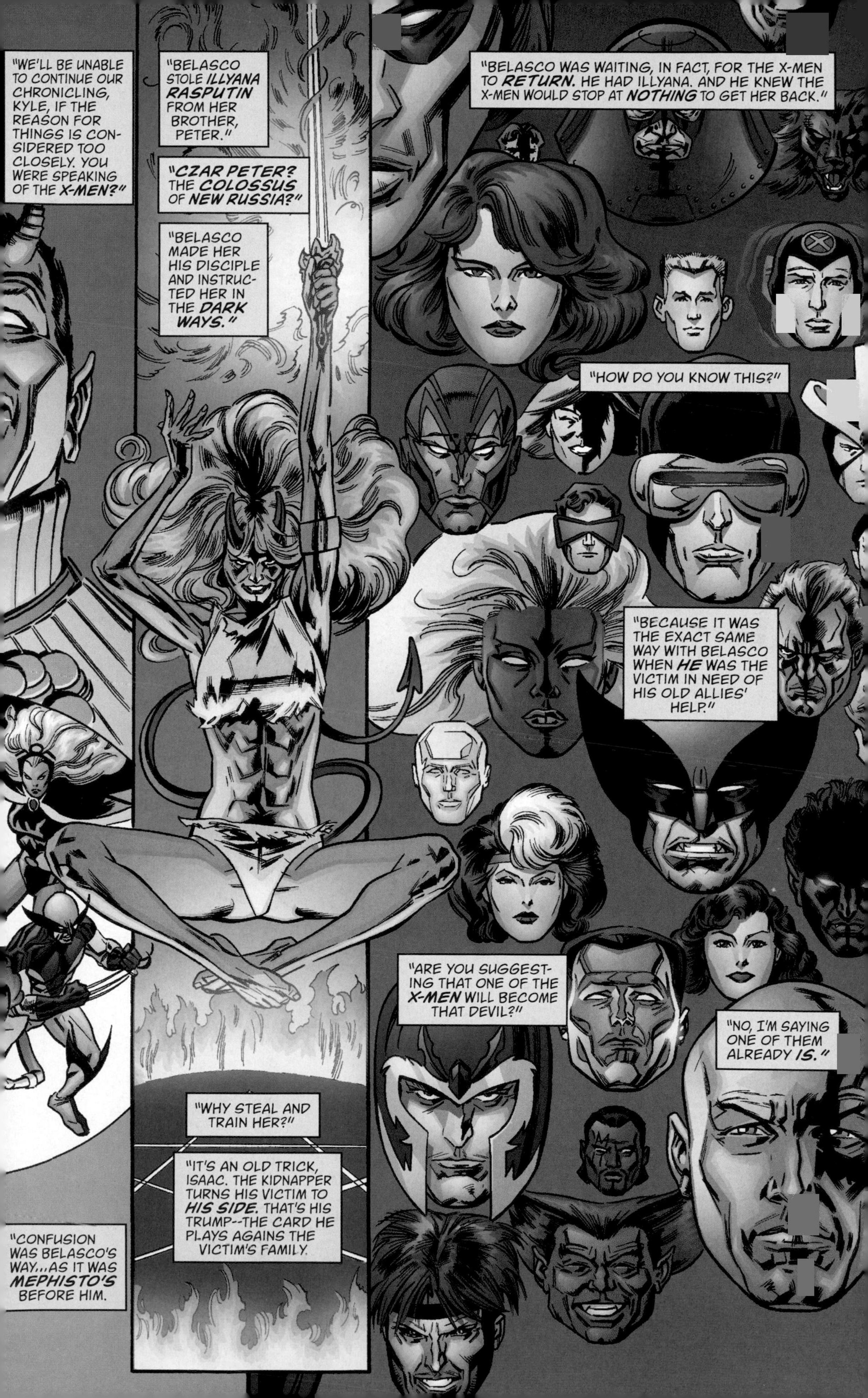
"WE'LL BE UNABLE TO CONTINUE OUR CHRONICLING, KYLE, IF THE REASON FOR THINGS IS CONSIDERED TOO CLOSELY. YOU WERE SPEAKING OF THE X-MEN?"
"BELASCO STOLE ILLYANA RASPUTIN FROM HER BROTHER, PETER."
"CZAR PETER? THE COLOSSUS OF NEW RUSSIA?"
"BELASCO MADE HER HIS DISCIPLE AND INSTRUCTED HER IN THE DARK WAYS."
"WHY STEAL AND TRAIN HER?"
"IT'S AN OLD TRICK, ISAAC. THE KIDNAPPER TURNS HIS VICTIM TO HIS SIDE. THAT'S HIS TRUMP--THE CARD HE PLAYS AGAINS THE VICTIM'S FAMILY.
"CONFUSION WAS BELASCO'S WAY...AS IT WAS MEPHISTO'S BEFORE HIM.
"BELASCO WAS WAITING, IN FACT, FOR THE X-MEN TO RETURN. HE HAD ILLYANA. AND HE KNEW THE X-MEN WOULD STOP AT NOTHING TO GET HER BACK."
"HOW DO YOU KNOW THIS?"
"BECAUSE IT WAS THE EXACT SAME WAY WITH BELASCO WHEN HE WAS THE VICTIM IN NEED OF HIS OLD ALLIES' HELP."
"ARE YOU SUGGESTING THAT ONE OF THE X-MEN WILL BECOME THAT DEVIL?"
"NO, I'M SAYING ONE OF THEM ALREADY IS."

"BUT THAT'S ANOTHER PAGE, ISAAC. SOMETIMES I WONDER IF THIS IS ALL WORTH IT."

"OF COURSE IT IS, KYLE. YOU AND I ARE JUST FORTUNATE THAT THERE'S A *BOOK BINDER* THAT LIVES BELOW US."

"A GOOD PORTENT, I WOULD HAVE TO SAY."

"THE *BLACK KNIGHT'S* ANNOUNCEMENT THAT HE WILL NOT BE KING OF THE INHUMAN WORLD HAS BEEN MET WITH MIXED APPLAUSE."

"HIS MOTHER, *MEDUSA,* AND HIS INTENDED WIFE, *LUNA,* HAVE LITTLE HOPE FOR THE STATURE THEY MIGHT HAVE ONCE COMMANDED."

WHY IS HE DOING THIS?

I'M SORRY, CHILD. PERHAPS THE SCIENCE COUNCIL WAS RIGHT AFTER ALL.

TO LEAVE THE *HIDDEN LAND* IS TO BE *POISONED* BY THIS WORLD. WE SHOULD HAVE NEVER LEFT.

OFF TO THE *SAVAGE LAND,* IS IT?

STEVE, WHAT'S *WRONG?*

IT WAS ONLY A LITTLE MORE THAN *THREE YEARS AGO* THAT I TOOK A CHILD'S LIFE, BRIAN.

AND NOW I'M SUPPOS TO BE WATCH OVER THE CH OF ALL O HUMANITY FUTURE CHILDREN

I'M NOT SURE IF I'M TO THIS.

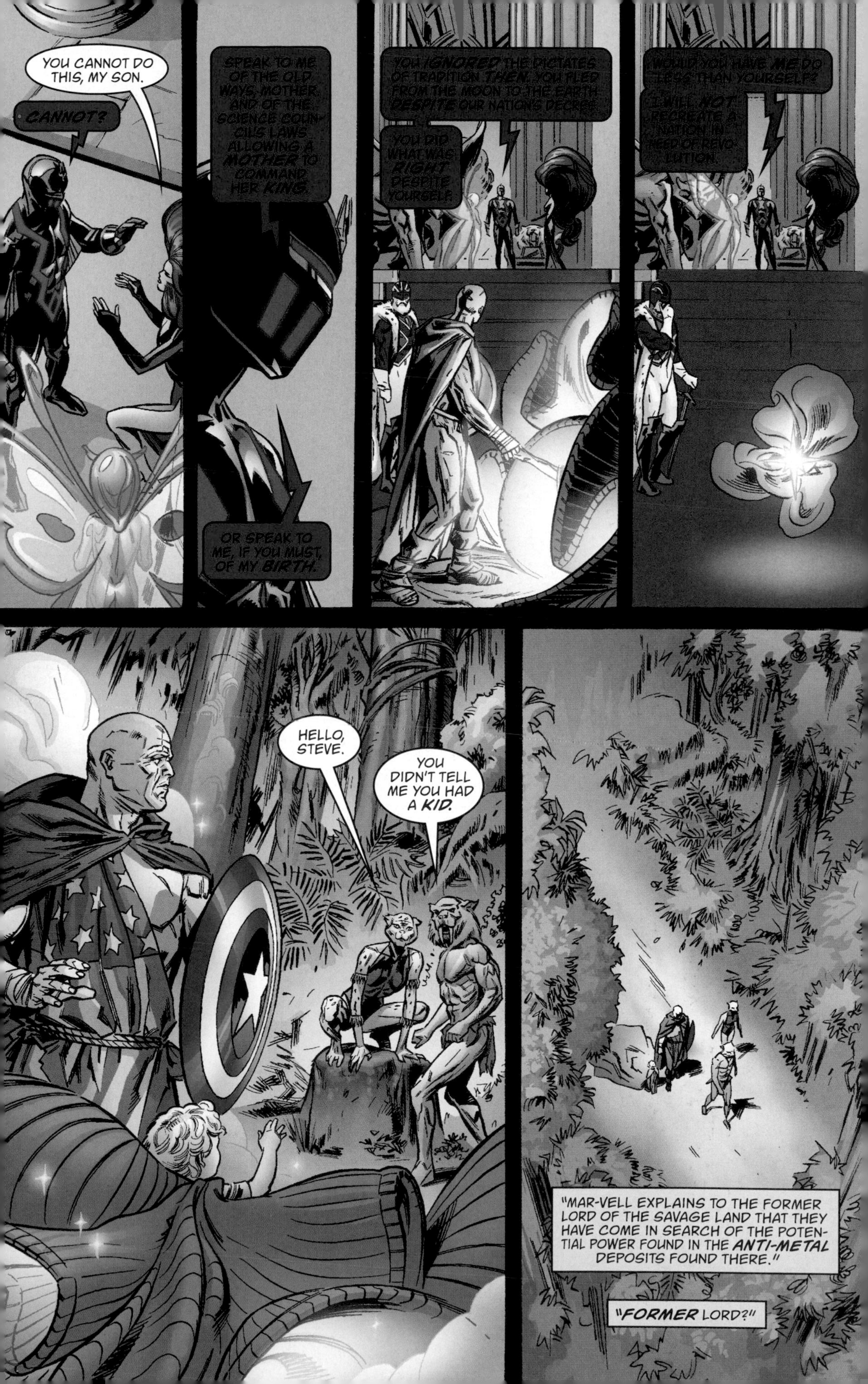
YOU CANNOT DO THIS, MY SON.
CANNOT?
SPEAK TO ME OF THE OLD WAYS, MOTHER, AND OF THE SCIENCE COUNCIL'S LAWS ALLOWING A MOTHER TO COMMAND HER KING.
OR SPEAK TO ME, IF YOU MUST, OF MY BIRTH.
YOU IGNORED THE DICTATES OF TRADITION THEN. YOU FLED FROM THE MOON TO THE EARTH DESPITE OUR NATION'S DECREE.
YOU DID WHAT WAS RIGHT DESPITE YOURSELF.
WOULD YOU HAVE ME DO LESS THAN YOURSELF?
I WILL NOT RECREATE A NATION IN NEED OF REVOLUTION.
HELLO, STEVE.
YOU DIDN'T TELL ME YOU HAD A KID.
"MAR-VELL EXPLAINS TO THE FORMER LORD OF THE SAVAGE LAND THAT THEY HAVE COME IN SEARCH OF THE POTENTIAL POWER FOUND IN THE ANTI-METAL DEPOSITS FOUND THERE."
"FORMER LORD?"

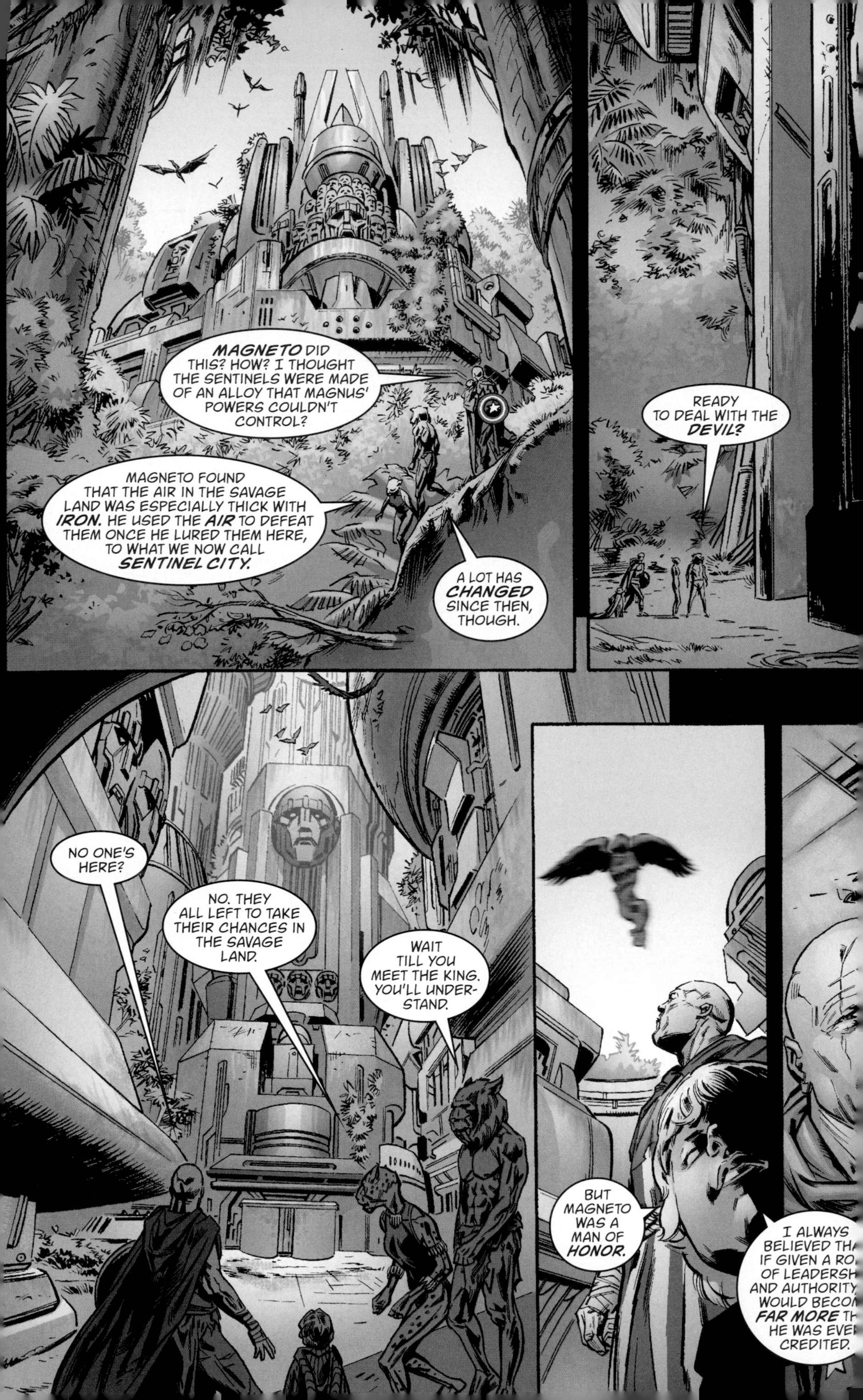
MAGNETO DID THIS? HOW? I THOUGHT THE SENTINELS WERE MADE OF AN ALLOY THAT MAGNUS' POWERS COULDN'T CONTROL?
MAGNETO FOUND THAT THE AIR IN THE SAVAGE LAND WAS ESPECIALLY THICK WITH IRON. HE USED THE AIR TO DEFEAT THEM ONCE HE LURED THEM HERE, TO WHAT WE NOW CALL SENTINEL CITY.
A LOT HAS CHANGED SINCE THEN, THOUGH.
READY TO DEAL WITH THE DEVIL?
NO ONE'S HERE?
NO. THEY ALL LEFT TO TAKE THEIR CHANCES IN THE SAVAGE LAND.
WAIT TILL YOU MEET THE KING. YOU'LL UNDERSTAND.
BUT MAGNETO WAS A MAN OF HONOR.
I ALWAYS BELIEVED THA IF GIVEN A RO OF LEADERSH AND AUTHORITY WOULD BECOM FAR MORE TH HE WAS EVE CREDITED.

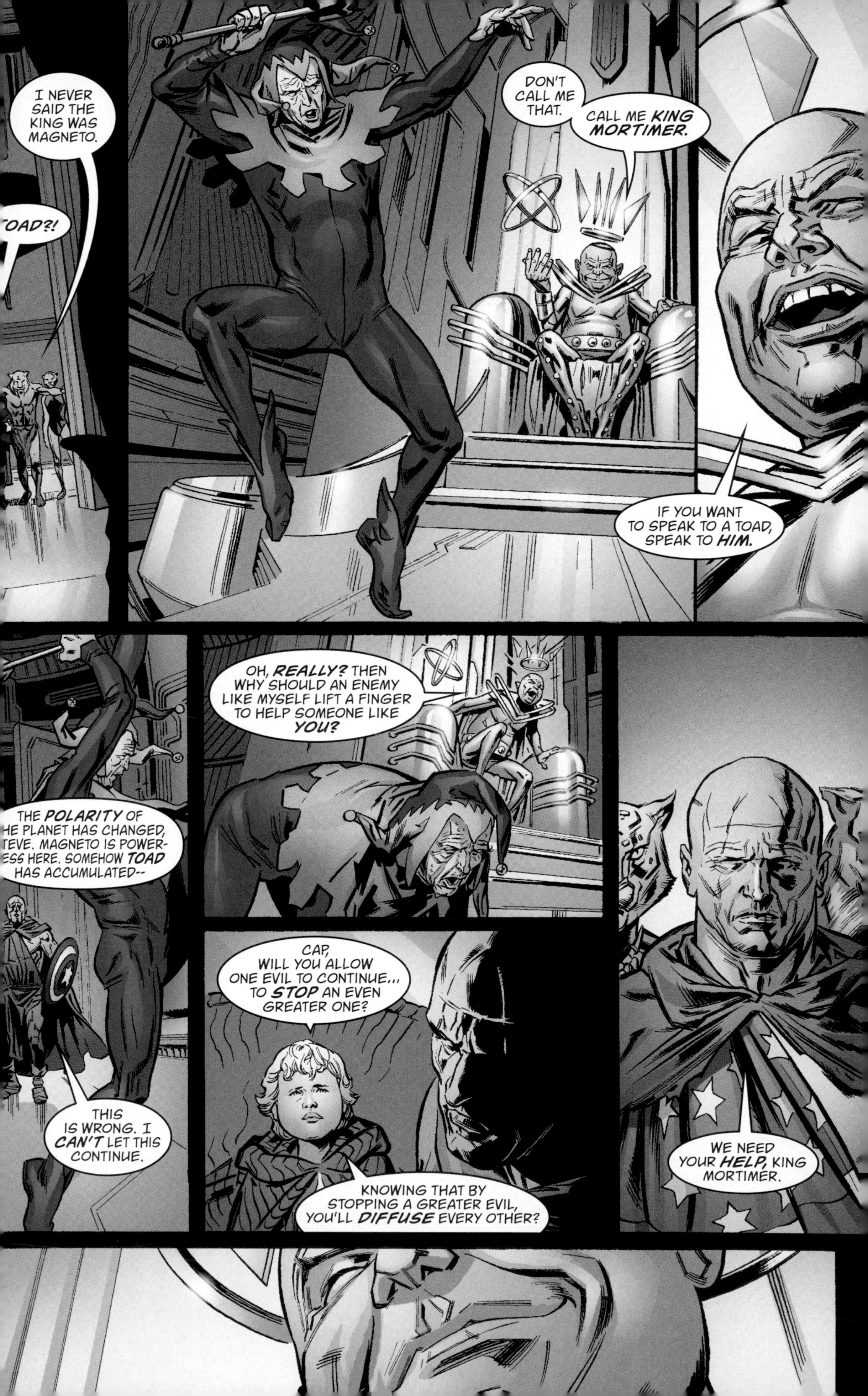
I NEVER SAID THE KING WAS MAGNETO.
TOAD?!
DON'T CALL ME THAT.
CALL ME KING MORTIMER.
IF YOU WANT TO SPEAK TO A TOAD, SPEAK TO HIM.
THE POLARITY OF HE PLANET HAS CHANGED, TEVE. MAGNETO IS POWER-ESS HERE. SOMEHOW TOAD HAS ACCUMULATED--
THIS IS WRONG. I CAN'T LET THIS CONTINUE.
OH, REALLY? THEN WHY SHOULD AN ENEMY LIKE MYSELF LIFT A FINGER TO HELP SOMEONE LIKE YOU?
CAP, WILL YOU ALLOW ONE EVIL TO CONTINUE... TO STOP AN EVEN GREATER ONE?
KNOWING THAT BY STOPPING A GREATER EVIL, YOU'LL DIFFUSE EVERY OTHER?
WE NEED YOUR HELP, KING MORTIMER.

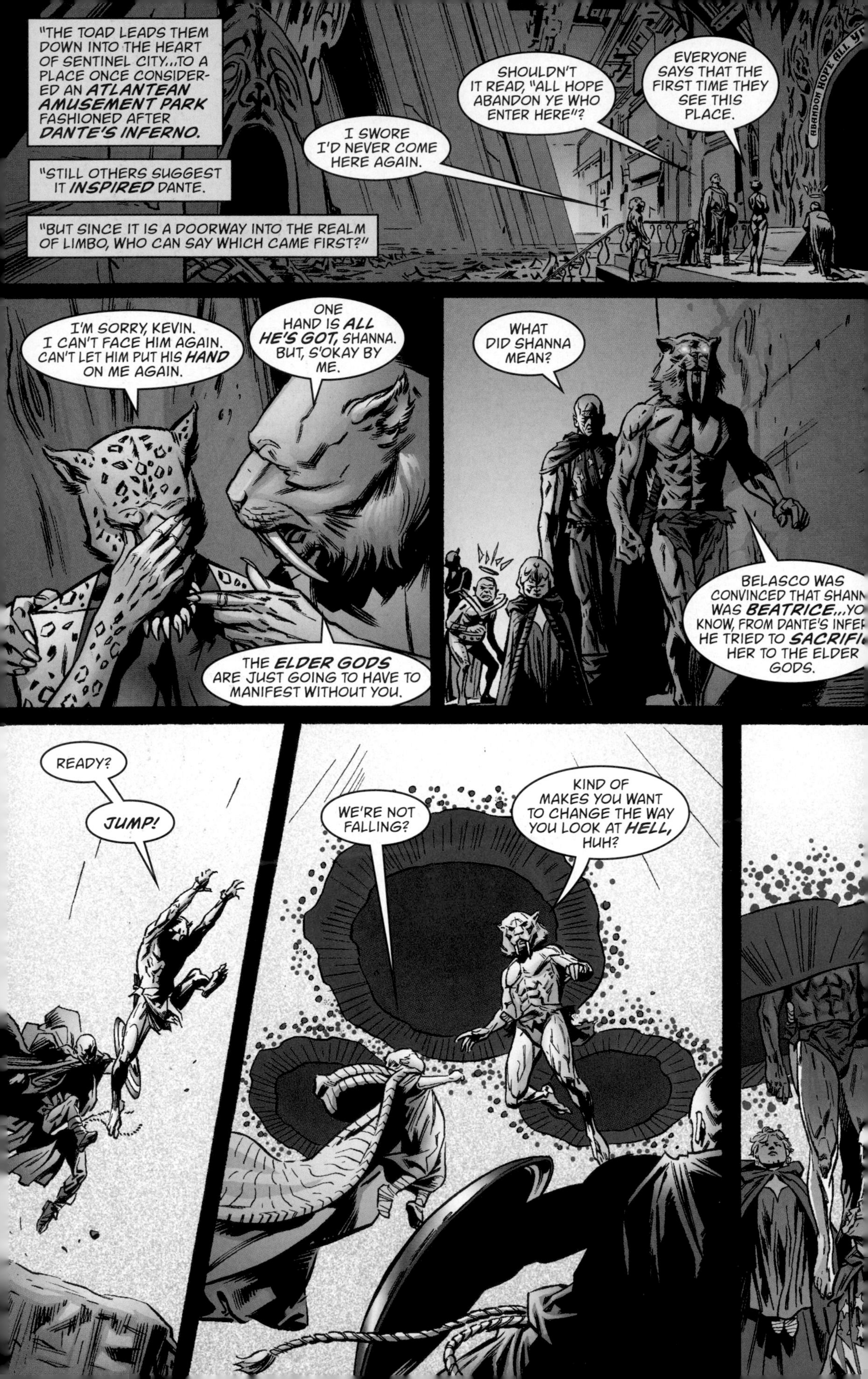
"THE TOAD LEADS THEM DOWN INTO THE HEART OF SENTINEL CITY...TO A PLACE ONCE CONSIDERED AN ATLANTEAN AMUSEMENT PARK FASHIONED AFTER DANTE'S INFERNO.
"STILL OTHERS SUGGEST IT INSPIRED DANTE.
"BUT SINCE IT IS A DOORWAY INTO THE REALM OF LIMBO, WHO CAN SAY WHICH CAME FIRST?"
I SWORE I'D NEVER COME HERE AGAIN.
SHOULDN'T IT READ, "ALL HOPE ABANDON YE WHO ENTER HERE"?
EVERYONE SAYS THAT THE FIRST TIME THEY SEE THIS PLACE.
I'M SORRY, KEVIN. I CAN'T FACE HIM AGAIN. CAN'T LET HIM PUT HIS HAND ON ME AGAIN.
ONE HAND IS ALL HE'S GOT, SHANNA. BUT, S'OKAY BY ME.
THE ELDER GODS ARE JUST GOING TO HAVE TO MANIFEST WITHOUT YOU.
WHAT DID SHANNA MEAN?
BELASCO WAS CONVINCED THAT SHANN WAS BEATRICE...YO KNOW, FROM DANTE'S INFEF HE TRIED TO SACRIFI HER TO THE ELDER GODS.
READY?
JUMP!
WE'RE NOT FALLING?
KIND OF MAKES YOU WANT TO CHANGE THE WAY YOU LOOK AT HELL, HUH?

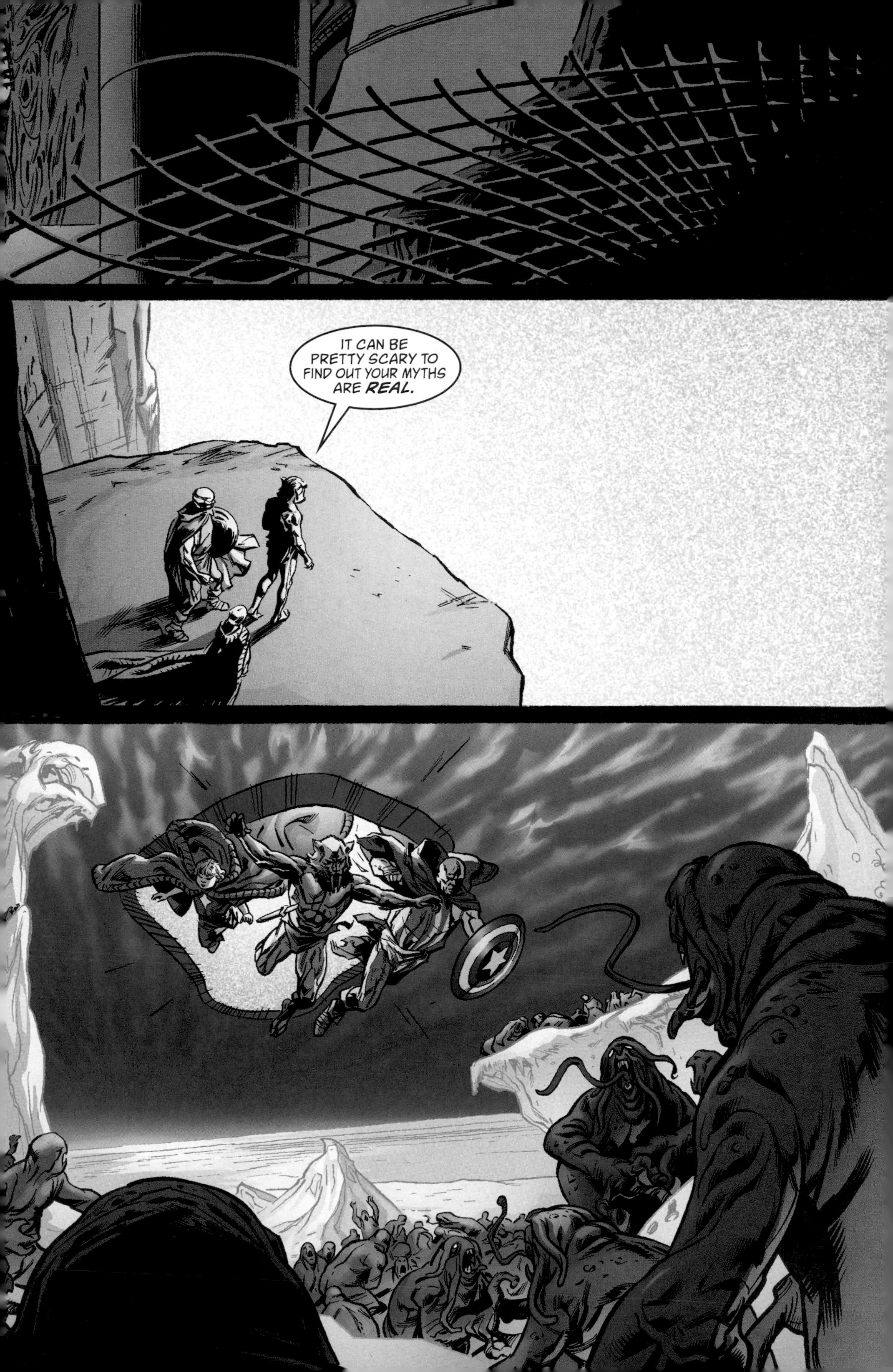
IT CAN BE PRETTY SCARY TO FIND OUT YOUR MYTHS ARE *REAL.*

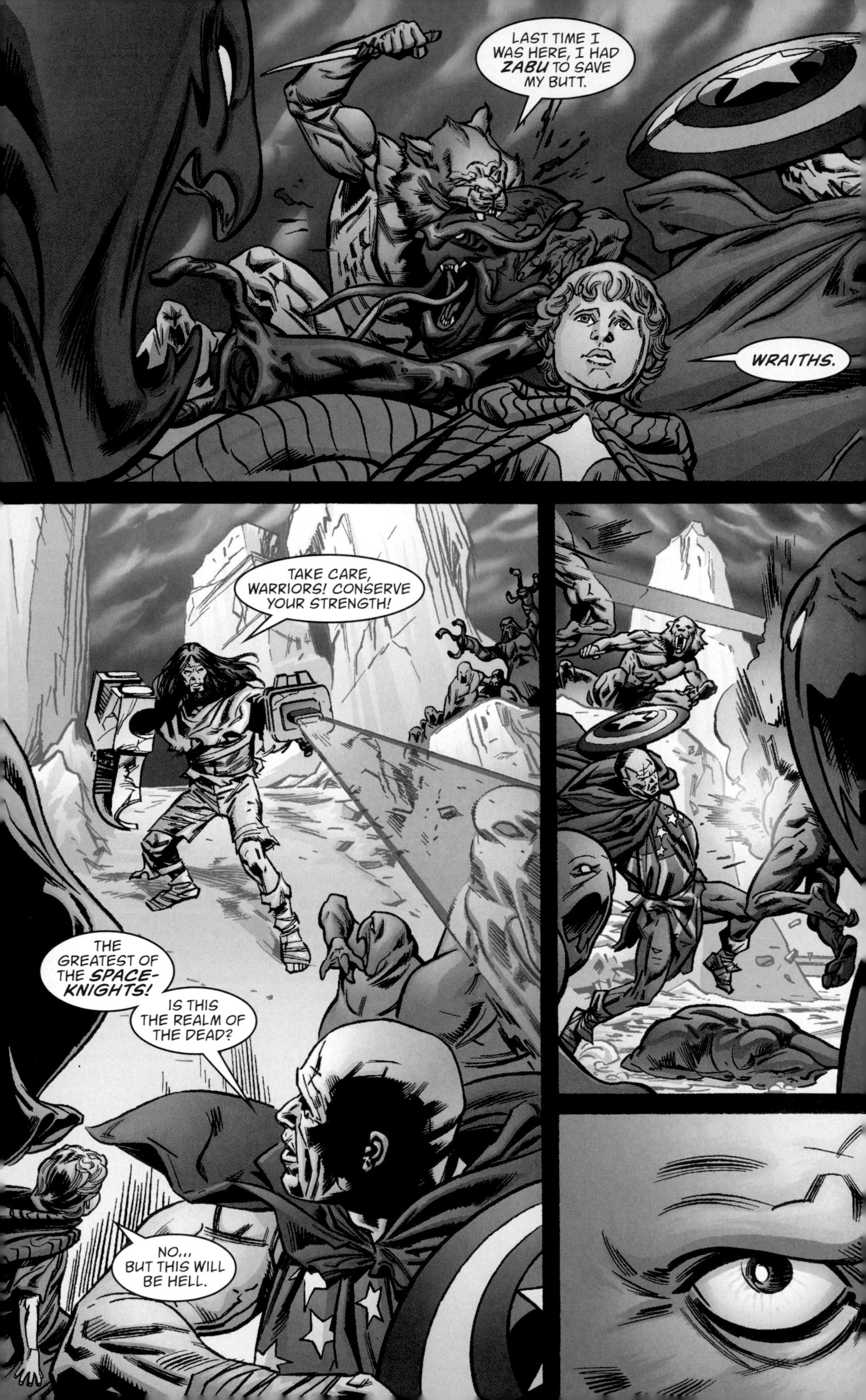
LAST TIME I WAS HERE, I HAD ZABU TO SAVE MY BUTT.
WRAITHS.
TAKE CARE, WARRIORS! CONSERVE YOUR STRENGTH!
THE GREATEST OF THE SPACE-KNIGHTS!
IS THIS THE REALM OF THE DEAD?
NO... BUT THIS WILL BE HELL.

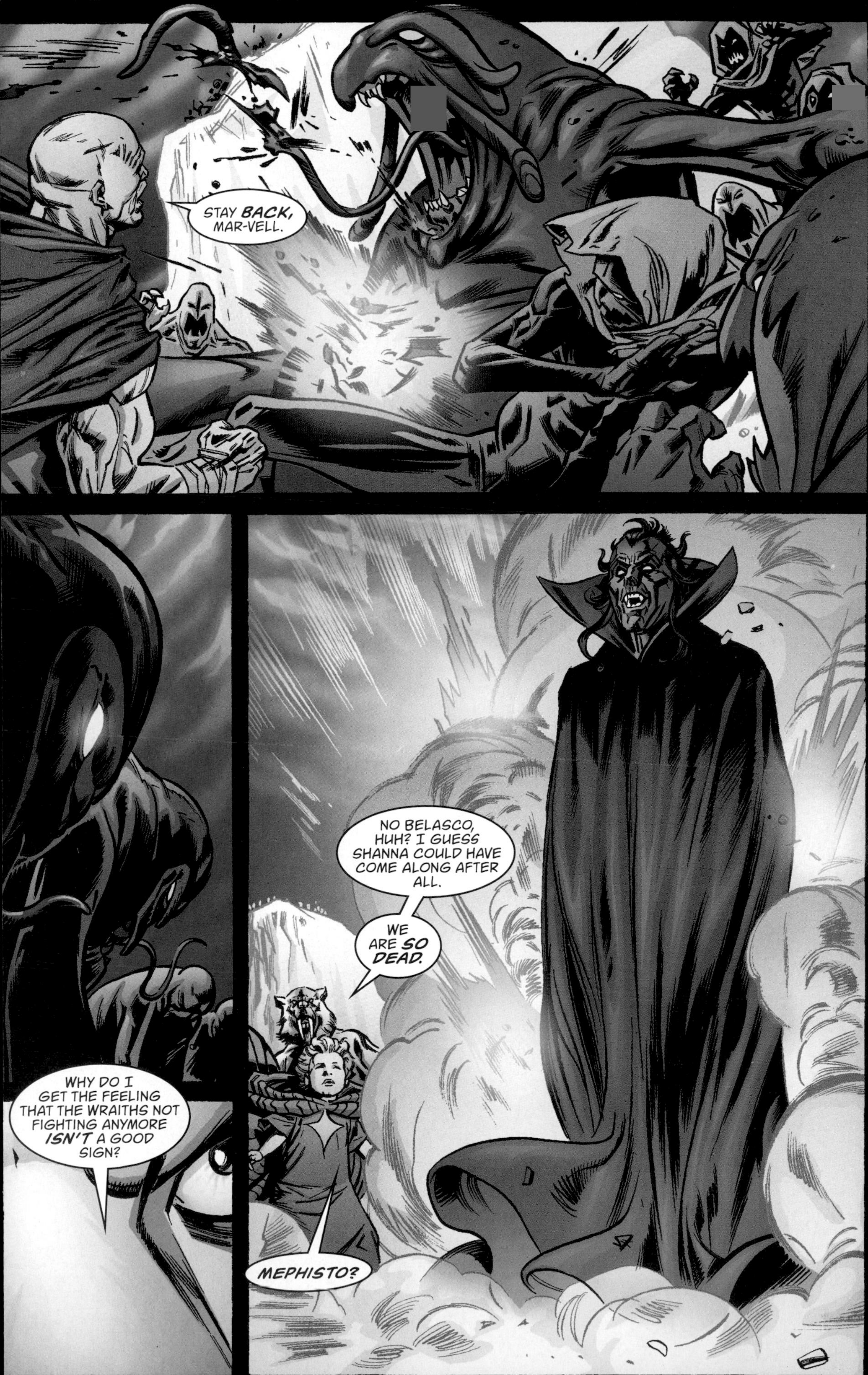
STAY BACK, MAR-VELL.
WHY DO I GET THE FEELING THAT THE WRAITHS NOT FIGHTING ANYMORE ISN'T A GOOD SIGN?
NO BELASCO, HUH? I GUESS SHANNA COULD HAVE COME ALONG AFTER ALL.
WE ARE SO DEAD.
MEPHISTO?

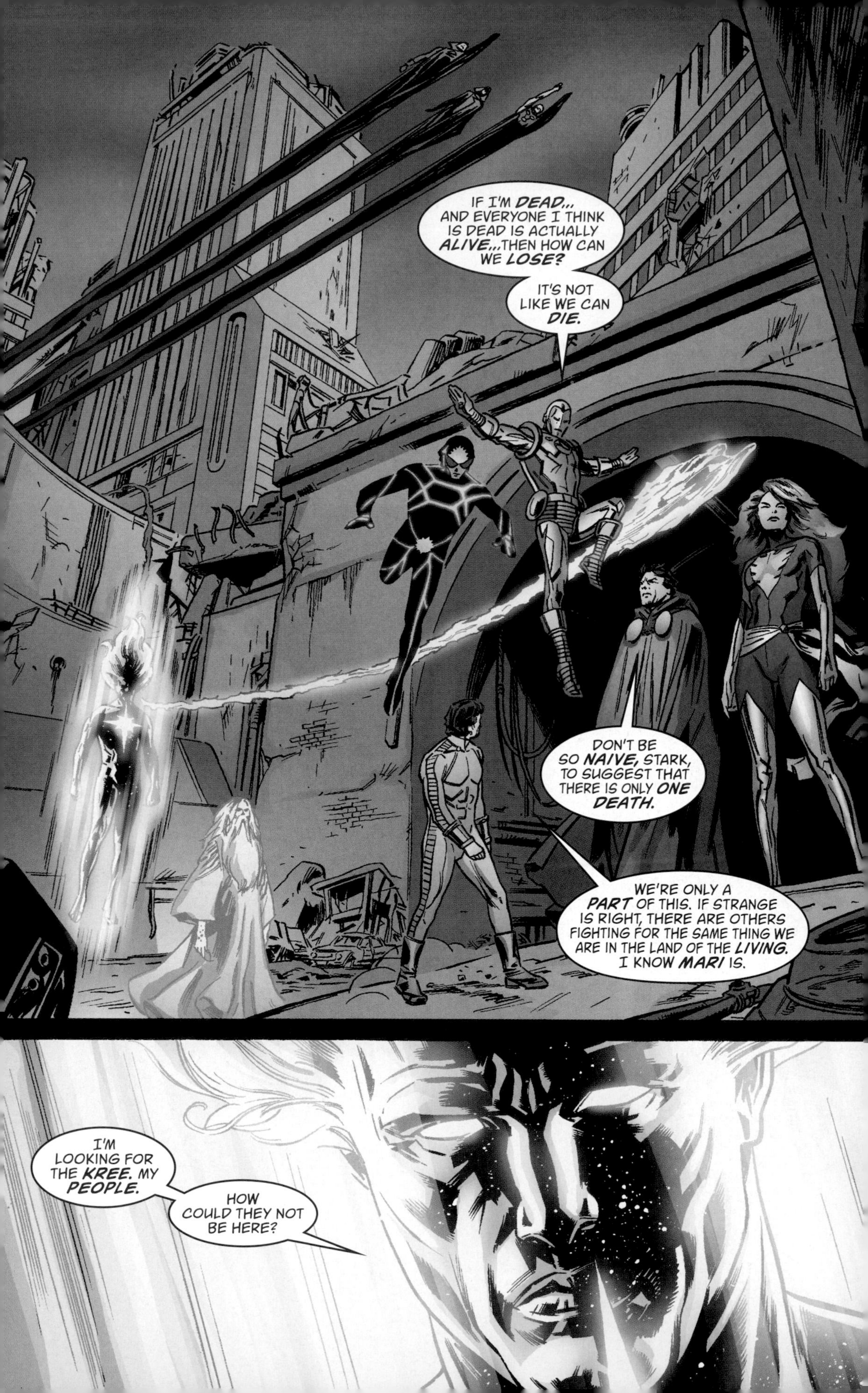
IF I'M DEAD... AND EVERYONE I THINK IS DEAD IS ACTUALLY ALIVE...THEN HOW CAN WE LOSE?
IT'S NOT LIKE WE CAN DIE.
DON'T BE SO NAIVE, STARK, TO SUGGEST THAT THERE IS ONLY ONE DEATH.
WE'RE ONLY A PART OF THIS. IF STRANGE IS RIGHT, THERE ARE OTHERS FIGHTING FOR THE SAME THING WE ARE IN THE LAND OF THE LIVING. I KNOW MARI IS.
I'M LOOKING FOR THE KREE. MY PEOPLE.
HOW COULD THEY NOT BE HERE?

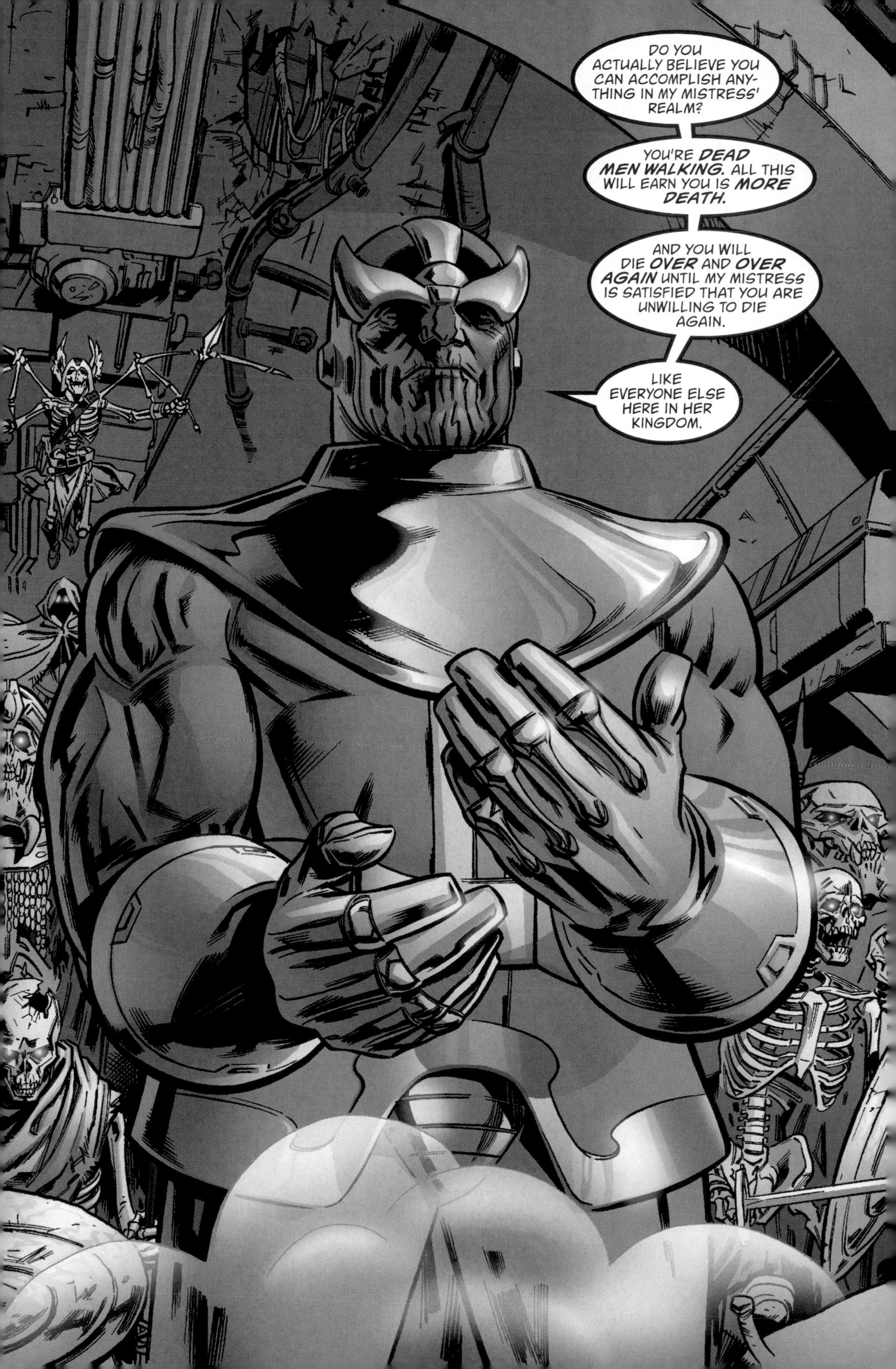
DO YOU ACTUALLY BELIEVE YOU CAN ACCOMPLISH ANY-THING IN MY MISTRESS' REALM?
YOU'RE **DEAD MEN WALKING.** ALL THIS WILL EARN YOU IS **MORE DEATH.**
AND YOU WILL DIE **OVER** AND **OVER AGAIN** UNTIL MY MISTRESS IS SATISFIED THAT YOU ARE UNWILLING TO DIE AGAIN.
LIKE EVERYONE ELSE HERE IN HER KINGDOM.

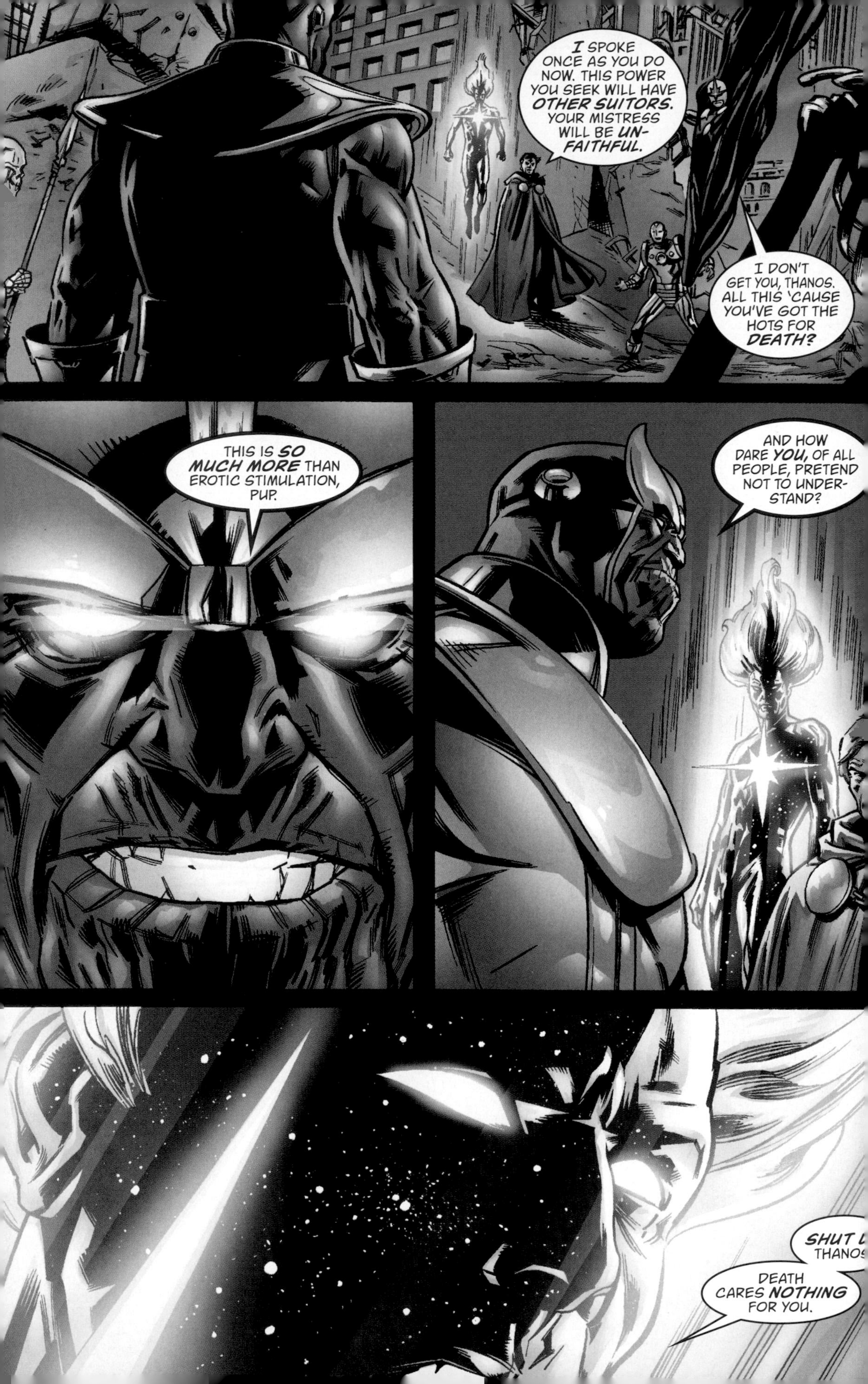

I SPOKE ONCE AS YOU DO NOW. THIS POWER YOU SEEK WILL HAVE OTHER SUITORS. YOUR MISTRESS WILL BE UN-FAITHFUL.
I DON'T GET YOU, THANOS. ALL THIS 'CAUSE YOU'VE GOT THE HOTS FOR DEATH?
THIS IS SO MUCH MORE THAN EROTIC STIMULATION, PUP.
AND HOW DARE YOU, OF ALL PEOPLE, PRETEND NOT TO UNDER-STAND?
DEATH CARES NOTHING FOR YOU.

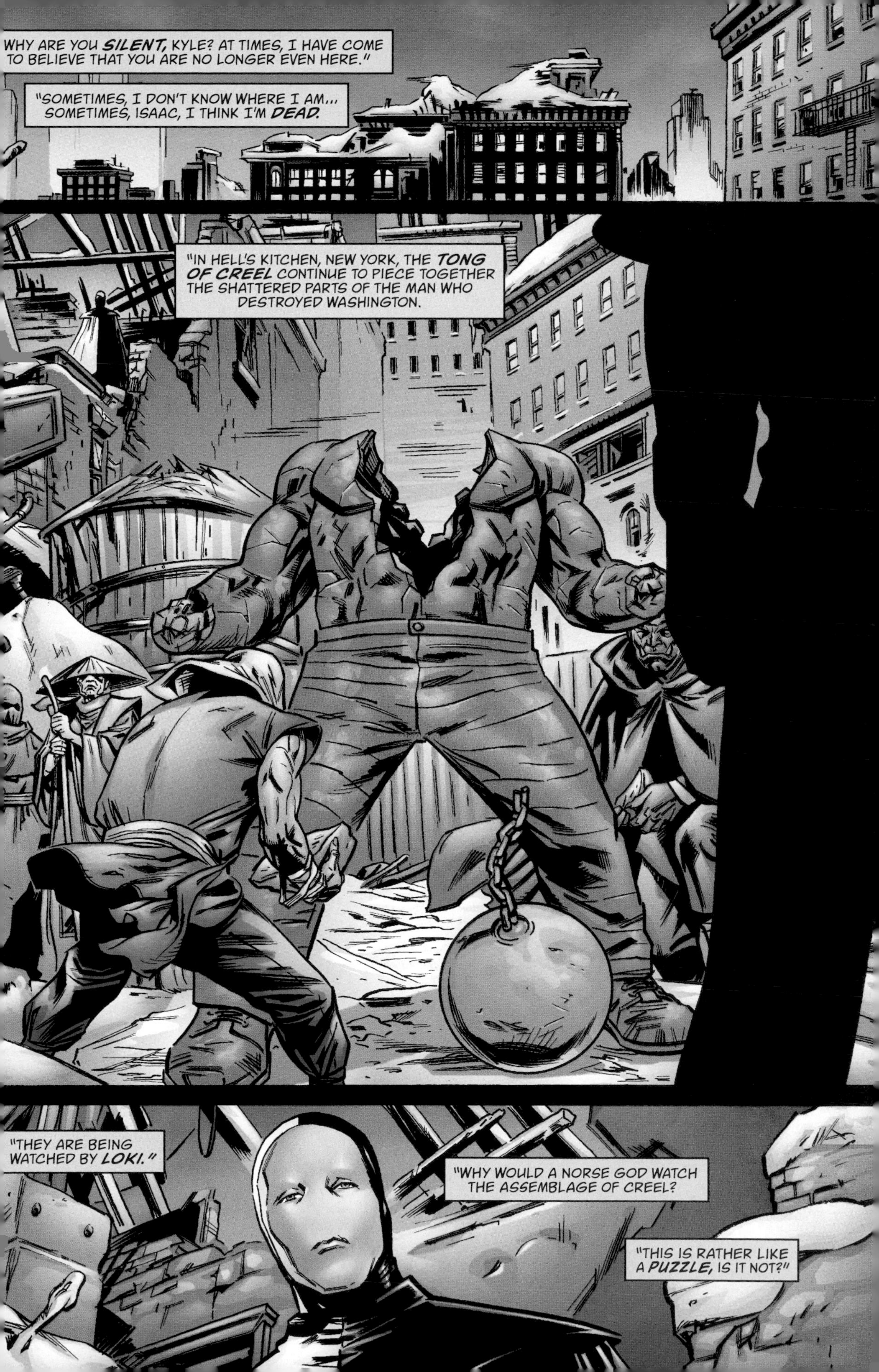
WHY ARE YOU *SILENT*, KYLE? AT TIMES, I HAVE COME TO BELIEVE THAT YOU ARE NO LONGER EVEN HERE."
"SOMETIMES, I DON'T KNOW WHERE I AM... SOMETIMES, ISAAC, I THINK I'M *DEAD*.
"IN HELL'S KITCHEN, NEW YORK, THE *TONG OF CREEL* CONTINUE TO PIECE TOGETHER THE SHATTERED PARTS OF THE MAN WHO DESTROYED WASHINGTON.
"THEY ARE BEING WATCHED BY *LOKI*."
"WHY WOULD A NORSE GOD WATCH THE ASSEMBLAGE OF CREEL?
"THIS IS RATHER LIKE A *PUZZLE*, IS IT NOT?"

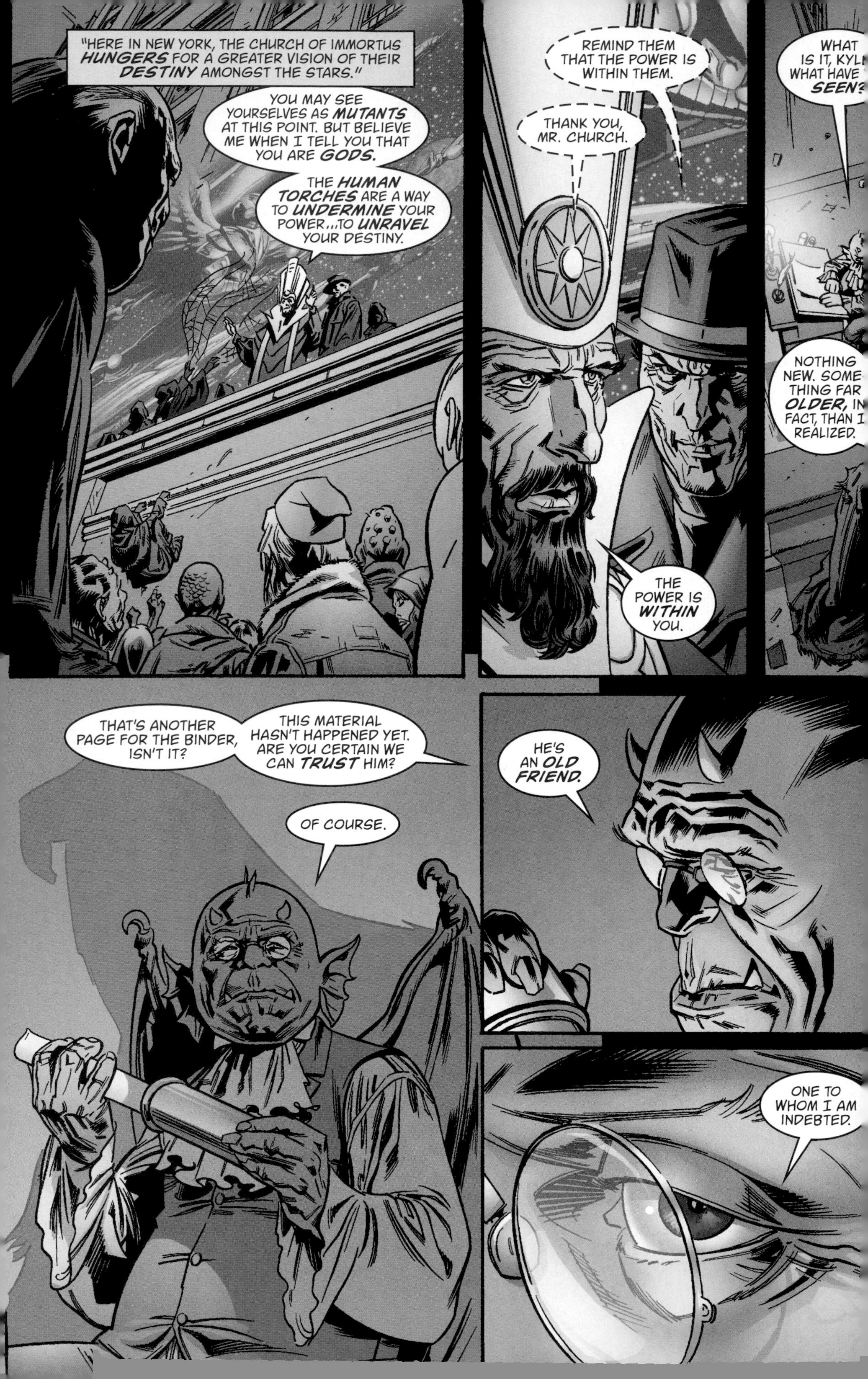
"HERE IN NEW YORK, THE CHURCH OF IMMORTUS HUNGERS FOR A GREATER VISION OF THEIR DESTINY AMONGST THE STARS."
YOU MAY SEE YOURSELVES AS MUTANTS AT THIS POINT. BUT BELIEVE ME WHEN I TELL YOU THAT YOU ARE GODS.
THE HUMAN TORCHES ARE A WAY TO UNDERMINE YOUR POWER...TO UNRAVEL YOUR DESTINY.
REMIND THEM THAT THE POWER IS WITHIN THEM.
THANK YOU, MR. CHURCH.
THE POWER IS WITHIN YOU.
WHAT IS IT, KYL WHAT HAVE SEEN?
NOTHING NEW. SOME THING FAR OLDER, IN FACT, THAN I REALIZED.
THAT'S ANOTHER PAGE FOR THE BINDER, ISN'T IT?
THIS MATERIAL HASN'T HAPPENED YET. ARE YOU CERTAIN WE CAN TRUST HIM?
OF COURSE.
HE'S AN OLD FRIEND.
ONE TO WHOM I AM INDEBTED.

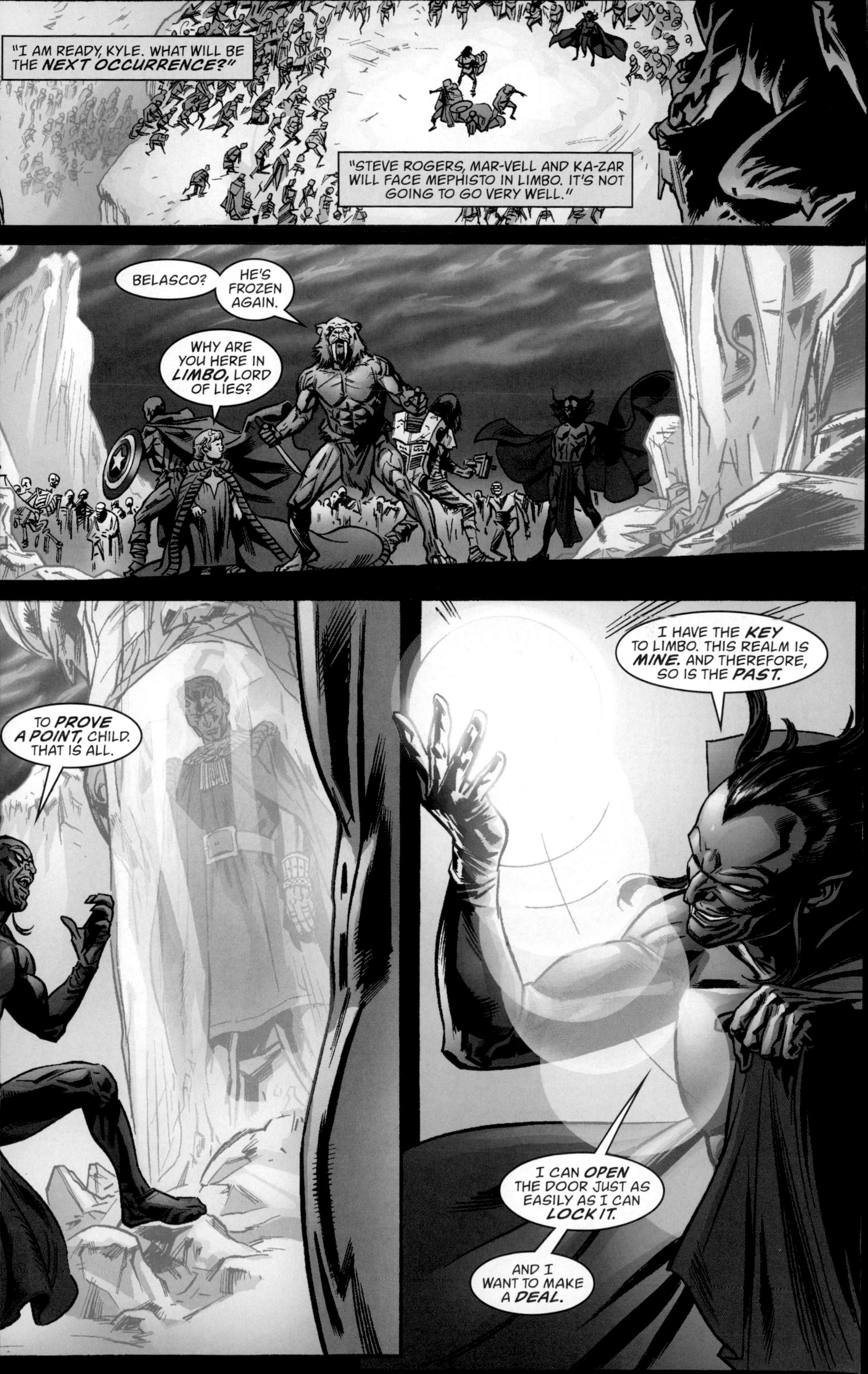
"I AM READY, KYLE. WHAT WILL BE THE NEXT OCCURRENCE?"
"STEVE ROGERS, MAR-VELL AND KA-ZAR WILL FACE MEPHISTO IN LIMBO. IT'S NOT GOING TO GO VERY WELL."
BELASCO?
HE'S FROZEN AGAIN.
WHY ARE YOU HERE IN LIMBO, LORD OF LIES?
TO PROVE A POINT, CHILD. THAT IS ALL.
I HAVE THE KEY TO LIMBO. THIS REALM IS MINE. AND THEREFORE, SO IS THE PAST.
I CAN OPEN THE DOOR JUST AS EASILY AS I CAN LOCK IT.
AND I WANT TO MAKE A DEAL.

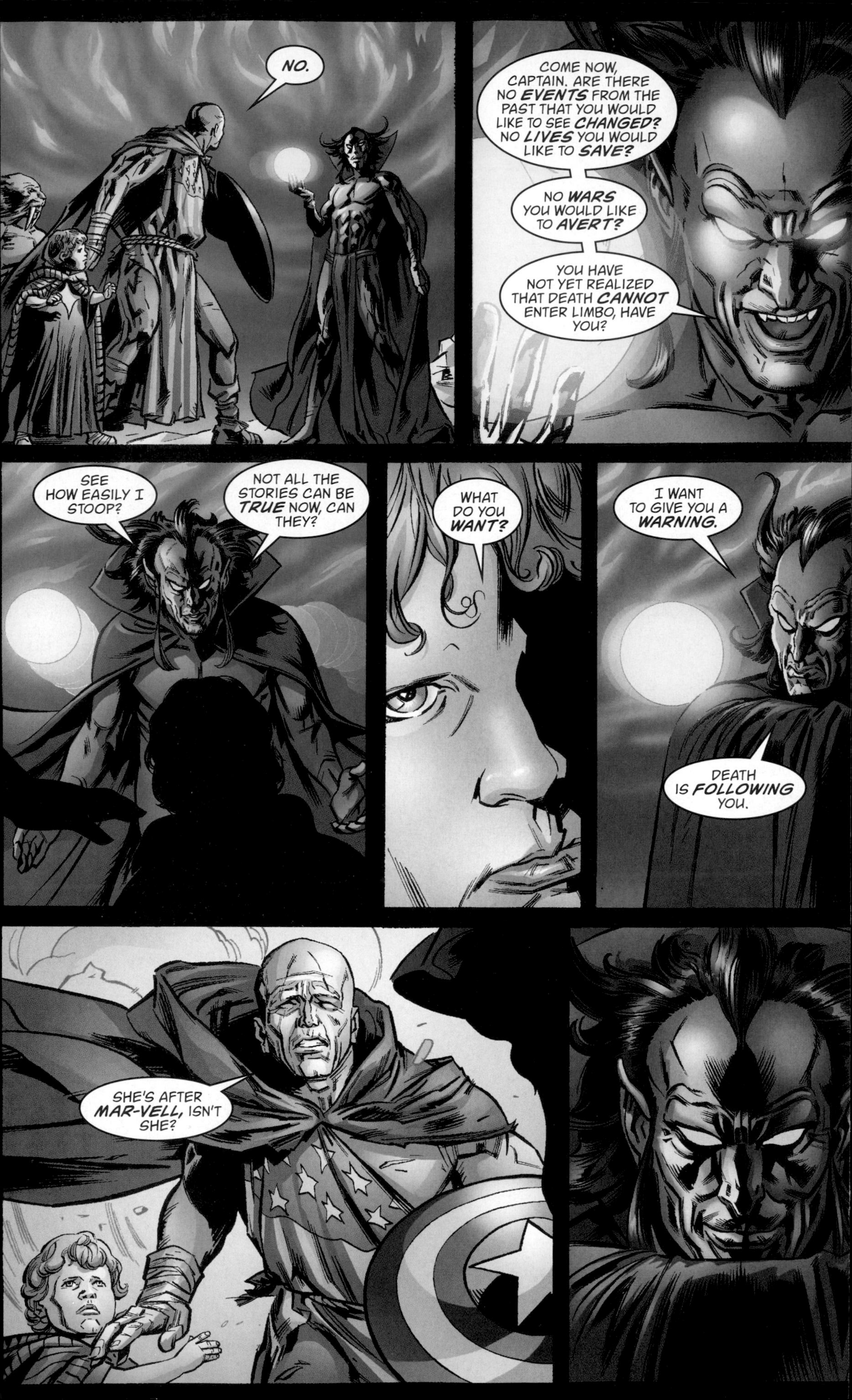
NO.
COME NOW, CAPTAIN. ARE THERE NO EVENTS FROM THE PAST THAT YOU WOULD LIKE TO SEE CHANGED? NO LIVES YOU WOULD LIKE TO SAVE?
NO WARS YOU WOULD LIKE TO AVERT?
YOU HAVE NOT YET REALIZED THAT DEATH CANNOT ENTER LIMBO, HAVE YOU?
SEE HOW EASILY I STOOP?
NOT ALL THE STORIES CAN BE TRUE NOW, CAN THEY?
WHAT DO YOU WANT?
I WANT TO GIVE YOU A WARNING.
DEATH IS FOLLOWING YOU.
SHE'S AFTER MAR-VELL, ISN'T SHE?

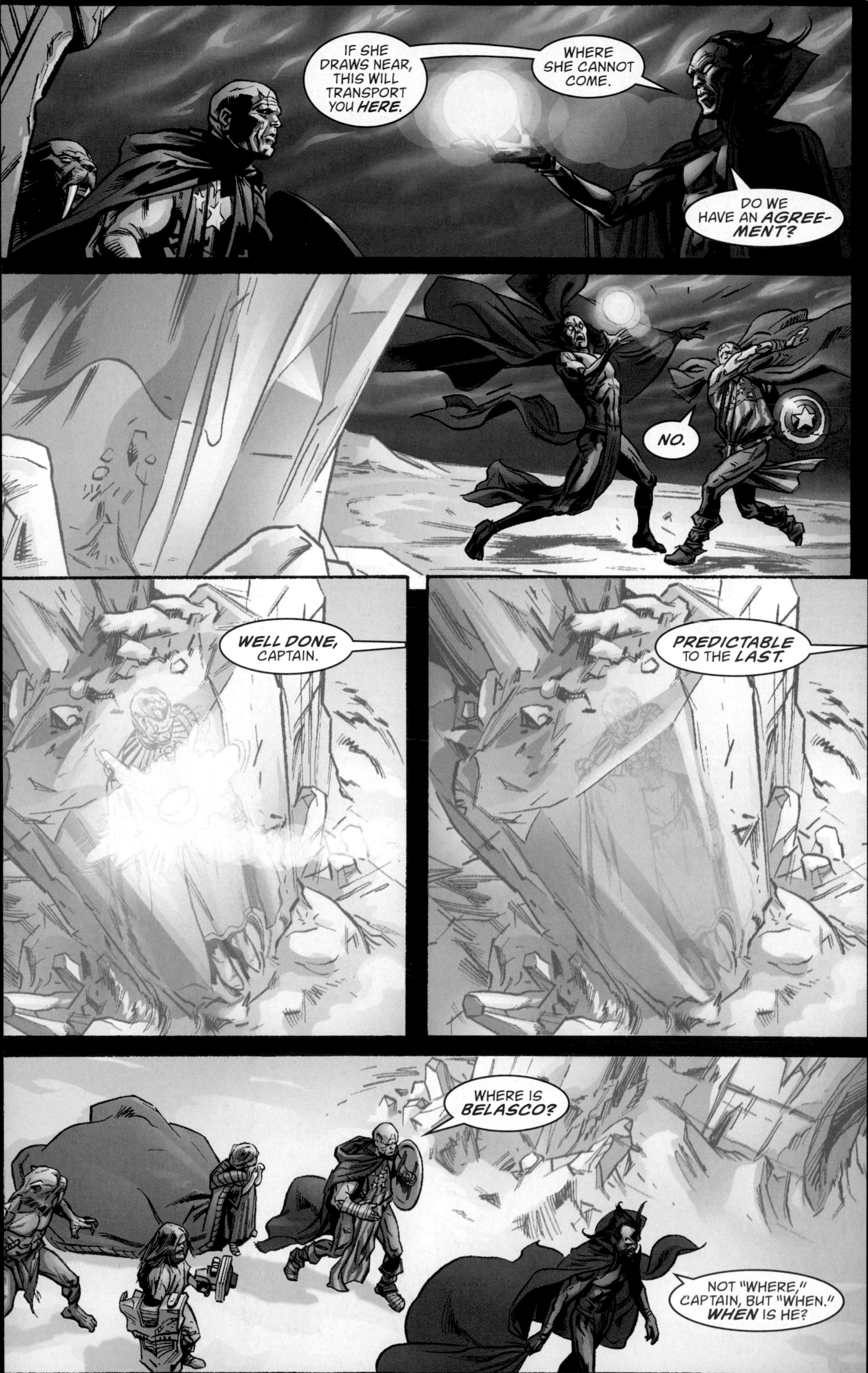
IF SHE DRAWS NEAR, THIS WILL TRANSPORT YOU HERE.
WHERE SHE CANNOT COME.
DO WE HAVE AN AGREE-MENT?
NO.
WELL DONE, CAPTAIN.
PREDICTABLE TO THE LAST.
WHERE IS BELASCO?
NOT "WHERE," CAPTAIN, BUT "WHEN." WHEN IS HE?

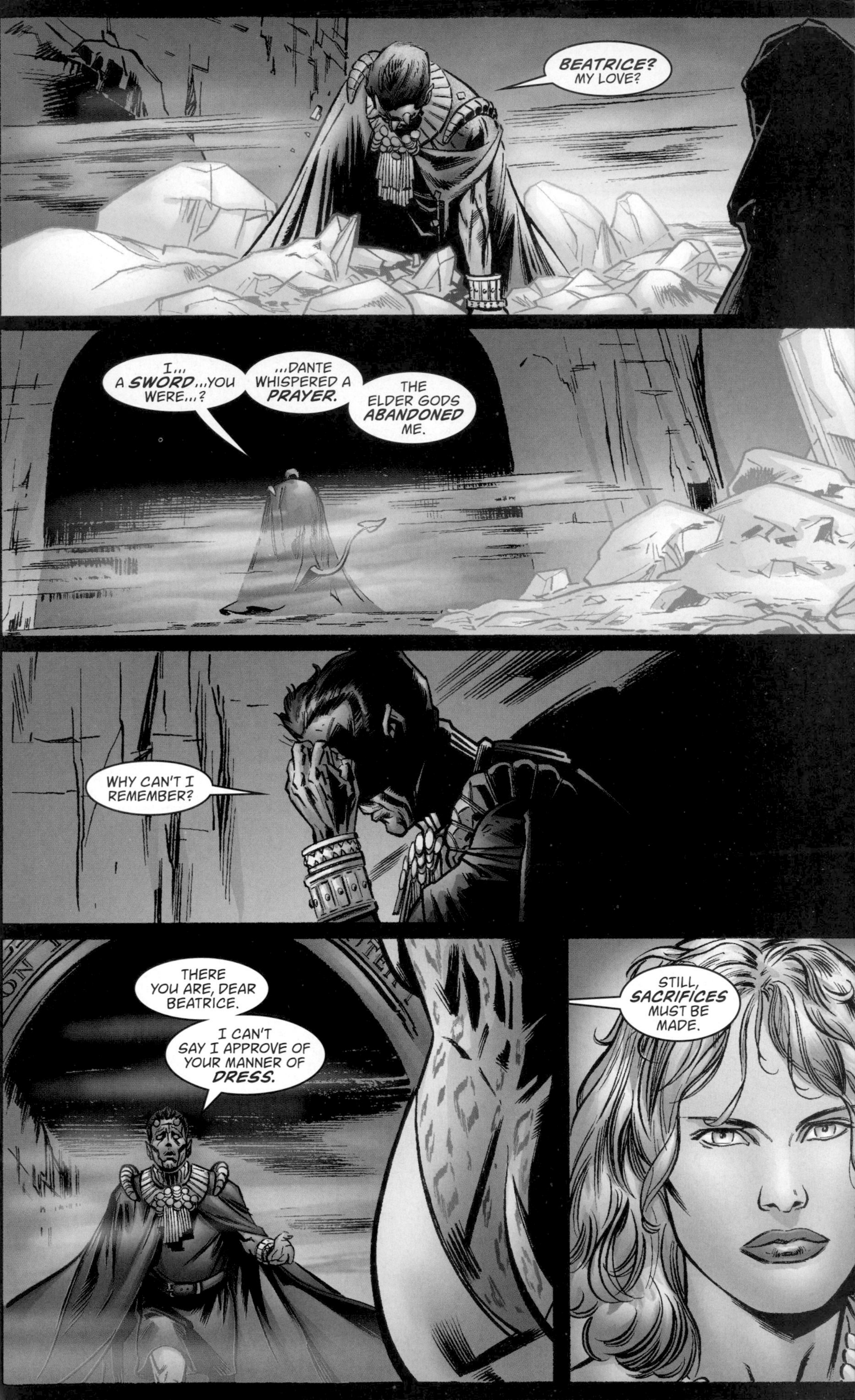
BEATRICE? MY LOVE?
I... A SWORD...YOU WERE...?
...DANTE WHISPERED A PRAYER.
THE ELDER GODS ABANDONED ME.
WHY CAN'T I REMEMBER?
THERE YOU ARE, DEAR BEATRICE.
I CAN'T SAY I APPROVE OF YOUR MANNER OF DRESS.
STILL, SACRIFICES MUST BE MADE.

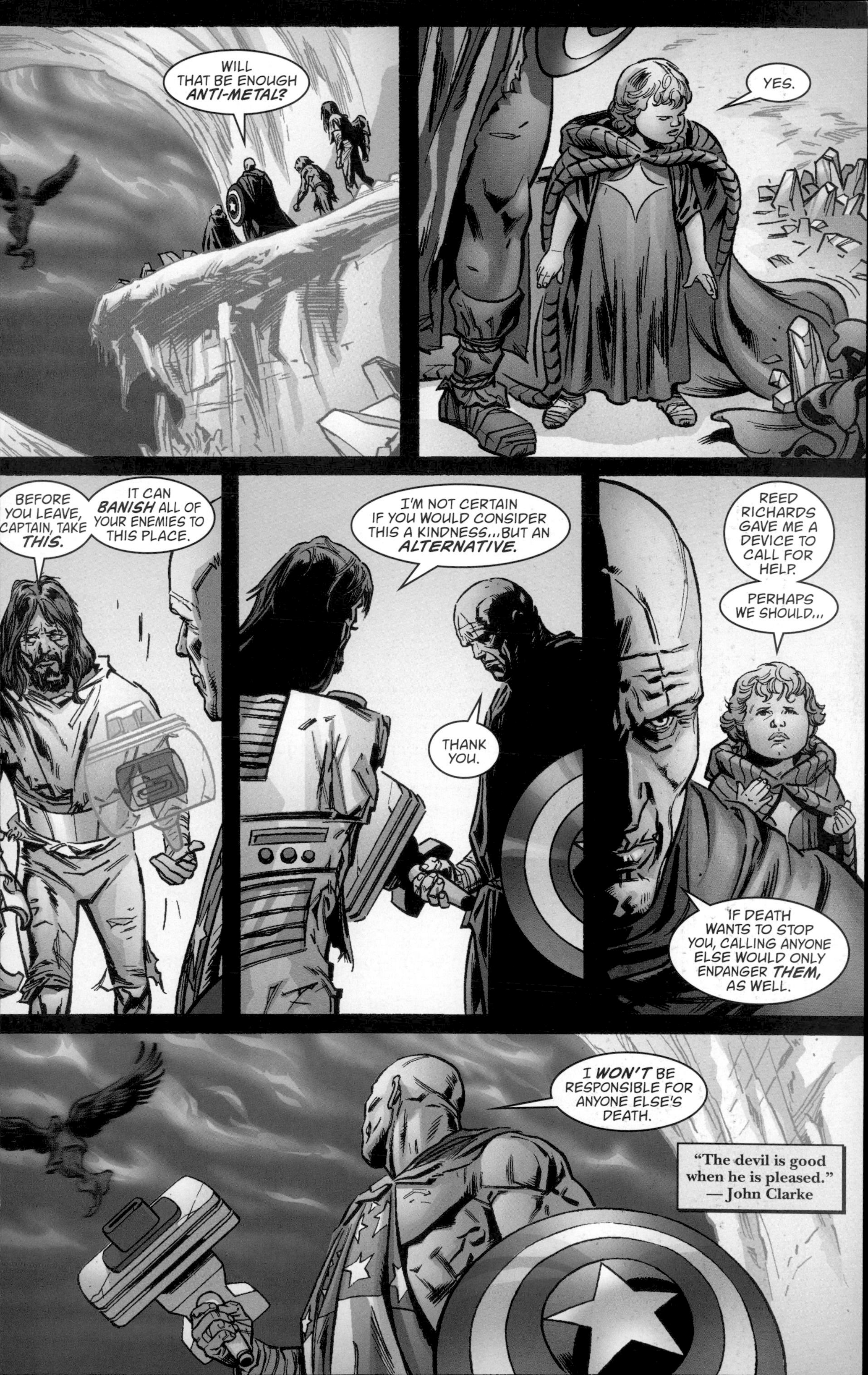

WILL THAT BE ENOUGH ANTI-METAL?
YES.
BEFORE YOU LEAVE, CAPTAIN, TAKE THIS.
IT CAN BANISH ALL OF YOUR ENEMIES TO THIS PLACE.
I'M NOT CERTAIN IF YOU WOULD CONSIDER THIS A KINDNESS... BUT AN ALTERNATIVE.
THANK YOU.
REED RICHARDS GAVE ME A DEVICE TO CALL FOR HELP.
PERHAPS WE SHOULD...
IF DEATH WANTS TO STOP YOU, CALLING ANYONE ELSE WOULD ONLY ENDANGER THEM, AS WELL.
I WON'T BE RESPONSIBLE FOR ANYONE ELSE'S DEATH.
"The devil is good when he is pleased." — John Clarke

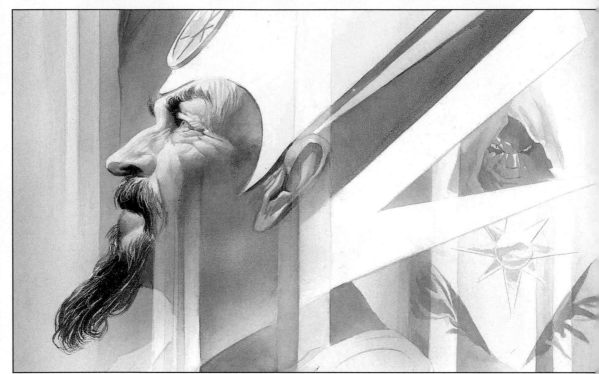

APPENDIX TO CHAPTER THREE

W R I T T E N B Y J I M K R U E G E R

"I would like to speak with you about the places your equipment cannot see into, Uatu."

"I was certain you would, robot. I cannot see into Limbo. As there are other worlds I am not privy to. In the past, I have looked upon Asgard through the eyes of another robot, known as the Recorder. But it was destroyed long ago."

"Is that why you thought I would comply with your wishes? Why you chose me?

"Yes. What have you learned by eavesdropping on the writings of Kyle Richmond?"

"I'm learning so much of what is going on, both in Limbo, and in the realm of the Dead.

"Interesting, isn't it, robot?"

"What?"

"That your only source of information seems to continue coming from one who has been blinded of sorts?"

"You're a funny guy, Uatu. I wish my father had programmed me with a sense of humor. I might enjoy your company more."

"Hmmm."

"I assume that Mephisto must have taken one of the X-Men and convinced him..."
"Him?"
"Belasco is male."

"As was Thor."

"Okay. Assuming Mephisto took one of the X-Men, convinced him... or her that he or she was indeed the demon, Belasco, and sent him or her back in time, certain that the rivalry between Belasco and Dante still exists. At which point Belasco mistakes Shanna for Beatrice, and his first clash with Ka-Zar begins. The question is why."

"There is a problem with this theory, robot. Where does it begin?"
"I know, according to your machinery Belasco did indeed appear to Shanna, and did indeed try to use her to call down the dark gods. "

"Unless."
"Unless we are already in a divergent timeline, changed by Belasco's trip to the past. What if everything from that point is, indeed, part of that divergent timeline? I've been watching Franklin die at the hands of the Sentinels believing that this was the echo of the true reality whereby Franklin goes on to become Galactus. But what if ours is the altered reality? What if Franklin is supposed to be dead? Or what if he's supposed to be alive – and not supposed to be Galactus, either?"
"The race you mock, robot, has through luck despite its own savagery, come to grips with the truth that the manipulation of time leads to the possibility of creating an alternate reality. For humanity, time is like a river that flows, yet due to certain mechanical manipulations, a tributary from this river leads back into the mainstream, creating a loop."
"What's wrong with that?"
"It assumes only one river. It assumes that it is a river. It assumes that it is a line. Something of merely two dimensions."
"Is it something else?"
"Yes. But what that is, is even hidden from the Watchers. The alternate realities are caused by more than a mutated mankind's manipulations. They are determined by the sum total of possibility."
"Every alternative becomes the recognition of a possibility? It's not our choices that determine us?"
"No."
"So... all of our options create these realities, and then those realities are multiplied by the realities of every other person who has ever lived or met any one else? And the way these realities intermingle creates new realities after this? And that has nothing to do with the clear manipulation of time as of yet?

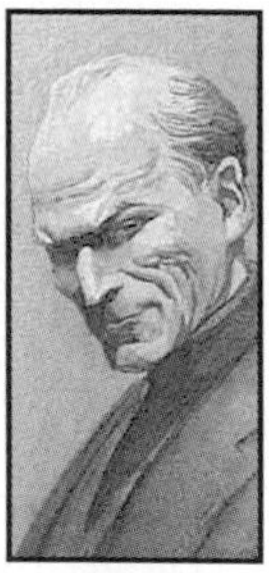

"No."
"The time manipulations reconfigure all those combinations. All purpose, all meaning, all reason, then..."
"Exactly, robot."
"All meaning is thrown into question."
"It is unfortunate that it has taken so long, that so much damage has been caused for the sake of you reaching this conclusion."
"But how could...?"
"I know what you are thinking – for what reason should I attempt to change anything at all? What purpose can a hero have? After all, in another world, in an alternative existence, the possibility of what you want to alter can already be seen to its conclusion in that reality. And in that reality, the very hope of salvation creates new problems and disasters. You are wondering why you should do anything at all. You are wondering if there is anything better to do that simply to watch."
"Watch?"
"Ah. Now we understand each other."
"You're right, Uatu. Our decisions, then, account for nothing, because the entire range of possibilities is given form and substance. For all history, we have wrestled with the possibility that we begin from nothingness, enter nothingness, and in between, I guess, consider the nature of the nothingness. But we were only half-correct. Everything-ness is the same as nothingness. I'm not certain which I prefer. Both result, in the end, in meaninglessness."
"Yes."
"But then, Uatu, can't the same be said about watching?"

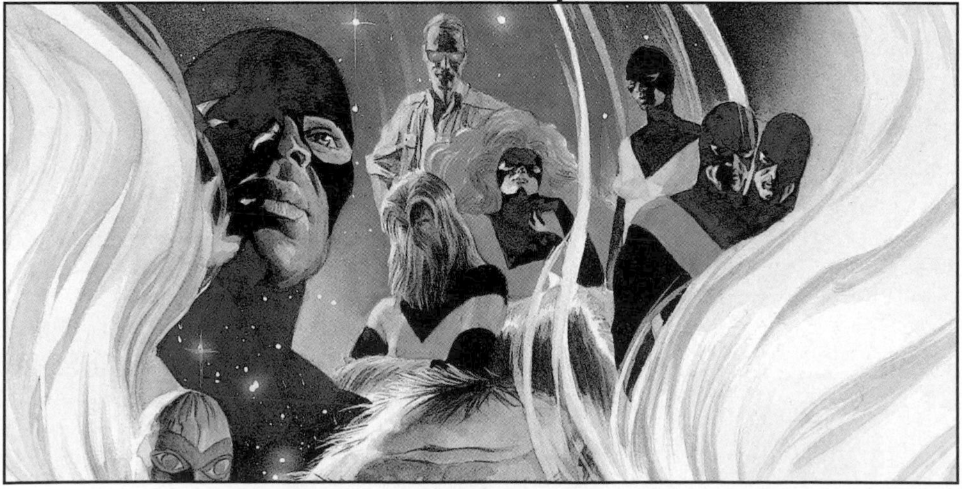

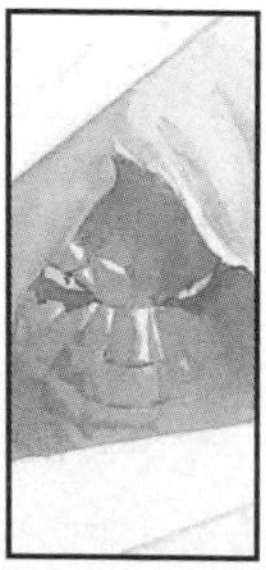

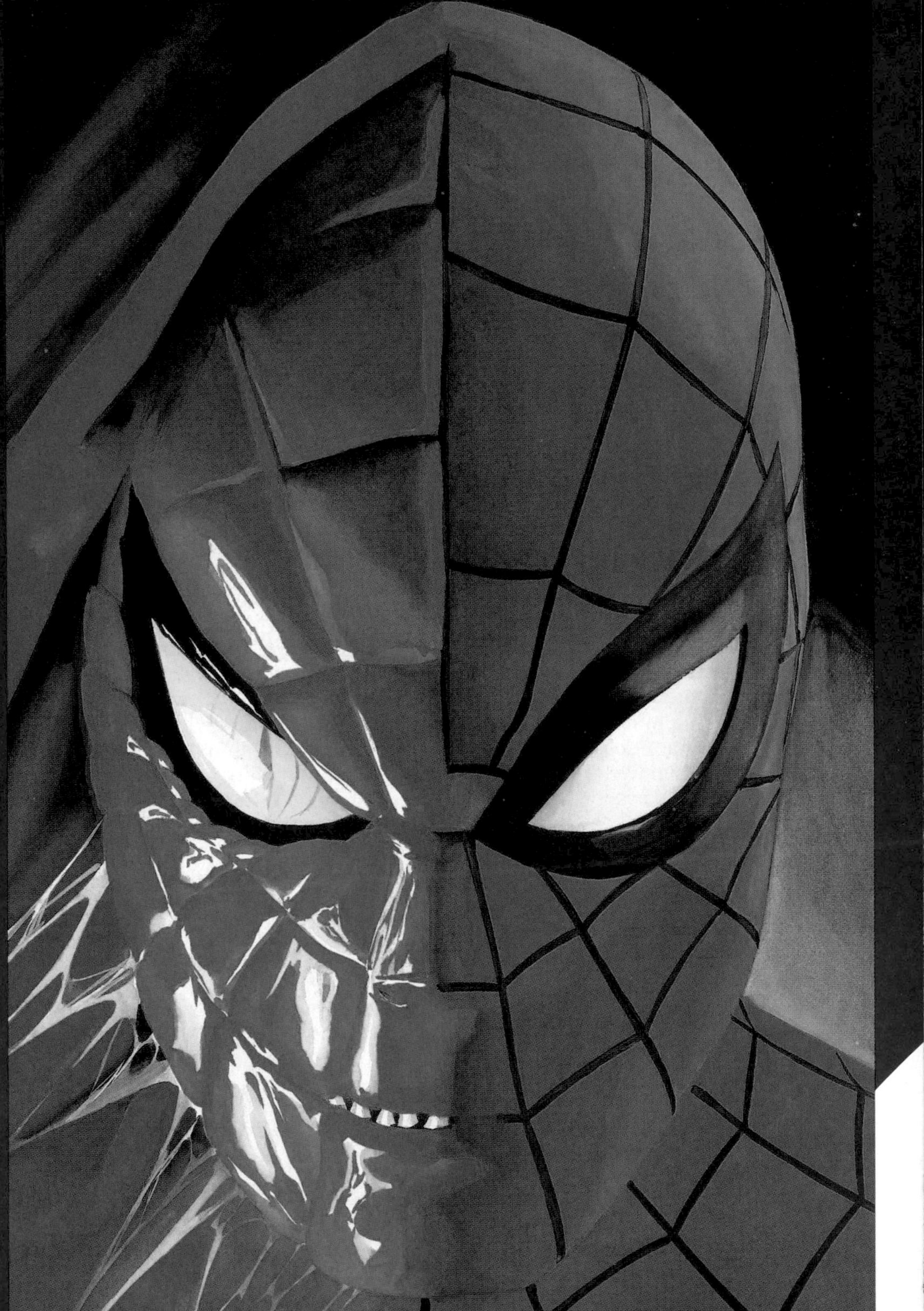

UNIVERSE X : SPIDEY

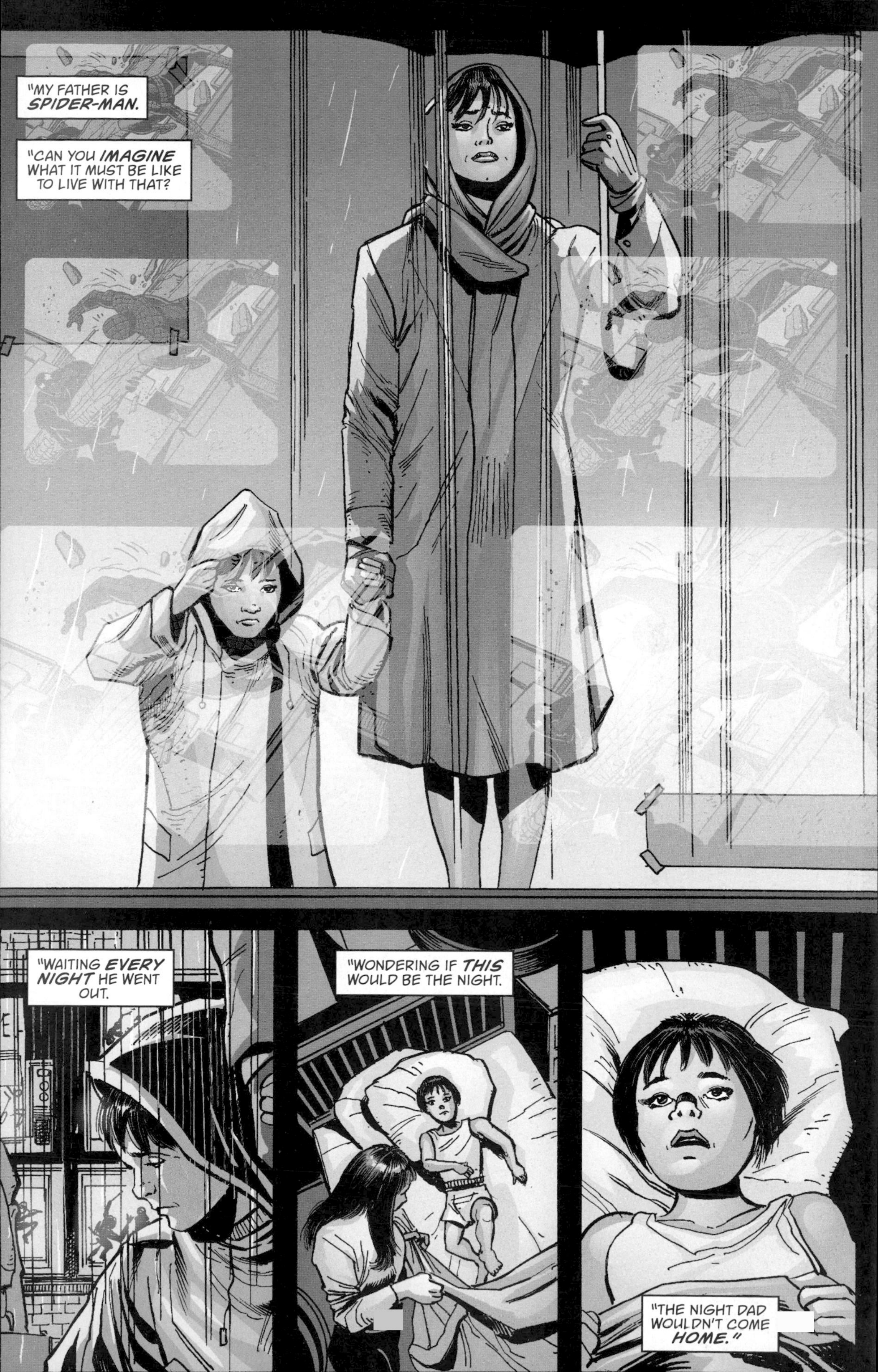
"MY FATHER IS SPIDER-MAN.
"CAN YOU IMAGINE WHAT IT MUST BE LIKE TO LIVE WITH THAT?
"WAITING EVERY NIGHT HE WENT OUT.
"WONDERING IF THIS WOULD BE THE NIGHT.
"THE NIGHT DAD WOULDN'T COME HOME."

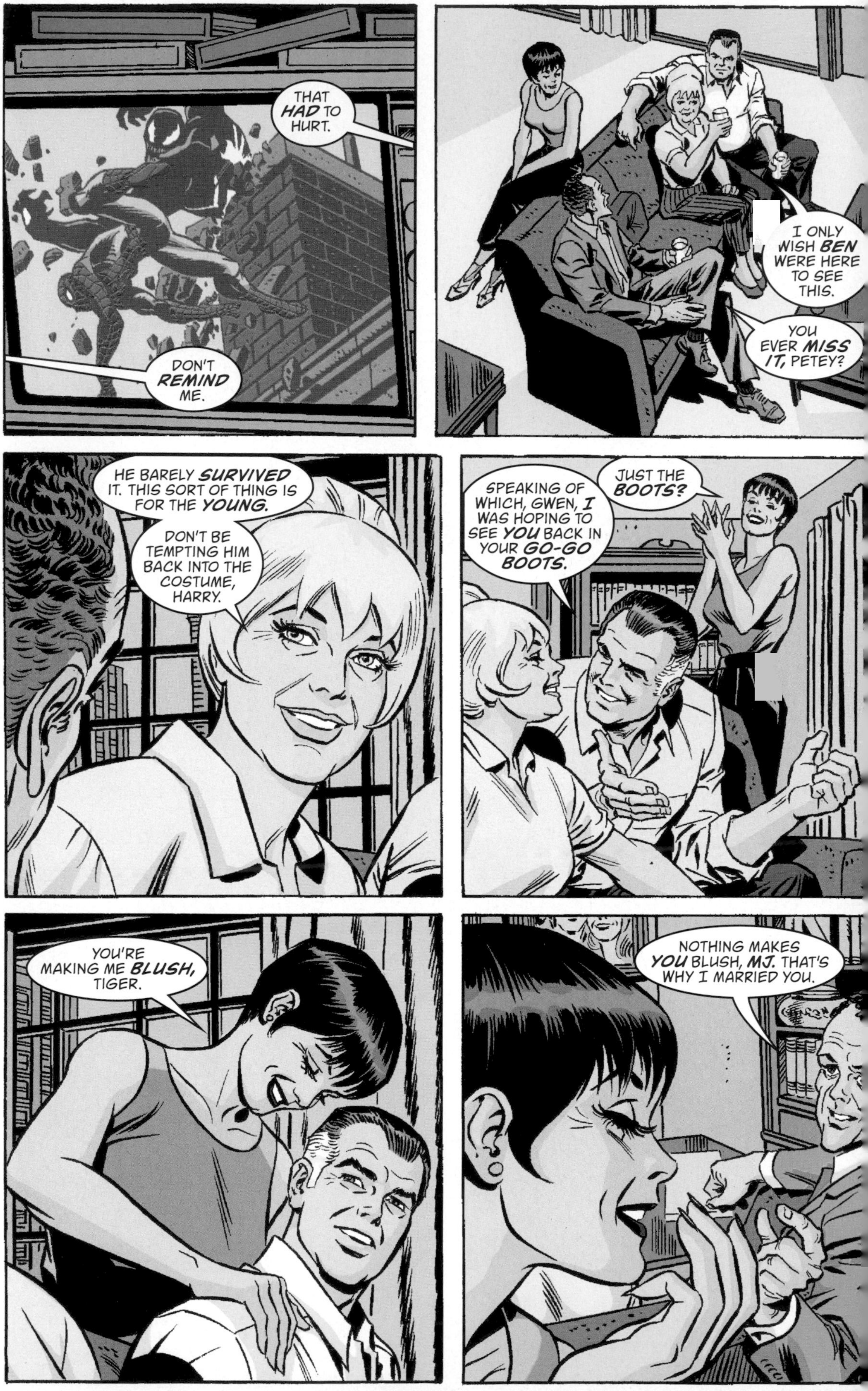
THAT HAD TO HURT.
DON'T REMIND ME.
I ONLY WISH BEN WERE HERE TO SEE THIS.
YOU EVER MISS IT, PETEY?
HE BARELY SURVIVED IT. THIS SORT OF THING IS FOR THE YOUNG.
DON'T BE TEMPTING HIM BACK INTO THE COSTUME, HARRY.
SPEAKING OF WHICH, GWEN, I WAS HOPING TO SEE YOU BACK IN YOUR GO-GO BOOTS.
JUST THE BOOTS?
YOU'RE MAKING ME BLUSH, TIGER.
NOTHING MAKES YOU BLUSH, MJ. THAT'S WHY I MARRIED YOU.

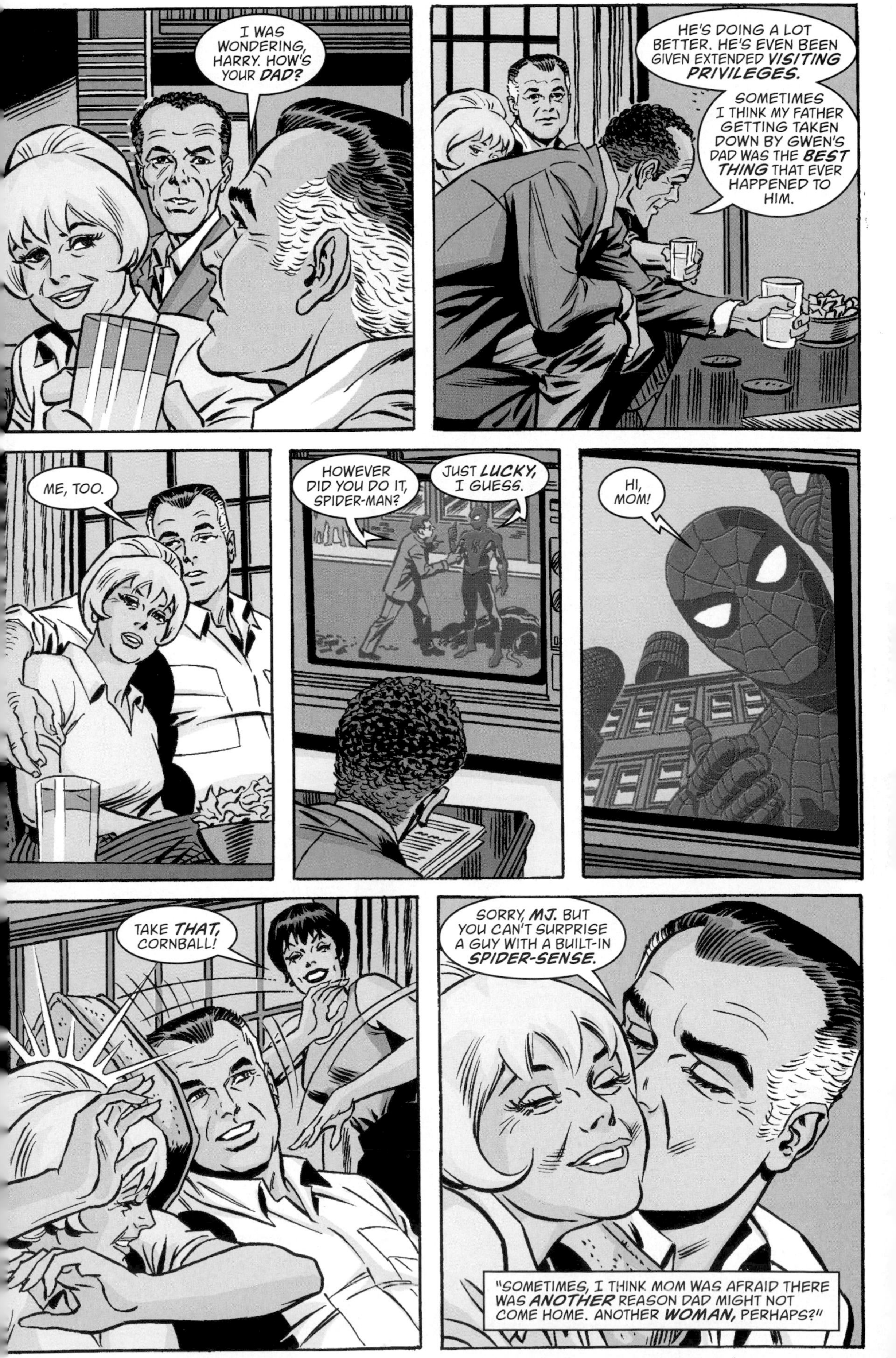
I WAS WONDERING, HARRY. HOW'S YOUR DAD?
HE'S DOING A LOT BETTER. HE'S EVEN BEEN GIVEN EXTENDED VISITING PRIVILEGES.
SOMETIMES I THINK MY FATHER GETTING TAKEN DOWN BY GWEN'S DAD WAS THE BEST THING THAT EVER HAPPENED TO HIM.
ME, TOO.
HOWEVER DID YOU DO IT, SPIDER-MAN?
JUST LUCKY, I GUESS.
HI, MOM!
TAKE THAT, CORNBALL!
SORRY, MJ. BUT YOU CAN'T SURPRISE A GUY WITH A BUILT-IN SPIDER-SENSE.
"SOMETIMES, I THINK MOM WAS AFRAID THERE WAS ANOTHER REASON DAD MIGHT NOT COME HOME. ANOTHER WOMAN, PERHAPS?"

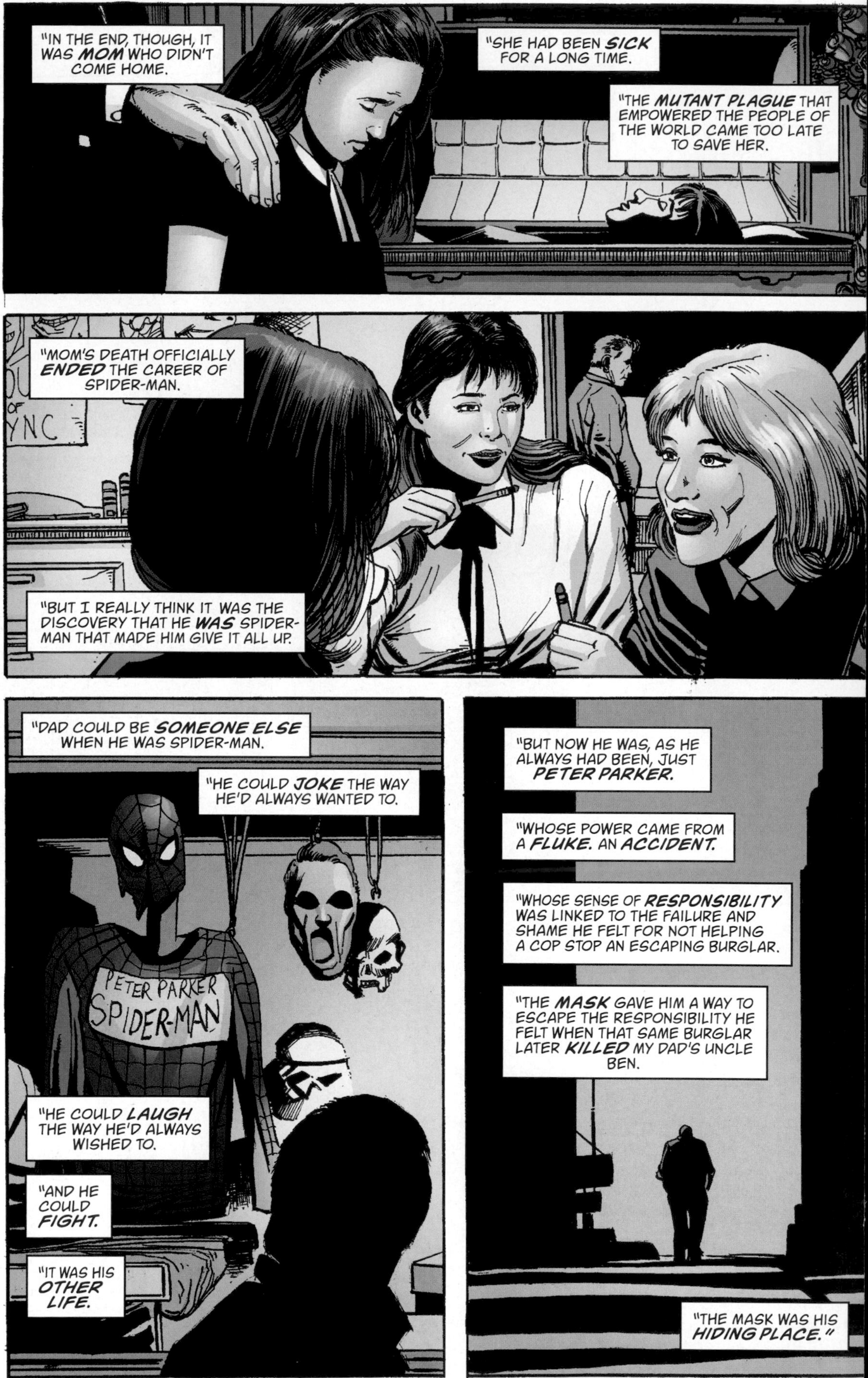
"IN THE END, THOUGH, IT WAS MOM WHO DIDN'T COME HOME.
"SHE HAD BEEN SICK FOR A LONG TIME.
"THE MUTANT PLAGUE THAT EMPOWERED THE PEOPLE OF THE WORLD CAME TOO LATE TO SAVE HER.
"MOM'S DEATH OFFICIALLY ENDED THE CAREER OF SPIDER-MAN.
"BUT I REALLY THINK IT WAS THE DISCOVERY THAT HE WAS SPIDER-MAN THAT MADE HIM GIVE IT ALL UP.
"DAD COULD BE SOMEONE ELSE WHEN HE WAS SPIDER-MAN.
"HE COULD JOKE THE WAY HE'D ALWAYS WANTED TO.
PETER PARKER SPIDER-MAN
"HE COULD LAUGH THE WAY HE'D ALWAYS WISHED TO.
"AND HE COULD FIGHT.
"IT WAS HIS OTHER LIFE.
"BUT NOW HE WAS, AS HE ALWAYS HAD BEEN, JUST PETER PARKER.
"WHOSE POWER CAME FROM A FLUKE. AN ACCIDENT.
"WHOSE SENSE OF RESPONSIBILITY WAS LINKED TO THE FAILURE AND SHAME HE FELT FOR NOT HELPING A COP STOP AN ESCAPING BURGLAR.
"THE MASK GAVE HIM A WAY TO ESCAPE THE RESPONSIBILITY HE FELT WHEN THAT SAME BURGLAR LATER KILLED MY DAD'S UNCLE BEN.
"THE MASK WAS HIS HIDING PLACE."

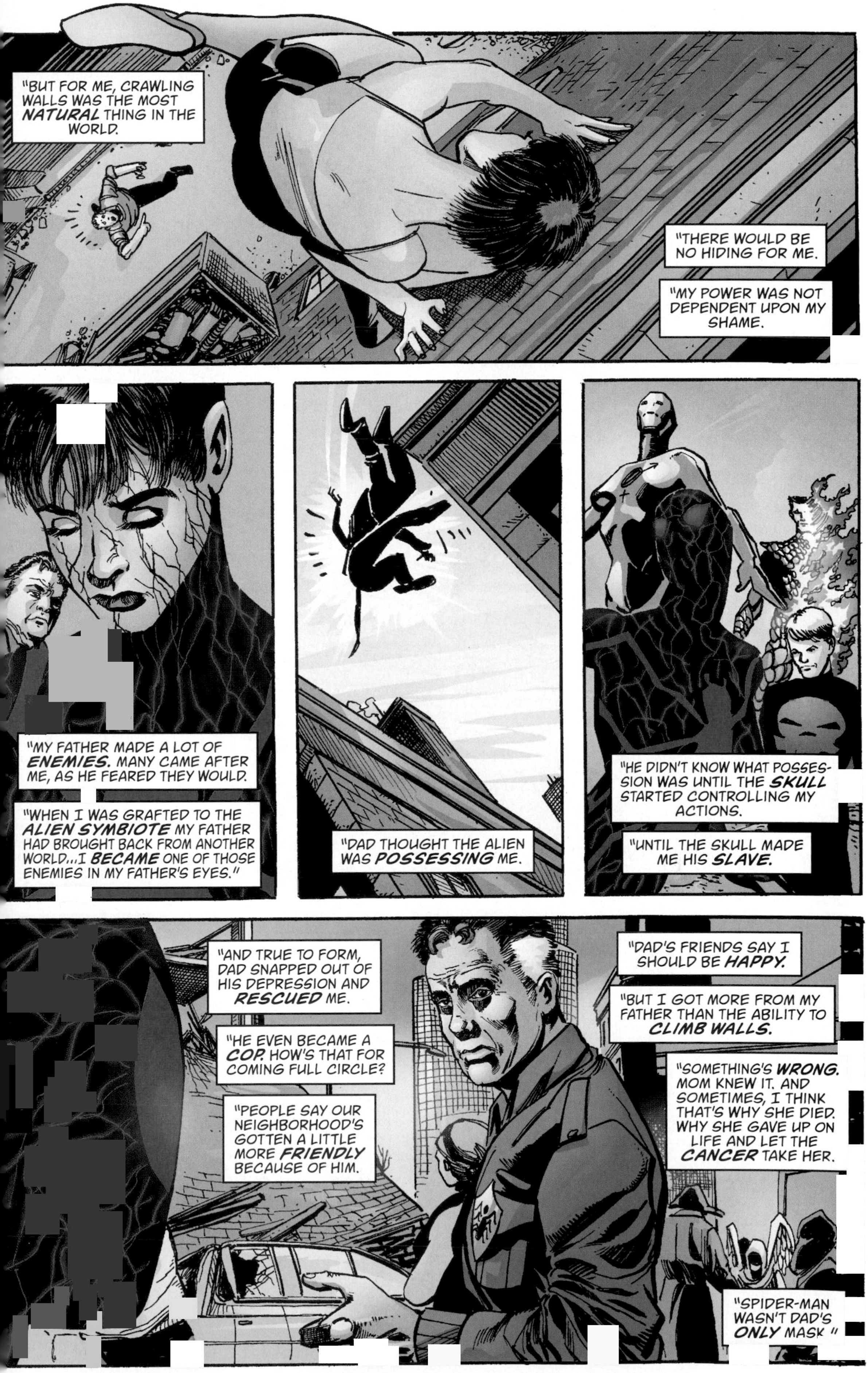
"BUT FOR ME, CRAWLING WALLS WAS THE MOST NATURAL THING IN THE WORLD.
"THERE WOULD BE NO HIDING FOR ME.
"MY POWER WAS NOT DEPENDENT UPON MY SHAME.
"MY FATHER MADE A LOT OF ENEMIES. MANY CAME AFTER ME, AS HE FEARED THEY WOULD.
"WHEN I WAS GRAFTED TO THE ALIEN SYMBIOTE MY FATHER HAD BROUGHT BACK FROM ANOTHER WORLD...I BECAME ONE OF THOSE ENEMIES IN MY FATHER'S EYES."
"DAD THOUGHT THE ALIEN WAS POSSESSING ME.
"HE DIDN'T KNOW WHAT POSSES-SION WAS UNTIL THE SKULL STARTED CONTROLLING MY ACTIONS.
"UNTIL THE SKULL MADE ME HIS SLAVE.
"AND TRUE TO FORM, DAD SNAPPED OUT OF HIS DEPRESSION AND RESCUED ME.
"HE EVEN BECAME A COP. HOW'S THAT FOR COMING FULL CIRCLE?
"PEOPLE SAY OUR NEIGHBORHOOD'S GOTTEN A LITTLE MORE FRIENDLY BECAUSE OF HIM.
"DAD'S FRIENDS SAY I SHOULD BE HAPPY.
"BUT I GOT MORE FROM MY FATHER THAN THE ABILITY TO CLIMB WALLS.
"SOMETHING'S WRONG. MOM KNEW IT. AND SOMETIMES, I THINK THAT'S WHY SHE DIED. WHY SHE GAVE UP ON LIFE AND LET THE CANCER TAKE HER.
"SPIDER-MAN WASN'T DAD'S ONLY MASK."

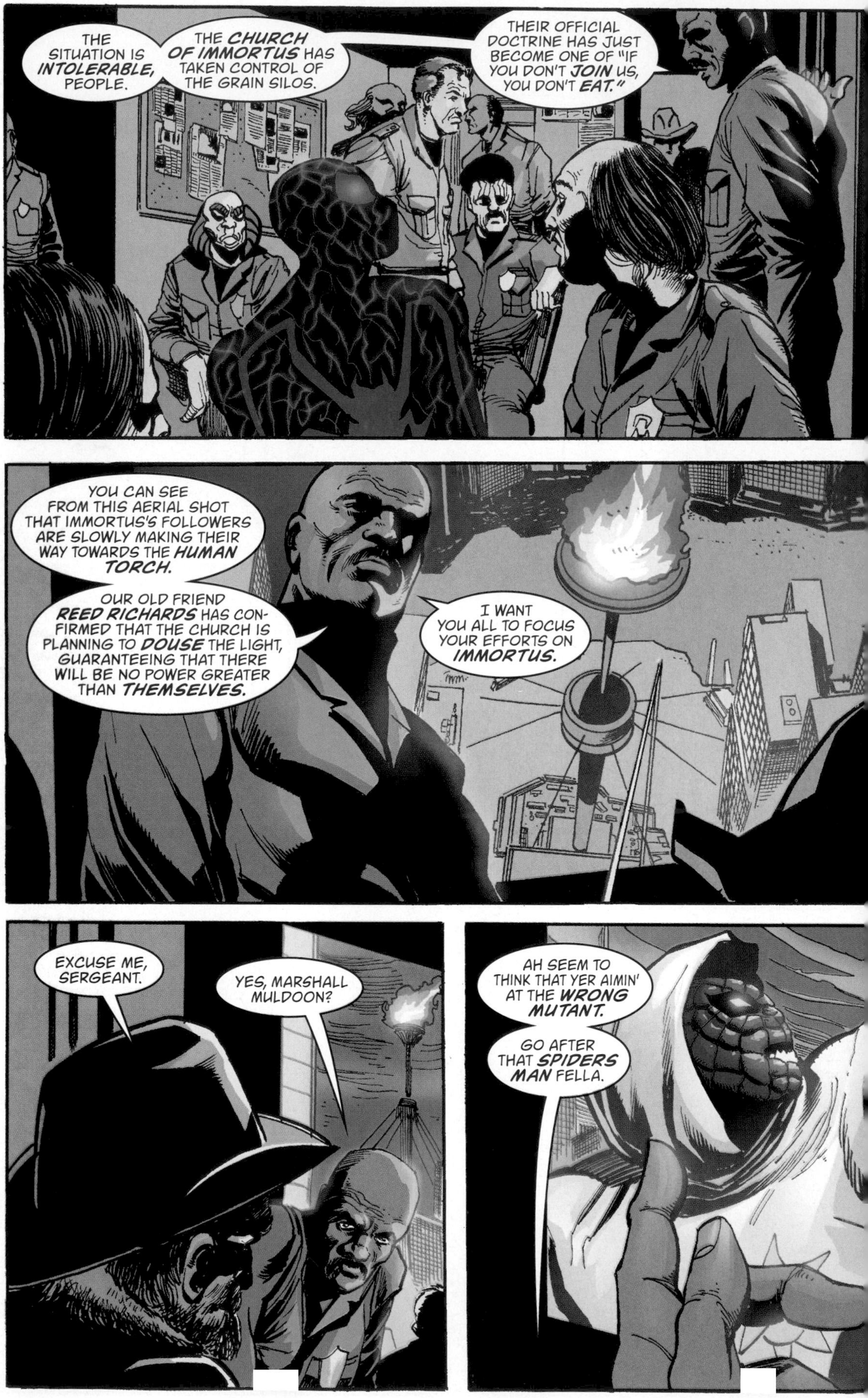
THE SITUATION IS INTOLERABLE, PEOPLE.
THE CHURCH OF IMMORTUS HAS TAKEN CONTROL OF THE GRAIN SILOS.
THEIR OFFICIAL DOCTRINE HAS JUST BECOME ONE OF "IF YOU DON'T JOIN US, YOU DON'T EAT."
YOU CAN SEE FROM THIS AERIAL SHOT THAT IMMORTUS'S FOLLOWERS ARE SLOWLY MAKING THEIR WAY TOWARDS THE HUMAN TORCH.
OUR OLD FRIEND REED RICHARDS HAS CONFIRMED THAT THE CHURCH IS PLANNING TO DOUSE THE LIGHT, GUARANTEEING THAT THERE WILL BE NO POWER GREATER THAN THEMSELVES.
I WANT YOU ALL TO FOCUS YOUR EFFORTS ON IMMORTUS.
EXCUSE ME, SERGEANT.
YES, MARSHALL MULDOON?
AH SEEM TO THINK THAT YER AIMIN' AT THE WRONG MUTANT.
GO AFTER THAT SPIDERS MAN FELLA.

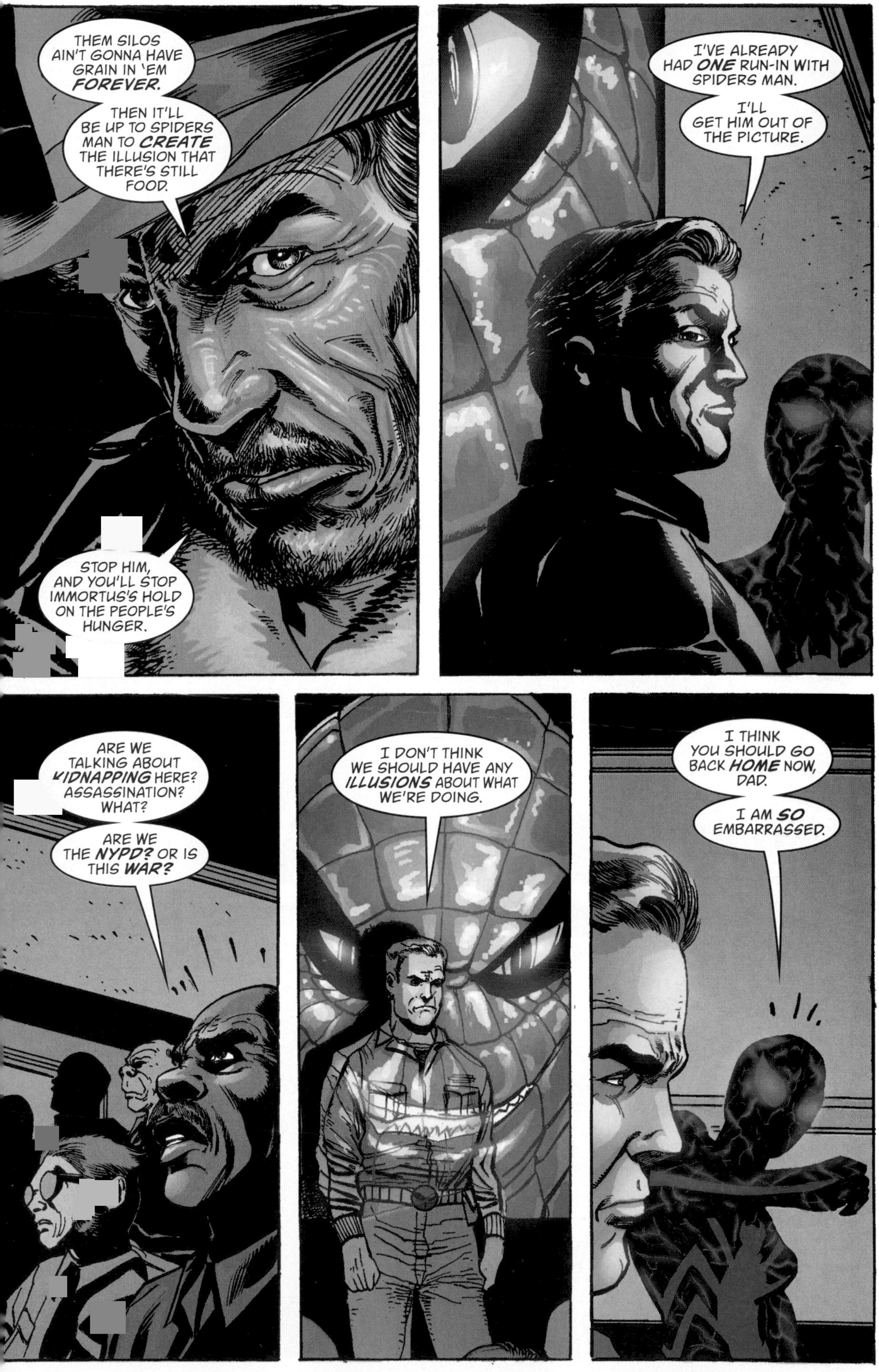
THEM SILOS AIN'T GONNA HAVE GRAIN IN 'EM FOREVER.
THEN IT'LL BE UP TO SPIDERS MAN TO CREATE THE ILLUSION THAT THERE'S STILL FOOD.
STOP HIM, AND YOU'LL STOP IMMORTUS'S HOLD ON THE PEOPLE'S HUNGER.
I'VE ALREADY HAD ONE RUN-IN WITH SPIDERS MAN.
I'LL GET HIM OUT OF THE PICTURE.
ARE WE TALKING ABOUT KIDNAPPING HERE? ASSASSINATION? WHAT?
ARE WE THE NYPD? OR IS THIS WAR?
I DON'T THINK WE SHOULD HAVE ANY ILLUSIONS ABOUT WHAT WE'RE DOING.
I THINK YOU SHOULD GO BACK HOME NOW, DAD.
I AM SO EMBARRASSED.

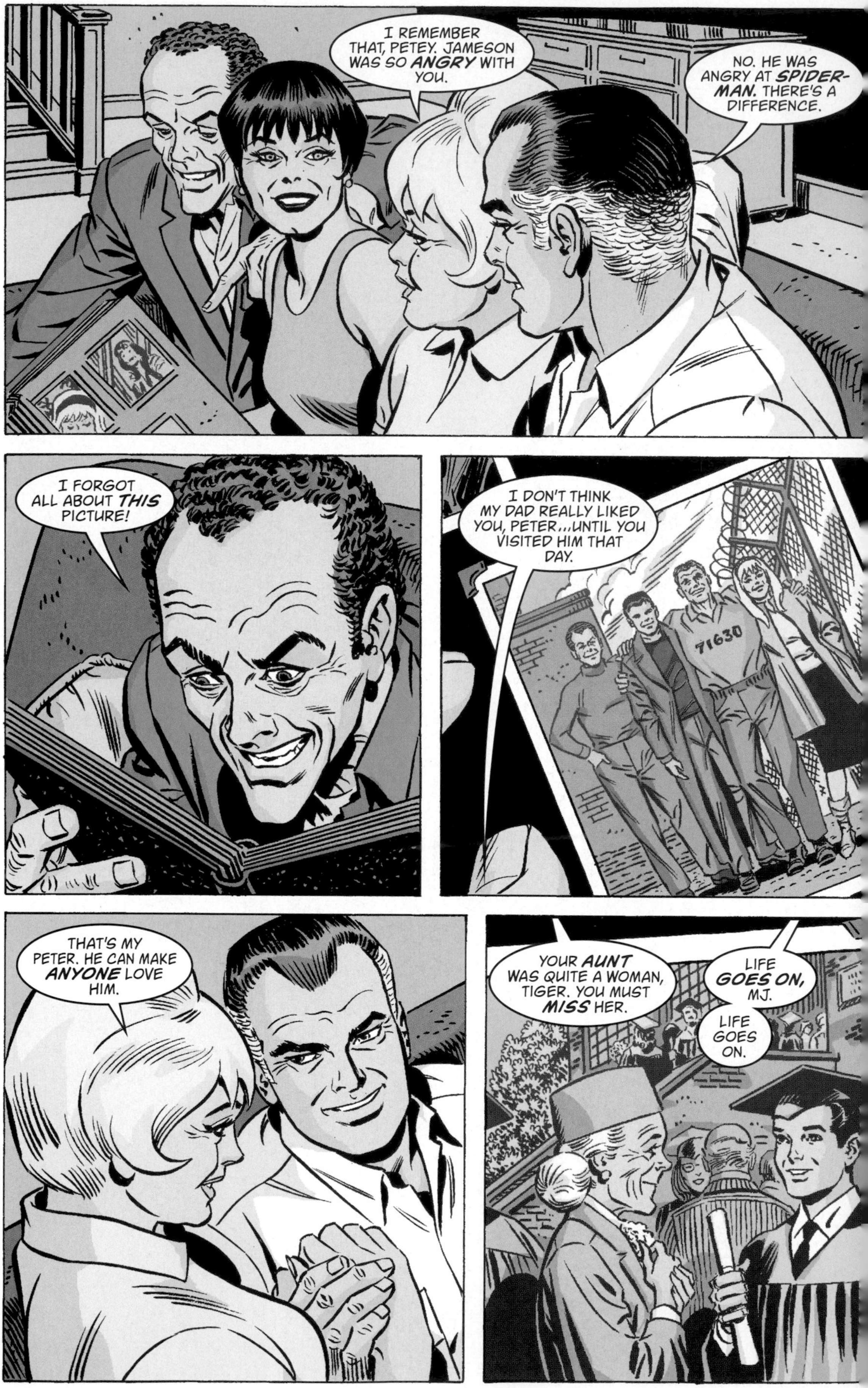
I REMEMBER THAT, PETEY. JAMESON WAS SO ANGRY WITH YOU.
NO. HE WAS ANGRY AT SPIDER-MAN. THERE'S A DIFFERENCE.
I FORGOT ALL ABOUT THIS PICTURE!
I DON'T THINK MY DAD REALLY LIKED YOU, PETER...UNTIL YOU VISITED HIM THAT DAY.
71630
THAT'S MY PETER. HE CAN MAKE ANYONE LOVE HIM.
YOUR AUNT WAS QUITE A WOMAN, TIGER. YOU MUST MISS HER.
LIFE GOES ON, MJ.
LIFE GOES ON.

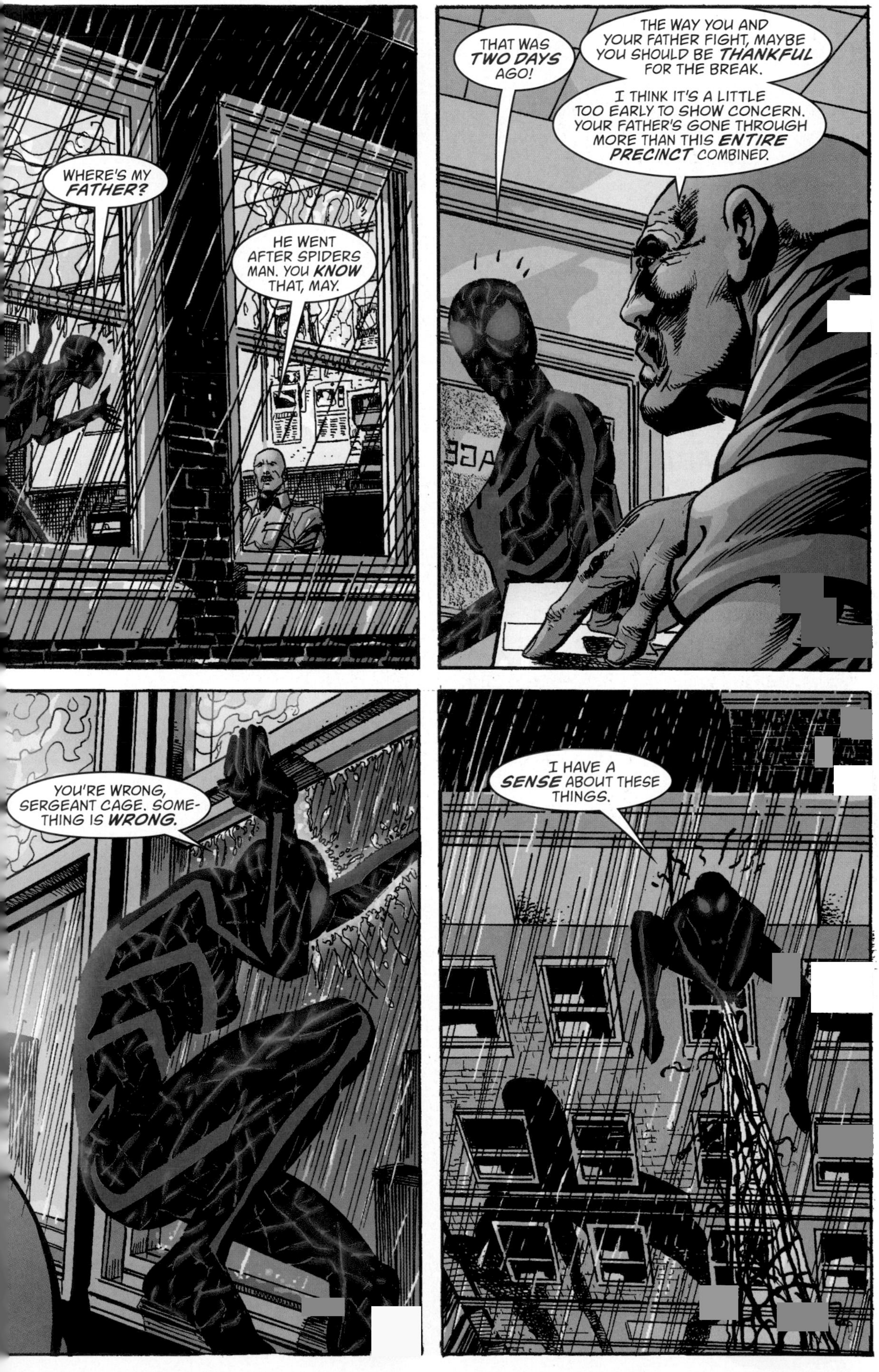
WHERE'S MY FATHER?
HE WENT AFTER SPIDERS MAN. YOU KNOW THAT, MAY.
THAT WAS TWO DAYS AGO!
THE WAY YOU AND YOUR FATHER FIGHT, MAYBE YOU SHOULD BE THANKFUL FOR THE BREAK.
I THINK IT'S A LITTLE TOO EARLY TO SHOW CONCERN. YOUR FATHER'S GONE THROUGH MORE THAN THIS ENTIRE PRECINCT COMBINED.
YOU'RE WRONG, SERGEANT CAGE. SOMETHING IS WRONG.
I HAVE A SENSE ABOUT THESE THINGS.

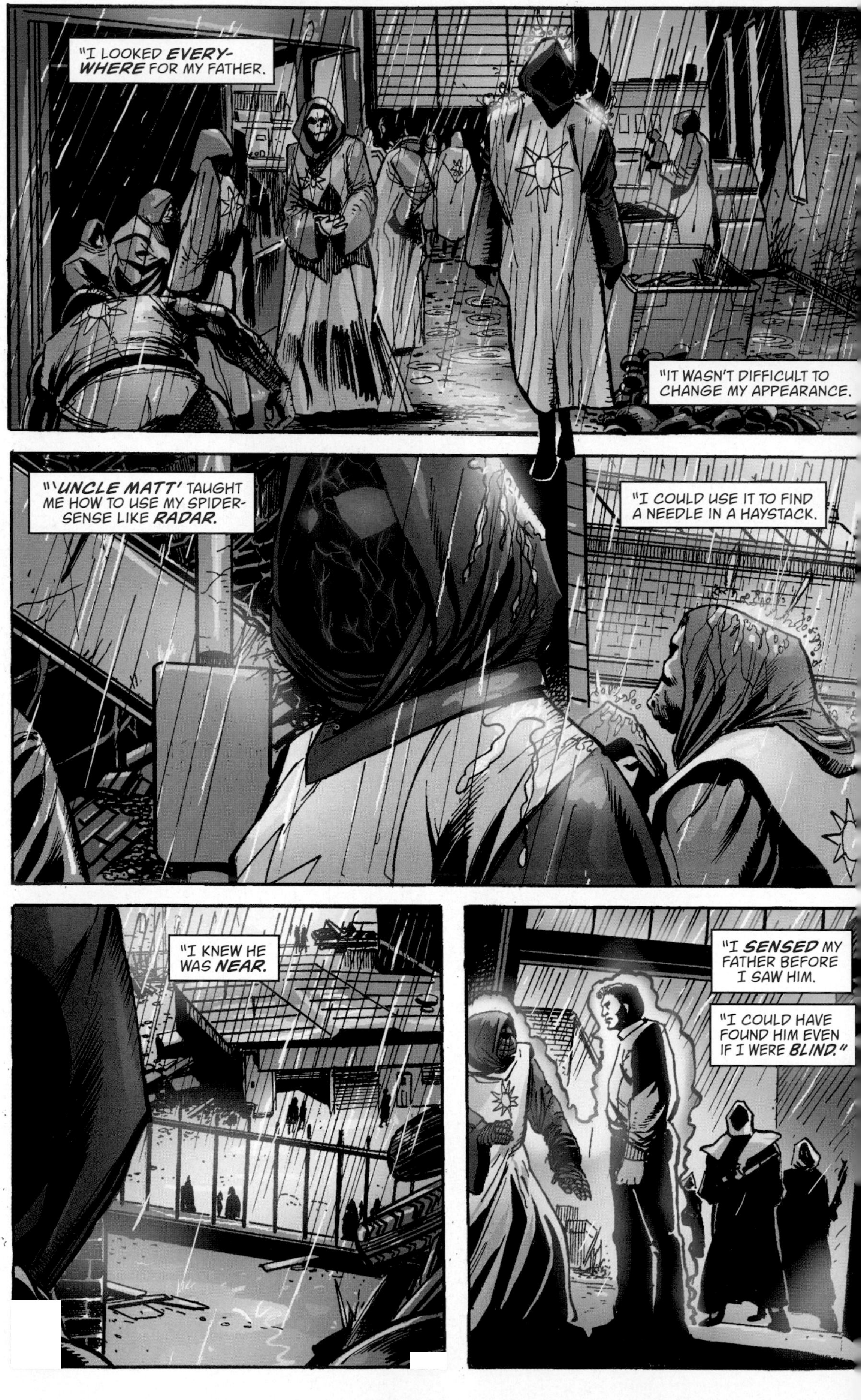
"I LOOKED EVERY-WHERE FOR MY FATHER.
"IT WASN'T DIFFICULT TO CHANGE MY APPEARANCE.
"'UNCLE MATT' TAUGHT ME HOW TO USE MY SPIDER-SENSE LIKE RADAR.
"I COULD USE IT TO FIND A NEEDLE IN A HAYSTACK.
"I KNEW HE WAS NEAR.
"I SENSED MY FATHER BEFORE I SAW HIM.
"I COULD HAVE FOUND HIM EVEN IF I WERE BLIND."

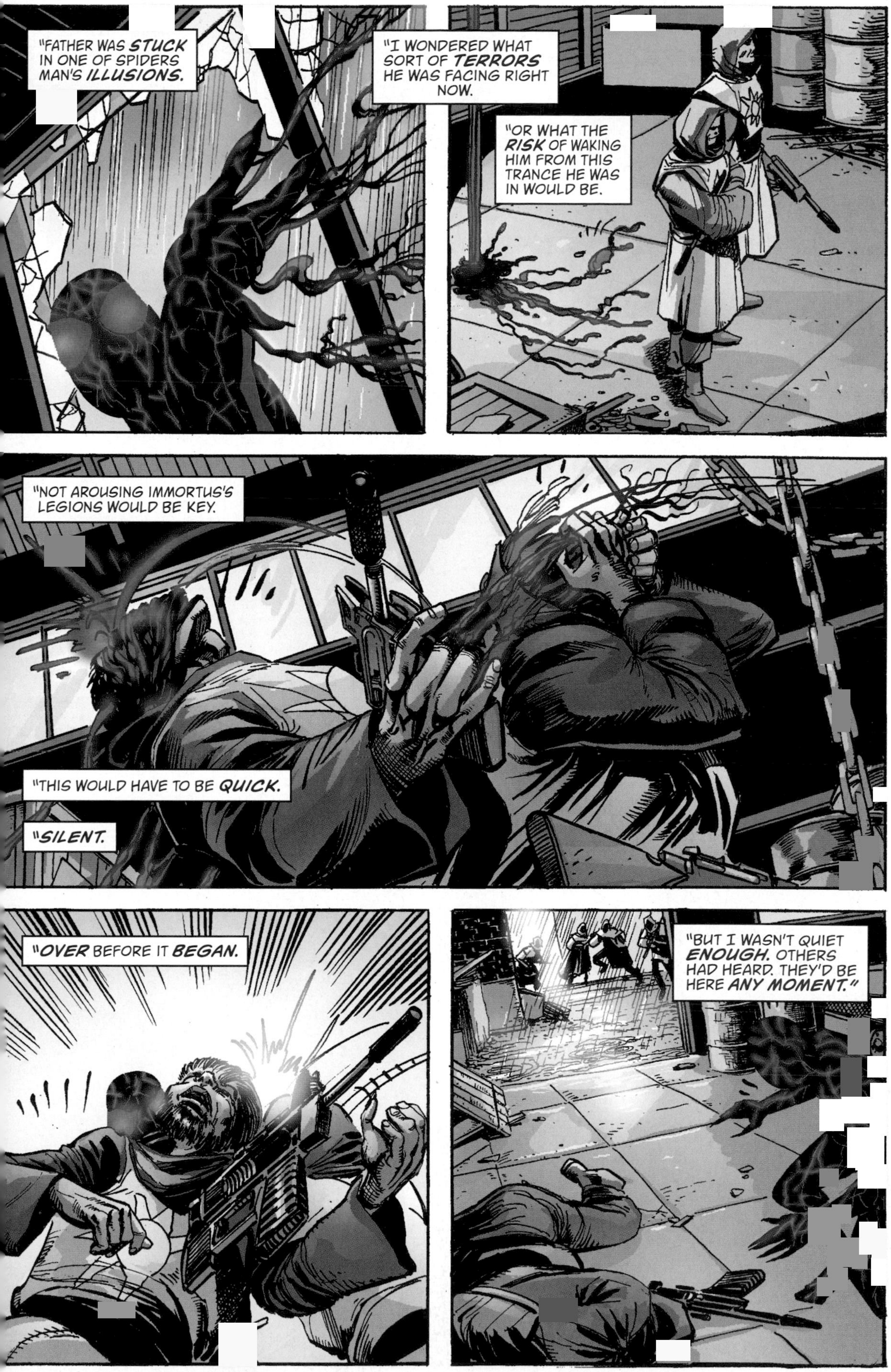
"FATHER WAS STUCK IN ONE OF SPIDERS MAN'S ILLUSIONS.
"I WONDERED WHAT SORT OF TERRORS HE WAS FACING RIGHT NOW.
"OR WHAT THE RISK OF WAKING HIM FROM THIS TRANCE HE WAS IN WOULD BE.
"NOT AROUSING IMMORTUS'S LEGIONS WOULD BE KEY.
"THIS WOULD HAVE TO BE QUICK.
"SILENT.
"OVER BEFORE IT BEGAN.
"BUT I WASN'T QUIET ENOUGH. OTHERS HAD HEARD. THEY'D BE HERE ANY MOMENT."

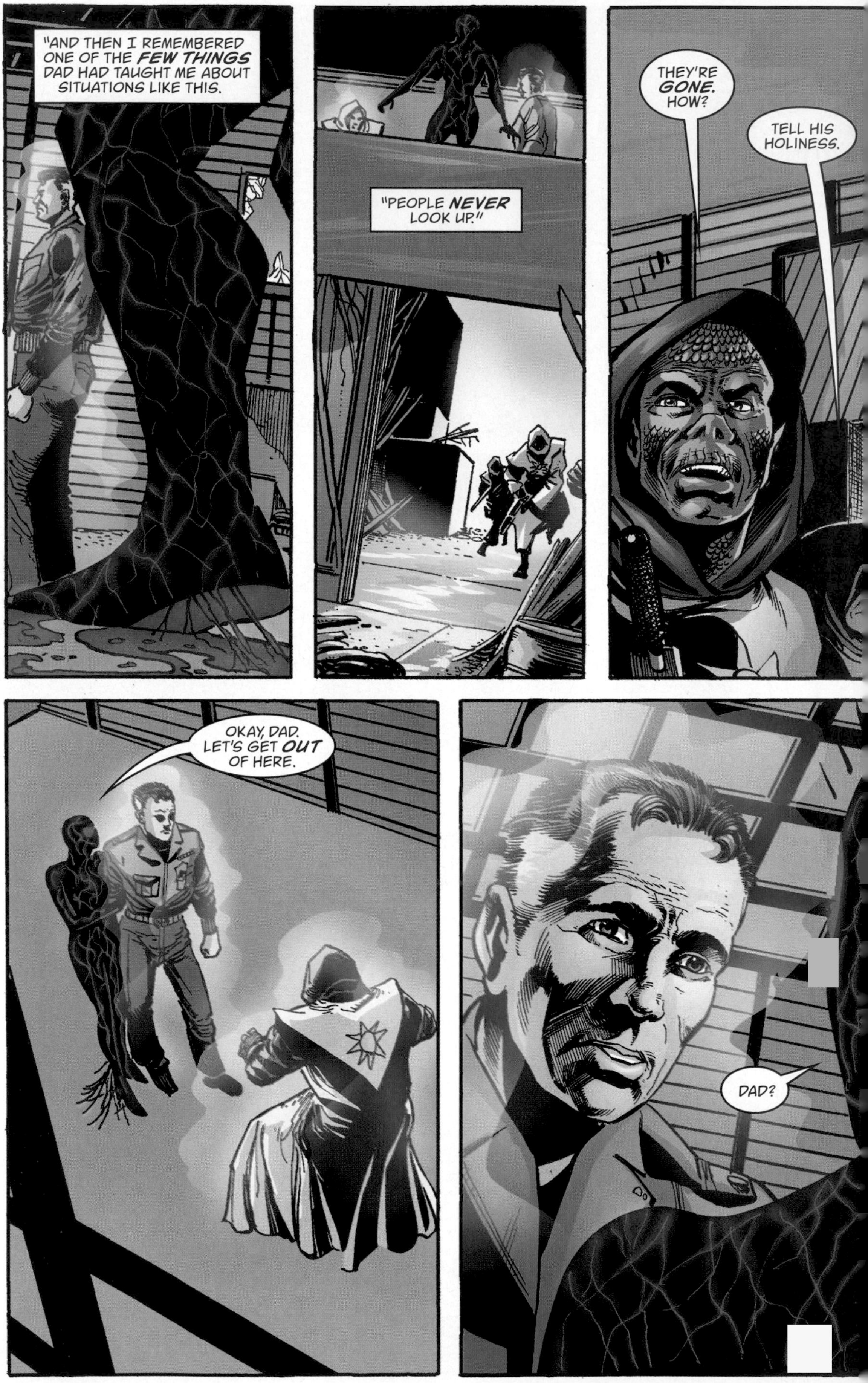
"AND THEN I REMEMBERED ONE OF THE FEW THINGS DAD HAD TAUGHT ME ABOUT SITUATIONS LIKE THIS.
"PEOPLE NEVER LOOK UP."
THEY'RE GONE. HOW?
TELL HIS HOLINESS.
OKAY, DAD. LET'S GET OUT OF HERE.
DAD?

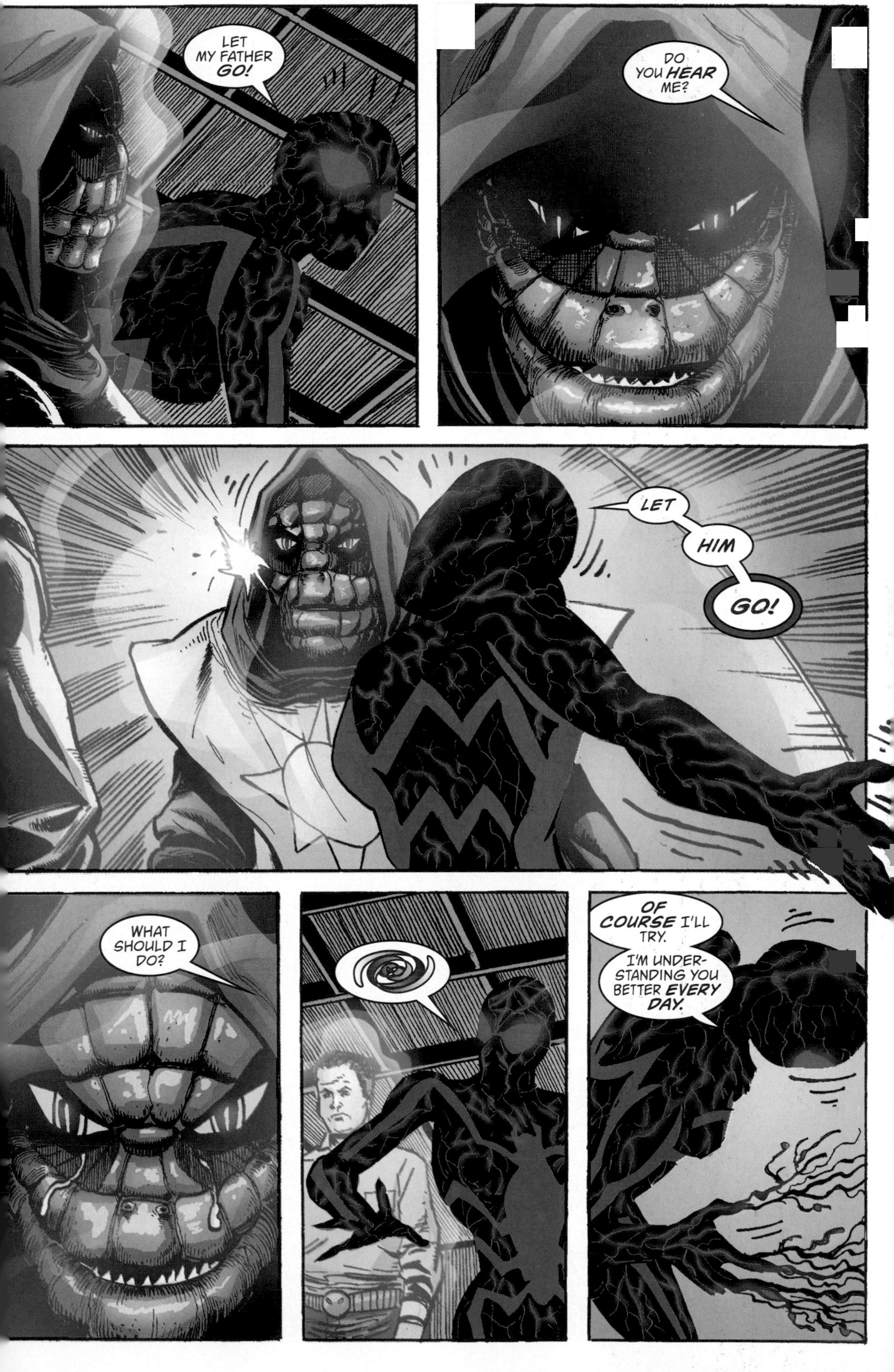
LET MY FATHER GO!
DO YOU HEAR ME?
LET
HIM
GO!
WHAT SHOULD I DO?
OF COURSE I'LL TRY.
I'M UNDER-STANDING YOU BETTER EVERY DAY.

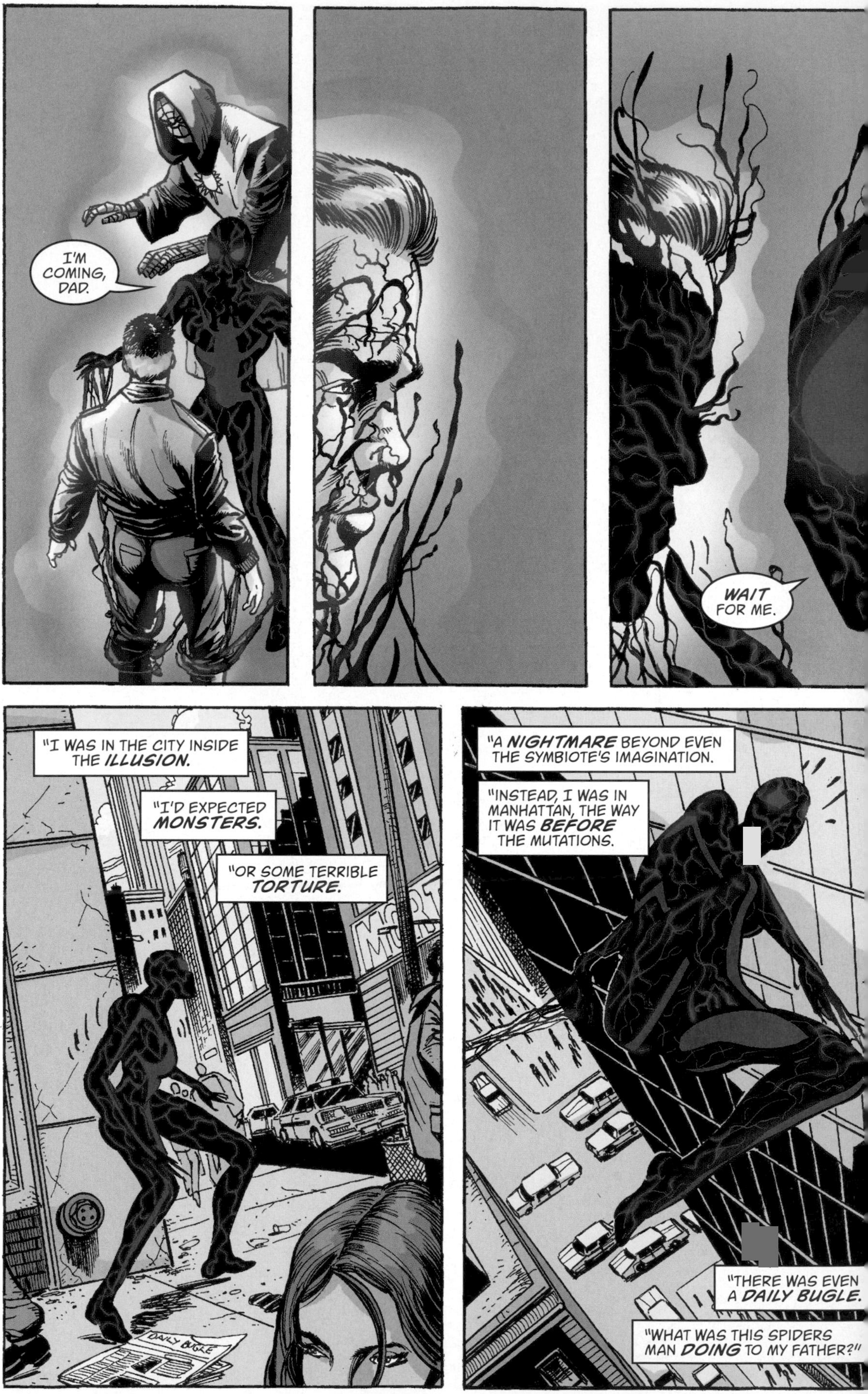
I'M COMING, DAD.
WAIT FOR ME.
"I WAS IN THE CITY INSIDE THE ILLUSION.
"I'D EXPECTED MONSTERS.
"OR SOME TERRIBLE TORTURE.
DAILY BUGLE
"A NIGHTMARE BEYOND EVEN THE SYMBIOTE'S IMAGINATION.
"INSTEAD, I WAS IN MANHATTAN, THE WAY IT WAS BEFORE THE MUTATIONS.
"THERE WAS EVEN A DAILY BUGLE.
"WHAT WAS THIS SPIDERS MAN DOING TO MY FATHER?"

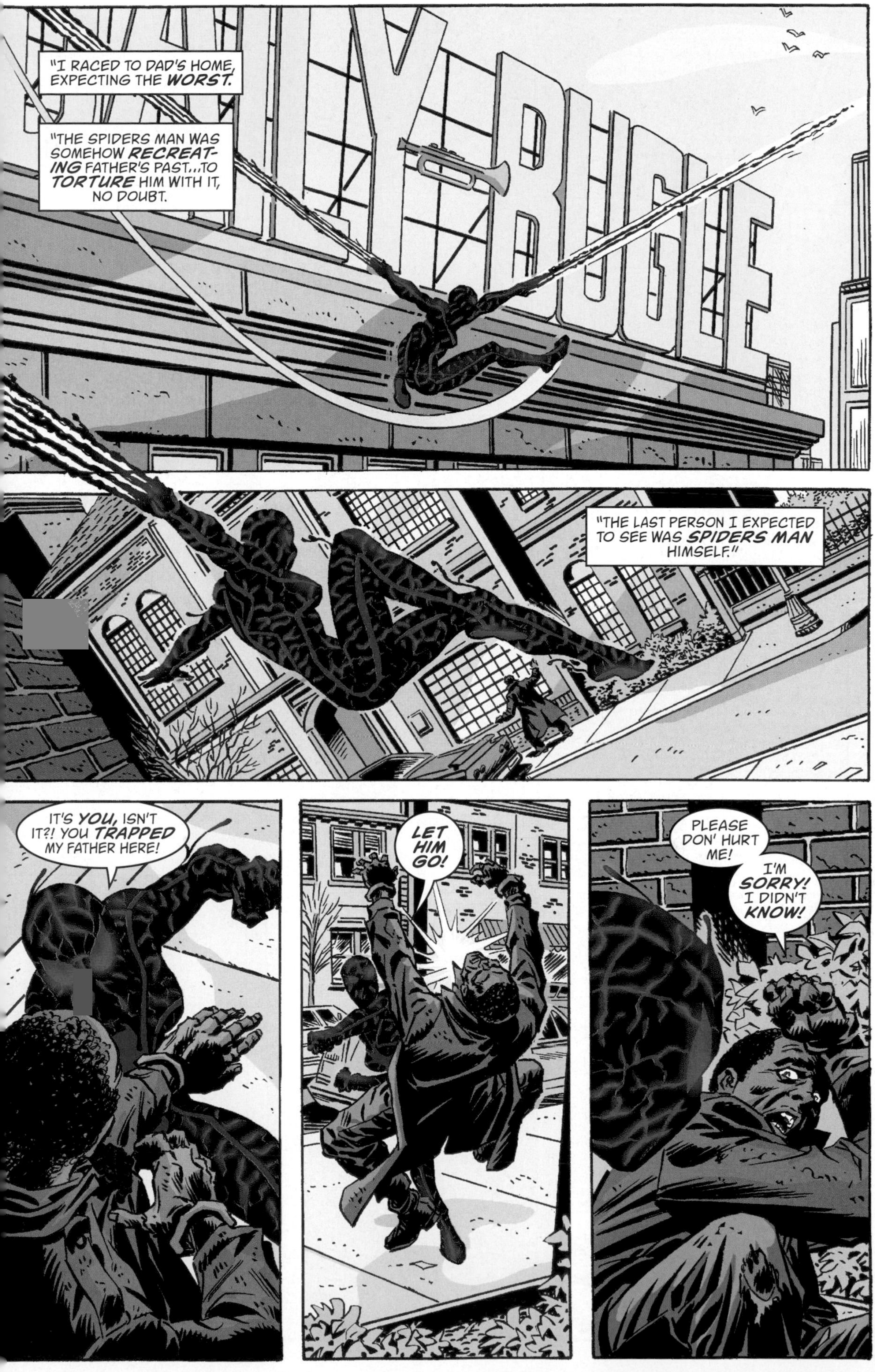
"I RACED TO DAD'S HOME, EXPECTING THE WORST.
"THE SPIDERS MAN WAS SOMEHOW RECREATING FATHER'S PAST...TO TORTURE HIM WITH IT, NO DOUBT.
"THE LAST PERSON I EXPECTED TO SEE WAS SPIDERS MAN HIMSELF."
IT'S YOU, ISN'T IT?! YOU TRAPPED MY FATHER HERE!
LET HIM GO!
PLEASE DON' HURT ME!
I'M SORRY! I DIDN'T KNOW!

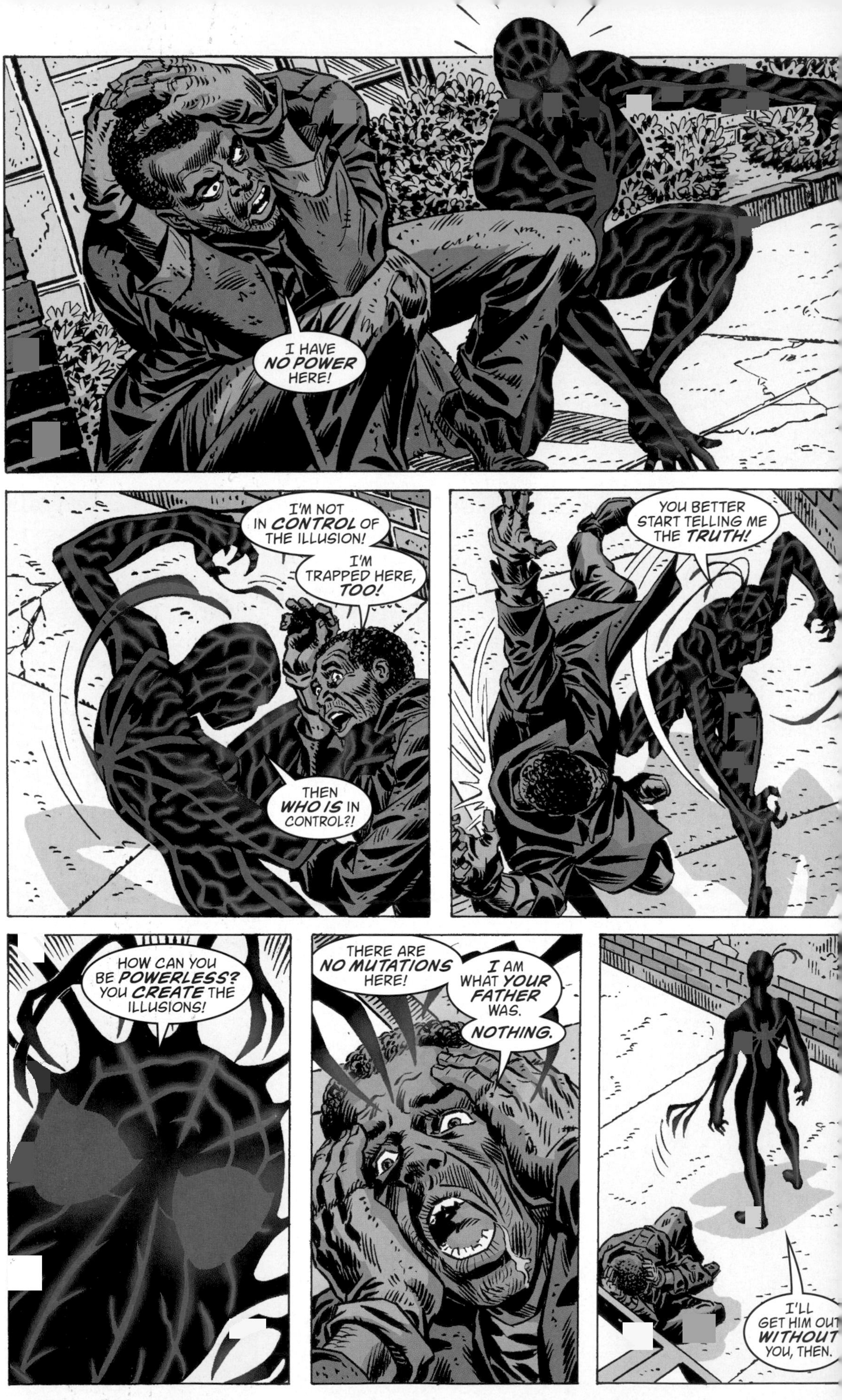
I HAVE NO POWER HERE!
I'M NOT IN CONTROL OF THE ILLUSION!
I'M TRAPPED HERE, TOO!
THEN WHO IS IN CONTROL?!
YOU BETTER START TELLING ME THE TRUTH!
HOW CAN YOU BE POWERLESS? YOU CREATE THE ILLUSIONS!
THERE ARE NO MUTATIONS HERE!
I AM WHAT YOUR FATHER WAS.
NOTHING.
I'LL GET HIM OUT WITHOUT YOU, THEN.

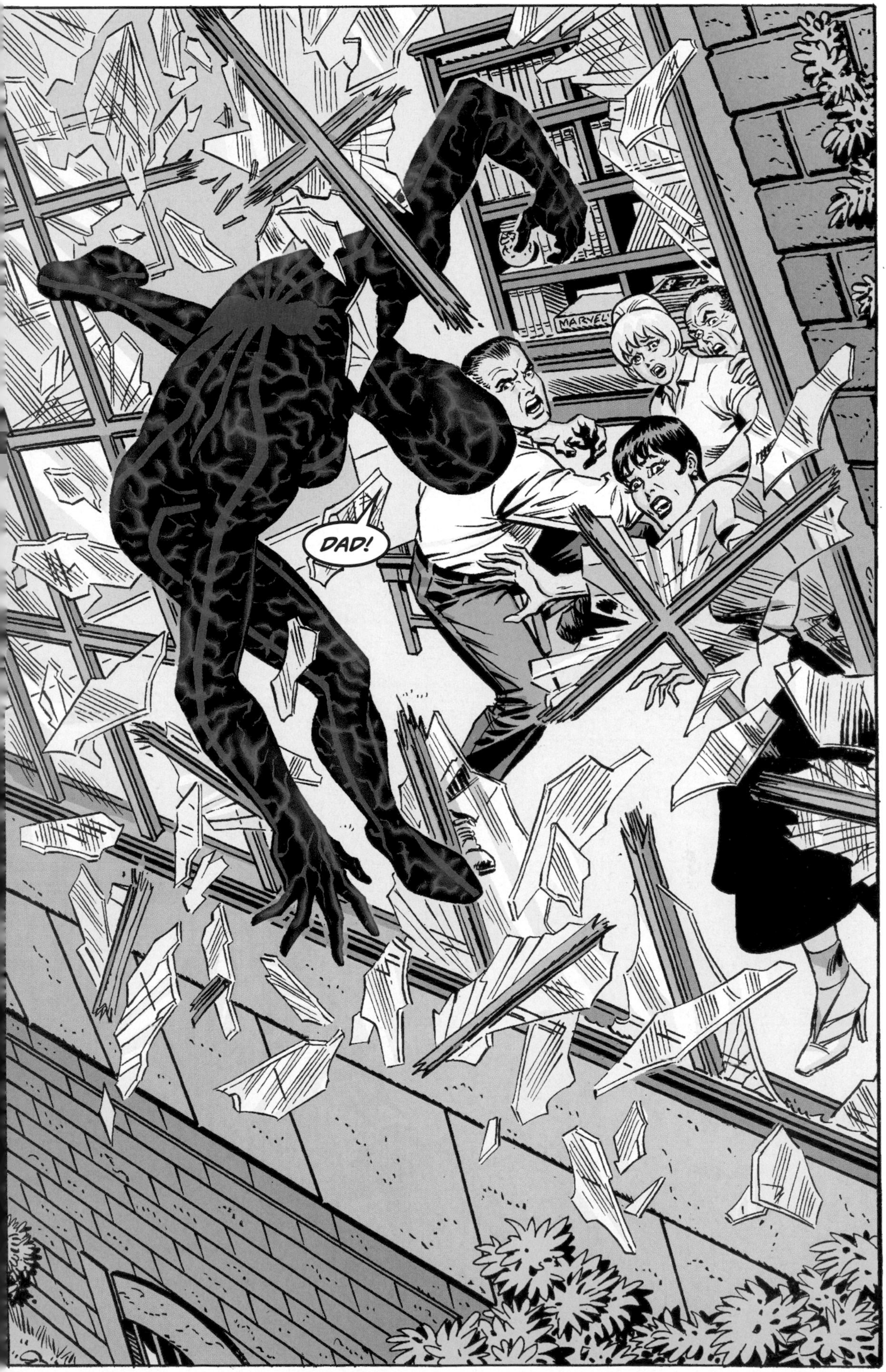
DAD!

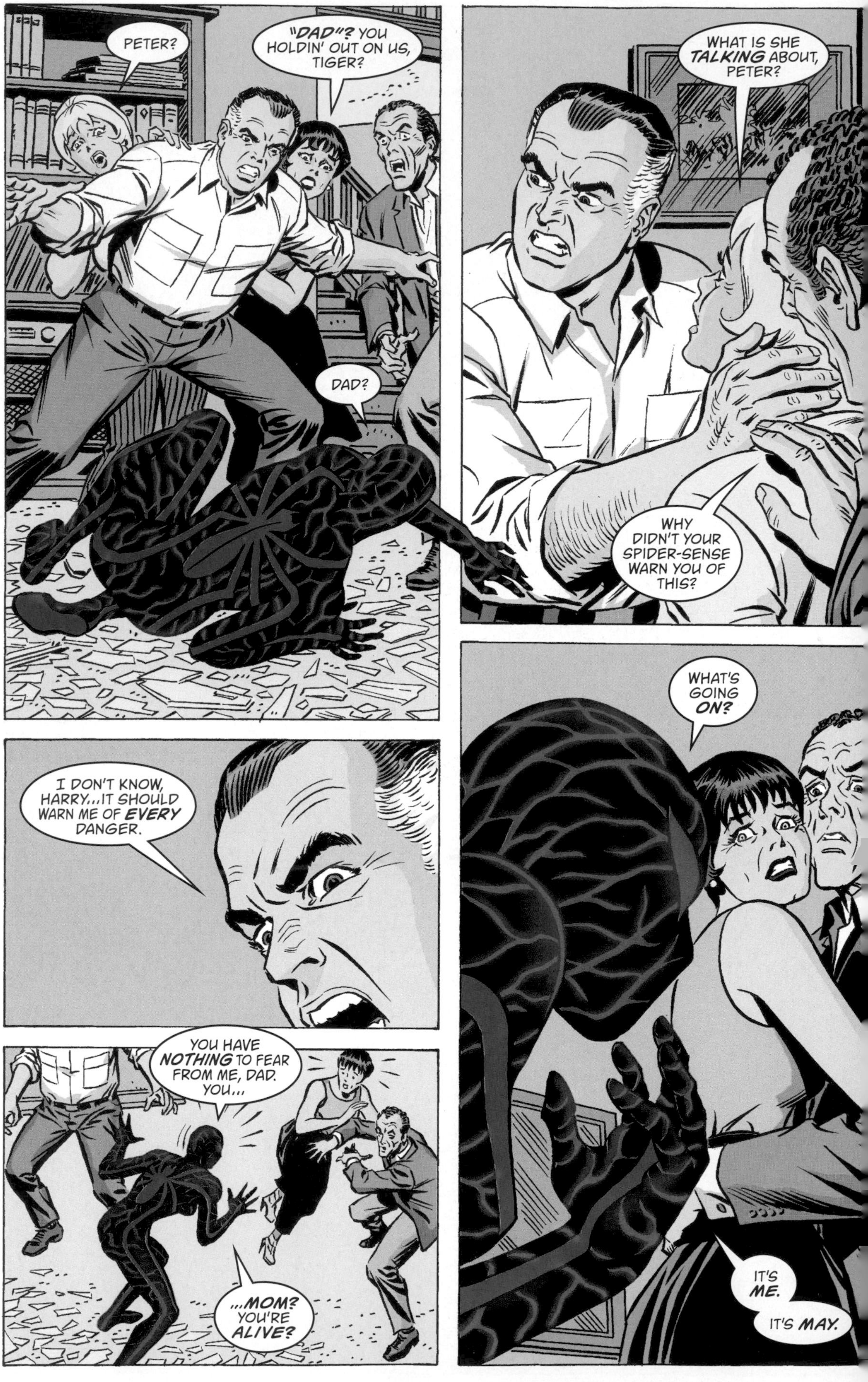
PETER?
"DAD"? YOU HOLDIN' OUT ON US, TIGER?
DAD?
WHAT IS SHE TALKING ABOUT, PETER?
WHY DIDN'T YOUR SPIDER-SENSE WARN YOU OF THIS?
I DON'T KNOW, HARRY...IT SHOULD WARN ME OF EVERY DANGER.
YOU HAVE NOTHING TO FEAR FROM ME, DAD. YOU...
...MOM? YOU'RE ALIVE?
WHAT'S GOING ON?
IT'S ME.
IT'S MAY.

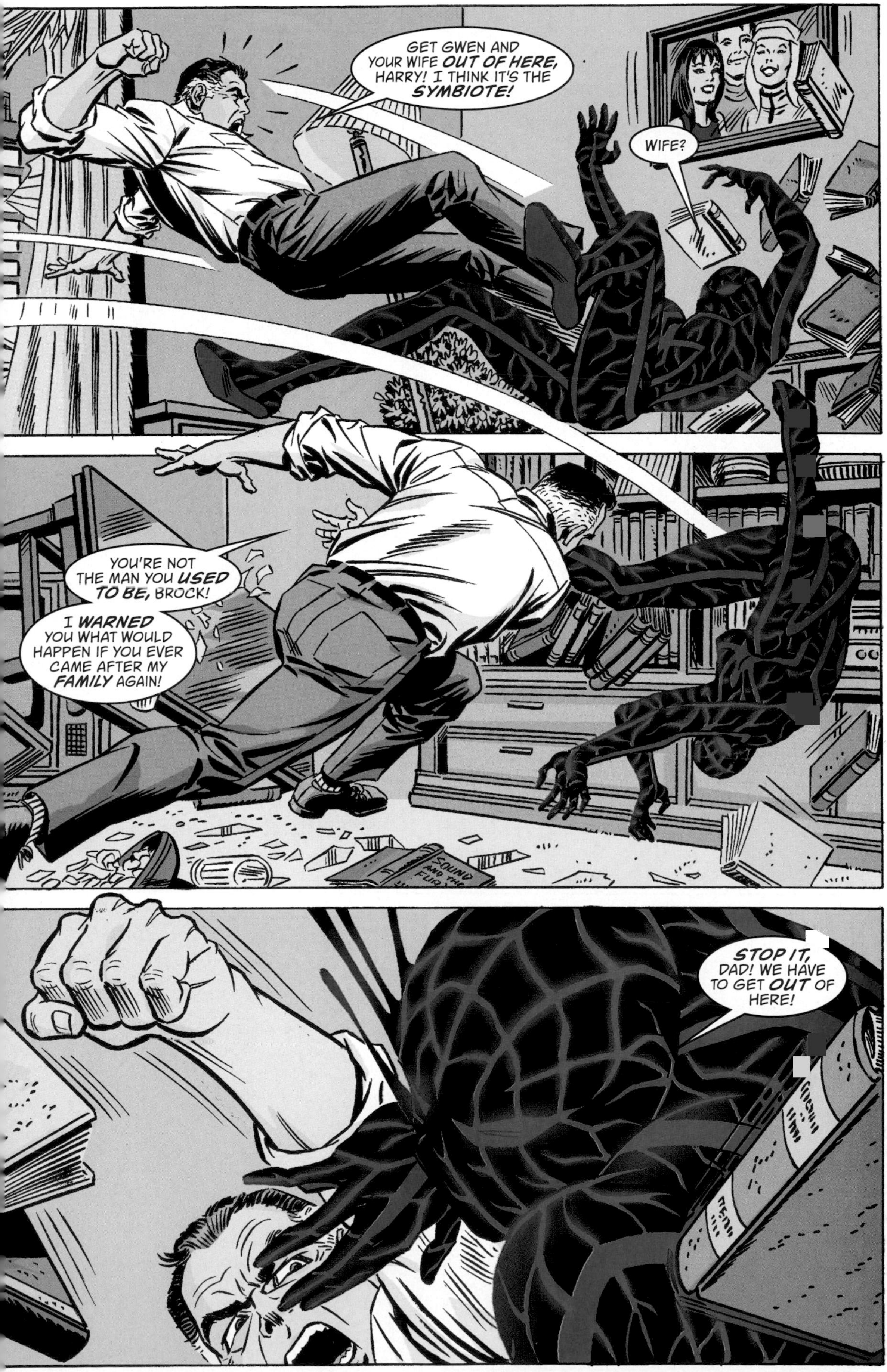
GET GWEN AND YOUR WIFE OUT OF HERE, HARRY! I THINK IT'S THE SYMBIOTE!
WIFE?
YOU'RE NOT THE MAN YOU USED TO BE, BROCK!
I WARNED YOU WHAT WOULD HAPPEN IF YOU EVER CAME AFTER MY FAMILY AGAIN!
STOP IT, DAD! WE HAVE TO GET OUT OF HERE!

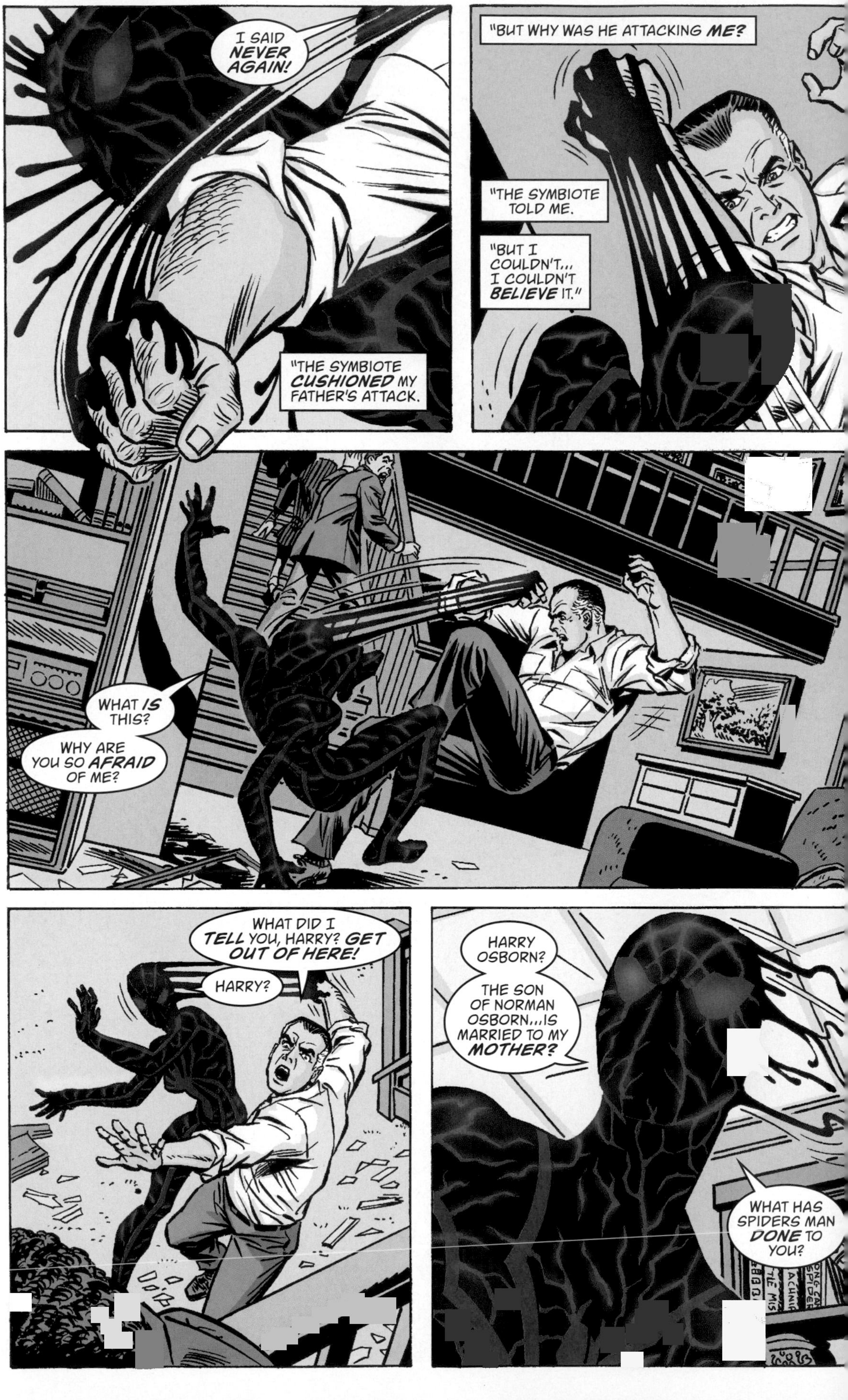
I SAID NEVER AGAIN!
"THE SYMBIOTE CUSHIONED MY FATHER'S ATTACK.
"BUT WHY WAS HE ATTACKING ME?
"THE SYMBIOTE TOLD ME.
"BUT I COULDN'T... I COULDN'T BELIEVE IT."
WHAT IS THIS?
WHY ARE YOU SO AFRAID OF ME?
WHAT DID I TELL YOU, HARRY? GET OUT OF HERE!
HARRY?
HARRY OSBORN?
THE SON OF NORMAN OSBORN...IS MARRIED TO MY MOTHER?
WHAT HAS SPIDERS MAN DONE TO YOU?

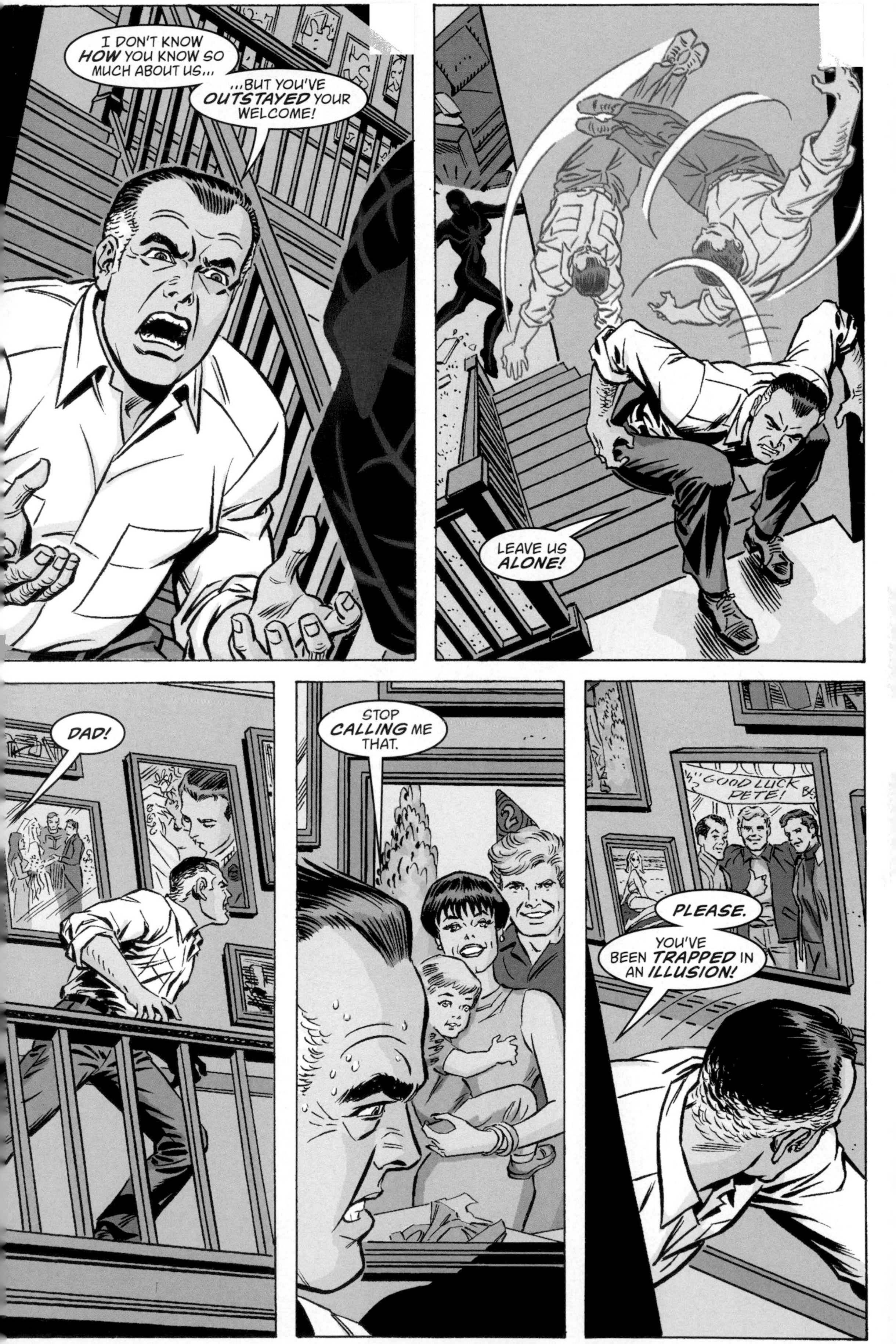
I DON'T KNOW HOW YOU KNOW SO MUCH ABOUT US...
...BUT YOU'VE OUTSTAYED YOUR WELCOME!
LEAVE US ALONE!
DAD!
STOP CALLING ME THAT.
GOOD LUCK PETE!
PLEASE.
YOU'VE BEEN TRAPPED IN AN ILLUSION!

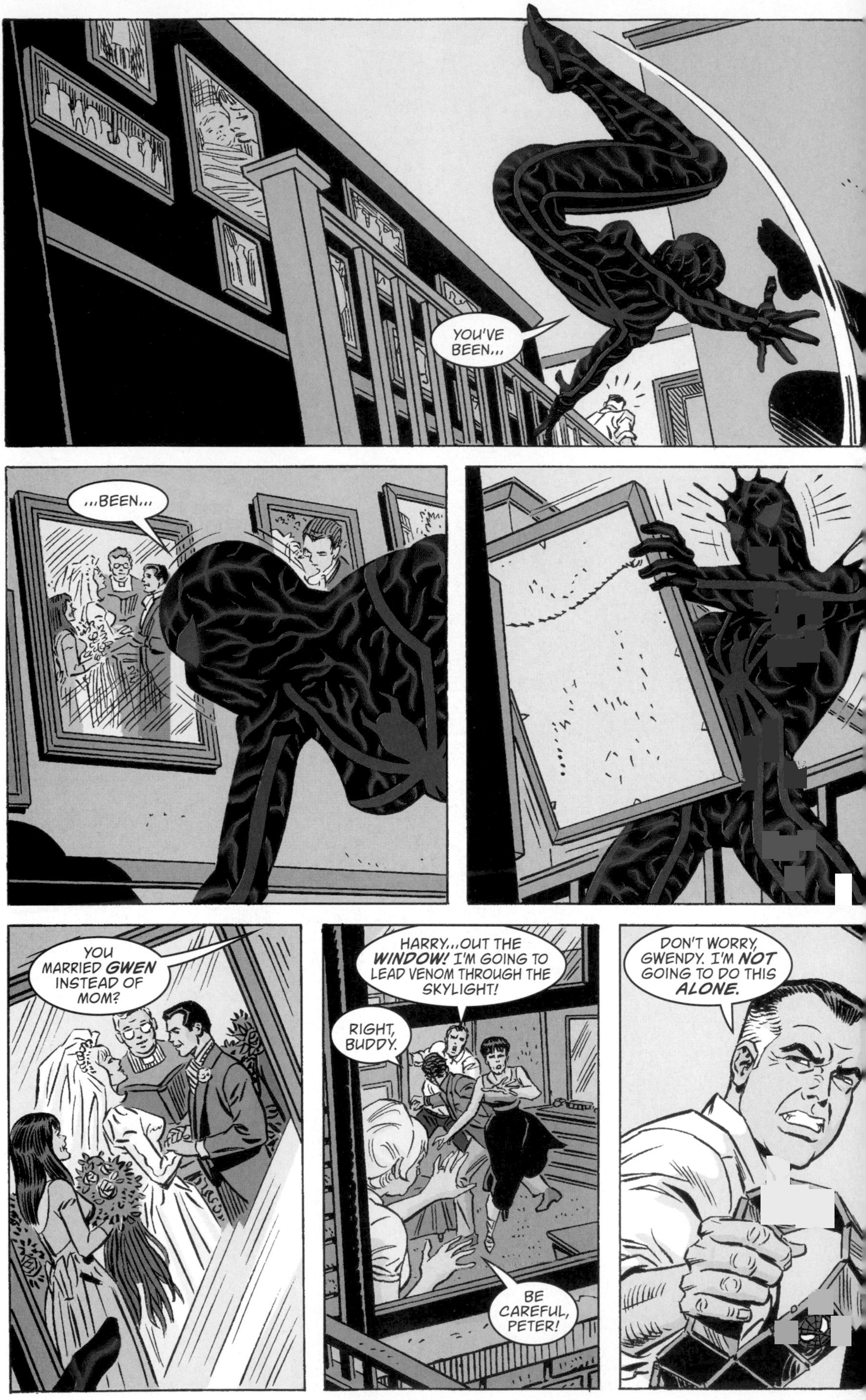
YOU'VE BEEN...
...BEEN...
YOU MARRIED GWEN INSTEAD OF MOM?
HARRY...OUT THE WINDOW! I'M GOING TO LEAD VENOM THROUGH THE SKYLIGHT!
RIGHT, BUDDY.
BE CAREFUL, PETER!
DON'T WORRY, GWENDY. I'M NOT GOING TO DO THIS ALONE.

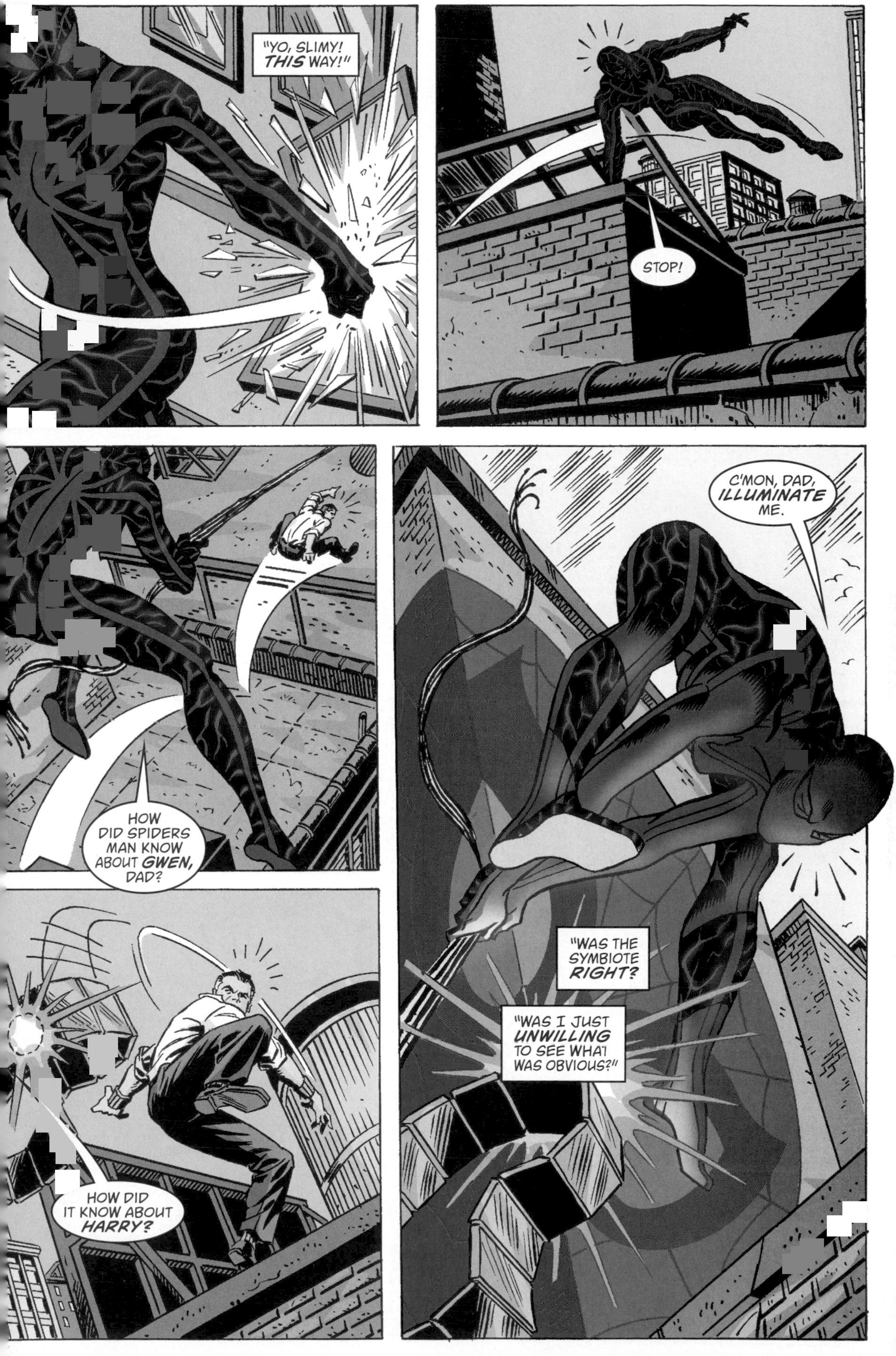

"YO, SLIMY! THIS WAY!"
STOP!
HOW DID SPIDERS MAN KNOW ABOUT GWEN, DAD?
HOW DID IT KNOW ABOUT HARRY?
C'MON, DAD, ILLUMINATE ME.
"WAS THE SYMBIOTE RIGHT?
"WAS I JUST UNWILLING TO SEE WHAT WAS OBVIOUS?"

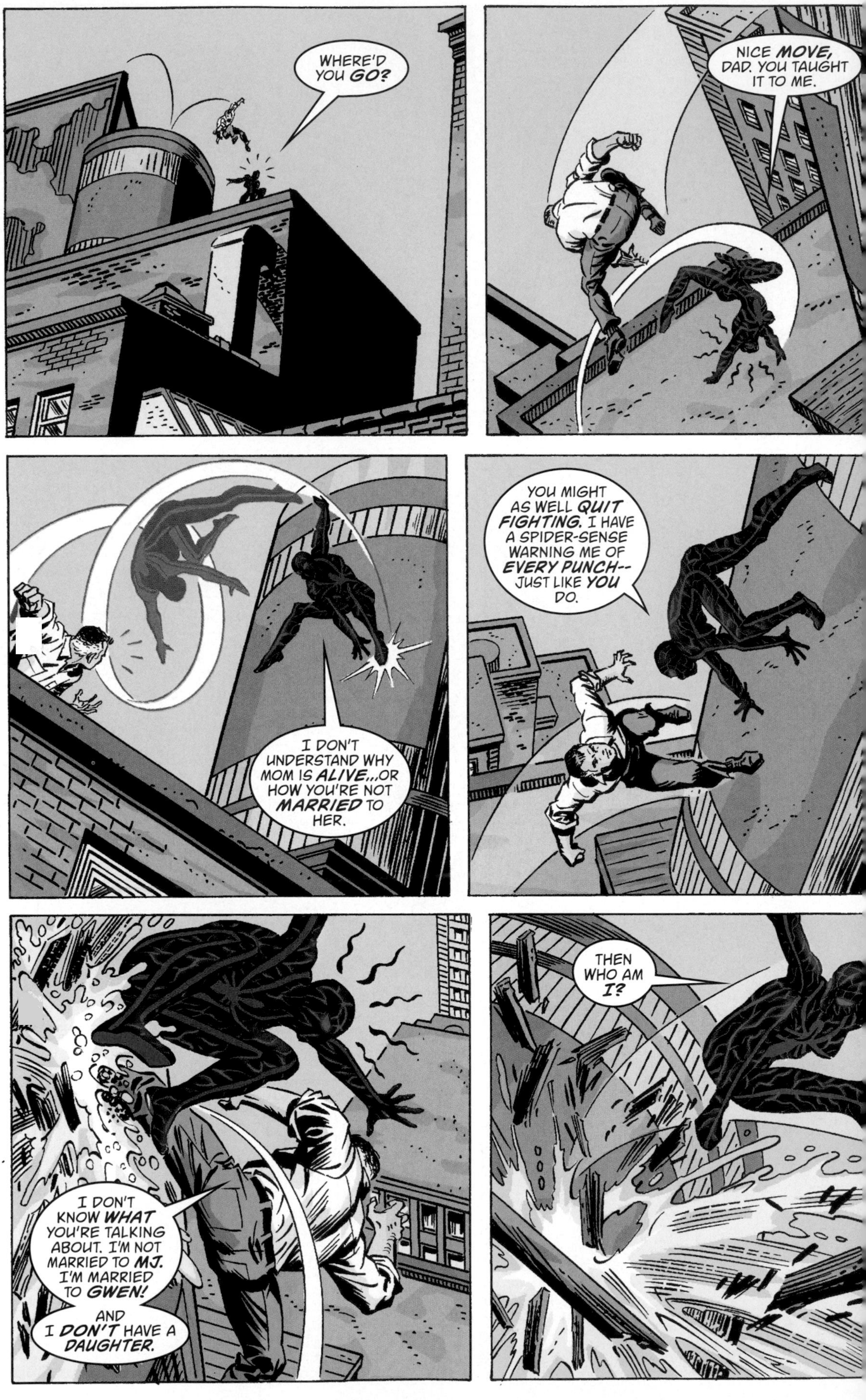
WHERE'D YOU GO?
NICE MOVE, DAD. YOU TAUGHT IT TO ME.
I DON'T UNDERSTAND WHY MOM IS ALIVE...OR HOW YOU'RE NOT MARRIED TO HER.
YOU MIGHT AS WELL QUIT FIGHTING. I HAVE A SPIDER-SENSE WARNING ME OF EVERY PUNCH-- JUST LIKE YOU DO.
I DON'T KNOW WHAT YOU'RE TALKING ABOUT. I'M NOT MARRIED TO MJ. I'M MARRIED TO GWEN!
AND I DON'T HAVE A DAUGHTER.
THEN WHO AM I?

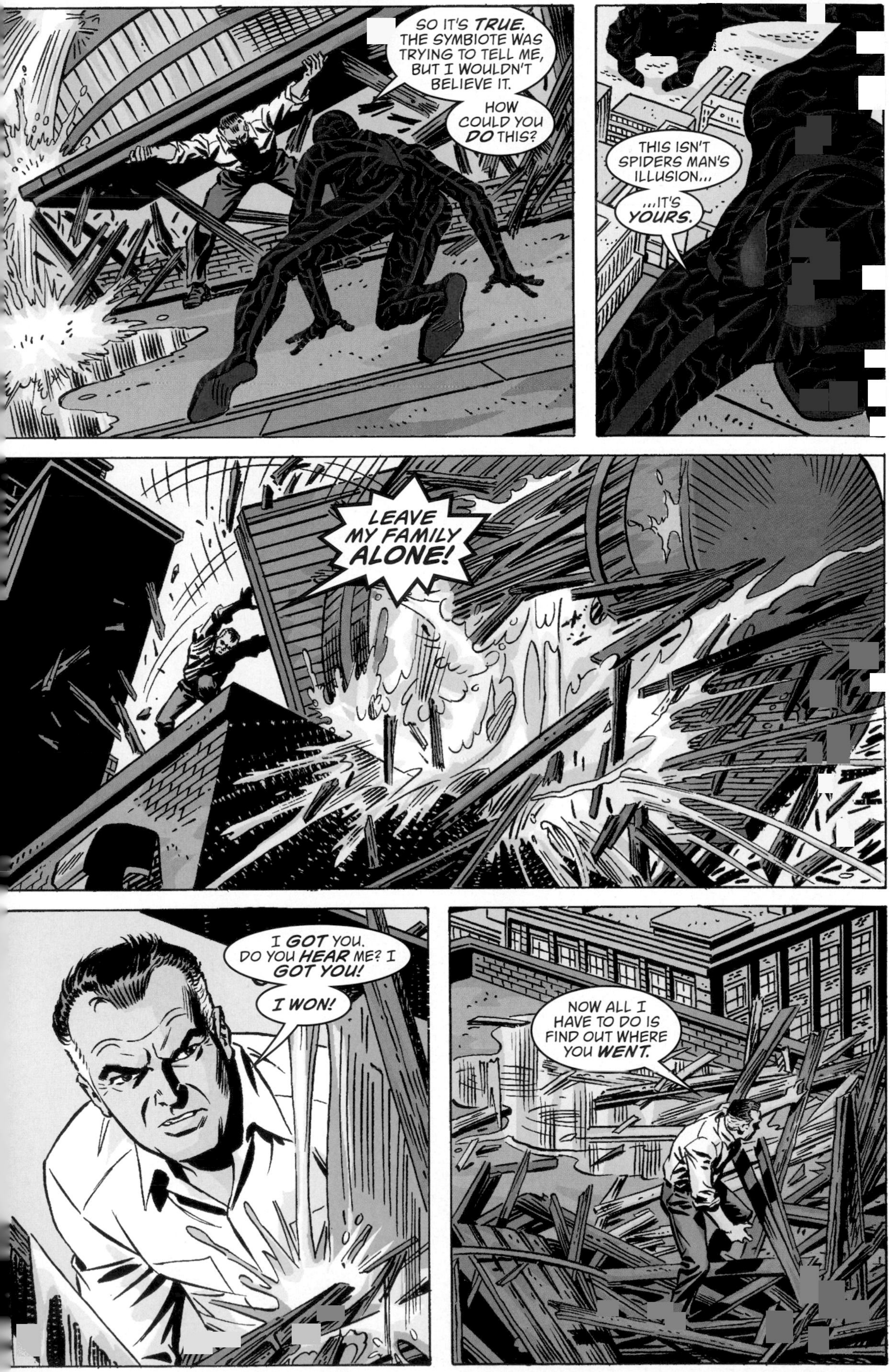
SO IT'S TRUE. THE SYMBIOTE WAS TRYING TO TELL ME, BUT I WOULDN'T BELIEVE IT.
HOW COULD YOU DO THIS?
THIS ISN'T SPIDERS MAN'S ILLUSION...
...IT'S YOURS.
LEAVE MY FAMILY ALONE!
I GOT YOU. DO YOU HEAR ME? I GOT YOU!
I WON!
NOW ALL I HAVE TO DO IS FIND OUT WHERE YOU WENT.

I CAN'T BELIEVE IT. **DAD'S** IN CONTROL.

WHAT AM I GOING TO DO **NOW?**

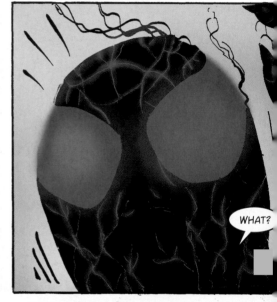

WHAT?

I CAN **TAKE OVER** THE ILLUSION?

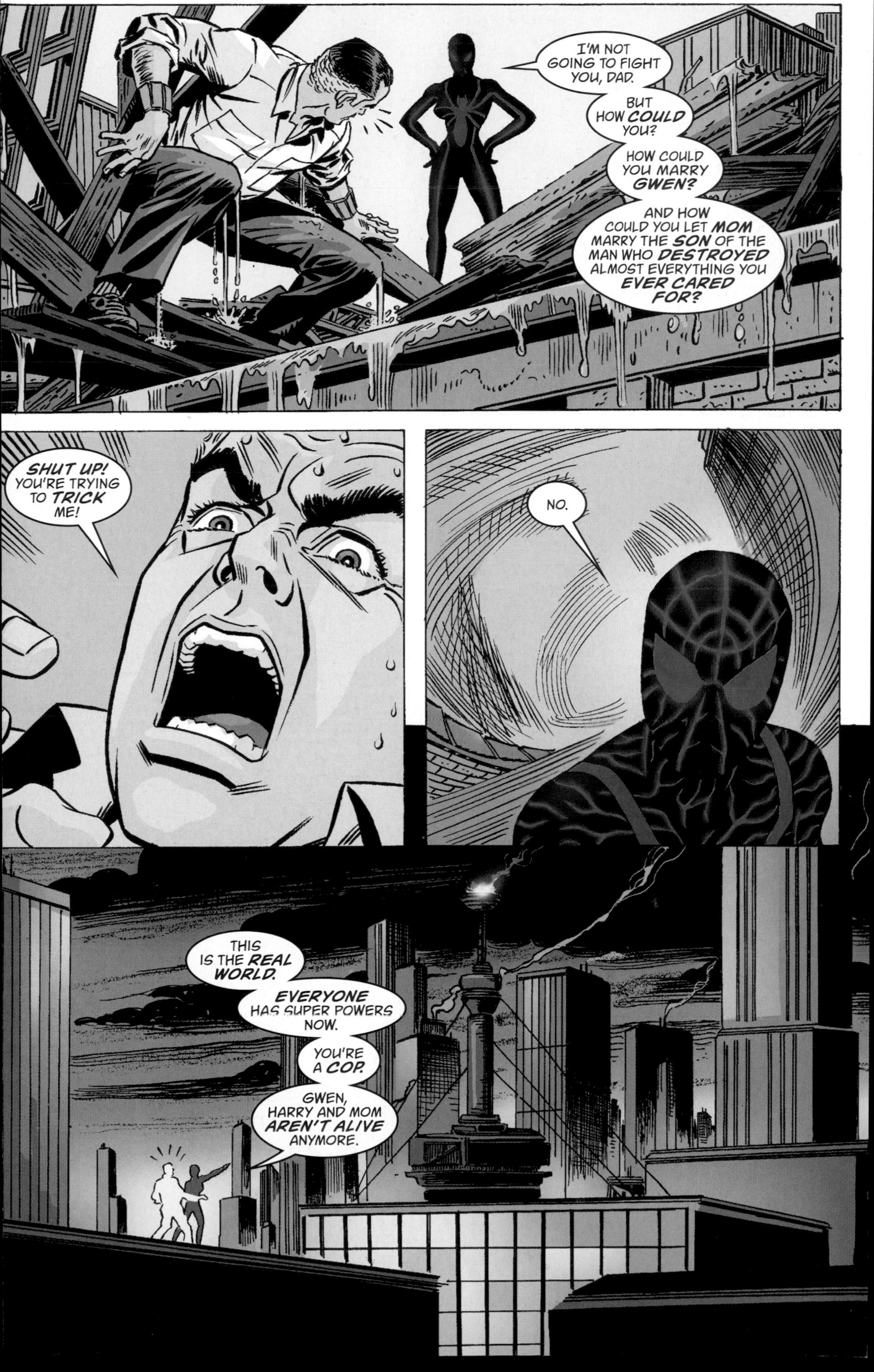
I'M NOT GOING TO FIGHT YOU, DAD.
BUT HOW COULD YOU?
HOW COULD YOU MARRY GWEN?
AND HOW COULD YOU LET MOM MARRY THE SON OF THE MAN WHO DESTROYED ALMOST EVERYTHING YOU EVER CARED FOR?
SHUT UP! YOU'RE TRYING TO TRICK ME!
NO.
THIS IS THE REAL WORLD.
EVERYONE HAS SUPER POWERS NOW.
YOU'RE A COP.
GWEN, HARRY AND MOM AREN'T ALIVE ANYMORE.

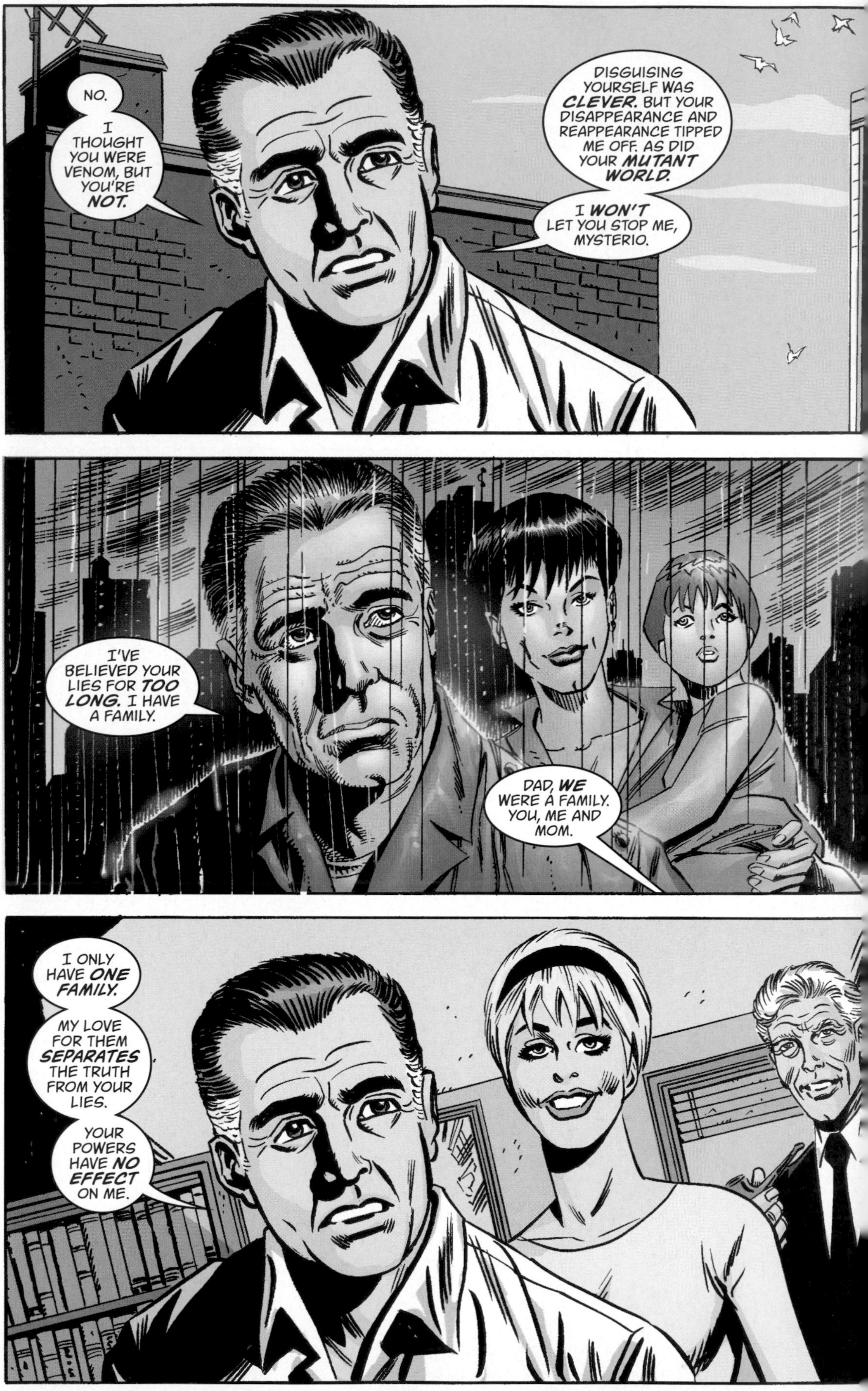
NO.
I THOUGHT YOU WERE VENOM, BUT YOU'RE NOT.
DISGUISING YOURSELF WAS CLEVER. BUT YOUR DISAPPEARANCE AND REAPPEARANCE TIPPED ME OFF. AS DID YOUR MUTANT WORLD.
I WON'T LET YOU STOP ME, MYSTERIO.
I'VE BELIEVED YOUR LIES FOR TOO LONG. I HAVE A FAMILY.
DAD, WE WERE A FAMILY. YOU, ME AND MOM.
I ONLY HAVE ONE FAMILY.
MY LOVE FOR THEM SEPARATES THE TRUTH FROM YOUR LIES.
YOUR POWERS HAVE NO EFFECT ON ME.

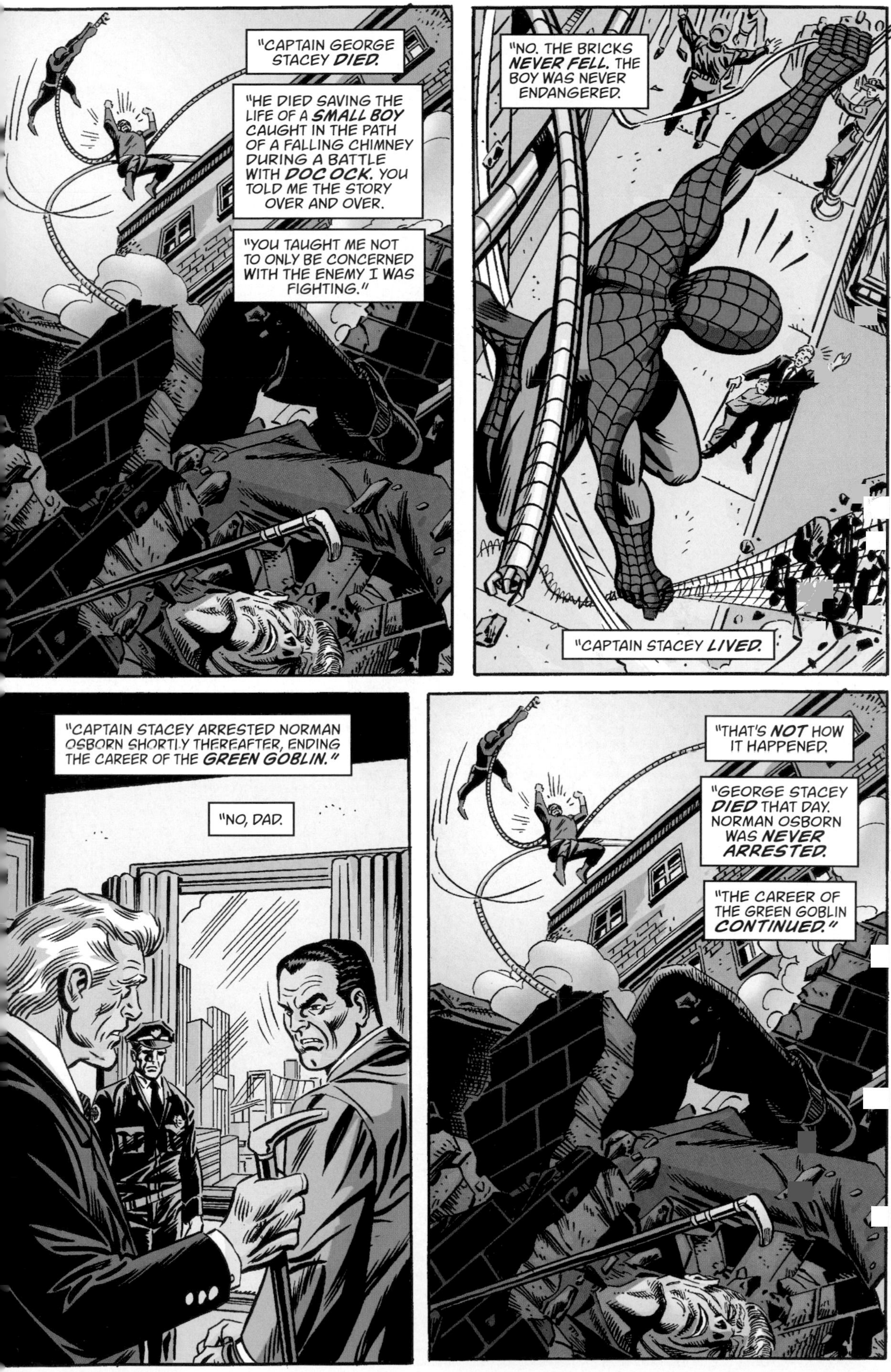
"CAPTAIN GEORGE STACEY DIED.
"HE DIED SAVING THE LIFE OF A SMALL BOY CAUGHT IN THE PATH OF A FALLING CHIMNEY DURING A BATTLE WITH DOC OCK. YOU TOLD ME THE STORY OVER AND OVER.
"YOU TAUGHT ME NOT TO ONLY BE CONCERNED WITH THE ENEMY I WAS FIGHTING."
"NO. THE BRICKS NEVER FELL. THE BOY WAS NEVER ENDANGERED.
"CAPTAIN STACEY LIVED.
"CAPTAIN STACEY ARRESTED NORMAN OSBORN SHORTLY THEREAFTER, ENDING THE CAREER OF THE GREEN GOBLIN."
"NO, DAD.
"THAT'S NOT HOW IT HAPPENED.
"GEORGE STACEY DIED THAT DAY. NORMAN OSBORN WAS NEVER ARRESTED.
"THE CAREER OF THE GREEN GOBLIN CONTINUED."

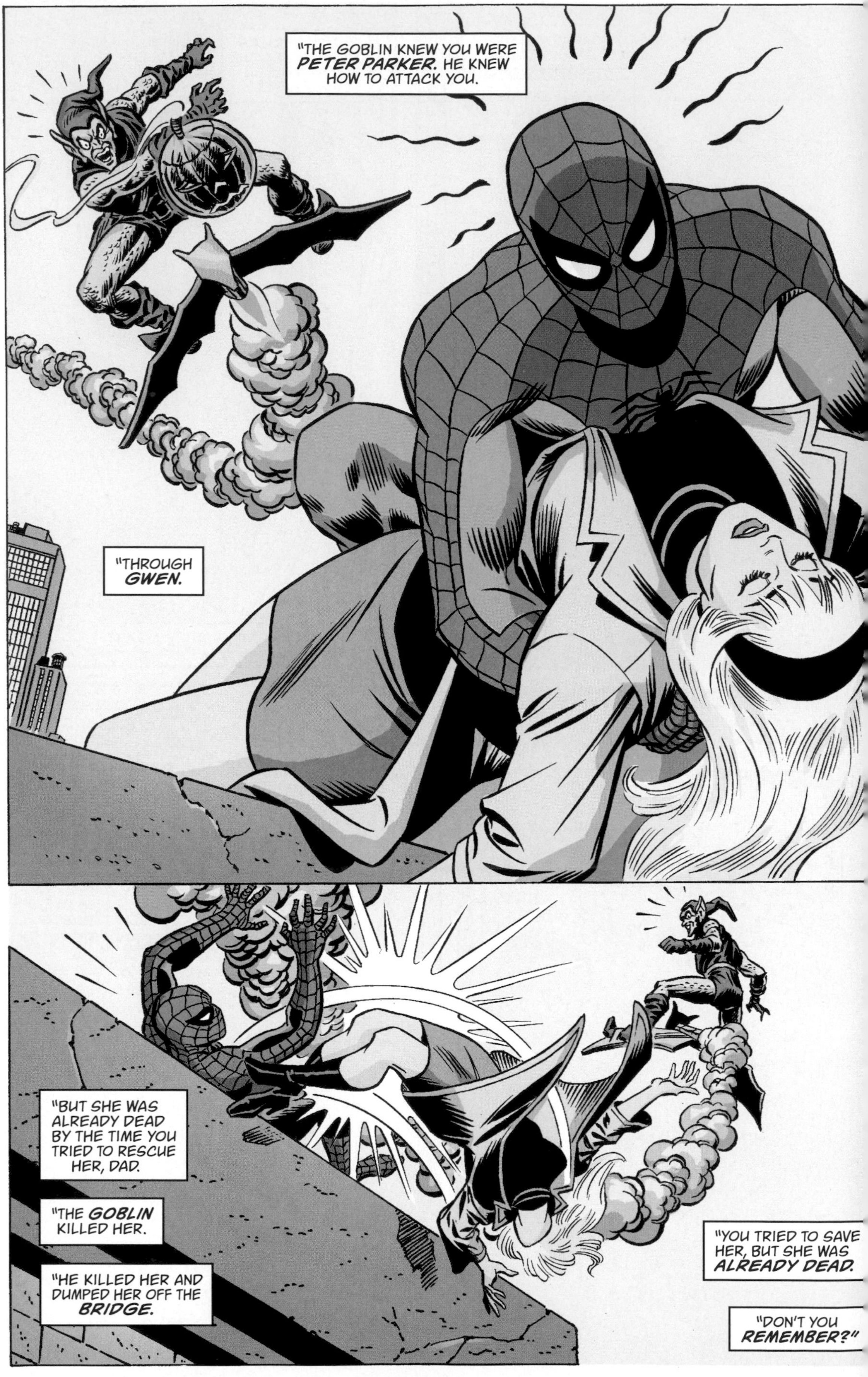
"THE GOBLIN KNEW YOU WERE PETER PARKER. HE KNEW HOW TO ATTACK YOU.
"THROUGH GWEN.
"BUT SHE WAS ALREADY DEAD BY THE TIME YOU TRIED TO RESCUE HER, DAD.
"THE GOBLIN KILLED HER.
"HE KILLED HER AND DUMPED HER OFF THE BRIDGE.
"YOU TRIED TO SAVE HER, BUT SHE WAS ALREADY DEAD.
"DON'T YOU REMEMBER?"

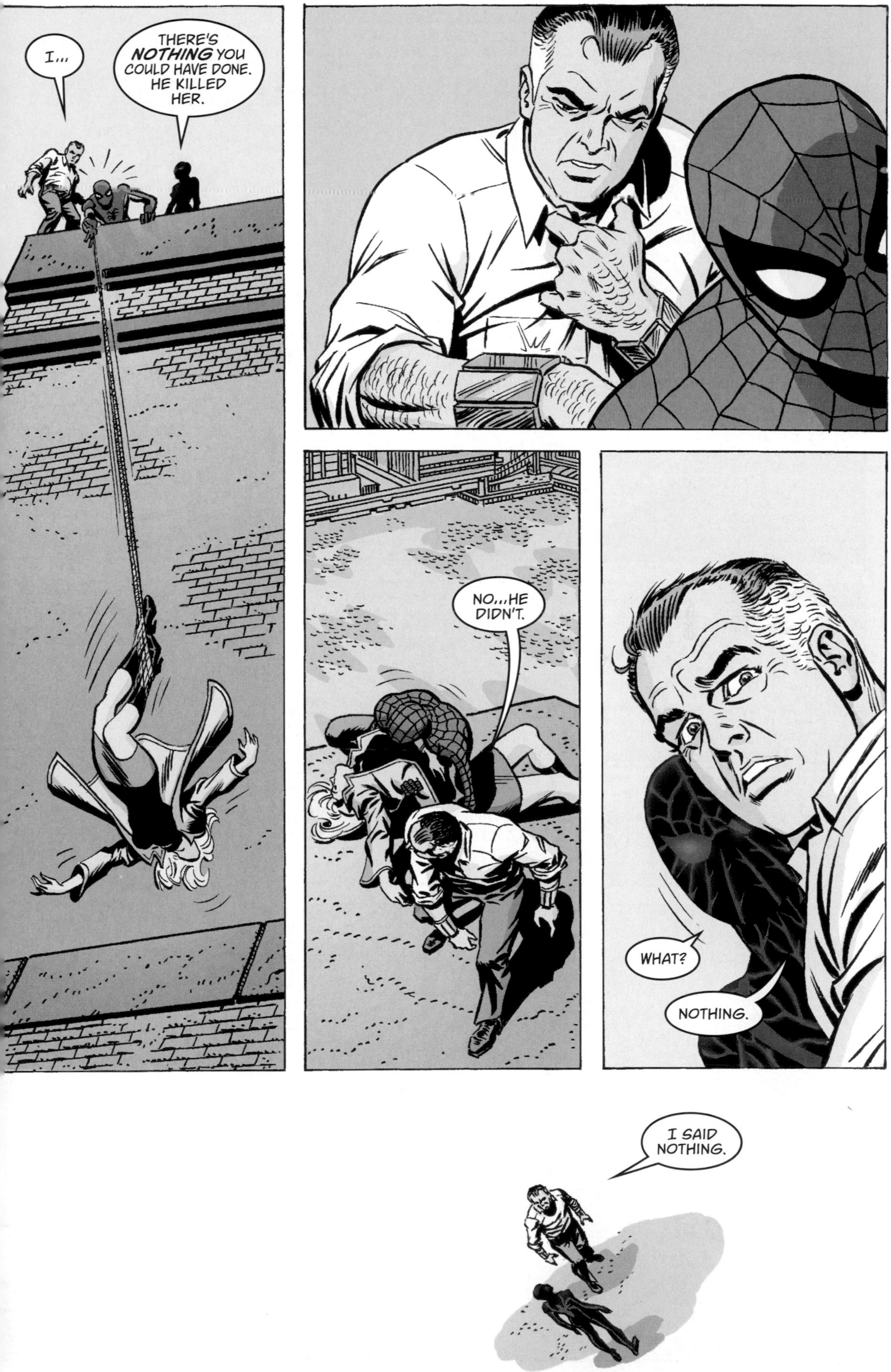
I...
THERE'S NOTHING YOU COULD HAVE DONE. HE KILLED HER.
NO...HE DIDN'T.
WHAT?
NOTHING.
I SAID NOTHING.

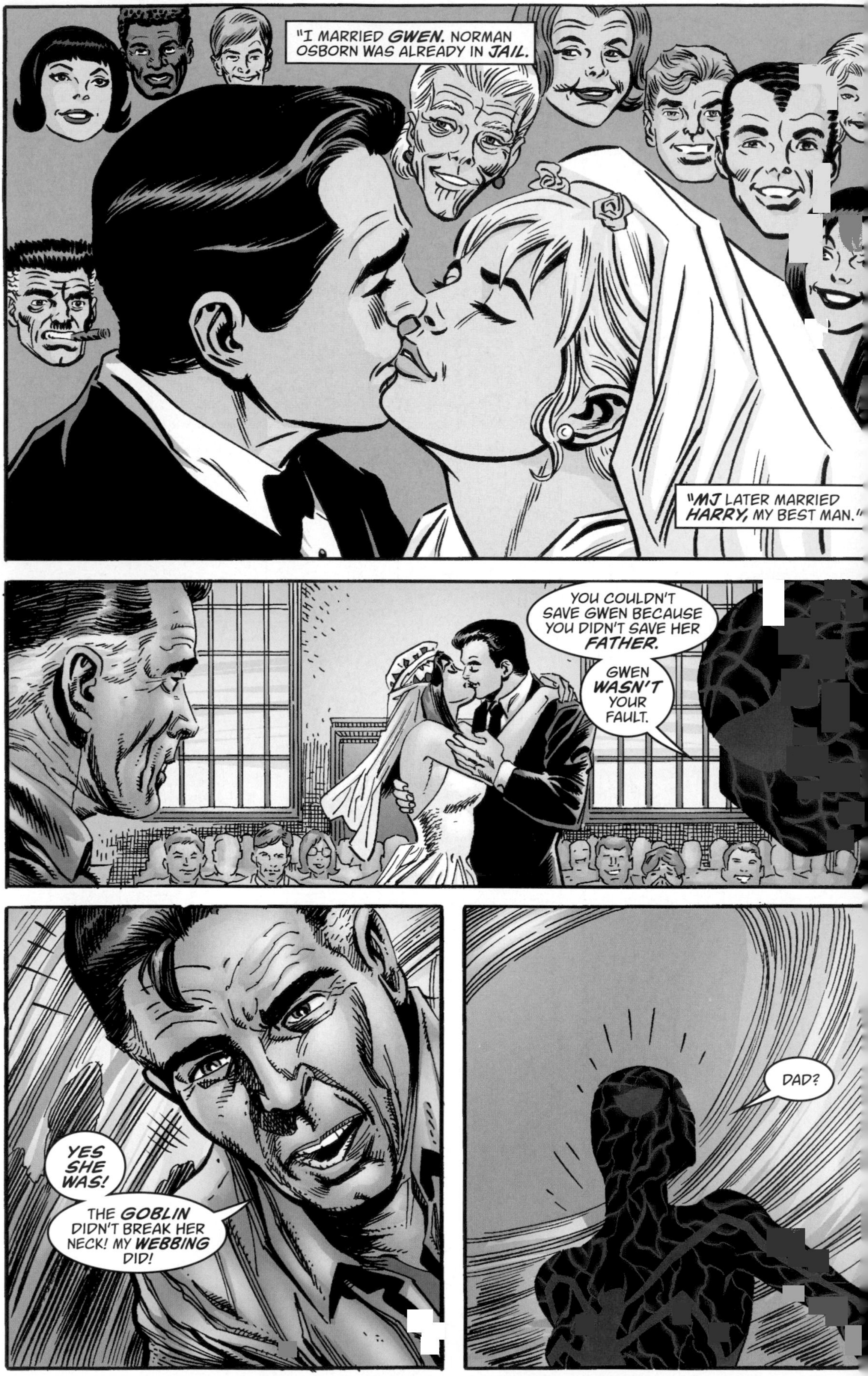
"I MARRIED GWEN. NORMAN OSBORN WAS ALREADY IN JAIL.
"MJ LATER MARRIED HARRY, MY BEST MAN."
YOU COULDN'T SAVE GWEN BECAUSE YOU DIDN'T SAVE HER FATHER.
GWEN WASN'T YOUR FAULT.
YES SHE WAS!
THE GOBLIN DIDN'T BREAK HER NECK! MY WEBBING DID!
DAD?

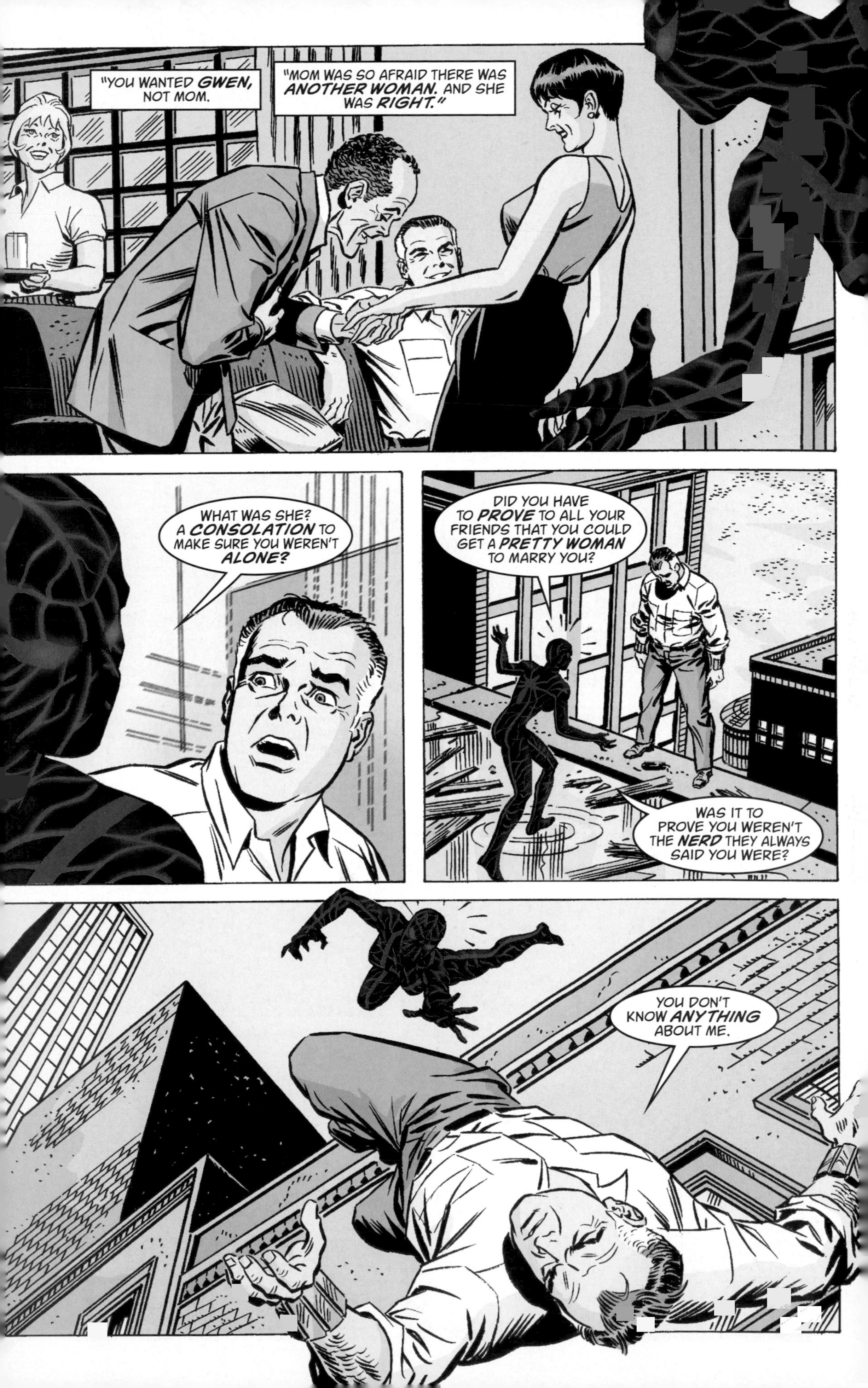
"YOU WANTED GWEN, NOT MOM.
"MOM WAS SO AFRAID THERE WAS ANOTHER WOMAN. AND SHE WAS RIGHT."
WHAT WAS SHE? A CONSOLATION TO MAKE SURE YOU WEREN'T ALONE?
DID YOU HAVE TO PROVE TO ALL YOUR FRIENDS THAT YOU COULD GET A PRETTY WOMAN TO MARRY YOU?
WAS IT TO PROVE YOU WEREN'T THE NERD THEY ALWAYS SAID YOU WERE?
YOU DON'T KNOW ANYTHING ABOUT ME.

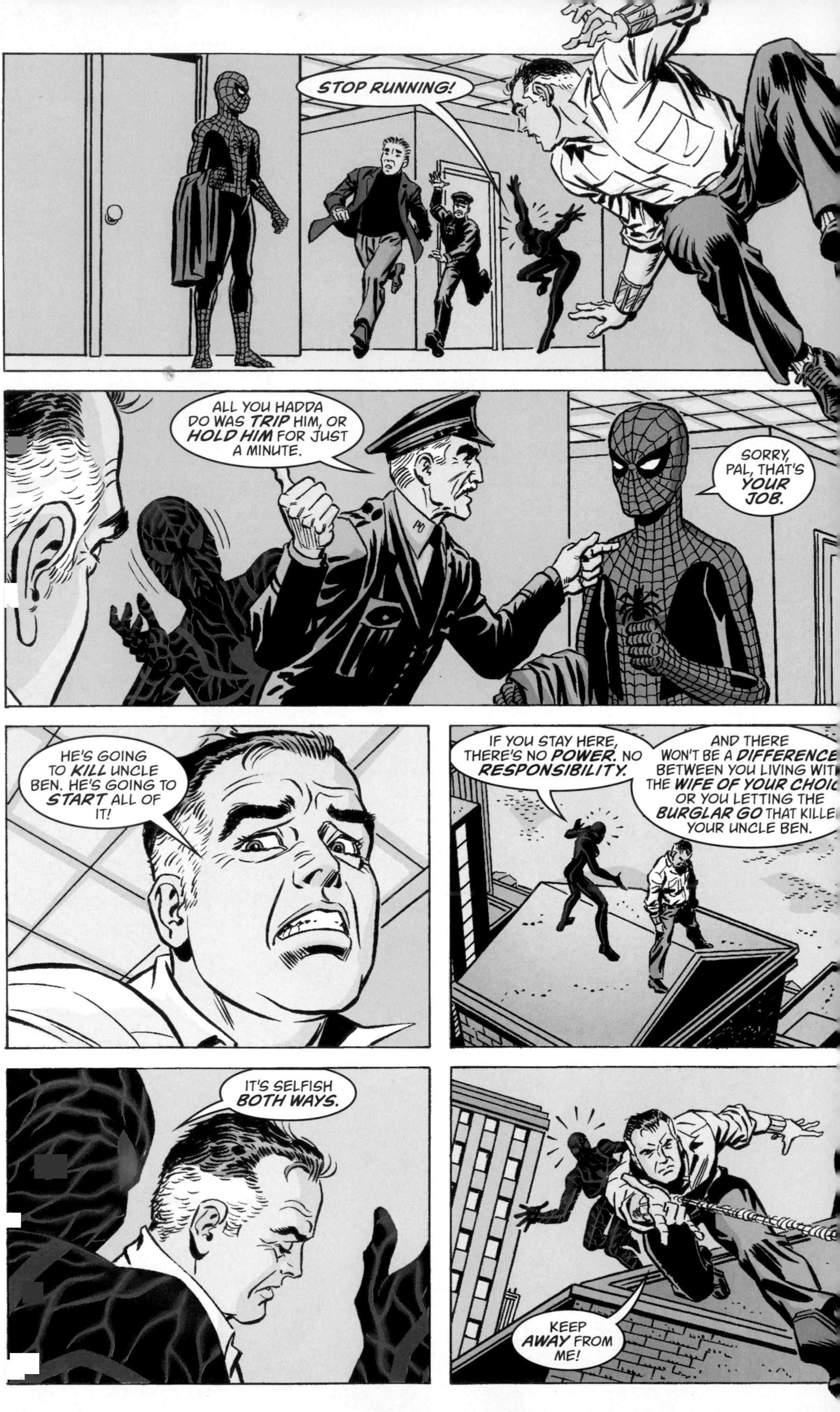
STOP RUNNING!
ALL YOU HADDA DO WAS TRIP HIM, OR HOLD HIM FOR JUST A MINUTE.
SORRY, PAL, THAT'S YOUR JOB.
HE'S GOING TO KILL UNCLE BEN. HE'S GOING TO START ALL OF IT!
IF YOU STAY HERE, THERE'S NO POWER. NO RESPONSIBILITY.
AND THERE WON'T BE A DIFFERENCE BETWEEN YOU LIVING WIT THE WIFE OF YOUR CHOI OR YOU LETTING THE BURGLAR GO THAT KILLE YOUR UNCLE BEN.
IT'S SELFISH BOTH WAYS.
KEEP AWAY FROM ME!

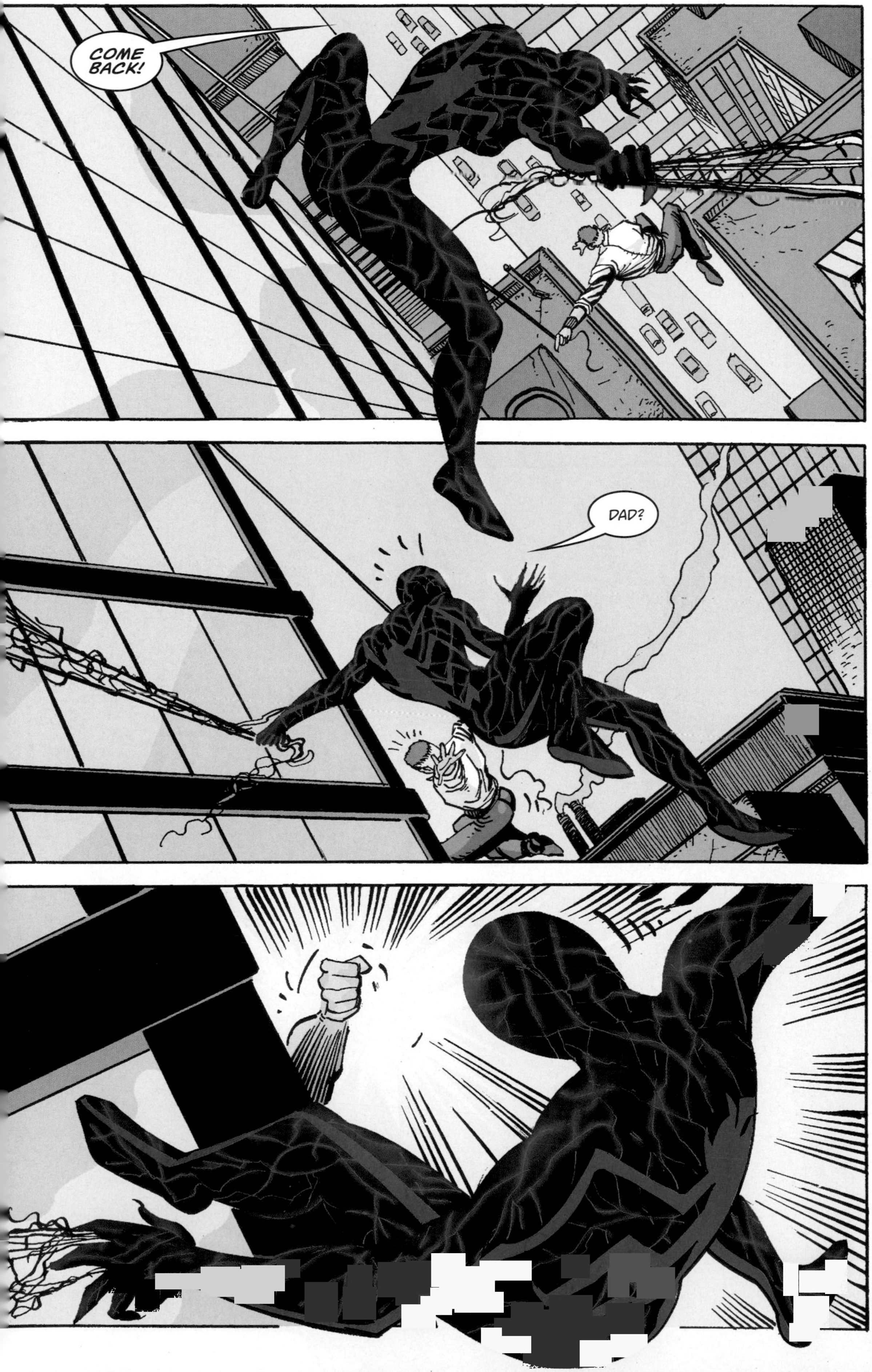
COME BACK!
DAD?

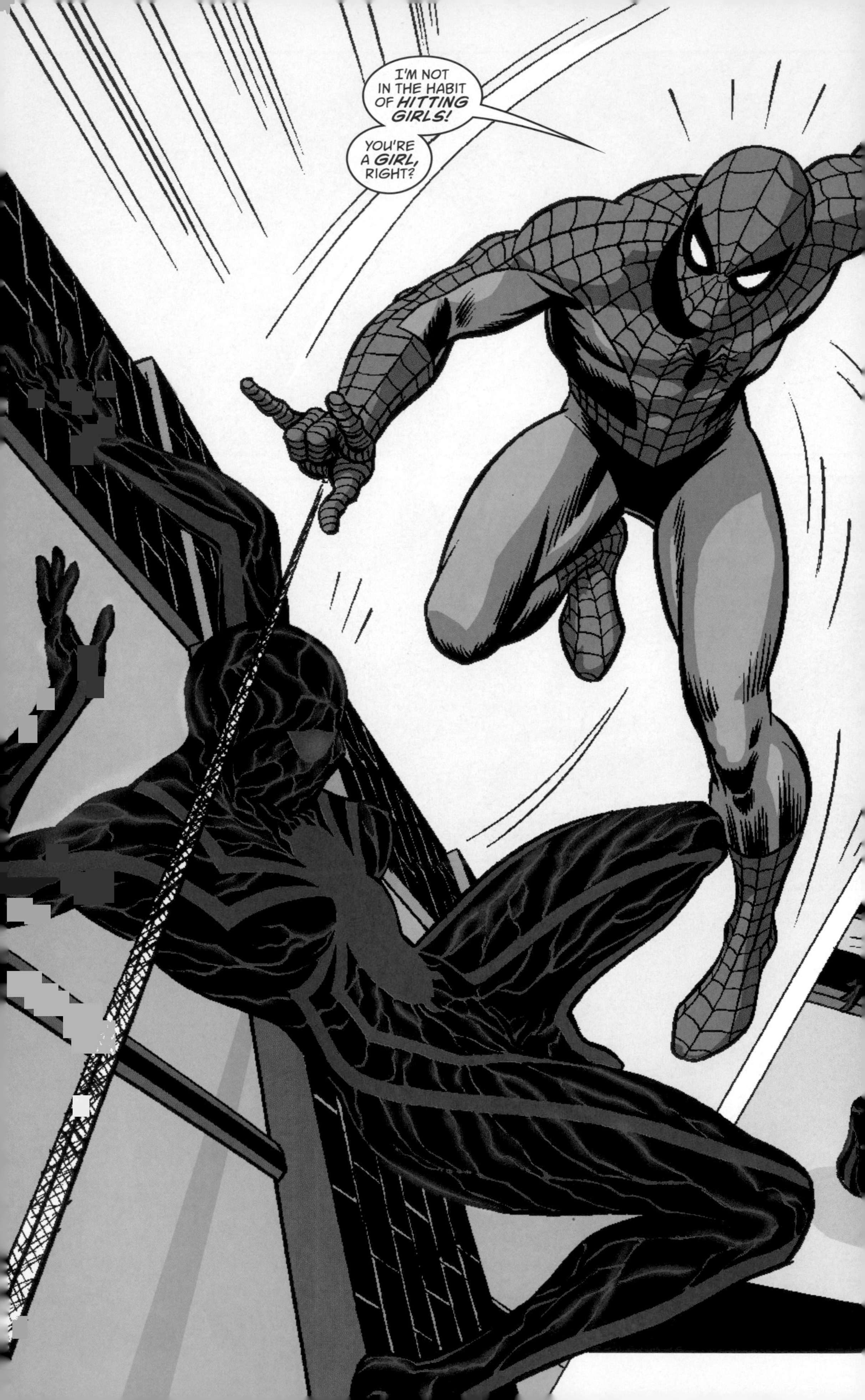
I'M NOT IN THE HABIT OF HITTING GIRLS!
YOU'RE A GIRL, RIGHT?

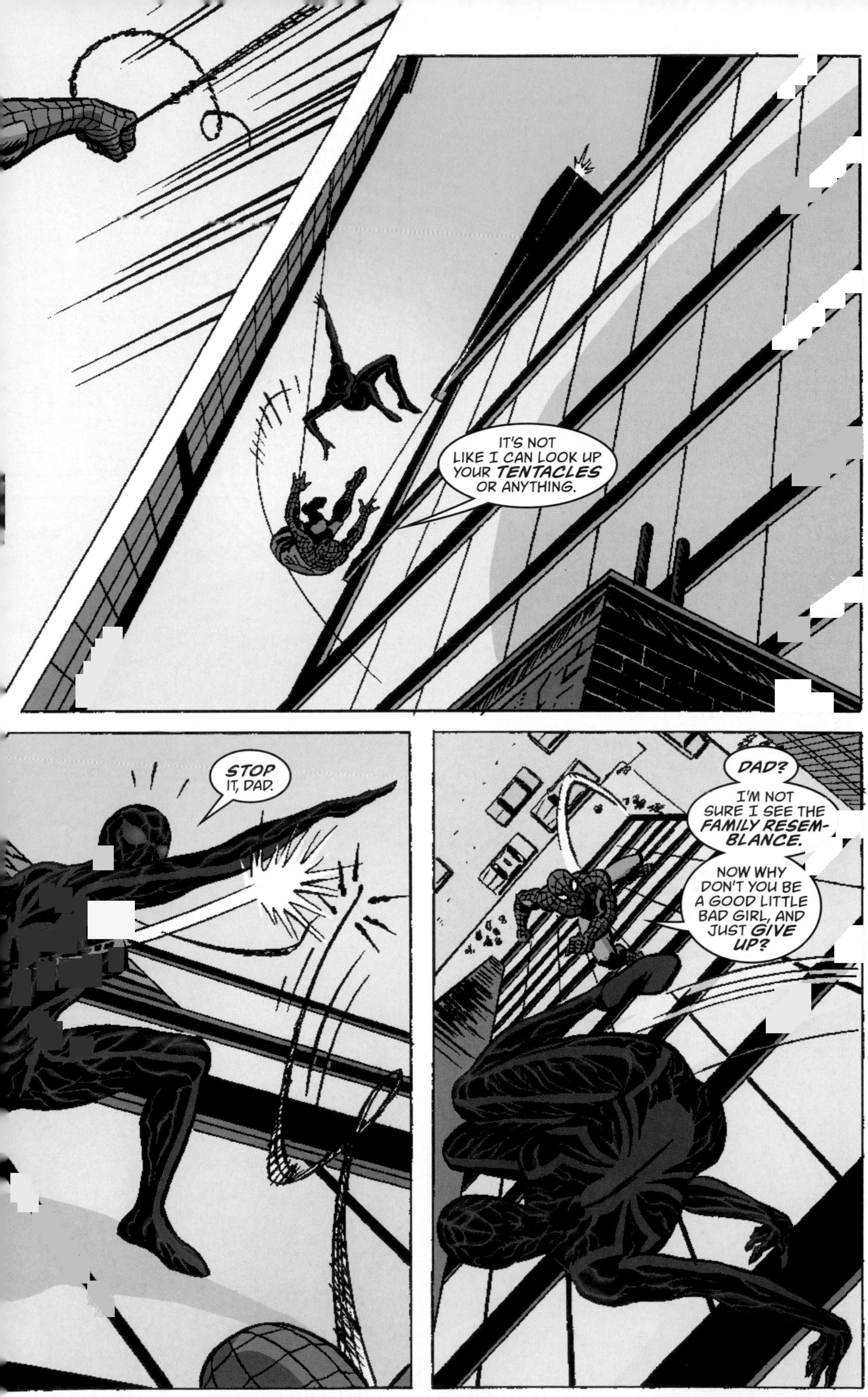
IT'S NOT LIKE I CAN LOOK UP YOUR TENTACLES OR ANYTHING.
STOP IT, DAD.
DAD?
I'M NOT SURE I SEE THE FAMILY RESEMBLANCE.
NOW WHY DON'T YOU BE A GOOD LITTLE BAD GIRL, AND JUST GIVE UP?

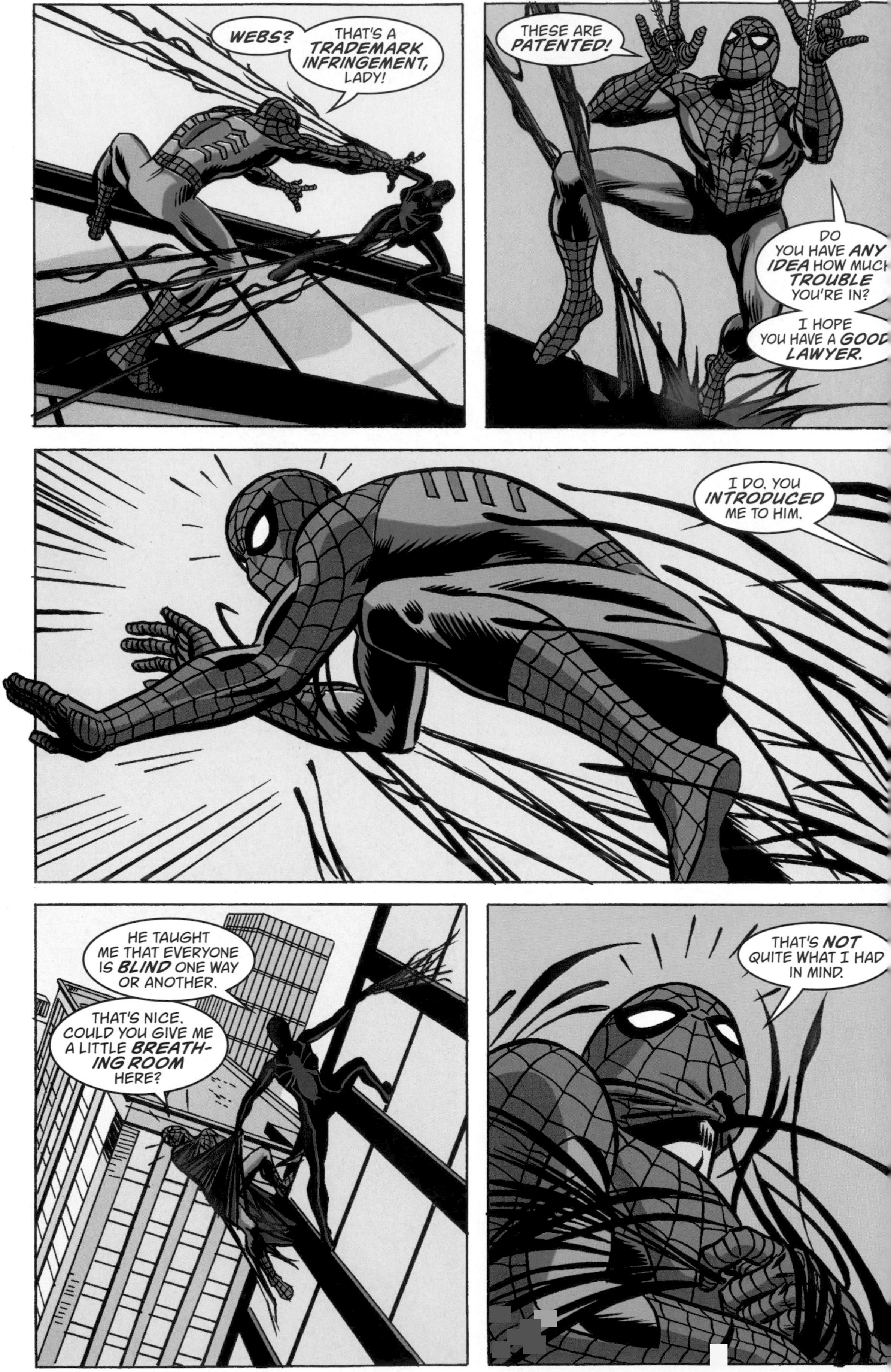
WEBS?
THAT'S A TRADEMARK INFRINGEMENT, LADY!
THESE ARE PATENTED!
DO YOU HAVE ANY IDEA HOW MUCH TROUBLE YOU'RE IN?
I HOPE YOU HAVE A GOOD LAWYER.
I DO. YOU INTRODUCED ME TO HIM.
HE TAUGHT ME THAT EVERYONE IS BLIND ONE WAY OR ANOTHER.
THAT'S NICE. COULD YOU GIVE ME A LITTLE BREATHING ROOM HERE?
THAT'S NOT QUITE WHAT I HAD IN MIND.

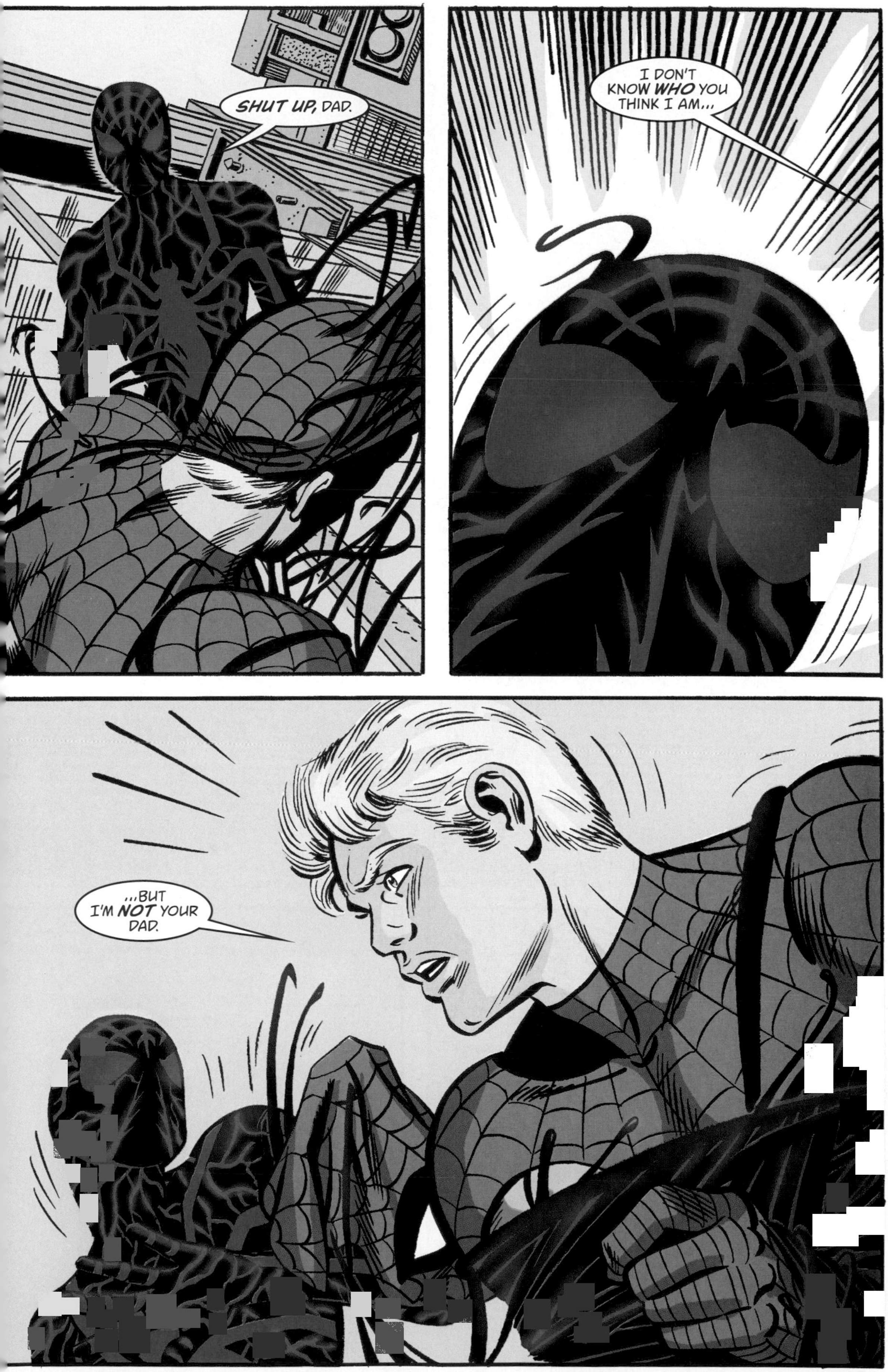
SHUT UP, DAD.
I DON'T KNOW WHO YOU THINK I AM...
...BUT I'M NOT YOUR DAD.

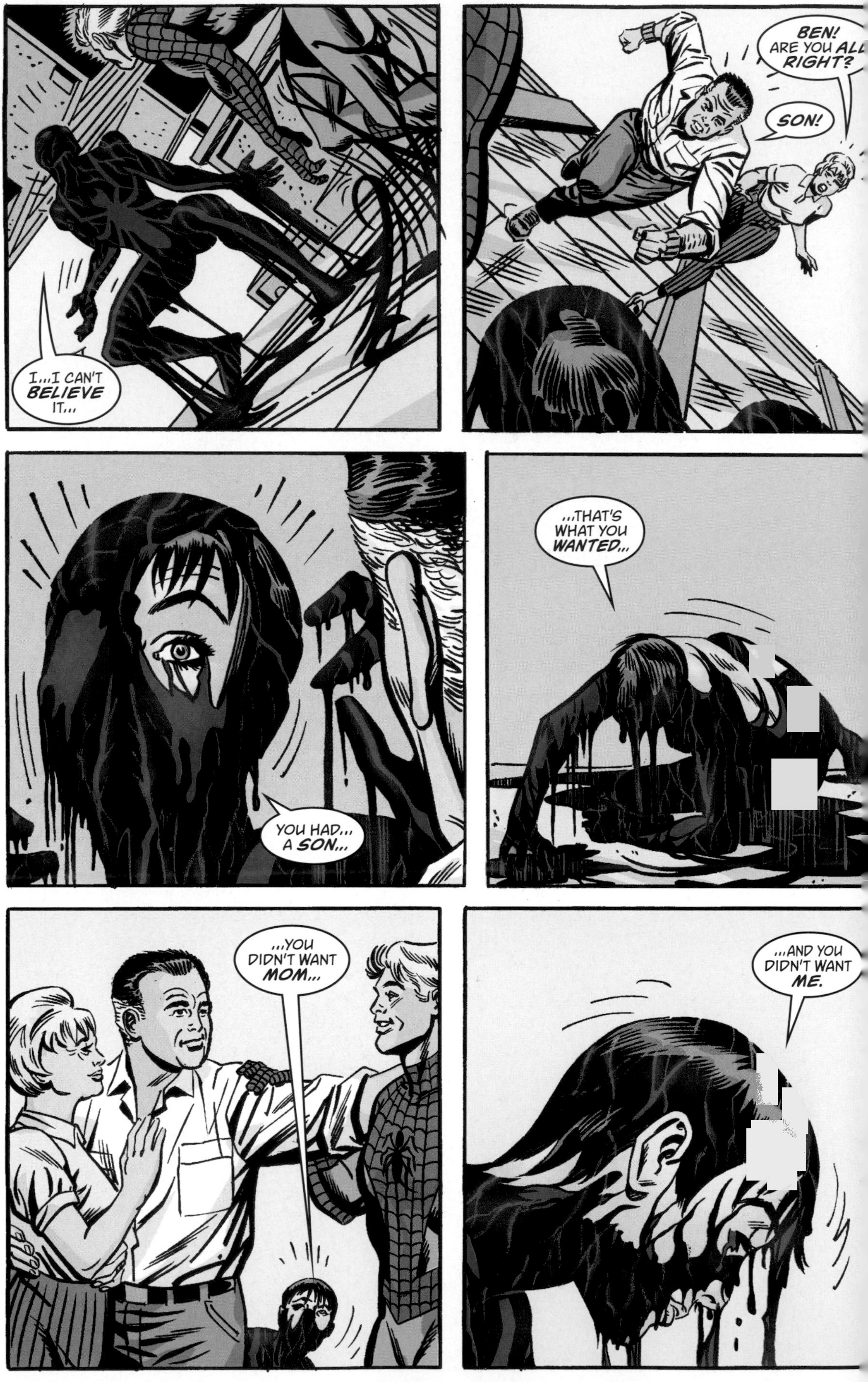
I...I CAN'T BELIEVE IT...
BEN! ARE YOU ALL RIGHT?
SON!
YOU HAD... A SON...
...THAT'S WHAT YOU WANTED...
...YOU DIDN'T WANT MOM...
...AND YOU DIDN'T WANT ME.

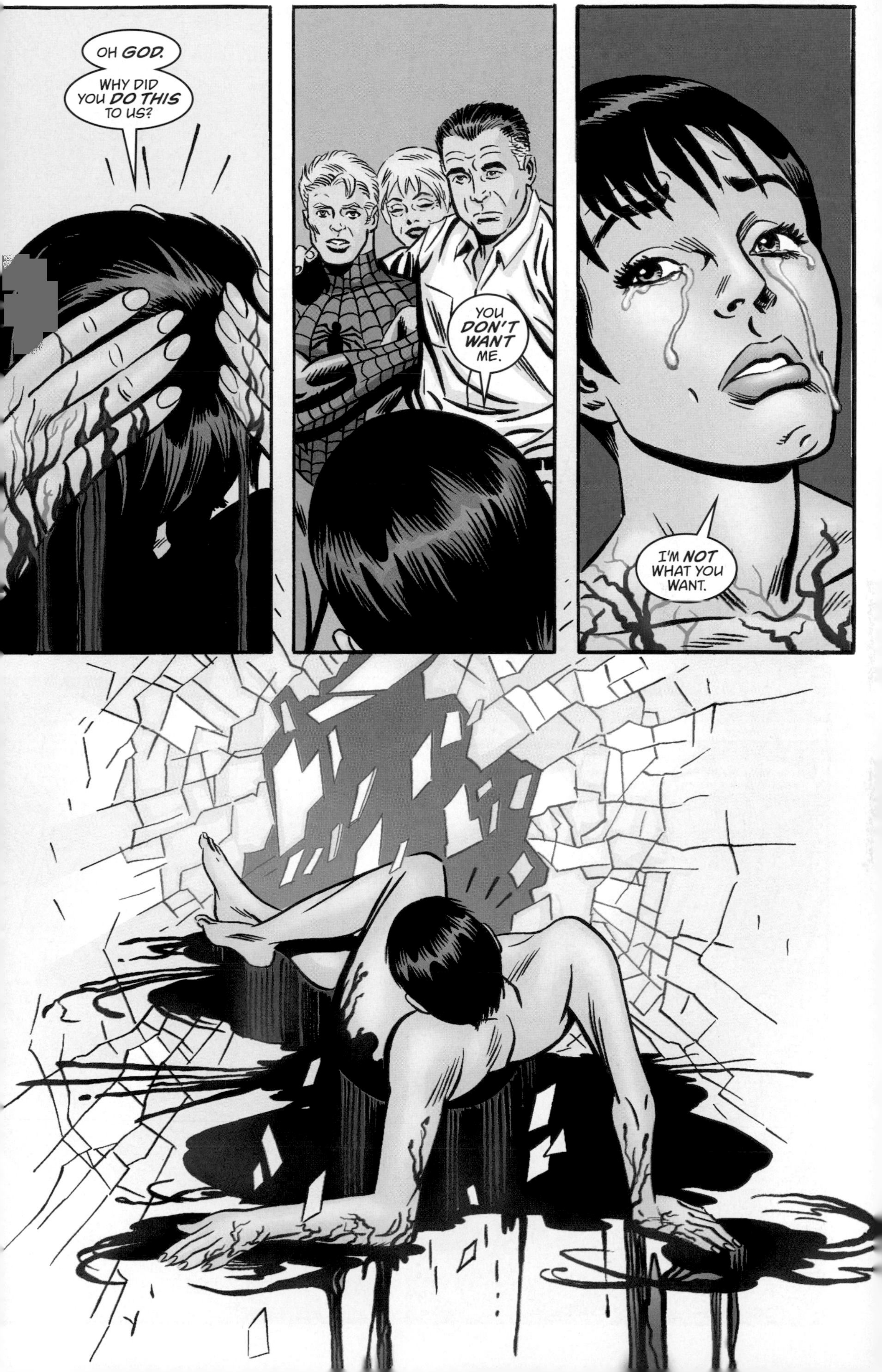
OH GOD.
WHY DID YOU DO THIS TO US?
YOU DON'T WANT ME.
I'M NOT WHAT YOU WANT.

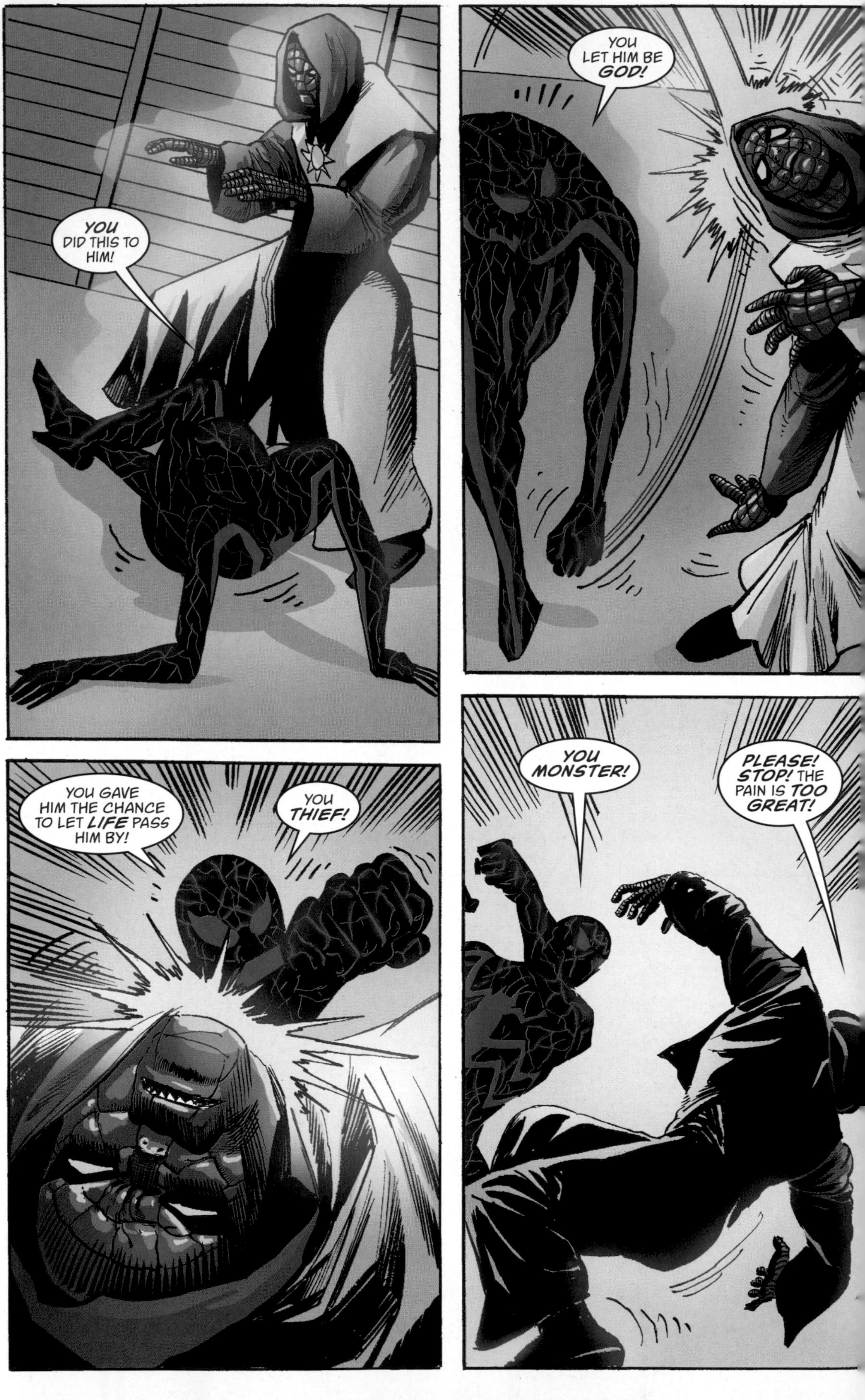
YOU DID THIS TO HIM!
YOU LET HIM BE GOD!
YOU GAVE HIM THE CHANCE TO LET LIFE PASS HIM BY!
YOU THIEF!
YOU MONSTER!
PLEASE! STOP! THE PAIN IS TOO GREAT!

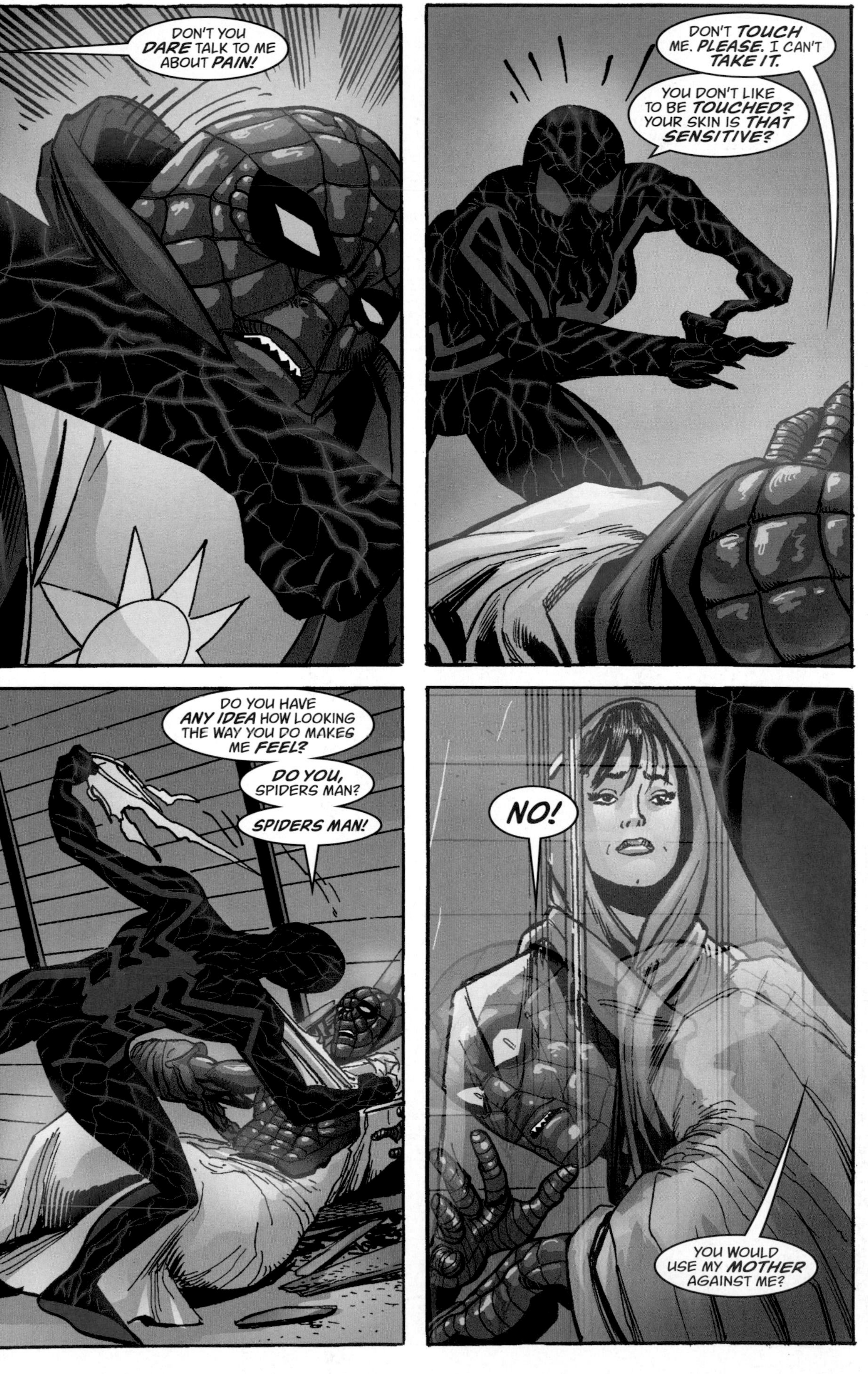
DON'T YOU DARE TALK TO ME ABOUT PAIN!
DON'T TOUCH ME. PLEASE. I CAN'T TAKE IT.
YOU DON'T LIKE TO BE TOUCHED? YOUR SKIN IS THAT SENSITIVE?
DO YOU HAVE ANY IDEA HOW LOOKING THE WAY YOU DO MAKES ME FEEL?
DO YOU, SPIDERS MAN?
SPIDERS MAN!
NO!
YOU WOULD USE MY MOTHER AGAINST ME?

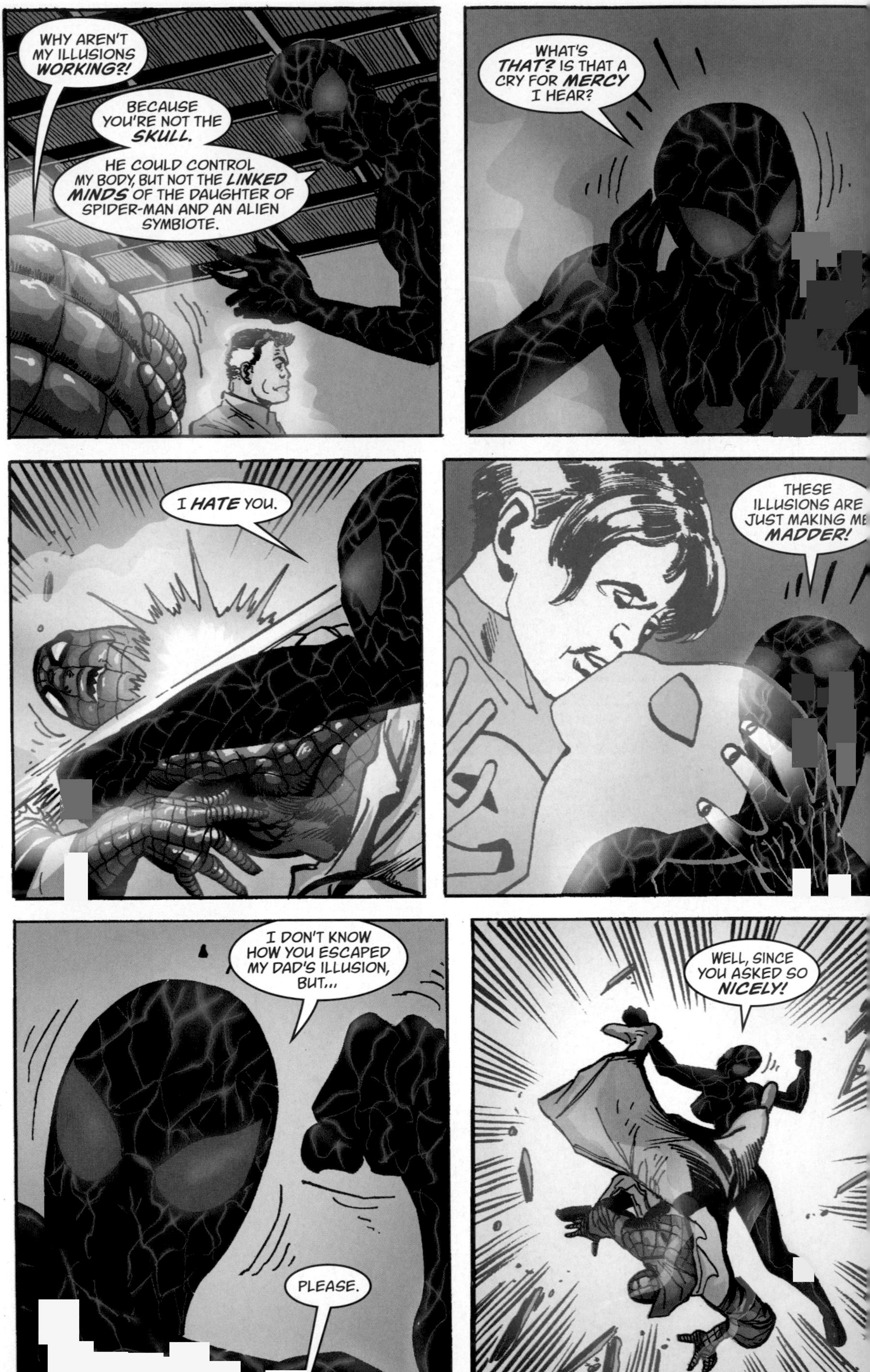
WHY AREN'T MY ILLUSIONS WORKING?!
BECAUSE YOU'RE NOT THE SKULL.
HE COULD CONTROL MY BODY, BUT NOT THE LINKED MINDS OF THE DAUGHTER OF SPIDER-MAN AND AN ALIEN SYMBIOTE.
WHAT'S THAT? IS THAT A CRY FOR MERCY I HEAR?
I HATE YOU.
THESE ILLUSIONS ARE JUST MAKING ME MADDER!
I DON'T KNOW HOW YOU ESCAPED MY DAD'S ILLUSION, BUT...
PLEASE.
WELL, SINCE YOU ASKED SO NICELY!

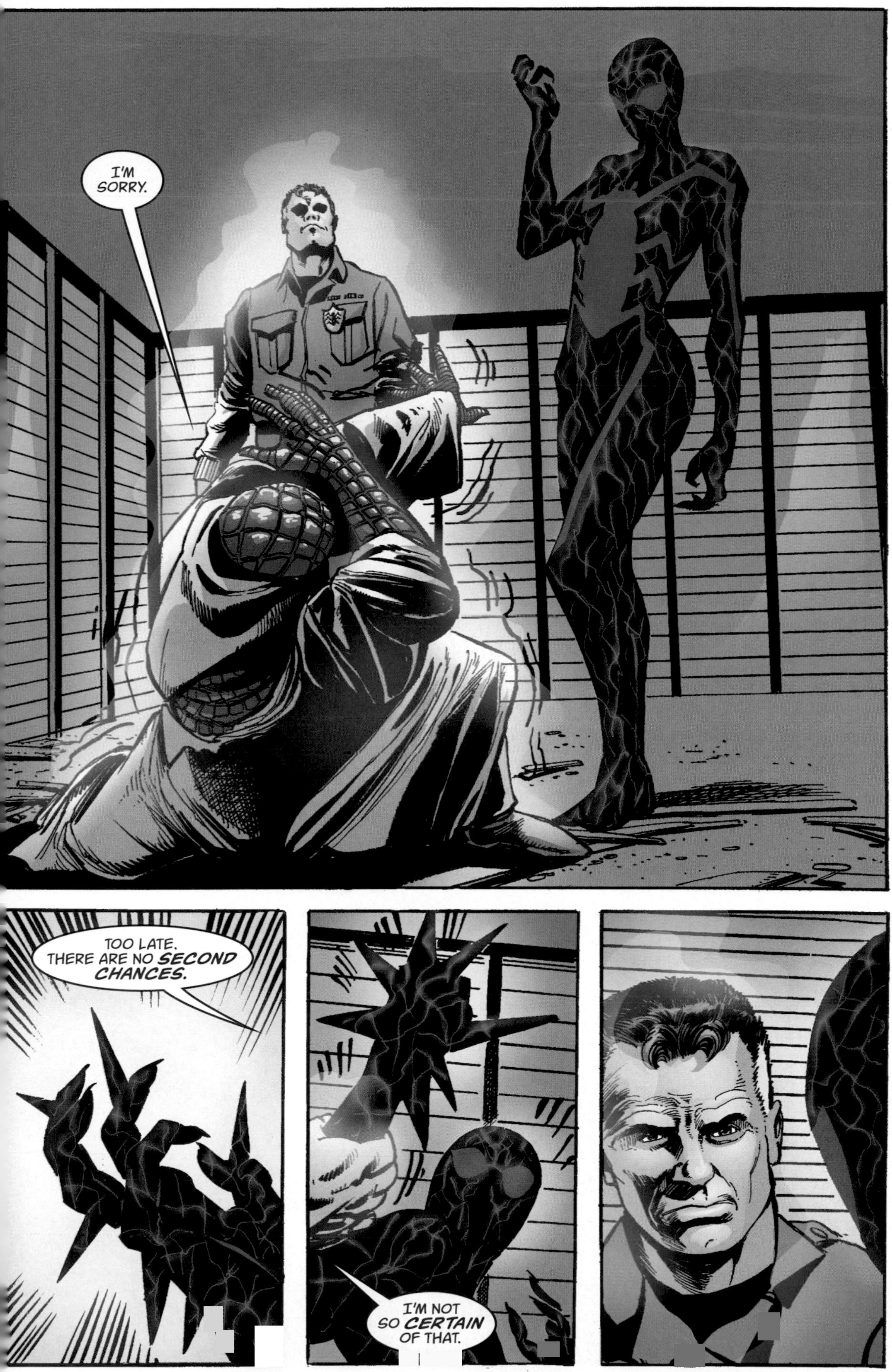
I'M SORRY.
TOO LATE. THERE ARE NO SECOND CHANCES.
I'M NOT SO CERTAIN OF THAT.

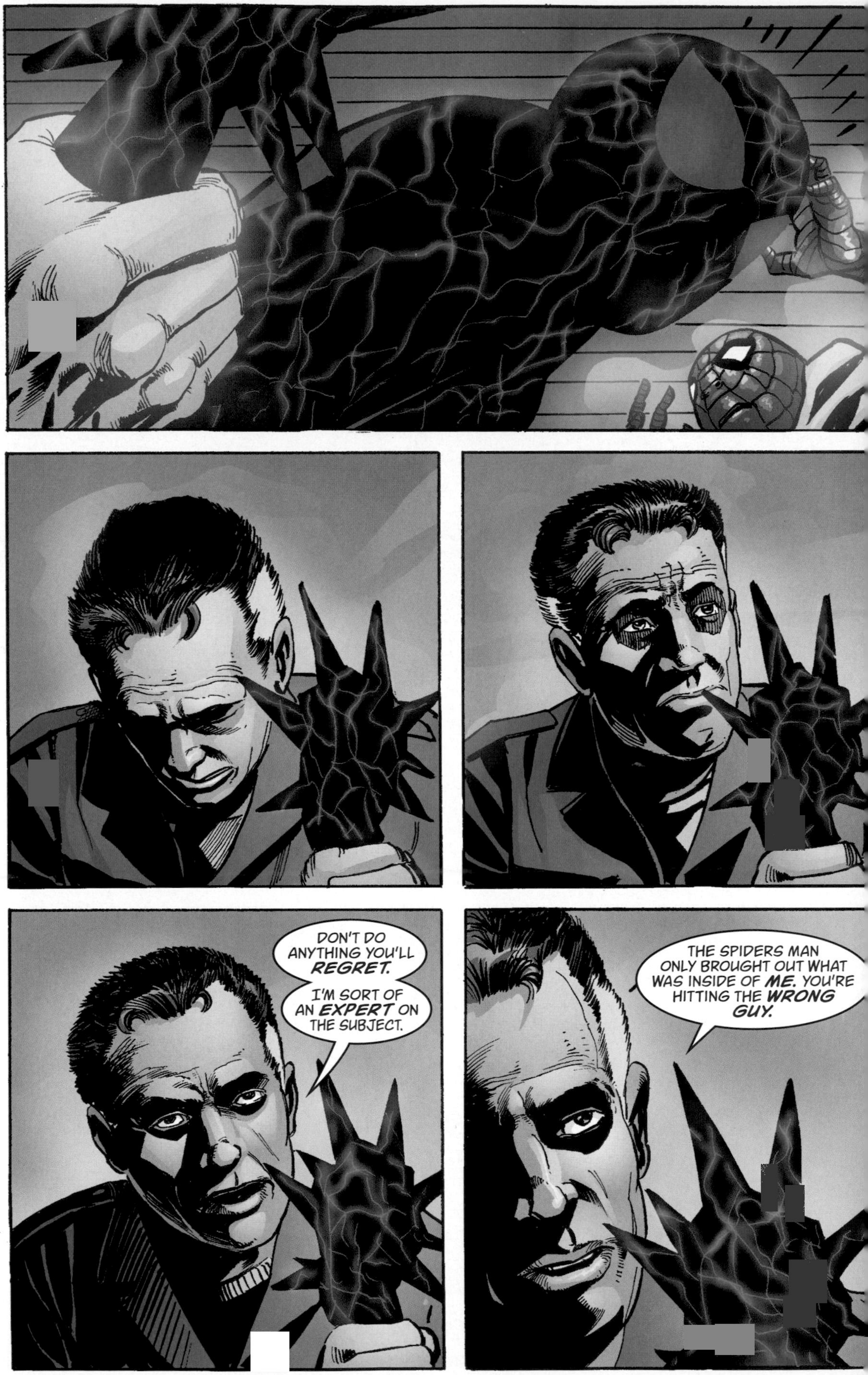
DON'T DO ANYTHING YOU'LL REGRET.
I'M SORT OF AN EXPERT ON THE SUBJECT.
THE SPIDERS MAN ONLY BROUGHT OUT WHAT WAS INSIDE OF ME. YOU'RE HITTING THE WRONG GUY.

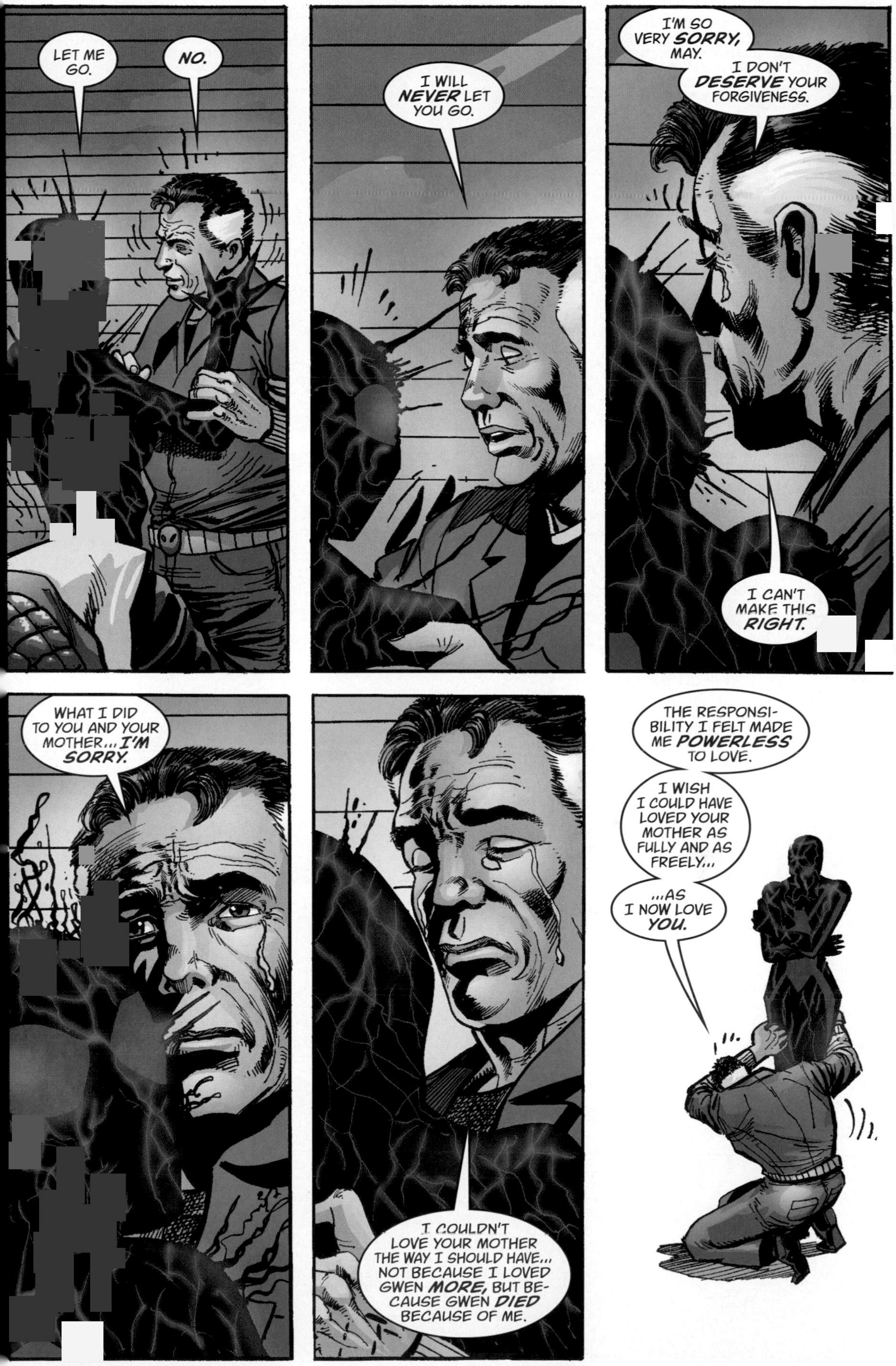
LET ME GO.
NO.
I WILL NEVER LET YOU GO.
I'M SO VERY SORRY, MAY.
I DON'T DESERVE YOUR FORGIVENESS.
I CAN'T MAKE THIS RIGHT.
WHAT I DID TO YOU AND YOUR MOTHER... I'M SORRY.
I COULDN'T LOVE YOUR MOTHER THE WAY I SHOULD HAVE... NOT BECAUSE I LOVED GWEN MORE, BUT BECAUSE GWEN DIED BECAUSE OF ME.
THE RESPONSIBILITY I FELT MADE ME POWERLESS TO LOVE.
I WISH I COULD HAVE LOVED YOUR MOTHER AS FULLY AND AS FREELY...
...AS I NOW LOVE YOU.

I'M JUST YOUR DAUGHTER, DAD.

WHY'D YOU COME OUT OF THE ILLUSION? YOU HAD *EVERYTHING* THERE. A WIFE. A FAMILY. FRIENDS.

EVERYTHING.

WHEN I SAW YOU, EVERYTHING WASN'T *ENOUGH.*

I KEPT ASKING MYSELF *WHY,* IF IT WAS ALL AN ILLUSION, WHY I STILL LET THE *BURGLAR* PASS BY?

WHY DID I LET *UNCLE BEN* DIE?

WHY DIDN'T I *CHANGE* THAT?

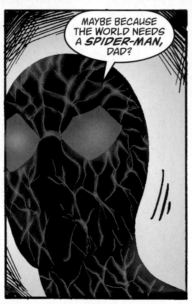

MAYBE BECAUSE THE WORLD NEEDS A *SPIDER-MAN,* DAD?

I *NEED* YOU, MAY. AND I DIDN'T KNOW *HOW MUCH* TILL NOW.

AND I HAVE *YOU* TO THANK, SPIDER-MAN.

WILL YOU COME WITH US?

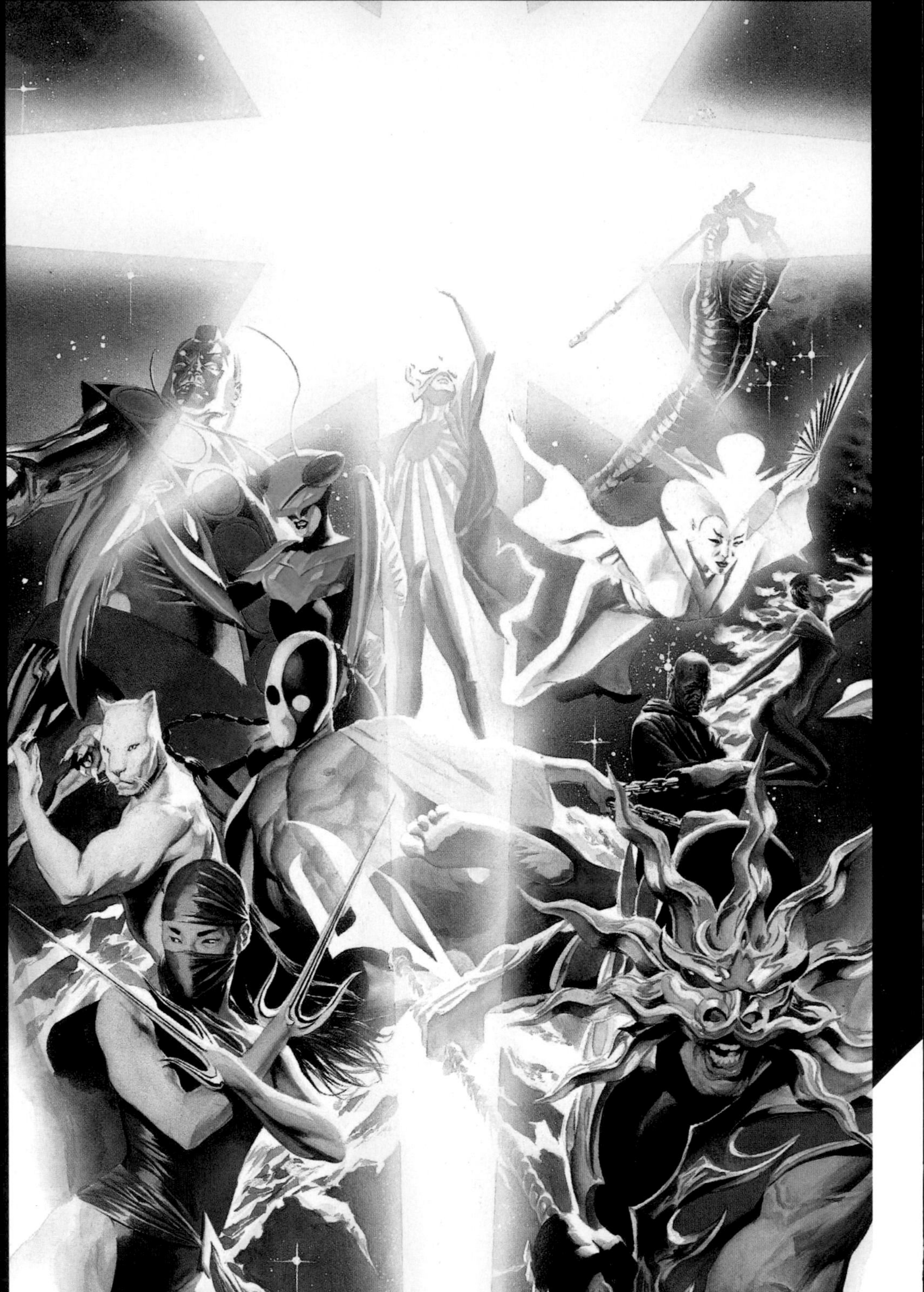

CHAPTER FOUR

"I'm hearing the rustling of papers, Isaac. Is something wrong with one of the pages I've dictated?"

"Certainly not, Kyle. It is merely a note I wrote to myself. A reminder of an errand I have planned for myself. I am curious as to why you cannot see the words on this page the same way you can predict other pregnant events of our day."

"I...don't know why. Sometimes things that are especially close to me are impossible to see. Like a blind spot or something. What did the note say?"

"That if we are now writing mankind's last days on planet Earth, I am going to need quite a bit more paper. Now continue..."

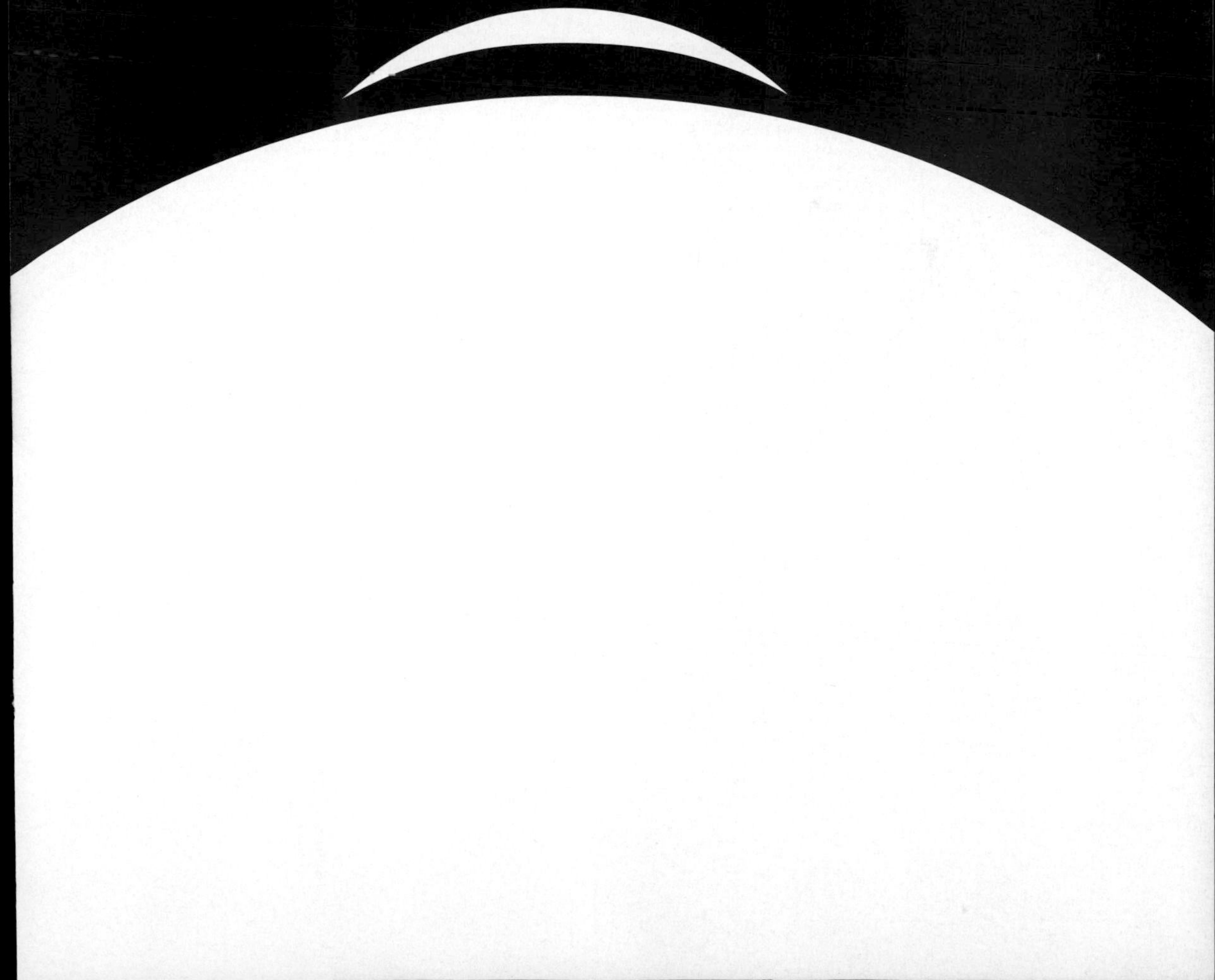

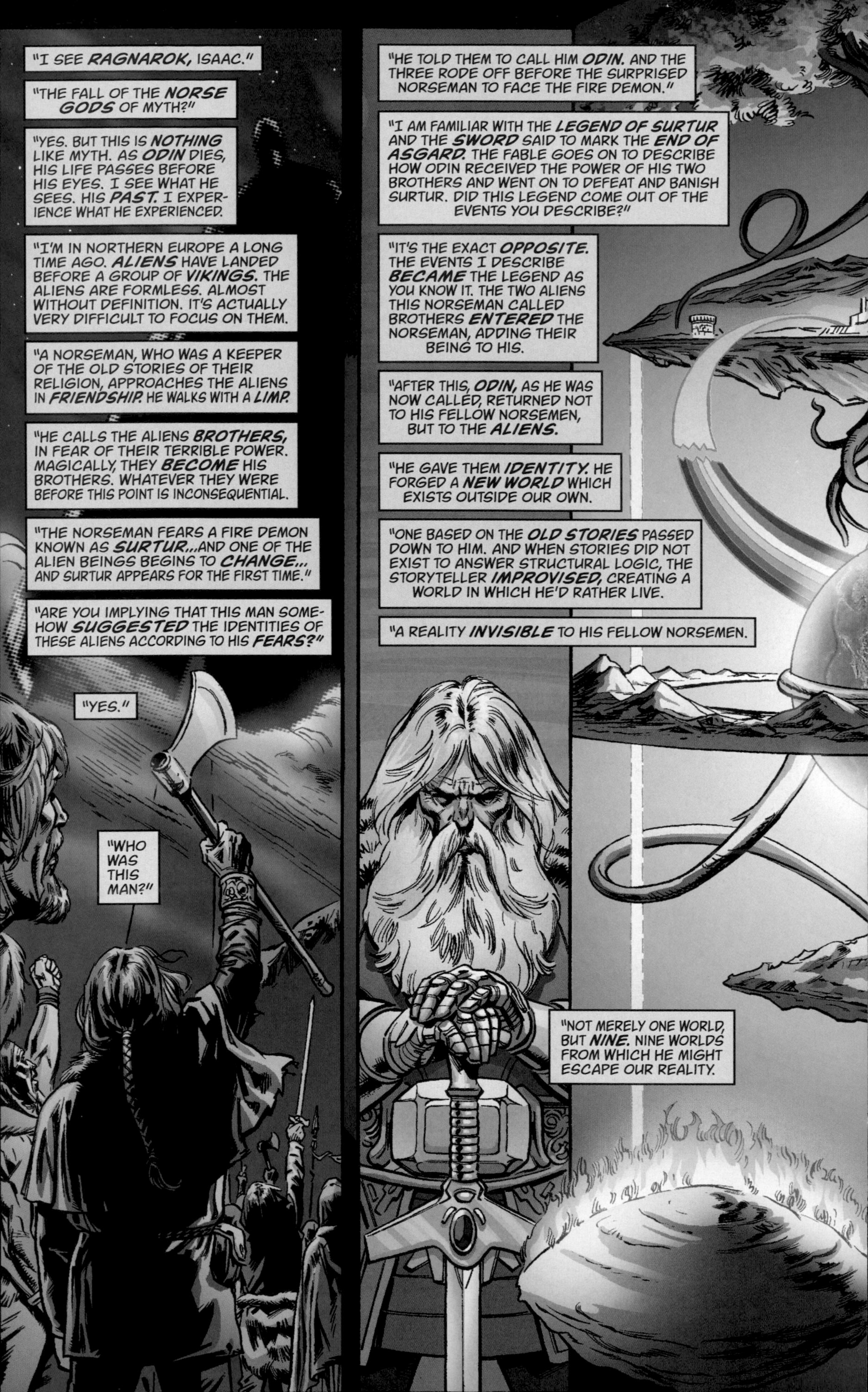
"I SEE RAGNAROK, ISAAC."
"THE FALL OF THE NORSE GODS OF MYTH?"
"YES. BUT THIS IS NOTHING LIKE MYTH. AS ODIN DIES, HIS LIFE PASSES BEFORE HIS EYES. I SEE WHAT HE SEES. HIS PAST. I EXPERIENCE WHAT HE EXPERIENCED.
"I'M IN NORTHERN EUROPE A LONG TIME AGO. ALIENS HAVE LANDED BEFORE A GROUP OF VIKINGS. THE ALIENS ARE FORMLESS. ALMOST WITHOUT DEFINITION. IT'S ACTUALLY VERY DIFFICULT TO FOCUS ON THEM.
"A NORSEMAN, WHO WAS A KEEPER OF THE OLD STORIES OF THEIR RELIGION, APPROACHES THE ALIENS IN FRIENDSHIP. HE WALKS WITH A LIMP.
"HE CALLS THE ALIENS BROTHERS, IN FEAR OF THEIR TERRIBLE POWER. MAGICALLY, THEY BECOME HIS BROTHERS. WHATEVER THEY WERE BEFORE THIS POINT IS INCONSEQUENTIAL.
"THE NORSEMAN FEARS A FIRE DEMON KNOWN AS SURTUR...AND ONE OF THE ALIEN BEINGS BEGINS TO CHANGE... AND SURTUR APPEARS FOR THE FIRST TIME."
"ARE YOU IMPLYING THAT THIS MAN SOMEHOW SUGGESTED THE IDENTITIES OF THESE ALIENS ACCORDING TO HIS FEARS?"
"YES."
"WHO WAS THIS MAN?"
"HE TOLD THEM TO CALL HIM ODIN. AND THE THREE RODE OFF BEFORE THE SURPRISED NORSEMAN TO FACE THE FIRE DEMON."
"I AM FAMILIAR WITH THE LEGEND OF SURTUR AND THE SWORD SAID TO MARK THE END OF ASGARD. THE FABLE GOES ON TO DESCRIBE HOW ODIN RECEIVED THE POWER OF HIS TWO BROTHERS AND WENT ON TO DEFEAT AND BANISH SURTUR. DID THIS LEGEND COME OUT OF THE EVENTS YOU DESCRIBE?"
"IT'S THE EXACT OPPOSITE. THE EVENTS I DESCRIBE BECAME THE LEGEND AS YOU KNOW IT. THE TWO ALIENS THIS NORSEMAN CALLED BROTHERS ENTERED THE NORSEMAN, ADDING THEIR BEING TO HIS.
"AFTER THIS, ODIN, AS HE WAS NOW CALLED, RETURNED NOT TO HIS FELLOW NORSEMEN, BUT TO THE ALIENS.
"HE GAVE THEM IDENTITY. HE FORGED A NEW WORLD WHICH EXISTS OUTSIDE OUR OWN.
"ONE BASED ON THE OLD STORIES PASSED DOWN TO HIM. AND WHEN STORIES DID NOT EXIST TO ANSWER STRUCTURAL LOGIC, THE STORYTELLER IMPROVISED, CREATING A WORLD IN WHICH HE'D RATHER LIVE.
"A REALITY INVISIBLE TO HIS FELLOW NORSEMEN.
"NOT MERELY ONE WORLD, BUT NINE. NINE WORLDS FROM WHICH HE MIGHT ESCAPE OUR REALITY.

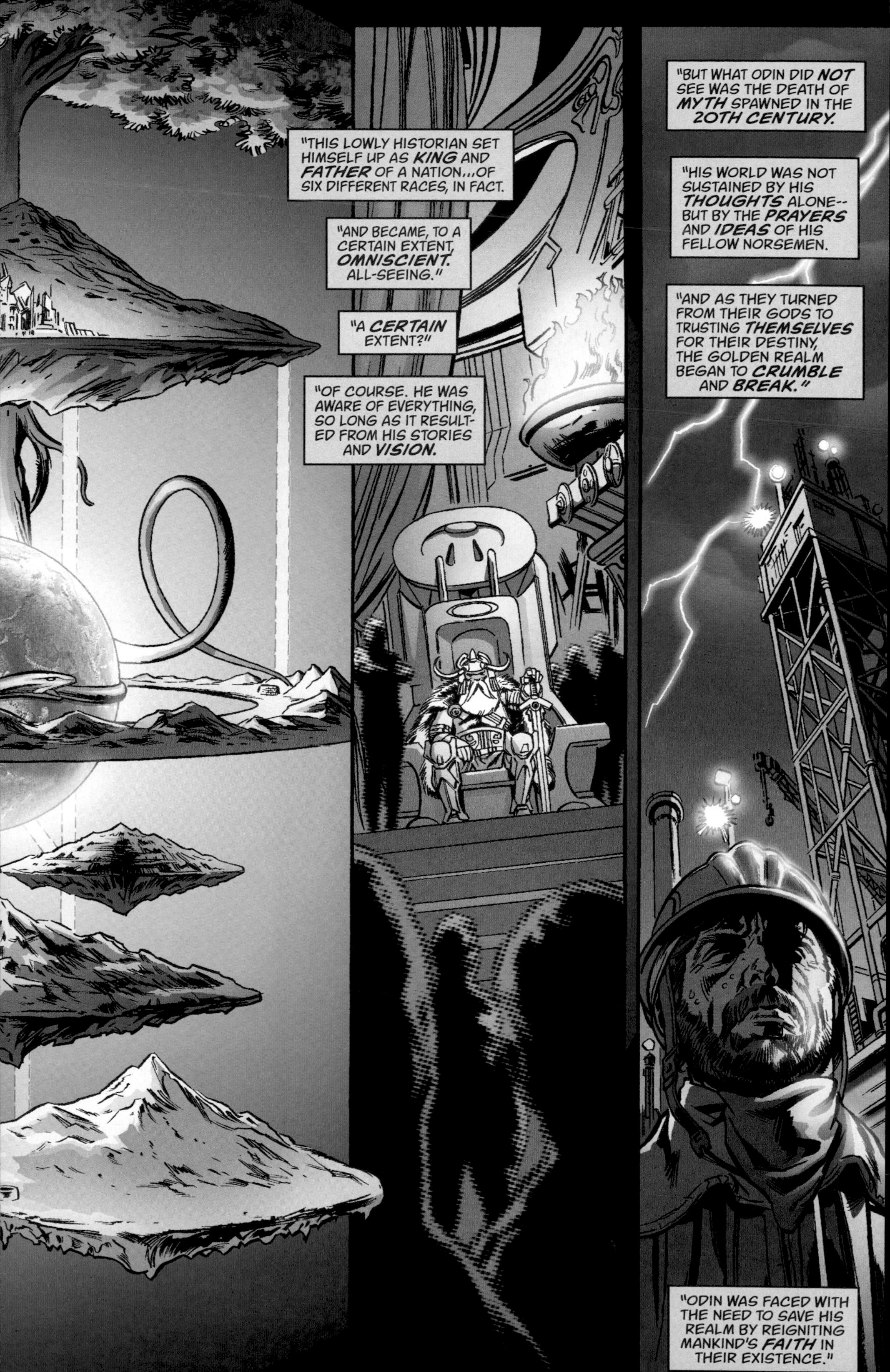
"THIS LOWLY HISTORIAN SET HIMSELF UP AS KING AND FATHER OF A NATION...OF SIX DIFFERENT RACES, IN FACT.
"AND BECAME, TO A CERTAIN EXTENT, OMNISCIENT. ALL-SEEING."
"A CERTAIN EXTENT?"
"OF COURSE. HE WAS AWARE OF EVERYTHING, SO LONG AS IT RESULTED FROM HIS STORIES AND VISION.
"BUT WHAT ODIN DID NOT SEE WAS THE DEATH OF MYTH SPAWNED IN THE 20TH CENTURY.
"HIS WORLD WAS NOT SUSTAINED BY HIS THOUGHTS ALONE--BUT BY THE PRAYERS AND IDEAS OF HIS FELLOW NORSEMEN.
"AND AS THEY TURNED FROM THEIR GODS TO TRUSTING THEMSELVES FOR THEIR DESTINY, THE GOLDEN REALM BEGAN TO CRUMBLE AND BREAK."
"ODIN WAS FACED WITH THE NEED TO SAVE HIS REALM BY REIGNITING MANKIND'S FAITH IN THEIR EXISTENCE."

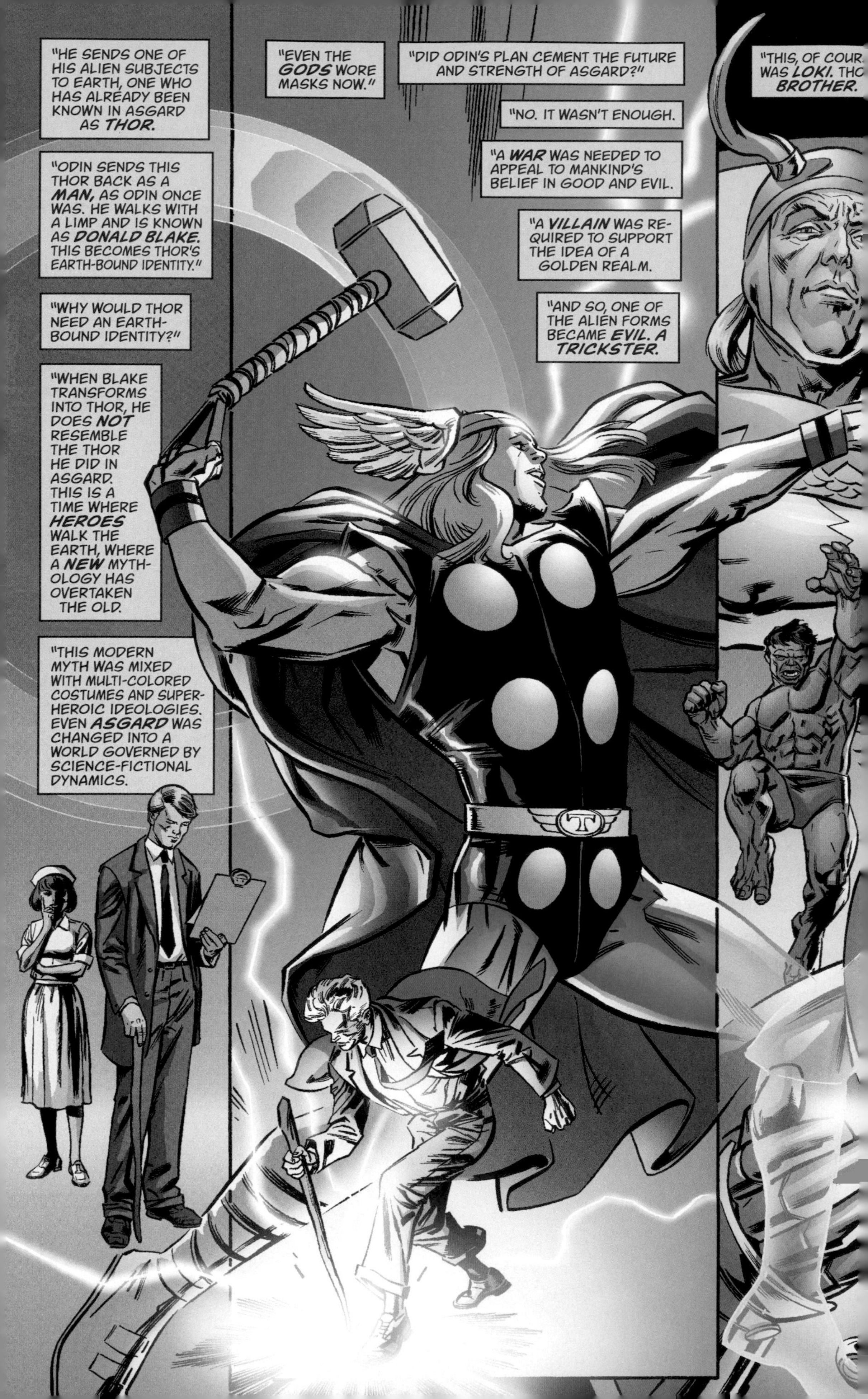
"HE SENDS ONE OF HIS ALIEN SUBJECTS TO EARTH, ONE WHO HAS ALREADY BEEN KNOWN IN ASGARD AS THOR.
"ODIN SENDS THIS THOR BACK AS A MAN, AS ODIN ONCE WAS. HE WALKS WITH A LIMP AND IS KNOWN AS DONALD BLAKE. THIS BECOMES THOR'S EARTH-BOUND IDENTITY."
"WHY WOULD THOR NEED AN EARTH-BOUND IDENTITY?"
"WHEN BLAKE TRANSFORMS INTO THOR, HE DOES NOT RESEMBLE THE THOR HE DID IN ASGARD. THIS IS A TIME WHERE HEROES WALK THE EARTH, WHERE A NEW MYTHOLOGY HAS OVERTAKEN THE OLD.
"THIS MODERN MYTH WAS MIXED WITH MULTI-COLORED COSTUMES AND SUPER-HEROIC IDEOLOGIES. EVEN ASGARD WAS CHANGED INTO A WORLD GOVERNED BY SCIENCE-FICTIONAL DYNAMICS.
"EVEN THE GODS WORE MASKS NOW."
"DID ODIN'S PLAN CEMENT THE FUTURE AND STRENGTH OF ASGARD?"
"NO. IT WASN'T ENOUGH.
"A WAR WAS NEEDED TO APPEAL TO MANKIND'S BELIEF IN GOOD AND EVIL.
"A VILLAIN WAS REQUIRED TO SUPPORT THE IDEA OF A GOLDEN REALM.
"AND SO, ONE OF THE ALIEN FORMS BECAME EVIL. A TRICKSTER.
"THIS, OF COUR
WAS LOKI. THO
BROTHER.

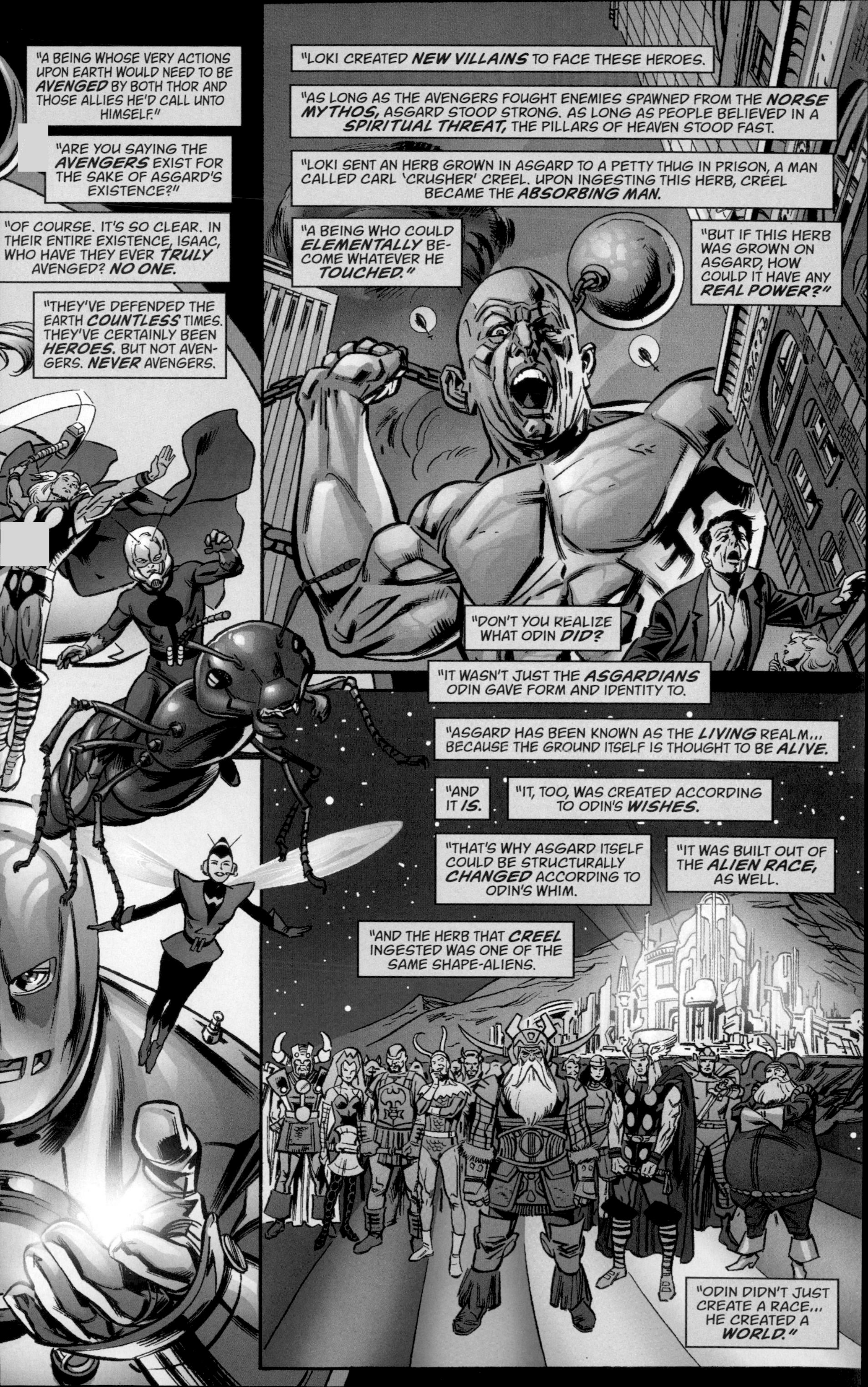
"A BEING WHOSE VERY ACTIONS UPON EARTH WOULD NEED TO BE AVENGED BY BOTH THOR AND THOSE ALLIES HE'D CALL UNTO HIMSELF."
"ARE YOU SAYING THE AVENGERS EXIST FOR THE SAKE OF ASGARD'S EXISTENCE?"
"OF COURSE. IT'S SO CLEAR. IN THEIR ENTIRE EXISTENCE, ISAAC, WHO HAVE THEY EVER TRULY AVENGED? NO ONE.
"THEY'VE DEFENDED THE EARTH COUNTLESS TIMES. THEY'VE CERTAINLY BEEN HEROES. BUT NOT AVENGERS. NEVER AVENGERS.
"LOKI CREATED NEW VILLAINS TO FACE THESE HEROES.
"AS LONG AS THE AVENGERS FOUGHT ENEMIES SPAWNED FROM THE NORSE MYTHOS, ASGARD STOOD STRONG. AS LONG AS PEOPLE BELIEVED IN A SPIRITUAL THREAT, THE PILLARS OF HEAVEN STOOD FAST.
"LOKI SENT AN HERB GROWN IN ASGARD TO A PETTY THUG IN PRISON, A MAN CALLED CARL 'CRUSHER' CREEL. UPON INGESTING THIS HERB, CREEL BECAME THE ABSORBING MAN.
"A BEING WHO COULD ELEMENTALLY BECOME WHATEVER HE TOUCHED."
"BUT IF THIS HERB WAS GROWN ON ASGARD, HOW COULD IT HAVE ANY REAL POWER?"
"DON'T YOU REALIZE WHAT ODIN DID?
"IT WASN'T JUST THE ASGARDIANS ODIN GAVE FORM AND IDENTITY TO.
"ASGARD HAS BEEN KNOWN AS THE LIVING REALM... BECAUSE THE GROUND ITSELF IS THOUGHT TO BE ALIVE.
"AND IT IS.
"IT, TOO, WAS CREATED ACCORDING TO ODIN'S WISHES.
"THAT'S WHY ASGARD ITSELF COULD BE STRUCTURALLY CHANGED ACCORDING TO ODIN'S WHIM.
"IT WAS BUILT OUT OF THE ALIEN RACE, AS WELL.
"AND THE HERB THAT CREEL INGESTED WAS ONE OF THE SAME SHAPE-ALIENS.
"ODIN DIDN'T JUST CREATE A RACE... HE CREATED A WORLD."

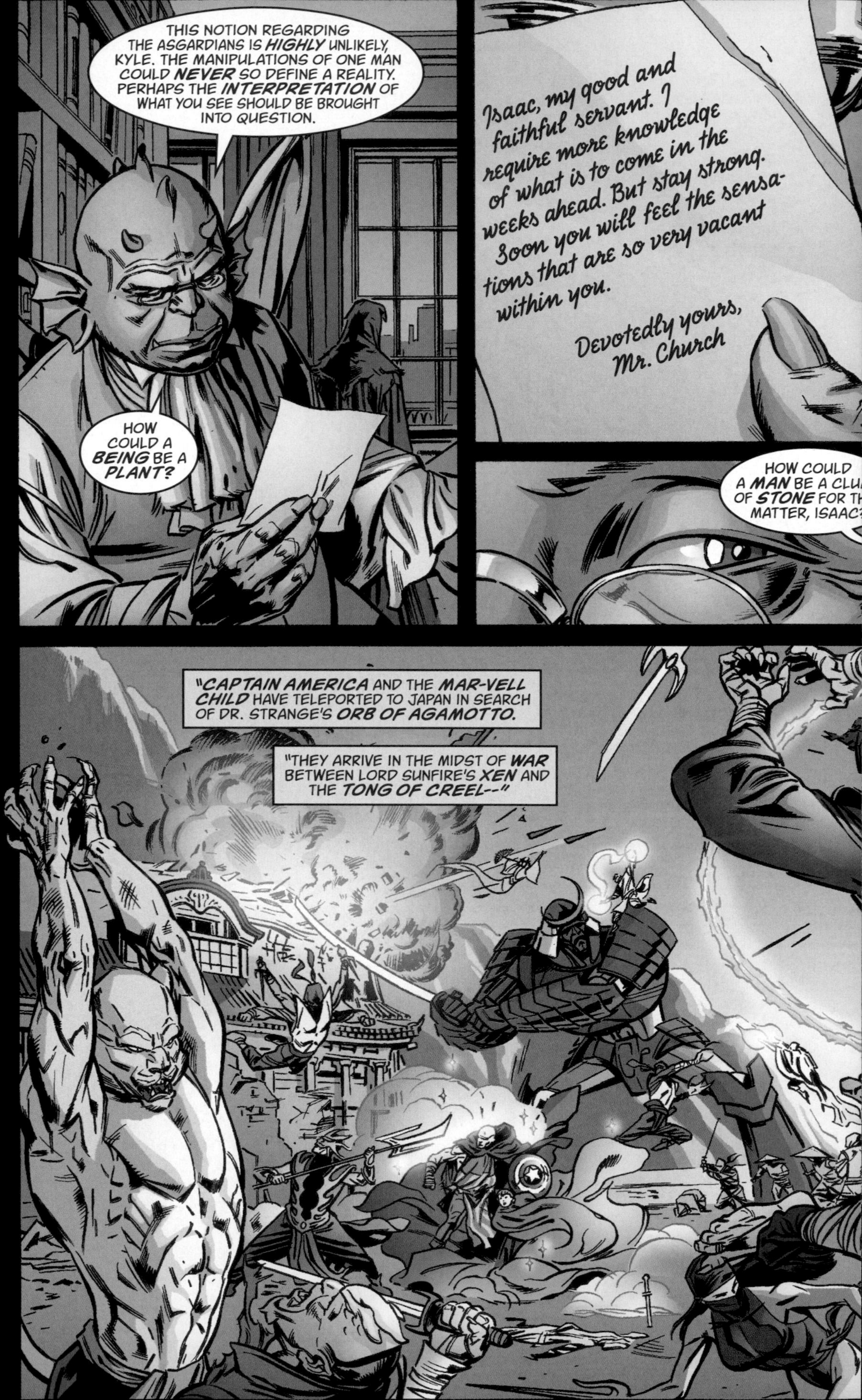
THIS NOTION REGARDING THE ASGARDIANS IS HIGHLY UNLIKELY, KYLE. THE MANIPULATIONS OF ONE MAN COULD NEVER SO DEFINE A REALITY. PERHAPS THE INTERPRETATION OF WHAT YOU SEE SHOULD BE BROUGHT INTO QUESTION.
Isaac, my good and faithful servant. I require more knowledge of what is to come in the weeks ahead. But stay strong. Soon you will feel the sensations that are so very vacant within you.
Devotedly yours, Mr. Church
HOW COULD A BEING BE A PLANT?
"CAPTAIN AMERICA AND THE MAR-VELL CHILD HAVE TELEPORTED TO JAPAN IN SEARCH OF DR. STRANGE'S ORB OF AGAMOTTO.
"THEY ARRIVE IN THE MIDST OF WAR BETWEEN LORD SUNFIRE'S XEN AND THE TONG OF CREEL--"

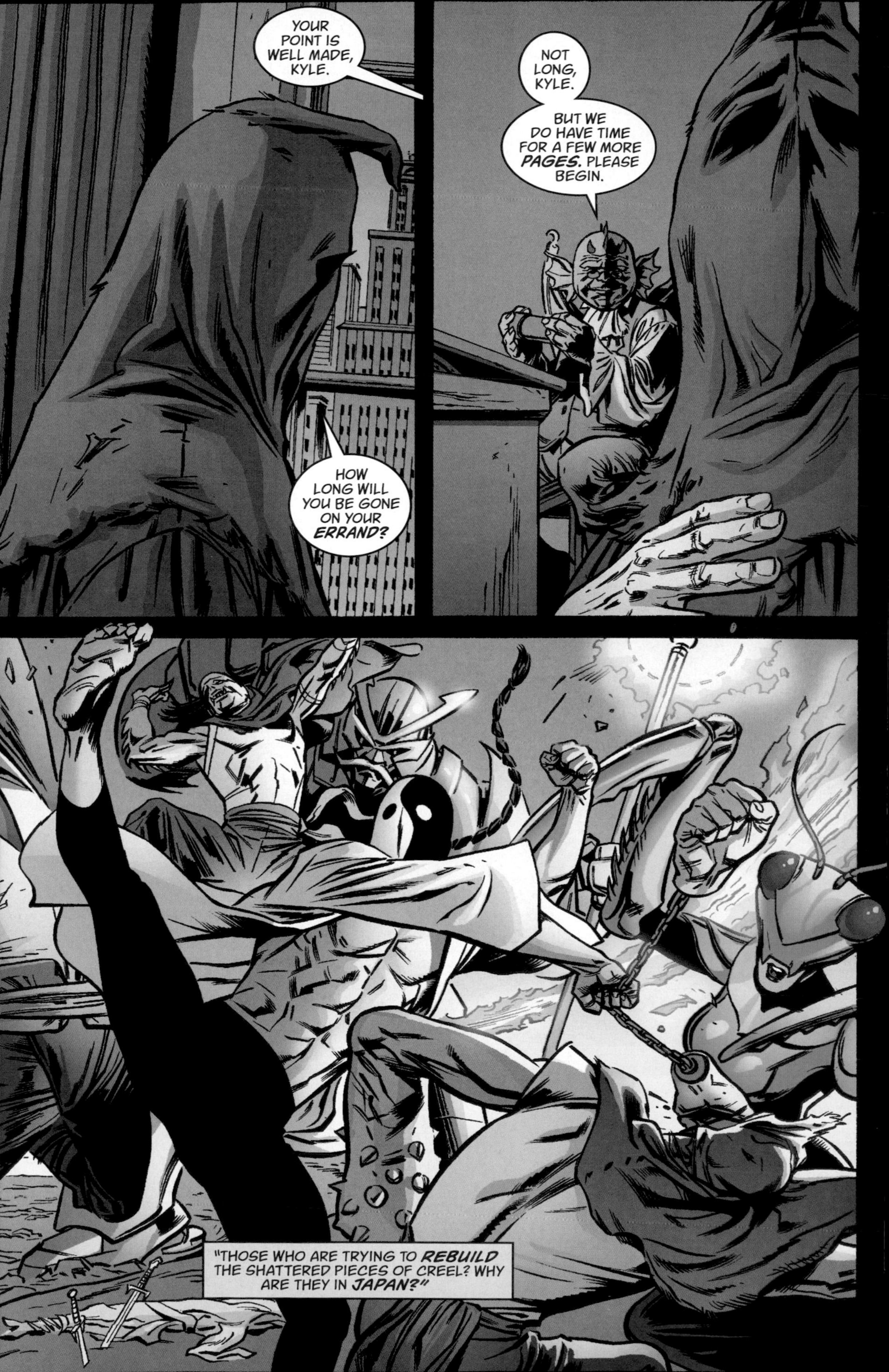
YOUR POINT IS WELL MADE, KYLE.
HOW LONG WILL YOU BE GONE ON YOUR ERRAND?
NOT LONG, KYLE.
BUT WE DO HAVE TIME FOR A FEW MORE PAGES. PLEASE BEGIN.
"THOSE WHO ARE TRYING TO REBUILD THE SHATTERED PIECES OF CREEL? WHY ARE THEY IN JAPAN?"

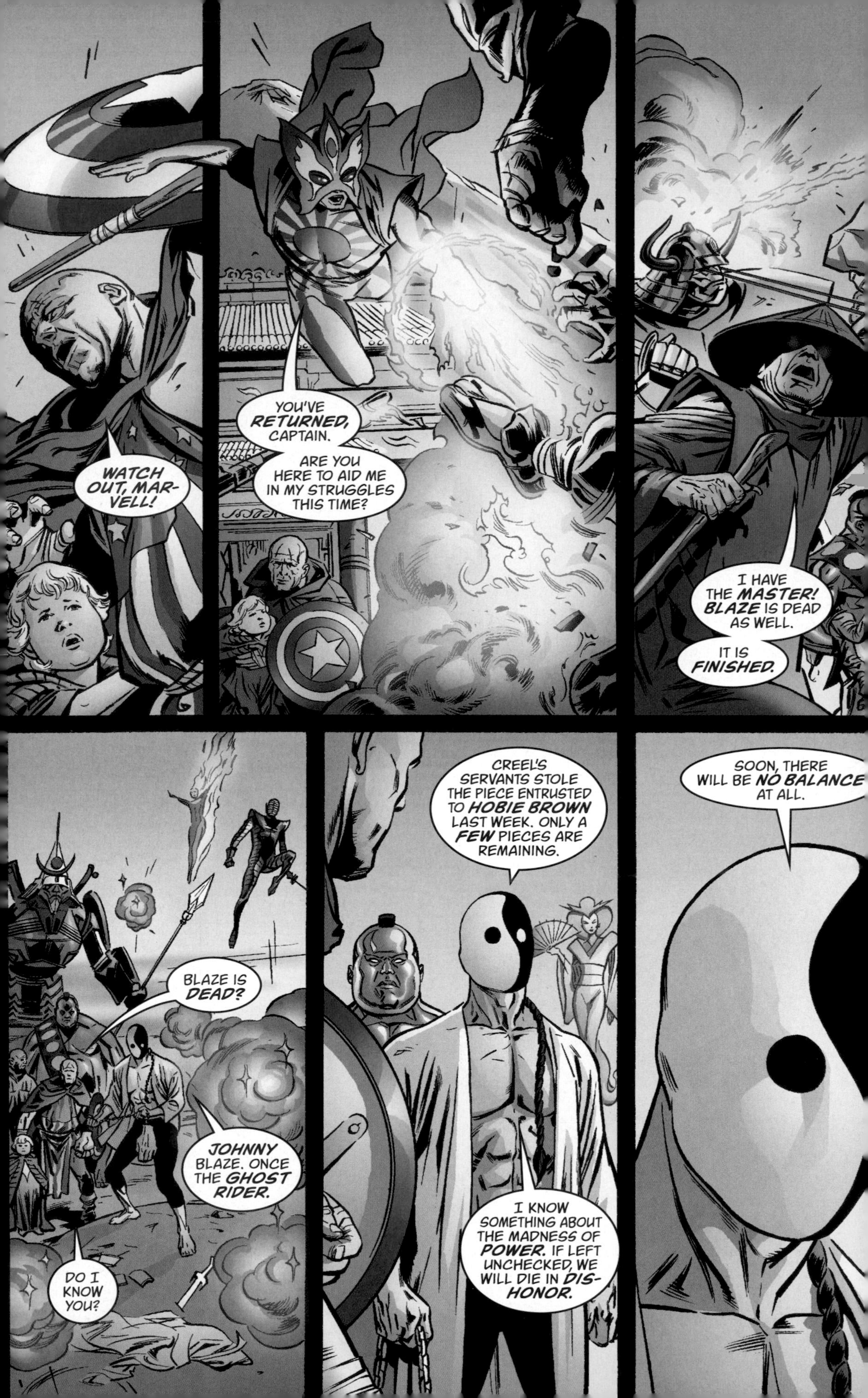
WATCH OUT, MAR-VELL!
YOU'VE RETURNED, CAPTAIN.
ARE YOU HERE TO AID ME IN MY STRUGGLES THIS TIME?
I HAVE THE MASTER! BLAZE IS DEAD AS WELL.
IT IS FINISHED.
BLAZE IS DEAD?
JOHNNY BLAZE. ONCE THE GHOST RIDER.
DO I KNOW YOU?
CREEL'S SERVANTS STOLE THE PIECE ENTRUSTED TO HOBIE BROWN LAST WEEK. ONLY A FEW PIECES ARE REMAINING.
I KNOW SOMETHING ABOUT THE MADNESS OF POWER. IF LEFT UNCHECKED, WE WILL DIE IN DIS-HONOR.
SOON, THERE WILL BE NO BALANCE AT ALL.

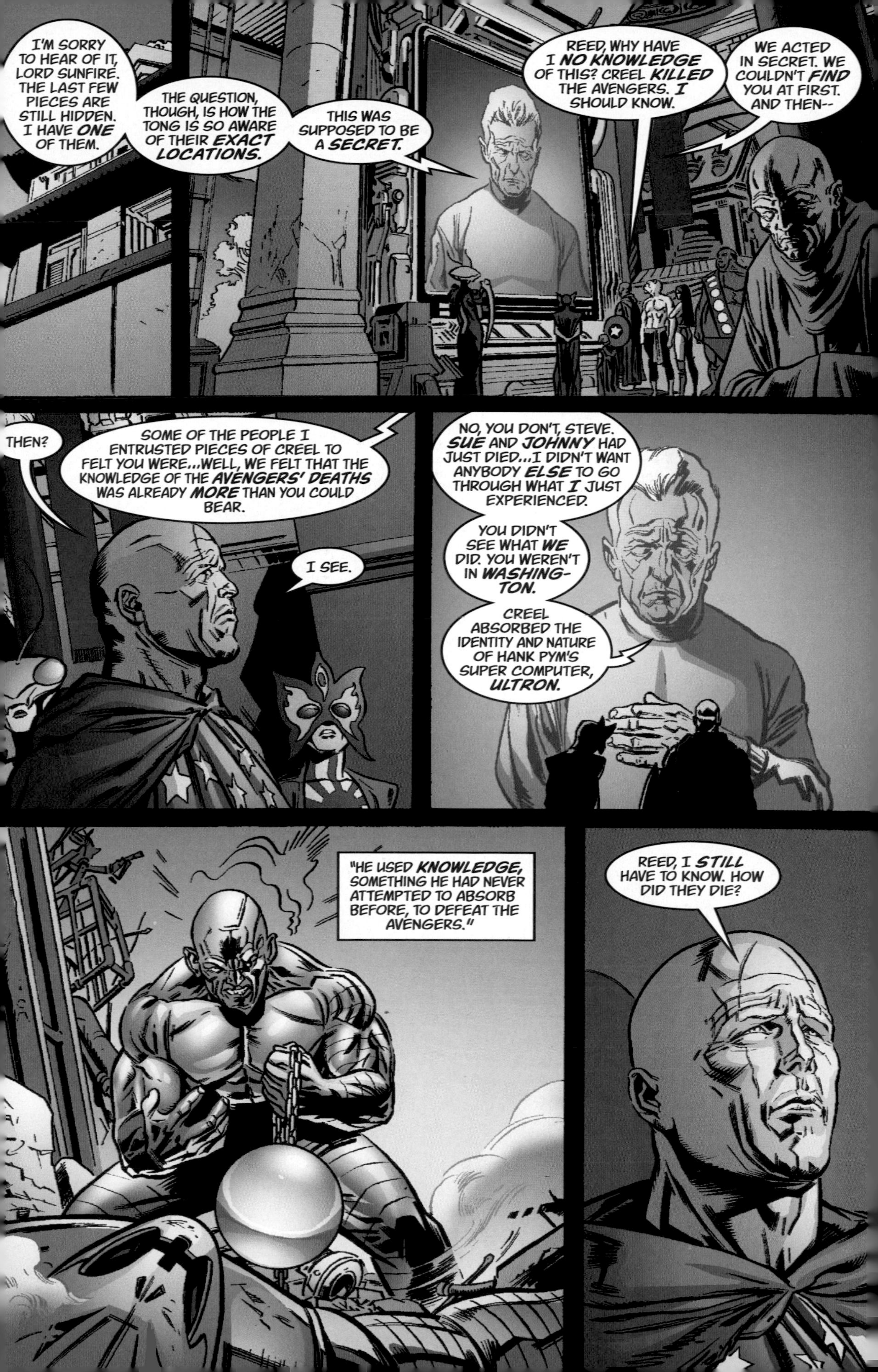
I'M SORRY TO HEAR OF IT, LORD SUNFIRE. THE LAST FEW PIECES ARE STILL HIDDEN. I HAVE ONE OF THEM.
THE QUESTION, THOUGH, IS HOW THE TONG IS SO AWARE OF THEIR EXACT LOCATIONS.
THIS WAS SUPPOSED TO BE A SECRET.
REED, WHY HAVE I NO KNOWLEDGE OF THIS? CREEL KILLED THE AVENGERS. I SHOULD KNOW.
WE ACTED IN SECRET. WE COULDN'T FIND YOU AT FIRST. AND THEN--
THEN?
SOME OF THE PEOPLE I ENTRUSTED PIECES OF CREEL TO FELT YOU WERE...WELL, WE FELT THAT THE KNOWLEDGE OF THE AVENGERS' DEATHS WAS ALREADY MORE THAN YOU COULD BEAR.
I SEE.
NO, YOU DON'T, STEVE. SUE AND JOHNNY HAD JUST DIED...I DIDN'T WANT ANYBODY ELSE TO GO THROUGH WHAT I JUST EXPERIENCED.
YOU DIDN'T SEE WHAT WE DID. YOU WEREN'T IN WASHINGTON.
CREEL ABSORBED THE IDENTITY AND NATURE OF HANK PYM'S SUPER COMPUTER, ULTRON.
"HE USED KNOWLEDGE, SOMETHING HE HAD NEVER ATTEMPTED TO ABSORB BEFORE, TO DEFEAT THE AVENGERS."
REED, I STILL HAVE TO KNOW. HOW DID THEY DIE?

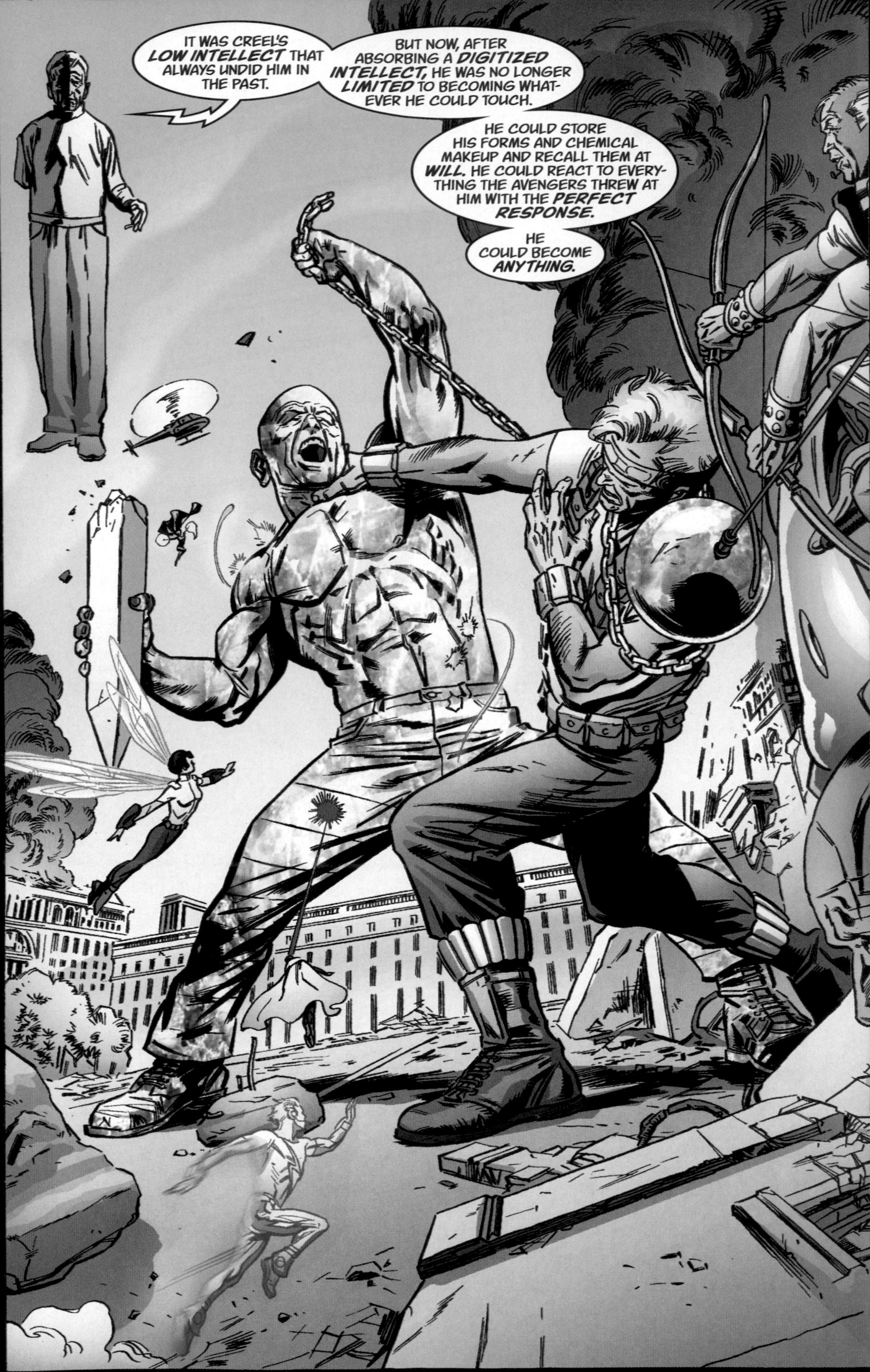
IT WAS CREEL'S LOW INTELLECT THAT ALWAYS UNDID HIM IN THE PAST.
BUT NOW, AFTER ABSORBING A DIGITIZED INTELLECT, HE WAS NO LONGER LIMITED TO BECOMING WHAT-EVER HE COULD TOUCH.
HE COULD STORE HIS FORMS AND CHEMICAL MAKEUP AND RECALL THEM AT WILL. HE COULD REACT TO EVERY-THING THE AVENGERS THREW AT HIM WITH THE PERFECT RESPONSE.
HE COULD BECOME ANYTHING.

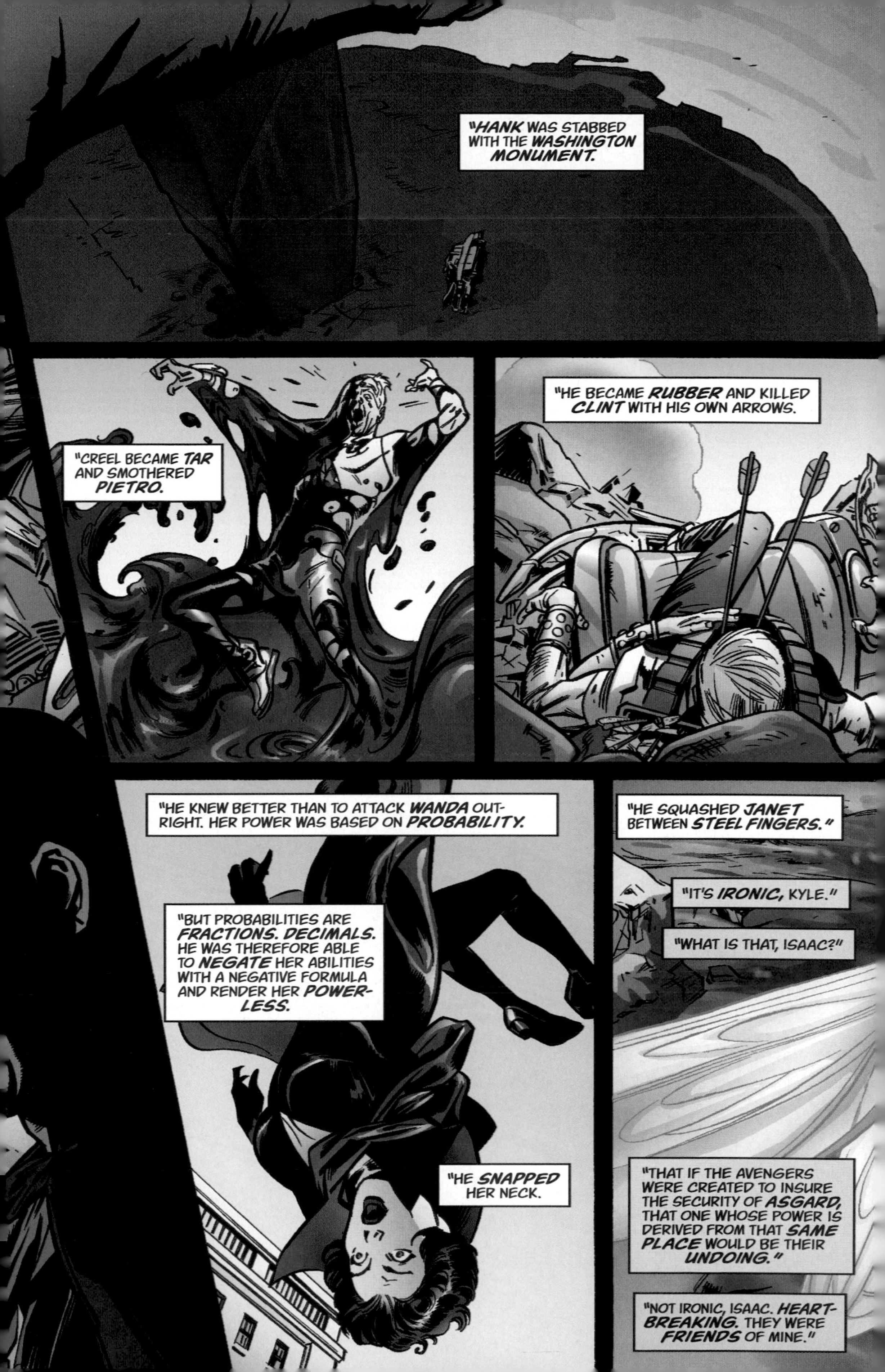
"HANK WAS STABBED WITH THE WASHINGTON MONUMENT.
"CREEL BECAME TAR AND SMOTHERED PIETRO.
"HE BECAME RUBBER AND KILLED CLINT WITH HIS OWN ARROWS.
"HE KNEW BETTER THAN TO ATTACK WANDA OUT-RIGHT. HER POWER WAS BASED ON PROBABILITY.
"BUT PROBABILITIES ARE FRACTIONS. DECIMALS. HE WAS THEREFORE ABLE TO NEGATE HER ABILITIES WITH A NEGATIVE FORMULA AND RENDER HER POWER-LESS.
"HE SNAPPED HER NECK.
"HE SQUASHED JANET BETWEEN STEEL FINGERS."
"IT'S IRONIC, KYLE."
"WHAT IS THAT, ISAAC?"
"THAT IF THE AVENGERS WERE CREATED TO INSURE THE SECURITY OF ASGARD, THAT ONE WHOSE POWER IS DERIVED FROM THAT SAME PLACE WOULD BE THEIR UNDOING."
"NOT IRONIC, ISAAC. HEART-BREAKING. THEY WERE FRIENDS OF MINE."

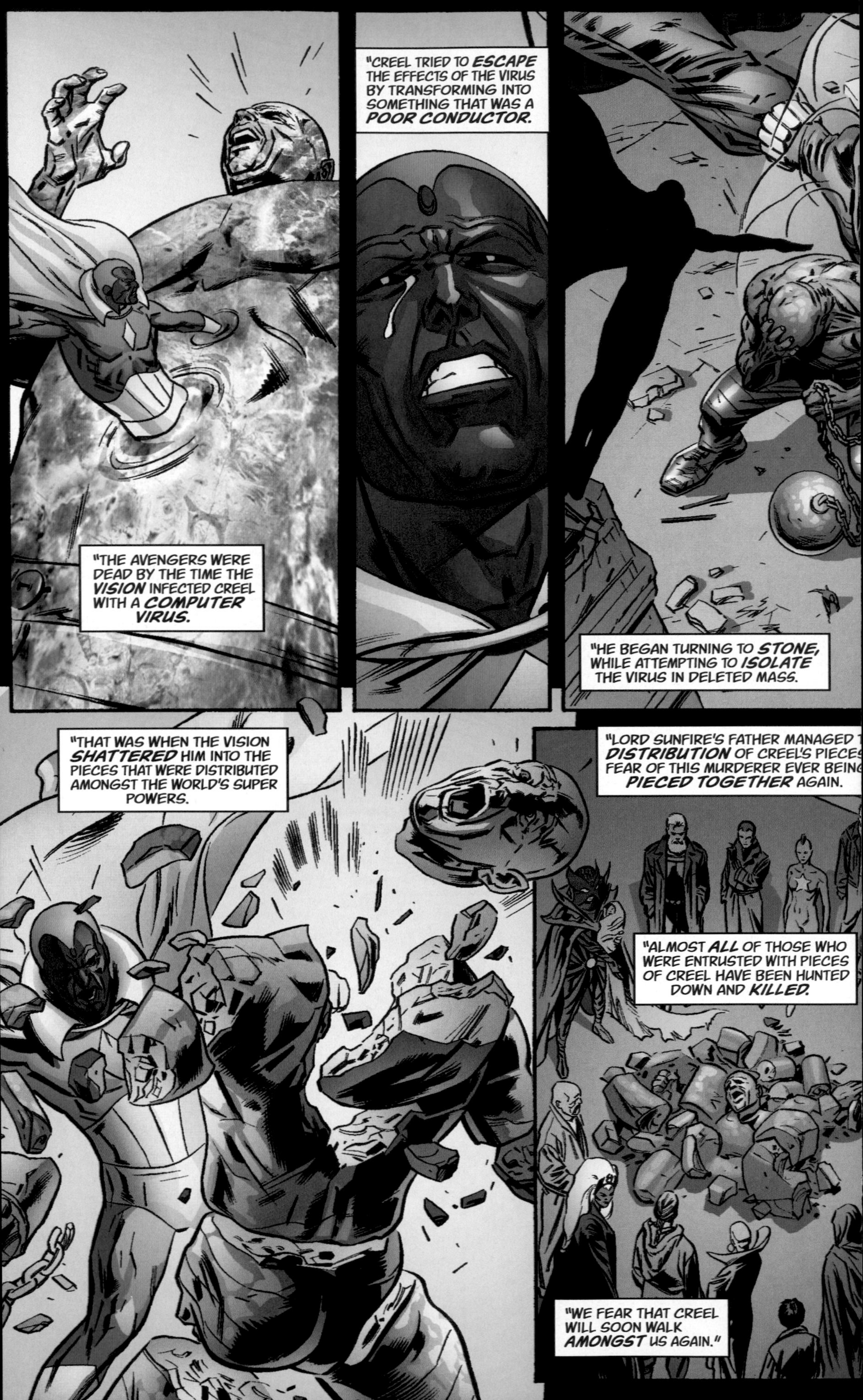
"THE AVENGERS WERE DEAD BY THE TIME THE VISION INFECTED CREEL WITH A COMPUTER VIRUS.
"CREEL TRIED TO ESCAPE THE EFFECTS OF THE VIRUS BY TRANSFORMING INTO SOMETHING THAT WAS A POOR CONDUCTOR.
"HE BEGAN TURNING TO STONE, WHILE ATTEMPTING TO ISOLATE THE VIRUS IN DELETED MASS.
"THAT WAS WHEN THE VISION SHATTERED HIM INTO THE PIECES THAT WERE DISTRIBUTED AMONGST THE WORLD'S SUPER POWERS.
"LORD SUNFIRE'S FATHER MANAGED T DISTRIBUTION OF CREEL'S PIECES FEAR OF THIS MURDERER EVER BEING PIECED TOGETHER AGAIN.
"ALMOST ALL OF THOSE WHO WERE ENTRUSTED WITH PIECES OF CREEL HAVE BEEN HUNTED DOWN AND KILLED.
"WE FEAR THAT CREEL WILL SOON WALK AMONGST US AGAIN."

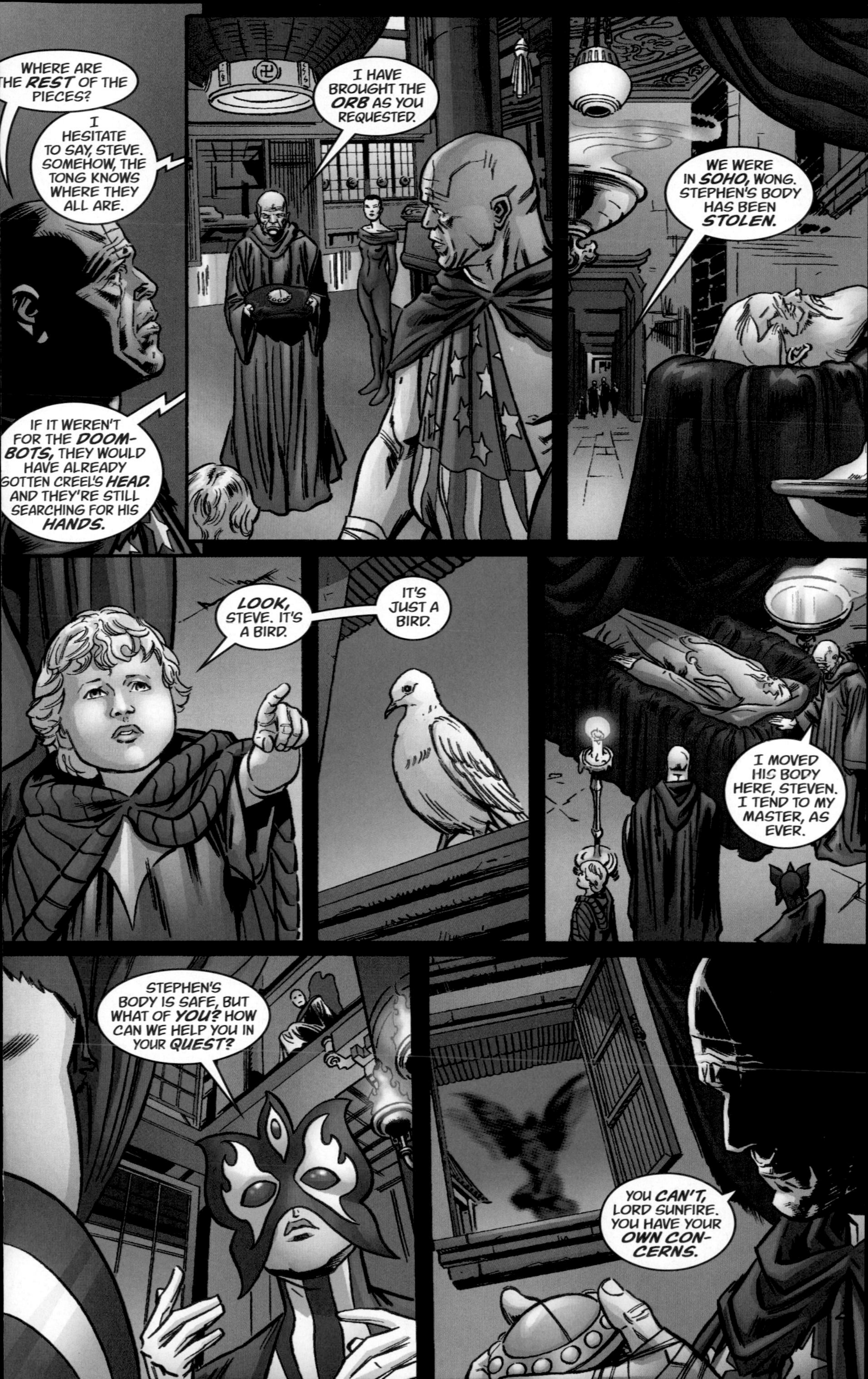

WHERE ARE THE REST OF THE PIECES?
I HESITATE TO SAY, STEVE. SOMEHOW, THE TONG KNOWS WHERE THEY ALL ARE.
IF IT WEREN'T FOR THE DOOM-BOTS, THEY WOULD HAVE ALREADY GOTTEN CREEL'S HEAD. AND THEY'RE STILL SEARCHING FOR HIS HANDS.
I HAVE BROUGHT THE ORB AS YOU REQUESTED.
WE WERE IN SOHO, WONG. STEPHEN'S BODY HAS BEEN STOLEN.
LOOK, STEVE. IT'S A BIRD.
IT'S JUST A BIRD.
I MOVED HIS BODY HERE, STEVEN. I TEND TO MY MASTER, AS EVER.
STEPHEN'S BODY IS SAFE, BUT WHAT OF YOU? HOW CAN WE HELP YOU IN YOUR QUEST?
YOU CAN'T, LORD SUNFIRE. YOU HAVE YOUR OWN CON-CERNS.

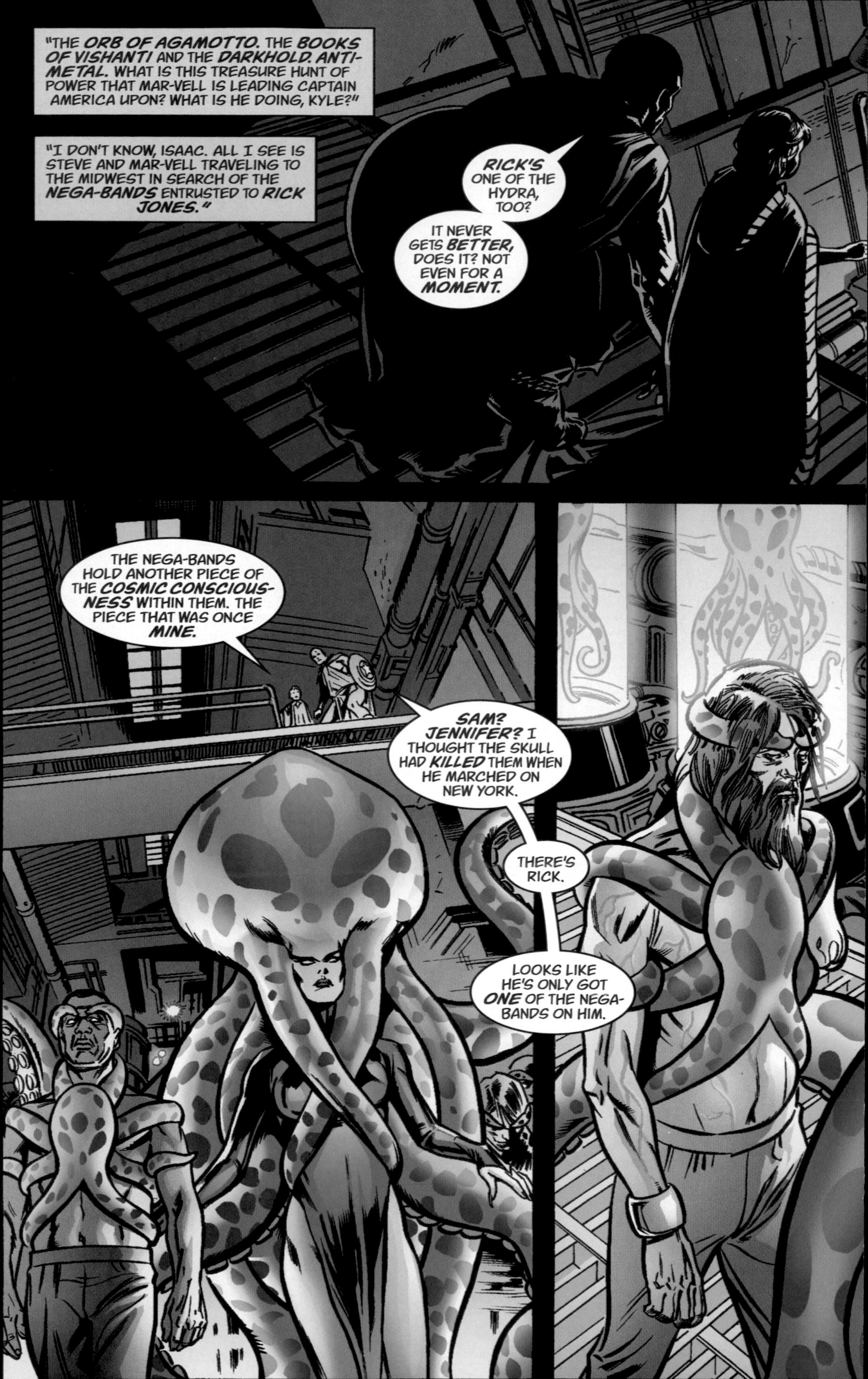
"THE ORB OF AGAMOTTO. THE BOOKS OF VISHANTI AND THE DARKHOLD. ANTI-METAL. WHAT IS THIS TREASURE HUNT OF POWER THAT MAR-VELL IS LEADING CAPTAIN AMERICA UPON? WHAT IS HE DOING, KYLE?"
"I DON'T KNOW, ISAAC. ALL I SEE IS STEVE AND MAR-VELL TRAVELING TO THE MIDWEST IN SEARCH OF THE NEGA-BANDS ENTRUSTED TO RICK JONES."
RICK'S ONE OF THE HYDRA, TOO?
IT NEVER GETS BETTER, DOES IT? NOT EVEN FOR A MOMENT.
THE NEGA-BANDS HOLD ANOTHER PIECE OF THE COSMIC CONSCIOUSNESS WITHIN THEM. THE PIECE THAT WAS ONCE MINE.
SAM? JENNIFER? I THOUGHT THE SKULL HAD KILLED THEM WHEN HE MARCHED ON NEW YORK.
THERE'S RICK.
LOOKS LIKE HE'S ONLY GOT ONE OF THE NEGA-BANDS ON HIM.

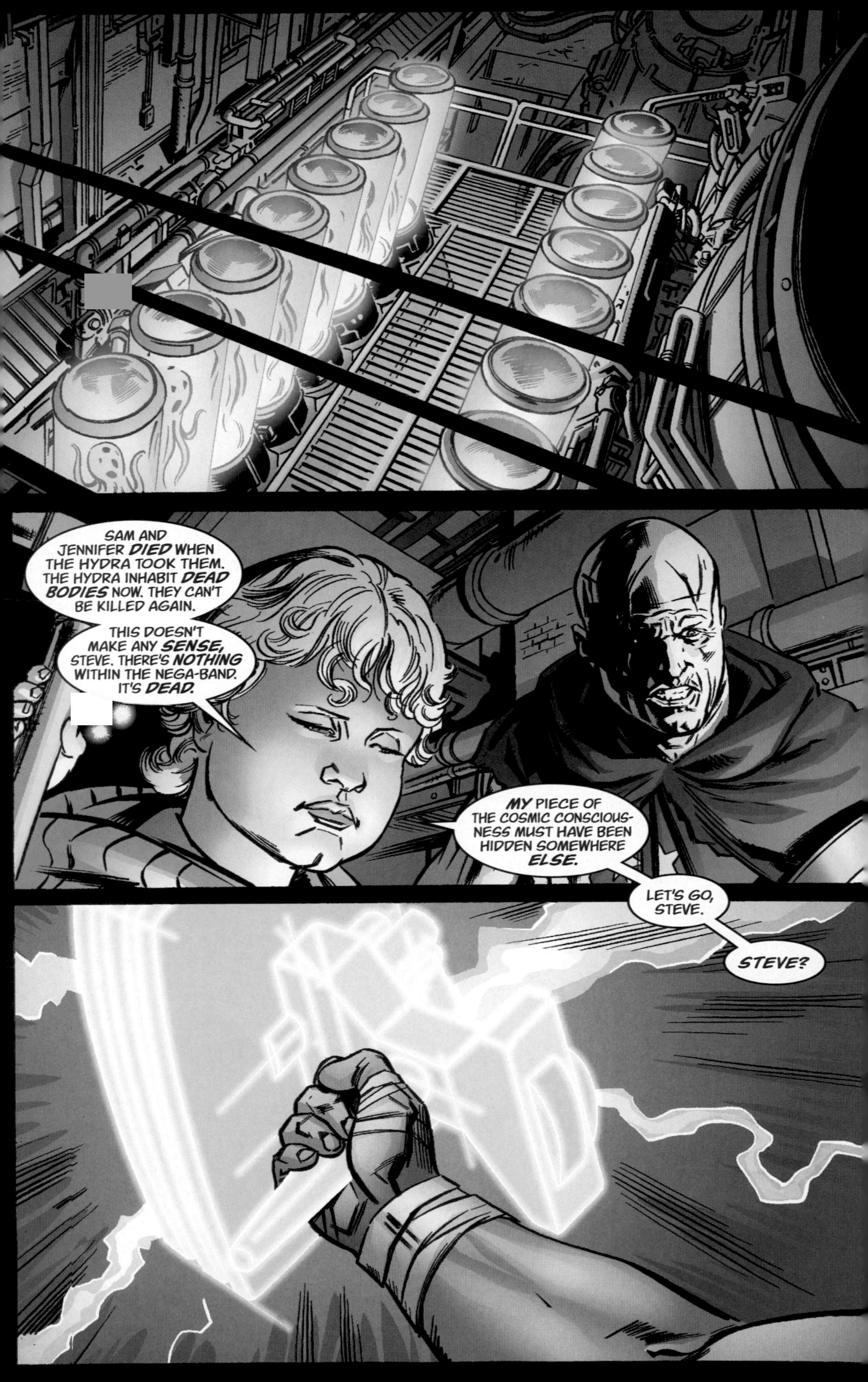
SAM AND JENNIFER *DIED* WHEN THE HYDRA TOOK THEM. THE HYDRA INHABIT *DEAD BODIES* NOW. THEY CAN'T BE KILLED AGAIN.
THIS DOESN'T MAKE ANY *SENSE*, STEVE. THERE'S *NOTHING* WITHIN THE NEGA-BAND. IT'S *DEAD*.
MY PIECE OF THE COSMIC CONSCIOUSNESS MUST HAVE BEEN HIDDEN SOMEWHERE *ELSE*.
LET'S GO, STEVE.
STEVE?

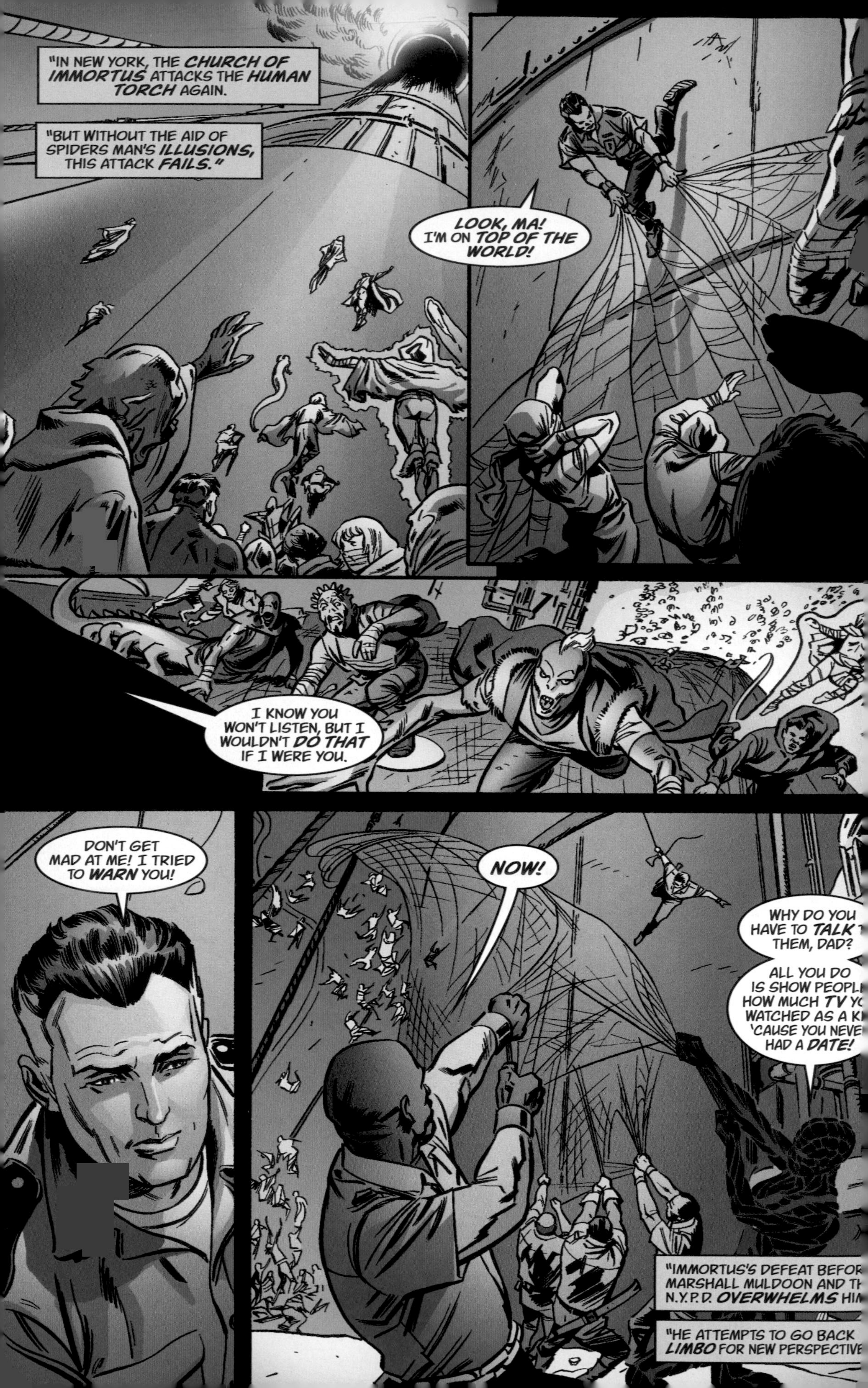
"IN NEW YORK, THE CHURCH OF IMMORTUS ATTACKS THE HUMAN TORCH AGAIN.
"BUT WITHOUT THE AID OF SPIDERS MAN'S ILLUSIONS, THIS ATTACK FAILS."
LOOK, MA! I'M ON TOP OF THE WORLD!
I KNOW YOU WON'T LISTEN, BUT I WOULDN'T DO THAT IF I WERE YOU.
DON'T GET MAD AT ME! I TRIED TO WARN YOU!
NOW!
WHY DO YOU HAVE TO TALK THEM, DAD?
ALL YOU DO IS SHOW PEOPL HOW MUCH TV Y WATCHED AS A K 'CAUSE YOU NEVE HAD A DATE!
"IMMORTUS'S DEFEAT BEFOR MARSHALL MULDOON AND TH N.Y.P.D. OVERWHELMS HIM
"HE ATTEMPTS TO GO BACK LIMBO FOR NEW PERSPECTIVE

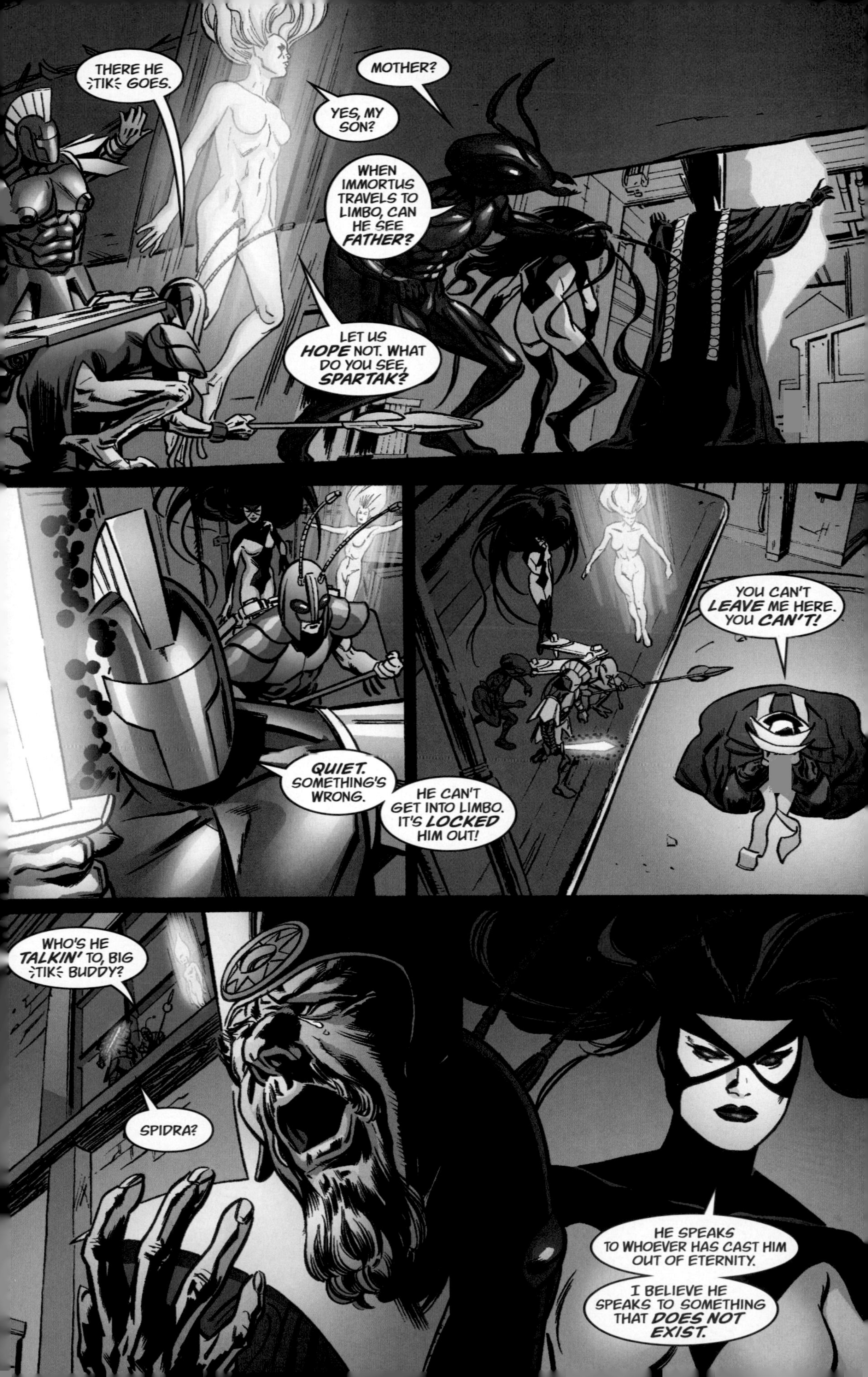
THERE HE ⁝TIK⁝ GOES.
MOTHER?
YES, MY SON?
WHEN IMMORTUS TRAVELS TO LIMBO, CAN HE SEE FATHER?
LET US HOPE NOT. WHAT DO YOU SEE, SPARTAK?
QUIET. SOMETHING'S WRONG.
HE CAN'T GET INTO LIMBO. IT'S LOCKED HIM OUT!
YOU CAN'T LEAVE ME HERE. YOU CAN'T!
WHO'S HE TALKIN' TO, BIG ⁝TIK⁝ BUDDY?
SPIDRA?
HE SPEAKS TO WHOEVER HAS CAST HIM OUT OF ETERNITY.
I BELIEVE HE SPEAKS TO SOMETHING THAT DOES NOT EXIST.

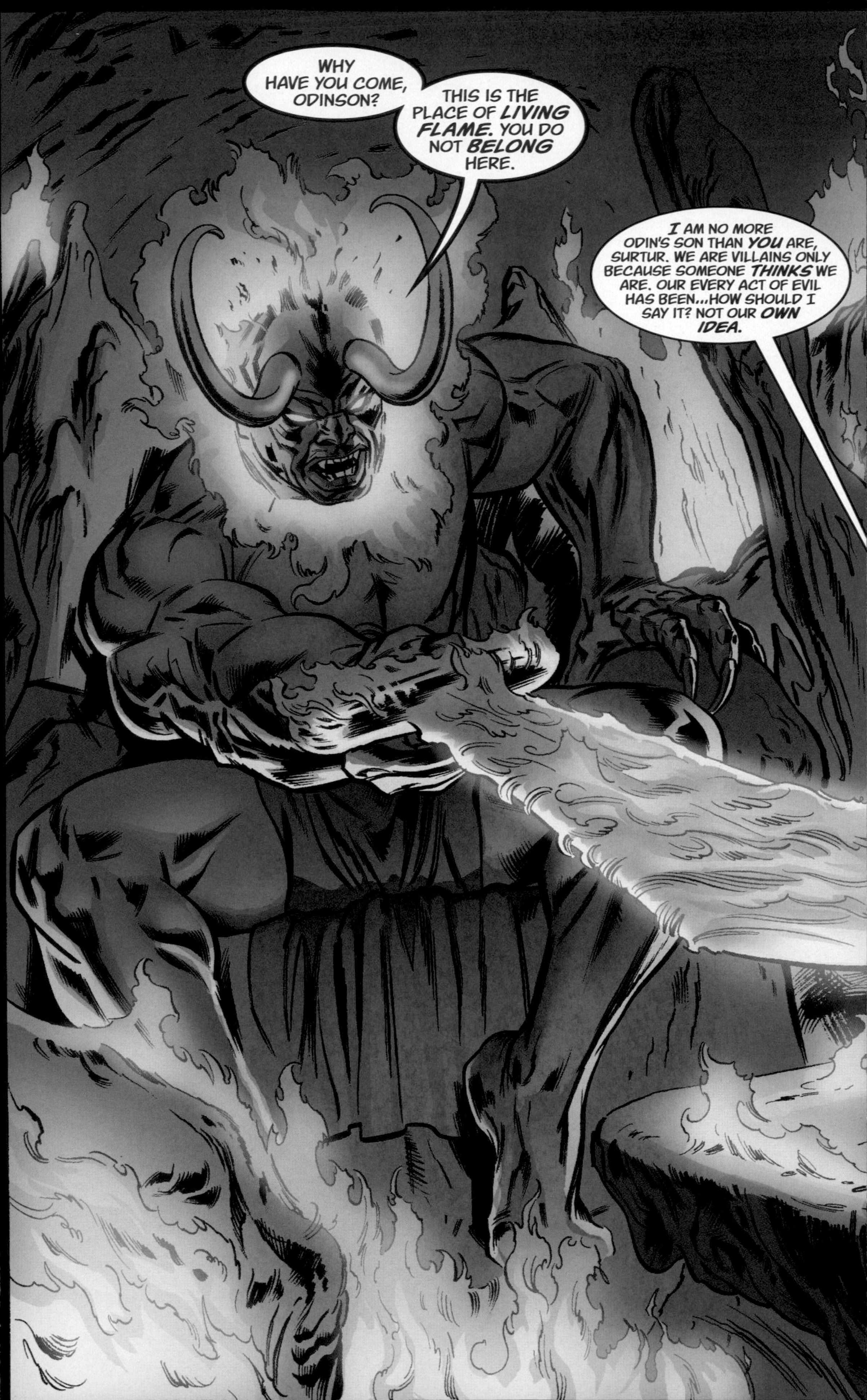
WHY HAVE YOU COME, ODINSON?
THIS IS THE PLACE OF LIVING FLAME. YOU DO NOT BELONG HERE.
I AM NO MORE ODIN'S SON THAN YOU ARE, SURTUR. WE ARE VILLAINS ONLY BECAUSE SOMEONE THINKS WE ARE. OUR EVERY ACT OF EVIL HAS BEEN...HOW SHOULD I SAY IT? NOT OUR OWN IDEA.

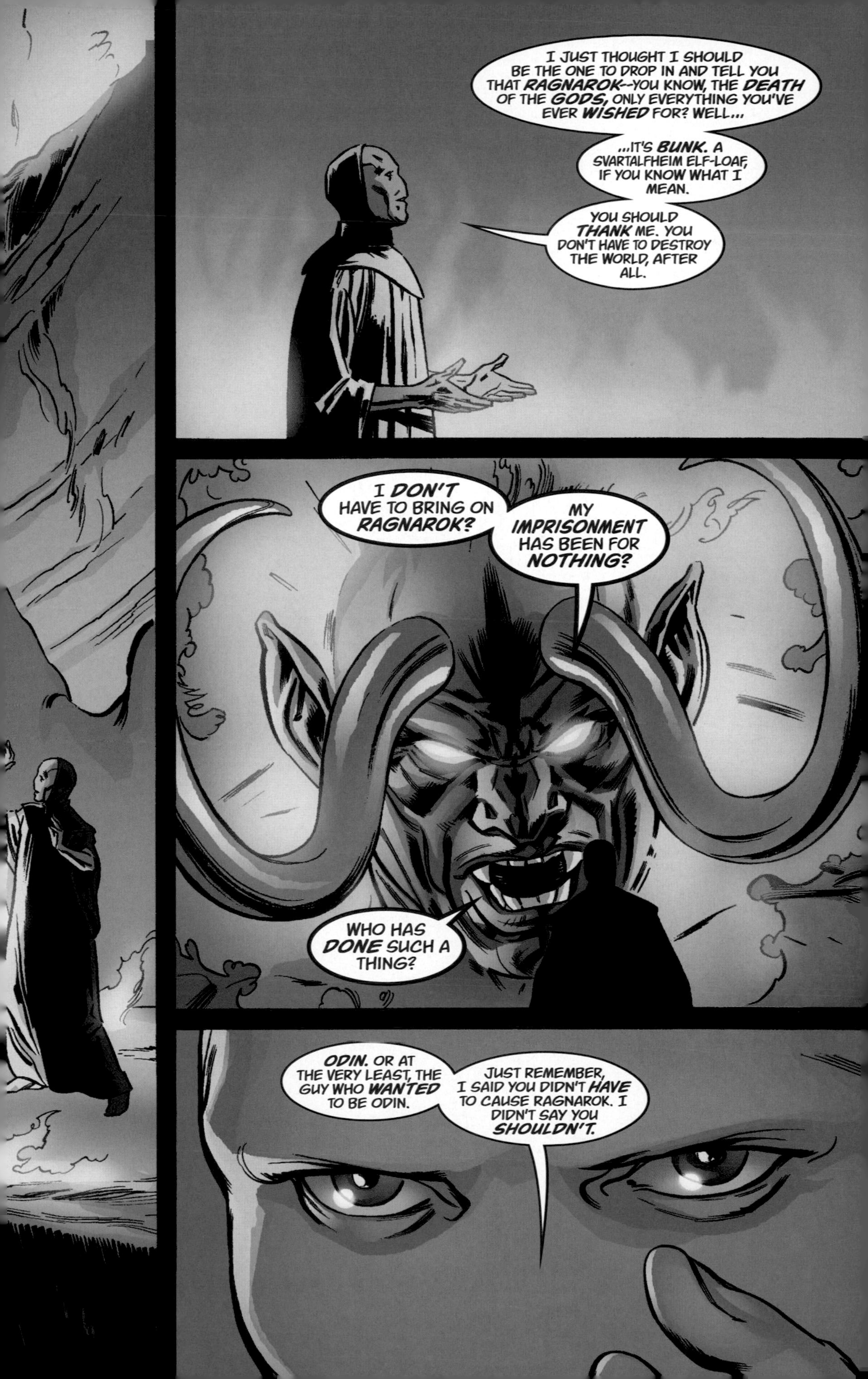
I JUST THOUGHT I SHOULD BE THE ONE TO DROP IN AND TELL YOU THAT RAGNAROK--YOU KNOW, THE DEATH OF THE GODS, ONLY EVERYTHING YOU'VE EVER WISHED FOR? WELL...
...IT'S BUNK. A SVARTALFHEIM ELF-LOAF, IF YOU KNOW WHAT I MEAN.
YOU SHOULD THANK ME. YOU DON'T HAVE TO DESTROY THE WORLD, AFTER ALL.
I DON'T HAVE TO BRING ON RAGNAROK?
MY IMPRISONMENT HAS BEEN FOR NOTHING?
WHO HAS DONE SUCH A THING?
ODIN. OR AT THE VERY LEAST, THE GUY WHO WANTED TO BE ODIN.
JUST REMEMBER, I SAID YOU DIDN'T HAVE TO CAUSE RAGNAROK. I DIDN'T SAY YOU SHOULDN'T.

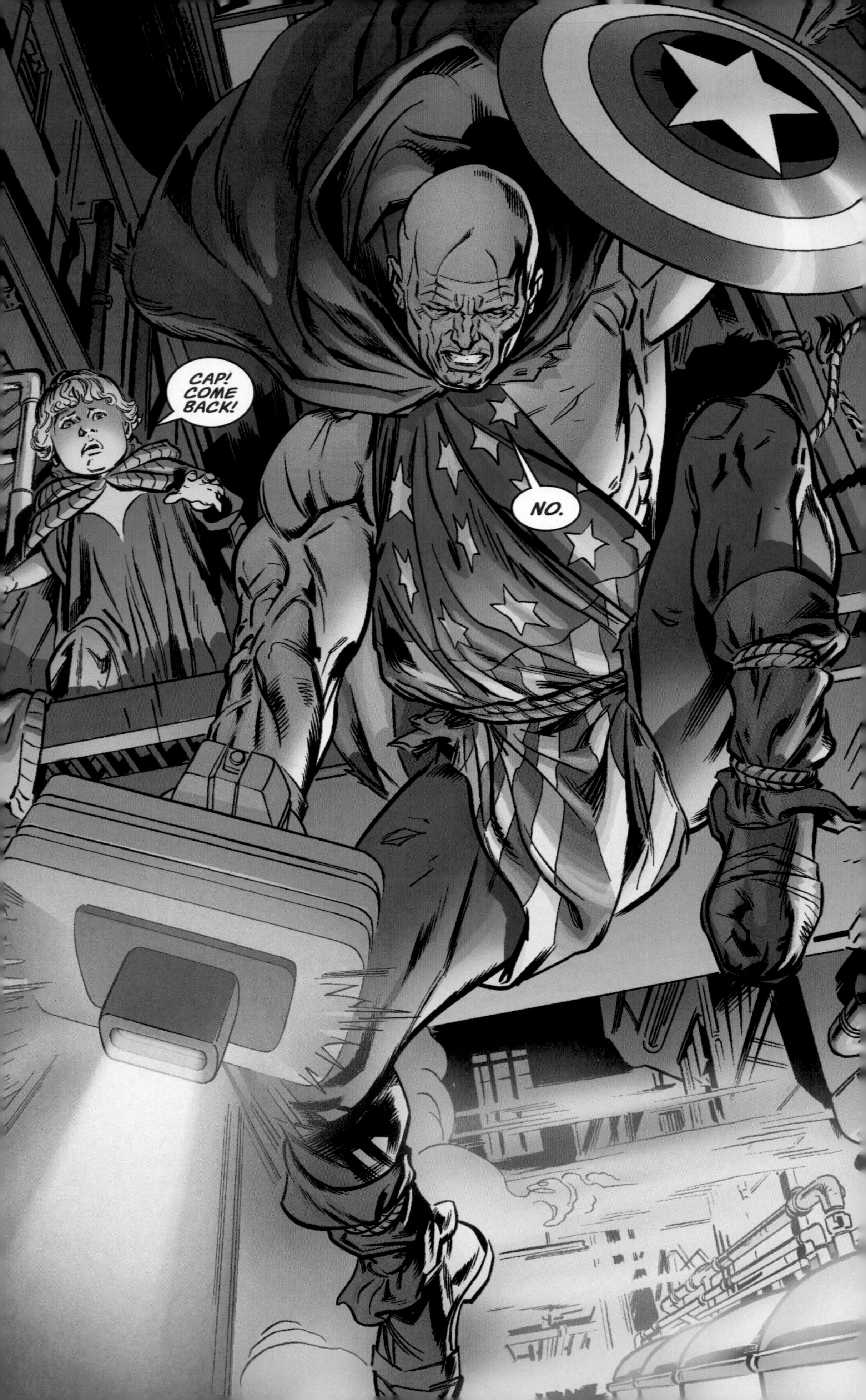
CAP! COME BACK!
NO.

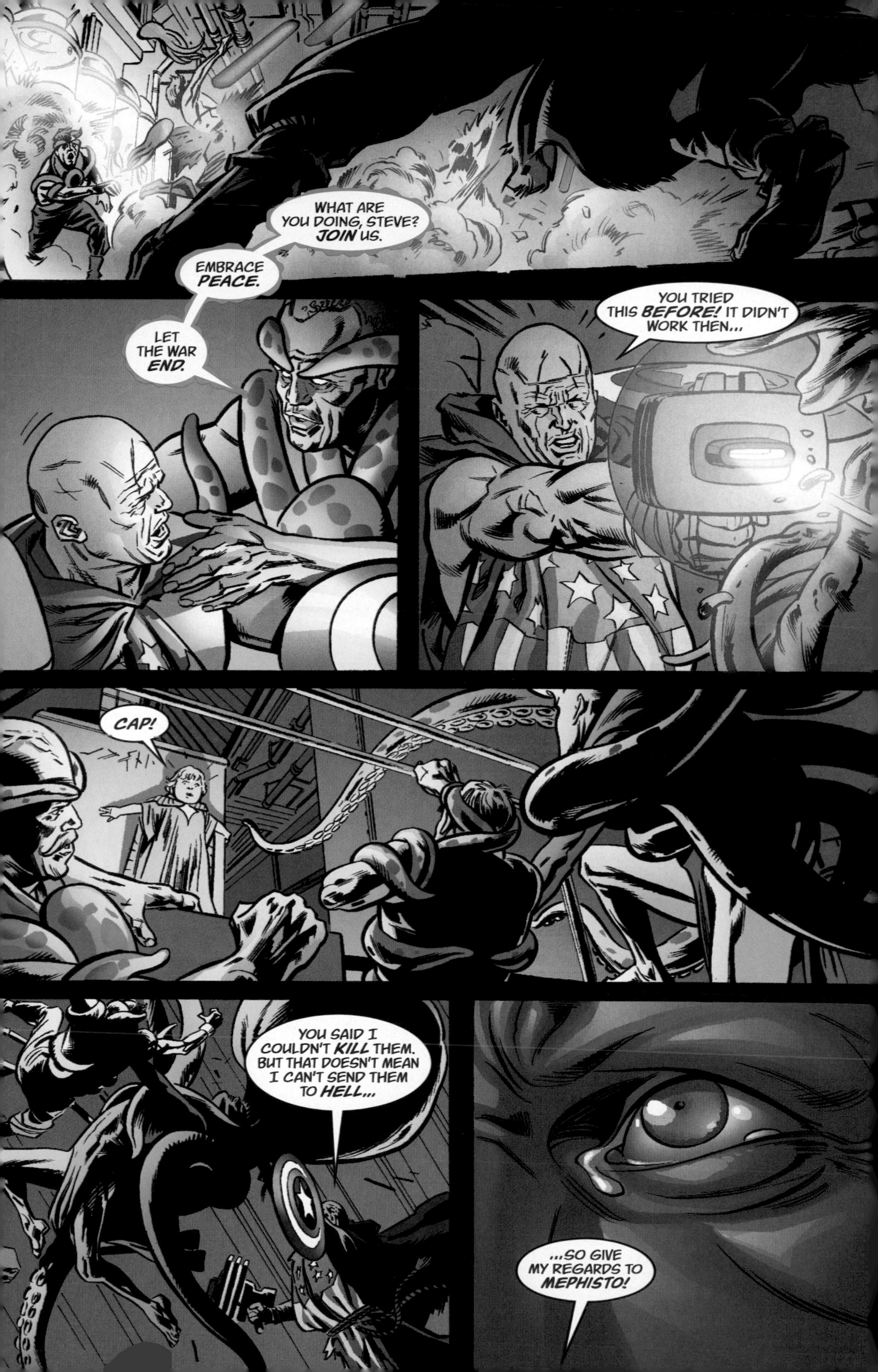
WHAT ARE YOU DOING, STEVE? JOIN US.
EMBRACE PEACE.
LET THE WAR END.
YOU TRIED THIS BEFORE! IT DIDN'T WORK THEN...
CAP!
YOU SAID I COULDN'T KILL THEM. BUT THAT DOESN'T MEAN I CAN'T SEND THEM TO HELL...
...SO GIVE MY REGARDS TO MEPHISTO!

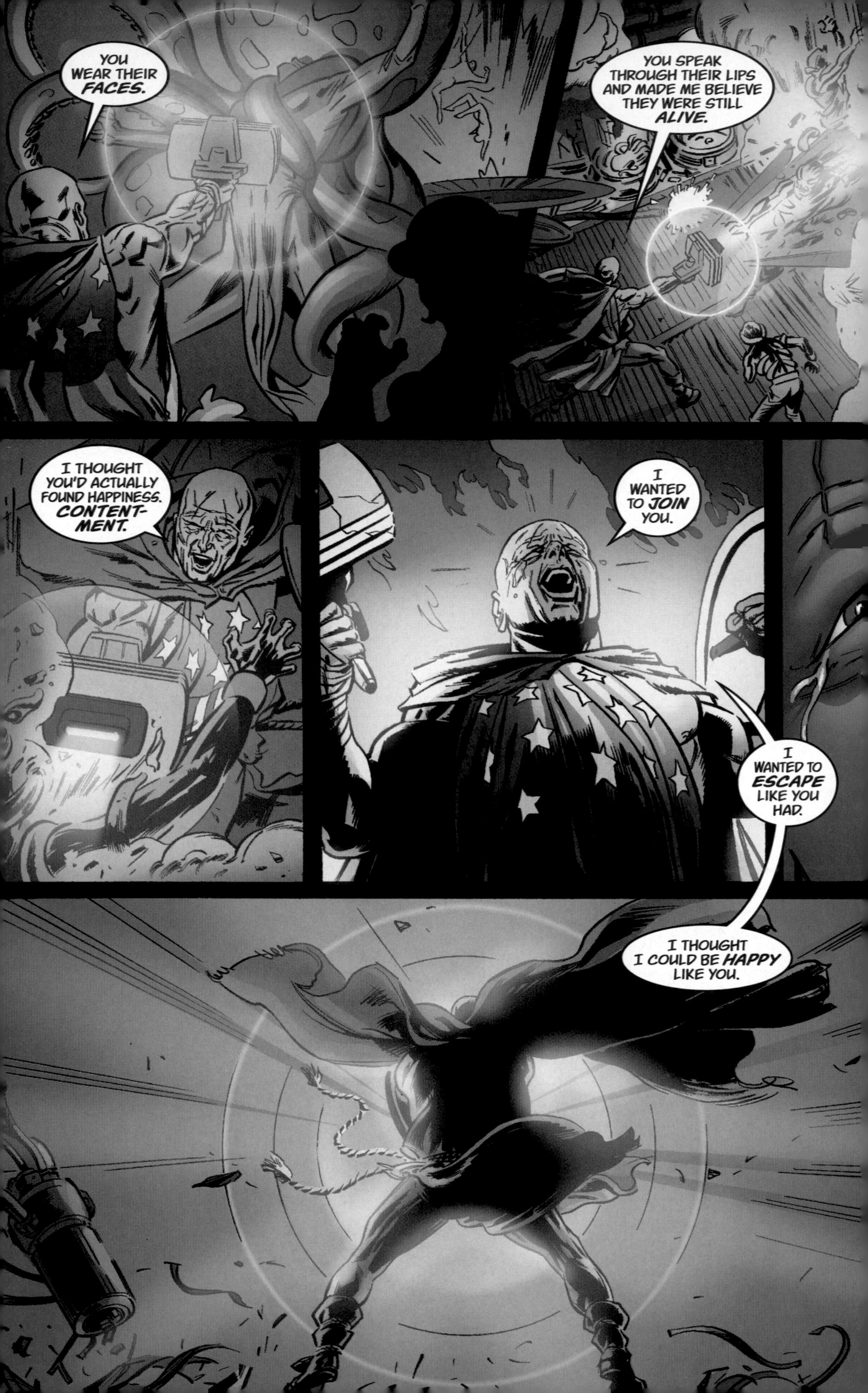
YOU WEAR THEIR *FACES.*
YOU SPEAK THROUGH THEIR LIPS AND MADE ME BELIEVE THEY WERE STILL *ALIVE.*
I THOUGHT YOU'D ACTUALLY FOUND HAPPINESS. *CONTENT-MENT.*
I WANTED TO *JOIN* YOU.
I WANTED TO *ESCAPE* LIKE YOU HAD.
I THOUGHT I COULD BE *HAPPY* LIKE YOU.

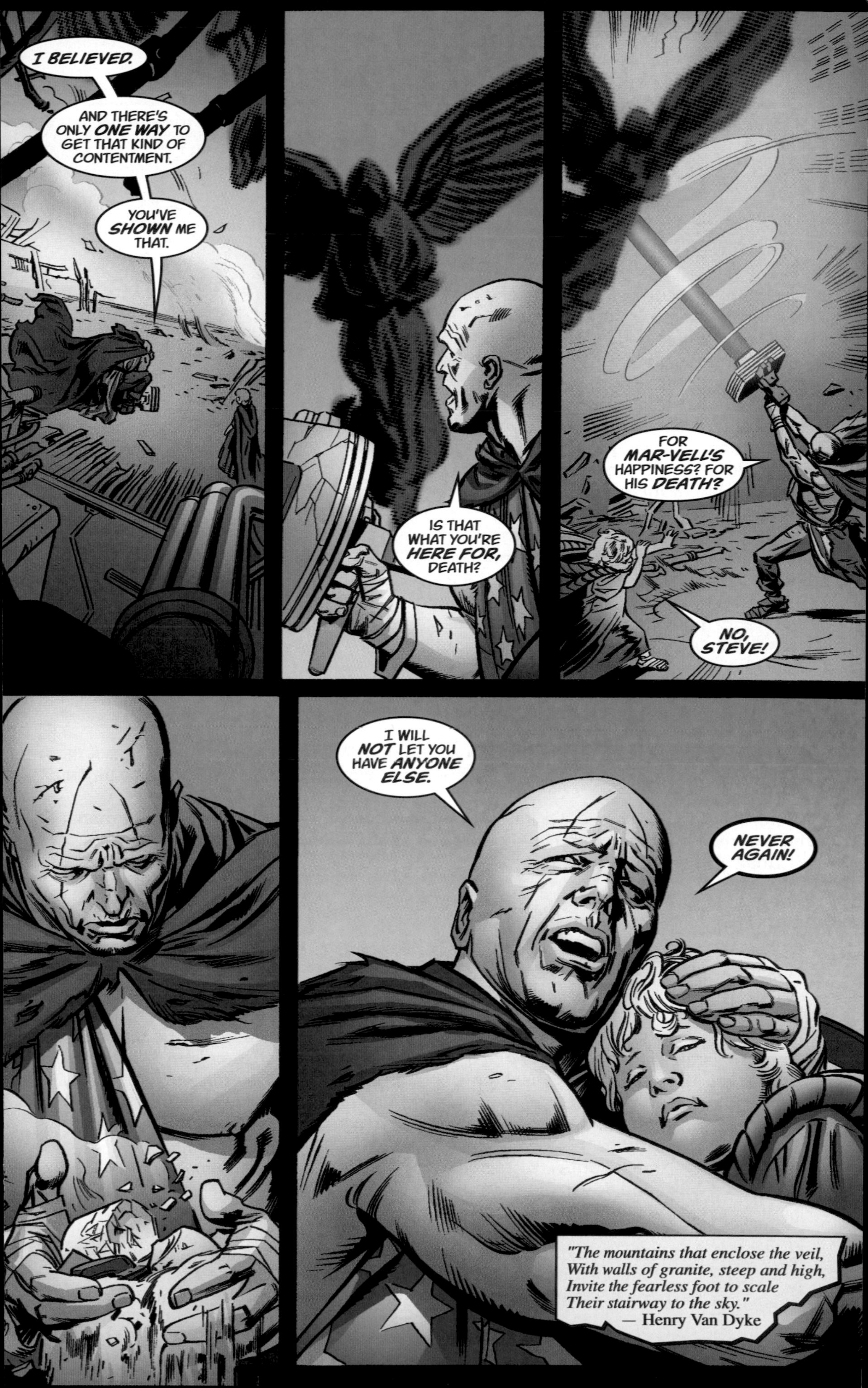
I BELIEVED.
AND THERE'S ONLY ONE WAY TO GET THAT KIND OF CONTENTMENT.
YOU'VE SHOWN ME THAT.
IS THAT WHAT YOU'RE HERE FOR, DEATH?
FOR MAR-VELL'S HAPPINESS? FOR HIS DEATH?
NO, STEVE!
I WILL NOT LET YOU HAVE ANYONE ELSE.
NEVER AGAIN!
"The mountains that enclose the veil,
With walls of granite, steep and high,
Invite the fearless foot to scale
Their stairway to the sky."
— Henry Van Dyke

UNIVERSE X

APPENDIX TO CHAPTER FOUR

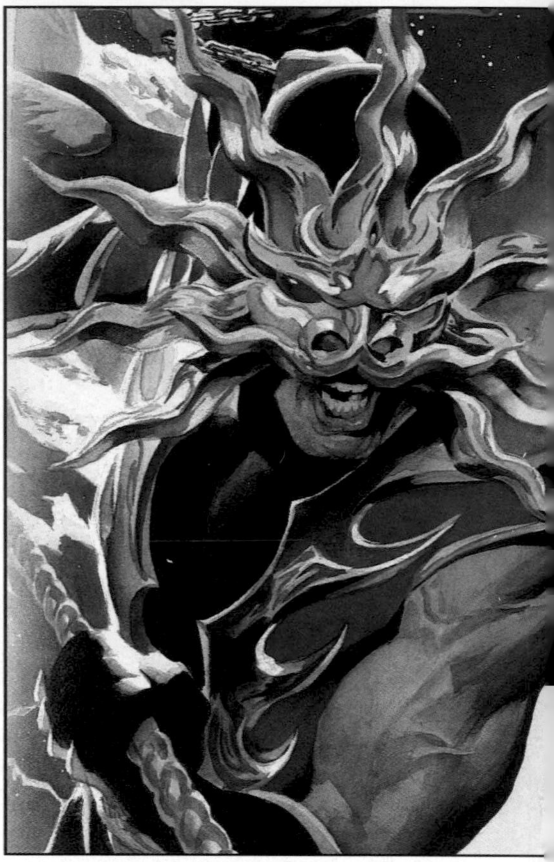

WRITTEN BY JIM KRUEGER

"Why is it, Uatu, that I can't shake the feeling that Death is not following Mar-Vell, but Steve Rogers... Captain America?"

"What leads you to this conclusion, robot?"

"I'm not certain. Call it a hunch."

"You are not capable of hunches, merely calculating probabilities."

"You don't have any idea what it's like to be human, alien. So your definitions of what I am capable or incapable of are little more than uninformed opinion."

"Your attempts at defensiveness need work, robot, if you are going to convince the population of Earth that you are one of them."

"Whatever you say, Uatu. But this is about whether or not Cap is defending Mar-Vell from Death, or if, indeed, he is the prey of Death."

"What concerns you?"

"Two things: the first is Cap himself."

"Yes?"

"I have just watched him swear with all the conviction and definition of the soldier he is, that no one would ever die again. That Death would not be allowed to take anyone."

"Madness."

"Perhaps so, but it must be the insanity that comes with perfect reason. Perhaps there comes a point at which all fighting, all death, seems meaningless."

"Death is natural. It comes to all men."

"Does it?"

"Yes."

"But why?"

"That is the natural order brought out of the chaos of being. Birth and Death. We have spoken of this."

"But why does Birth necessitate Death?"

"What are you saying?"

"If the plague that cursed man to be mutated was brought about by the Celestial tampering with mankind, who is to say that Death itself is not some sort of a curse as well? There is a being who is chasing Captain America and Mar-Vell whose touch will spirit one or both of them to a netherworld where another war is being fought according to the prophesying eyes of Kyle Richmond."

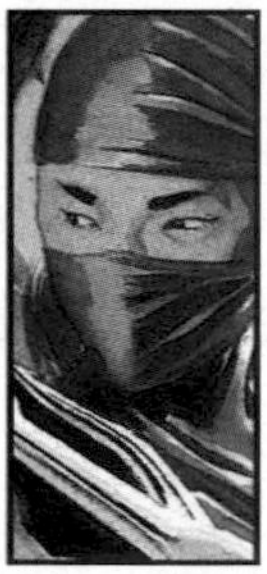

"And so this Death is a curse?"

"I don't know. You have said that all of life is biological. That it is merely birth and death and birth again."

"It is."

"Then why does Death come on wings? Or in the form of a skeleton? Or in the form of a teenage girl? Why does death seem to have a personification?"

"I myself, have not seen Death, but merely witnessed it from a distance. Perhaps humanity is guilty once again of anthropomorphizing your own destruction just as your invention of God is a animation of the concept of birth and creation."

"But Uatu. It's not. Not if you would have us think of the Celestials as our gods. Then our memories of beings being responsible for who we are, are not the fabrications of a superstitious people, but a belief in personalities very real."

"I will concede this, robot. It seems you have learned something of the nature of existence, after all."

"So what if Death is a personality? Was there an originator of life on Earth prior to the Celestials' coming? Prior to the day, perhaps, that you were set here upon the moon to play midwife for the growing Celestial child within Earth? What if, Watcher? What if there were things done upon Earth you did not see?"

"Make your point, robot."

"What if you only accept Death as natural because you were not witness to a world upon which Death did not reign supreme?"

"Then I would be a fool to have assumed so much."

"Thank you."

"But I am not a fool, X-51, just as it is foolish to suggest as much. Death is not merely a commonality for the humanity you try so hard to mock. It is a common element to all of the planets in the universe. Every world knows it. No land is alien to its entropic nature."

"But what if Earth was the conduit to Death entering the Universe? What if all the universe became prey to entropy as a result of Earth?"

"I would say that you have been watching Sunday School lessons far more than the lives of those heroes you claim to care so much for."

"Did the Celestials create Death's Realm?"

"What?"

"What explanation is there for this place we hear Kyle Richmond speak about?"

"Why must there be an explanation? Perhaps these are only the dreams of the dead. Or perhaps this child who claims to be Mar-Vell has a sort of different effect on the mind than did the child Captain America killed."

"The Skull?"

"Yes. Perhaps the Mar-Vell child merely affects the beliefs of one's mind and convinces all he comes upon with a sort of hallucination or shared perspective upon a world that does not exist at all? Perhaps this Mar-Vell child has mutant abilities after all."

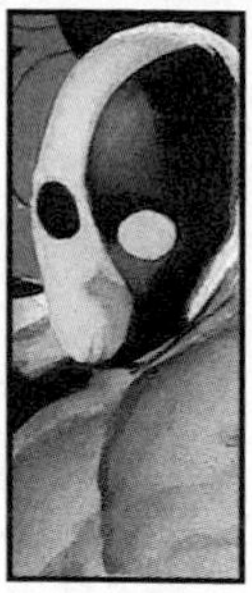

"How can you say that? Didn't he bring Sue Richards back from the dead?"

"I doubt it."

"What do you mean?

"The Richards woman was formed out of Reed Richards arm. Richards himself was already a second-tier mutation. Perhaps her existence is like that of the Asgardians and Galactus himself. Maybe Sue Richards now lives only as long as Richards believes that that is her identity."

"No..."

"Why not, X-51? Is it because what I am saying could not possibly be true, or is it because you don't want it to be? It's a matter of perspective, isn't it?"

"So what you're saying is that we have invented these dreams of Death to suggest that there is something after life to look forward to? That Mar-Vell's quest and Captain America's belief that this will somehow end war, are an illusion?"

"Why not?"

"I... I... don't..."

"I thought not. You see, X-51, knowledge is a danger to humanity. It promises hope in its unanswered questions and at the same time damns humanity when the unanswered becomes revealed."

"What about Mephisto?"

"What?"

"What about the Devil?"

"There is no devil, except, of course, for your referral to myself for not lifting a finger to help your miserable species."

"No. I'm talking about Mephisto."

"There is no Mephisto."

"You're certain of that?"

"Yes."

"That almost confirms, though, that there are beings and places that you cannot see. It almost proves that your explanations are only limited to your experiences and those of the rest of your species."

"It does indeed. But we have seen so much more than you."

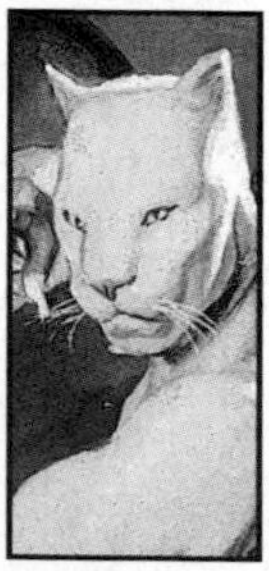

"Still..."

"Have you ever thought, robot, why my equipment is capable to witnessing "Death" yet requires a Recorder to witness the realms of Asgard? Have you ever thought of what that says about Death?"

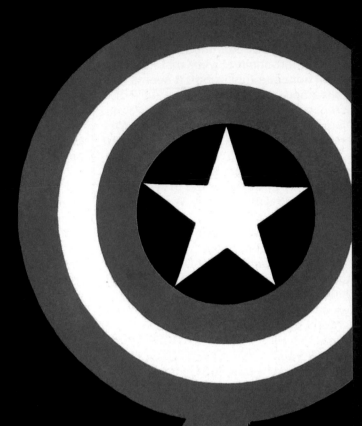

UNIVERSE X: CAP

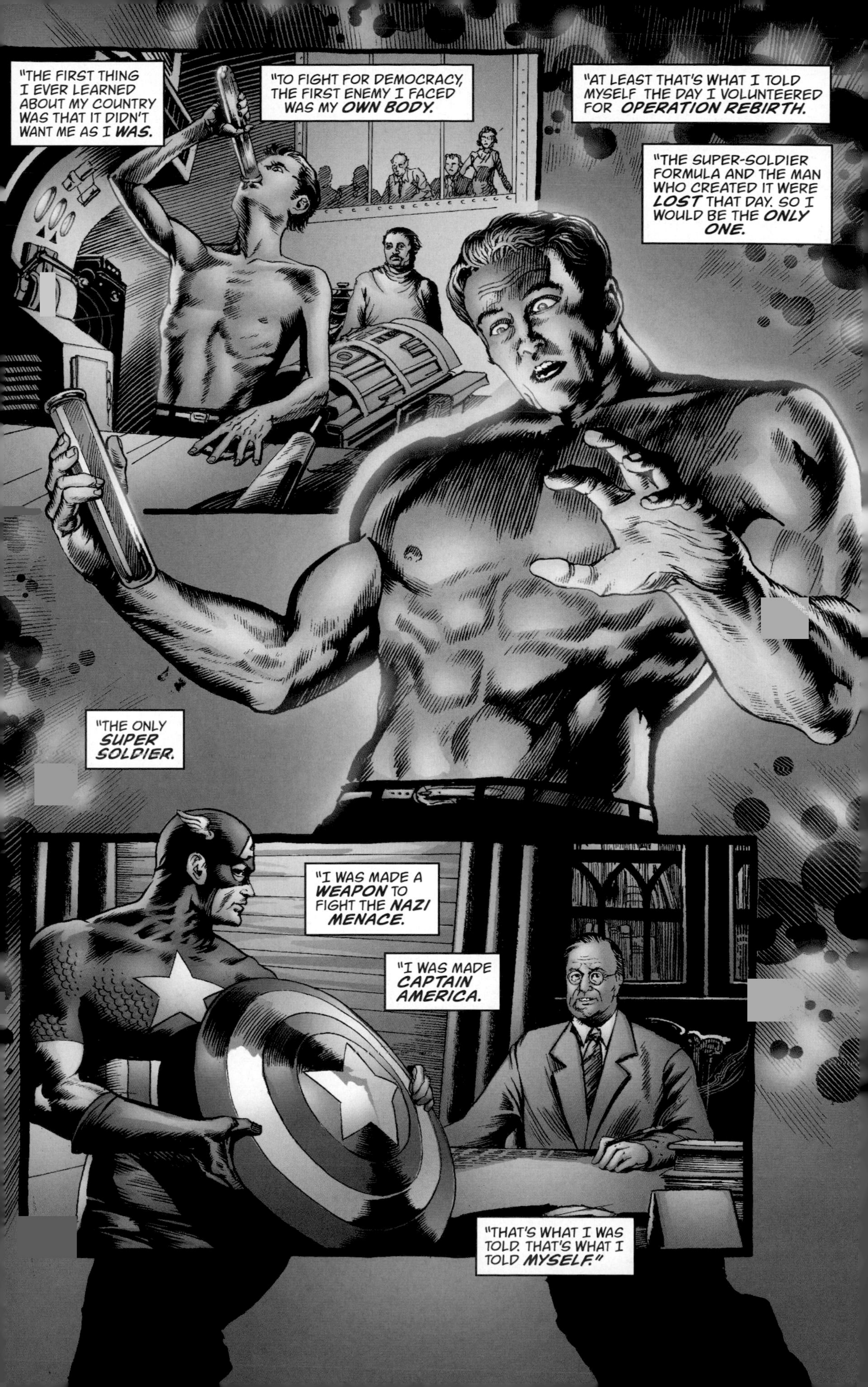
"THE FIRST THING I EVER LEARNED ABOUT MY COUNTRY WAS THAT IT DIDN'T WANT ME AS I WAS.
"TO FIGHT FOR DEMOCRACY, THE FIRST ENEMY I FACED WAS MY OWN BODY.
"AT LEAST THAT'S WHAT I TOLD MYSELF THE DAY I VOLUNTEERED FOR OPERATION REBIRTH.
"THE SUPER-SOLDIER FORMULA AND THE MAN WHO CREATED IT WERE LOST THAT DAY. SO I WOULD BE THE ONLY ONE.
"THE ONLY SUPER SOLDIER.
"I WAS MADE A WEAPON TO FIGHT THE NAZI MENACE.
"I WAS MADE CAPTAIN AMERICA.
"THAT'S WHAT I WAS TOLD. THAT'S WHAT I TOLD MYSELF."

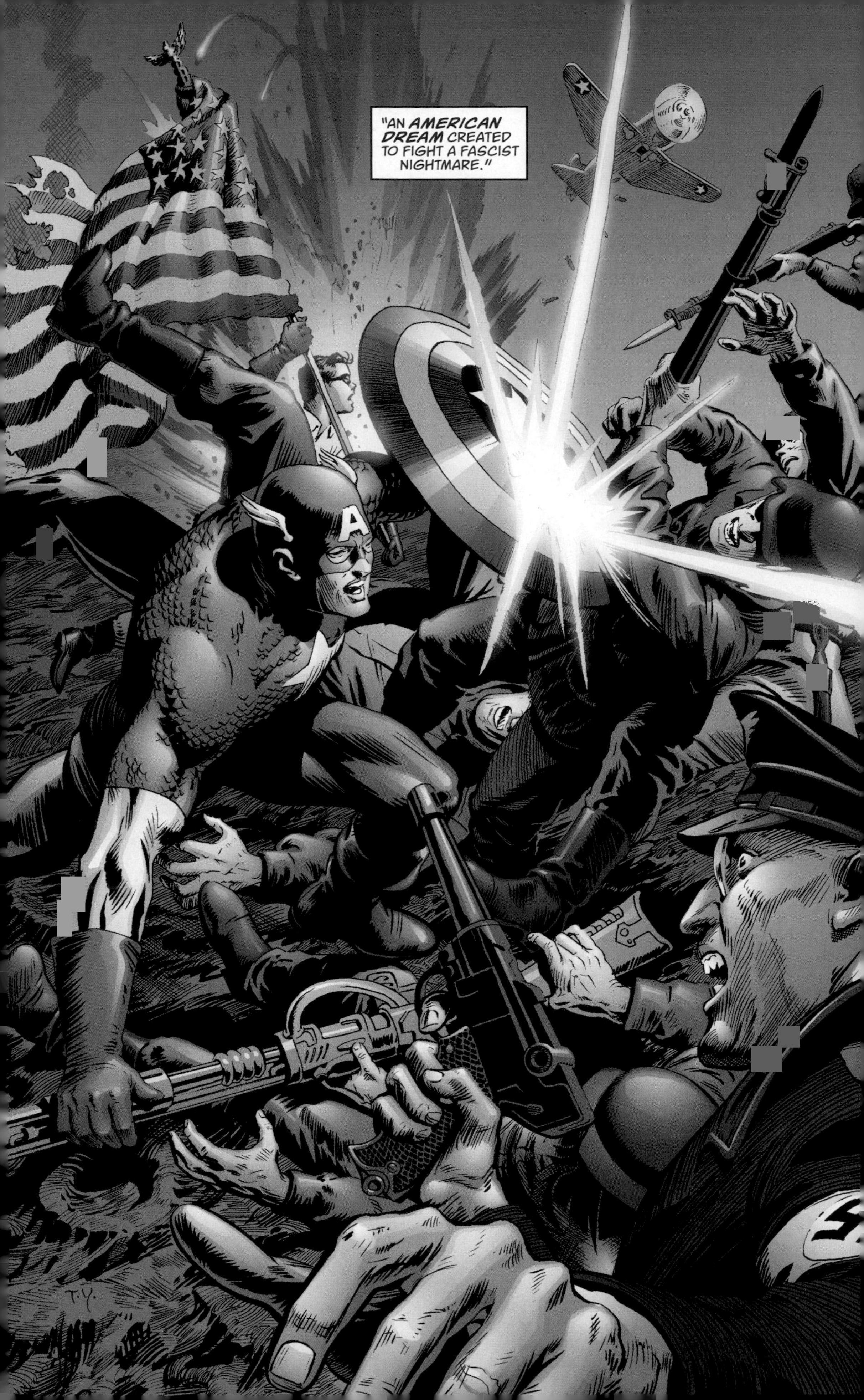
"AN AMERICAN DREAM CREATED TO FIGHT A FASCIST NIGHTMARE."
T.Y.

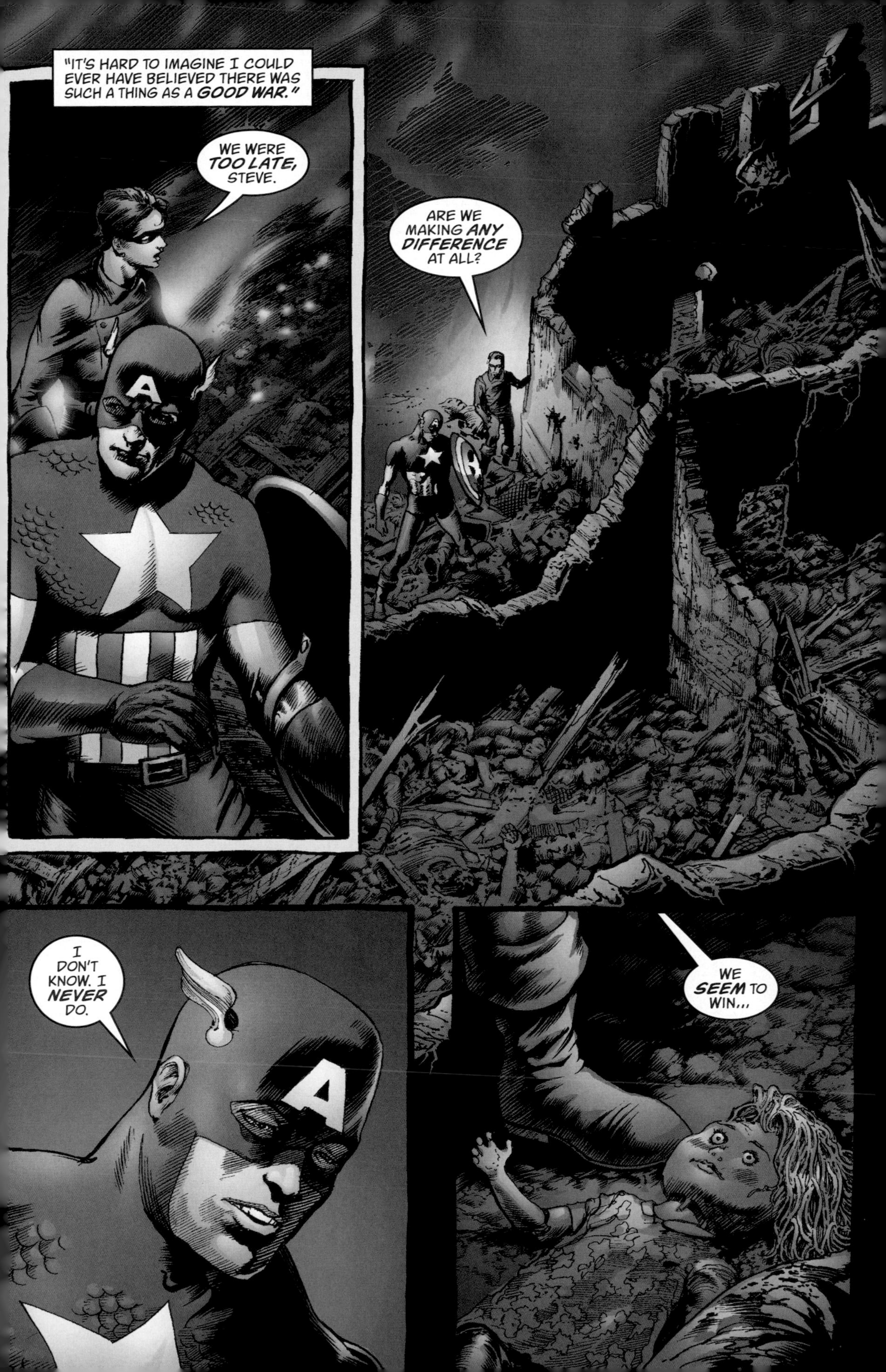
"IT'S HARD TO IMAGINE I COULD EVER HAVE BELIEVED THERE WAS SUCH A THING AS A GOOD WAR."
WE WERE TOO LATE, STEVE.
ARE WE MAKING ANY DIFFERENCE AT ALL?
I DON'T KNOW. I NEVER DO.
WE SEEM TO WIN...

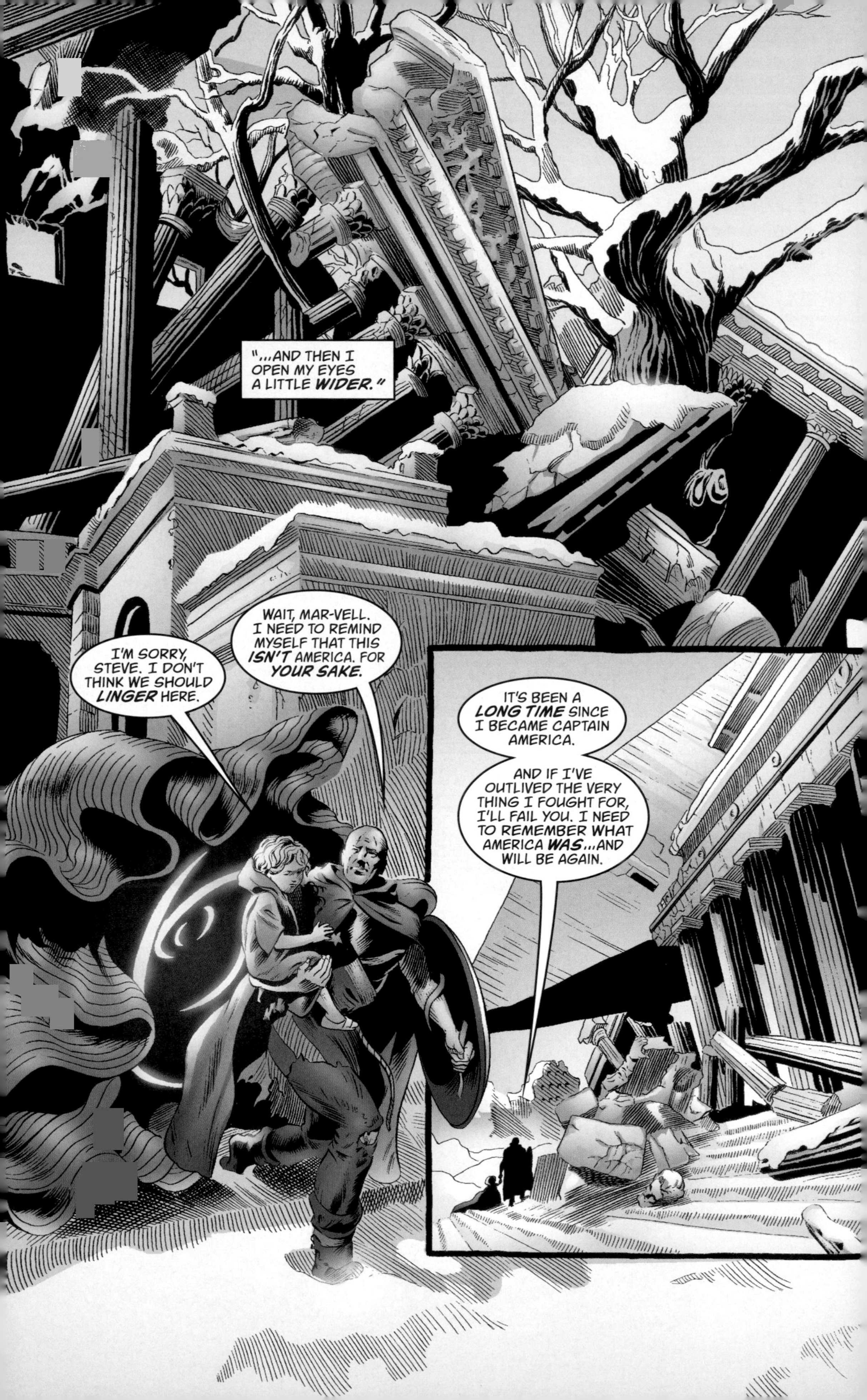
"...AND THEN I OPEN MY EYES A LITTLE WIDER."
I'M SORRY, STEVE. I DON'T THINK WE SHOULD LINGER HERE.
WAIT, MAR-VELL. I NEED TO REMIND MYSELF THAT THIS ISN'T AMERICA. FOR YOUR SAKE.
IT'S BEEN A LONG TIME SINCE I BECAME CAPTAIN AMERICA.
AND IF I'VE OUTLIVED THE VERY THING I FOUGHT FOR, I'LL FAIL YOU. I NEED TO REMEMBER WHAT AMERICA WAS...AND WILL BE AGAIN.

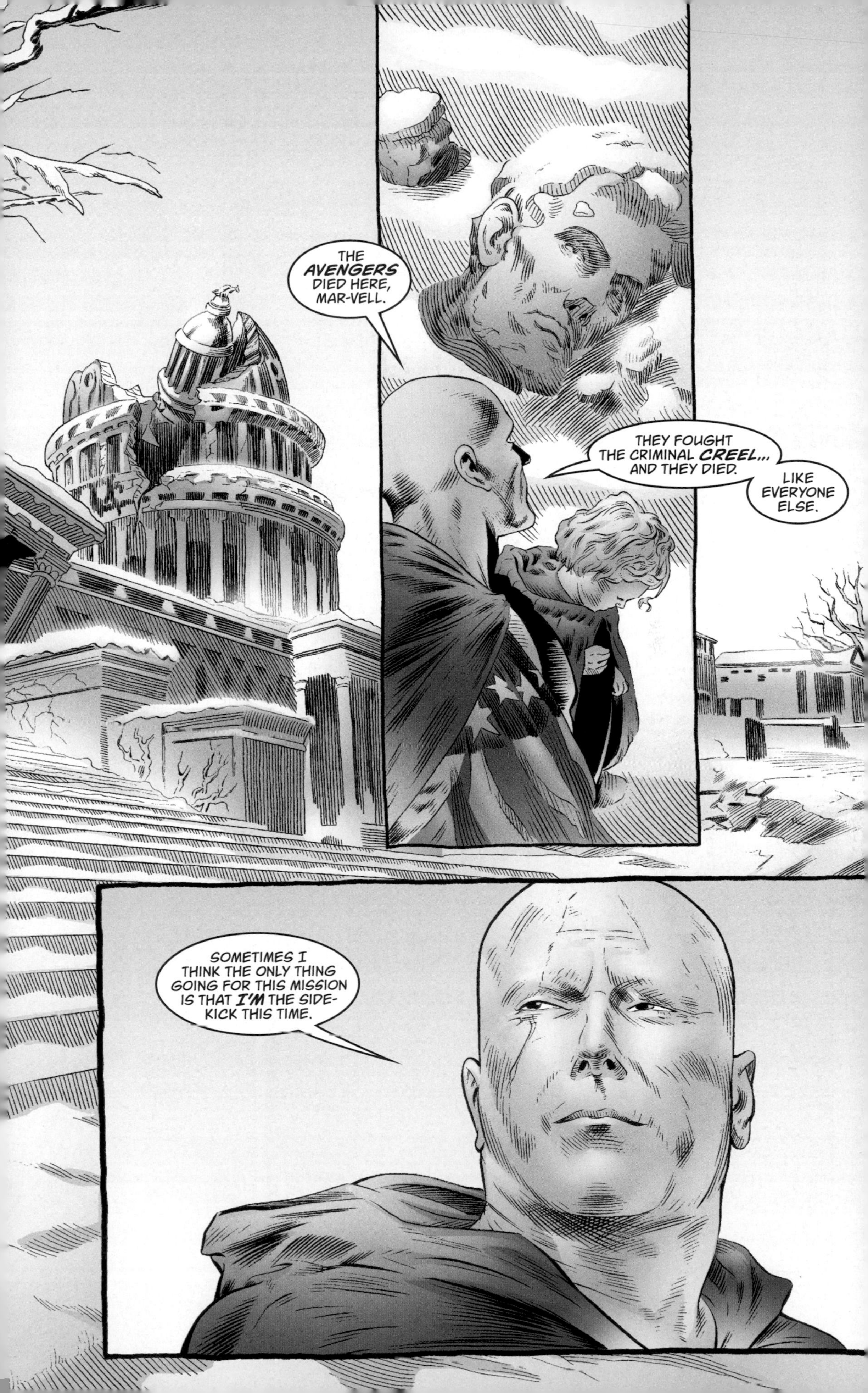

THE *AVENGERS* DIED HERE, MAR-VELL.
THEY FOUGHT THE CRIMINAL *CREEL*... AND THEY DIED.
LIKE EVERYONE ELSE.
SOMETIMES I THINK THE ONLY THING GOING FOR THIS MISSION IS THAT *I'M* THE SIDE-KICK THIS TIME.

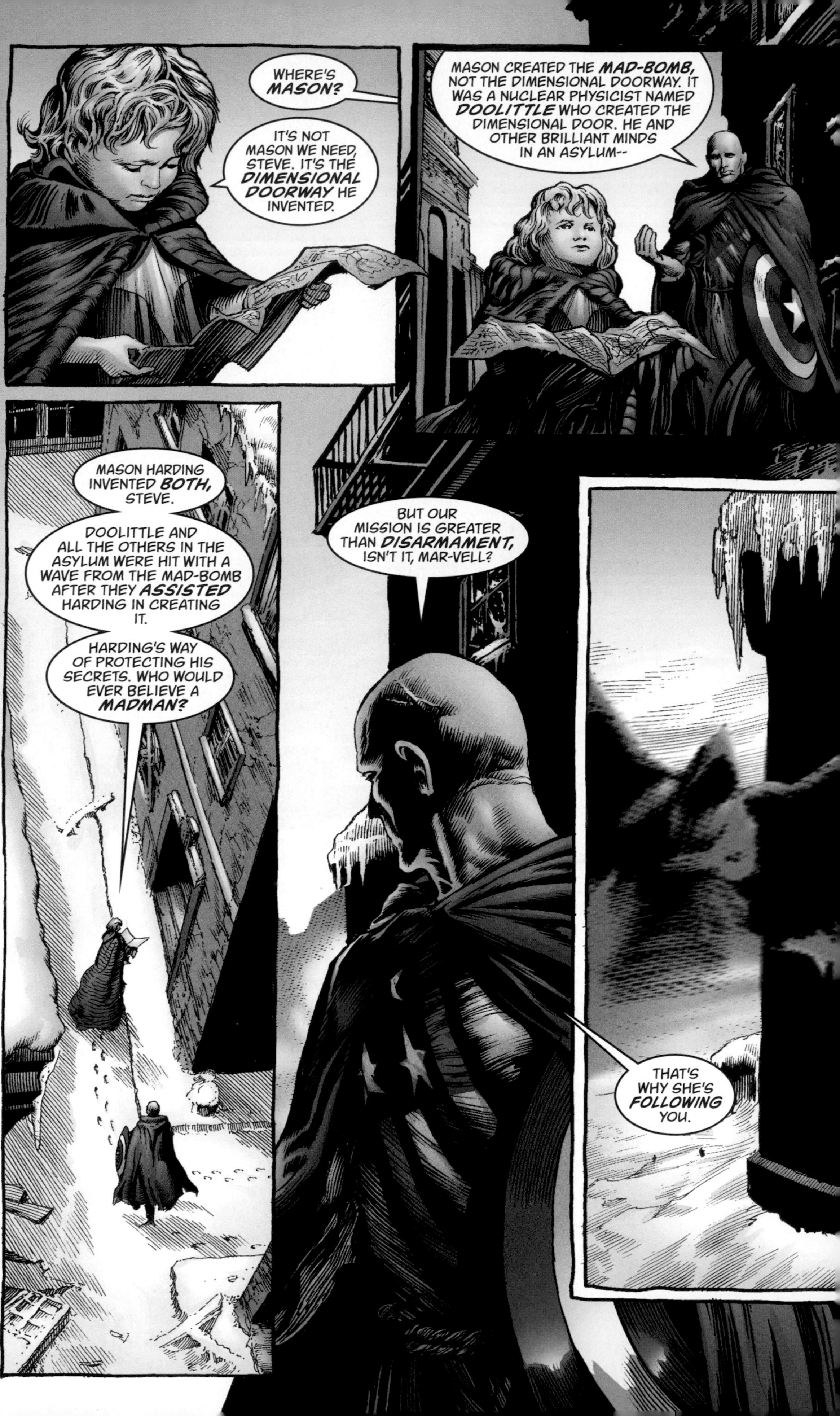

WHERE'S MASON?
IT'S NOT MASON WE NEED, STEVE. IT'S THE DIMENSIONAL DOORWAY HE INVENTED.
MASON CREATED THE MAD-BOMB, NOT THE DIMENSIONAL DOORWAY. IT WAS A NUCLEAR PHYSICIST NAMED DOOLITTLE WHO CREATED THE DIMENSIONAL DOOR. HE AND OTHER BRILLIANT MINDS IN AN ASYLUM--
MASON HARDING INVENTED BOTH, STEVE.
DOOLITTLE AND ALL THE OTHERS IN THE ASYLUM WERE HIT WITH A WAVE FROM THE MAD-BOMB AFTER THEY ASSISTED HARDING IN CREATING IT.
HARDING'S WAY OF PROTECTING HIS SECRETS. WHO WOULD EVER BELIEVE A MADMAN?
BUT OUR MISSION IS GREATER THAN DISARMAMENT, ISN'T IT, MAR-VELL?
THAT'S WHY SHE'S FOLLOWING YOU.

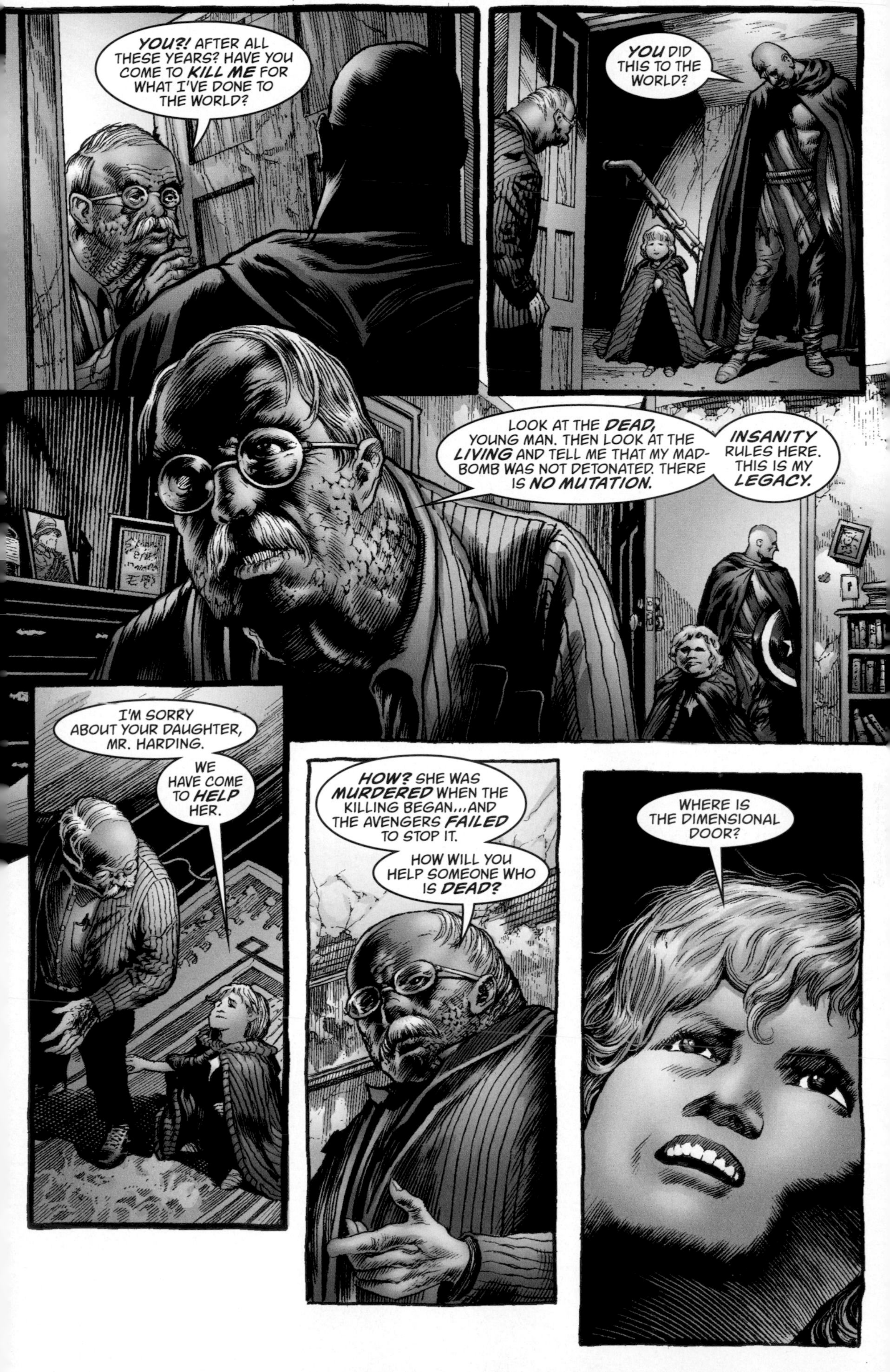
YOU?! AFTER ALL THESE YEARS? HAVE YOU COME TO KILL ME FOR WHAT I'VE DONE TO THE WORLD?
YOU DID THIS TO THE WORLD?
LOOK AT THE DEAD, YOUNG MAN. THEN LOOK AT THE LIVING AND TELL ME THAT MY MAD-BOMB WAS NOT DETONATED. THERE IS NO MUTATION.
INSANITY RULES HERE. THIS IS MY LEGACY.
I'M SORRY ABOUT YOUR DAUGHTER, MR. HARDING.
WE HAVE COME TO HELP HER.
HOW? SHE WAS MURDERED WHEN THE KILLING BEGAN...AND THE AVENGERS FAILED TO STOP IT.
HOW WILL YOU HELP SOMEONE WHO IS DEAD?
WHERE IS THE DIMENSIONAL DOOR?

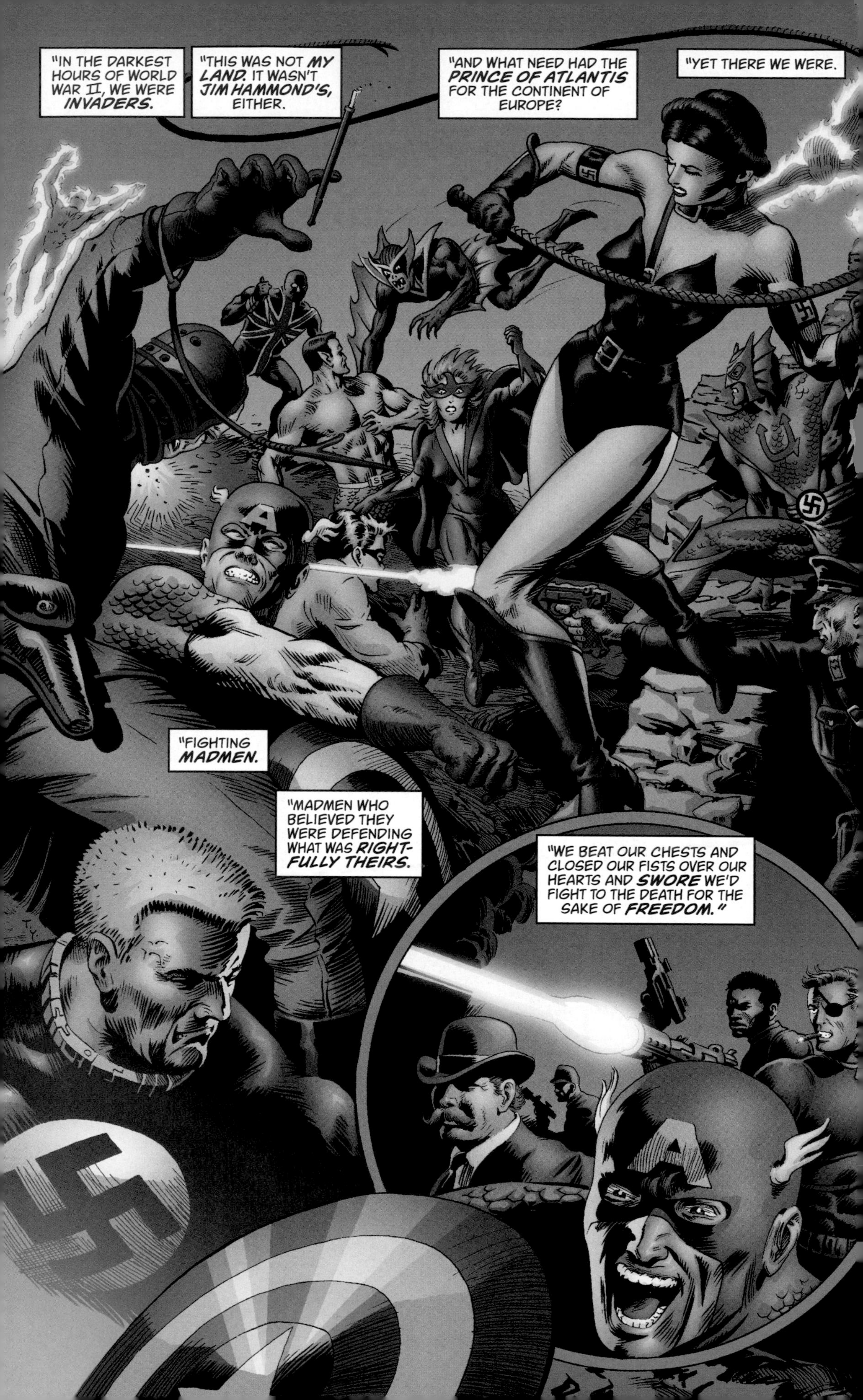
"IN THE DARKEST HOURS OF WORLD WAR II, WE WERE INVADERS.
"THIS WAS NOT MY LAND. IT WASN'T JIM HAMMOND'S, EITHER.
"AND WHAT NEED HAD THE PRINCE OF ATLANTIS FOR THE CONTINENT OF EUROPE?
"YET THERE WE WERE.
"FIGHTING MADMEN.
"MADMEN WHO BELIEVED THEY WERE DEFENDING WHAT WAS RIGHTFULLY THEIRS.
"WE BEAT OUR CHESTS AND CLOSED OUR FISTS OVER OUR HEARTS AND SWORE WE'D FIGHT TO THE DEATH FOR THE SAKE OF FREEDOM."

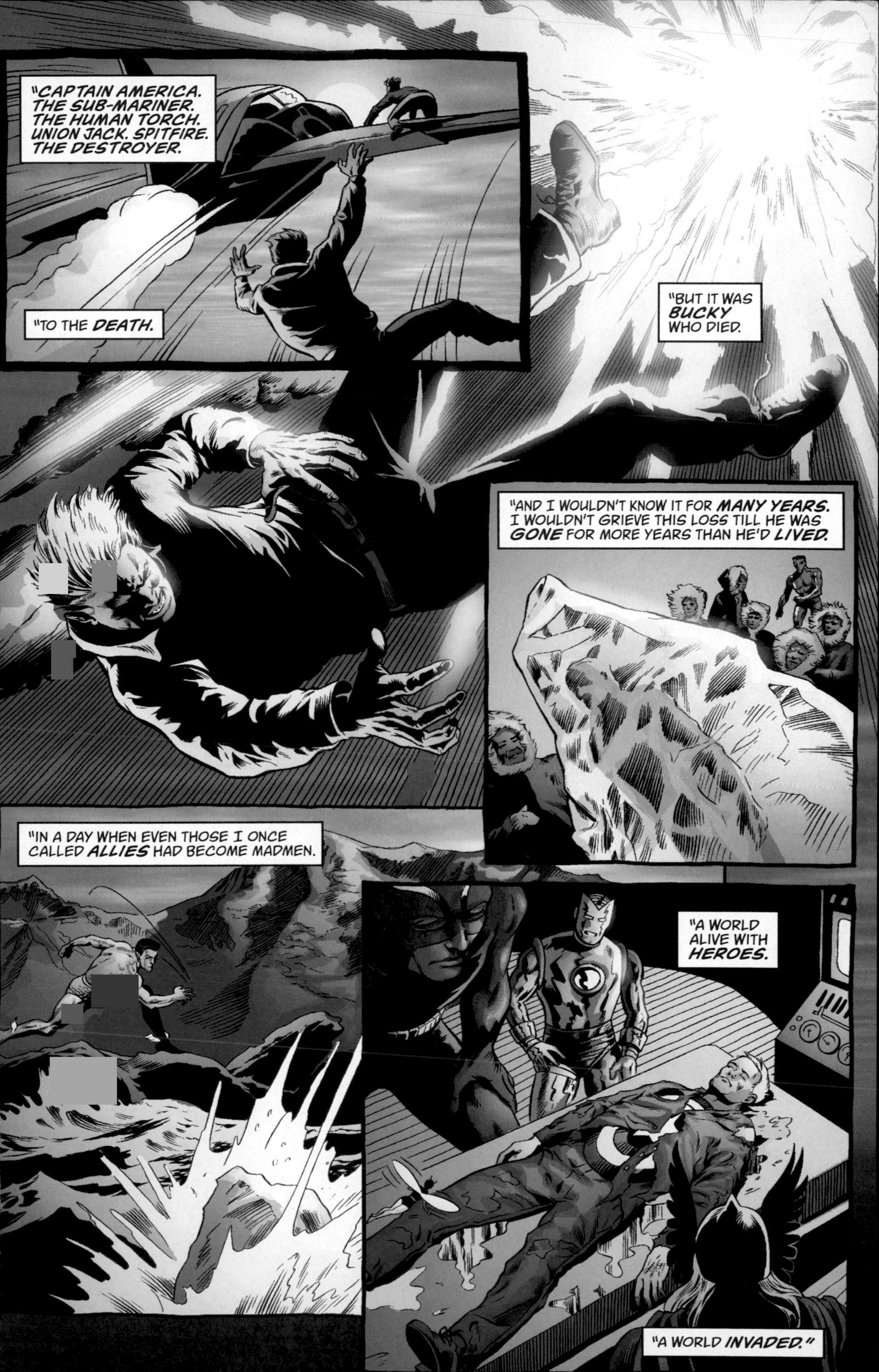
"CAPTAIN AMERICA. THE SUB-MARINER. THE HUMAN TORCH. UNION JACK. SPITFIRE. THE DESTROYER.
"TO THE DEATH.
"BUT IT WAS BUCKY WHO DIED.
"AND I WOULDN'T KNOW IT FOR MANY YEARS. I WOULDN'T GRIEVE THIS LOSS TILL HE WAS GONE FOR MORE YEARS THAN HE'D LIVED.
"IN A DAY WHEN EVEN THOSE I ONCE CALLED ALLIES HAD BECOME MADMEN.
"A WORLD ALIVE WITH HEROES.
"A WORLD INVADED."

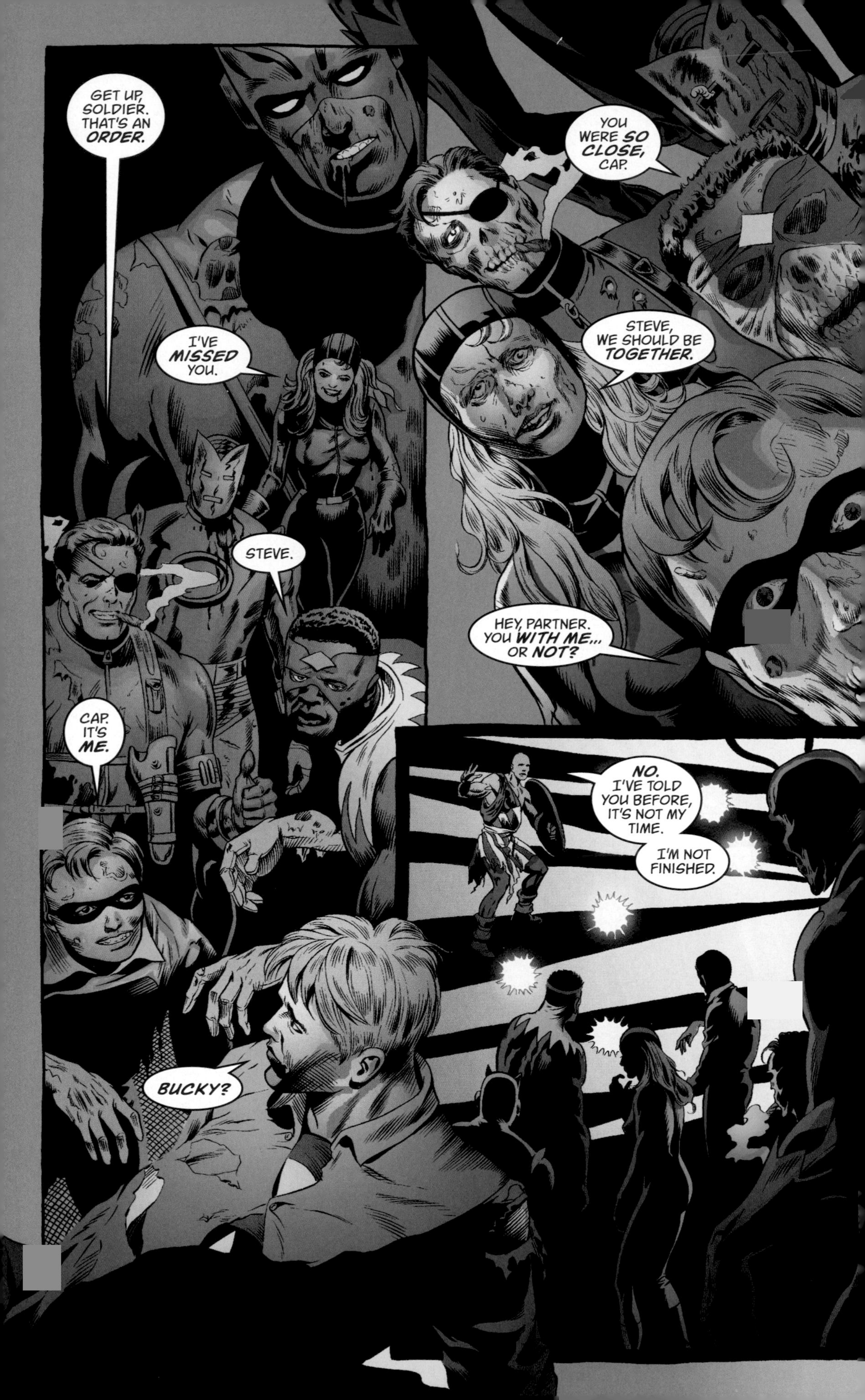
GET UP, SOLDIER. THAT'S AN ORDER.
YOU WERE SO CLOSE, CAP.
I'VE MISSED YOU.
STEVE, WE SHOULD BE TOGETHER.
STEVE.
HEY, PARTNER. YOU WITH ME... OR NOT?
CAP. IT'S ME.
BUCKY?
NO. I'VE TOLD YOU BEFORE, IT'S NOT MY TIME.
I'M NOT FINISHED.

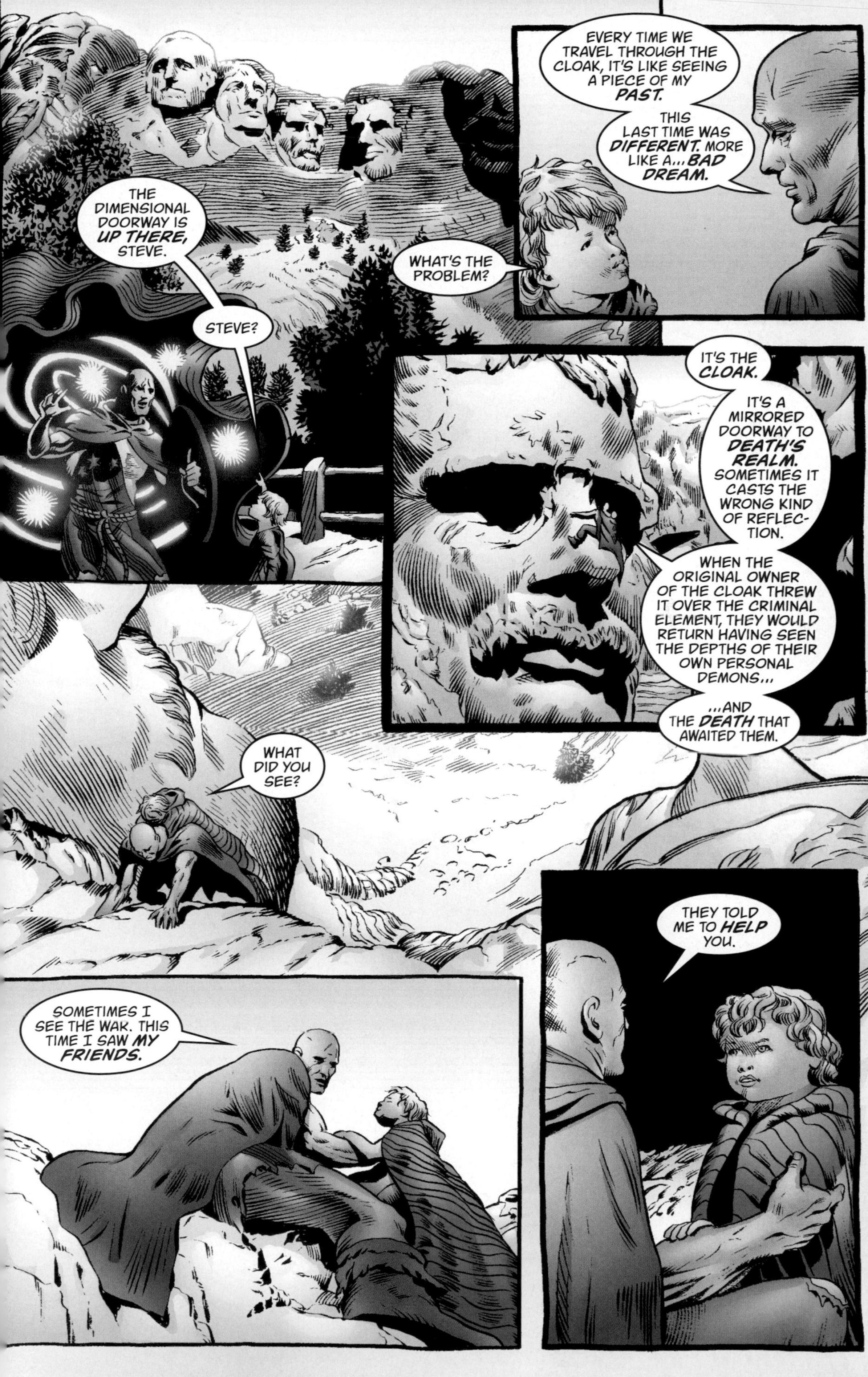
THE DIMENSIONAL DOORWAY IS UP THERE, STEVE.
STEVE?
WHAT'S THE PROBLEM?
EVERY TIME WE TRAVEL THROUGH THE CLOAK, IT'S LIKE SEEING A PIECE OF MY PAST.
THIS LAST TIME WAS DIFFERENT. MORE LIKE A... BAD DREAM.
IT'S THE CLOAK.
IT'S A MIRRORED DOORWAY TO DEATH'S REALM. SOMETIMES IT CASTS THE WRONG KIND OF REFLEC-TION.
WHEN THE ORIGINAL OWNER OF THE CLOAK THREW IT OVER THE CRIMINAL ELEMENT, THEY WOULD RETURN HAVING SEEN THE DEPTHS OF THEIR OWN PERSONAL DEMONS...
...AND THE DEATH THAT AWAITED THEM.
WHAT DID YOU SEE?
SOMETIMES I SEE THE WAR. THIS TIME I SAW MY FRIENDS.
THEY TOLD ME TO HELP YOU.

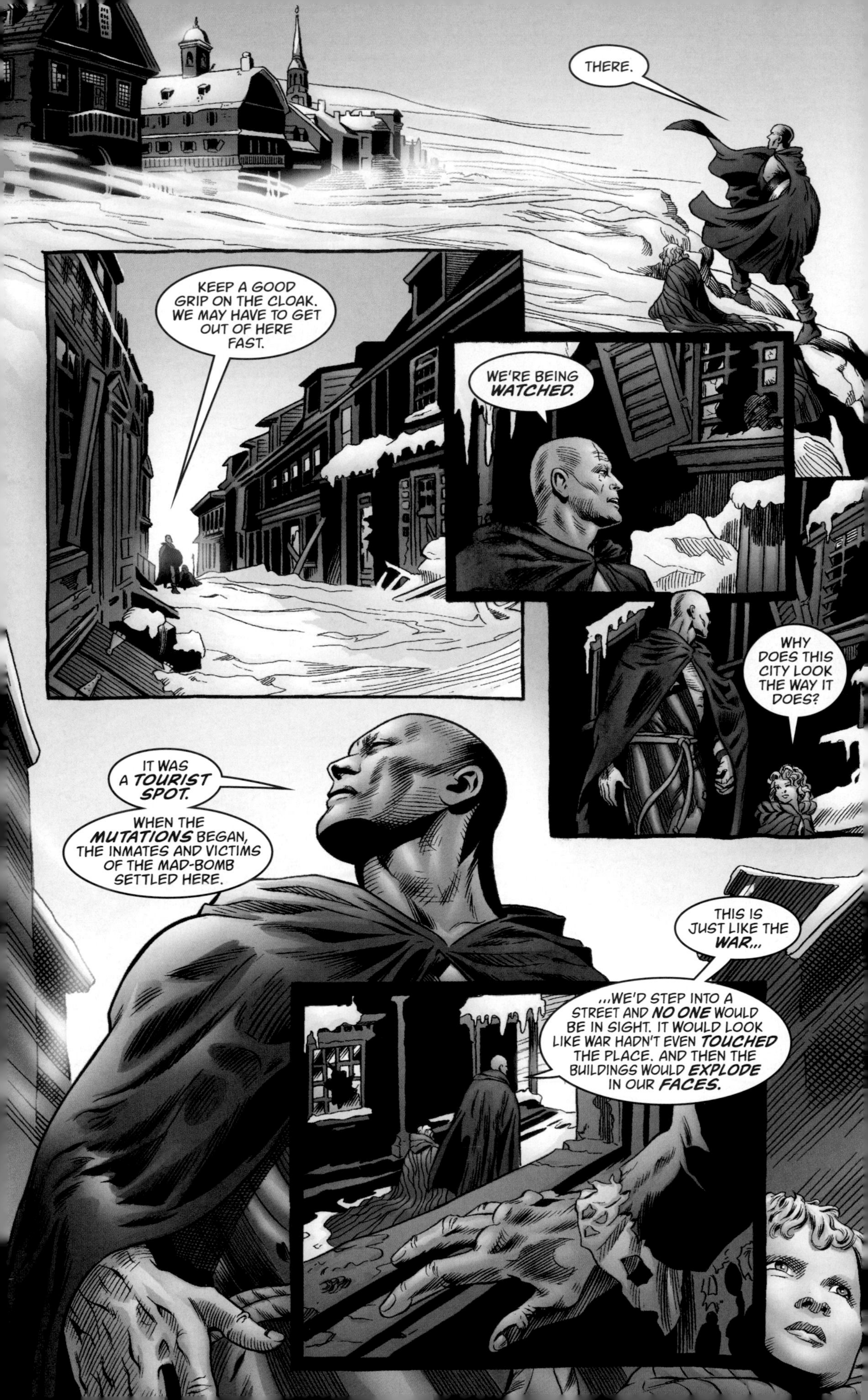
THERE.
KEEP A GOOD GRIP ON THE CLOAK. WE MAY HAVE TO GET OUT OF HERE FAST.
WE'RE BEING *WATCHED.*
WHY DOES THIS CITY LOOK THE WAY IT DOES?
IT WAS A *TOURIST SPOT.*
WHEN THE *MUTATIONS* BEGAN, THE INMATES AND VICTIMS OF THE MAD-BOMB SETTLED HERE.
THIS IS JUST LIKE THE *WAR...*
...WE'D STEP INTO A STREET AND *NO ONE* WOULD BE IN SIGHT. IT WOULD LOOK LIKE WAR HADN'T EVEN *TOUCHED* THE PLACE. AND THEN THE BUILDINGS WOULD *EXPLODE* IN OUR *FACES.*

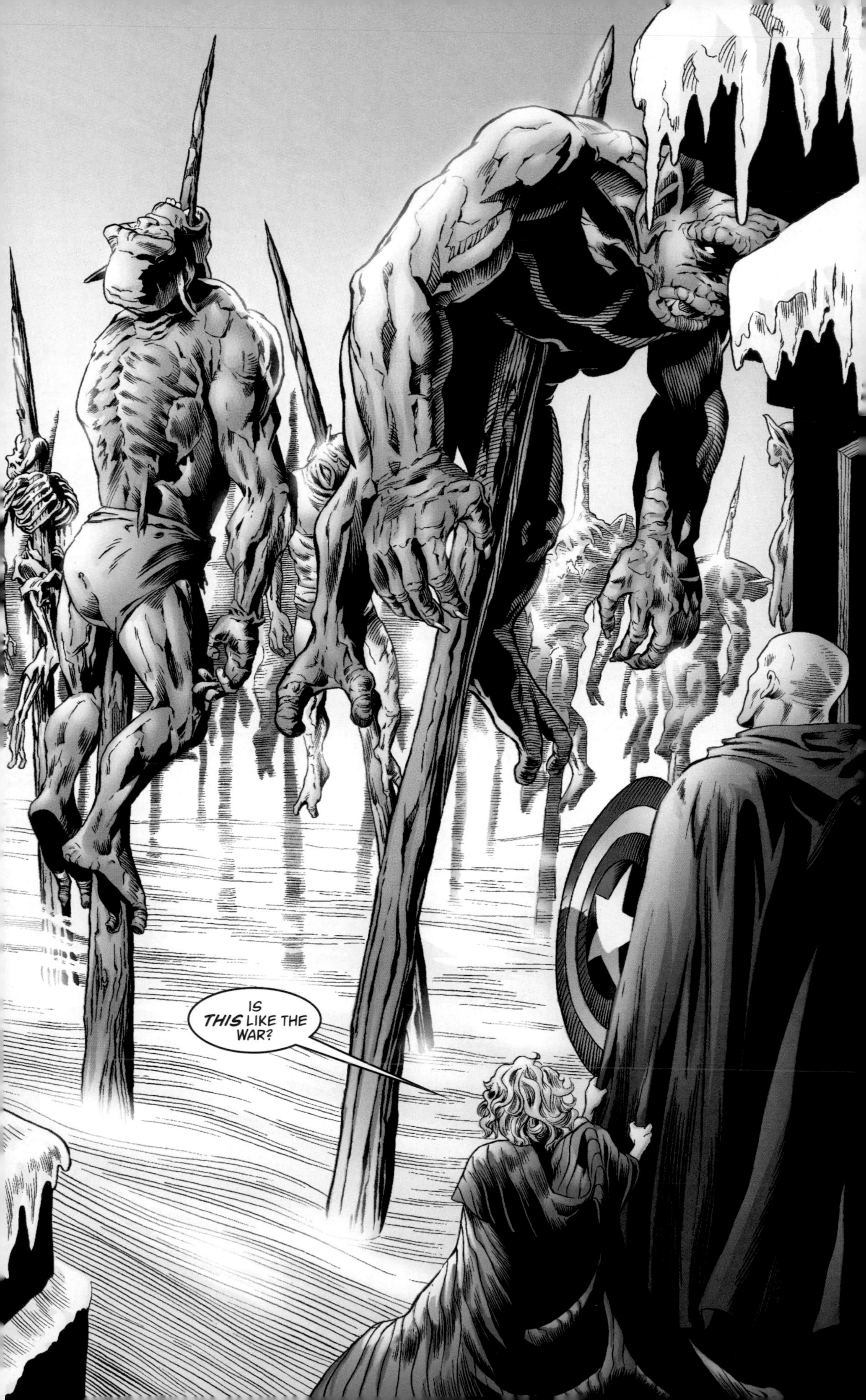
IS *THIS* LIKE THE WAR?

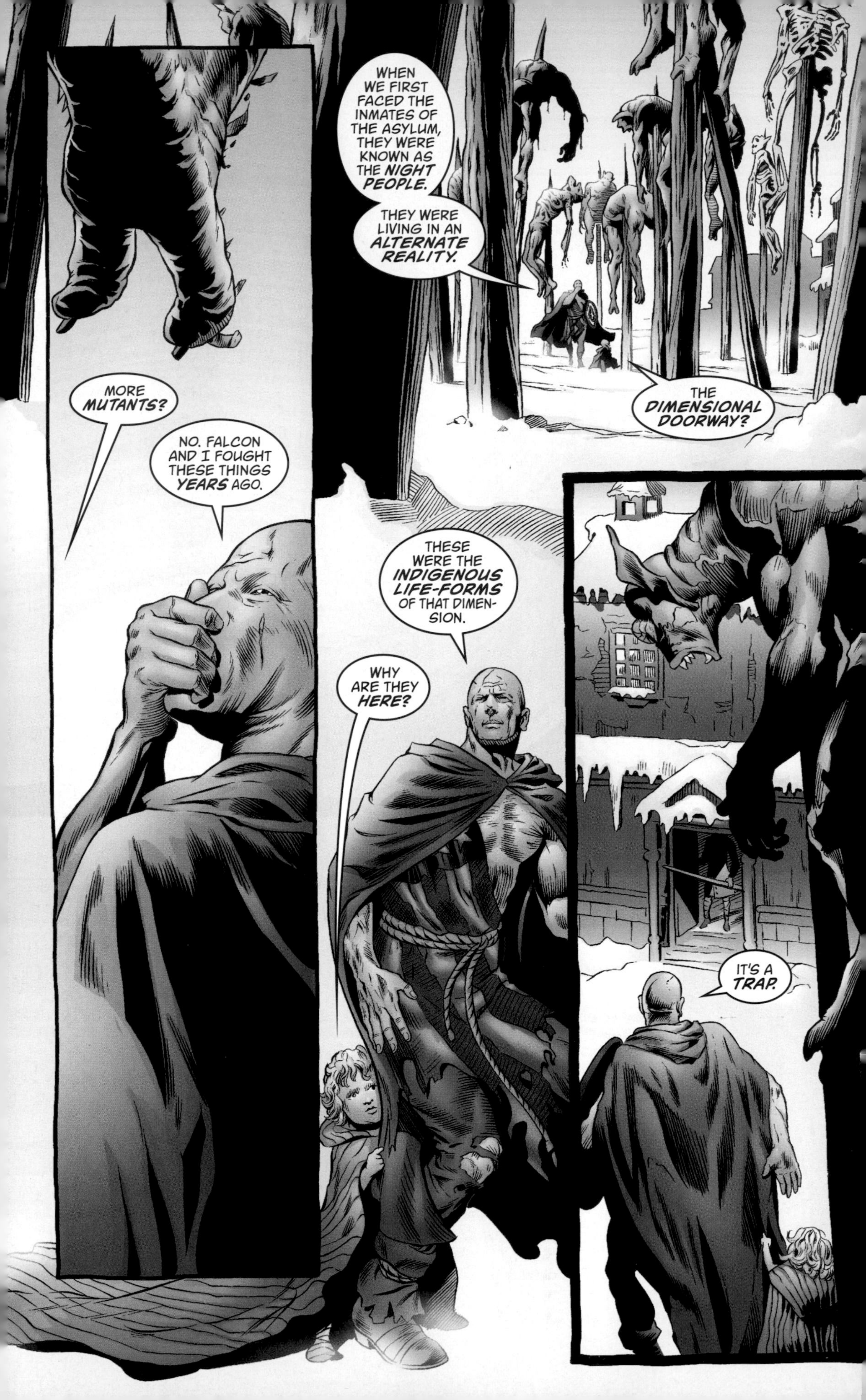
WHEN WE FIRST FACED THE INMATES OF THE ASYLUM, THEY WERE KNOWN AS THE NIGHT PEOPLE.
THEY WERE LIVING IN AN ALTERNATE REALITY.
THE DIMENSIONAL DOORWAY?
MORE MUTANTS?
NO. FALCON AND I FOUGHT THESE THINGS YEARS AGO.
THESE WERE THE INDIGENOUS LIFE-FORMS OF THAT DIMEN-SION.
WHY ARE THEY HERE?
IT'S A TRAP.

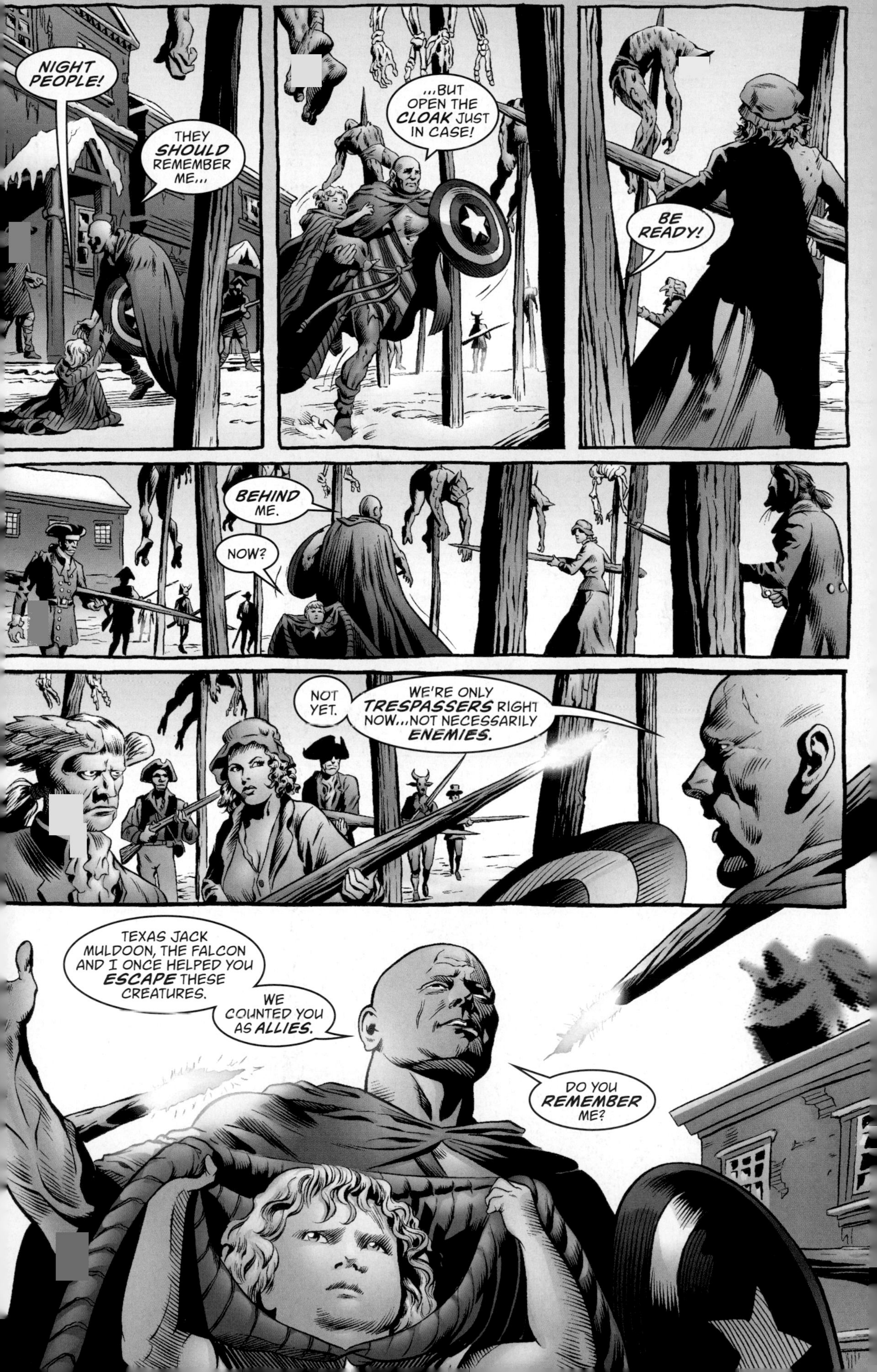
NIGHT PEOPLE!
THEY SHOULD REMEMBER ME...
...BUT OPEN THE CLOAK JUST IN CASE!
BE READY!
BEHIND ME.
NOW?
NOT YET.
WE'RE ONLY TRESPASSERS RIGHT NOW...NOT NECESSARILY ENEMIES.
TEXAS JACK MULDOON, THE FALCON AND I ONCE HELPED YOU ESCAPE THESE CREATURES.
WE COUNTED YOU AS ALLIES.
DO YOU REMEMBER ME?

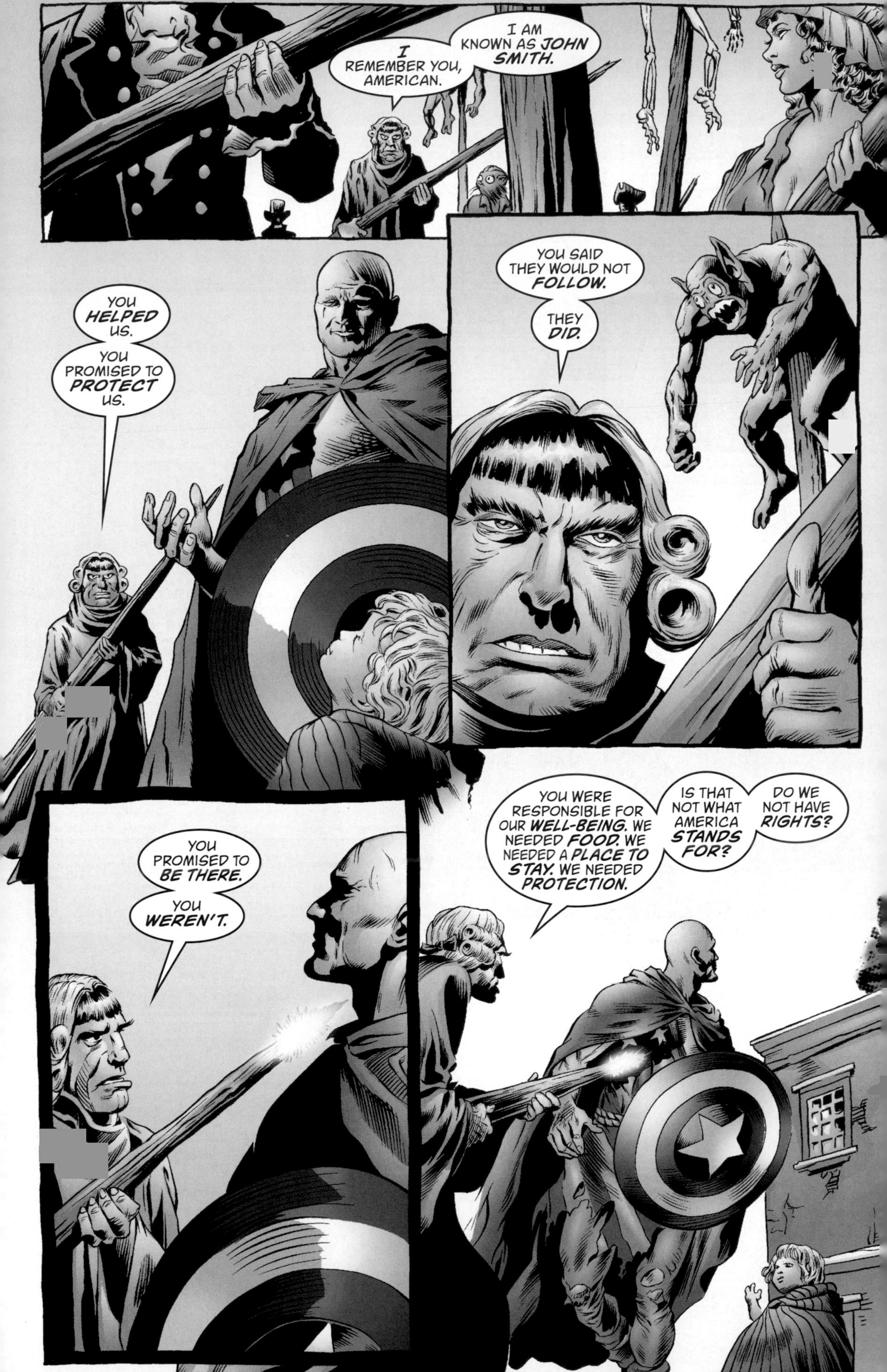

I REMEMBER YOU, AMERICAN.
I AM KNOWN AS JOHN SMITH.
YOU HELPED US.
YOU PROMISED TO PROTECT US.
YOU SAID THEY WOULD NOT FOLLOW.
THEY DID.
YOU PROMISED TO BE THERE.
YOU WEREN'T.
YOU WERE RESPONSIBLE FOR OUR WELL-BEING. WE NEEDED FOOD. WE NEEDED A PLACE TO STAY. WE NEEDED PROTECTION.
IS THAT NOT WHAT AMERICA STANDS FOR?
DO WE NOT HAVE RIGHTS?

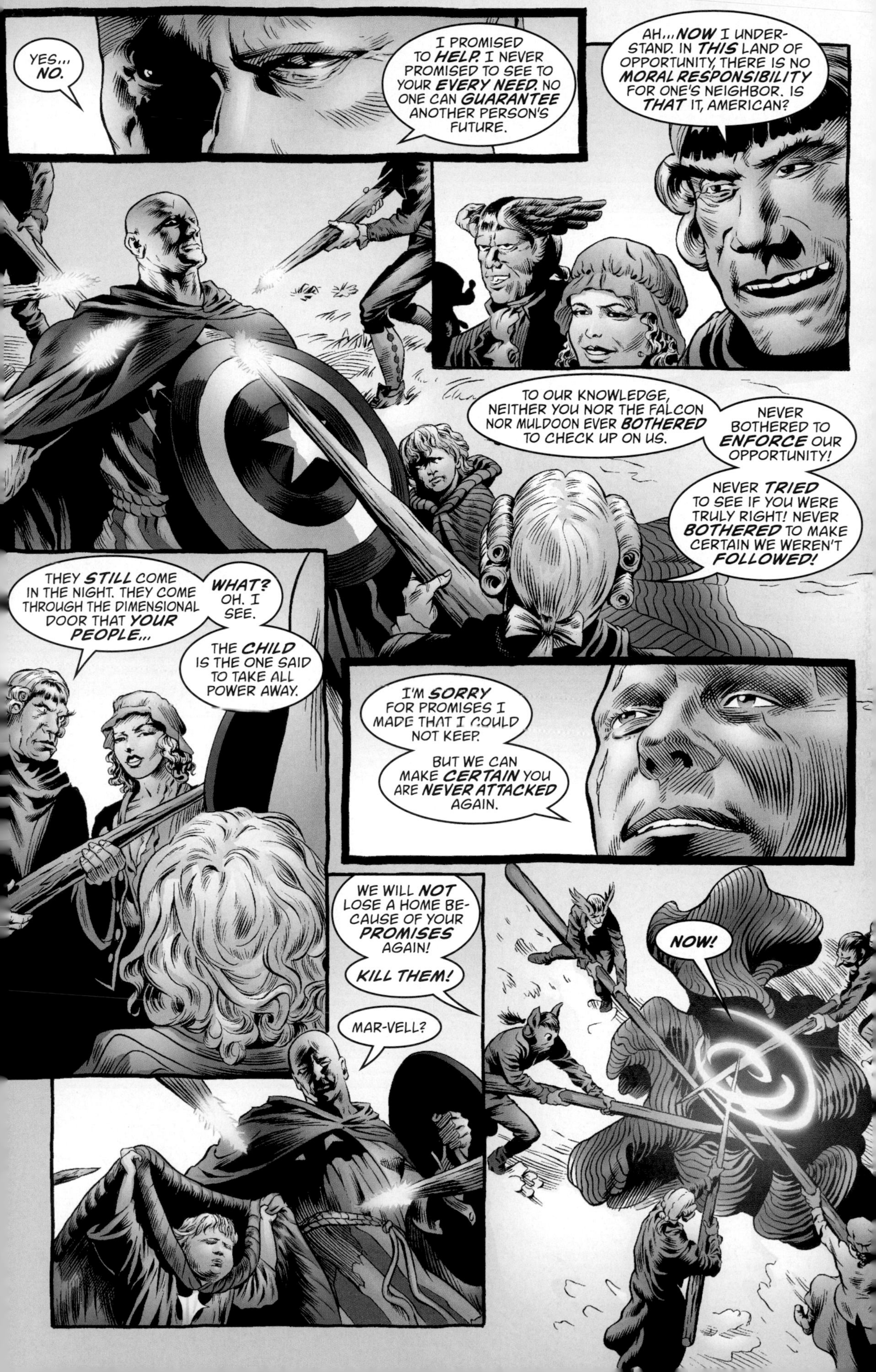
YES... NO.
I PROMISED TO HELP. I NEVER PROMISED TO SEE TO YOUR EVERY NEED. NO ONE CAN GUARANTEE ANOTHER PERSON'S FUTURE.
AH... NOW I UNDERSTAND. IN THIS LAND OF OPPORTUNITY, THERE IS NO MORAL RESPONSIBILITY FOR ONE'S NEIGHBOR. IS THAT IT, AMERICAN?
TO OUR KNOWLEDGE, NEITHER YOU NOR THE FALCON NOR MULDOON EVER BOTHERED TO CHECK UP ON US.
NEVER BOTHERED TO ENFORCE OUR OPPORTUNITY!
NEVER TRIED TO SEE IF YOU WERE TRULY RIGHT! NEVER BOTHERED TO MAKE CERTAIN WE WEREN'T FOLLOWED!
THEY STILL COME IN THE NIGHT. THEY COME THROUGH THE DIMENSIONAL DOOR THAT YOUR PEOPLE...
WHAT? OH. I SEE.
THE CHILD IS THE ONE SAID TO TAKE ALL POWER AWAY.
I'M SORRY FOR PROMISES I MADE THAT I COULD NOT KEEP.
BUT WE CAN MAKE CERTAIN YOU ARE NEVER ATTACKED AGAIN.
WE WILL NOT LOSE A HOME BECAUSE OF YOUR PROMISES AGAIN!
KILL THEM!
MAR-VELL?
NOW!

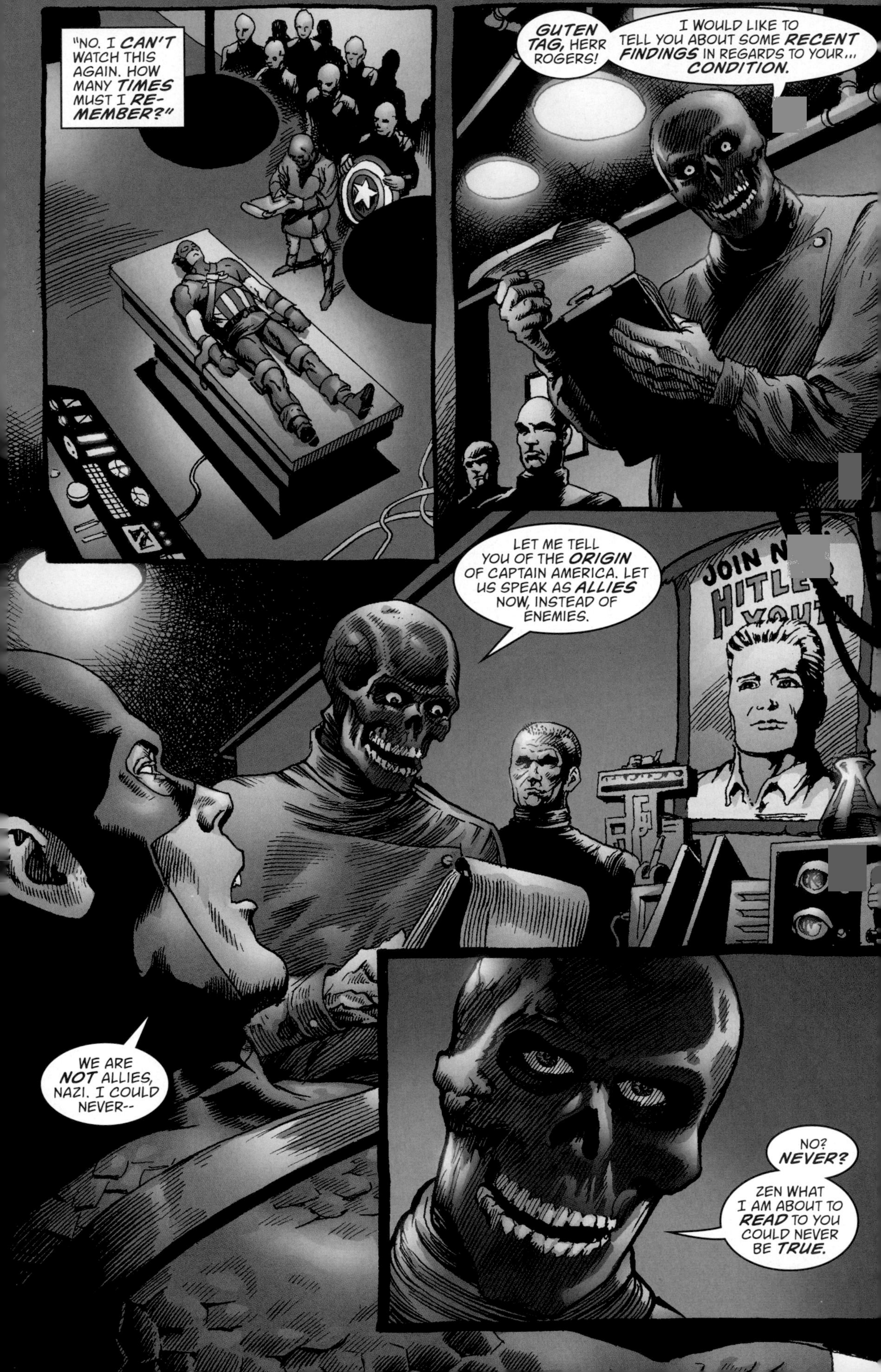
"NO. I CAN'T WATCH THIS AGAIN. HOW MANY TIMES MUST I RE-MEMBER?"
GUTEN TAG, HERR ROGERS!
I WOULD LIKE TO TELL YOU ABOUT SOME RECENT FINDINGS IN REGARDS TO YOUR... CONDITION.
LET ME TELL YOU OF THE ORIGIN OF CAPTAIN AMERICA. LET US SPEAK AS ALLIES NOW, INSTEAD OF ENEMIES.
WE ARE NOT ALLIES, NAZI. I COULD NEVER--
NO? NEVER?
ZEN WHAT I AM ABOUT TO READ TO YOU COULD NEVER BE TRUE.

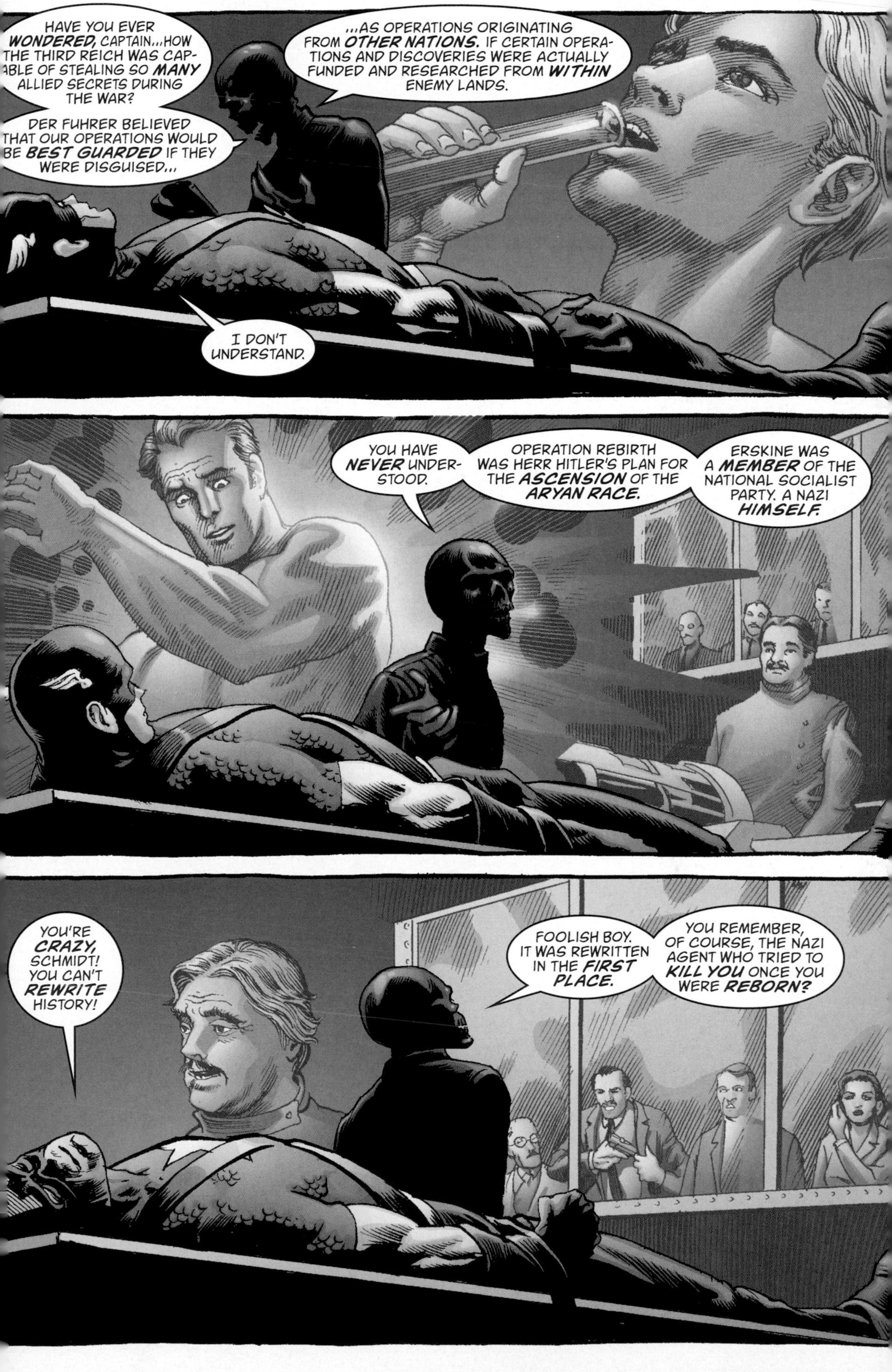
HAVE YOU EVER WONDERED, CAPTAIN...HOW THE THIRD REICH WAS CAPABLE OF STEALING SO MANY ALLIED SECRETS DURING THE WAR?
DER FUHRER BELIEVED THAT OUR OPERATIONS WOULD BE BEST GUARDED IF THEY WERE DISGUISED...
...AS OPERATIONS ORIGINATING FROM OTHER NATIONS. IF CERTAIN OPERATIONS AND DISCOVERIES WERE ACTUALLY FUNDED AND RESEARCHED FROM WITHIN ENEMY LANDS.
I DON'T UNDERSTAND.
YOU HAVE NEVER UNDERSTOOD.
OPERATION REBIRTH WAS HERR HITLER'S PLAN FOR THE ASCENSION OF THE ARYAN RACE.
ERSKINE WAS A MEMBER OF THE NATIONAL SOCIALIST PARTY. A NAZI HIMSELF.
YOU'RE CRAZY, SCHMIDT! YOU CAN'T REWRITE HISTORY!
FOOLISH BOY. IT WAS REWRITTEN IN THE FIRST PLACE.
YOU REMEMBER, OF COURSE, THE NAZI AGENT WHO TRIED TO KILL YOU ONCE YOU WERE REBORN?

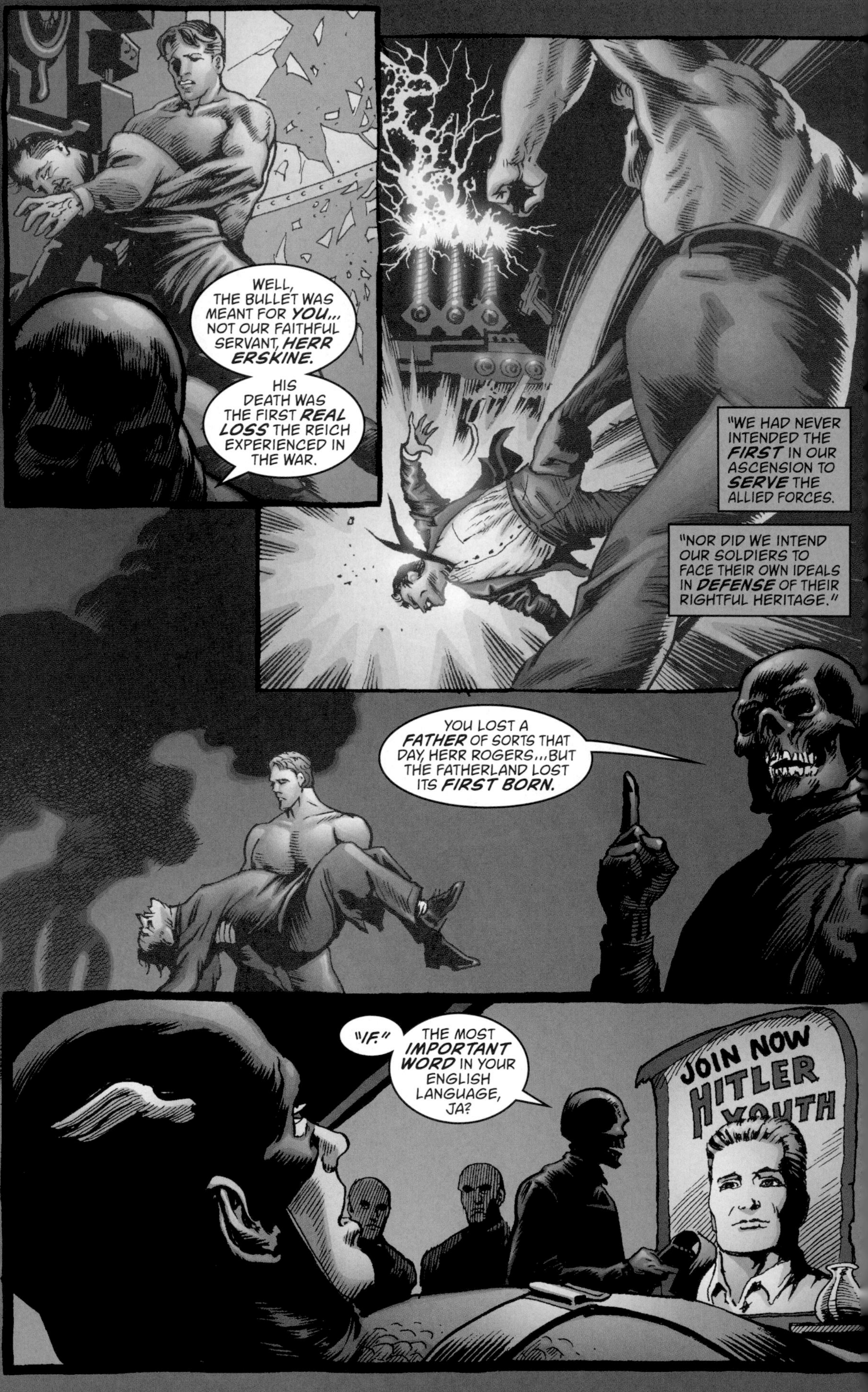
WELL, THE BULLET WAS MEANT FOR YOU... NOT OUR FAITHFUL SERVANT, HERR ERSKINE.
HIS DEATH WAS THE FIRST REAL LOSS THE REICH EXPERIENCED IN THE WAR.
"WE HAD NEVER INTENDED THE FIRST IN OUR ASCENSION TO SERVE THE ALLIED FORCES.
"NOR DID WE INTEND OUR SOLDIERS TO FACE THEIR OWN IDEALS IN DEFENSE OF THEIR RIGHTFUL HERITAGE."
YOU LOST A FATHER OF SORTS THAT DAY, HERR ROGERS...BUT THE FATHERLAND LOST ITS FIRST BORN.
"IF."
THE MOST IMPORTANT WORD IN YOUR ENGLISH LANGUAGE, JA?
JOIN NOW
HITLER
YOUTH

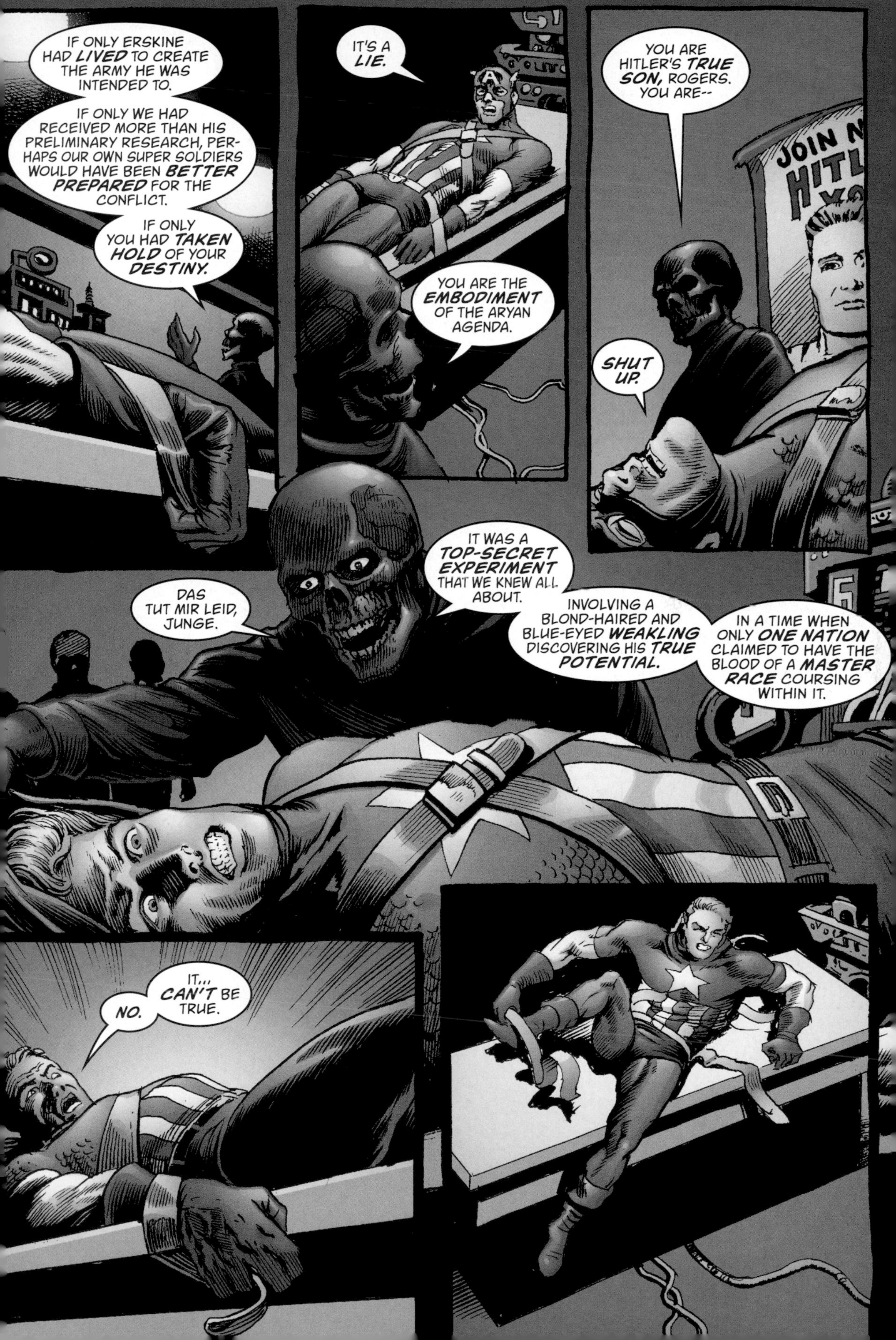

IF ONLY ERSKINE HAD LIVED TO CREATE THE ARMY HE WAS INTENDED TO.
IF ONLY WE HAD RECEIVED MORE THAN HIS PRELIMINARY RESEARCH, PERHAPS OUR OWN SUPER SOLDIERS WOULD HAVE BEEN BETTER PREPARED FOR THE CONFLICT.
IF ONLY YOU HAD TAKEN HOLD OF YOUR DESTINY.
IT'S A LIE.
YOU ARE THE EMBODIMENT OF THE ARYAN AGENDA.
YOU ARE HITLER'S TRUE SON, ROGERS. YOU ARE--
JOIN
HITL
SHUT UP.
DAS TUT MIR LEID, JUNGE.
IT WAS A TOP-SECRET EXPERIMENT THAT WE KNEW ALL ABOUT.
INVOLVING A BLOND-HAIRED AND BLUE-EYED WEAKLING DISCOVERING HIS TRUE POTENTIAL.
IN A TIME WHEN ONLY ONE NATION CLAIMED TO HAVE THE BLOOD OF A MASTER RACE COURSING WITHIN IT.
NO.
IT... CAN'T BE TRUE.

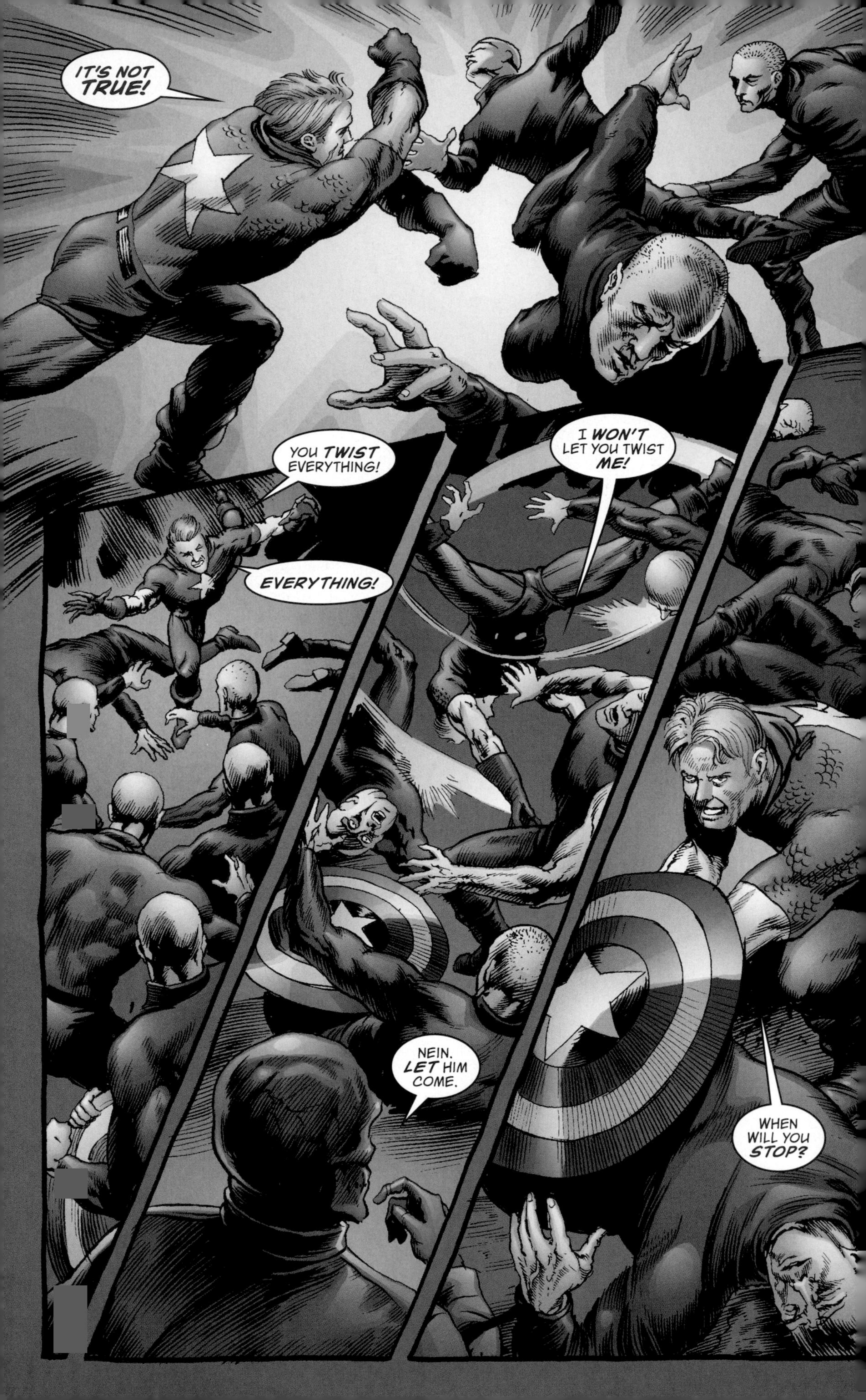
IT'S NOT TRUE!
YOU TWIST EVERYTHING!
EVERYTHING!
I WON'T LET YOU TWIST ME!
NEIN. LET HIM COME.
WHEN WILL YOU STOP?

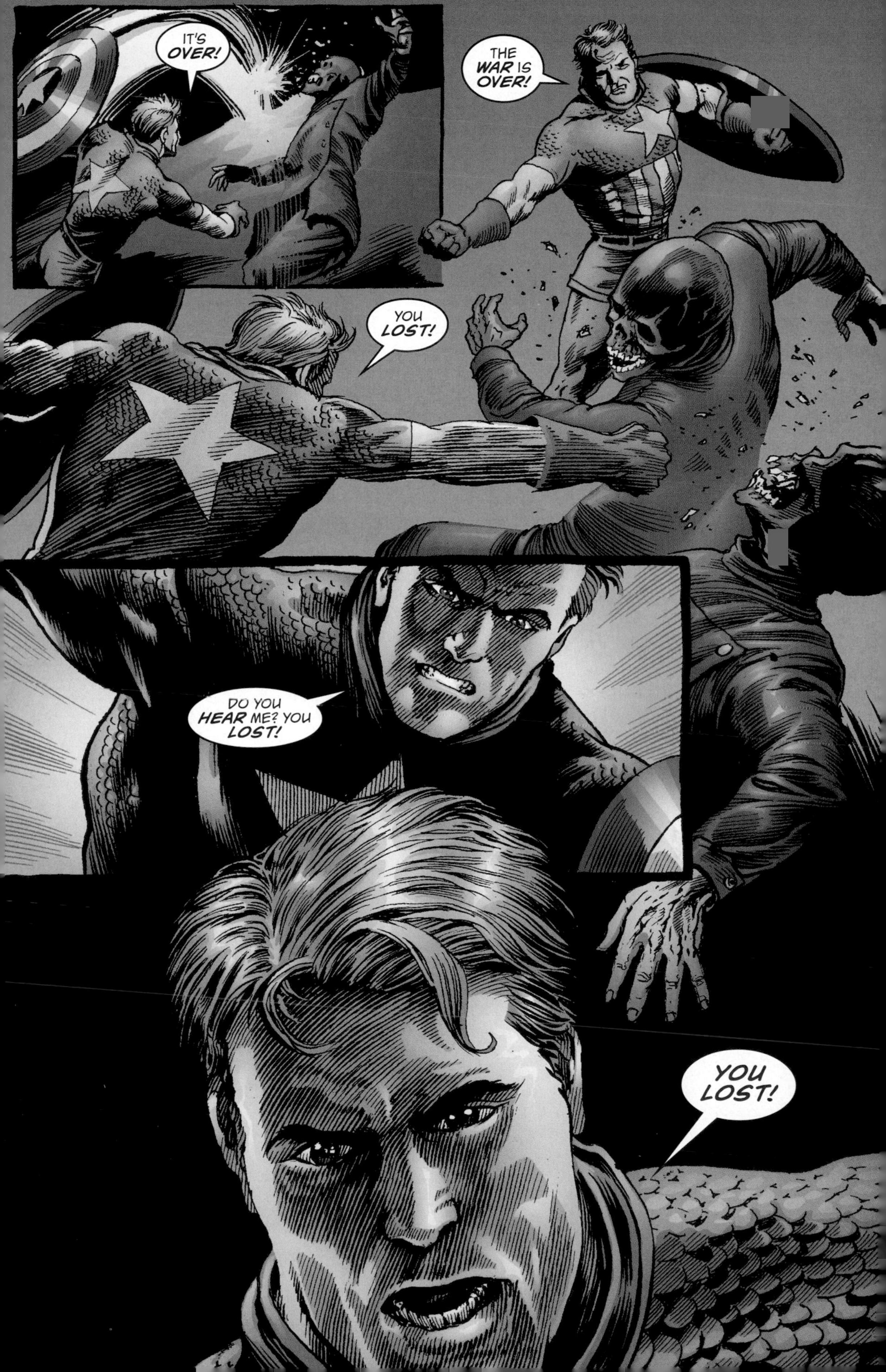
IT'S OVER!
THE WAR IS OVER!
YOU LOST!
DO YOU HEAR ME? YOU LOST!
YOU LOST!

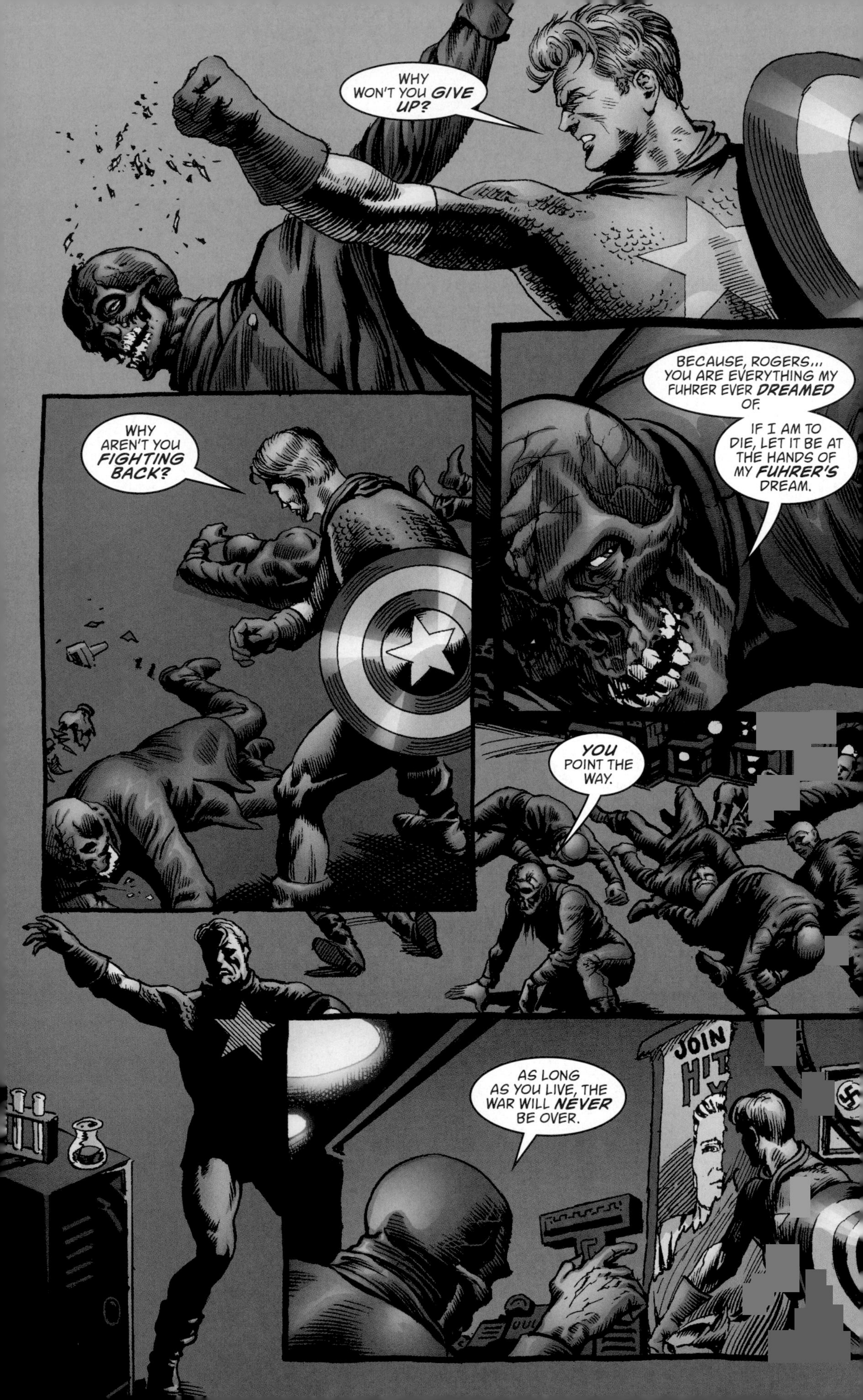

WHY WON'T YOU GIVE UP?
BECAUSE, ROGERS... YOU ARE EVERYTHING MY FUHRER EVER DREAMED OF.
IF I AM TO DIE, LET IT BE AT THE HANDS OF MY FUHRER'S DREAM.
WHY AREN'T YOU FIGHTING BACK?
YOU POINT THE WAY.
AS LONG AS YOU LIVE, THE WAR WILL NEVER BE OVER.
JOIN

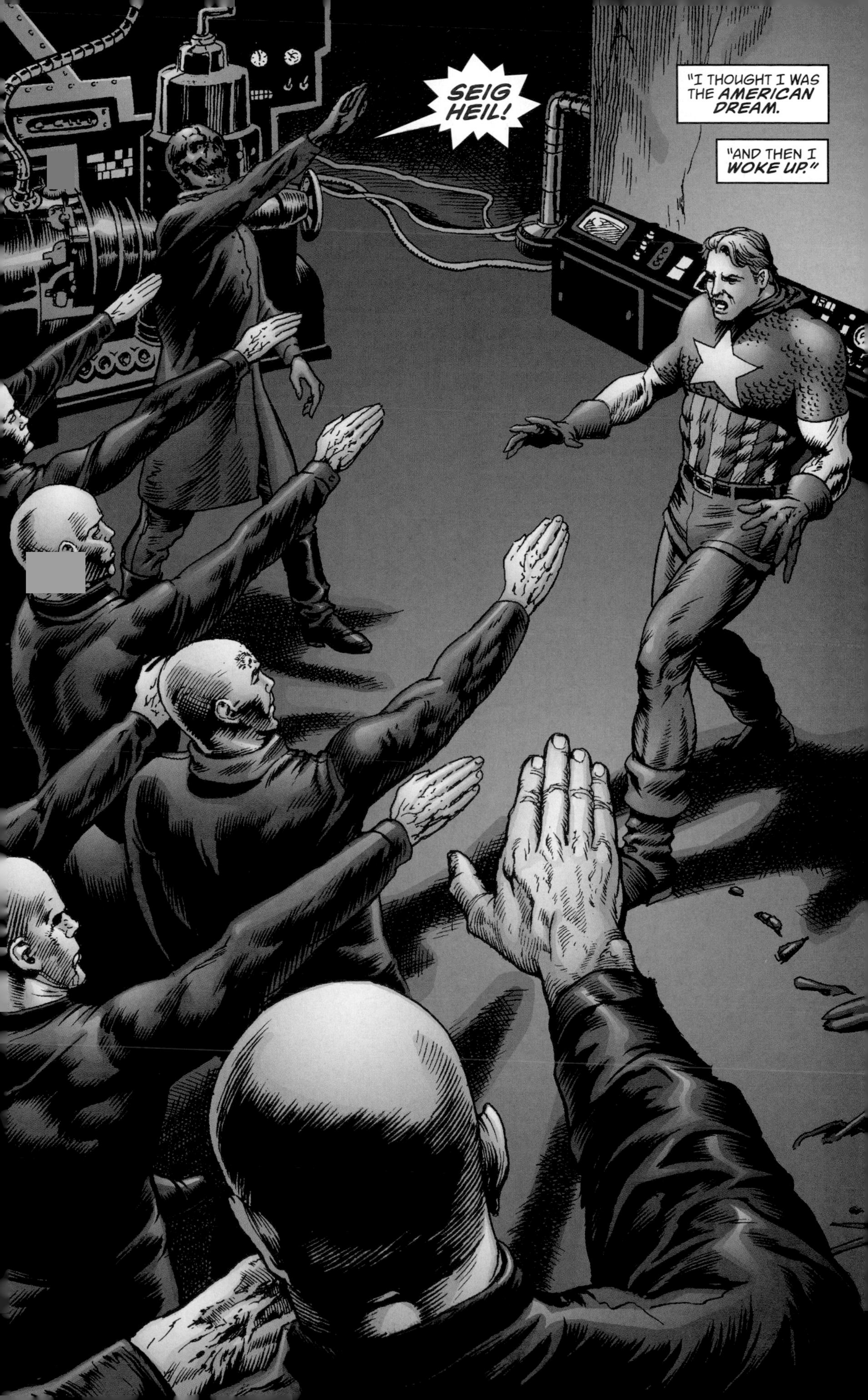
SEIG HEIL!
"I THOUGHT I WAS THE AMERICAN DREAM.
"AND THEN I WOKE UP."

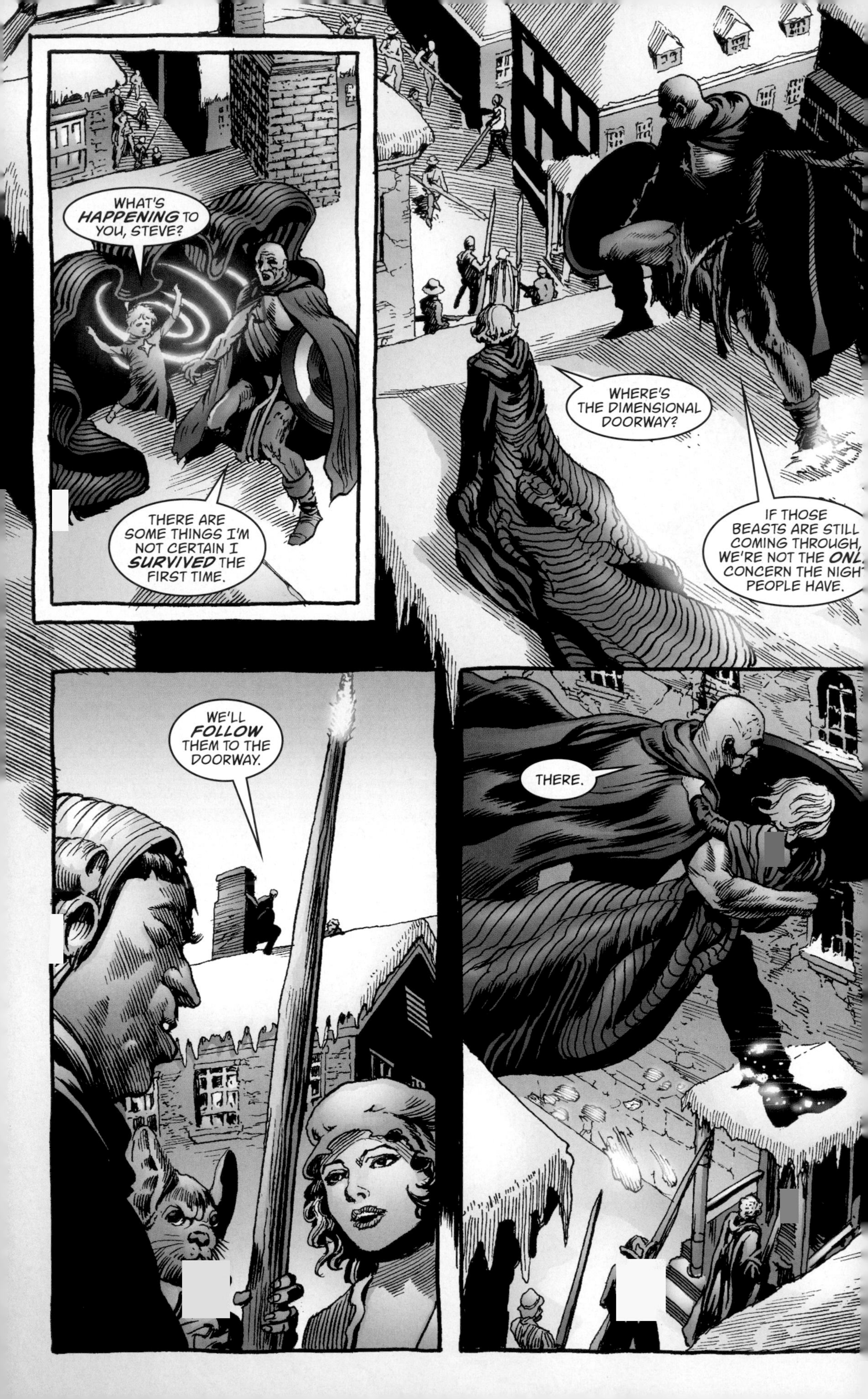
WHAT'S HAPPENING TO YOU, STEVE?
THERE ARE SOME THINGS I'M NOT CERTAIN I SURVIVED THE FIRST TIME.
WHERE'S THE DIMENSIONAL DOORWAY?
IF THOSE BEASTS ARE STILL COMING THROUGH, WE'RE NOT THE ONL CONCERN THE NIGH PEOPLE HAVE.
WE'LL FOLLOW THEM TO THE DOORWAY.
THERE.

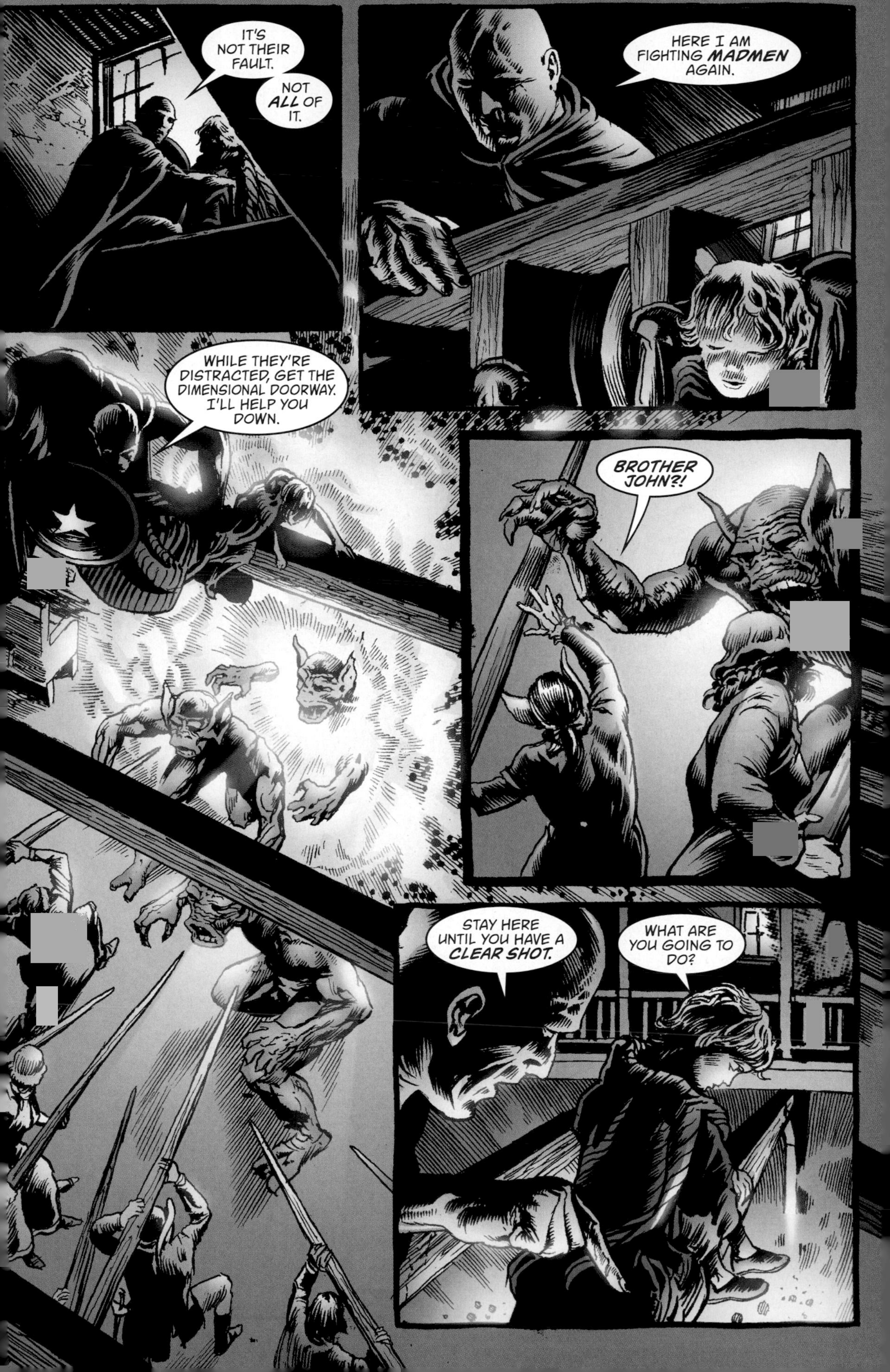
IT'S NOT THEIR FAULT.
NOT ALL OF IT.
HERE I AM FIGHTING MADMEN AGAIN.
WHILE THEY'RE DISTRACTED, GET THE DIMENSIONAL DOORWAY. I'LL HELP YOU DOWN.
BROTHER JOHN?!
STAY HERE UNTIL YOU HAVE A CLEAR SHOT.
WHAT ARE YOU GOING TO DO?

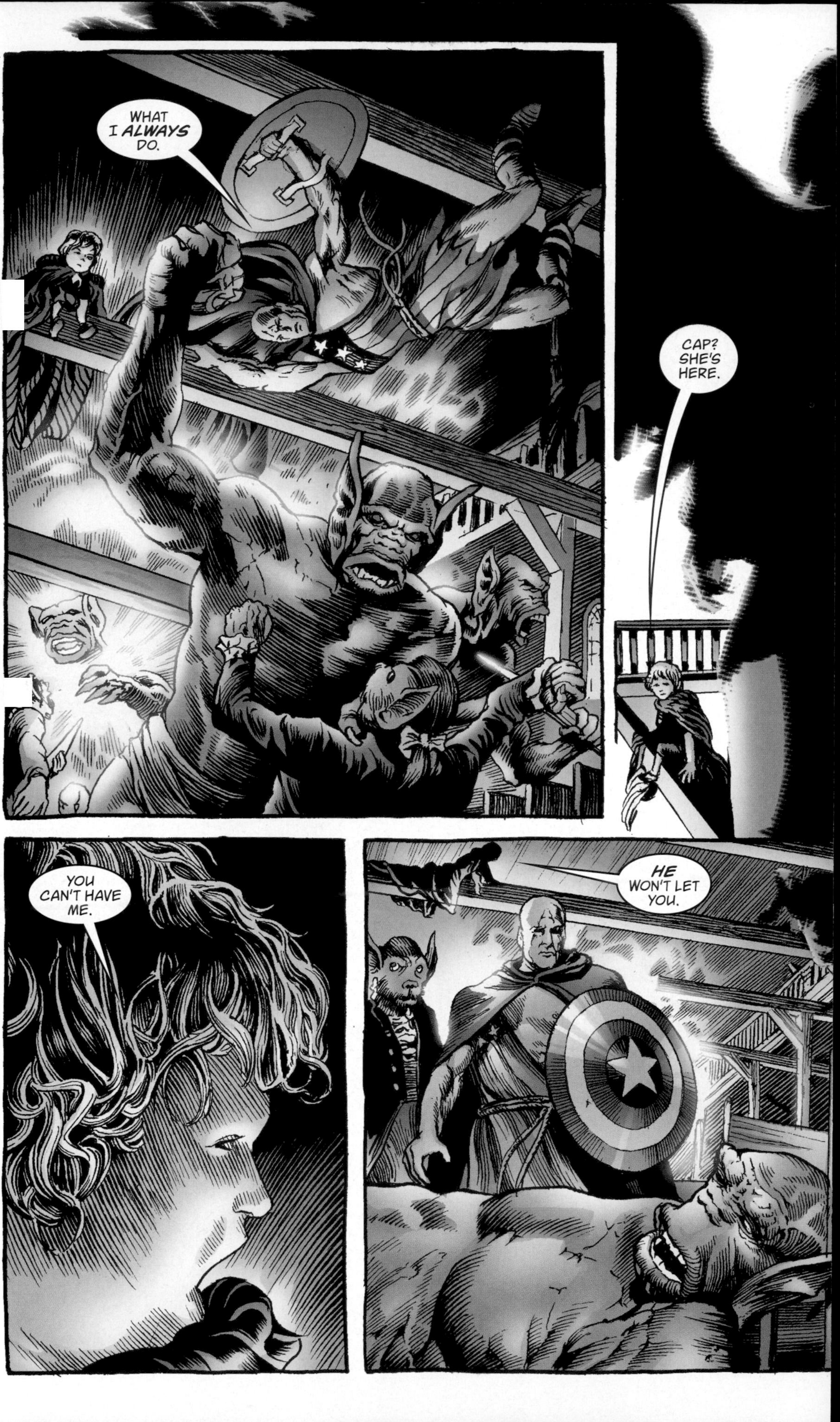
WHAT I *ALWAYS* DO.
CAP? SHE'S HERE.
YOU CAN'T HAVE ME.
HE WON'T LET YOU.

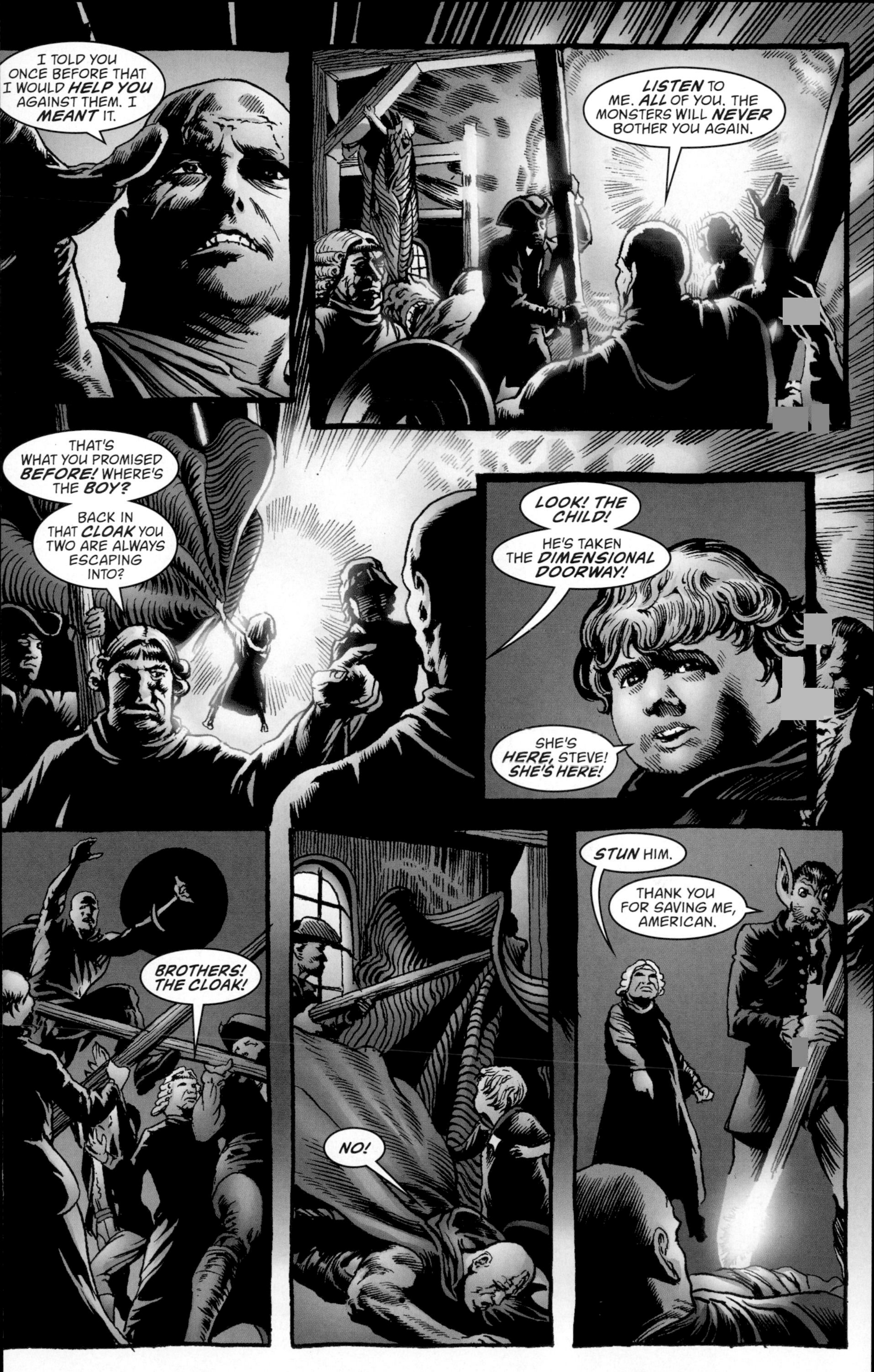
I TOLD YOU ONCE BEFORE THAT I WOULD HELP YOU AGAINST THEM. I MEANT IT.
LISTEN TO ME. ALL OF YOU. THE MONSTERS WILL NEVER BOTHER YOU AGAIN.
THAT'S WHAT YOU PROMISED BEFORE! WHERE'S THE BOY?
BACK IN THAT CLOAK YOU TWO ARE ALWAYS ESCAPING INTO?
LOOK! THE CHILD!
HE'S TAKEN THE DIMENSIONAL DOORWAY!
SHE'S HERE, STEVE! SHE'S HERE!
BROTHERS! THE CLOAK!
NO!
STUN HIM.
THANK YOU FOR SAVING ME, AMERICAN.

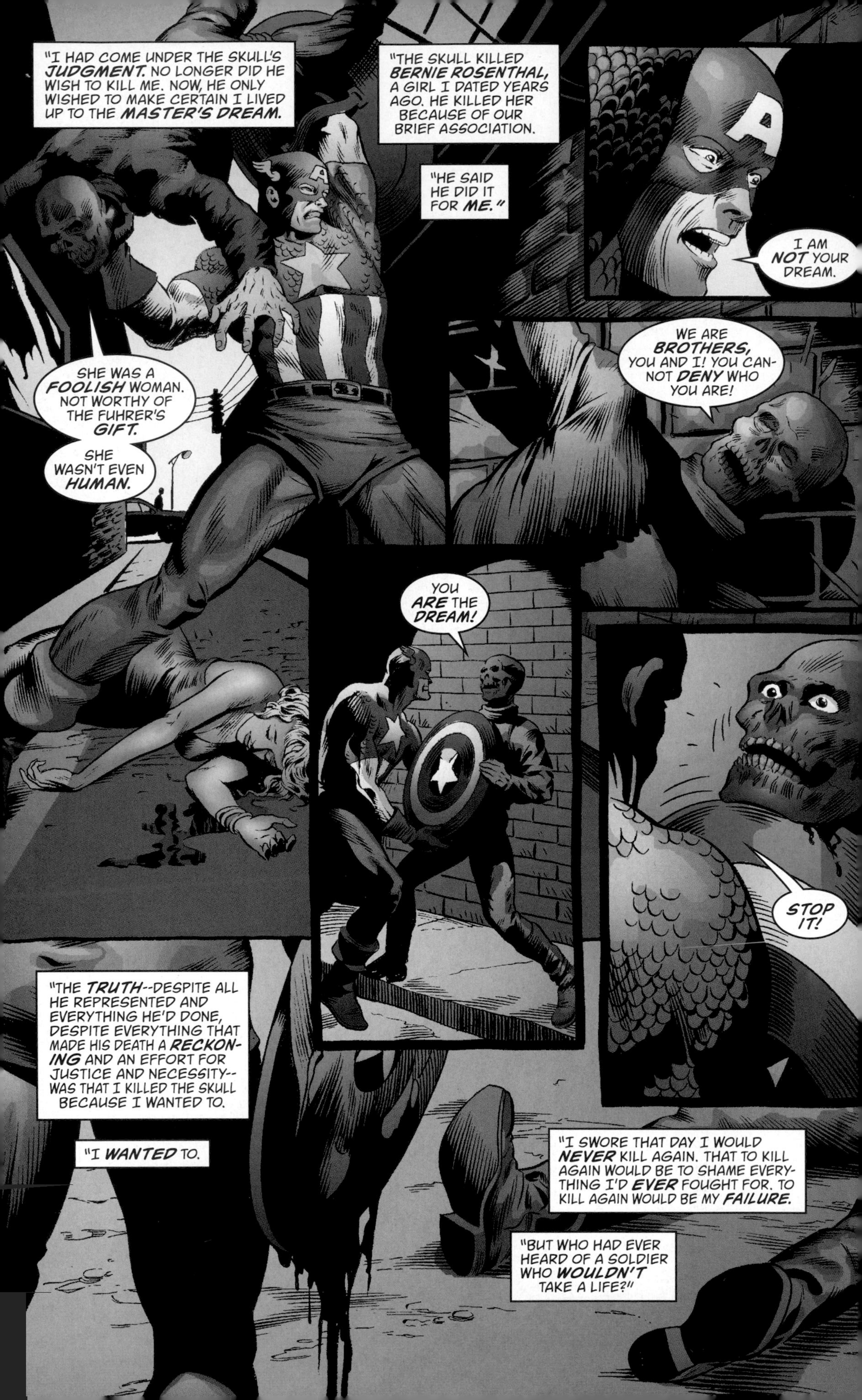
"I HAD COME UNDER THE SKULL'S JUDGMENT. NO LONGER DID HE WISH TO KILL ME. NOW, HE ONLY WISHED TO MAKE CERTAIN I LIVED UP TO THE MASTER'S DREAM.
"THE SKULL KILLED BERNIE ROSENTHAL, A GIRL I DATED YEARS AGO. HE KILLED HER BECAUSE OF OUR BRIEF ASSOCIATION.
"HE SAID HE DID IT FOR ME."
SHE WAS A FOOLISH WOMAN. NOT WORTHY OF THE FUHRER'S GIFT.
SHE WASN'T EVEN HUMAN.
I AM NOT YOUR DREAM.
WE ARE BROTHERS, YOU AND I! YOU CAN-NOT DENY WHO YOU ARE!
YOU ARE THE DREAM!
STOP IT!
"THE TRUTH--DESPITE ALL HE REPRESENTED AND EVERYTHING HE'D DONE, DESPITE EVERYTHING THAT MADE HIS DEATH A RECKON-ING AND AN EFFORT FOR JUSTICE AND NECESSITY--WAS THAT I KILLED THE SKULL BECAUSE I WANTED TO.
"I WANTED TO.
"I SWORE THAT DAY I WOULD NEVER KILL AGAIN. THAT TO KILL AGAIN WOULD BE TO SHAME EVERY-THING I'D EVER FOUGHT FOR. TO KILL AGAIN WOULD BE MY FAILURE.
"BUT WHO HAD EVER HEARD OF A SOLDIER WHO WOULDN'T TAKE A LIFE?"

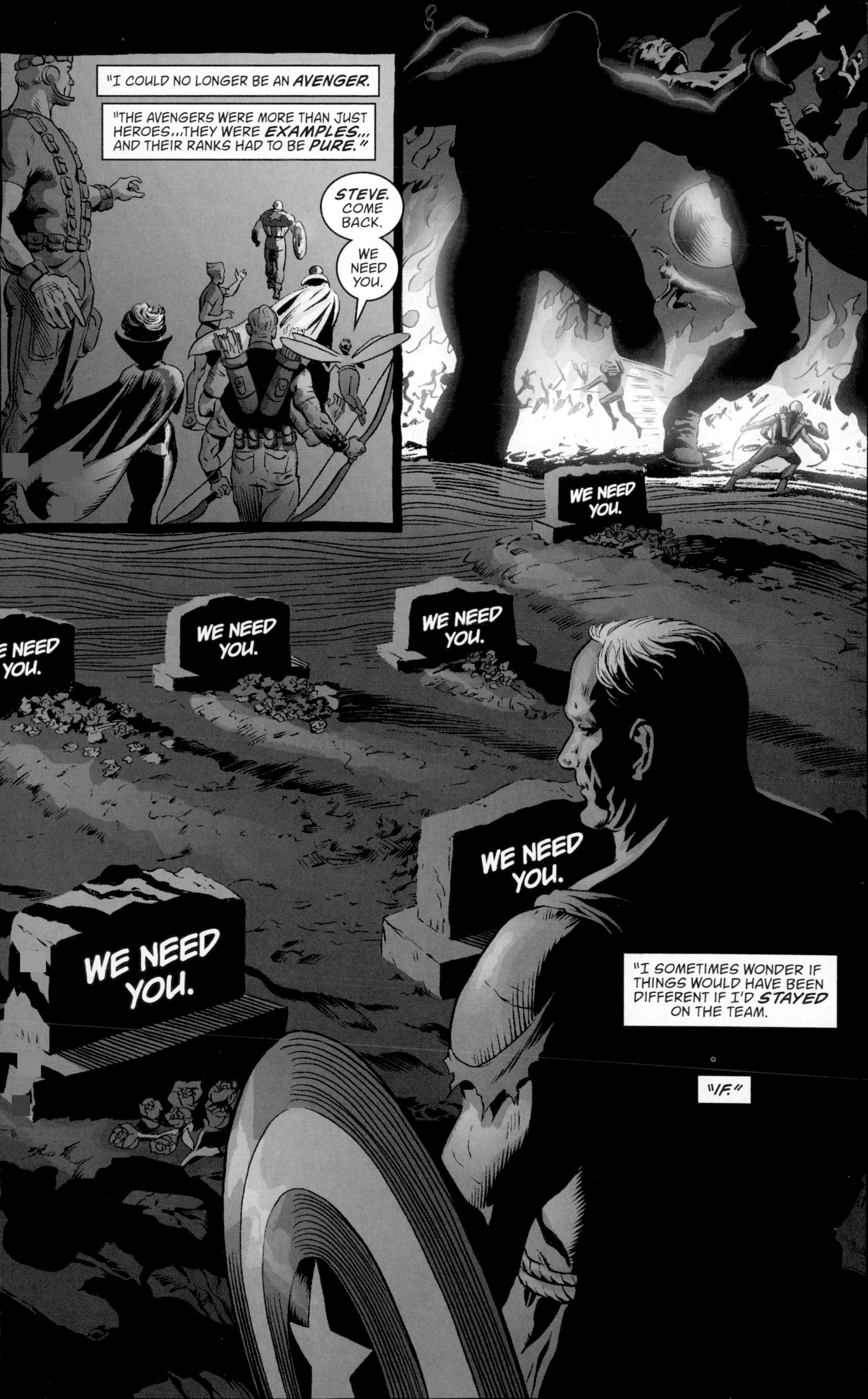
"I COULD NO LONGER BE AN AVENGER.
"THE AVENGERS WERE MORE THAN JUST HEROES...THEY WERE EXAMPLES... AND THEIR RANKS HAD TO BE PURE."
STEVE. COME BACK.
WE NEED YOU.
WE NEED YOU.
WE NEED YOU.
WE NEED YOU.
WE NEED YOU.
WE NEED YOU.
WE NEED YOU.
"I SOMETIMES WONDER IF THINGS WOULD HAVE BEEN DIFFERENT IF I'D STAYED ON THE TEAM.
"IF."

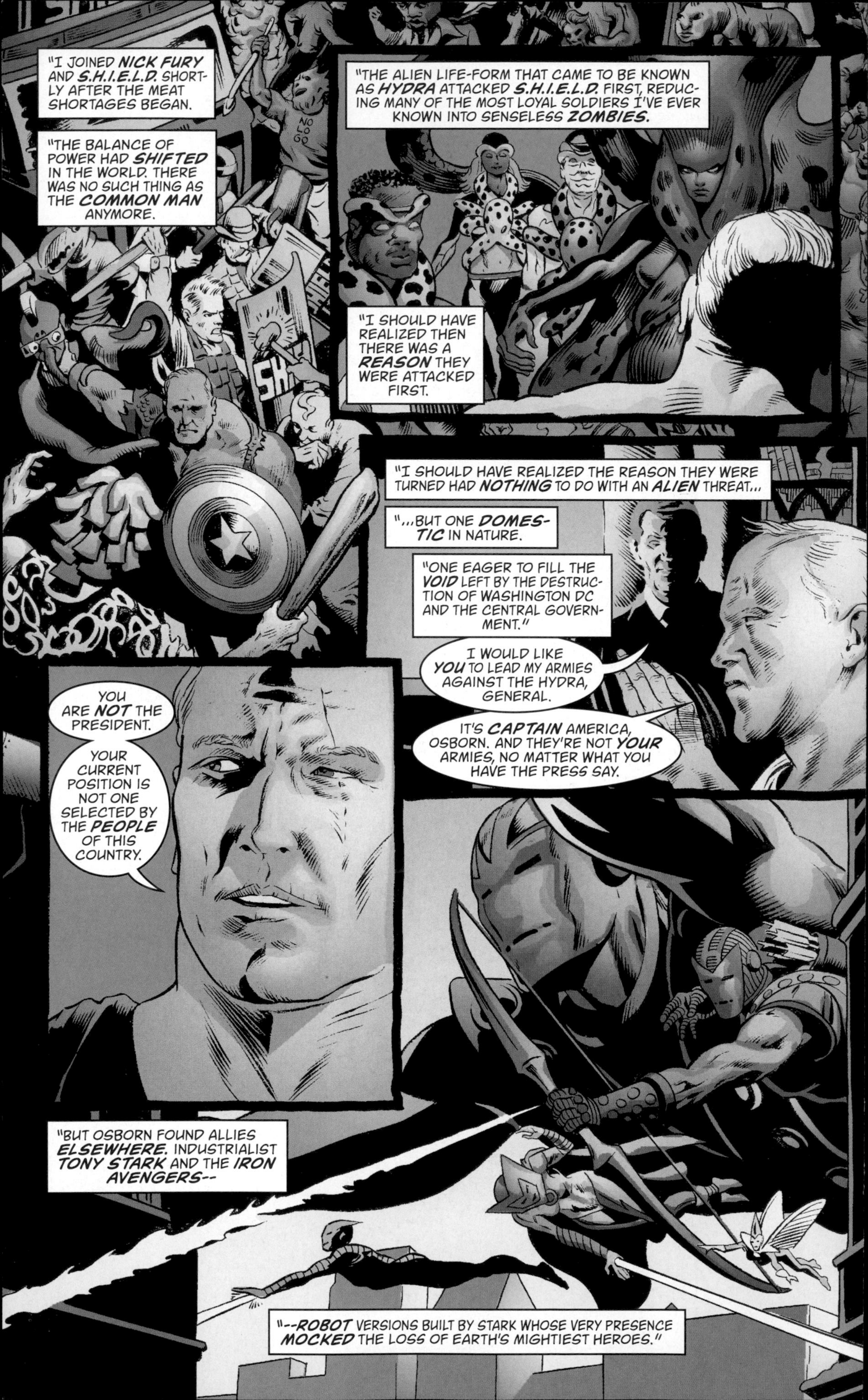
"I JOINED NICK FURY AND S.H.I.E.L.D. SHORTLY AFTER THE MEAT SHORTAGES BEGAN.
"THE BALANCE OF POWER HAD SHIFTED IN THE WORLD. THERE WAS NO SUCH THING AS THE COMMON MAN ANYMORE.
NO LO GO
"THE ALIEN LIFE-FORM THAT CAME TO BE KNOWN AS HYDRA ATTACKED S.H.I.E.L.D. FIRST, REDUCING MANY OF THE MOST LOYAL SOLDIERS I'VE EVER KNOWN INTO SENSELESS ZOMBIES.
"I SHOULD HAVE REALIZED THEN THERE WAS A REASON THEY WERE ATTACKED FIRST.
"I SHOULD HAVE REALIZED THE REASON THEY WERE TURNED HAD NOTHING TO DO WITH AN ALIEN THREAT...
"...BUT ONE DOMESTIC IN NATURE.
"ONE EAGER TO FILL THE VOID LEFT BY THE DESTRUCTION OF WASHINGTON DC AND THE CENTRAL GOVERNMENT."
I WOULD LIKE YOU TO LEAD MY ARMIES AGAINST THE HYDRA, GENERAL.
IT'S CAPTAIN AMERICA, OSBORN. AND THEY'RE NOT YOUR ARMIES, NO MATTER WHAT YOU HAVE THE PRESS SAY.
YOU ARE NOT THE PRESIDENT.
YOUR CURRENT POSITION IS NOT ONE SELECTED BY THE PEOPLE OF THIS COUNTRY.
"BUT OSBORN FOUND ALLIES ELSEWHERE. INDUSTRIALIST TONY STARK AND THE IRON AVENGERS--
"--ROBOT VERSIONS BUILT BY STARK WHOSE VERY PRESENCE MOCKED THE LOSS OF EARTH'S MIGHTIEST HEROES."

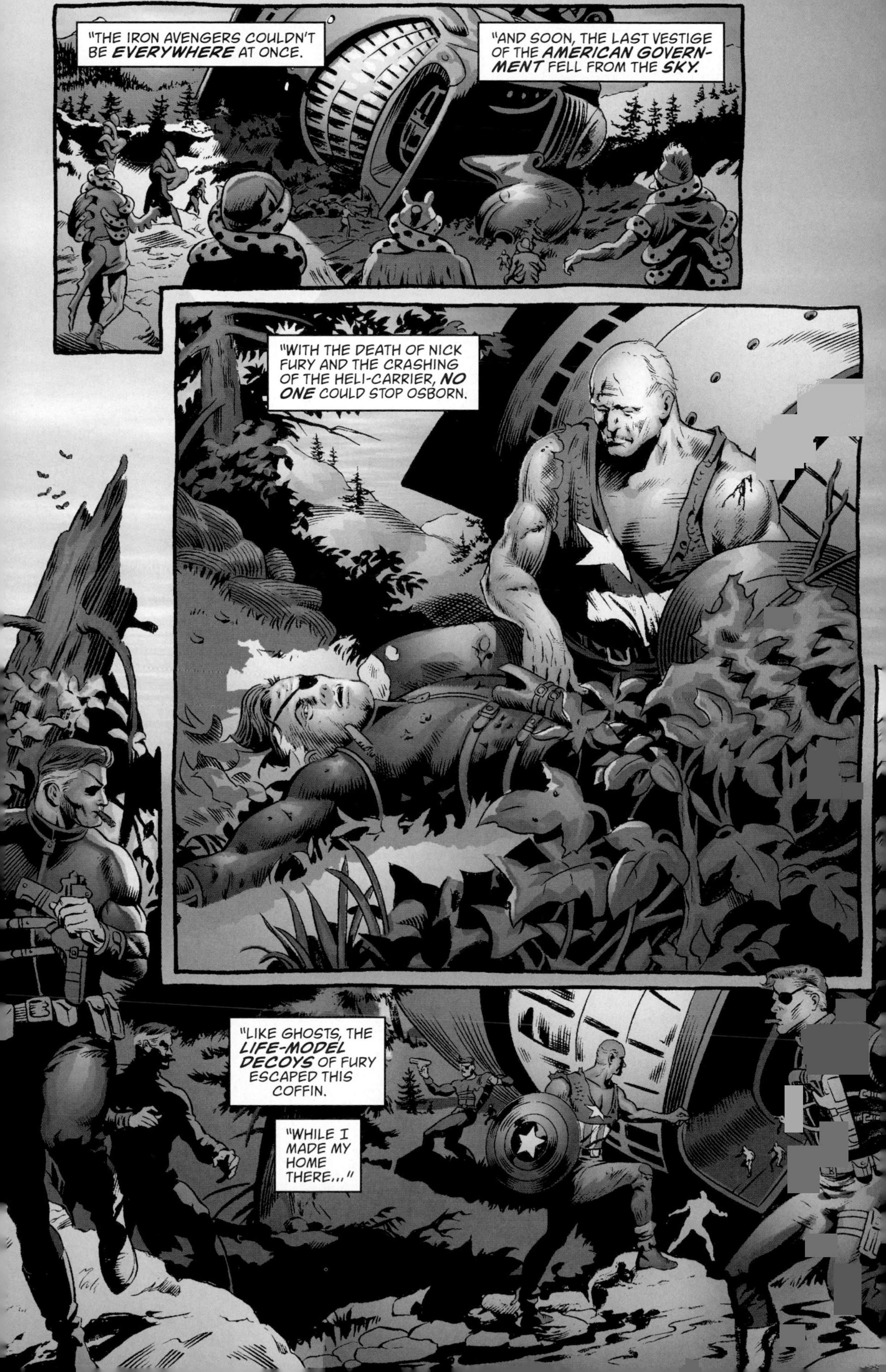
"THE IRON AVENGERS COULDN'T BE EVERYWHERE AT ONCE.
"AND SOON, THE LAST VESTIGE OF THE AMERICAN GOVERNMENT FELL FROM THE SKY.
"WITH THE DEATH OF NICK FURY AND THE CRASHING OF THE HELI-CARRIER, NO ONE COULD STOP OSBORN.
"LIKE GHOSTS, THE LIFE-MODEL DECOYS OF FURY ESCAPED THIS COFFIN.
"WHILE I MADE MY HOME THERE..."

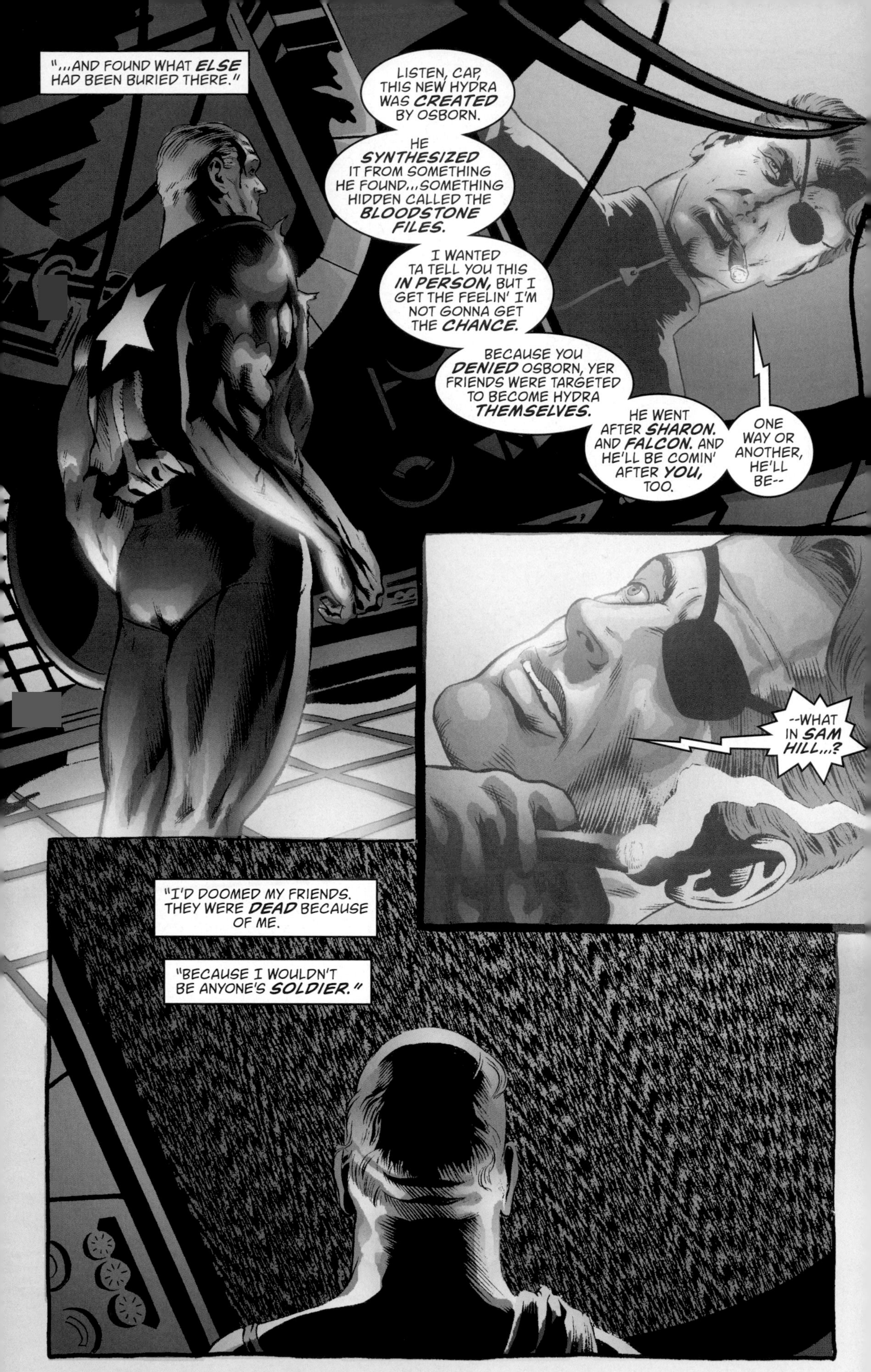
"...AND FOUND WHAT ELSE HAD BEEN BURIED THERE."
LISTEN, CAP, THIS NEW HYDRA WAS CREATED BY OSBORN.
HE SYNTHESIZED IT FROM SOMETHING HE FOUND...SOMETHING HIDDEN CALLED THE BLOODSTONE FILES.
I WANTED TA TELL YOU THIS IN PERSON, BUT I GET THE FEELIN' I'M NOT GONNA GET THE CHANCE.
BECAUSE YOU DENIED OSBORN, YER FRIENDS WERE TARGETED TO BECOME HYDRA THEMSELVES.
HE WENT AFTER SHARON. AND FALCON. AND HE'LL BE COMIN' AFTER YOU, TOO.
ONE WAY OR ANOTHER, HE'LL BE--
--WHAT IN SAM HILL...?
"I'D DOOMED MY FRIENDS. THEY WERE DEAD BECAUSE OF ME.
"BECAUSE I WOULDN'T BE ANYONE'S SOLDIER."

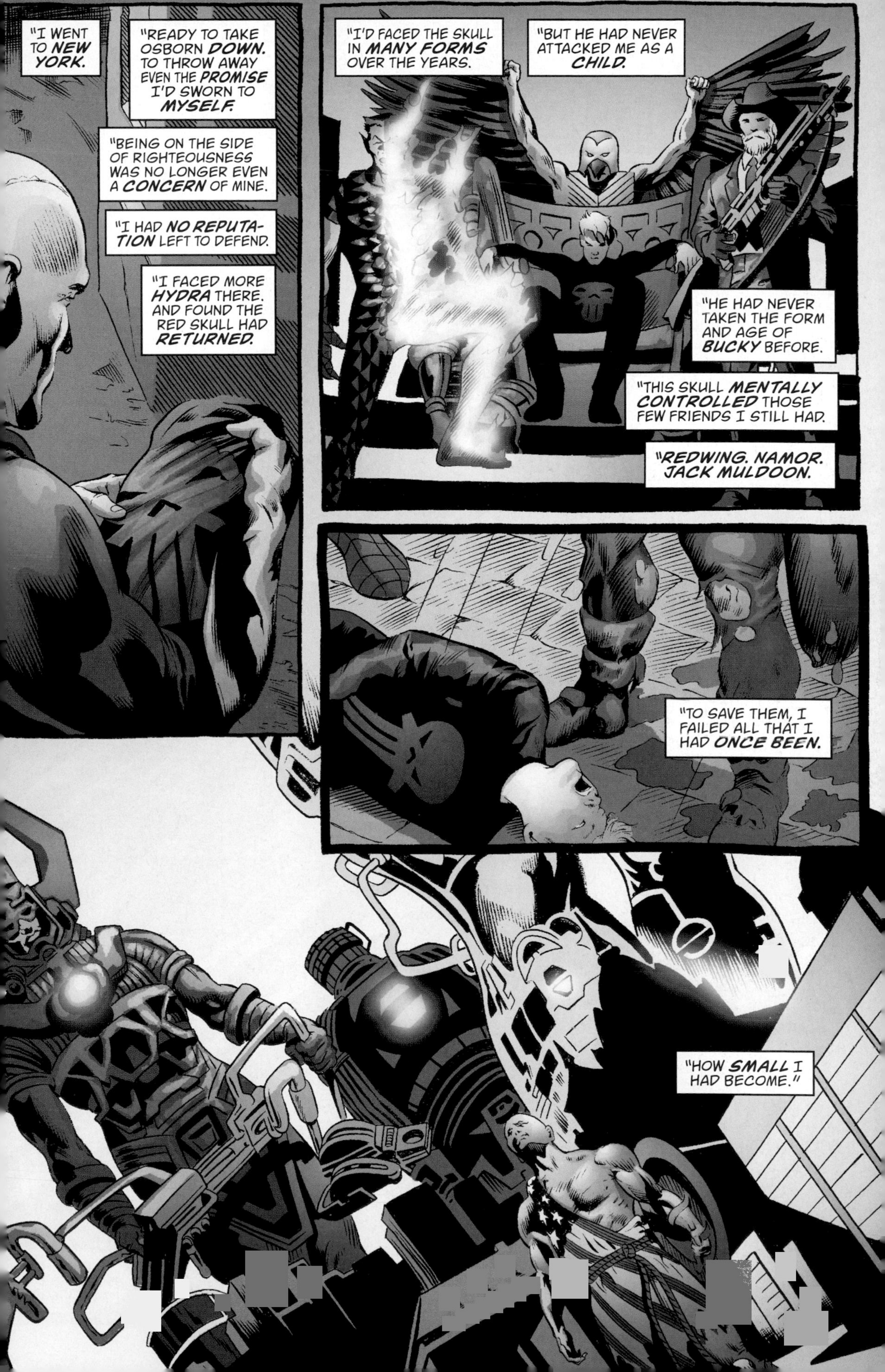
"I WENT TO NEW YORK.
"READY TO TAKE OSBORN DOWN. TO THROW AWAY EVEN THE PROMISE I'D SWORN TO MYSELF.
"BEING ON THE SIDE OF RIGHTEOUSNESS WAS NO LONGER EVEN A CONCERN OF MINE.
"I HAD NO REPUTATION LEFT TO DEFEND.
"I FACED MORE HYDRA THERE. AND FOUND THE RED SKULL HAD RETURNED.
"I'D FACED THE SKULL IN MANY FORMS OVER THE YEARS.
"BUT HE HAD NEVER ATTACKED ME AS A CHILD.
"HE HAD NEVER TAKEN THE FORM AND AGE OF BUCKY BEFORE.
"THIS SKULL MENTALLY CONTROLLED THOSE FEW FRIENDS I STILL HAD.
"REDWING. NAMOR. JACK MULDOON.
"TO SAVE THEM, I FAILED ALL THAT I HAD ONCE BEEN.
"HOW SMALL I HAD BECOME."

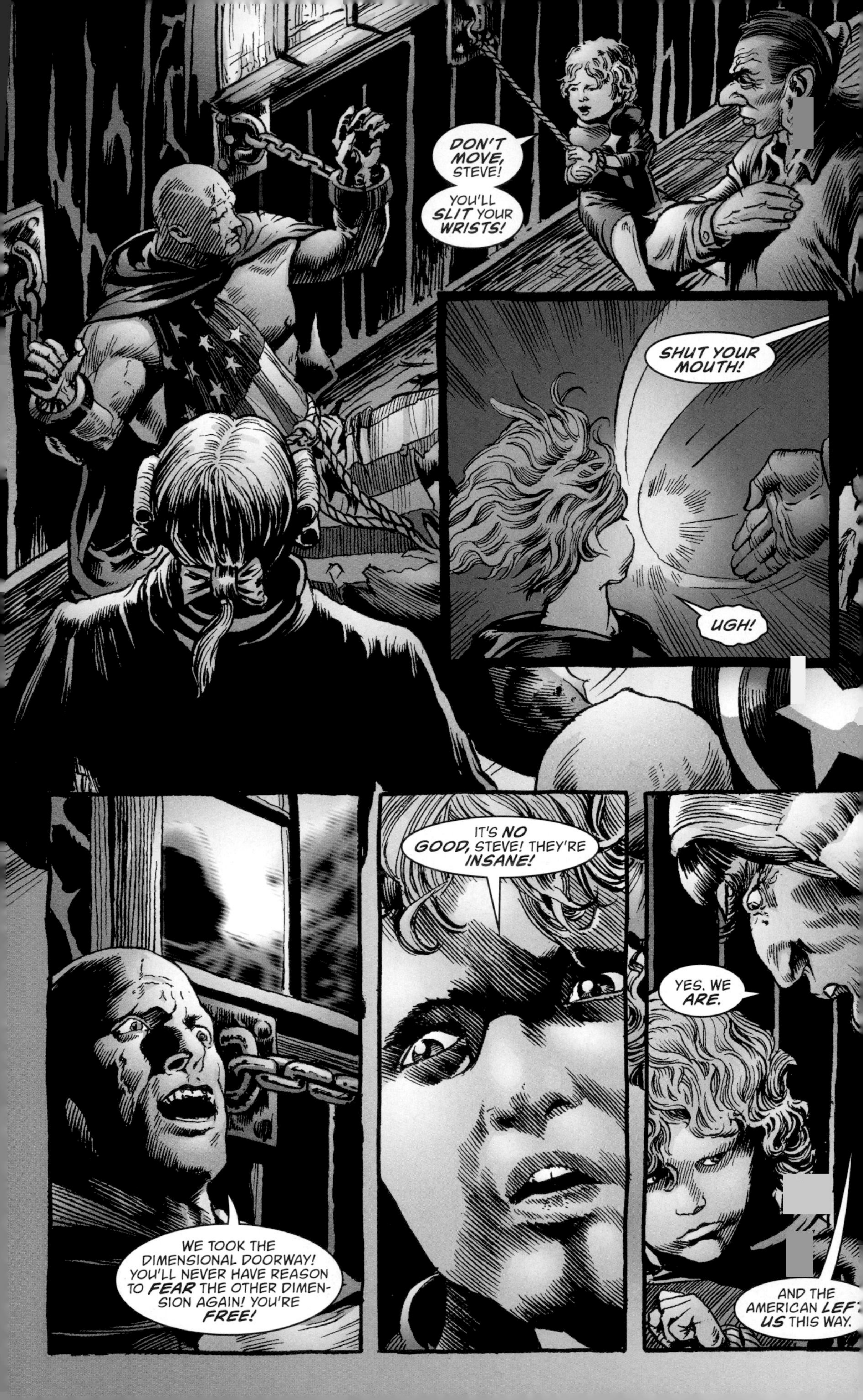
DON'T MOVE, STEVE!
YOU'LL SLIT YOUR WRISTS!
SHUT YOUR MOUTH!
UGH!
WE TOOK THE DIMENSIONAL DOORWAY! YOU'LL NEVER HAVE REASON TO FEAR THE OTHER DIMEN-SION AGAIN! YOU'RE FREE!
IT'S NO GOOD, STEVE! THEY'RE INSANE!
YES. WE ARE.
AND THE AMERICAN LEF US THIS WAY.

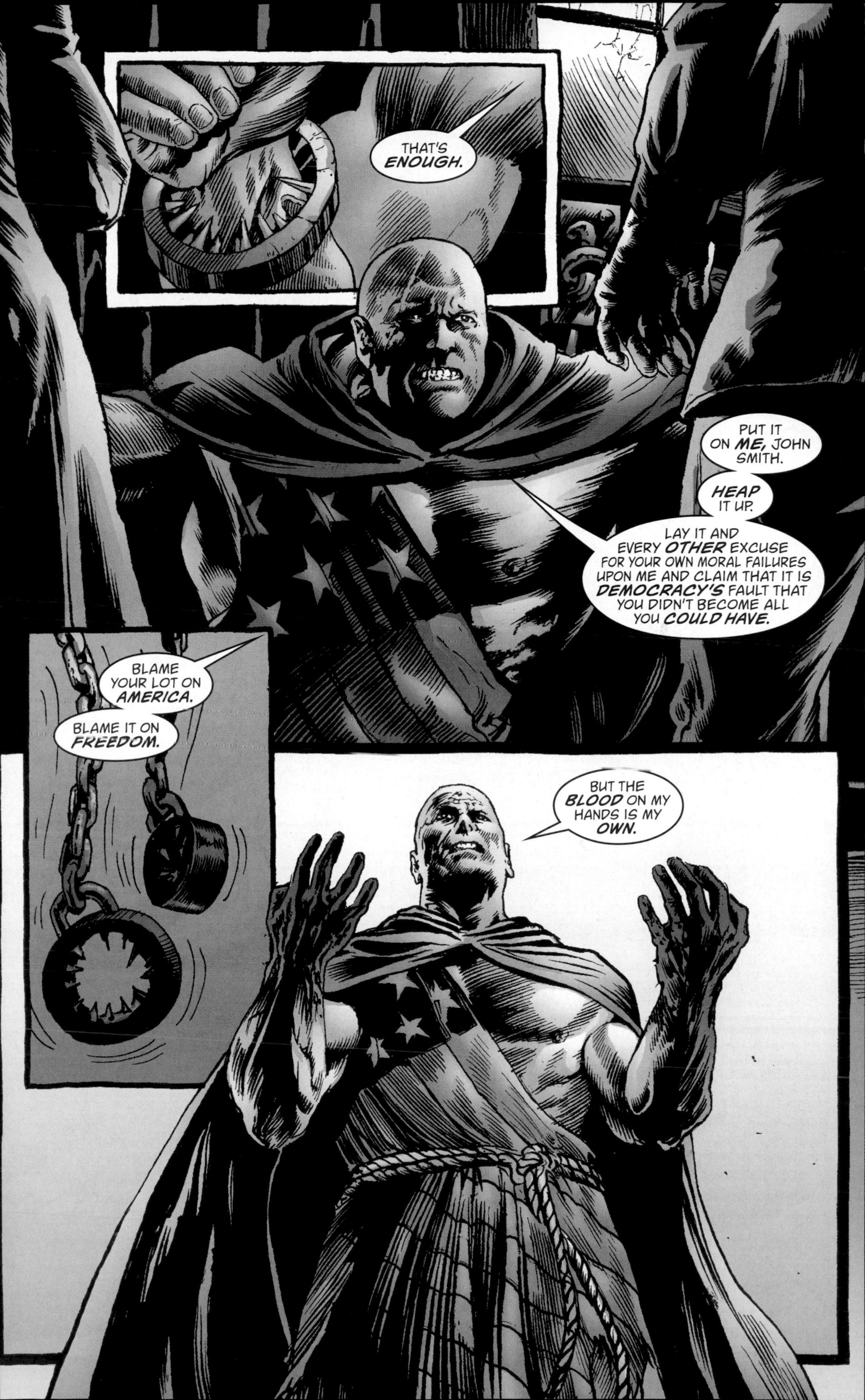
THAT'S ENOUGH.
PUT IT ON ME, JOHN SMITH.
HEAP IT UP.
LAY IT AND EVERY OTHER EXCUSE FOR YOUR OWN MORAL FAILURES UPON ME AND CLAIM THAT IT IS DEMOCRACY'S FAULT THAT YOU DIDN'T BECOME ALL YOU COULD HAVE.
BLAME YOUR LOT ON AMERICA.
BLAME IT ON FREEDOM.
BUT THE BLOOD ON MY HANDS IS MY OWN.

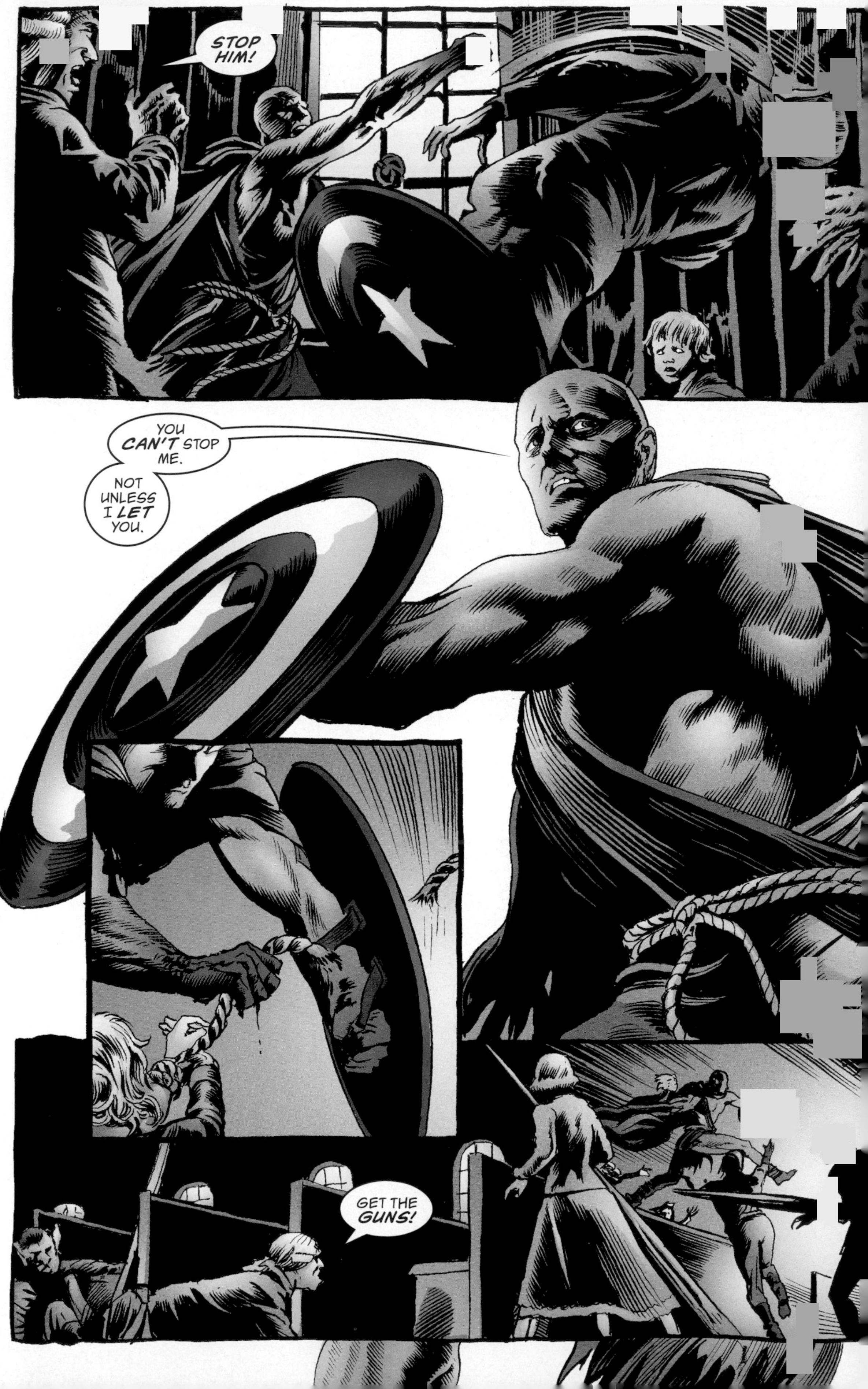
STOP HIM!
YOU CAN'T STOP ME.
NOT UNLESS I LET YOU.
GET THE GUNS!

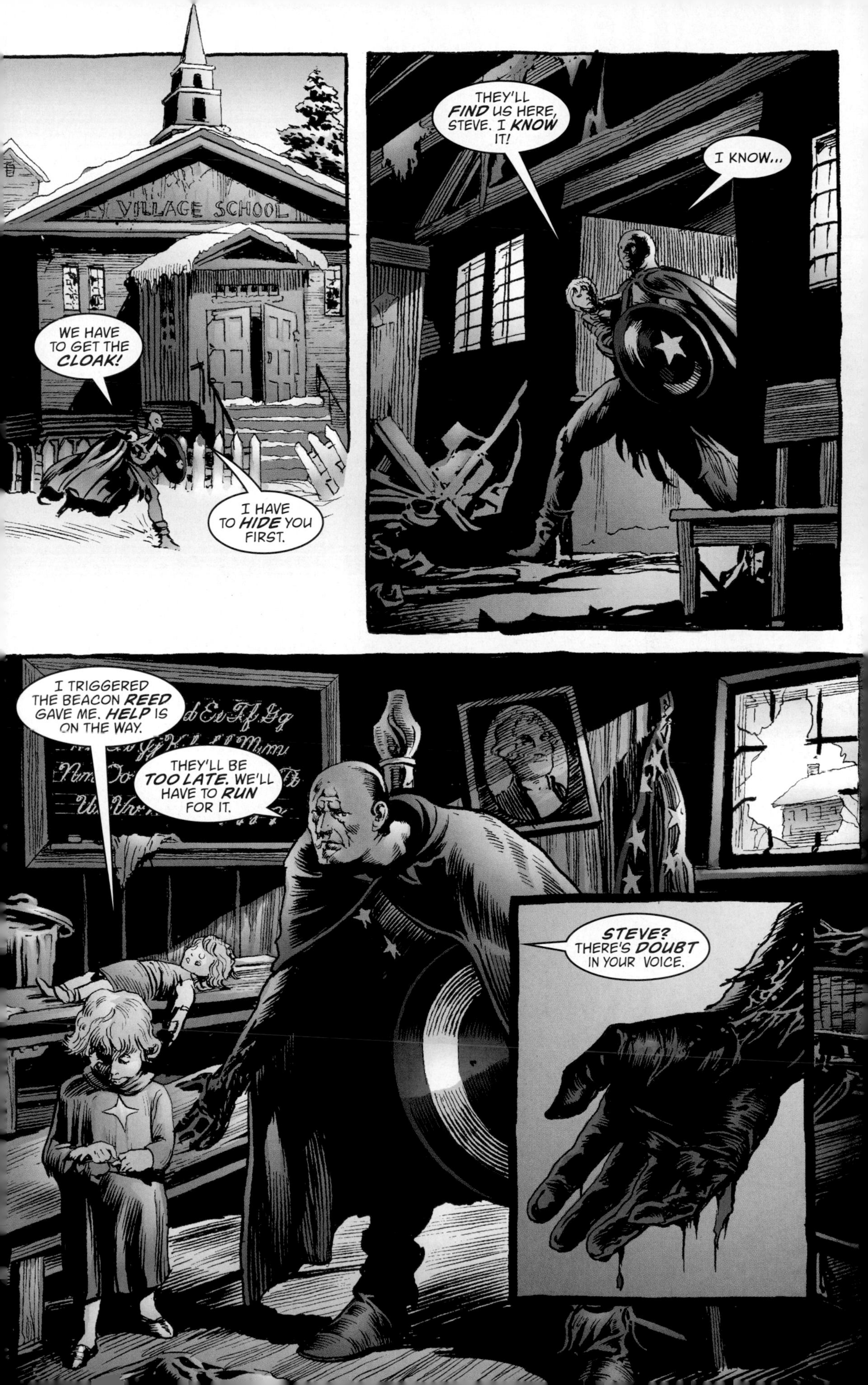
VILLAGE SCHOOL
WE HAVE TO GET THE CLOAK!
I HAVE TO HIDE YOU FIRST.
THEY'LL FIND US HERE, STEVE. I KNOW IT!
I KNOW...
I TRIGGERED THE BEACON REED GAVE ME. HELP IS ON THE WAY.
THEY'LL BE TOO LATE. WE'LL HAVE TO RUN FOR IT.
STEVE? THERE'S DOUBT IN YOUR VOICE.

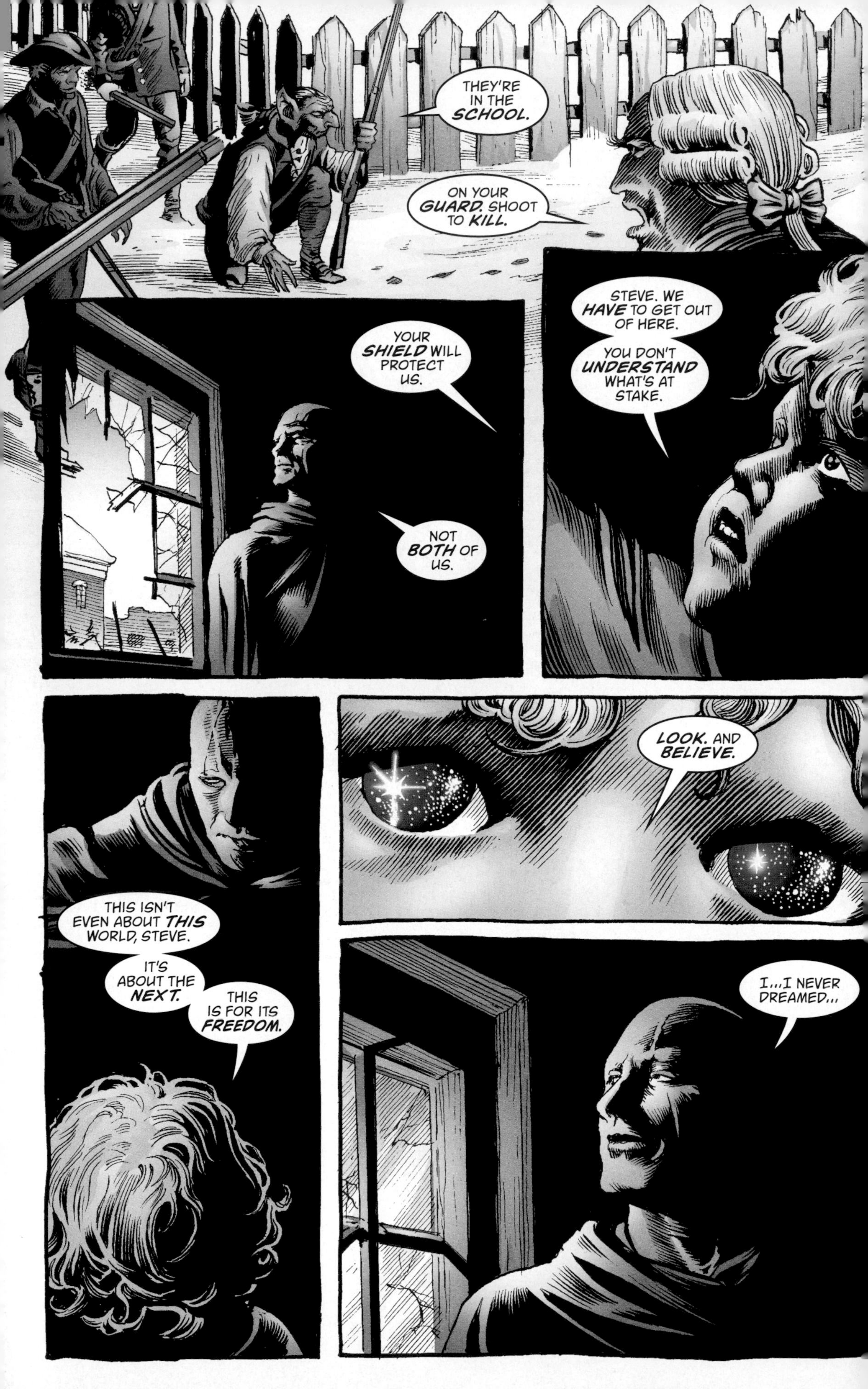
THEY'RE IN THE SCHOOL.
ON YOUR GUARD. SHOOT TO KILL.
YOUR SHIELD WILL PROTECT US.
NOT BOTH OF US.
STEVE. WE HAVE TO GET OUT OF HERE.
YOU DON'T UNDERSTAND WHAT'S AT STAKE.
THIS ISN'T EVEN ABOUT THIS WORLD, STEVE.
IT'S ABOUT THE NEXT.
THIS IS FOR ITS FREEDOM.
LOOK. AND BELIEVE.
I...I NEVER DREAMED...

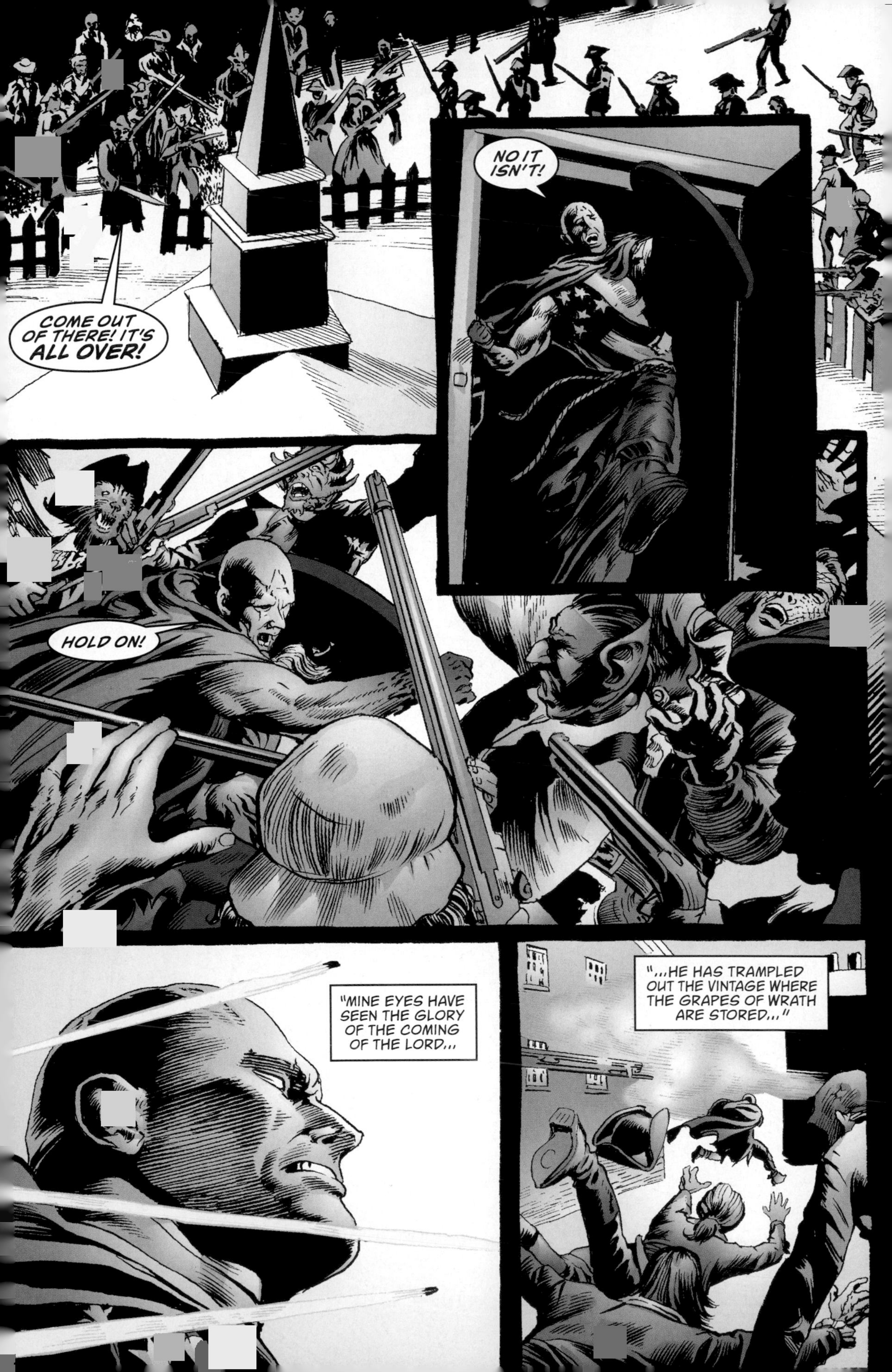
COME OUT OF THERE! IT'S ALL OVER!
NO IT ISN'T!
HOLD ON!
"MINE EYES HAVE SEEN THE GLORY OF THE COMING OF THE LORD...
"...HE HAS TRAMPLED OUT THE VINTAGE WHERE THE GRAPES OF WRATH ARE STORED..."

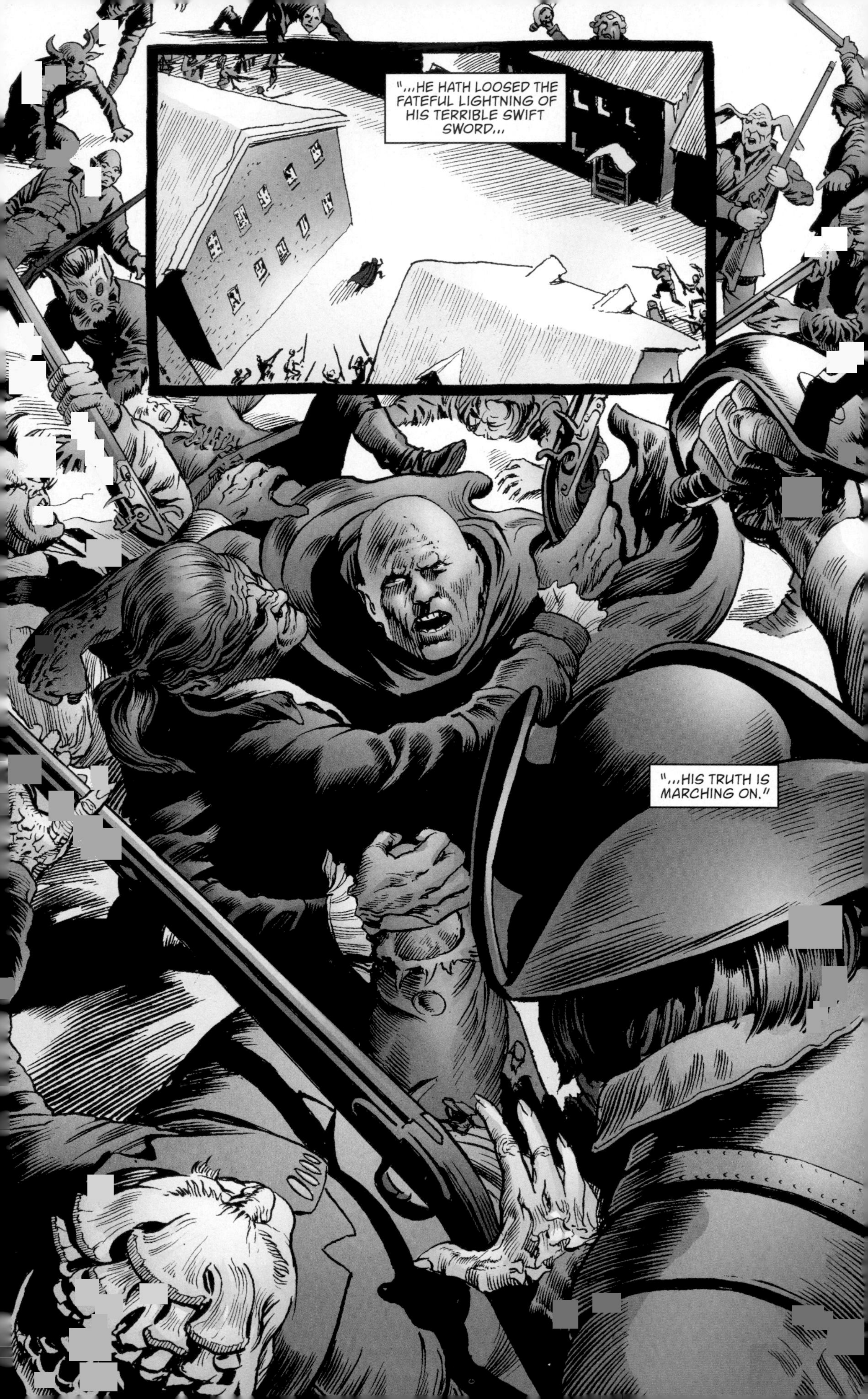
"...HE HATH LOOSED THE FATEFUL LIGHTNING OF HIS TERRIBLE SWIFT SWORD...
"...HIS TRUTH IS MARCHING ON."

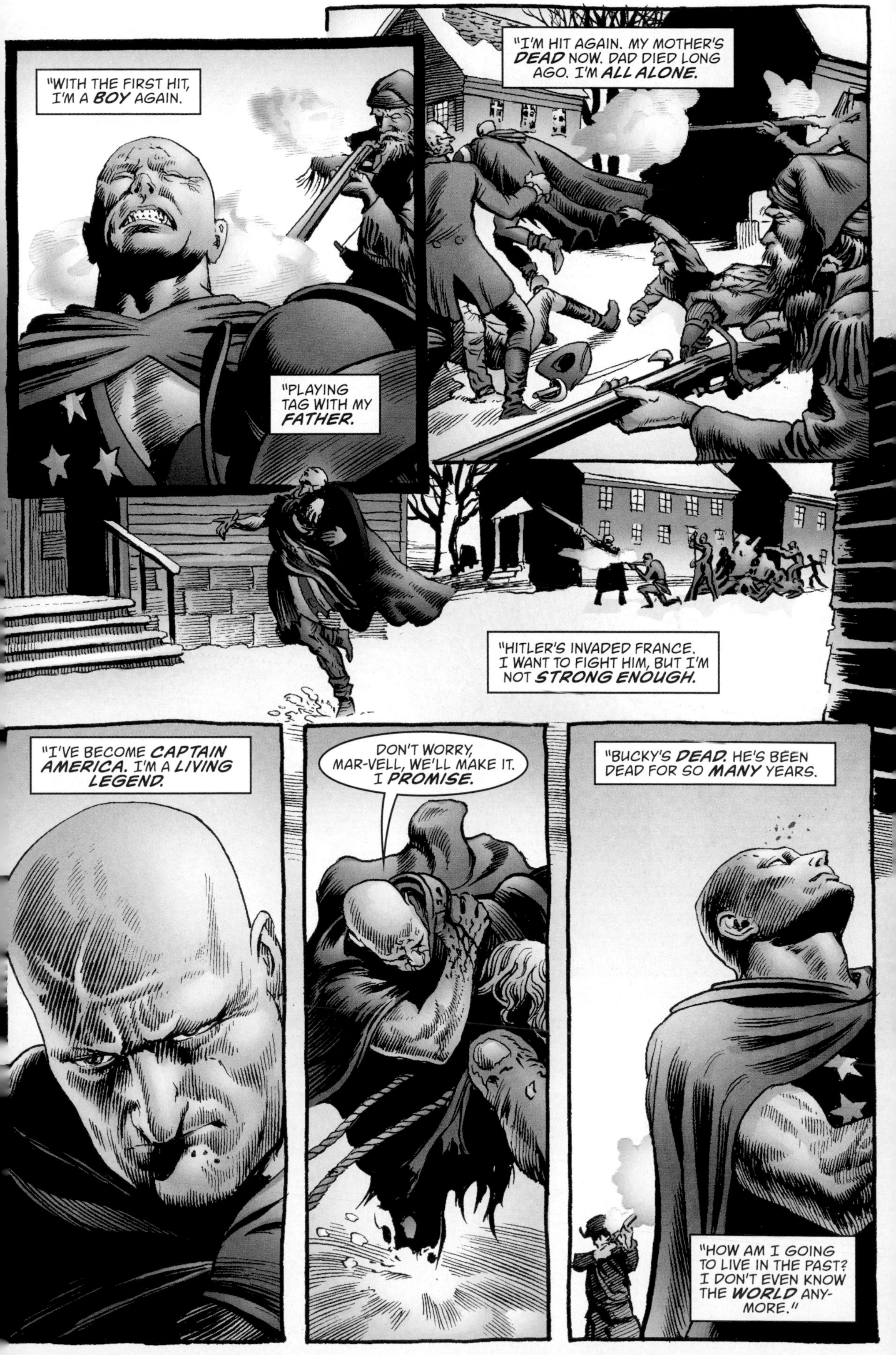
"WITH THE FIRST HIT, I'M A BOY AGAIN.
"PLAYING TAG WITH MY FATHER.
"I'M HIT AGAIN. MY MOTHER'S DEAD NOW. DAD DIED LONG AGO. I'M ALL ALONE.
"HITLER'S INVADED FRANCE. I WANT TO FIGHT HIM, BUT I'M NOT STRONG ENOUGH.
"I'VE BECOME CAPTAIN AMERICA. I'M A LIVING LEGEND.
DON'T WORRY, MAR-VELL, WE'LL MAKE IT. I PROMISE.
"BUCKY'S DEAD. HE'S BEEN DEAD FOR SO MANY YEARS.
"HOW AM I GOING TO LIVE IN THE PAST? I DON'T EVEN KNOW THE WORLD ANY-MORE."

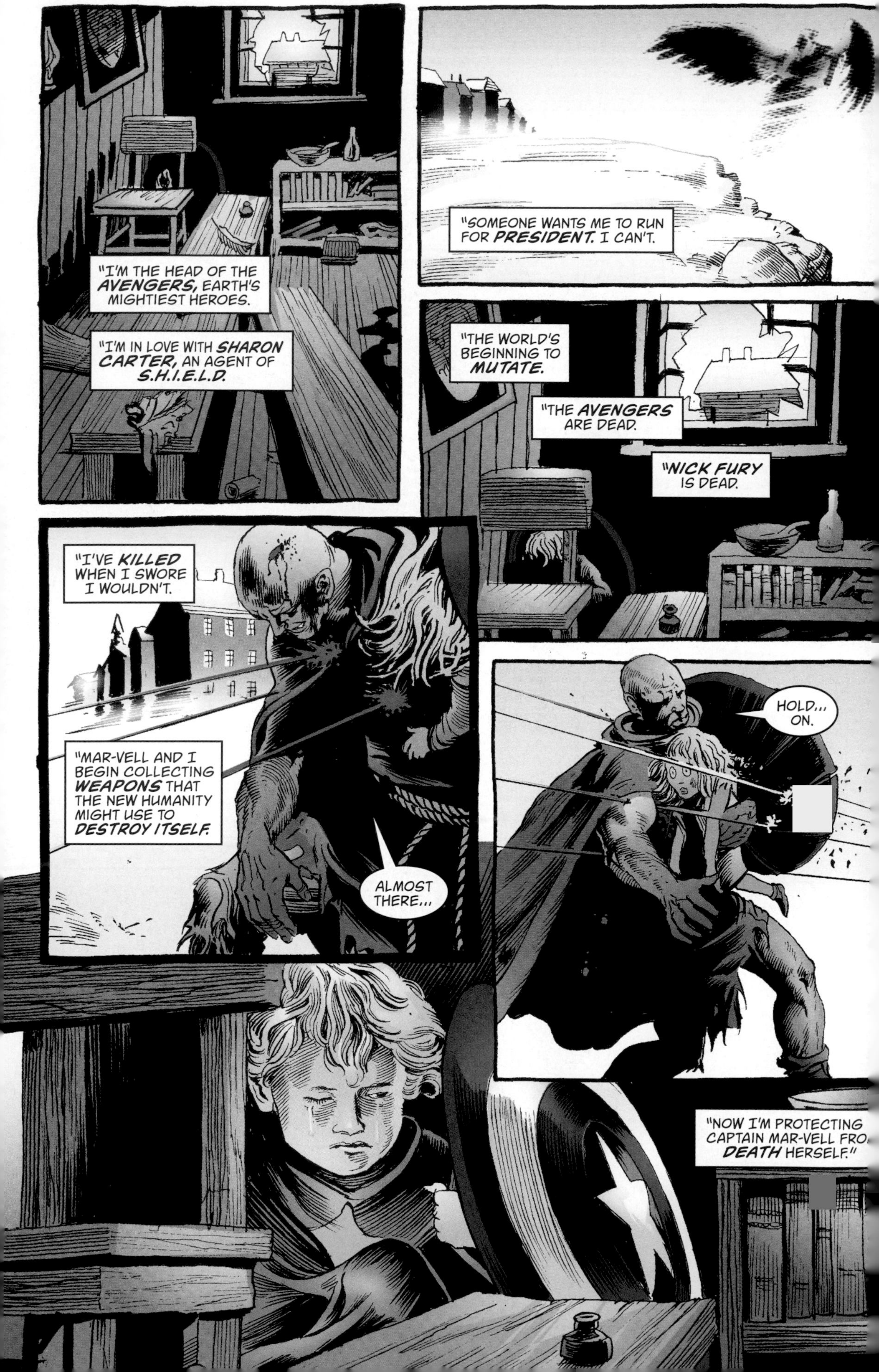

"I'M THE HEAD OF THE AVENGERS, EARTH'S MIGHTIEST HEROES.
"I'M IN LOVE WITH SHARON CARTER, AN AGENT OF S.H.I.E.L.D.
"SOMEONE WANTS ME TO RUN FOR PRESIDENT. I CAN'T.
"THE WORLD'S BEGINNING TO MUTATE.
"THE AVENGERS ARE DEAD.
"NICK FURY IS DEAD.
"I'VE KILLED WHEN I SWORE I WOULDN'T.
"MAR-VELL AND I BEGIN COLLECTING WEAPONS THAT THE NEW HUMANITY MIGHT USE TO DESTROY ITSELF.
ALMOST THERE...
HOLD... ON.
"NOW I'M PROTECTING CAPTAIN MAR-VELL FRO DEATH HERSELF."

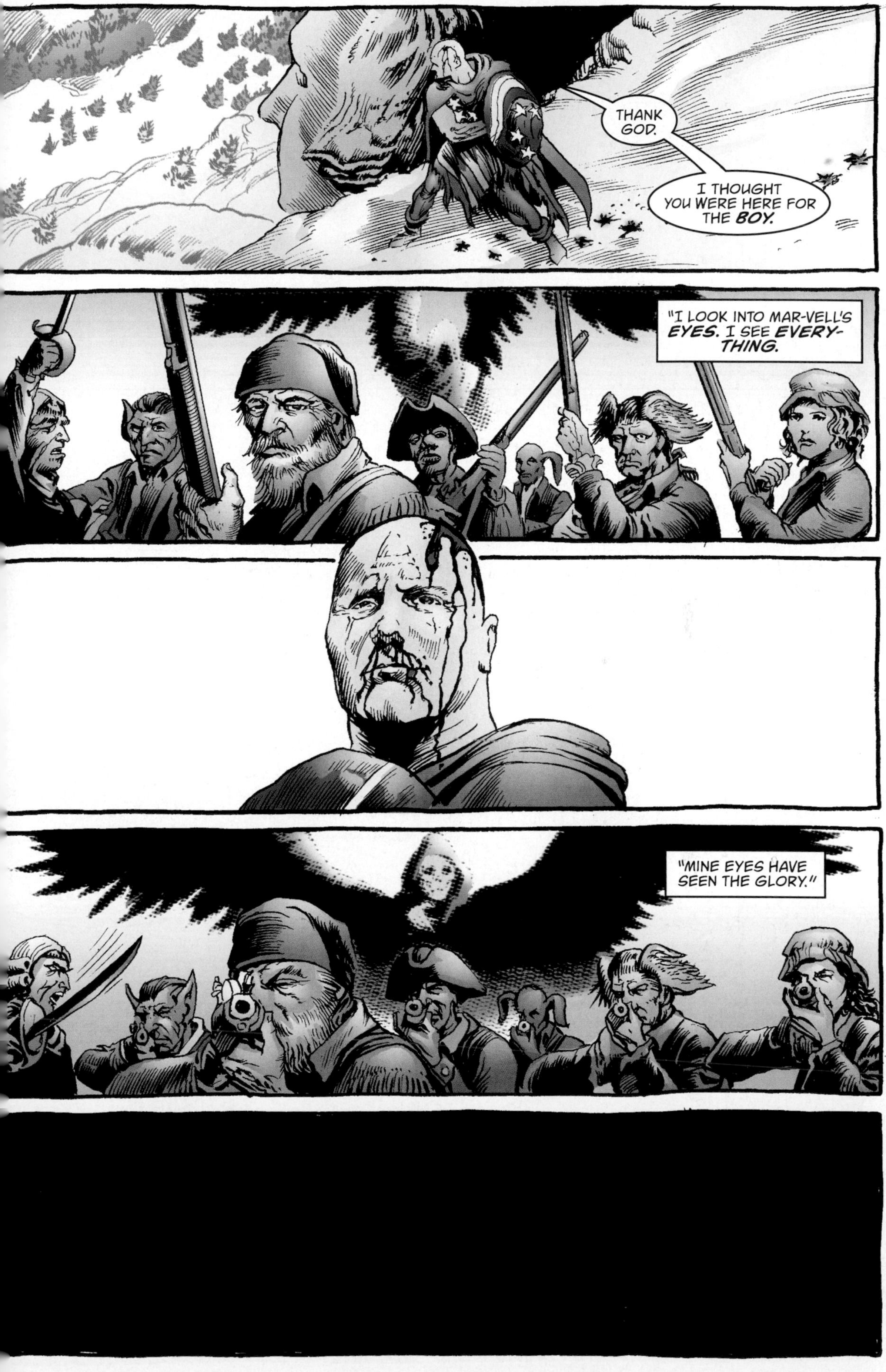
THANK GOD.
I THOUGHT YOU WERE HERE FOR THE BOY.
"I LOOK INTO MAR-VELL'S EYES. I SEE EVERY-THING.
"MINE EYES HAVE SEEN THE GLORY."

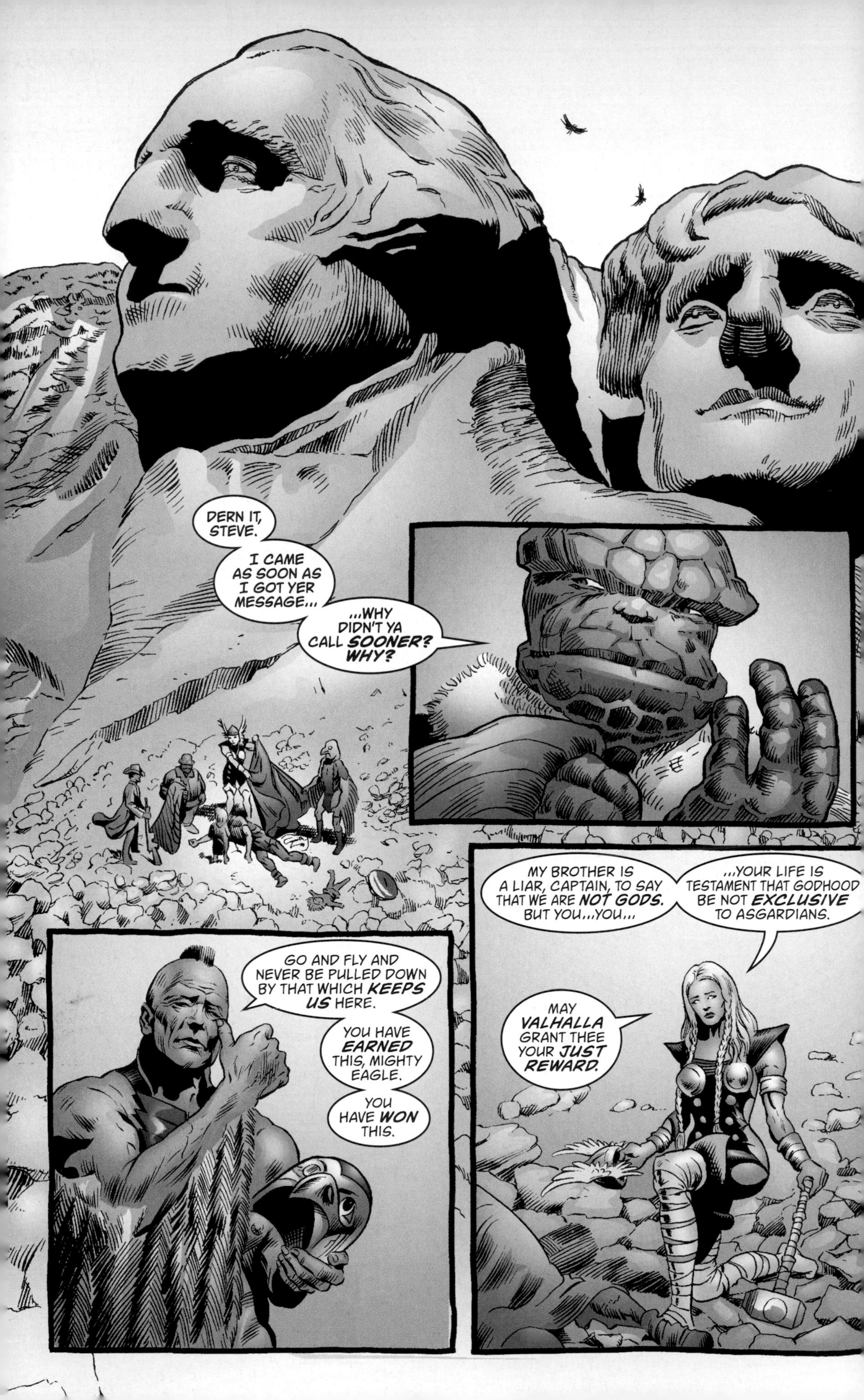
DERN IT, STEVE.
I CAME AS SOON AS I GOT YER MESSAGE...
...WHY DIDN'T YA CALL SOONER? WHY?
MY BROTHER IS A LIAR, CAPTAIN, TO SAY THAT WE ARE NOT GODS. BUT YOU...YOU...
...YOUR LIFE IS TESTAMENT THAT GODHOOD BE NOT EXCLUSIVE TO ASGARDIANS.
GO AND FLY AND NEVER BE PULLED DOWN BY THAT WHICH KEEPS US HERE.
YOU HAVE EARNED THIS, MIGHTY EAGLE.
YOU HAVE WON THIS.
MAY VALHALLA GRANT THEE YOUR JUST REWARD.

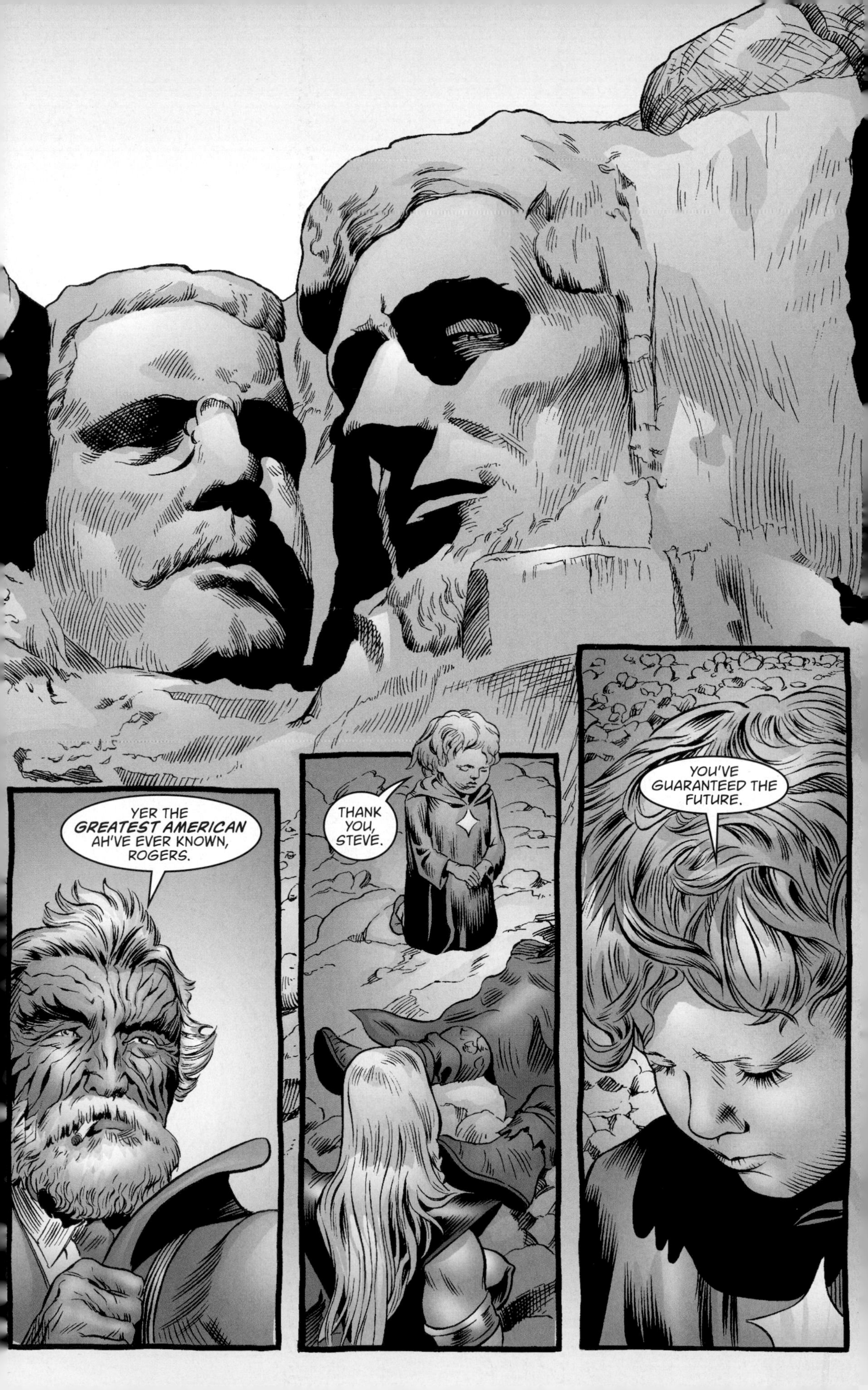
YER THE **GREATEST AMERICAN** AH'VE EVER KNOWN, ROGERS.
THANK YOU, STEVE.
YOU'VE GUARANTEED THE FUTURE.

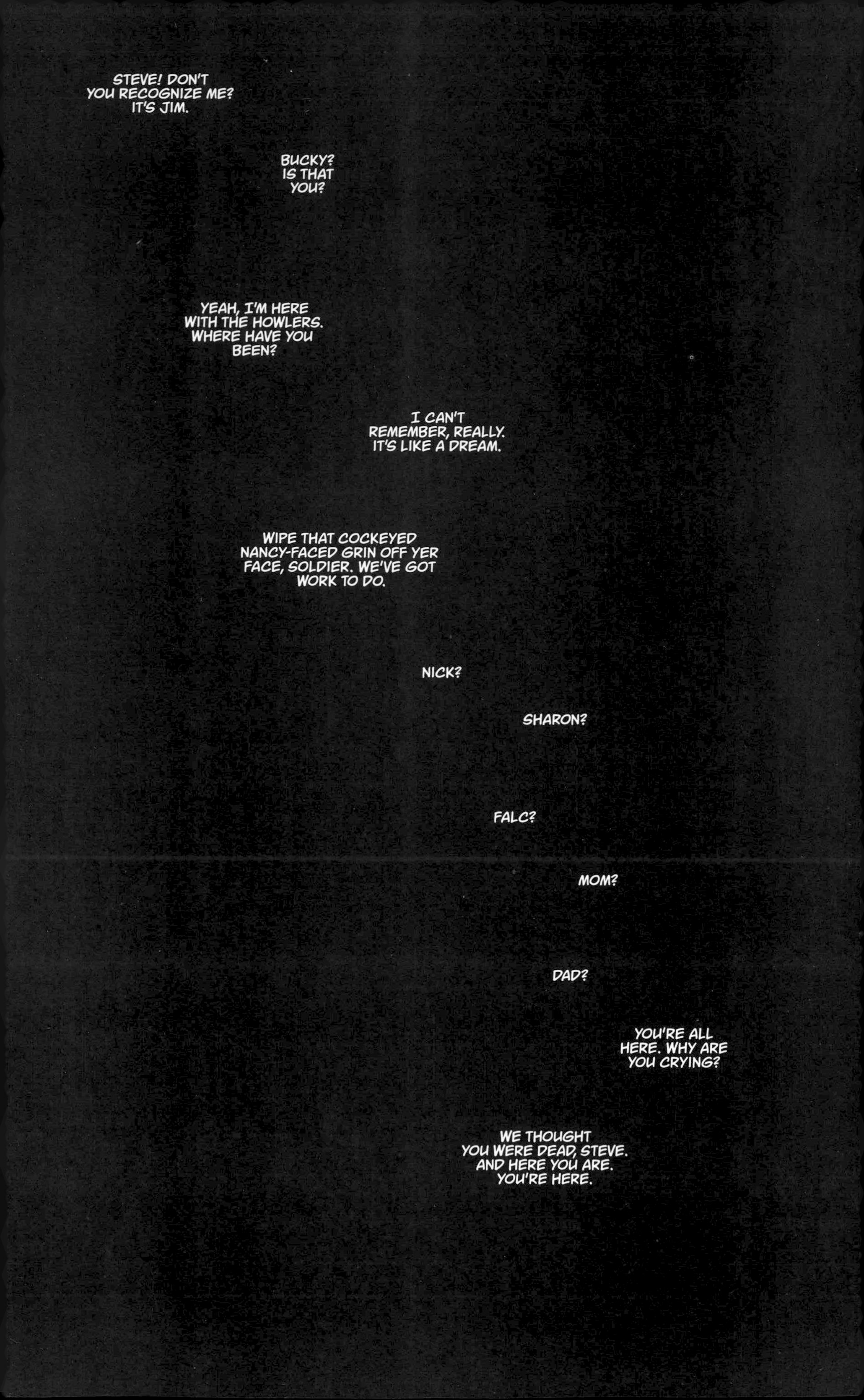
STEVE! DON'T YOU RECOGNIZE ME? IT'S JIM.
BUCKY? IS THAT YOU?
YEAH, I'M HERE WITH THE HOWLERS. WHERE HAVE YOU BEEN?
I CAN'T REMEMBER, REALLY. IT'S LIKE A DREAM.
WIPE THAT COCKEYED NANCY-FACED GRIN OFF YER FACE, SOLDIER. WE'VE GOT WORK TO DO.
NICK?
SHARON?
FALC?
MOM?
DAD?
YOU'RE ALL HERE. WHY ARE YOU CRYING?
WE THOUGHT YOU WERE DEAD, STEVE. AND HERE YOU ARE. YOU'RE HERE.

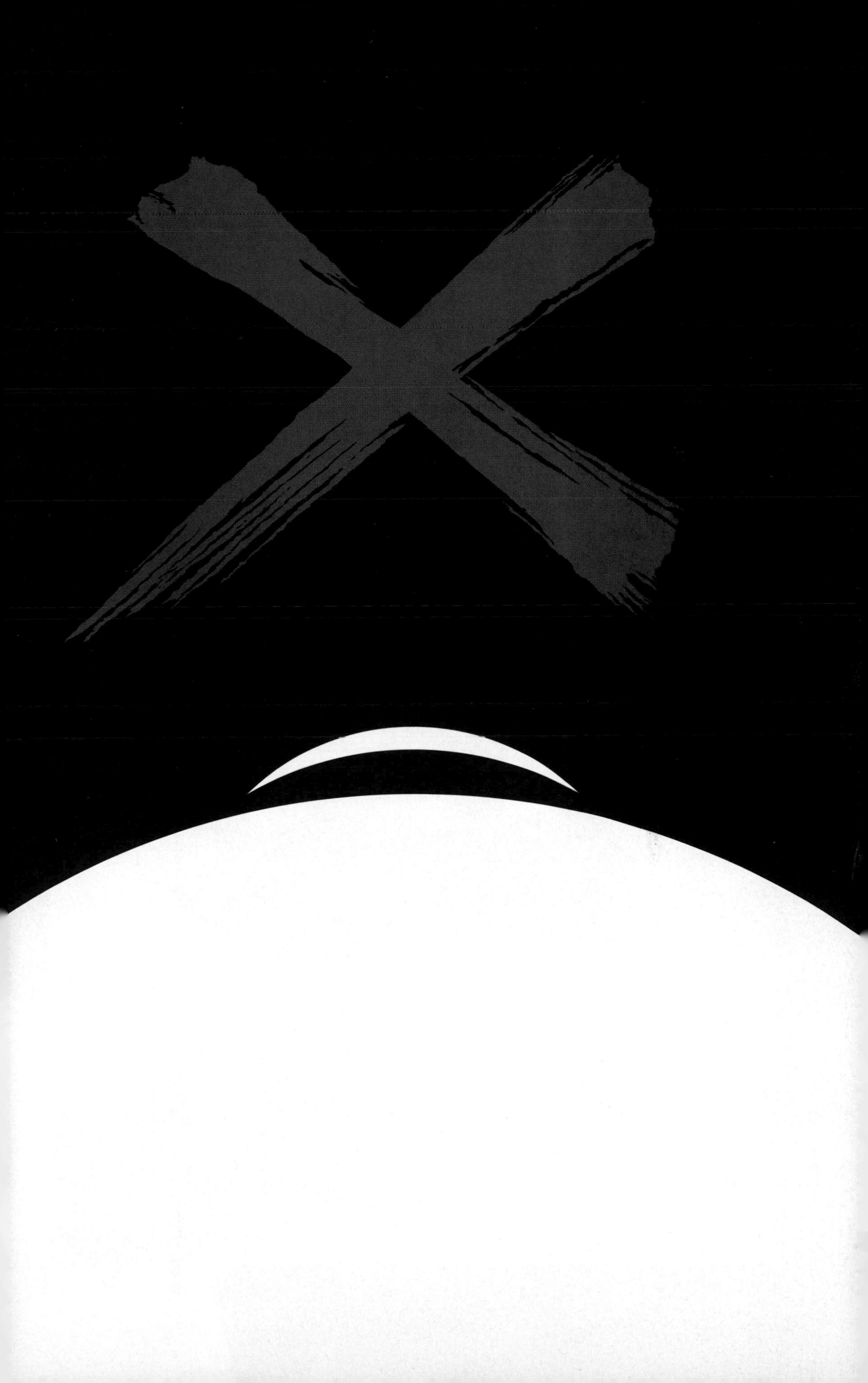

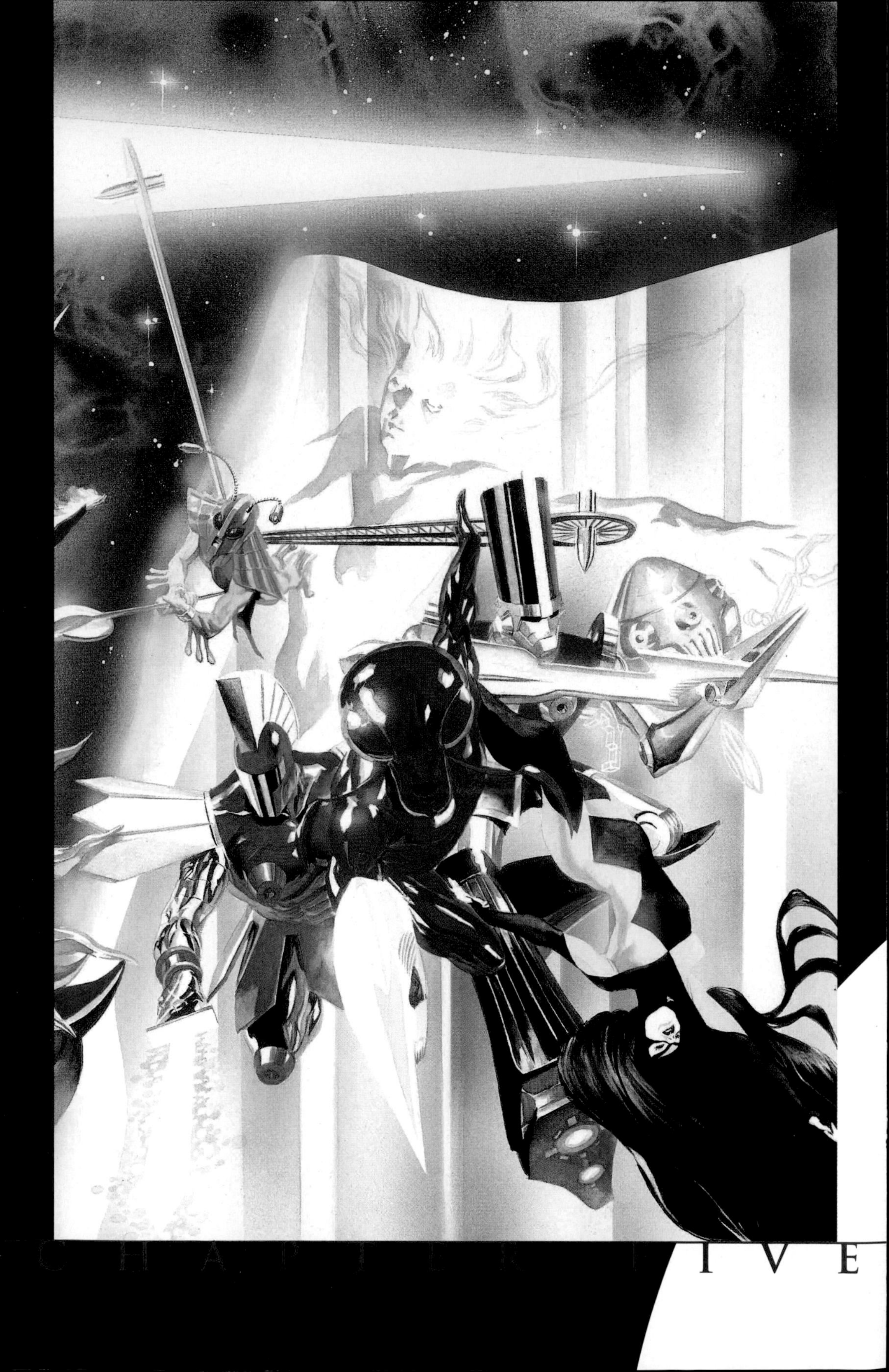

CHAPTER FIVE

"I am seeing the future, Isaac."

"Yes. Of course you are. And I write it down."

"You don't understand. This may explain why I am able to
see so much of what happened on other worlds."

"You are correct, Kyle. I don't understand."

"Okay. I am seeing the future Immortus promises the followers of his church."

"The destiny whereby mankind leaves Earth and migrates throughout the stars?"

"Exactly. But this colonization leads to disunity amongst mankind. Each colony begins to war
against the others. It's not a step forward. It's a step into hostility and barbarism — exactly as
Reed Richards now warns Immortus. Don't you see? Both men's notions about the future
become fact."

"Excuse me, Kyle, but how does this explain your
ability to see the past? Or other worlds?"

"Because mankind will someday return to Earth, Isaac."

"I was under the impression that Earth's destruction was imminent?"

"When mankind comes home to Earth — it's not the Earth of the future — but a time before
the Celestials even set foot on our world. I can see the past because it's the future. We live
our lives over and over again, Isaac. What's happening now has all
happened before."

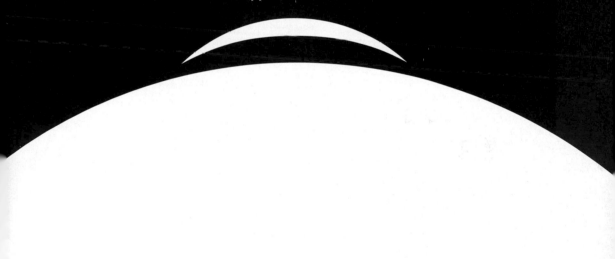

"SOMEHOW, THE POWER MAR-VELL RECEIVED TO ESCAPE THE REALM OF DEATH AND BE REBORN AMONGST THE LIVING IS *RELATED* TO HUMANITY'S *DISTANT FUTURE.*

"I SEE A *PRINCE* BEING TOLD BY HIS DYING FATHER THAT HE WILL *NEVER* BE A KING.

"WHAT IS THE *NAME* OF THIS PRINCE?"

"*WAYFINDER.*"

"DOES HE *FIND* THIS SWORD?"

"YES. BUT THE DISCOVERY *BLINDS* HIM. THE SWORD IS *IMBEDDED* IN A STAR.

"IT...GUIDES PRINCE WAYFINDER BACK TO *EARTH*, ALONG WITH THOUSANDS OF OTHERS FROM ALL THE PLANETS HIS QUEST TOOK HIM ON.

"BUT IT'S THE EARTH (THE *FAR PAST.* AN EARTH OF DINOSAURS AND *DEMONS.*"

"*DEMONS,* KYLE?"

"WAYFINDER AND HIS FOLLOWERS CAN'T DEFEAT THE DEMONS AND SO THE STAR, SKEWERED AS IT WAS CREATES A WORLD *WITHIN* OUR WORLD LIVE UPON. A WHOLE *UNIVERSE* OF WORLD THE *SUBATOMICA.*

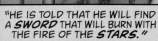

"BUT INSTEAD, WOULD ONE DAY SEE WITH *MORE* THAN HIS *EYES.*

"HE IS TOLD THAT HE WILL FIND A *SWORD* THAT WILL BURN WITH THE FIRE OF THE *STARS.*"

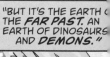

"A *SWORD* DID THA

"...YES.

"IT ALSO *TRANS-FORMED* WAYFINDE INTO THE FIRST BEIN TO EVER WIELD THE *ENIGMA FORCE.*

"BUT WHEN WAYFINDE AND THOSE CLOSES TO HIM DIED, THE SWO WAS *HIDDEN*...AND T ENIGMA FORCE SEARCH FOR *ANOTHER BEIN* TO REST UPON.

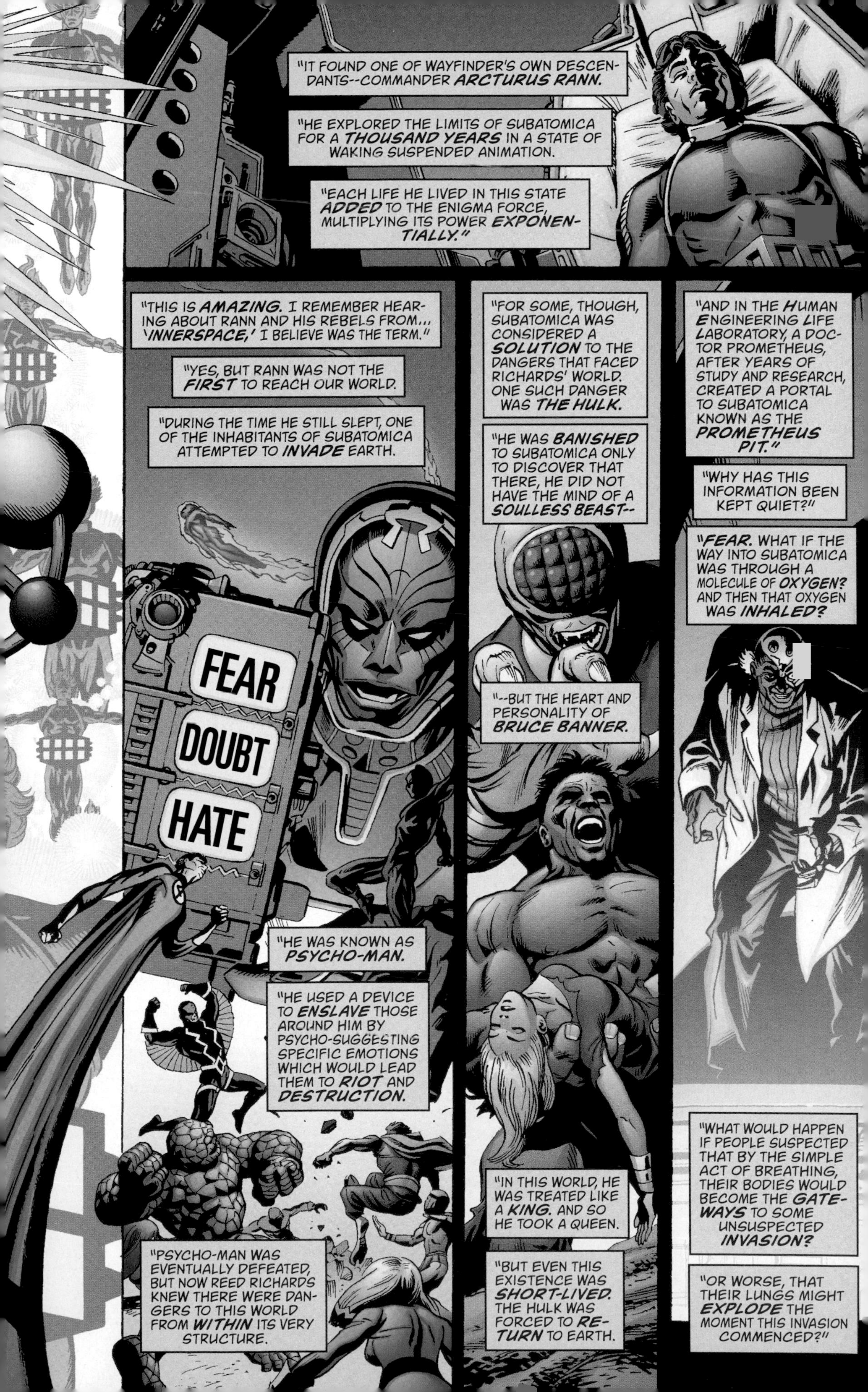
"IT FOUND ONE OF WAYFINDER'S OWN DESCENDANTS--COMMANDER ARCTURUS RANN.
"HE EXPLORED THE LIMITS OF SUBATOMICA FOR A THOUSAND YEARS IN A STATE OF WAKING SUSPENDED ANIMATION.
"EACH LIFE HE LIVED IN THIS STATE ADDED TO THE ENIGMA FORCE, MULTIPLYING ITS POWER EXPONENTIALLY."
"THIS IS AMAZING. I REMEMBER HEARING ABOUT RANN AND HIS REBELS FROM... 'INNERSPACE,' I BELIEVE WAS THE TERM."
"YES, BUT RANN WAS NOT THE FIRST TO REACH OUR WORLD.
"DURING THE TIME HE STILL SLEPT, ONE OF THE INHABITANTS OF SUBATOMICA ATTEMPTED TO INVADE EARTH.
FEAR
DOUBT
HATE
"HE WAS KNOWN AS PSYCHO-MAN.
"HE USED A DEVICE TO ENSLAVE THOSE AROUND HIM BY PSYCHO-SUGGESTING SPECIFIC EMOTIONS WHICH WOULD LEAD THEM TO RIOT AND DESTRUCTION.
"PSYCHO-MAN WAS EVENTUALLY DEFEATED, BUT NOW REED RICHARDS KNEW THERE WERE DANGERS TO THIS WORLD FROM WITHIN ITS VERY STRUCTURE.
"FOR SOME, THOUGH, SUBATOMICA WAS CONSIDERED A SOLUTION TO THE DANGERS THAT FACED RICHARDS' WORLD. ONE SUCH DANGER WAS THE HULK.
"HE WAS BANISHED TO SUBATOMICA ONLY TO DISCOVER THAT THERE, HE DID NOT HAVE THE MIND OF A SOULLESS BEAST--
"--BUT THE HEART AND PERSONALITY OF BRUCE BANNER.
"IN THIS WORLD, HE WAS TREATED LIKE A KING. AND SO HE TOOK A QUEEN.
"BUT EVEN THIS EXISTENCE WAS SHORT-LIVED. THE HULK WAS FORCED TO RETURN TO EARTH.
"AND IN THE HUMAN ENGINEERING LIFE LABORATORY, A DOCTOR PROMETHEUS, AFTER YEARS OF STUDY AND RESEARCH, CREATED A PORTAL TO SUBATOMICA KNOWN AS THE PROMETHEUS PIT."
"WHY HAS THIS INFORMATION BEEN KEPT QUIET?"
"FEAR. WHAT IF THE WAY INTO SUBATOMICA WAS THROUGH A MOLECULE OF OXYGEN? AND THEN THAT OXYGEN WAS INHALED?
"WHAT WOULD HAPPEN IF PEOPLE SUSPECTED THAT BY THE SIMPLE ACT OF BREATHING, THEIR BODIES WOULD BECOME THE GATEWAYS TO SOME UNSUSPECTED INVASION?
"OR WORSE, THAT THEIR LUNGS MIGHT EXPLODE THE MOMENT THIS INVASION COMMENCED?"

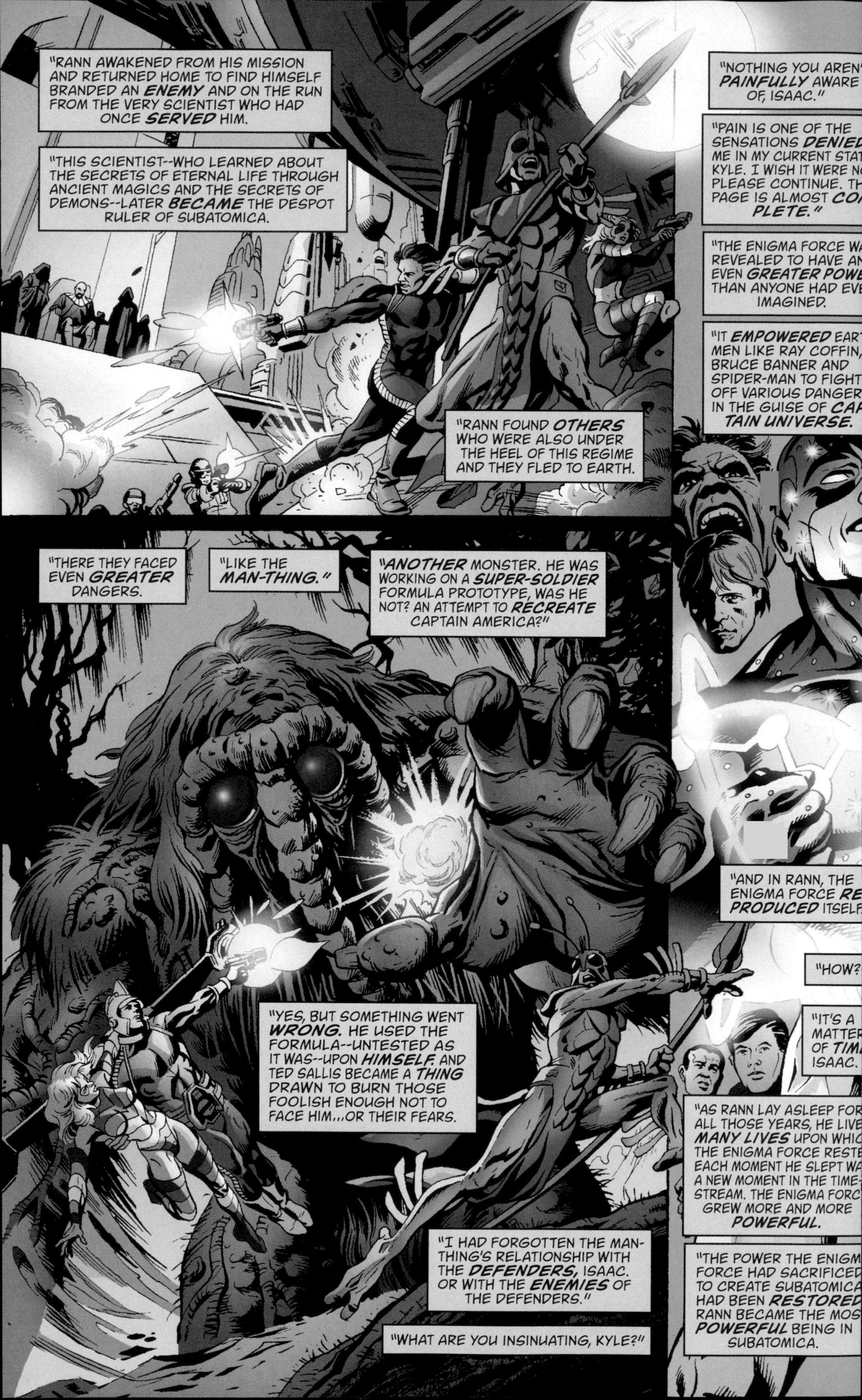
"RANN AWAKENED FROM HIS MISSION AND RETURNED HOME TO FIND HIMSELF BRANDED AN ENEMY AND ON THE RUN FROM THE VERY SCIENTIST WHO HAD ONCE SERVED HIM.
"THIS SCIENTIST--WHO LEARNED ABOUT THE SECRETS OF ETERNAL LIFE THROUGH ANCIENT MAGICS AND THE SECRETS OF DEMONS--LATER BECAME THE DESPOT RULER OF SUBATOMICA.
"RANN FOUND OTHERS WHO WERE ALSO UNDER THE HEEL OF THIS REGIME AND THEY FLED TO EARTH.
"THERE THEY FACED EVEN GREATER DANGERS.
"LIKE THE MAN-THING."
"ANOTHER MONSTER. HE WAS WORKING ON A SUPER-SOLDIER FORMULA PROTOTYPE, WAS HE NOT? AN ATTEMPT TO RECREATE CAPTAIN AMERICA?"
"YES, BUT SOMETHING WENT WRONG. HE USED THE FORMULA--UNTESTED AS IT WAS--UPON HIMSELF. AND TED SALLIS BECAME A THING DRAWN TO BURN THOSE FOOLISH ENOUGH NOT TO FACE HIM...OR THEIR FEARS.
"I HAD FORGOTTEN THE MAN-THING'S RELATIONSHIP WITH THE DEFENDERS, ISAAC. OR WITH THE ENEMIES OF THE DEFENDERS."
"WHAT ARE YOU INSINUATING, KYLE?"
"PAIN IS ONE OF THE SENSATIONS DENIED ME IN MY CURRENT STAT KYLE. I WISH IT WERE NO PLEASE CONTINUE. TH PAGE IS ALMOST COM PLETE."
"THE ENIGMA FORCE WA REVEALED TO HAVE AN EVEN GREATER POWE THAN ANYONE HAD EVE IMAGINED.
"IT EMPOWERED EART MEN LIKE RAY COFFIN, BRUCE BANNER AND SPIDER-MAN TO FIGHT OFF VARIOUS DANGER IN THE GUISE OF CAP TAIN UNIVERSE.
"AND IN RANN, THE ENIGMA FORCE RE PRODUCED ITSELF.
"HOW?
"IT'S A MATTER OF TIM ISAAC.
"AS RANN LAY ASLEEP FOR ALL THOSE YEARS, HE LIVE MANY LIVES UPON WHIC THE ENIGMA FORCE RESTE EACH MOMENT HE SLEPT WA A NEW MOMENT IN THE TIME-STREAM. THE ENIGMA FORC GREW MORE AND MORE POWERFUL.
"THE POWER THE ENIGM FORCE HAD SACRIFICED TO CREATE SUBATOMICA HAD BEEN RESTORED RANN BECAME THE MOS POWERFUL BEING IN SUBATOMICA.

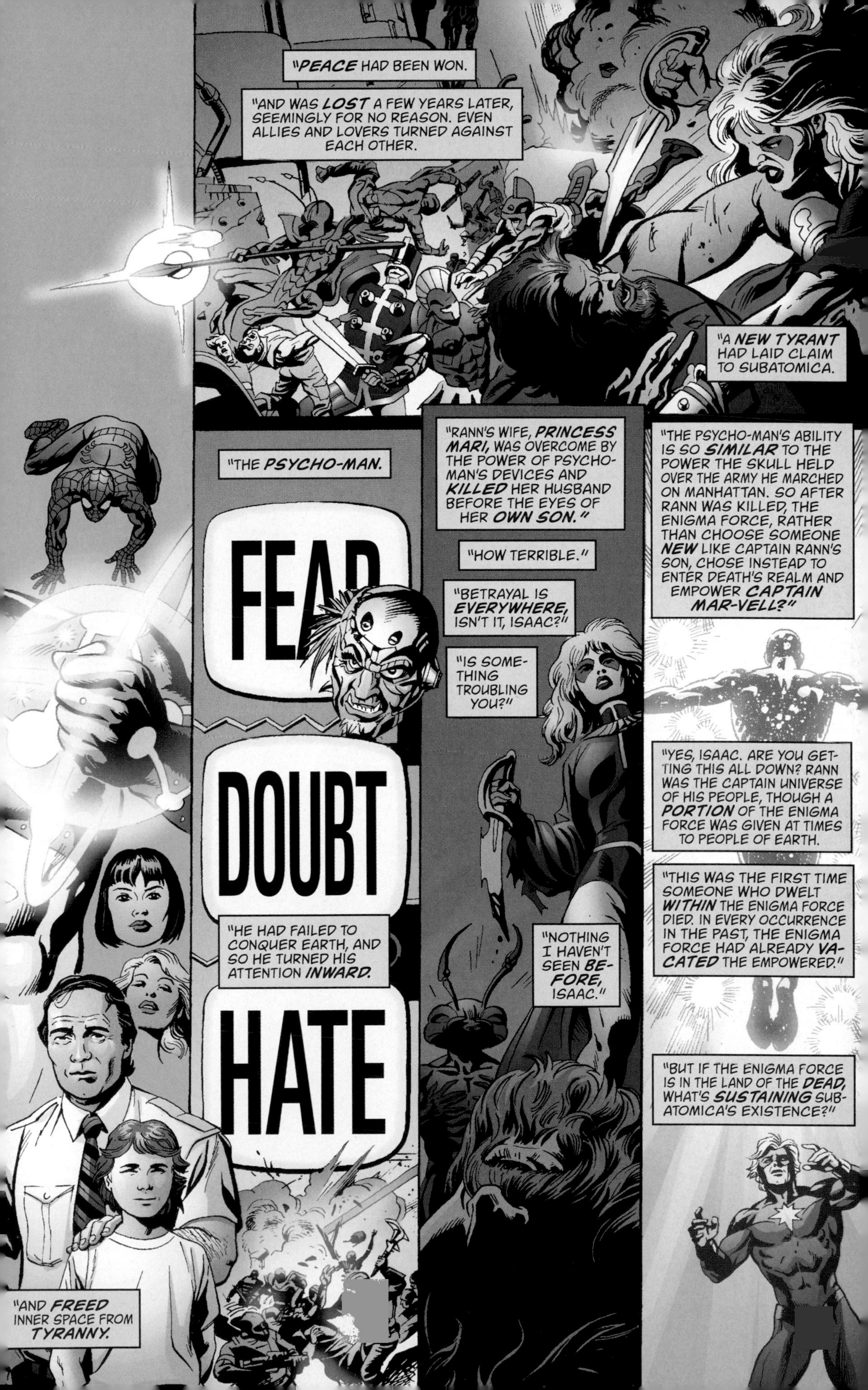

"AND FREED INNER SPACE FROM TYRANNY.
"PEACE HAD BEEN WON.
"AND WAS LOST A FEW YEARS LATER, SEEMINGLY FOR NO REASON. EVEN ALLIES AND LOVERS TURNED AGAINST EACH OTHER.
"A NEW TYRANT HAD LAID CLAIM TO SUBATOMICA.
"THE PSYCHO-MAN.
FEAR
DOUBT
HATE
"HE HAD FAILED TO CONQUER EARTH, AND SO HE TURNED HIS ATTENTION INWARD.
"RANN'S WIFE, PRINCESS MARI, WAS OVERCOME BY THE POWER OF PSYCHO-MAN'S DEVICES AND KILLED HER HUSBAND BEFORE THE EYES OF HER OWN SON."
"HOW TERRIBLE."
"BETRAYAL IS EVERYWHERE, ISN'T IT, ISAAC?"
"IS SOMETHING TROUBLING YOU?"
"NOTHING I HAVEN'T SEEN BEFORE, ISAAC."
"THE PSYCHO-MAN'S ABILITY IS SO SIMILAR TO THE POWER THE SKULL HELD OVER THE ARMY HE MARCHED ON MANHATTAN. SO AFTER RANN WAS KILLED, THE ENIGMA FORCE, RATHER THAN CHOOSE SOMEONE NEW LIKE CAPTAIN RANN'S SON, CHOSE INSTEAD TO ENTER DEATH'S REALM AND EMPOWER CAPTAIN MAR-VELL?"
"YES, ISAAC. ARE YOU GETTING THIS ALL DOWN? RANN WAS THE CAPTAIN UNIVERSE OF HIS PEOPLE, THOUGH A PORTION OF THE ENIGMA FORCE WAS GIVEN AT TIMES TO PEOPLE OF EARTH.
"THIS WAS THE FIRST TIME SOMEONE WHO DWELT WITHIN THE ENIGMA FORCE DIED. IN EVERY OCCURRENCE IN THE PAST, THE ENIGMA FORCE HAD ALREADY VACATED THE EMPOWERED."
"BUT IF THE ENIGMA FORCE IS IN THE LAND OF THE DEAD, WHAT'S SUSTAINING SUBATOMICA'S EXISTENCE?"

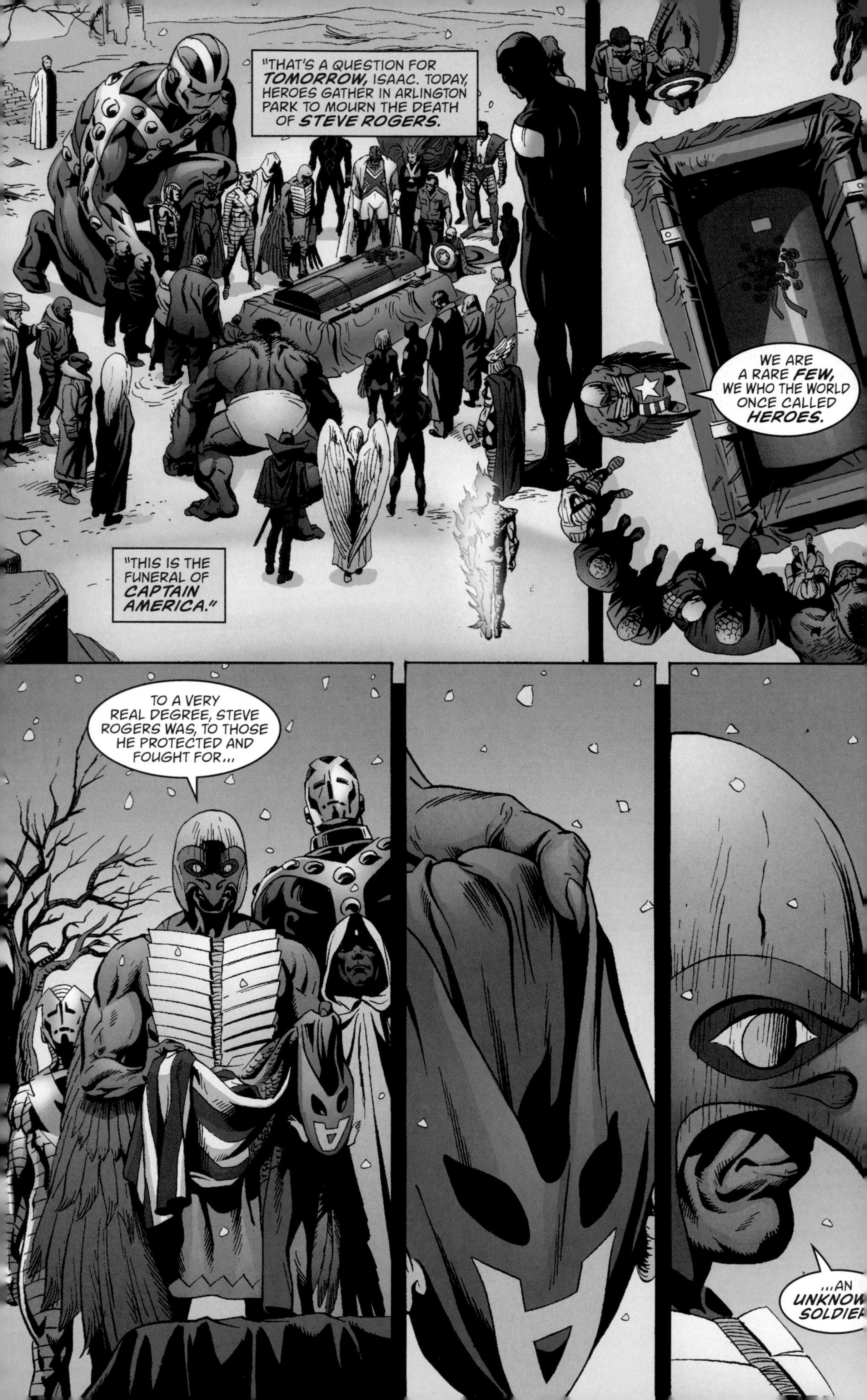
"THAT'S A QUESTION FOR TOMORROW, ISAAC. TODAY, HEROES GATHER IN ARLINGTON PARK TO MOURN THE DEATH OF STEVE ROGERS.
"THIS IS THE FUNERAL OF CAPTAIN AMERICA."
WE ARE A RARE FEW, WE WHO THE WORLD ONCE CALLED HEROES.
TO A VERY REAL DEGREE, STEVE ROGERS WAS, TO THOSE HE PROTECTED AND FOUGHT FOR...
...AN UNKNOW SOLDIE

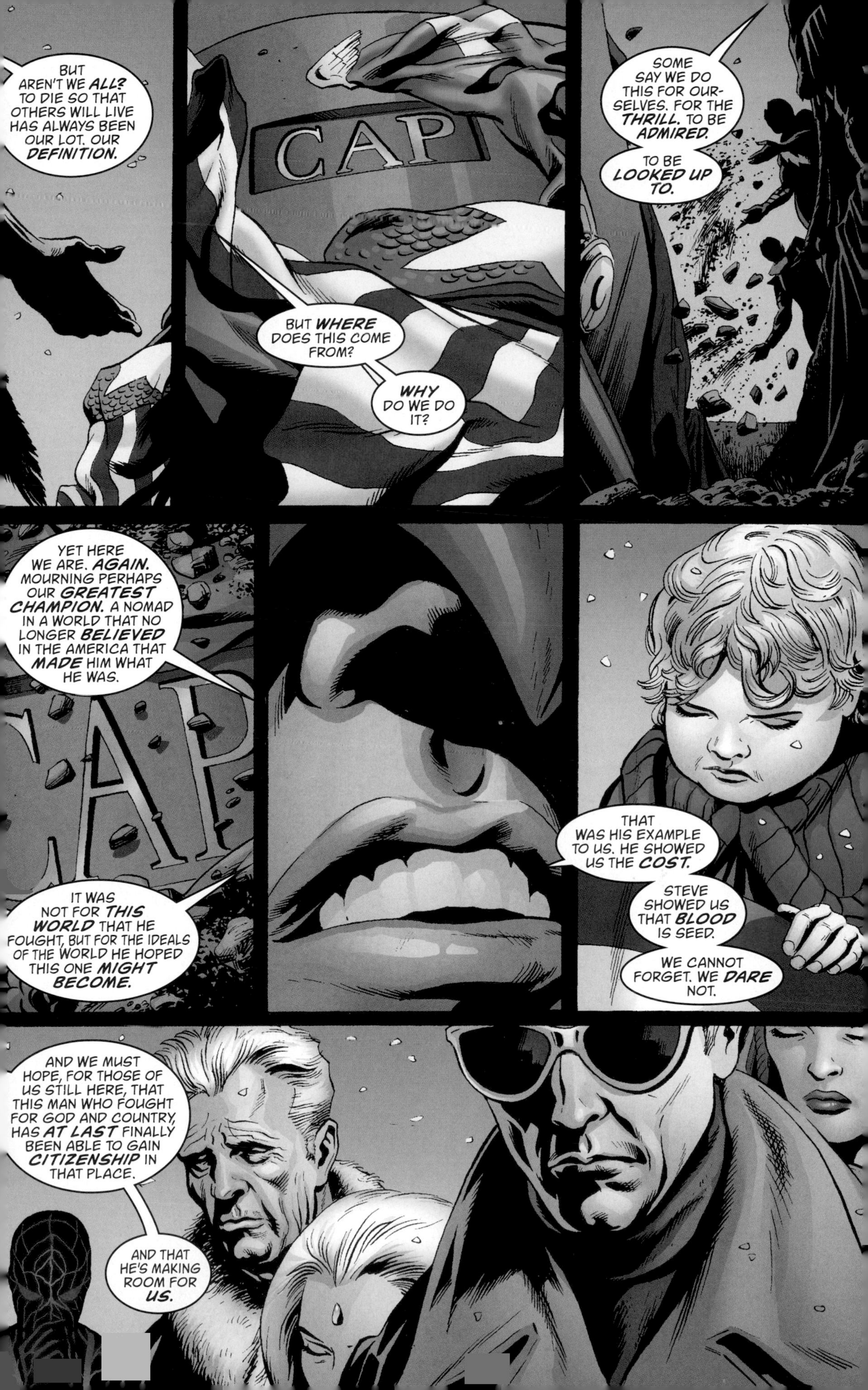
BUT AREN'T WE ALL? TO DIE SO THAT OTHERS WILL LIVE HAS ALWAYS BEEN OUR LOT. OUR DEFINITION.
CAP
BUT WHERE DOES THIS COME FROM?
WHY DO WE DO IT?
SOME SAY WE DO THIS FOR OURSELVES. FOR THE THRILL. TO BE ADMIRED.
TO BE LOOKED UP TO.
YET HERE WE ARE. AGAIN. MOURNING PERHAPS OUR GREATEST CHAMPION. A NOMAD IN A WORLD THAT NO LONGER BELIEVED IN THE AMERICA THAT MADE HIM WHAT HE WAS.
IT WAS NOT FOR THIS WORLD THAT HE FOUGHT, BUT FOR THE IDEALS OF THE WORLD HE HOPED THIS ONE MIGHT BECOME.
THAT WAS HIS EXAMPLE TO US. HE SHOWED US THE COST.
STEVE SHOWED US THAT BLOOD IS SEED.
WE CANNOT FORGET. WE DARE NOT.
AND WE MUST HOPE, FOR THOSE OF US STILL HERE, THAT THIS MAN WHO FOUGHT FOR GOD AND COUNTRY, HAS AT LAST FINALLY BEEN ABLE TO GAIN CITIZENSHIP IN THAT PLACE.
AND THAT HE'S MAKING ROOM FOR US.

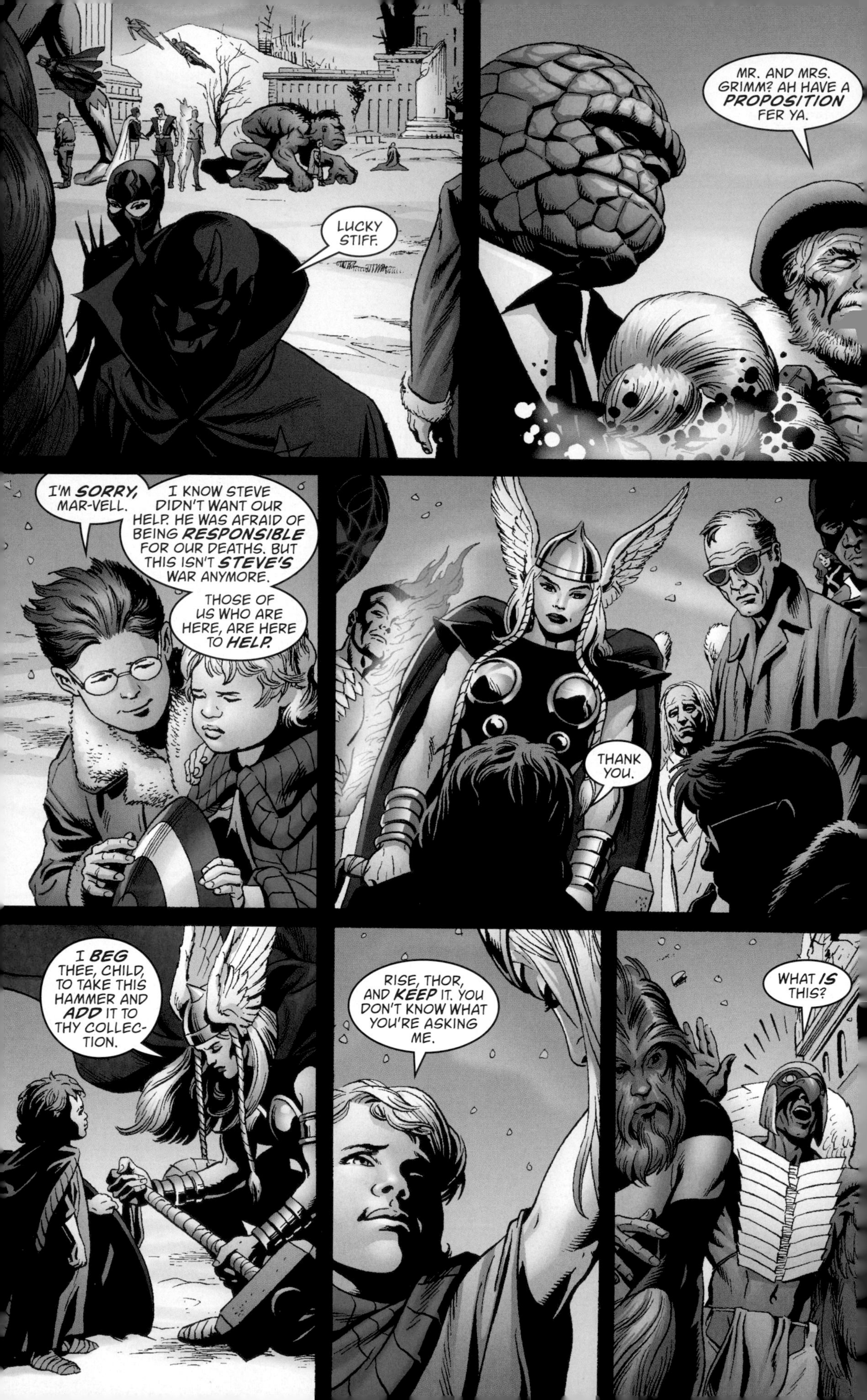
LUCKY STIFF.
MR. AND MRS. GRIMM? AH HAVE A PROPOSITION FER YA.
I'M SORRY, MAR-VELL.
I KNOW STEVE DIDN'T WANT OUR HELP. HE WAS AFRAID OF BEING RESPONSIBLE FOR OUR DEATHS. BUT THIS ISN'T STEVE'S WAR ANYMORE.
THOSE OF US WHO ARE HERE, ARE HERE TO HELP.
THANK YOU.
I BEG THEE, CHILD, TO TAKE THIS HAMMER AND ADD IT TO THY COLLEC-TION.
RISE, THOR, AND KEEP IT. YOU DON'T KNOW WHAT YOU'RE ASKING ME.
WHAT IS THIS?

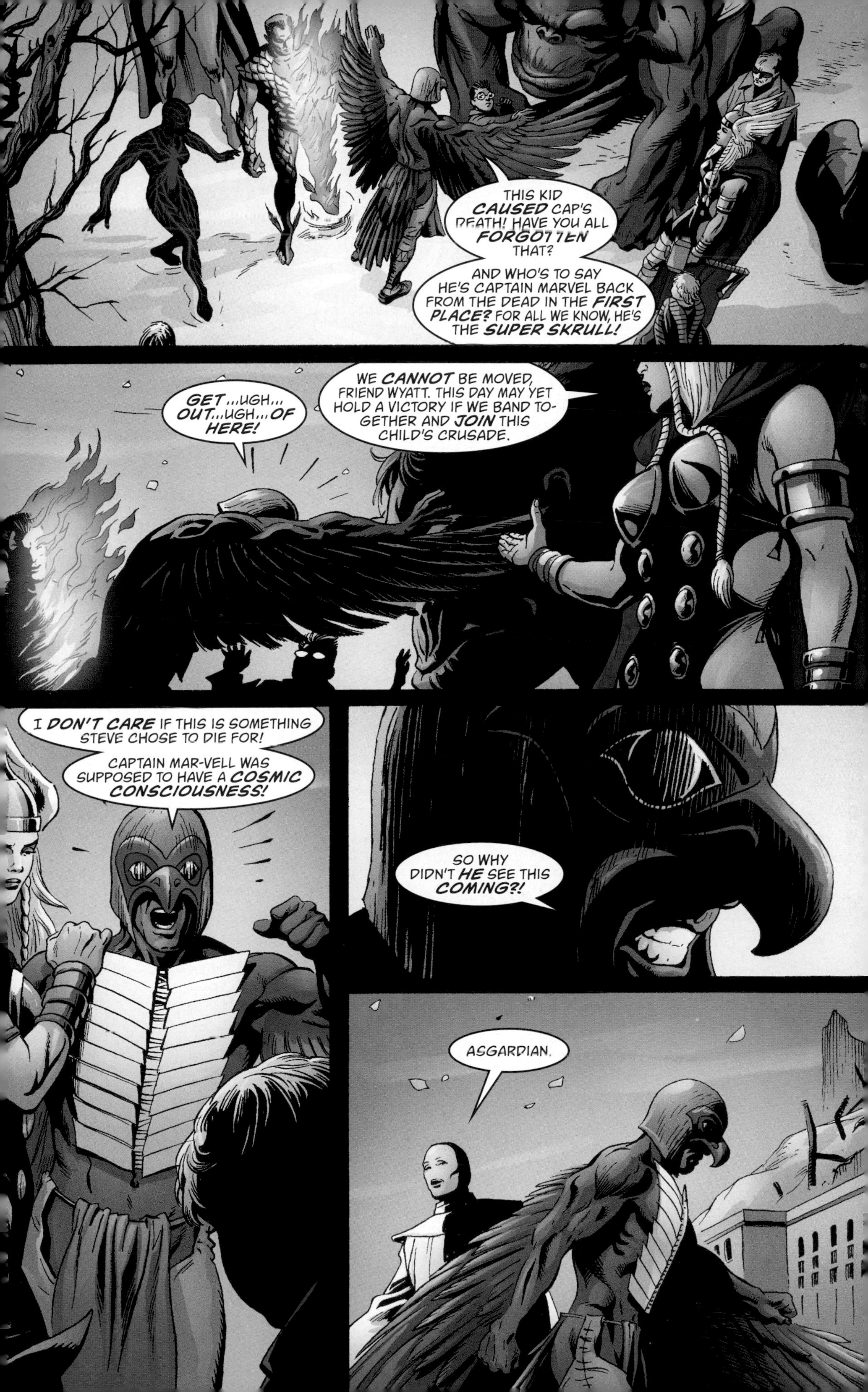
THIS KID CAUSED CAP'S DEATH! HAVE YOU ALL FORGOTTEN THAT?
AND WHO'S TO SAY HE'S CAPTAIN MARVEL BACK FROM THE DEAD IN THE FIRST PLACE? FOR ALL WE KNOW, HE'S THE SUPER SKRULL!
WE CANNOT BE MOVED, FRIEND WYATT. THIS DAY MAY YET HOLD A VICTORY IF WE BAND TO-GETHER AND JOIN THIS CHILD'S CRUSADE.
GET...UGH... OUT...UGH...OF HERE!
I DON'T CARE IF THIS IS SOMETHING STEVE CHOSE TO DIE FOR!
CAPTAIN MAR-VELL WAS SUPPOSED TO HAVE A COSMIC CONSCIOUSNESS!
SO WHY DIDN'T HE SEE THIS COMING?!
ASGARDIAN.

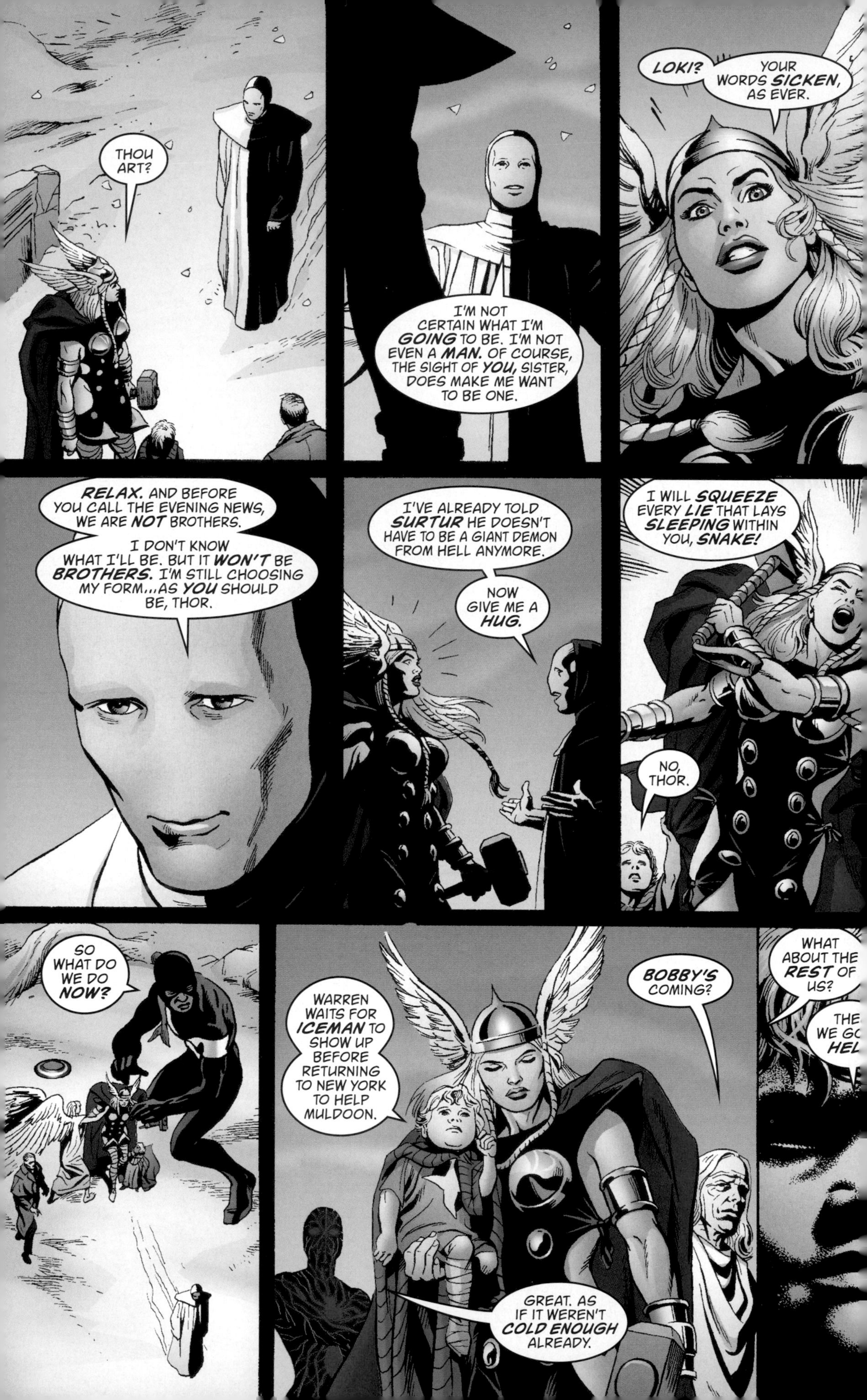
THOU ART?
I'M NOT CERTAIN WHAT I'M GOING TO BE. I'M NOT EVEN A MAN. OF COURSE, THE SIGHT OF YOU, SISTER, DOES MAKE ME WANT TO BE ONE.
LOKI?
YOUR WORDS SICKEN, AS EVER.
RELAX. AND BEFORE YOU CALL THE EVENING NEWS, WE ARE NOT BROTHERS.
I DON'T KNOW WHAT I'LL BE. BUT IT WON'T BE BROTHERS. I'M STILL CHOOSING MY FORM...AS YOU SHOULD BE, THOR.
I'VE ALREADY TOLD SURTUR HE DOESN'T HAVE TO BE A GIANT DEMON FROM HELL ANYMORE.
NOW GIVE ME A HUG.
I WILL SQUEEZE EVERY LIE THAT LAYS SLEEPING WITHIN YOU, SNAKE!
NO, THOR.
SO WHAT DO WE DO NOW?
WARREN WAITS FOR ICEMAN TO SHOW UP BEFORE RETURNING TO NEW YORK TO HELP MULDOON.
BOBBY'S COMING?
GREAT. AS IF IT WEREN'T COLD ENOUGH ALREADY.
WHAT ABOUT THE REST OF US?

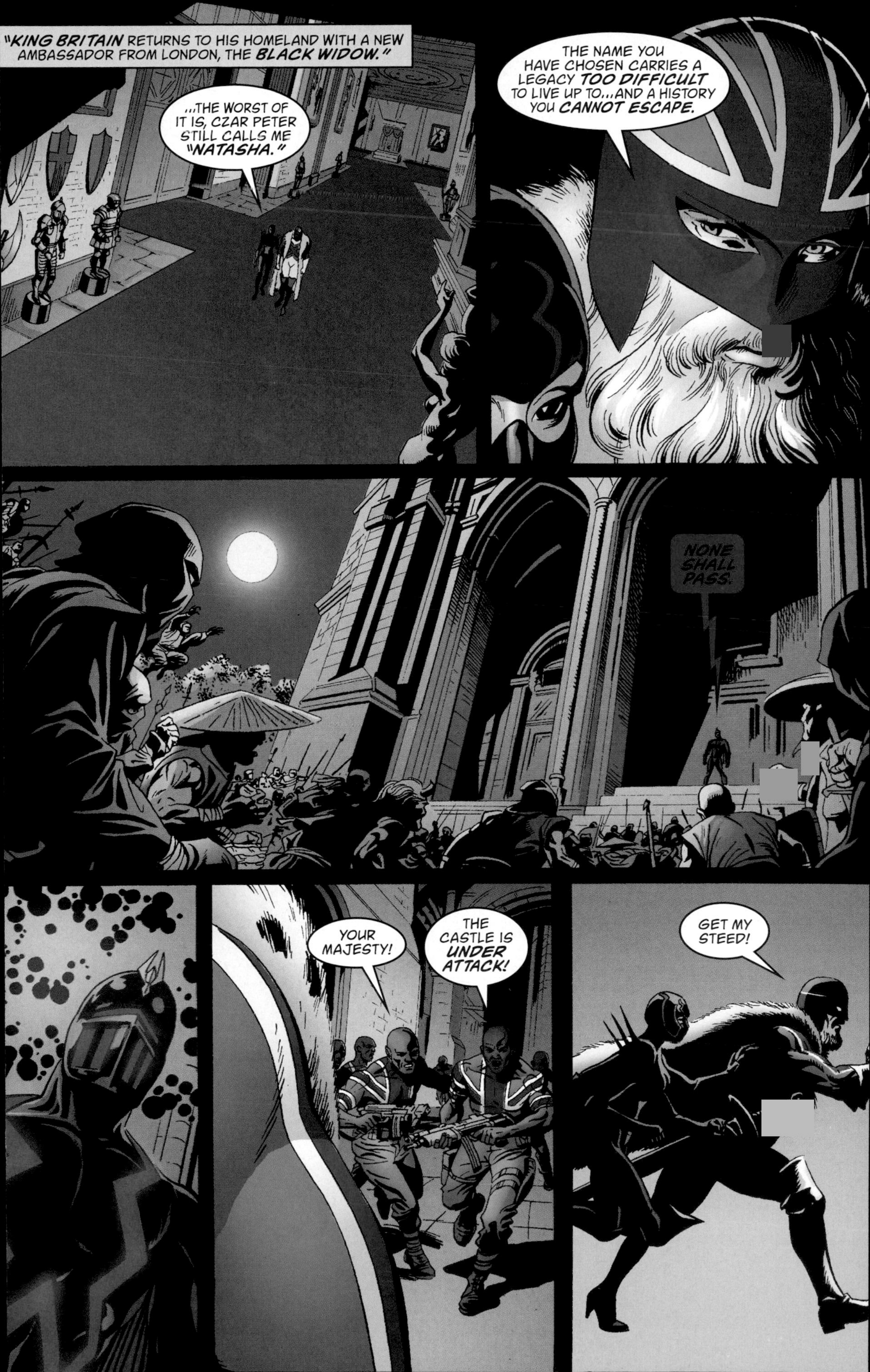
"KING BRITAIN RETURNS TO HIS HOMELAND WITH A NEW AMBASSADOR FROM LONDON, THE BLACK WIDOW."
...THE WORST OF IT IS, CZAR PETER STILL CALLS ME "NATASHA."
THE NAME YOU HAVE CHOSEN CARRIES A LEGACY TOO DIFFICULT TO LIVE UP TO...AND A HISTORY YOU CANNOT ESCAPE.
NONE SHALL PASS.
YOUR MAJESTY!
THE CASTLE IS UNDER ATTACK!
GET MY STEED!

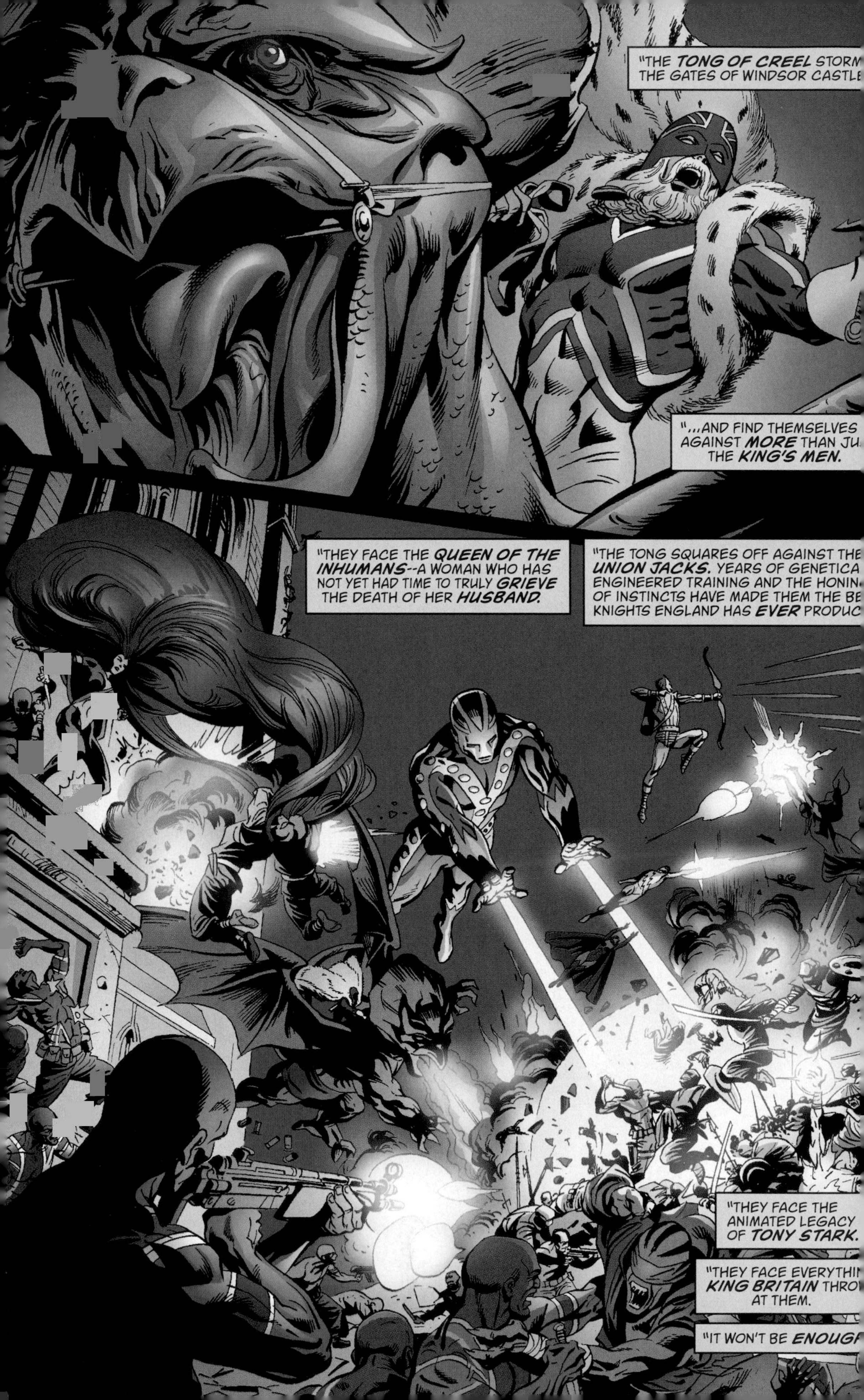
"THE TONG OF CREEL STORM
THE GATES OF WINDSOR CASTLE
"...AND FIND THEMSELVES
AGAINST MORE THAN JU
THE KING'S MEN.
"THEY FACE THE QUEEN OF THE INHUMANS--A WOMAN WHO HAS NOT YET HAD TIME TO TRULY GRIEVE THE DEATH OF HER HUSBAND.
"THE TONG SQUARES OFF AGAINST THE UNION JACKS. YEARS OF GENETICA ENGINEERED TRAINING AND THE HONIN OF INSTINCTS HAVE MADE THEM THE BE KNIGHTS ENGLAND HAS EVER PRODUC
"THEY FACE THE ANIMATED LEGACY OF TONY STARK.
"THEY FACE EVERYTHI KING BRITAIN THRO AT THEM.
"IT WON'T BE ENOUG

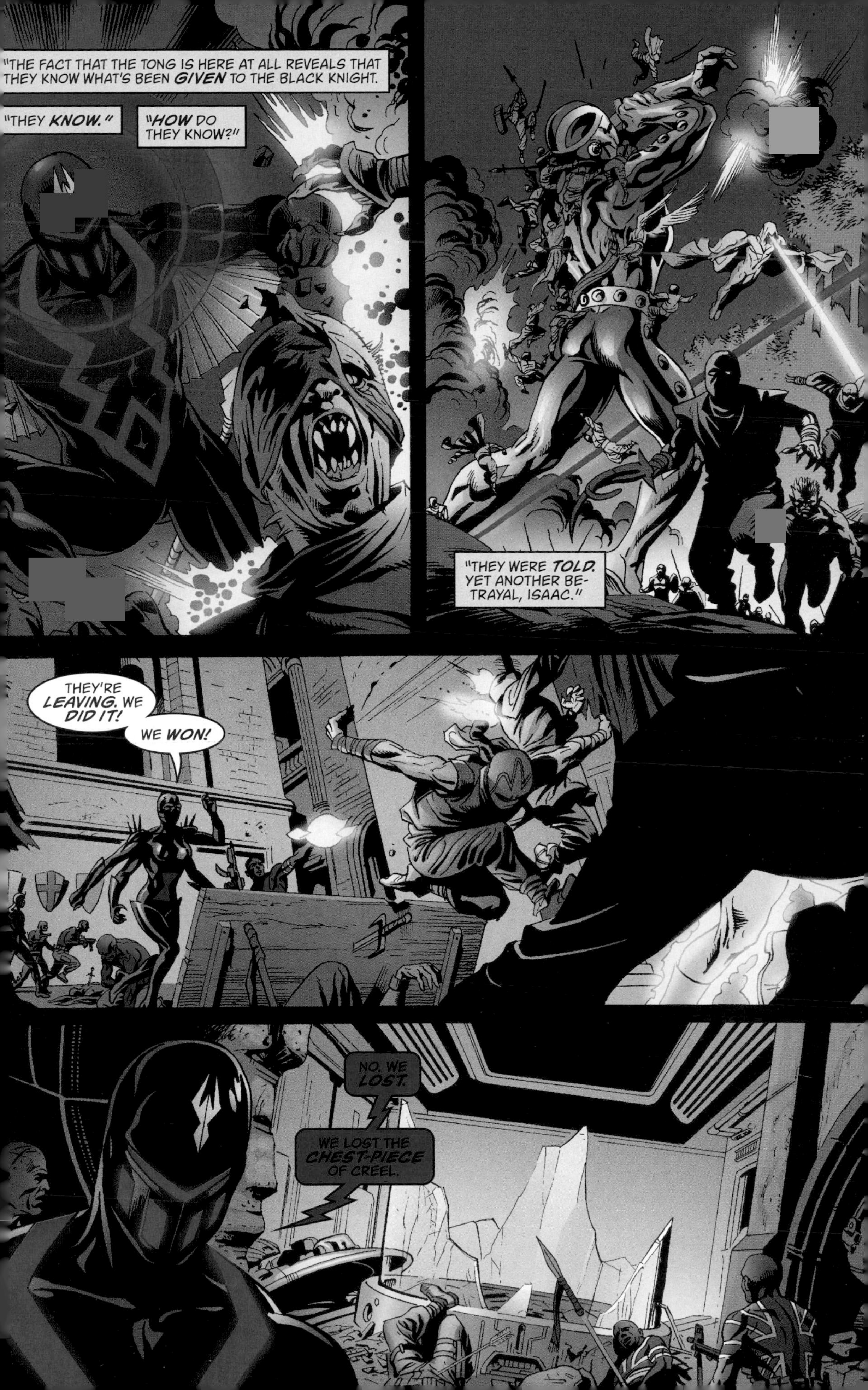
"THE FACT THAT THE TONG IS HERE AT ALL REVEALS THAT THEY KNOW WHAT'S BEEN GIVEN TO THE BLACK KNIGHT.
"THEY KNOW."
"HOW DO THEY KNOW?"
"THEY WERE TOLD. YET ANOTHER BE-TRAYAL, ISAAC."
THEY'RE LEAVING. WE DID IT!
WE WON!
NO, WE LOST.
WE LOST THE CHEST-PIECE OF CREEL.

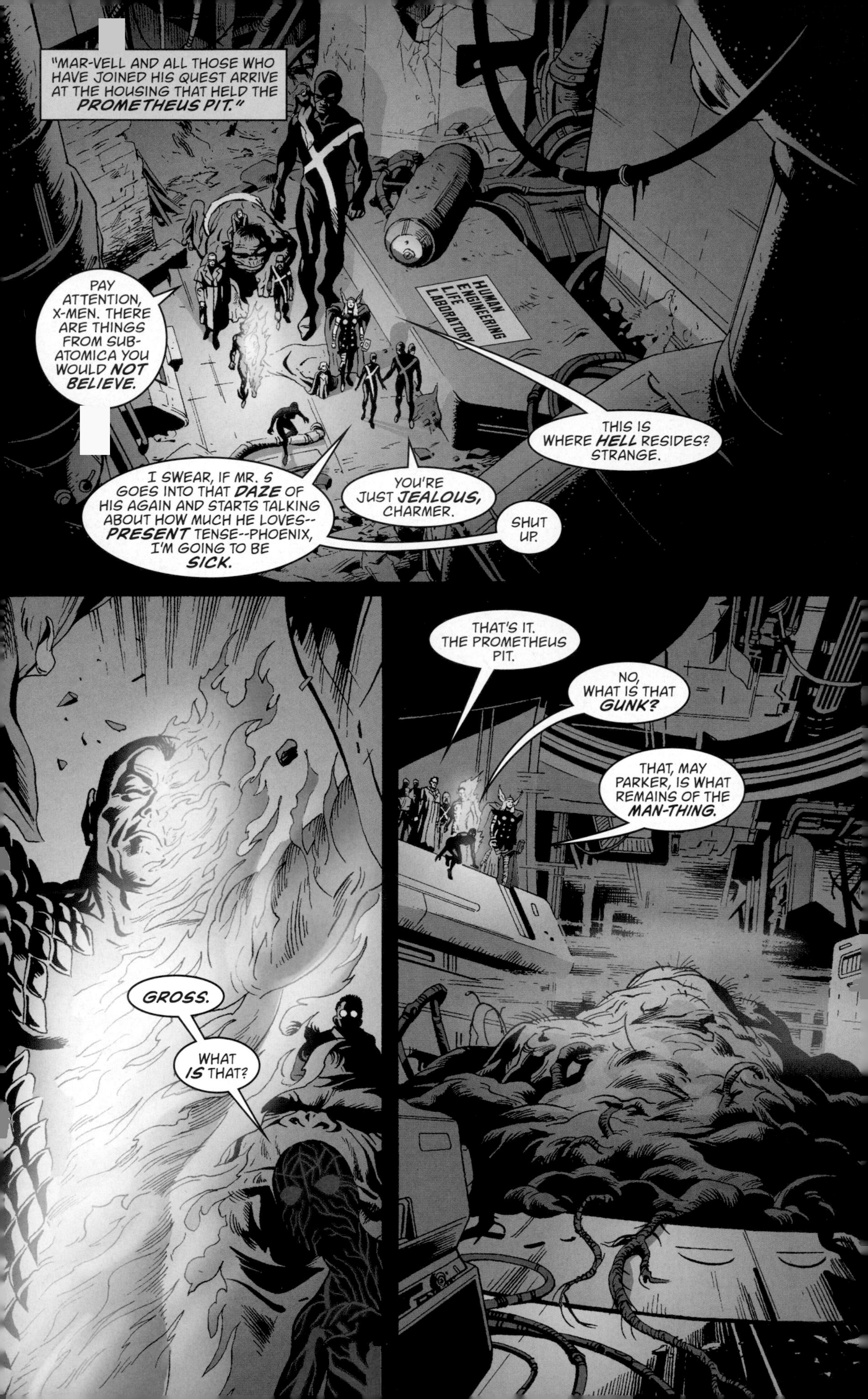
"MAR-VELL AND ALL THOSE WHO HAVE JOINED HIS QUEST ARRIVE AT THE HOUSING THAT HELD THE PROMETHEUS PIT."
PAY ATTENTION, X-MEN. THERE ARE THINGS FROM SUB-ATOMICA YOU WOULD NOT BELIEVE.
HUMAN ENGINEERING LIFE LABORATORY
THIS IS WHERE HELL RESIDES? STRANGE.
I SWEAR, IF MR. S GOES INTO THAT DAZE OF HIS AGAIN AND STARTS TALKING ABOUT HOW MUCH HE LOVES--PRESENT TENSE--PHOENIX, I'M GOING TO BE SICK.
YOU'RE JUST JEALOUS, CHARMER.
SHUT UP.
GROSS.
WHAT IS THAT?
THAT'S IT. THE PROMETHEUS PIT.
NO, WHAT IS THAT GUNK?
THAT, MAY PARKER, IS WHAT REMAINS OF THE MAN-THING.

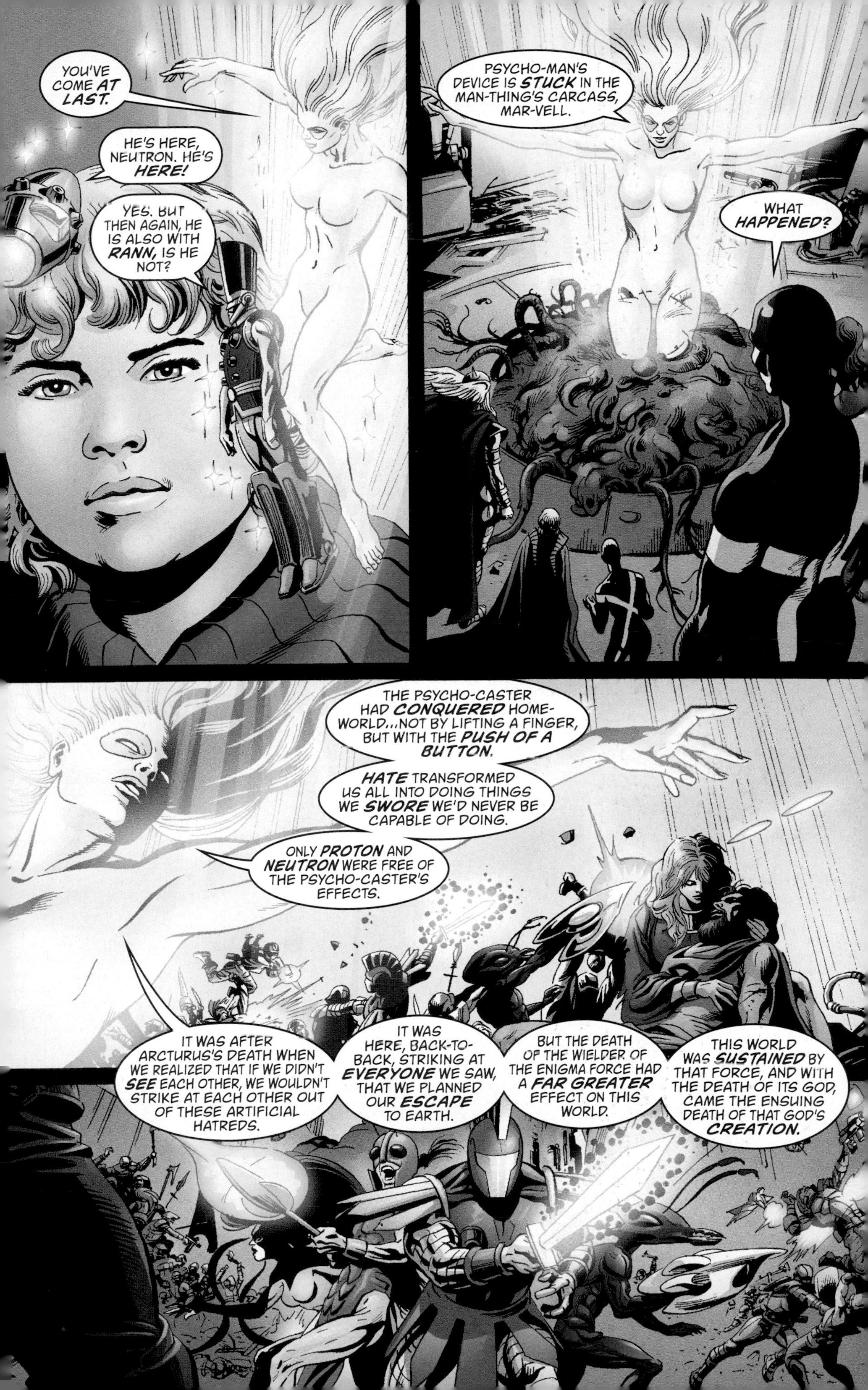
YOU'VE COME AT LAST.
HE'S HERE, NEUTRON. HE'S HERE!
YES. BUT THEN AGAIN, HE IS ALSO WITH RANN, IS HE NOT?
PSYCHO-MAN'S DEVICE IS STUCK IN THE MAN-THING'S CARCASS, MAR-VELL.
WHAT HAPPENED?
THE PSYCHO-CASTER HAD CONQUERED HOME-WORLD...NOT BY LIFTING A FINGER, BUT WITH THE PUSH OF A BUTTON.
HATE TRANSFORMED US ALL INTO DOING THINGS WE SWORE WE'D NEVER BE CAPABLE OF DOING.
ONLY PROTON AND NEUTRON WERE FREE OF THE PSYCHO-CASTER'S EFFECTS.
IT WAS AFTER ARCTURUS'S DEATH WHEN WE REALIZED THAT IF WE DIDN'T SEE EACH OTHER, WE WOULDN'T STRIKE AT EACH OTHER OUT OF THESE ARTIFICIAL HATREDS.
IT WAS HERE, BACK-TO-BACK, STRIKING AT EVERYONE WE SAW, THAT WE PLANNED OUR ESCAPE TO EARTH.
BUT THE DEATH OF THE WIELDER OF THE ENIGMA FORCE HAD A FAR GREATER EFFECT ON THIS WORLD.
THIS WORLD WAS SUSTAINED BY THAT FORCE, AND WITH THE DEATH OF ITS GOD, CAME THE ENSUING DEATH OF THAT GOD'S CREATION.

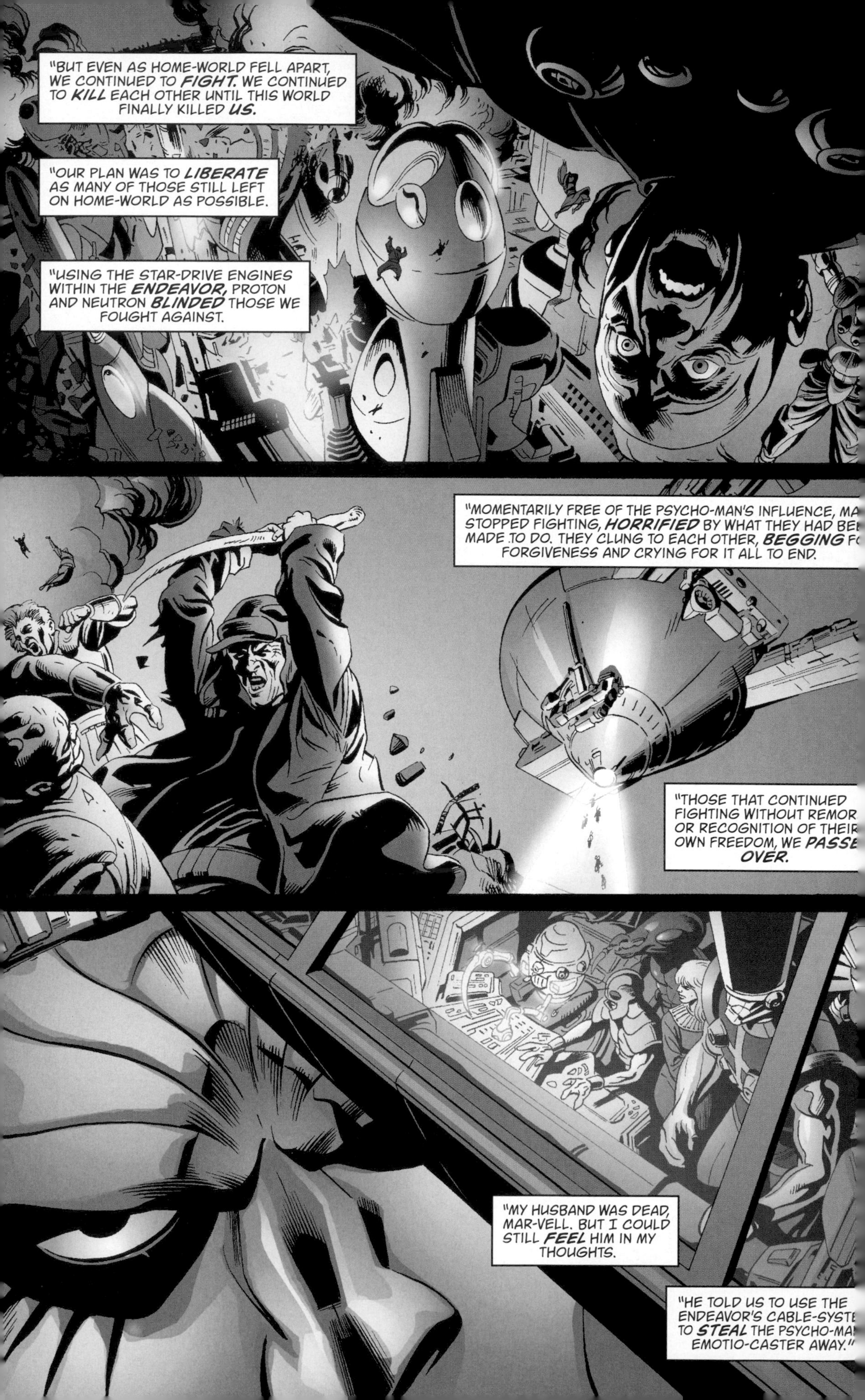
"BUT EVEN AS HOME-WORLD FELL APART, WE CONTINUED TO FIGHT. WE CONTINUED TO KILL EACH OTHER UNTIL THIS WORLD FINALLY KILLED US.
"OUR PLAN WAS TO LIBERATE AS MANY OF THOSE STILL LEFT ON HOME-WORLD AS POSSIBLE.
"USING THE STAR-DRIVE ENGINES WITHIN THE ENDEAVOR, PROTON AND NEUTRON BLINDED THOSE WE FOUGHT AGAINST.
"MOMENTARILY FREE OF THE PSYCHO-MAN'S INFLUENCE, MA STOPPED FIGHTING, HORRIFIED BY WHAT THEY HAD BE MADE TO DO. THEY CLUNG TO EACH OTHER, BEGGING F FORGIVENESS AND CRYING FOR IT ALL TO END.
"THOSE THAT CONTINUED FIGHTING WITHOUT REMOR OR RECOGNITION OF THEIR OWN FREEDOM, WE PASSE OVER.
"MY HUSBAND WAS DEAD, MAR-VELL. BUT I COULD STILL FEEL HIM IN MY THOUGHTS.
"HE TOLD US TO USE THE ENDEAVOR'S CABLE-SYSTE TO STEAL THE PSYCHO-MA EMOTIO-CASTER AWAY."

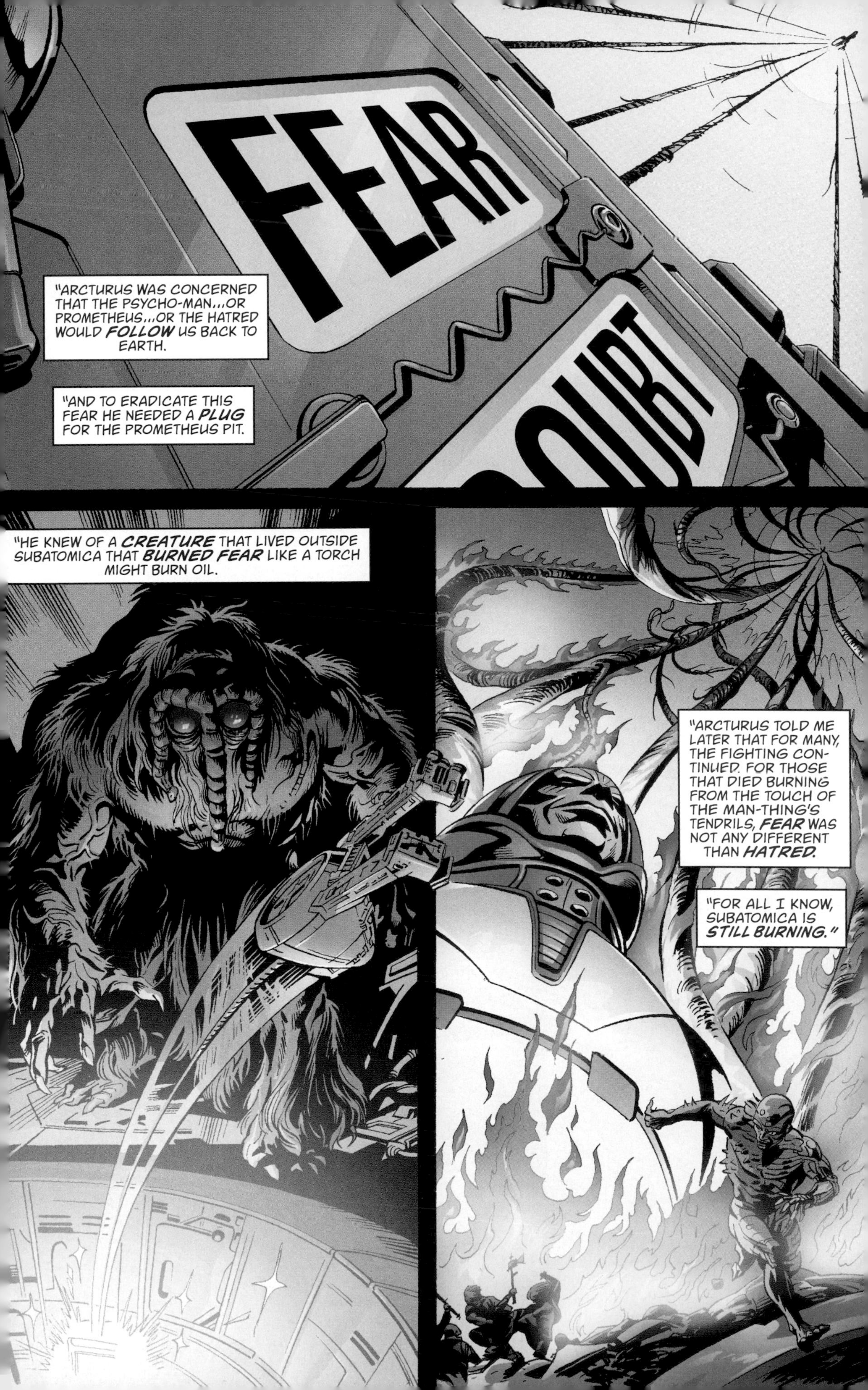
FEAR
DOUBT
"ARCTURUS WAS CONCERNED THAT THE PSYCHO-MAN...OR PROMETHEUS...OR THE HATRED WOULD FOLLOW US BACK TO EARTH.
"AND TO ERADICATE THIS FEAR HE NEEDED A PLUG FOR THE PROMETHEUS PIT.
"HE KNEW OF A CREATURE THAT LIVED OUTSIDE SUBATOMICA THAT BURNED FEAR LIKE A TORCH MIGHT BURN OIL.
"ARCTURUS TOLD ME LATER THAT FOR MANY, THE FIGHTING CONTINUED. FOR THOSE THAT DIED BURNING FROM THE TOUCH OF THE MAN-THING'S TENDRILS, FEAR WAS NOT ANY DIFFERENT THAN HATRED.
"FOR ALL I KNOW, SUBATOMICA IS STILL BURNING."

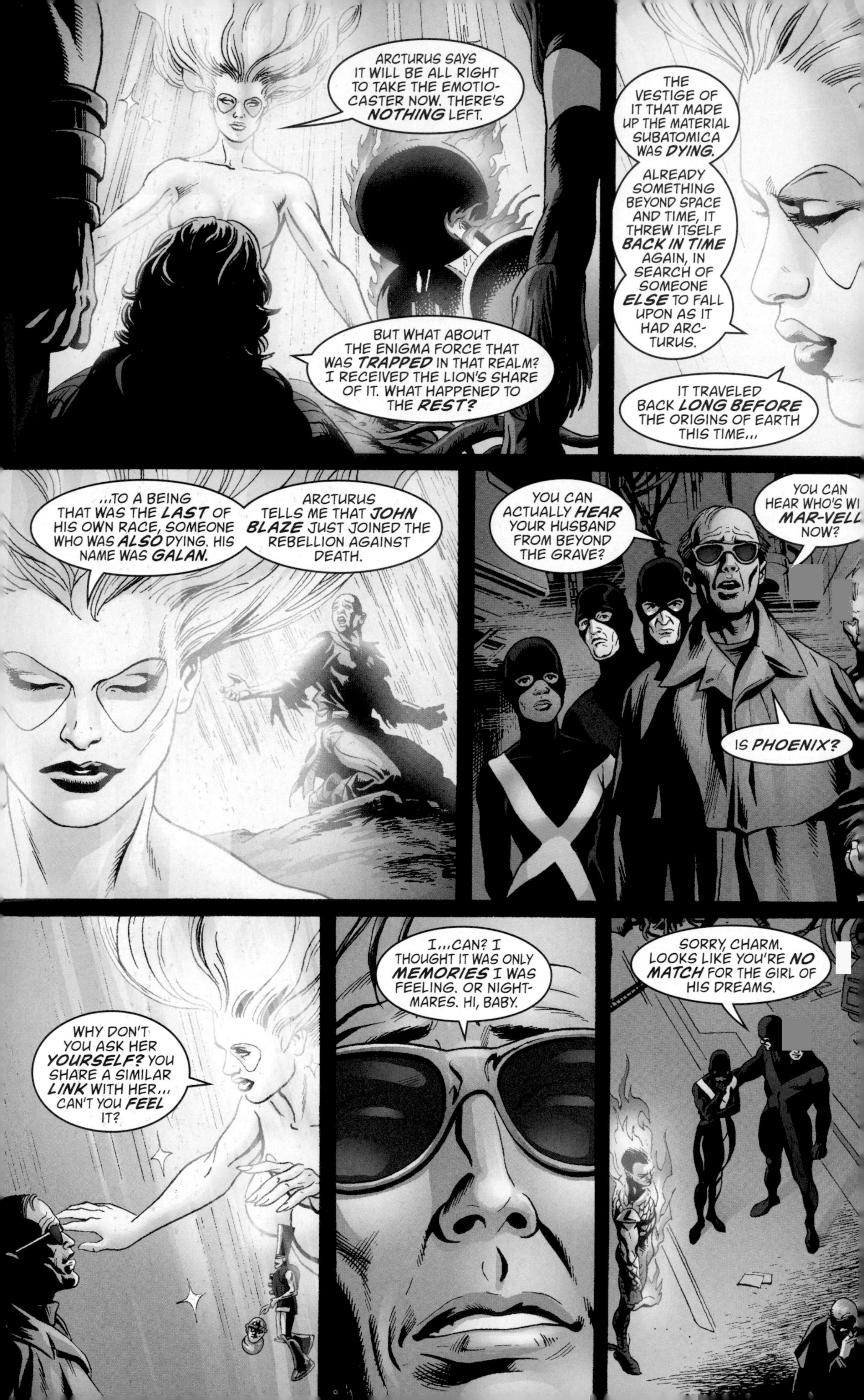

ARCTURUS SAYS IT WILL BE ALL RIGHT TO TAKE THE EMOTIO-CASTER NOW. THERE'S NOTHING LEFT.
BUT WHAT ABOUT THE ENIGMA FORCE THAT WAS TRAPPED IN THAT REALM? I RECEIVED THE LION'S SHARE OF IT. WHAT HAPPENED TO THE REST?
THE VESTIGE OF IT THAT MADE UP THE MATERIAL SUBATOMICA WAS DYING.
ALREADY SOMETHING BEYOND SPACE AND TIME, IT THREW ITSELF BACK IN TIME AGAIN, IN SEARCH OF SOMEONE ELSE TO FALL UPON AS IT HAD ARC-TURUS.
IT TRAVELED BACK LONG BEFORE THE ORIGINS OF EARTH THIS TIME...
...TO A BEING THAT WAS THE LAST OF HIS OWN RACE, SOMEONE WHO WAS ALSO DYING. HIS NAME WAS GALAN.
ARCTURUS TELLS ME THAT JOHN BLAZE JUST JOINED THE REBELLION AGAINST DEATH.
YOU CAN ACTUALLY HEAR YOUR HUSBAND FROM BEYOND THE GRAVE?
YOU CAN HEAR WHO'S WI MAR-VELL NOW?
IS PHOENIX?
WHY DON'T YOU ASK HER YOURSELF? YOU SHARE A SIMILAR LINK WITH HER... CAN'T YOU FEEL IT?
I...CAN? I THOUGHT IT WAS ONLY MEMORIES I WAS FEELING. OR NIGHT-MARES. HI, BABY.
SORRY, CHARM. LOOKS LIKE YOU'RE NO MATCH FOR THE GIRL OF HIS DREAMS.

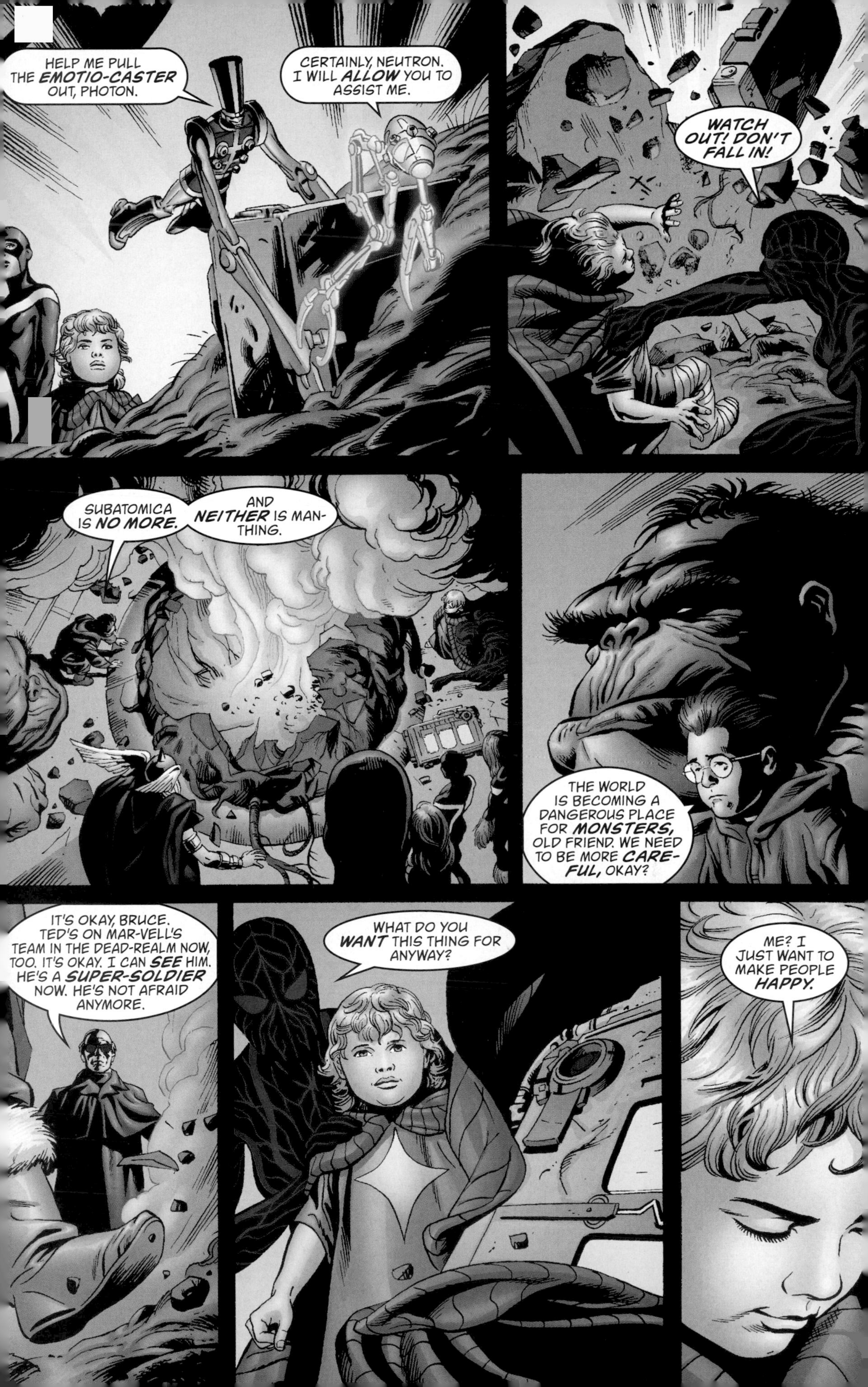

HELP ME PULL THE EMOTIO-CASTER OUT, PHOTON.
CERTAINLY, NEUTRON. I WILL ALLOW YOU TO ASSIST ME.
WATCH OUT! DON'T FALL IN!
SUBATOMICA IS NO MORE.
AND NEITHER IS MAN-THING.
THE WORLD IS BECOMING A DANGEROUS PLACE FOR MONSTERS, OLD FRIEND. WE NEED TO BE MORE CARE-FUL, OKAY?
IT'S OKAY, BRUCE. TED'S ON MAR-VELL'S TEAM IN THE DEAD-REALM NOW, TOO. IT'S OKAY. I CAN SEE HIM. HE'S A SUPER-SOLDIER NOW. HE'S NOT AFRAID ANYMORE.
WHAT DO YOU WANT THIS THING FOR ANYWAY?
ME? I JUST WANT TO MAKE PEOPLE HAPPY.

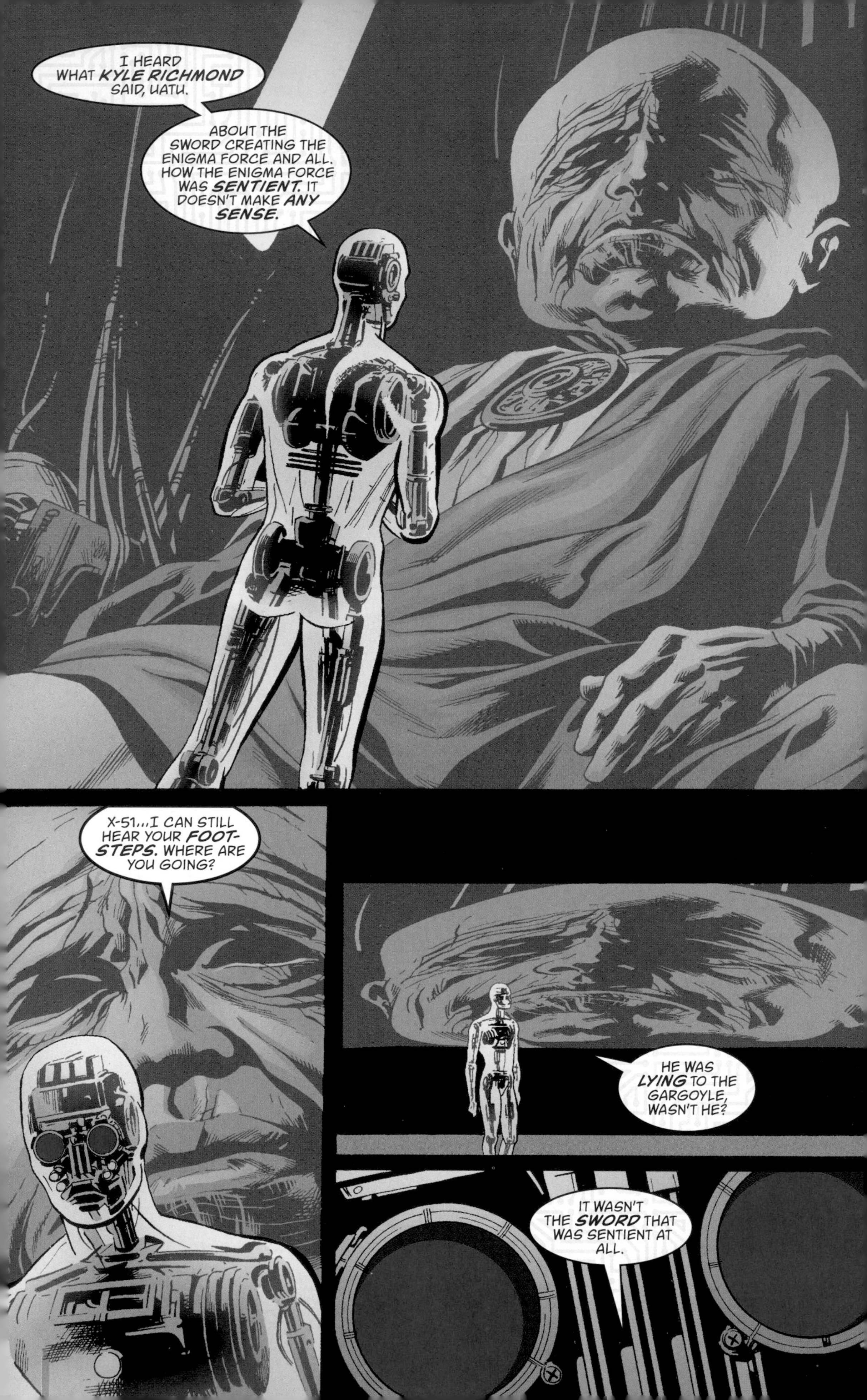
I HEARD WHAT KYLE RICHMOND SAID, UATU.
ABOUT THE SWORD CREATING THE ENIGMA FORCE AND ALL. HOW THE ENIGMA FORCE WAS SENTIENT. IT DOESN'T MAKE ANY SENSE.
X-51...I CAN STILL HEAR YOUR FOOT-STEPS. WHERE ARE YOU GOING?
HE WAS LYING TO THE GARGOYLE, WASN'T HE?
IT WASN'T THE SWORD THAT WAS SENTIENT AT ALL.

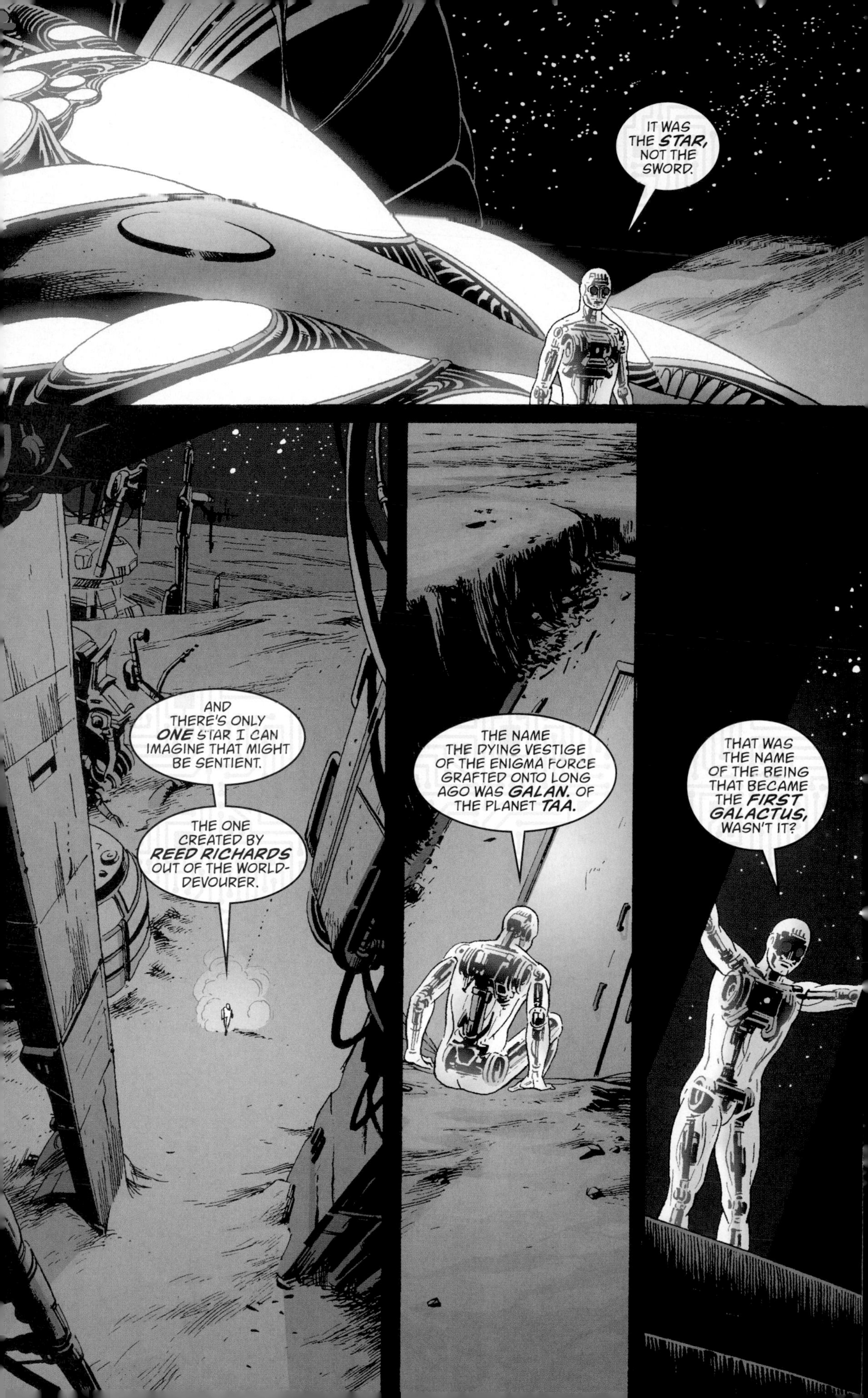
IT WAS THE STAR, NOT THE SWORD.
AND THERE'S ONLY ONE STAR I CAN IMAGINE THAT MIGHT BE SENTIENT.
THE ONE CREATED BY REED RICHARDS OUT OF THE WORLD-DEVOURER.
THE NAME THE DYING VESTIGE OF THE ENIGMA FORCE GRAFTED ONTO LONG AGO WAS GALAN. OF THE PLANET TAA.
THAT WAS THE NAME OF THE BEING THAT BECAME THE FIRST GALACTUS, WASN'T IT?

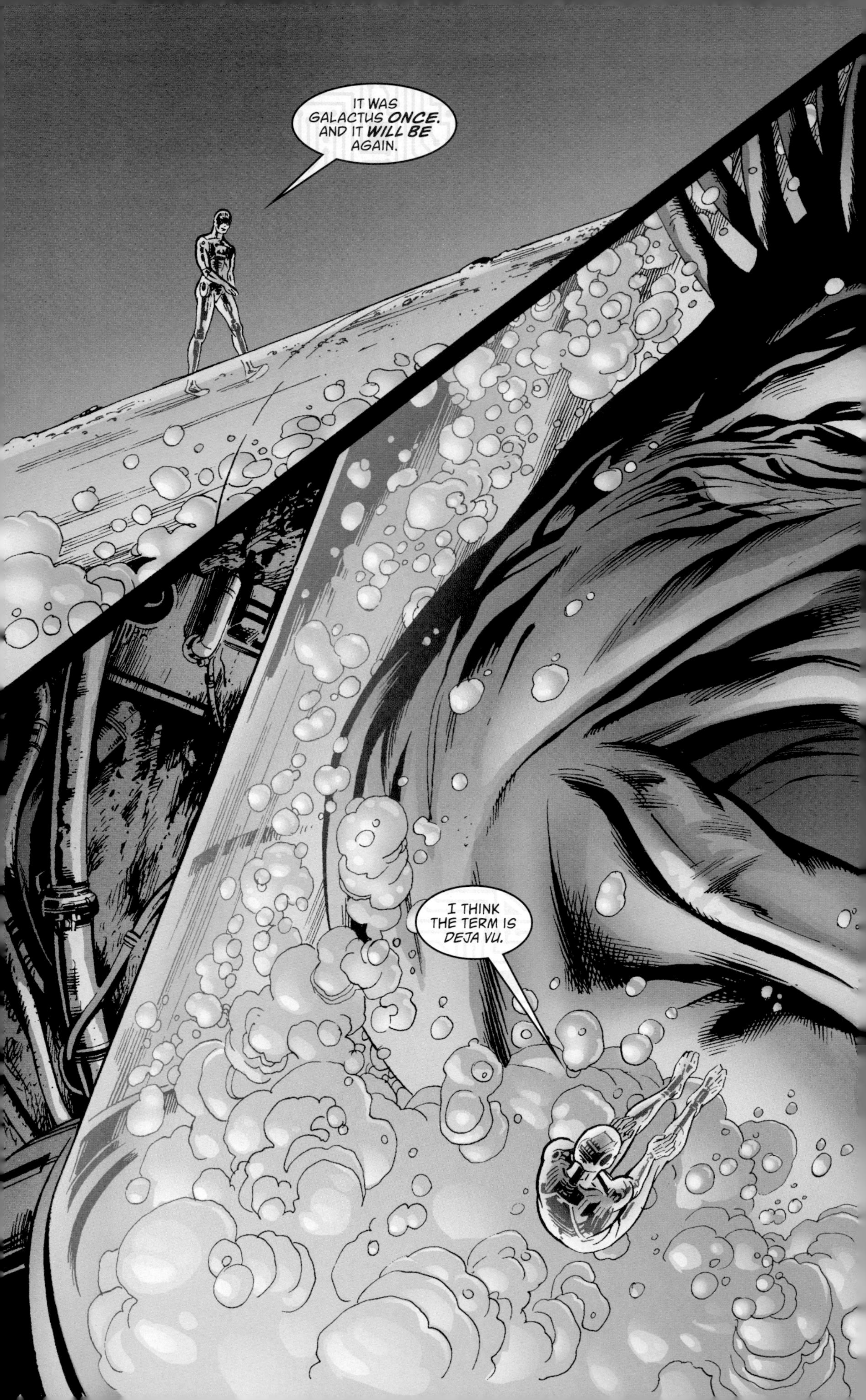
IT WAS GALACTUS ONCE. AND IT WILL BE AGAIN.
I THINK THE TERM IS DEJA VU.

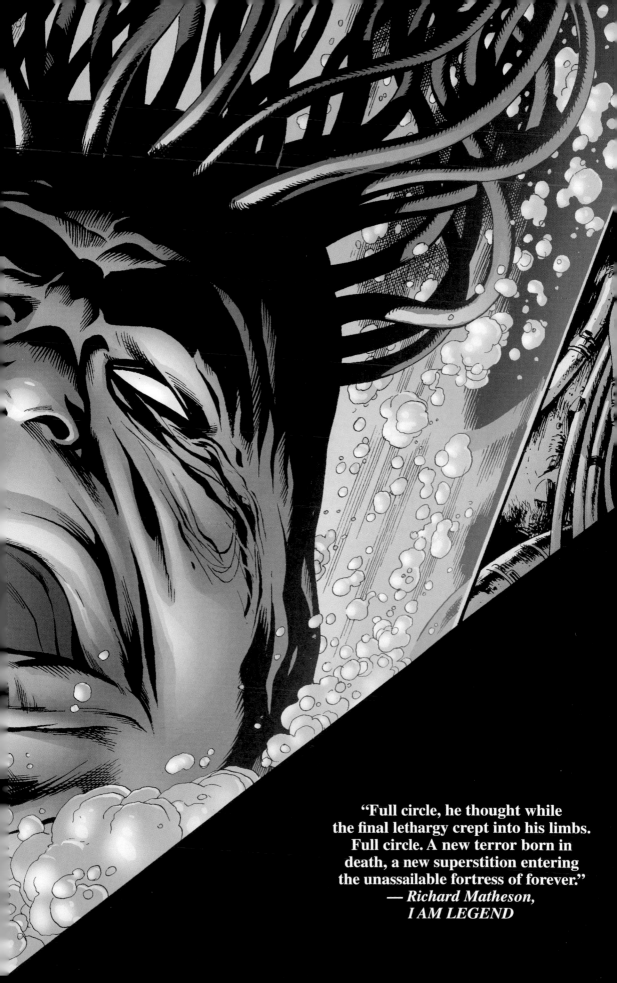

"Full circle, he thought while
the final lethargy crept into his limbs.
Full circle. A new terror born in
death, a new superstition entering
the unassailable fortress of forever."
— *Richard Matheson,*
I AM LEGEND

UNIVERSE X

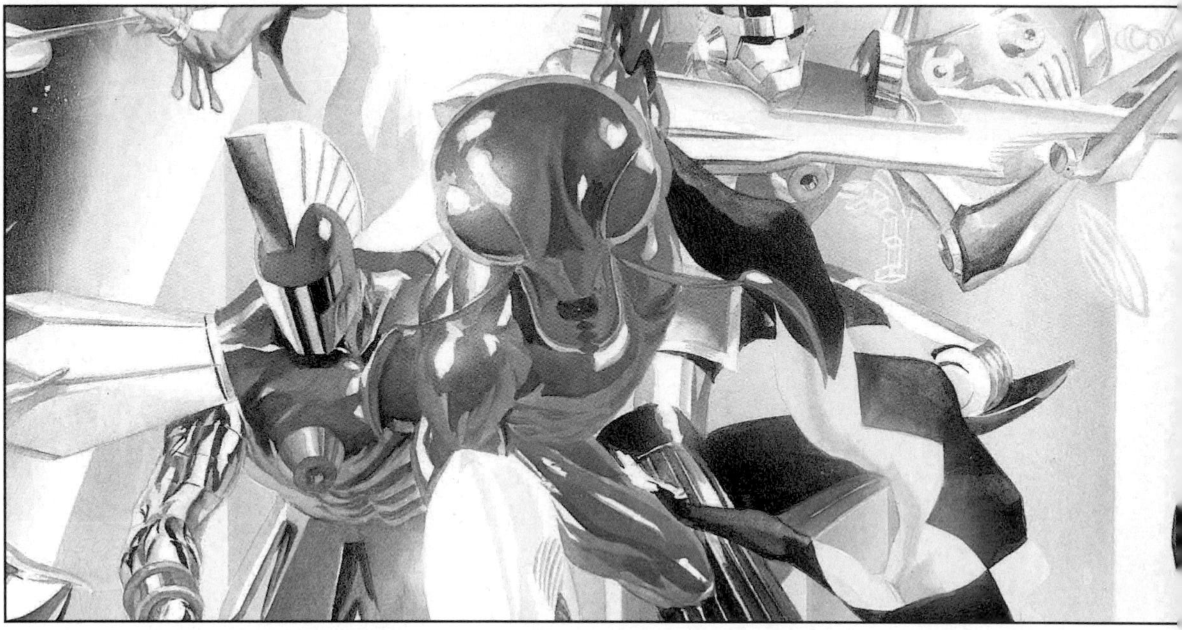

APPENDIX TO CHAPTER FIVE

WRITTEN BY JIM KRUEGER

"Again, this is an internal monologue being recorded in the event that this reality is destroyed. I am not suggesting at all that there is some enemy or threat to Earth that might result in its destruction, but because of the nature of these alternate realities and time cycles that seem to circle through all of human history.

"There was something in Mar-Vell's eyes that Captain America saw that gave him the courage to face Death and see her touch as a relief. What was that?

"The discovery of Supremor on the moon's surface leads to more questions than answers. Why would the Supreme Intelligence, with all its power and scope choose the moon of all places to wait?

"And why do I have a sense of such "wrong" when it comes to the existence of alternate realities?"

"Uatu, the former alien Watcher of Earth, a chronicler of not our history, but the growth and health of the Celestial that once grew in the heart of planet Earth, has little to say. In reality, inclinations towards fear and concern mean little to him. Things are as they are. Alternate realities exist because of the potential choices a being is capable of making... or the possibility of one event falling like a domino into another, changing the path of that event's fall.

"I will consider Peter Parker as an exercise to illustrate this problem.

"What if Peter Parker had stopped the thief who killed his Uncle Ben? Would he have made the same mistakes he did so early in his career? Or would Spider-Man exist at all? The death of his uncle was the catalyst for the creation of the hero know as Spider-Man."

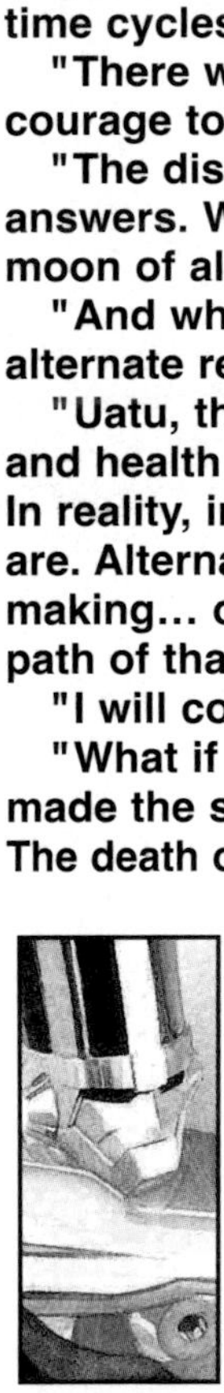

"What if Spider-Man joined the Fantastic Four? Would he have continued in the path that he had? Would he have been able to save the son of J. Jonah Jameson is he had been off-world with Reed Richards? What would that have meant for the rest of the world?

"Or what if he had remained an entertainer? Would this have somehow impacted the fear people have of mutants if they were now seen as entertainers. Would these 'powers' now only be seen as 'talents' or 'special effects'?

"Or what if someone else in Peter Parker's class had been bitten by the spider that gave him his wall-crawling abilities? Would Peter have been killed by the same thief that killed his Uncle Ben?

"Or what if Gwen Stacey had lived? There would be no May Parker. No Venom to distract the Skull those months before. No reason for Peter to even remain a hero. After all, it was in the emptiness caused by his Uncle Ben's death that created the need for responsibility. If Peter had new responsibilities that were not born out of tragedy, how would that change him?

"Or if Mary Jane had not died? Perhaps there would never have been the wall between Peter and May. Perhaps the Spiders Man would never have gotten control of Peter.

"Or if Peter Parker had not joined the fight against the Skull?

"This does not even consider all the different ways Peter's life affects others.

"All these possible scenarios create new histories, new continuities, new possibilities. But do they not also suggest a loss of character? Don't they create a dispersion of being? After all, if the range of my choices exist on other worlds, do I ever truly make a choice at all?

"Uatu has said that I do not. That this is why he is not concerned with even the death of the Celestial Embryo at the Earth's core. He says that on at least one other world, I did not rebel against Uatu and I did not send warning to Reed Richards on Earth. I am pained to think this is true. That is, regardless of utilitarian capability, I would betray the very people I was built to protect and live alongside.

"I suppose the real problem with this is the loss of individual freedom. It suggests that I don't make choices at all, but only satisfy and fulfill some cosmic niche in the realm of possibility.

"I am most concerned with how these worlds intermix with time manipulations. The creation of Galactus seems now to be a direct loop that runs from this universe's far future to its ancient past.

"And what of Franklin Richards, the new Galactus? What if he did not choose to become Galactus when his predecessor was transformed into a star? What if Reed Richards discovered the nature of the embryo within Earth before he transformed Galactus into a star?

"The problems faced with these questions is this. The choices mankind makes in large part determines the direction humanity will go in the future. If all choices are, to some extent, lived out, than there is no direction at all.

"Forget time. It's a loop, a cycle. Man is going nowhere.

"But, of course, this creates new difficulties, because there is growth. There is progress. It is not as Uatu states, an endless cycle of civilizations rising and falling. Surely the mere fact that we can now record what has gone before suggests some sort of hope for the future. Surely some.

"No. These alternate worlds cannot be merely the existence and collection of humanity's combined possibilities.

"Have there… or perhaps this needs to be stated differently, will there be at some point in the future the possibility of so many time manipulations that this is what has caused the differing worlds that I and Uatu have peered into?

"But are all these trips random? Or is there some sort of design to the multiverse, some motivation behind its being?

"I feel like I am once again debating with Uatu about whether good or evil exist. Meaning. How does this come about. Must an object's design suggest a designer? Does chaos have to demand an accidental origin?

"The key to these problems, I now believe, somehow rests in the eyes of Kyle Richmond. He can see things I cannot. Into places Uatu's equipment cannot peer. I must meet him, speak to him. If only to know what is to become of the rest of us."

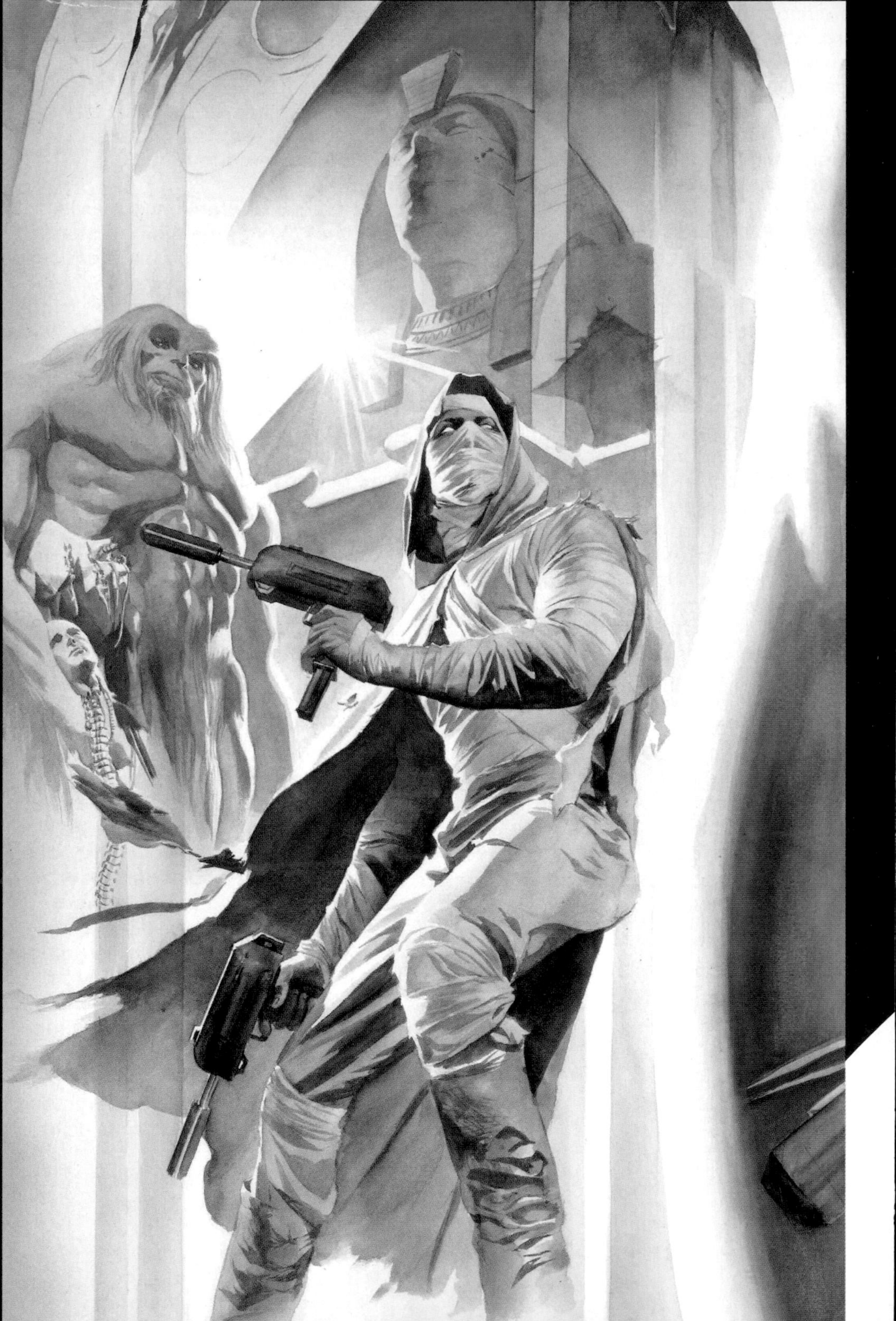

C H A P T E R S I X

"Kyle?"

" Yes, my friend?"

"What have I done, Kyle?"

"I'm thinking about what I've been in the past, Isaac. I was a villain once, you know."

"That was a long time ago."

"Not so long that I don't remember. I remember that girl I put in a wheelchair. I remember the people I killed. Even the people I thought I killed. And I'm asking myself if that's any worse..."

" Worse than what?"

" Worse than what's about to happen."

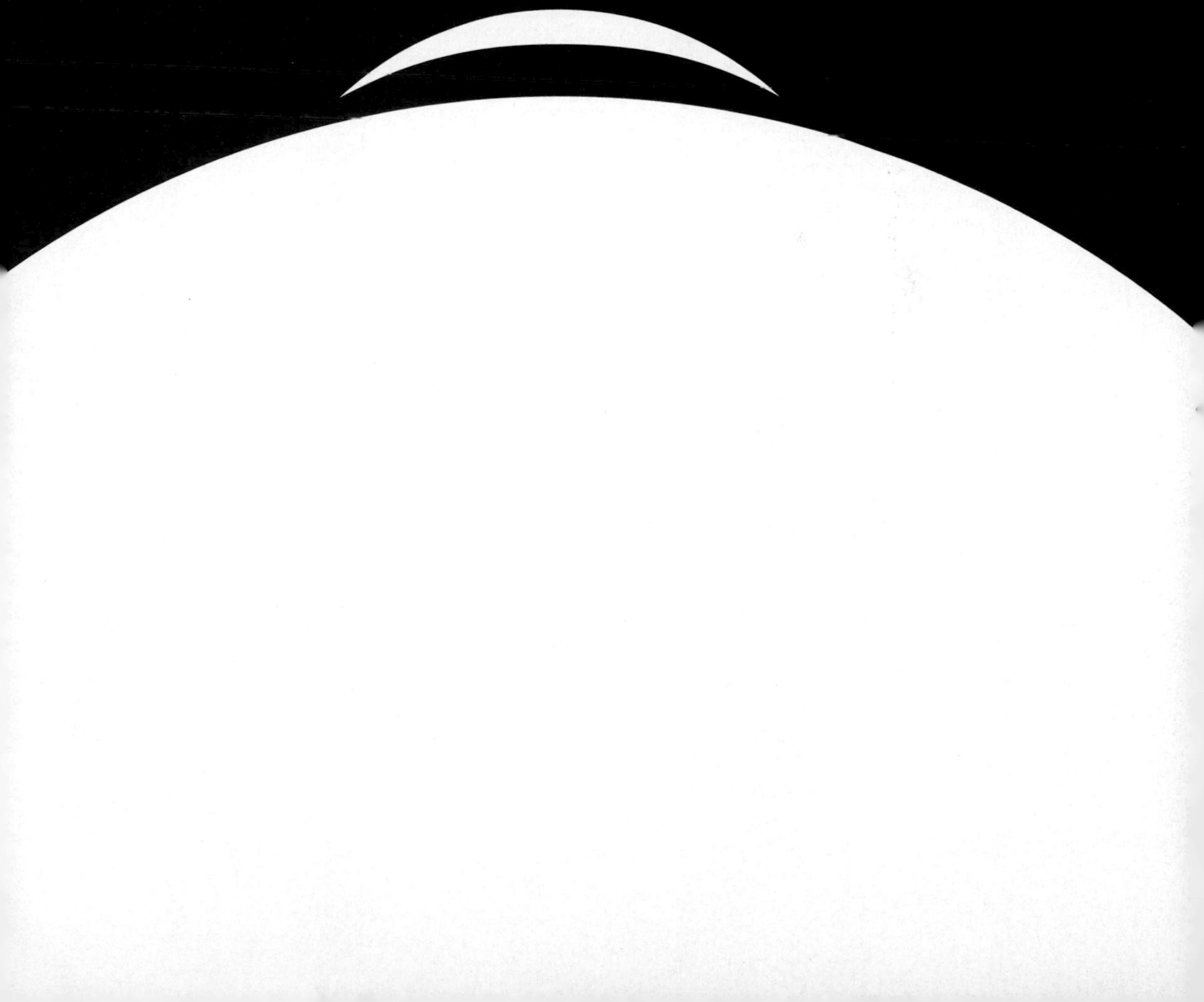

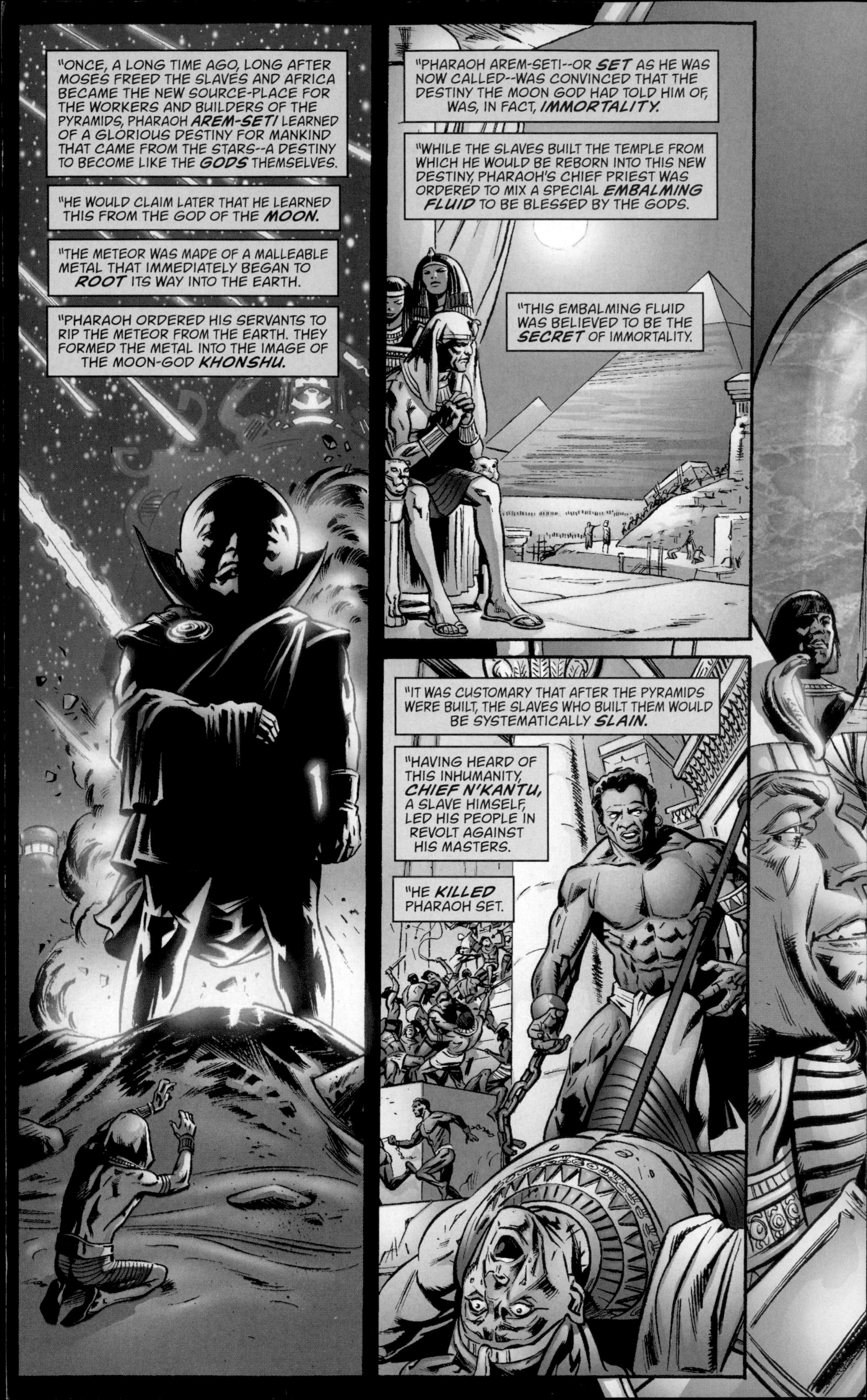
"ONCE, A LONG TIME AGO, LONG AFTER MOSES FREED THE SLAVES AND AFRICA BECAME THE NEW SOURCE-PLACE FOR THE WORKERS AND BUILDERS OF THE PYRAMIDS, PHARAOH AREM-SETI LEARNED OF A GLORIOUS DESTINY FOR MANKIND THAT CAME FROM THE STARS--A DESTINY TO BECOME LIKE THE GODS THEMSELVES.
"HE WOULD CLAIM LATER THAT HE LEARNED THIS FROM THE GOD OF THE MOON.
"THE METEOR WAS MADE OF A MALLEABLE METAL THAT IMMEDIATELY BEGAN TO ROOT ITS WAY INTO THE EARTH.
"PHARAOH ORDERED HIS SERVANTS TO RIP THE METEOR FROM THE EARTH. THEY FORMED THE METAL INTO THE IMAGE OF THE MOON-GOD KHONSHU.
"PHARAOH AREM-SETI--OR SET AS HE WAS NOW CALLED--WAS CONVINCED THAT THE DESTINY THE MOON GOD HAD TOLD HIM OF, WAS, IN FACT, IMMORTALITY.
"WHILE THE SLAVES BUILT THE TEMPLE FROM WHICH HE WOULD BE REBORN INTO THIS NEW DESTINY, PHARAOH'S CHIEF PRIEST WAS ORDERED TO MIX A SPECIAL EMBALMING FLUID TO BE BLESSED BY THE GODS.
"THIS EMBALMING FLUID WAS BELIEVED TO BE THE SECRET OF IMMORTALITY.
"IT WAS CUSTOMARY THAT AFTER THE PYRAMIDS WERE BUILT, THE SLAVES WHO BUILT THEM WOULD BE SYSTEMATICALLY SLAIN.
"HAVING HEARD OF THIS INHUMANITY, CHIEF N'KANTU, A SLAVE HIMSELF, LED HIS PEOPLE IN REVOLT AGAINST HIS MASTERS.
"HE KILLED PHARAOH SET.

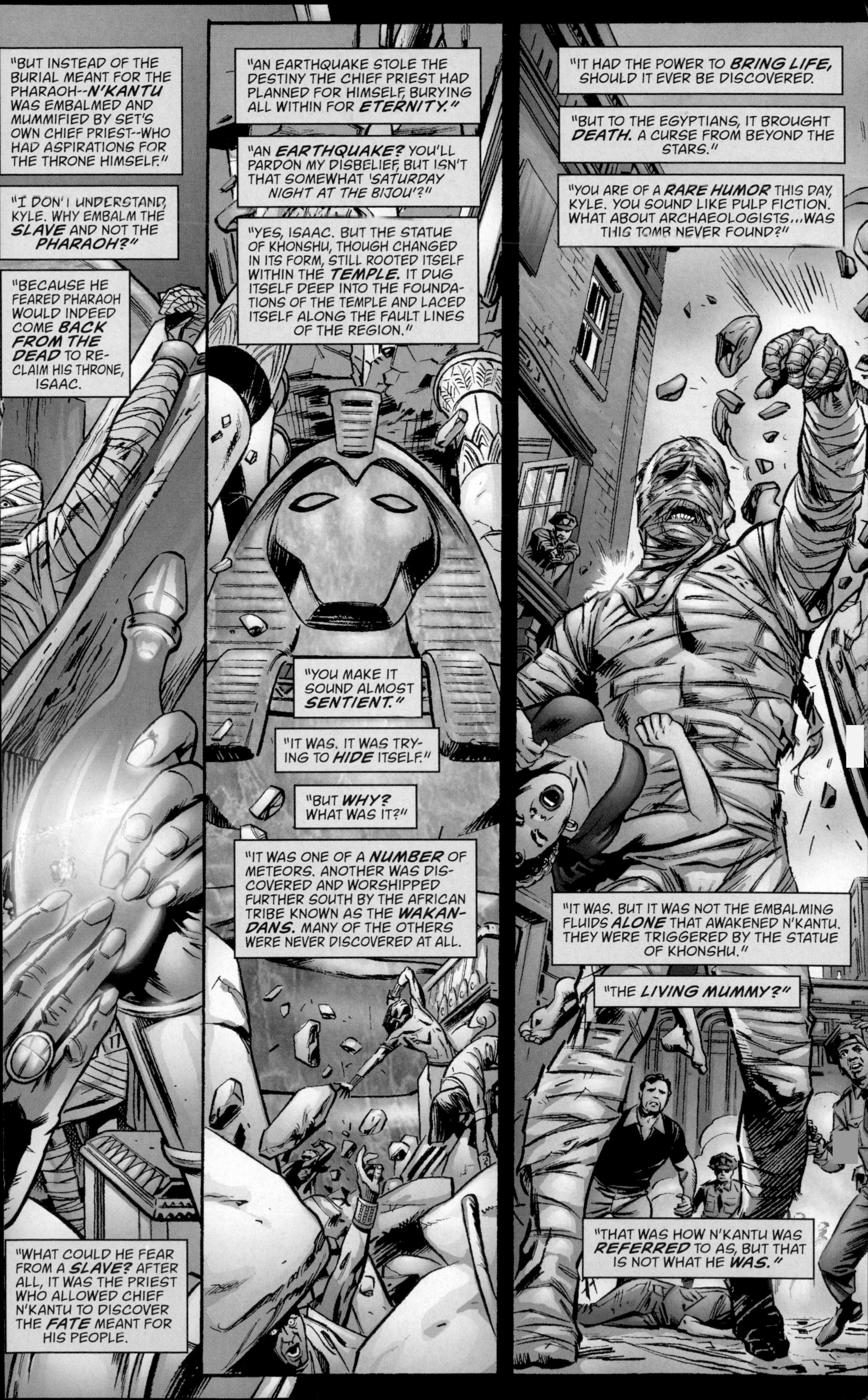
"BUT INSTEAD OF THE BURIAL MEANT FOR THE PHARAOH--N'KANTU WAS EMBALMED AND MUMMIFIED BY SET'S OWN CHIEF PRIEST--WHO HAD ASPIRATIONS FOR THE THRONE HIMSELF."
"I DON'T UNDERSTAND, KYLE. WHY EMBALM THE SLAVE AND NOT THE PHARAOH?"
"BECAUSE HE FEARED PHARAOH WOULD INDEED COME BACK FROM THE DEAD TO RE-CLAIM HIS THRONE, ISAAC.
"WHAT COULD HE FEAR FROM A SLAVE? AFTER ALL, IT WAS THE PRIEST WHO ALLOWED CHIEF N'KANTU TO DISCOVER THE FATE MEANT FOR HIS PEOPLE.
"AN EARTHQUAKE STOLE THE DESTINY THE CHIEF PRIEST HAD PLANNED FOR HIMSELF, BURYING ALL WITHIN FOR ETERNITY."
"AN EARTHQUAKE? YOU'LL PARDON MY DISBELIEF, BUT ISN'T THAT SOMEWHAT 'SATURDAY NIGHT AT THE BIJOU'?"
"YES, ISAAC. BUT THE STATUE OF KHONSHU, THOUGH CHANGED IN ITS FORM, STILL ROOTED ITSELF WITHIN THE TEMPLE. IT DUG ITSELF DEEP INTO THE FOUNDA-TIONS OF THE TEMPLE AND LACED ITSELF ALONG THE FAULT LINES OF THE REGION."
"YOU MAKE IT SOUND ALMOST SENTIENT."
"IT WAS. IT WAS TRY-ING TO HIDE ITSELF."
"BUT WHY? WHAT WAS IT?"
"IT WAS ONE OF A NUMBER OF METEORS. ANOTHER WAS DIS-COVERED AND WORSHIPPED FURTHER SOUTH BY THE AFRICAN TRIBE KNOWN AS THE WAKAN-DANS. MANY OF THE OTHERS WERE NEVER DISCOVERED AT ALL.
"IT HAD THE POWER TO BRING LIFE, SHOULD IT EVER BE DISCOVERED.
"BUT TO THE EGYPTIANS, IT BROUGHT DEATH. A CURSE FROM BEYOND THE STARS."
"YOU ARE OF A RARE HUMOR THIS DAY, KYLE. YOU SOUND LIKE PULP FICTION. WHAT ABOUT ARCHAEOLOGISTS...WAS THIS TOMB NEVER FOUND?"
"IT WAS. BUT IT WAS NOT THE EMBALMING FLUIDS ALONE THAT AWAKENED N'KANTU. THEY WERE TRIGGERED BY THE STATUE OF KHONSHU."
"THE LIVING MUMMY?"
"THAT WAS HOW N'KANTU WAS REFERRED TO AS, BUT THAT IS NOT WHAT HE WAS."

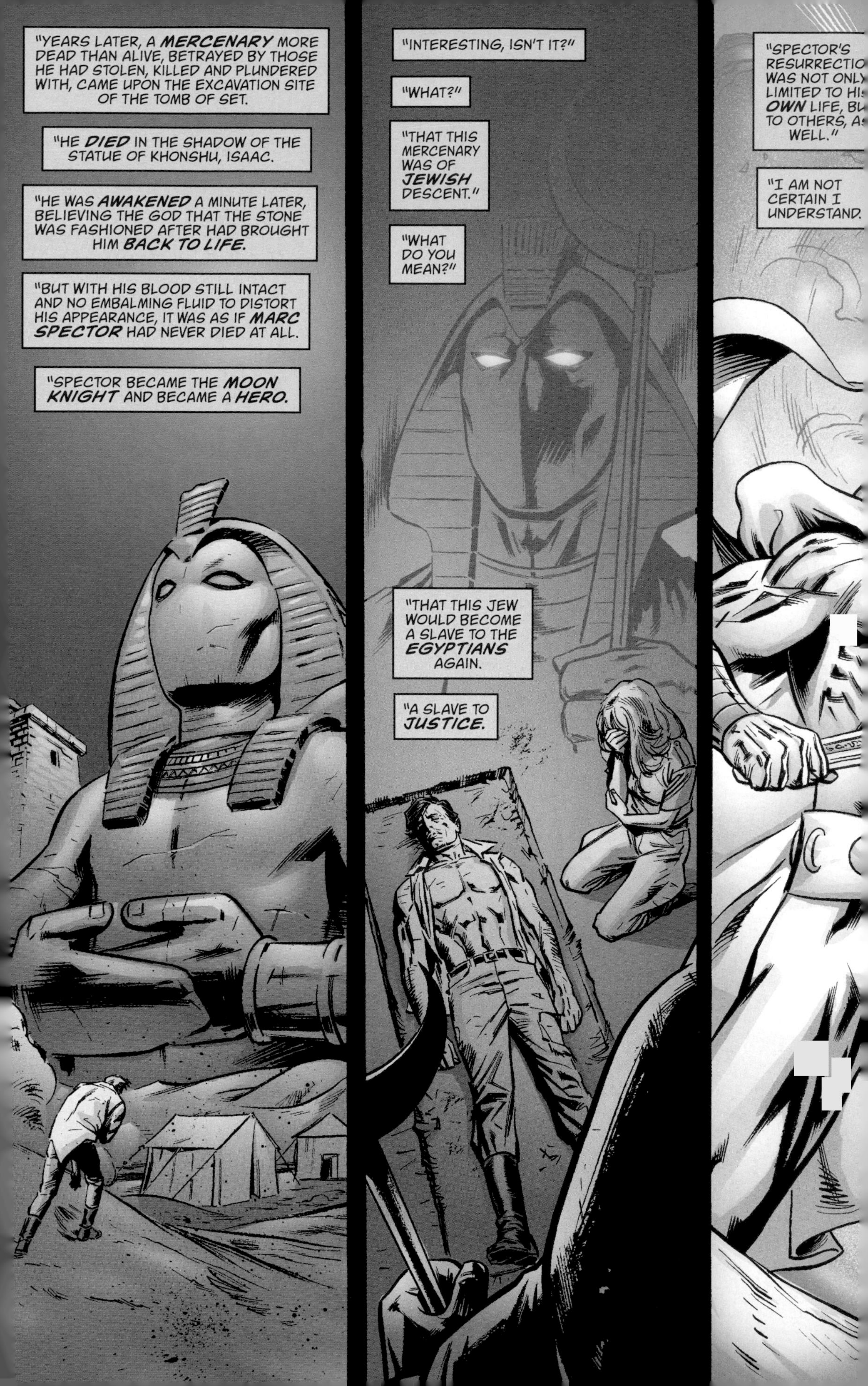
"YEARS LATER, A MERCENARY MORE DEAD THAN ALIVE, BETRAYED BY THOSE HE HAD STOLEN, KILLED AND PLUNDERED WITH, CAME UPON THE EXCAVATION SITE OF THE TOMB OF SET.
"HE DIED IN THE SHADOW OF THE STATUE OF KHONSHU, ISAAC.
"HE WAS AWAKENED A MINUTE LATER, BELIEVING THE GOD THAT THE STONE WAS FASHIONED AFTER HAD BROUGHT HIM BACK TO LIFE.
"BUT WITH HIS BLOOD STILL INTACT AND NO EMBALMING FLUID TO DISTORT HIS APPEARANCE, IT WAS AS IF MARC SPECTOR HAD NEVER DIED AT ALL.
"SPECTOR BECAME THE MOON KNIGHT AND BECAME A HERO.
"INTERESTING, ISN'T IT?"
"WHAT?"
"THAT THIS MERCENARY WAS OF JEWISH DESCENT."
"WHAT DO YOU MEAN?"
"THAT THIS JEW WOULD BECOME A SLAVE TO THE EGYPTIANS AGAIN.
"A SLAVE TO JUSTICE.
"SPECTOR'S RESURRECTIO WAS NOT ONLY LIMITED TO HI OWN LIFE, BU TO OTHERS, A WELL."
"I AM NOT CERTAIN I UNDERSTAND.

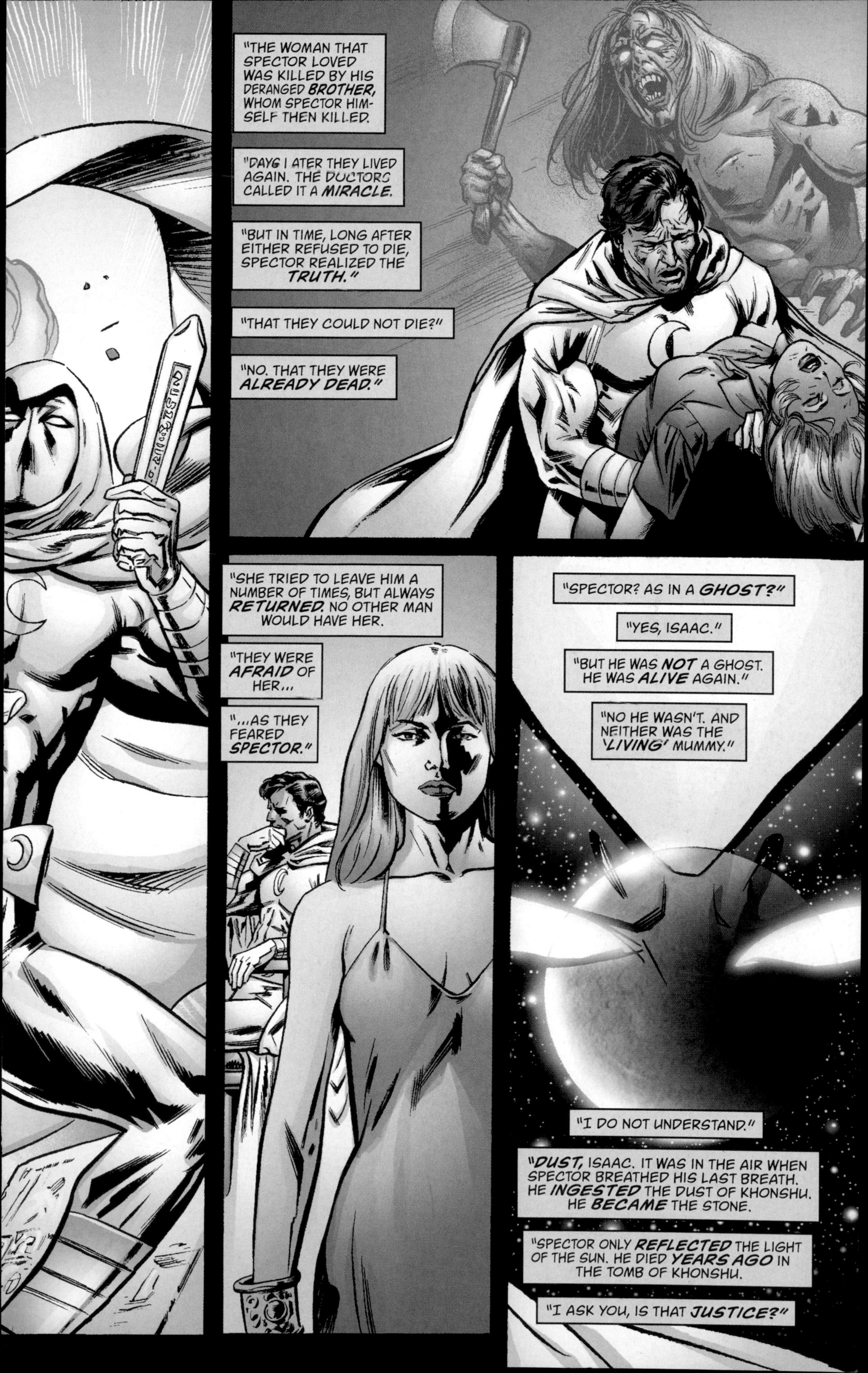
"THE WOMAN THAT SPECTOR LOVED WAS KILLED BY HIS DERANGED BROTHER, WHOM SPECTOR HIMSELF THEN KILLED.
"DAYS LATER THEY LIVED AGAIN. THE DOCTORS CALLED IT A MIRACLE.
"BUT IN TIME, LONG AFTER EITHER REFUSED TO DIE, SPECTOR REALIZED THE TRUTH."
"THAT THEY COULD NOT DIE?"
"NO. THAT THEY WERE ALREADY DEAD."
"SHE TRIED TO LEAVE HIM A NUMBER OF TIMES, BUT ALWAYS RETURNED. NO OTHER MAN WOULD HAVE HER.
"THEY WERE AFRAID OF HER...
"...AS THEY FEARED SPECTOR."
"SPECTOR? AS IN A GHOST?"
"YES, ISAAC."
"BUT HE WAS NOT A GHOST. HE WAS ALIVE AGAIN."
"NO HE WASN'T. AND NEITHER WAS THE 'LIVING' MUMMY."
"I DO NOT UNDERSTAND."
"DUST, ISAAC. IT WAS IN THE AIR WHEN SPECTOR BREATHED HIS LAST BREATH. HE INGESTED THE DUST OF KHONSHU. HE BECAME THE STONE.
"SPECTOR ONLY REFLECTED THE LIGHT OF THE SUN. HE DIED YEARS AGO IN THE TOMB OF KHONSHU.
"I ASK YOU, IS THAT JUSTICE?"

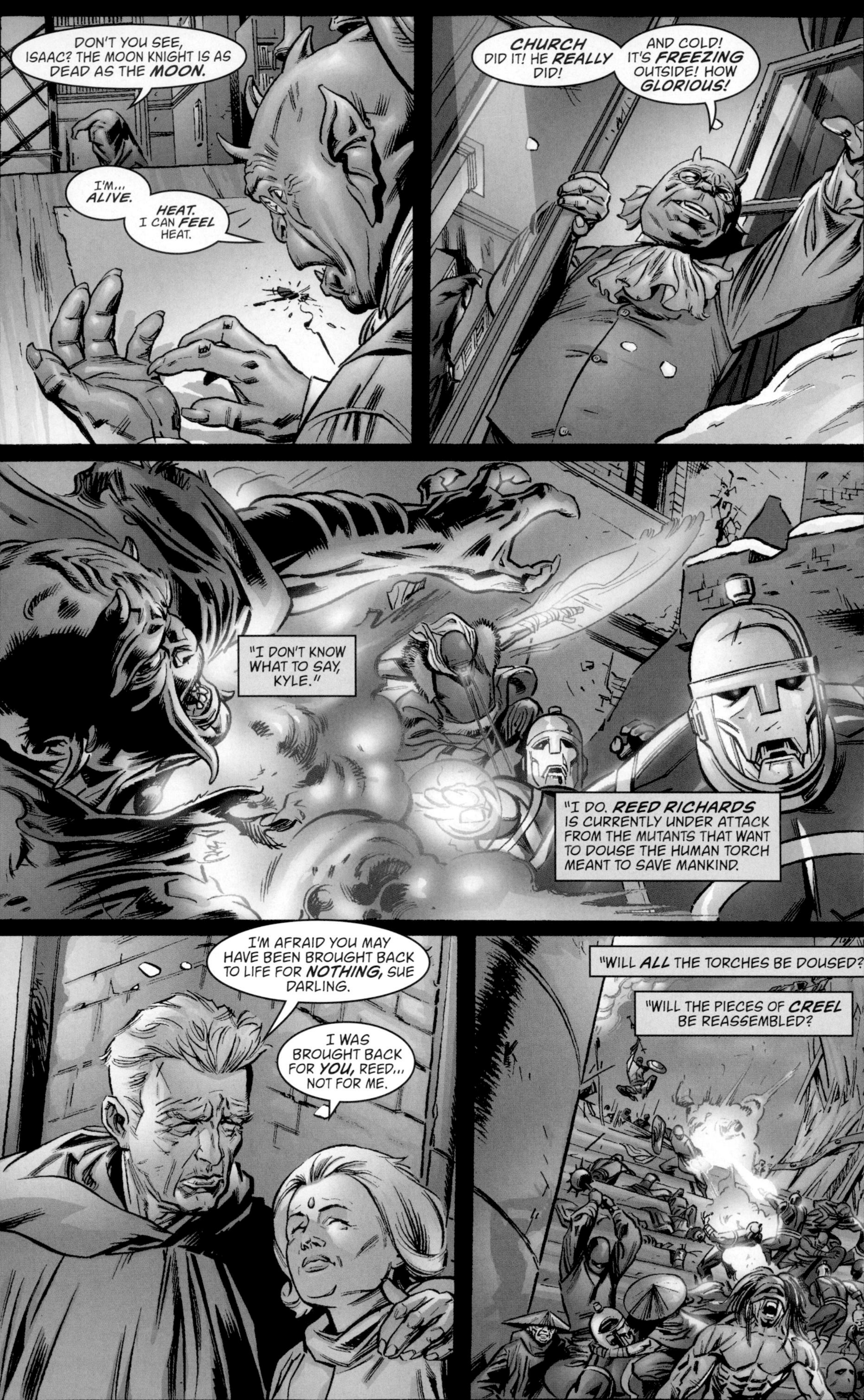
DON'T YOU SEE, ISAAC? THE MOON KNIGHT IS AS DEAD AS THE MOON.
I'M... ALIVE.
HEAT. I CAN FEEL HEAT.
CHURCH DID IT! HE REALLY DID!
AND COLD! IT'S FREEZING OUTSIDE! HOW GLORIOUS!
"I DON'T KNOW WHAT TO SAY, KYLE."
"I DO. REED RICHARDS IS CURRENTLY UNDER ATTACK FROM THE MUTANTS THAT WANT TO DOUSE THE HUMAN TORCH MEANT TO SAVE MANKIND.
I'M AFRAID YOU MAY HAVE BEEN BROUGHT BACK TO LIFE FOR NOTHING, SUE DARLING.
I WAS BROUGHT BACK FOR YOU, REED... NOT FOR ME.
"WILL ALL THE TORCHES BE DOUSED?
"WILL THE PIECES OF CREEL BE REASSEMBLED?

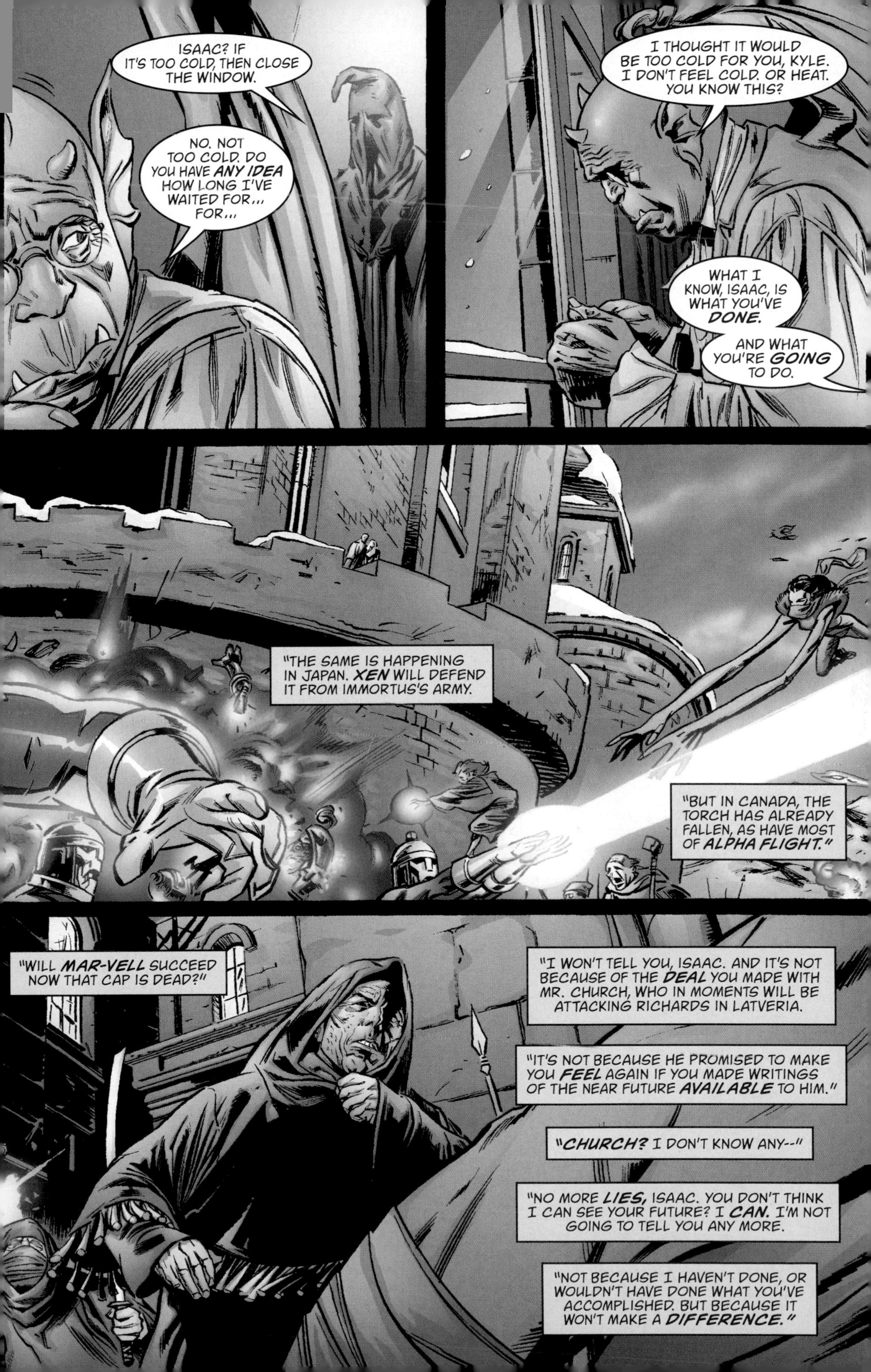
ISAAC? IF IT'S TOO COLD, THEN CLOSE THE WINDOW.
NO. NOT TOO COLD. DO YOU HAVE ANY IDEA HOW LONG I'VE WAITED FOR... FOR...
I THOUGHT IT WOULD BE TOO COLD FOR YOU, KYLE. I DON'T FEEL COLD. OR HEAT. YOU KNOW THIS?
WHAT I KNOW, ISAAC, IS WHAT YOU'VE DONE.
AND WHAT YOU'RE GOING TO DO.
"THE SAME IS HAPPENING IN JAPAN. XEN WILL DEFEND IT FROM IMMORTUS'S ARMY.
"BUT IN CANADA, THE TORCH HAS ALREADY FALLEN, AS HAVE MOST OF ALPHA FLIGHT."
"WILL MAR-VELL SUCCEED NOW THAT CAP IS DEAD?"
"I WON'T TELL YOU, ISAAC. AND IT'S NOT BECAUSE OF THE DEAL YOU MADE WITH MR. CHURCH, WHO IN MOMENTS WILL BE ATTACKING RICHARDS IN LATVERIA.
"IT'S NOT BECAUSE HE PROMISED TO MAKE YOU FEEL AGAIN IF YOU MADE WRITINGS OF THE NEAR FUTURE AVAILABLE TO HIM."
"CHURCH? I DON'T KNOW ANY--"
"NO MORE LIES, ISAAC. YOU DON'T THINK I CAN SEE YOUR FUTURE? I CAN. I'M NOT GOING TO TELL YOU ANY MORE.
"NOT BECAUSE I HAVEN'T DONE, OR WOULDN'T HAVE DONE WHAT YOU'VE ACCOMPLISHED. BUT BECAUSE IT WON'T MAKE A DIFFERENCE."

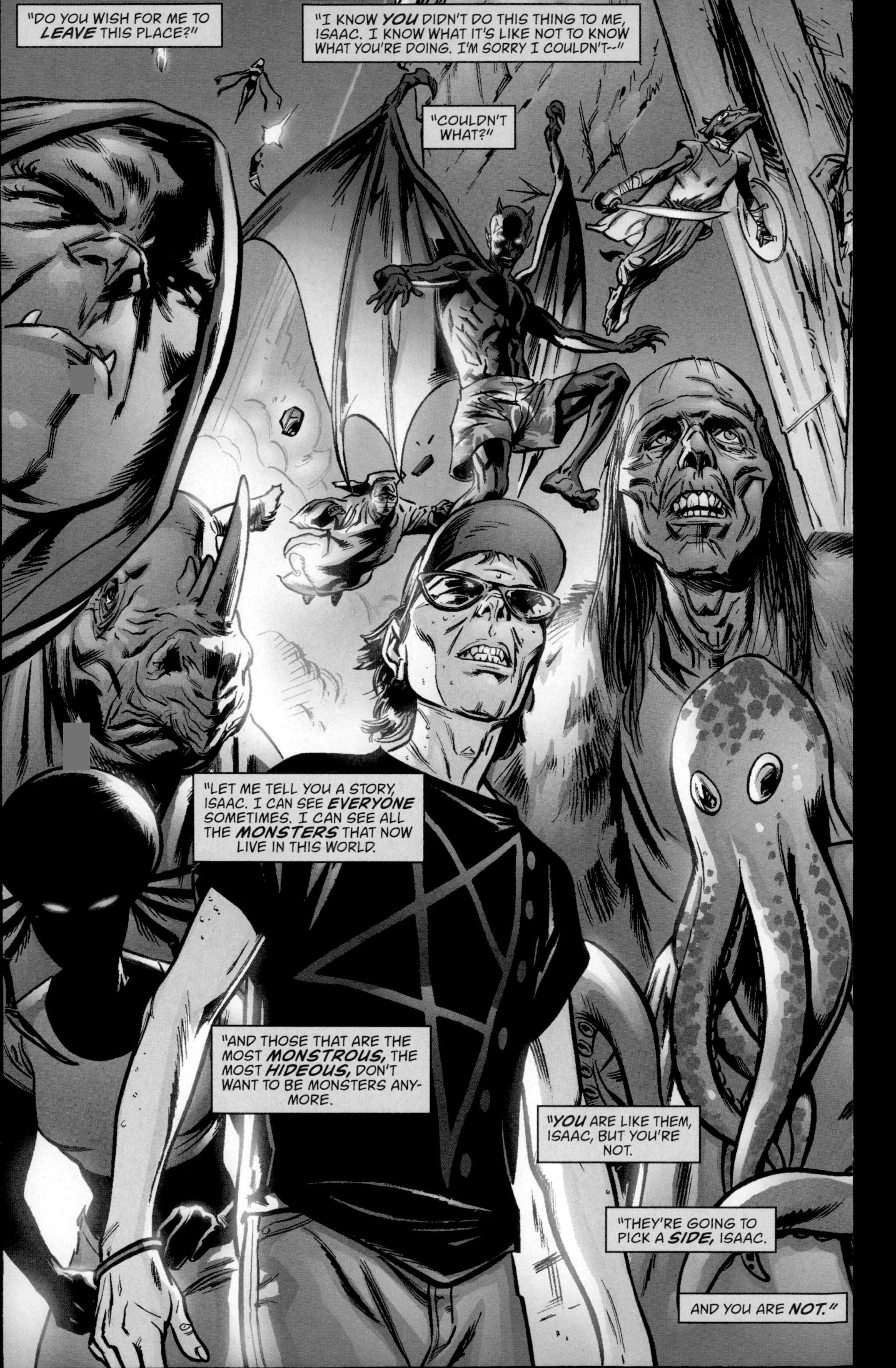
"DO YOU WISH FOR ME TO LEAVE THIS PLACE?"
"I KNOW YOU DIDN'T DO THIS THING TO ME, ISAAC. I KNOW WHAT IT'S LIKE NOT TO KNOW WHAT YOU'RE DOING. I'M SORRY I COULDN'T--"
"COULDN'T WHAT?"
"LET ME TELL YOU A STORY, ISAAC. I CAN SEE EVERYONE SOMETIMES. I CAN SEE ALL THE MONSTERS THAT NOW LIVE IN THIS WORLD.
"AND THOSE THAT ARE THE MOST MONSTROUS, THE MOST HIDEOUS, DON'T WANT TO BE MONSTERS ANY-MORE.
"YOU ARE LIKE THEM, ISAAC, BUT YOU'RE NOT.
"THEY'RE GOING TO PICK A SIDE, ISAAC.
AND YOU ARE NOT."

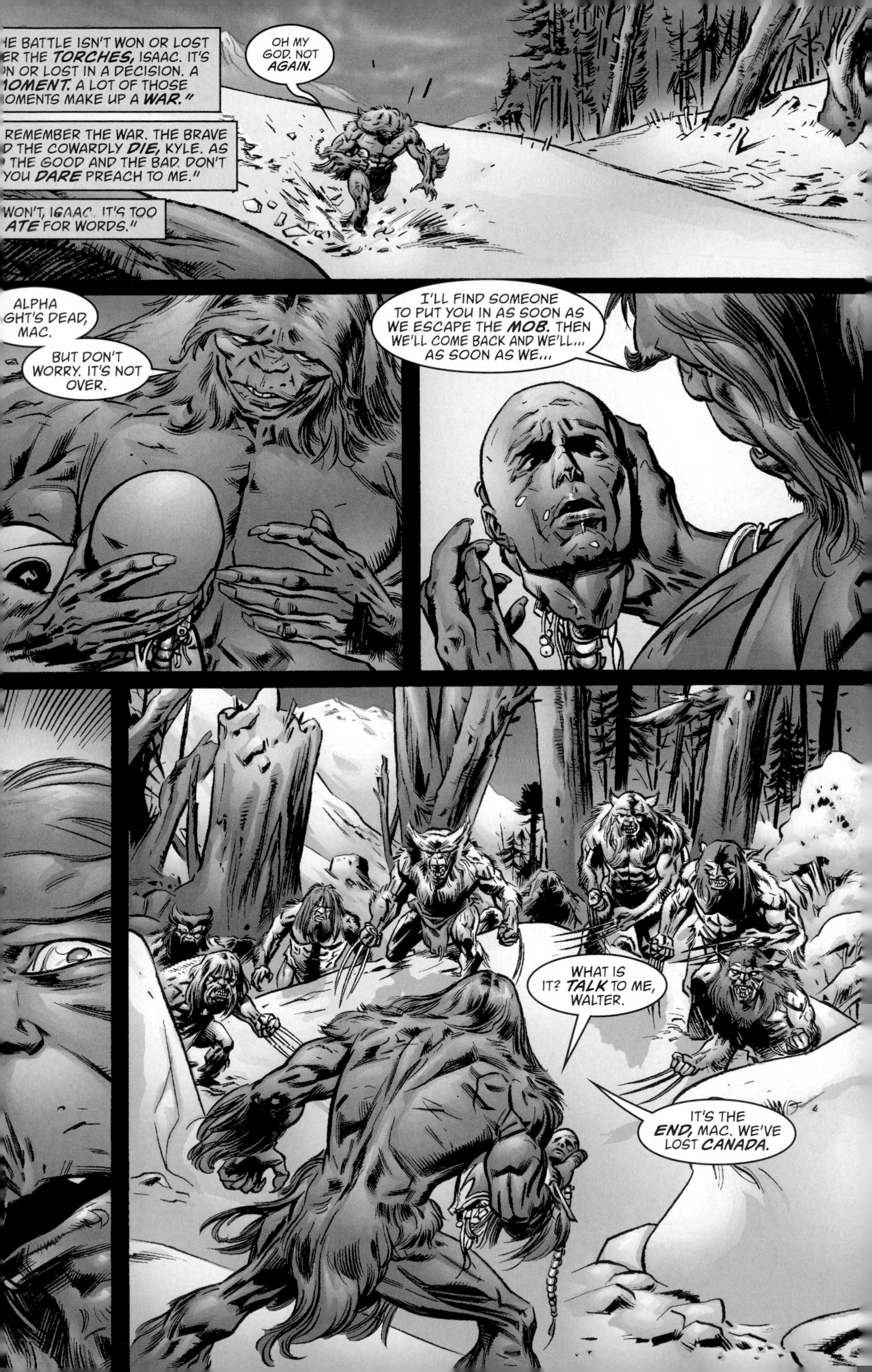

HE BATTLE ISN'T WON OR LOST ER THE TORCHES, ISAAC. IT'S N OR LOST IN A DECISION. A MOMENT. A LOT OF THOSE OMENTS MAKE UP A WAR."
OH MY GOD. NOT AGAIN.
REMEMBER THE WAR. THE BRAVE D THE COWARDLY DIE, KYLE. AS THE GOOD AND THE BAD. DON'T YOU DARE PREACH TO ME."
WON'T, ISAAC. IT'S TOO ATE FOR WORDS."
ALPHA GHT'S DEAD, MAC.
BUT DON'T WORRY. IT'S NOT OVER.
I'LL FIND SOMEONE TO PUT YOU IN AS SOON AS WE ESCAPE THE MOB. THEN WE'LL COME BACK AND WE'LL... AS SOON AS WE...
WHAT IS IT? TALK TO ME, WALTER.
IT'S THE END, MAC. WE'VE LOST CANADA.

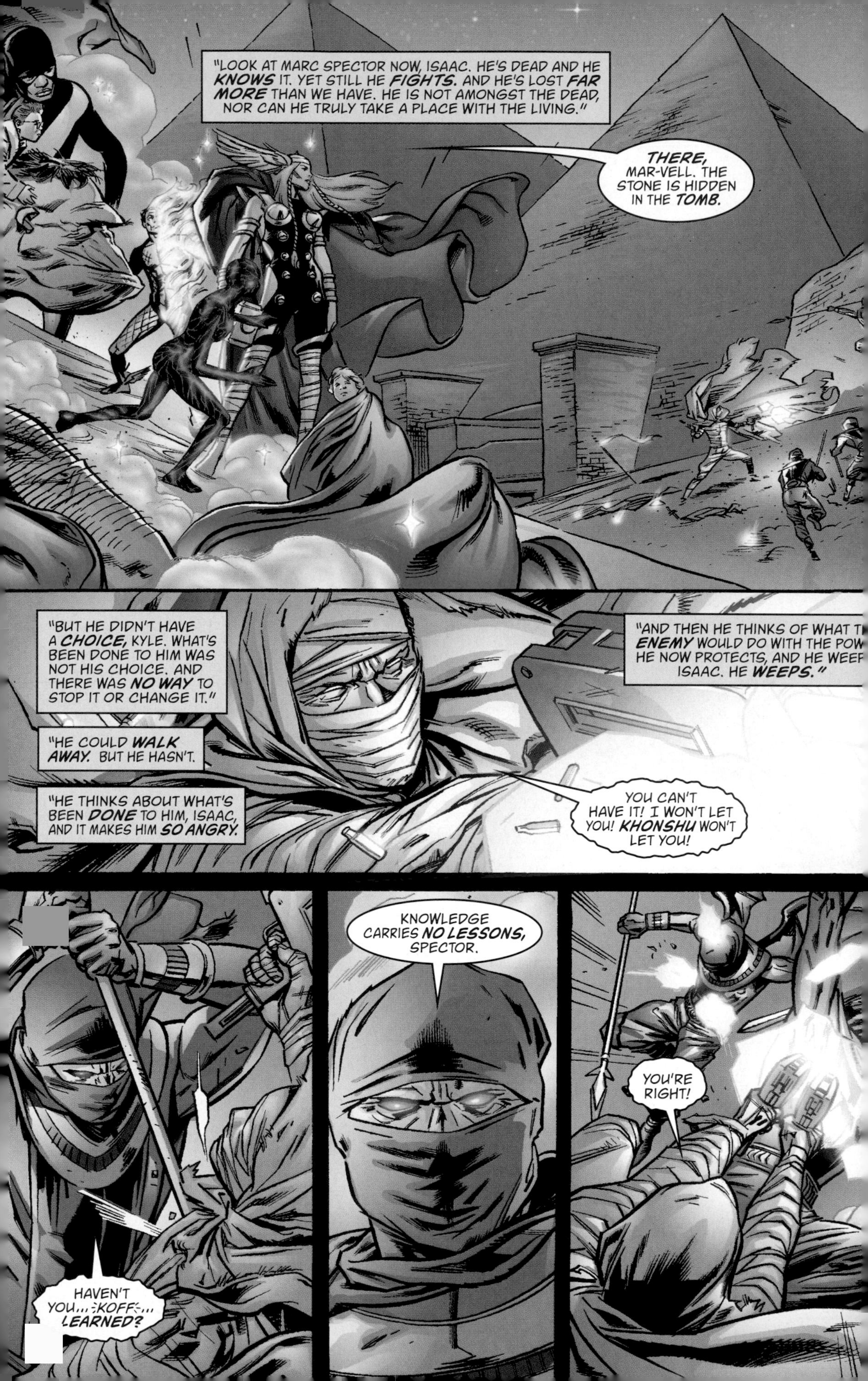
"LOOK AT MARC SPECTOR NOW, ISAAC. HE'S DEAD AND HE KNOWS IT. YET STILL HE FIGHTS. AND HE'S LOST FAR MORE THAN WE HAVE. HE IS NOT AMONGST THE DEAD, NOR CAN HE TRULY TAKE A PLACE WITH THE LIVING."
THERE, MAR-VELL. THE STONE IS HIDDEN IN THE TOMB.
"BUT HE DIDN'T HAVE A CHOICE, KYLE. WHAT'S BEEN DONE TO HIM WAS NOT HIS CHOICE. AND THERE WAS NO WAY TO STOP IT OR CHANGE IT."
"HE COULD WALK AWAY. BUT HE HASN'T.
"HE THINKS ABOUT WHAT'S BEEN DONE TO HIM, ISAAC, AND IT MAKES HIM SO ANGRY.
"AND THEN HE THINKS OF WHAT T ENEMY WOULD DO WITH THE POW HE NOW PROTECTS, AND HE WEEP ISAAC. HE WEEPS."
YOU CAN'T HAVE IT! I WON'T LET YOU! KHONSHU WON'T LET YOU!
HAVEN'T YOU... KOFF... LEARNED?
KNOWLEDGE CARRIES NO LESSONS, SPECTOR.
YOU'RE RIGHT!

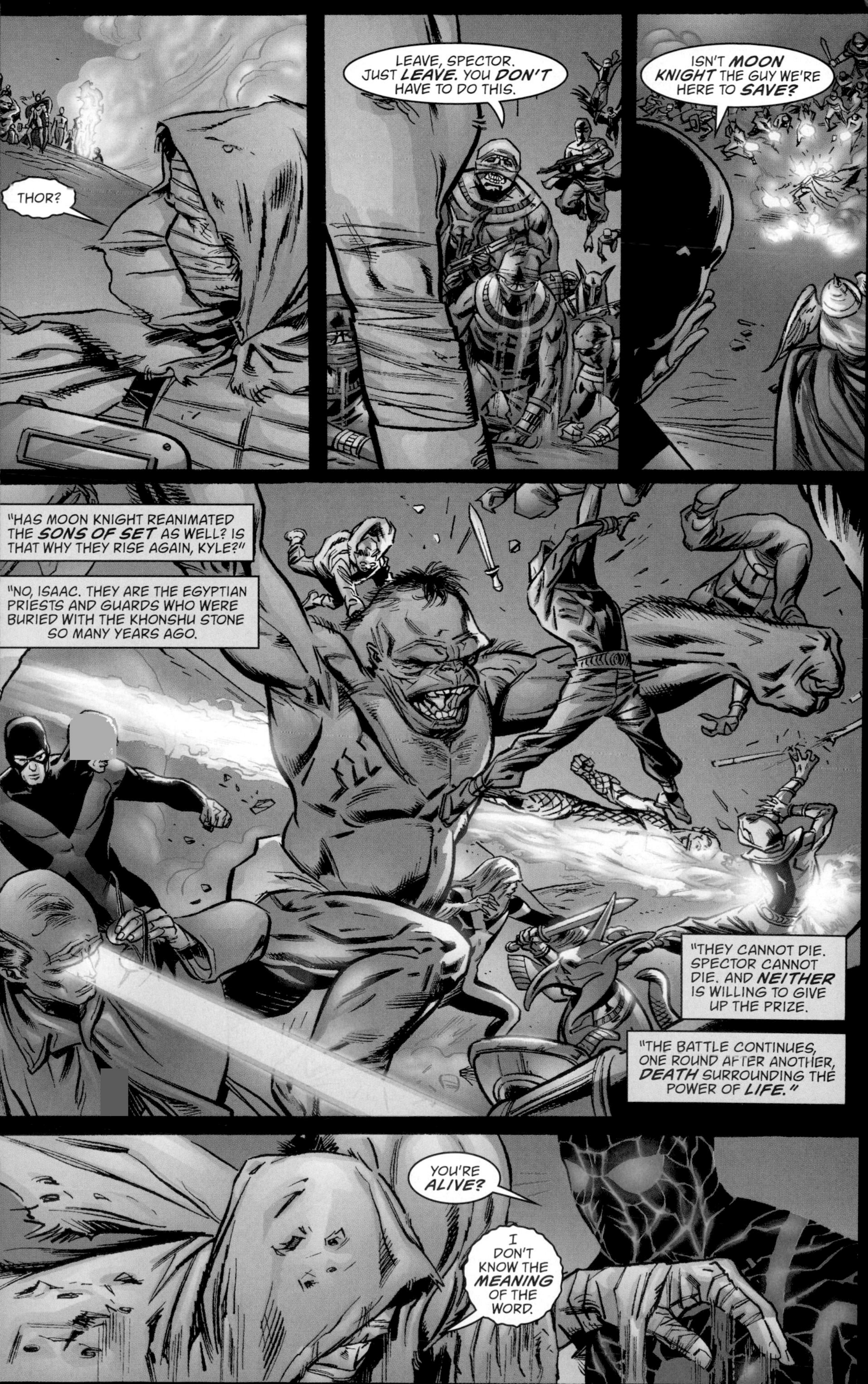
THOR?
LEAVE, SPECTOR. JUST LEAVE. YOU DON'T HAVE TO DO THIS.
ISN'T MOON KNIGHT THE GUY WE'RE HERE TO SAVE?
"HAS MOON KNIGHT REANIMATED THE SONS OF SET AS WELL? IS THAT WHY THEY RISE AGAIN, KYLE?"
"NO, ISAAC. THEY ARE THE EGYPTIAN PRIESTS AND GUARDS WHO WERE BURIED WITH THE KHONSHU STONE SO MANY YEARS AGO.
"THEY CANNOT DIE. SPECTOR CANNOT DIE. AND NEITHER IS WILLING TO GIVE UP THE PRIZE.
"THE BATTLE CONTINUES, ONE ROUND AFTER ANOTHER, DEATH SURROUNDING THE POWER OF LIFE."
YOU'RE ALIVE?
I DON'T KNOW THE MEANING OF THE WORD.

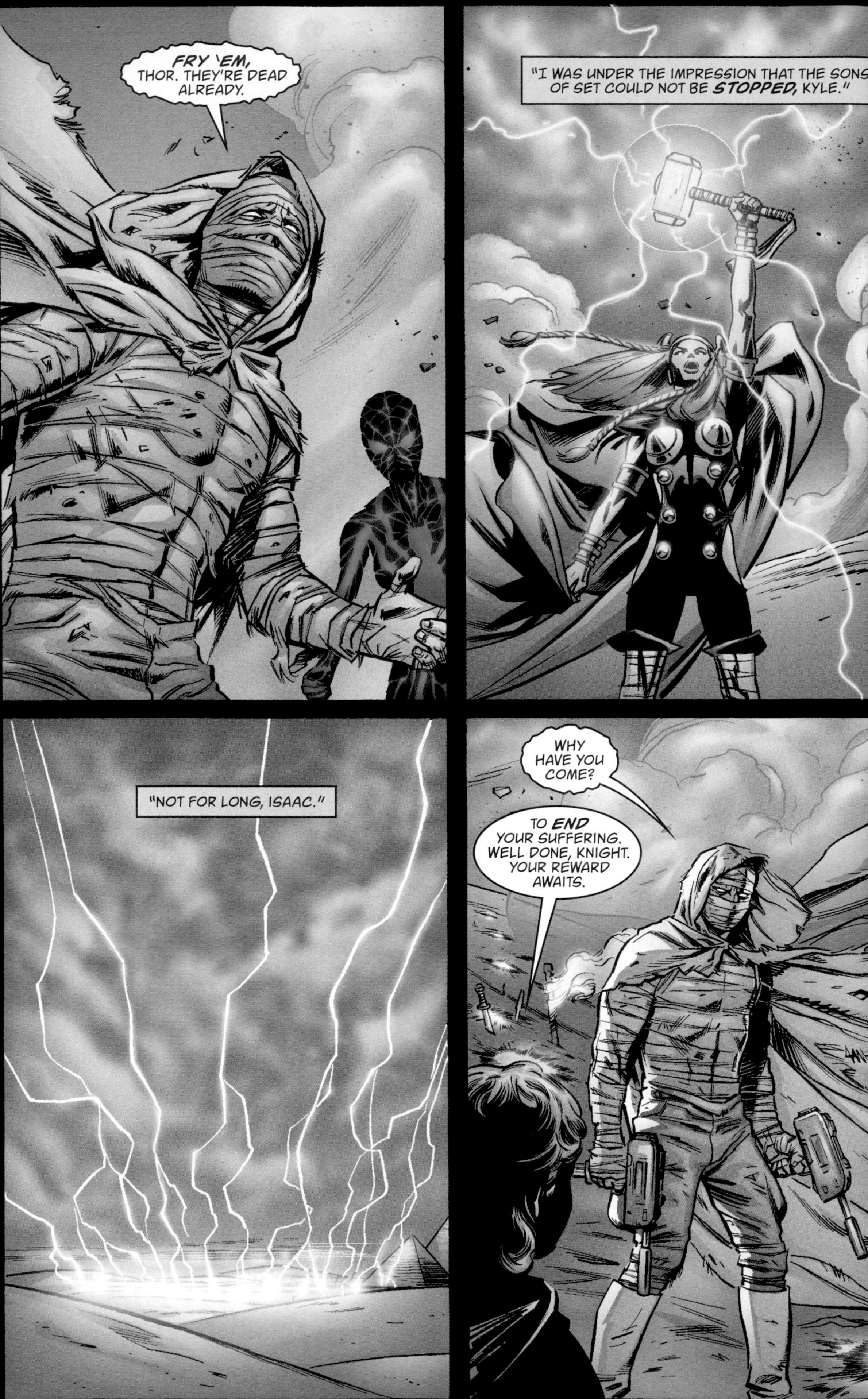
FRY 'EM, THOR. THEY'RE DEAD ALREADY.
"I WAS UNDER THE IMPRESSION THAT THE SONS OF SET COULD NOT BE STOPPED, KYLE."
"NOT FOR LONG, ISAAC."
WHY HAVE YOU COME?
TO END YOUR SUFFERING. WELL DONE, KNIGHT. YOUR REWARD AWAITS.

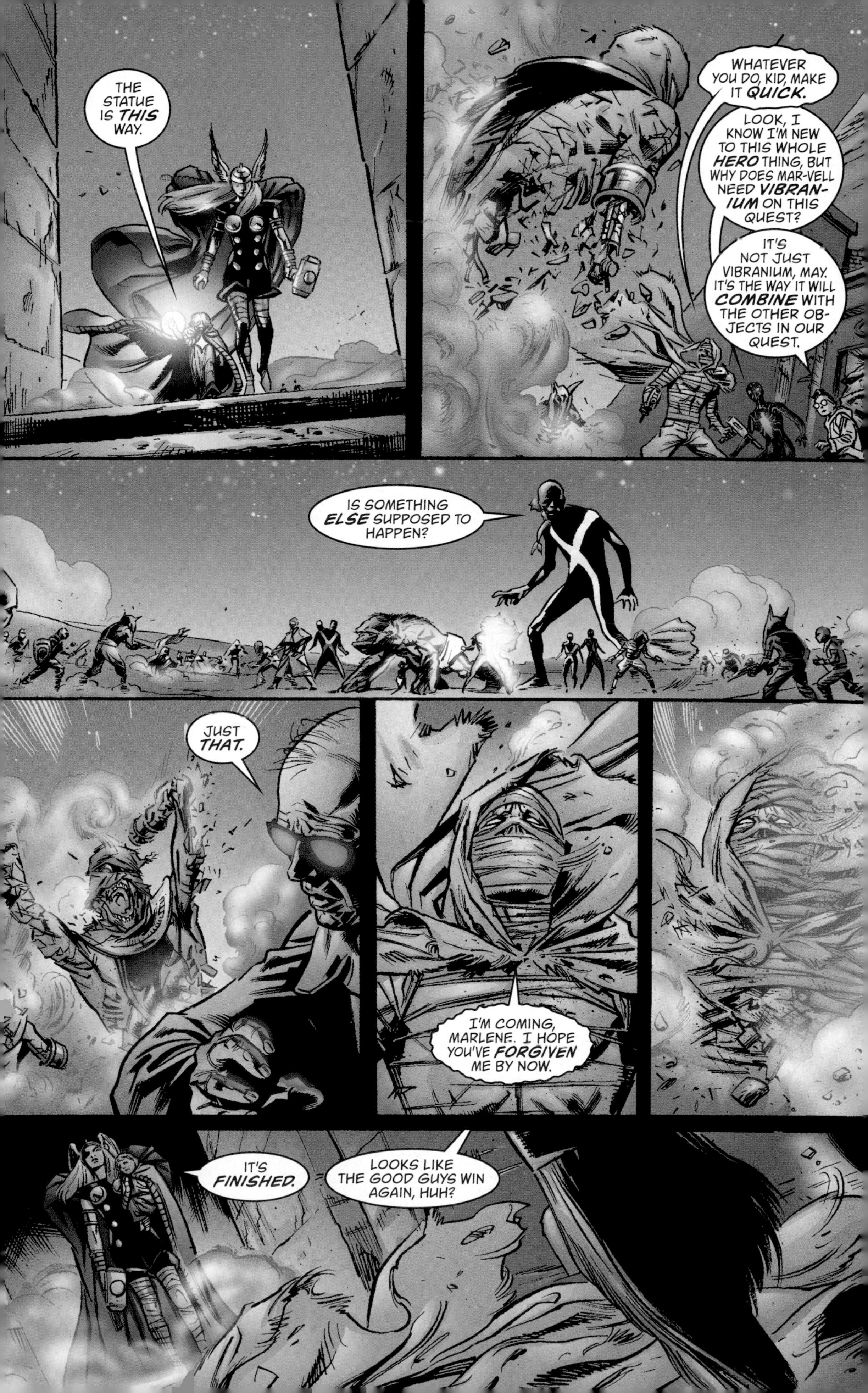
THE STATUE IS THIS WAY.
WHATEVER YOU DO, KID, MAKE IT QUICK.
LOOK, I KNOW I'M NEW TO THIS WHOLE HERO THING, BUT WHY DOES MAR-VELL NEED VIBRANIUM ON THIS QUEST?
IT'S NOT JUST VIBRANIUM, MAY. IT'S THE WAY IT WILL COMBINE WITH THE OTHER OBJECTS IN OUR QUEST.
IS SOMETHING ELSE SUPPOSED TO HAPPEN?
JUST THAT.
I'M COMING, MARLENE. I HOPE YOU'VE FORGIVEN ME BY NOW.
IT'S FINISHED.
LOOKS LIKE THE GOOD GUYS WIN AGAIN, HUH?

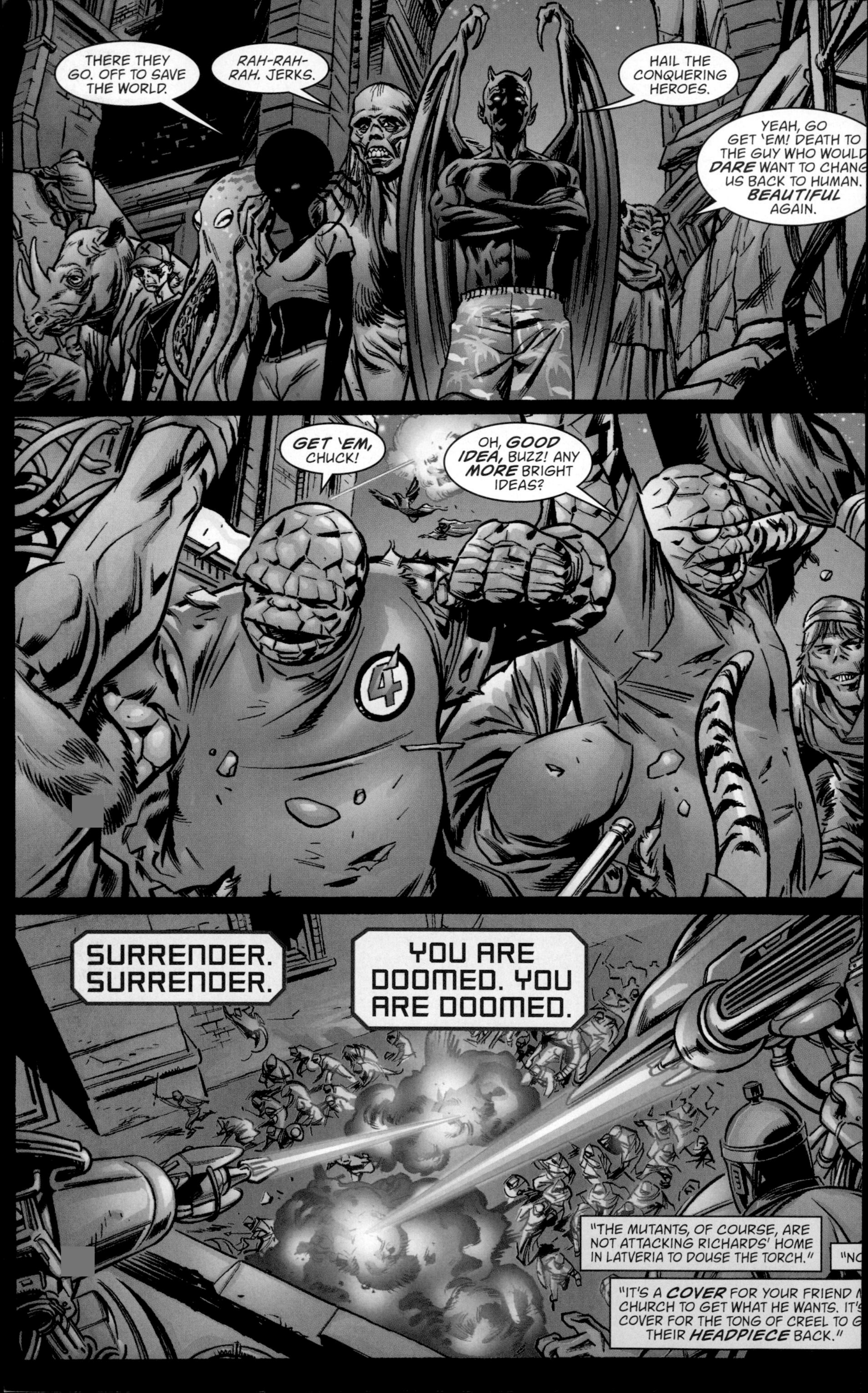

THERE THEY GO. OFF TO SAVE THE WORLD.
RAH-RAH-RAH. JERKS.
HAIL THE CONQUERING HEROES.
YEAH, GO GET 'EM! DEATH TO THE GUY WHO WOULD DARE WANT TO CHANG US BACK TO HUMAN. BEAUTIFUL AGAIN.
GET 'EM, CHUCK!
OH, GOOD IDEA, BUZZ! ANY MORE BRIGHT IDEAS?
SURRENDER. SURRENDER.
YOU ARE DOOMED. YOU ARE DOOMED.
"THE MUTANTS, OF COURSE, ARE NOT ATTACKING RICHARDS' HOME IN LATVERIA TO DOUSE THE TORCH."
"IT'S A COVER FOR YOUR FRIEND CHURCH TO GET WHAT HE WANTS. IT'S COVER FOR THE TONG OF CREEL TO G THEIR HEADPIECE BACK."

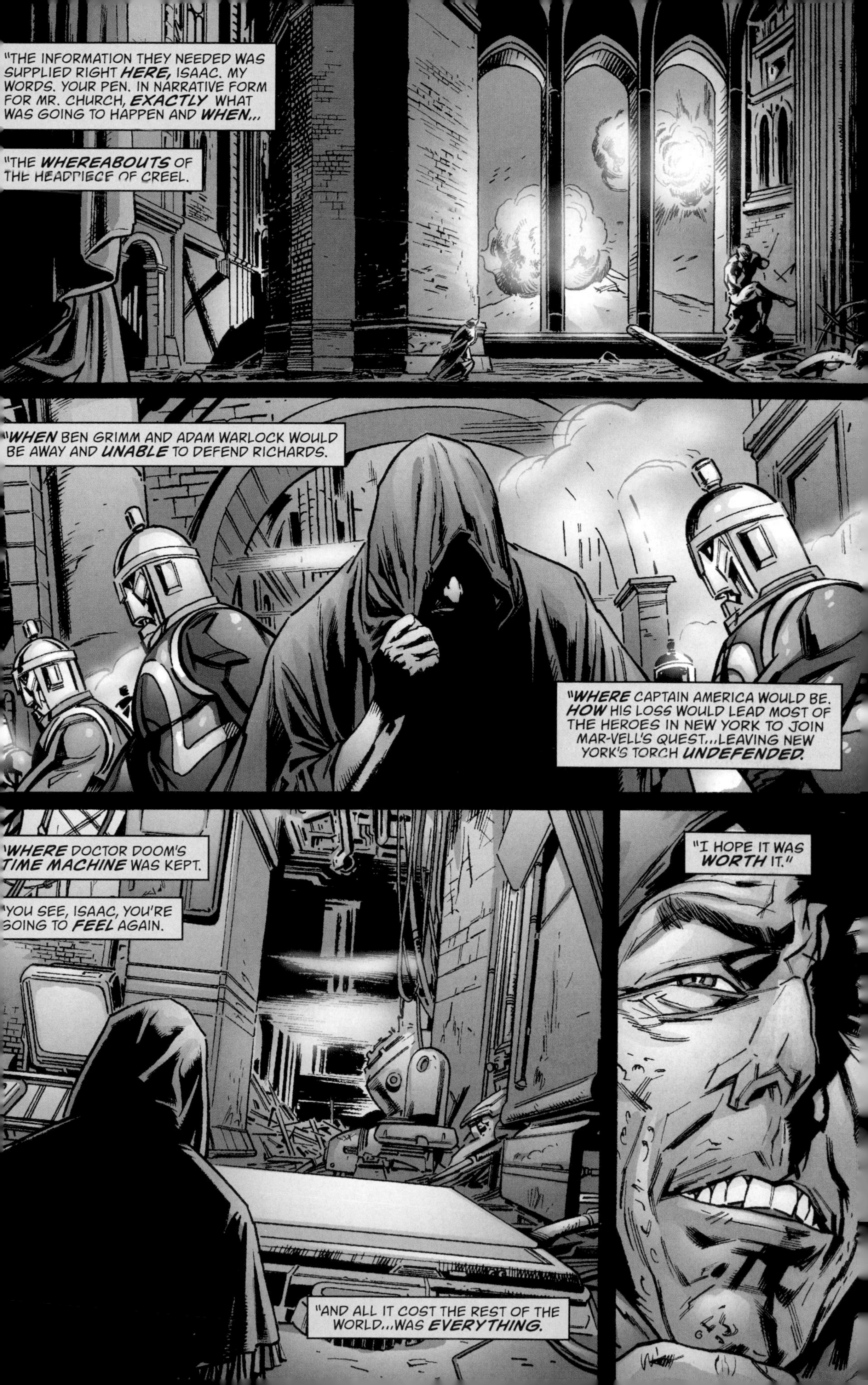
"THE INFORMATION THEY NEEDED WAS SUPPLIED RIGHT HERE, ISAAC. MY WORDS. YOUR PEN. IN NARRATIVE FORM FOR MR. CHURCH, EXACTLY WHAT WAS GOING TO HAPPEN AND WHEN...
"THE WHEREABOUTS OF THE HEADPIECE OF CREEL.
"WHEN BEN GRIMM AND ADAM WARLOCK WOULD BE AWAY AND UNABLE TO DEFEND RICHARDS.
"WHERE CAPTAIN AMERICA WOULD BE. HOW HIS LOSS WOULD LEAD MOST OF THE HEROES IN NEW YORK TO JOIN MAR-VELL'S QUEST...LEAVING NEW YORK'S TORCH UNDEFENDED.
"WHERE DOCTOR DOOM'S TIME MACHINE WAS KEPT.
"YOU SEE, ISAAC, YOU'RE GOING TO FEEL AGAIN.
"AND ALL IT COST THE REST OF THE WORLD...WAS EVERYTHING.
"I HOPE IT WAS WORTH IT."

WERE YOU ABLE TO GET THE *MANDARIN'S RINGS,* LORD SUNFIRE?

YES. AND WHAT OF THE *RE-ANIMATOR STONE?*

SHWUF

GROSS.

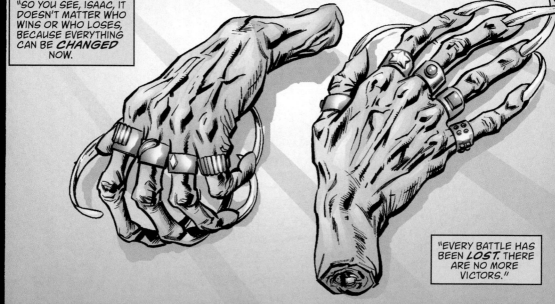

"SO YOU SEE, ISAAC, IT DOESN'T MATTER WHO WINS OR WHO LOSES, BECAUSE EVERYTHING CAN BE *CHANGED* NOW.

"EVERY BATTLE HAS BEEN *LOST.* THERE ARE NO MORE VICTORS."

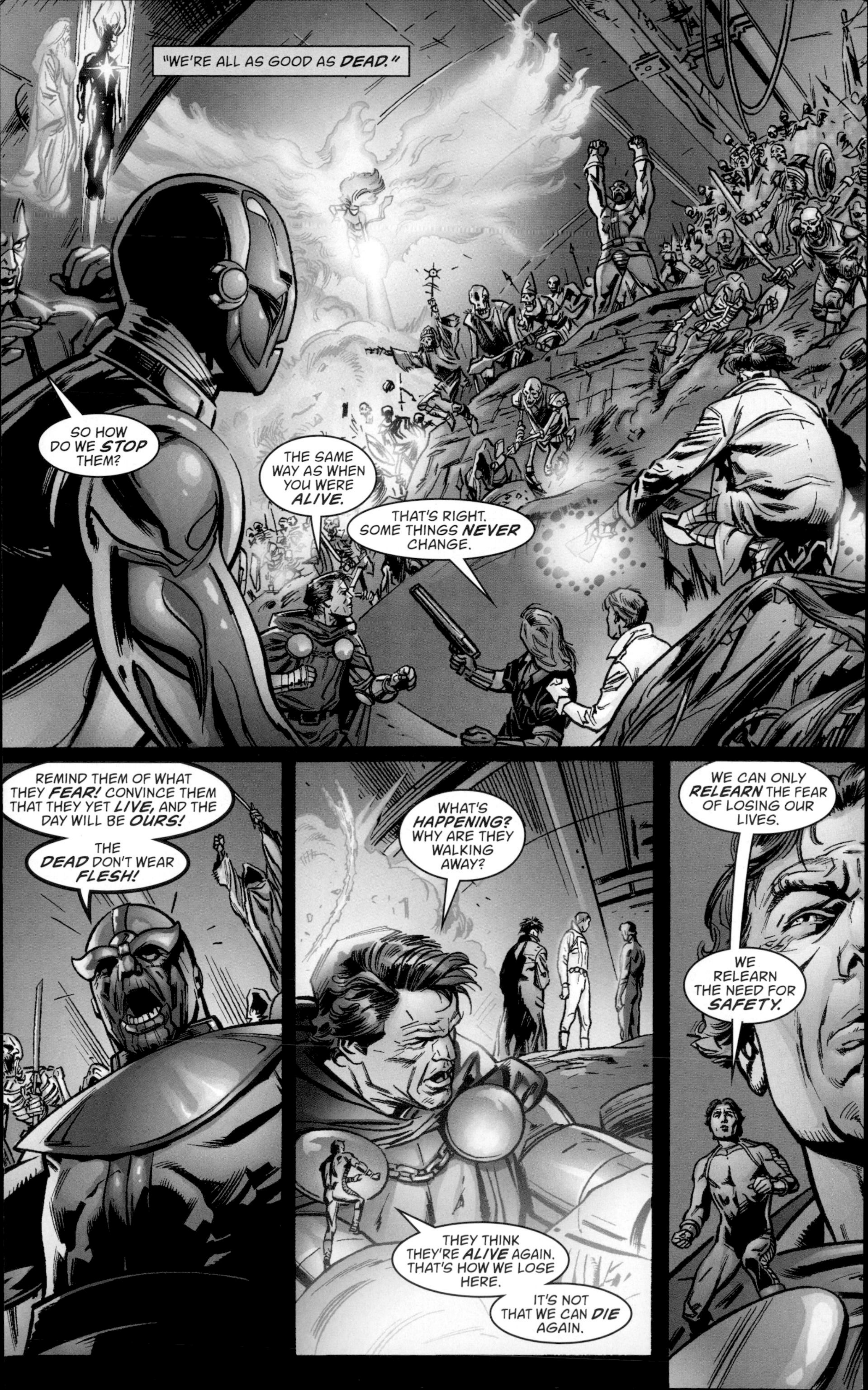
"WE'RE ALL AS GOOD AS DEAD."
SO HOW DO WE STOP THEM?
THE SAME WAY AS WHEN YOU WERE ALIVE.
THAT'S RIGHT. SOME THINGS NEVER CHANGE.
REMIND THEM OF WHAT THEY FEAR! CONVINCE THEM THAT THEY YET LIVE, AND THE DAY WILL BE OURS!
THE DEAD DON'T WEAR FLESH!
WHAT'S HAPPENING? WHY ARE THEY WALKING AWAY?
THEY THINK THEY'RE ALIVE AGAIN. THAT'S HOW WE LOSE HERE.
IT'S NOT THAT WE CAN DIE AGAIN.
WE CAN ONLY RELEARN THE FEAR OF LOSING OUR LIVES.
WE RELEARN THE NEED FOR SAFETY.

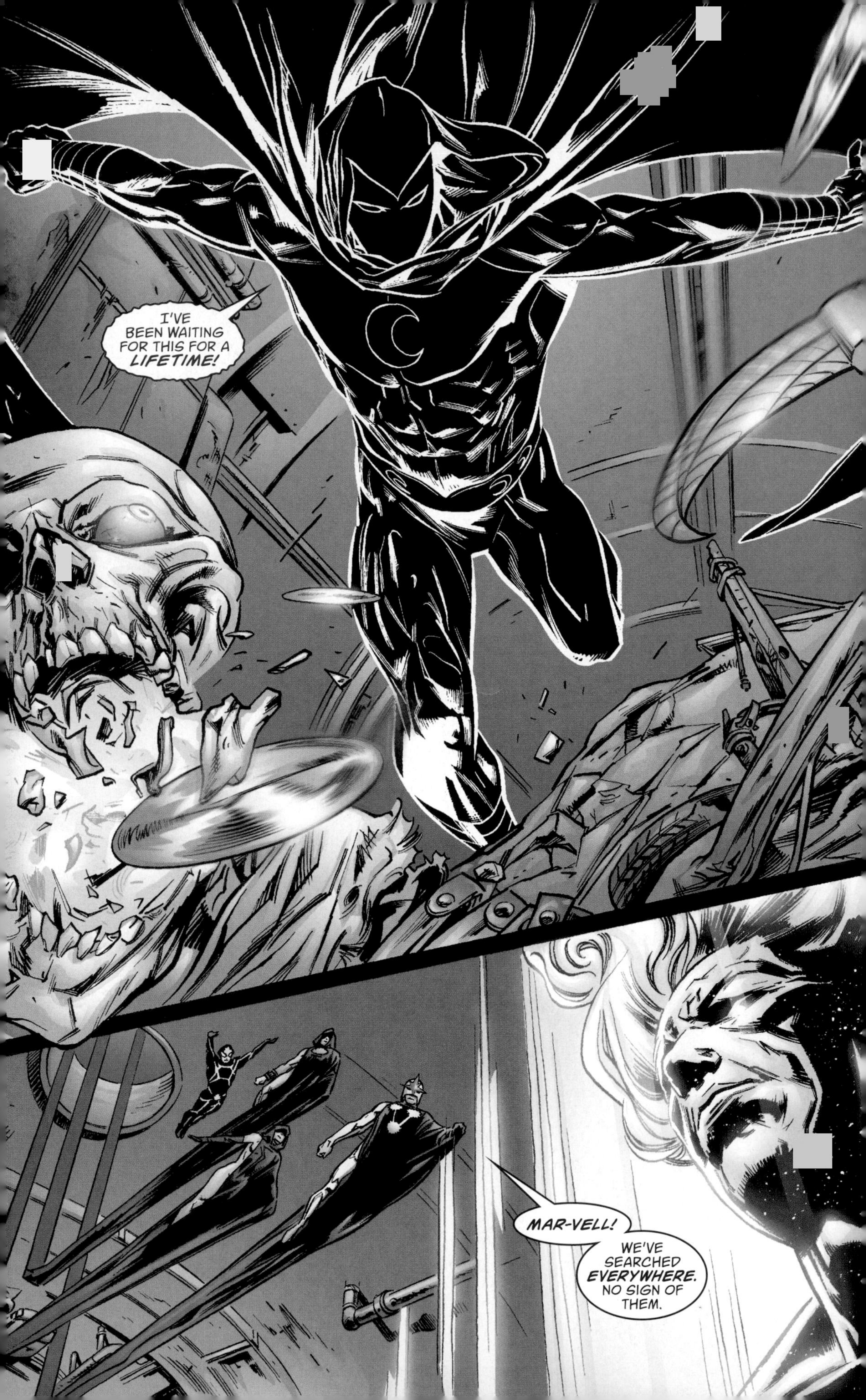
I'VE BEEN WAITING FOR THIS FOR A *LIFETIME!*
MAR-VELL!
WE'VE SEARCHED *EVERYWHERE.* NO SIGN OF THEM.

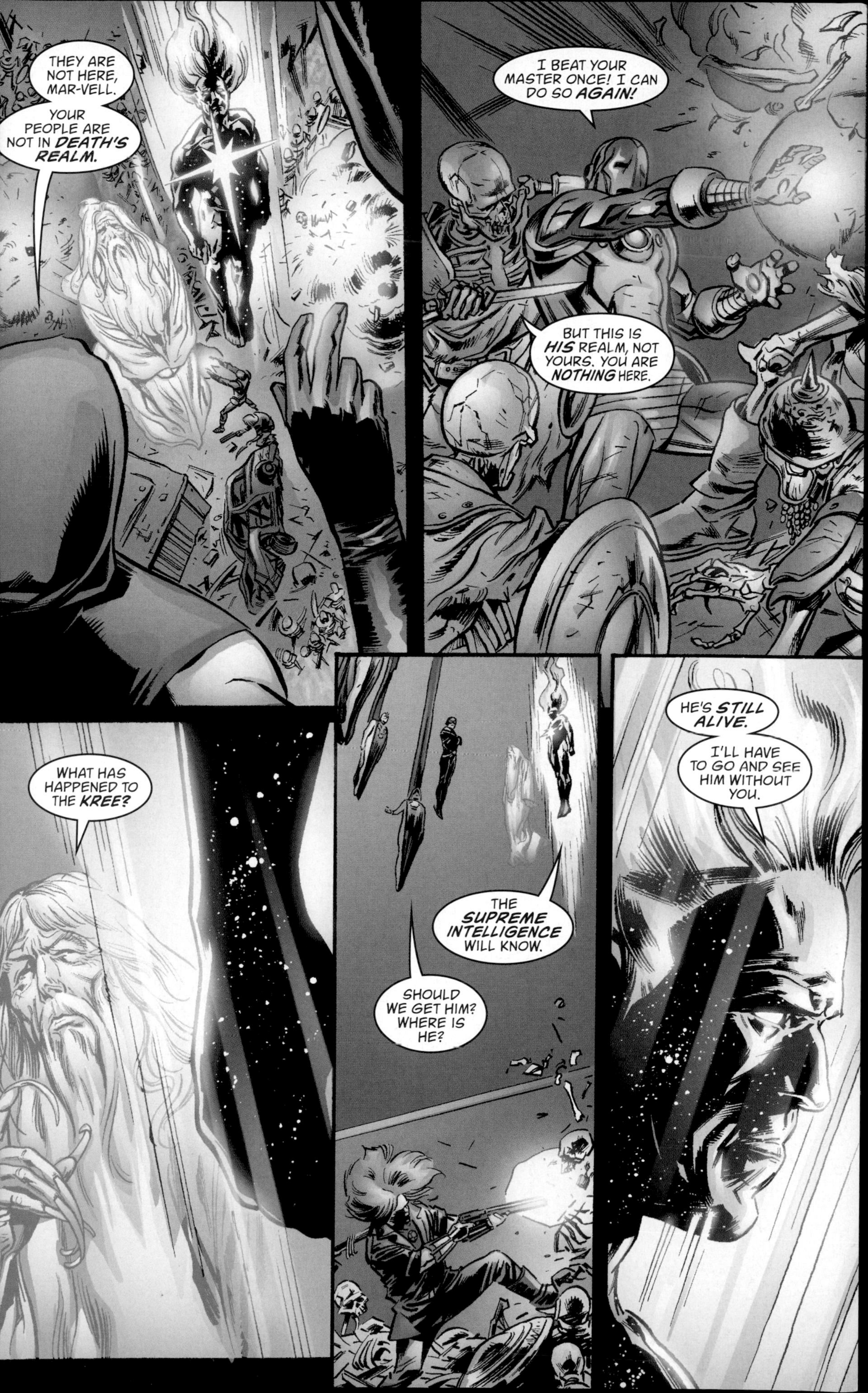
THEY ARE NOT HERE, MAR-VELL.
YOUR PEOPLE ARE NOT IN DEATH'S REALM.
I BEAT YOUR MASTER ONCE! I CAN DO SO AGAIN!
BUT THIS IS HIS REALM, NOT YOURS. YOU ARE NOTHING HERE.
WHAT HAS HAPPENED TO THE KREE?
THE SUPREME INTELLIGENCE WILL KNOW.
SHOULD WE GET HIM? WHERE IS HE?
HE'S STILL ALIVE.
I'LL HAVE TO GO AND SEE HIM WITHOUT YOU.

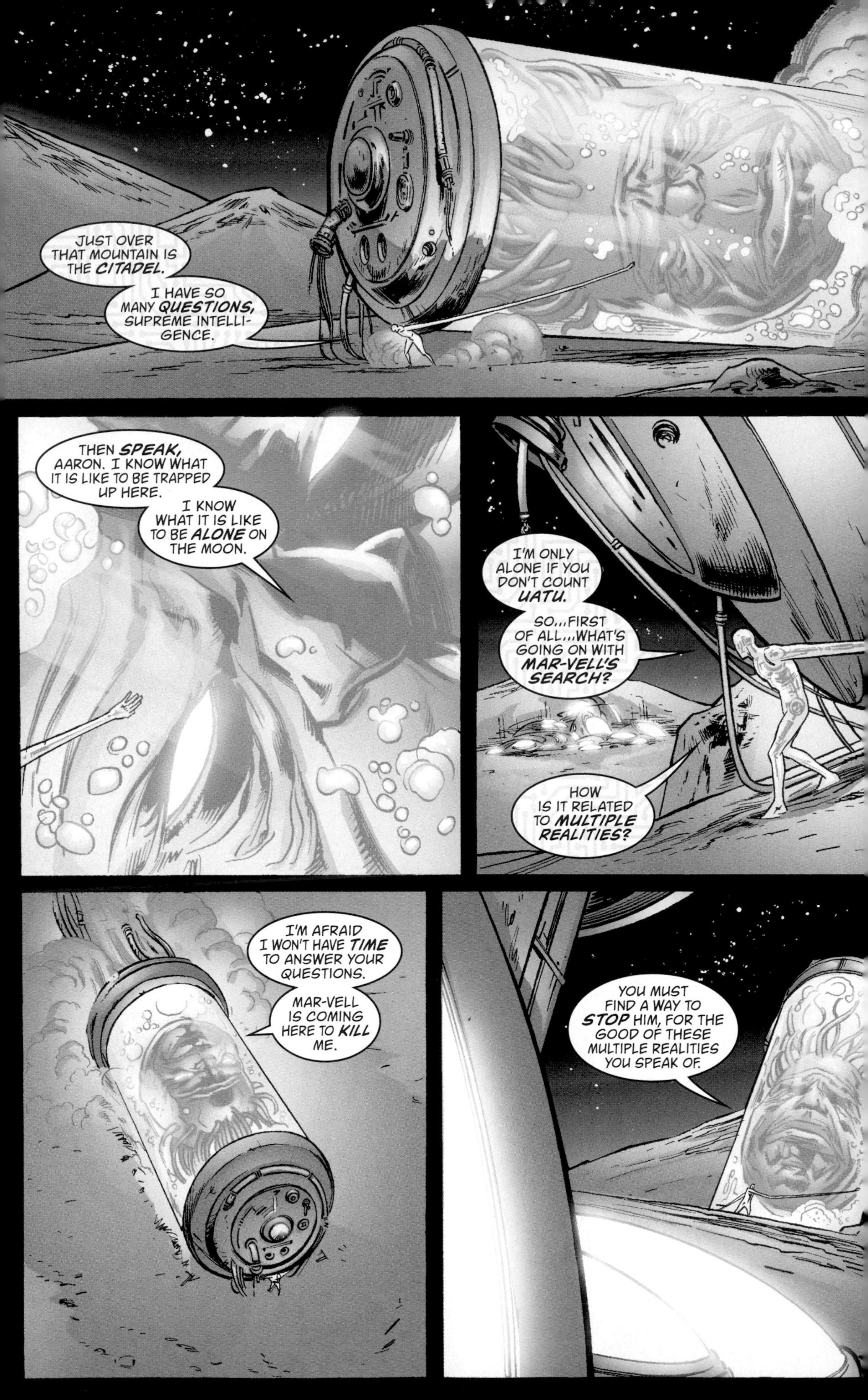

JUST OVER THAT MOUNTAIN IS THE CITADEL.
I HAVE SO MANY QUESTIONS, SUPREME INTELLI-GENCE.
THEN SPEAK, AARON. I KNOW WHAT IT IS LIKE TO BE TRAPPED UP HERE.
I KNOW WHAT IT IS LIKE TO BE ALONE ON THE MOON.
I'M ONLY ALONE IF YOU DON'T COUNT UATU.
SO...FIRST OF ALL...WHAT'S GOING ON WITH MAR-VELL'S SEARCH?
HOW IS IT RELATED TO MULTIPLE REALITIES?
I'M AFRAID I WON'T HAVE TIME TO ANSWER YOUR QUESTIONS.
MAR-VELL IS COMING HERE TO KILL ME.
YOU MUST FIND A WAY TO STOP HIM, FOR THE GOOD OF THESE MULTIPLE REALITIES YOU SPEAK OF.

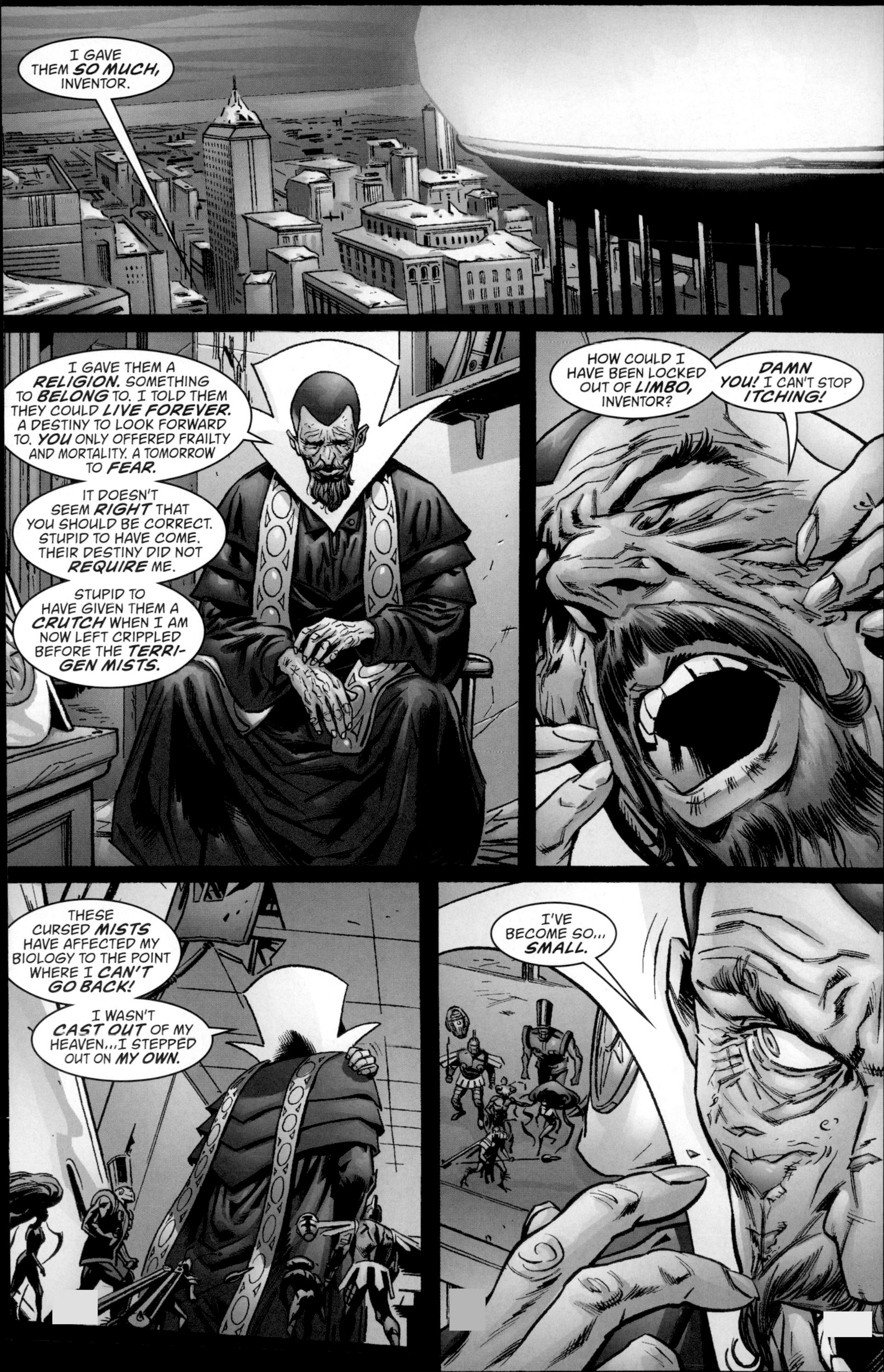
I GAVE THEM SO MUCH, INVENTOR.
I GAVE THEM A RELIGION. SOMETHING TO BELONG TO. I TOLD THEM THEY COULD LIVE FOREVER. A DESTINY TO LOOK FORWARD TO. YOU ONLY OFFERED FRAILTY AND MORTALITY. A TOMORROW TO FEAR.
IT DOESN'T SEEM RIGHT THAT YOU SHOULD BE CORRECT. STUPID TO HAVE COME. THEIR DESTINY DID NOT REQUIRE ME.
STUPID TO HAVE GIVEN THEM A CRUTCH WHEN I AM NOW LEFT CRIPPLED BEFORE THE TERRI-GEN MISTS.
HOW COULD I HAVE BEEN LOCKED OUT OF LIMBO, INVENTOR?
DAMN YOU! I CAN'T STOP ITCHING!
THESE CURSED MISTS HAVE AFFECTED MY BIOLOGY TO THE POINT WHERE I CAN'T GO BACK!
I WASN'T CAST OUT OF MY HEAVEN...I STEPPED OUT ON MY OWN.
I'VE BECOME SO... SMALL.

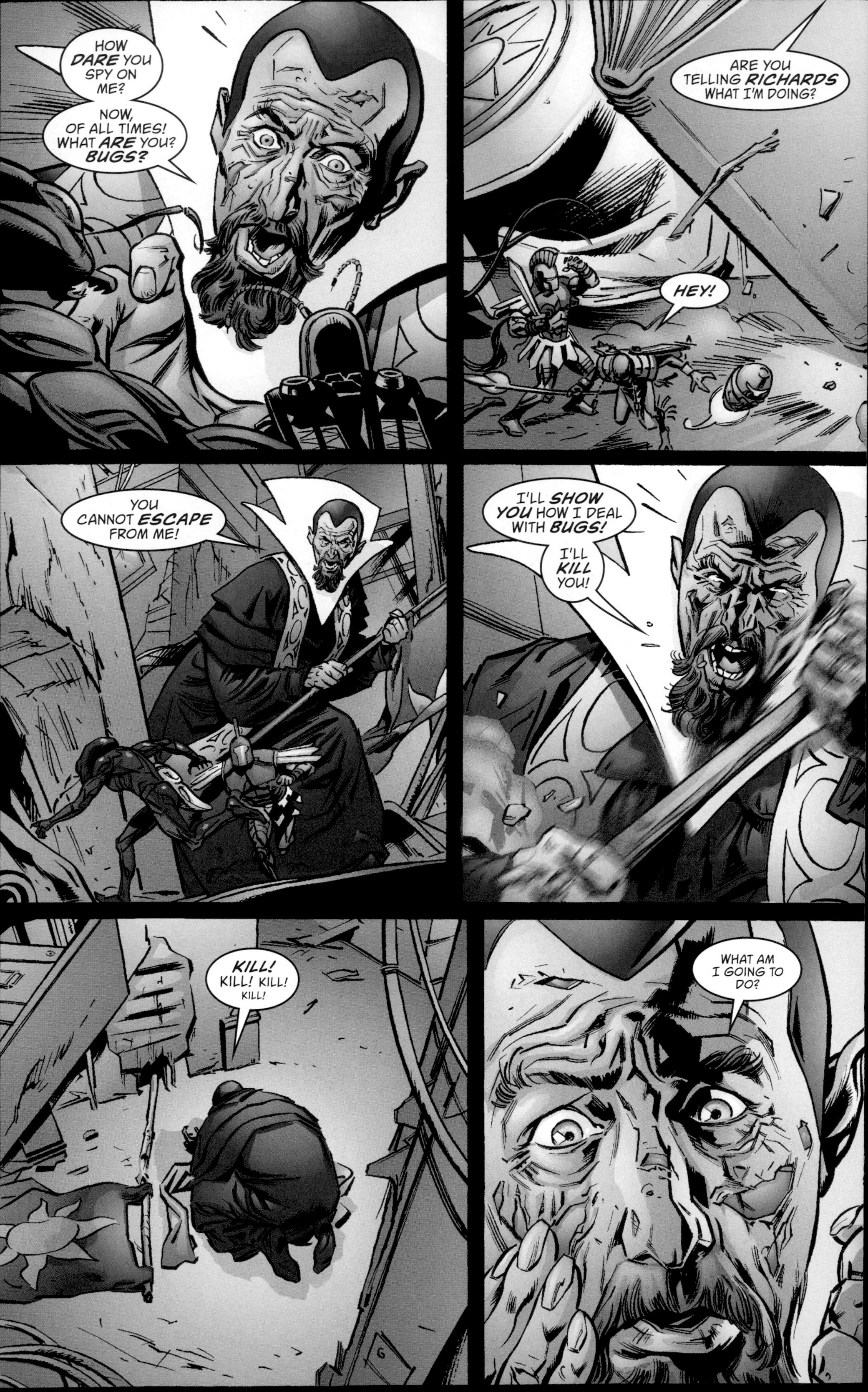
HOW DARE YOU SPY ON ME?
NOW, OF ALL TIMES! WHAT ARE YOU? BUGS?
ARE YOU TELLING RICHARDS WHAT I'M DOING?
HEY!
YOU CANNOT ESCAPE FROM ME!
I'LL SHOW YOU HOW I DEAL WITH BUGS!
I'LL KILL YOU!
KILL! KILL! KILL! KILL!
WHAT AM I GOING TO DO?

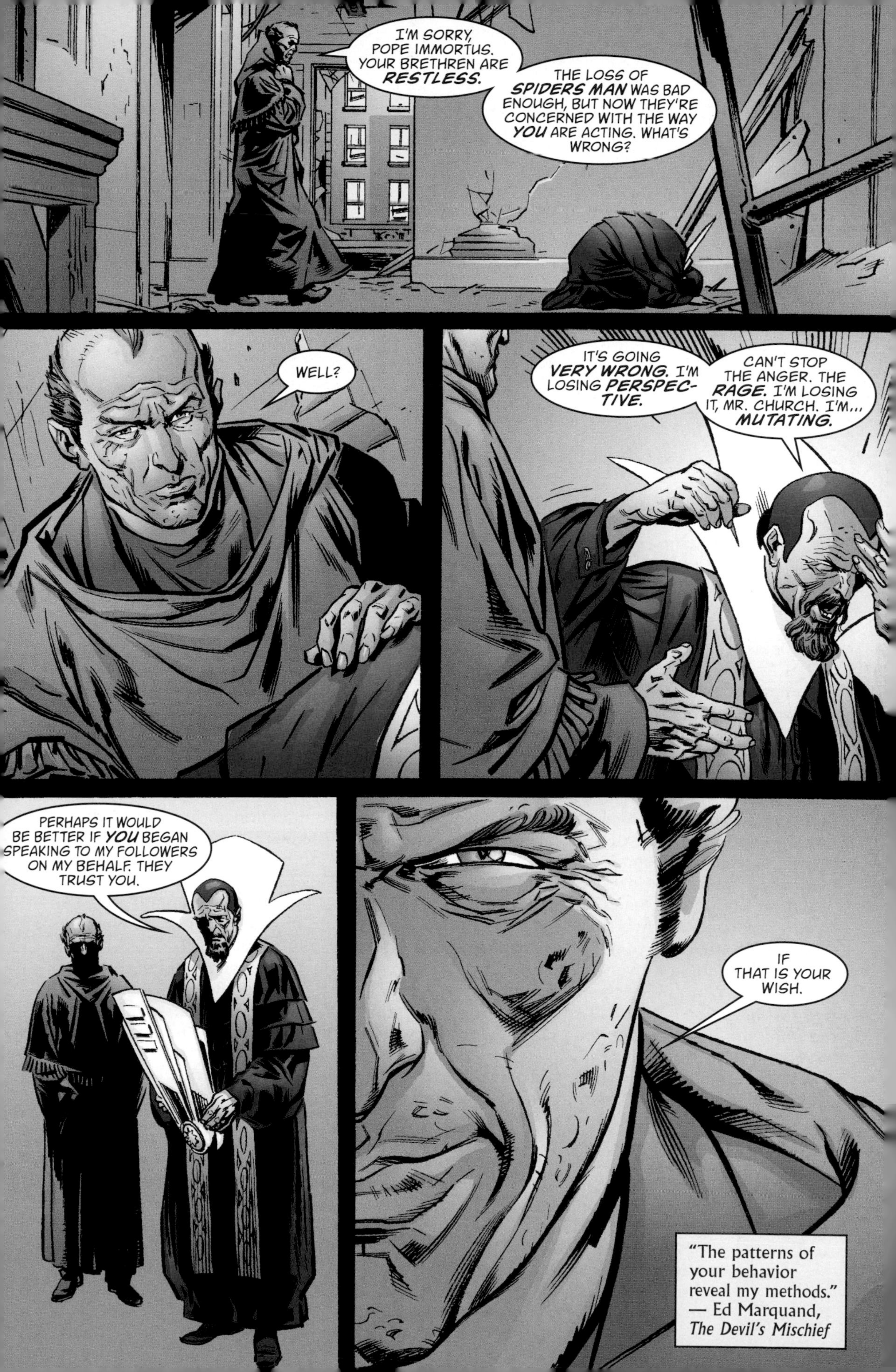
I'M SORRY, POPE IMMORTUS. YOUR BRETHREN ARE RESTLESS.
THE LOSS OF SPIDERS MAN WAS BAD ENOUGH, BUT NOW THEY'RE CONCERNED WITH THE WAY YOU ARE ACTING. WHAT'S WRONG?
WELL?
IT'S GOING VERY WRONG. I'M LOSING PERSPEC-TIVE.
CAN'T STOP THE ANGER. THE RAGE. I'M LOSING IT, MR. CHURCH. I'M... MUTATING.
PERHAPS IT WOULD BE BETTER IF YOU BEGAN SPEAKING TO MY FOLLOWERS ON MY BEHALF. THEY TRUST YOU.
IF THAT IS YOUR WISH.
"The patterns of your behavior reveal my methods."
— Ed Marquand, *The Devil's Mischief*

U N I V E R S E X

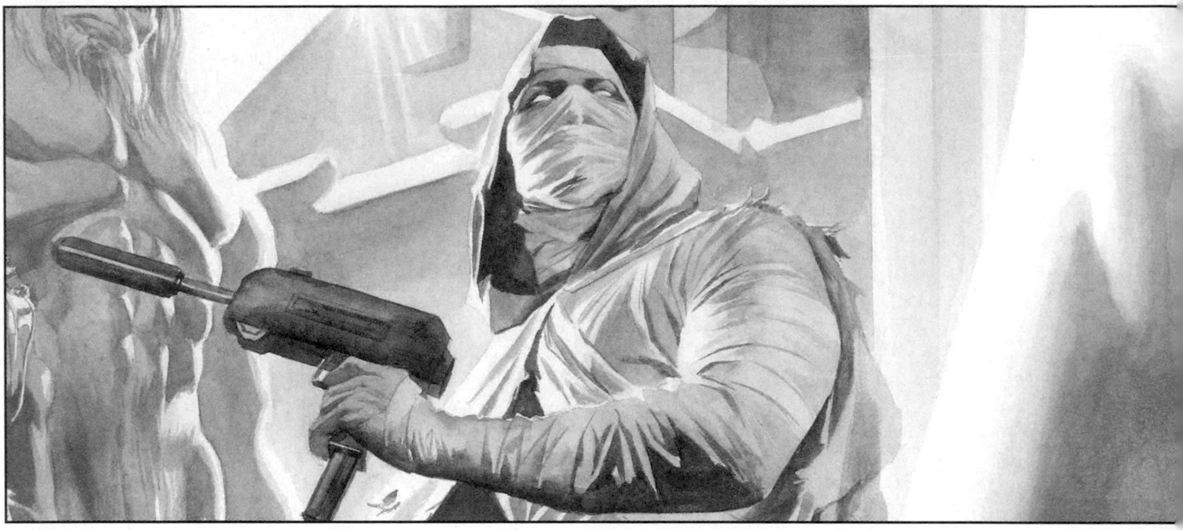

APPENDIX TO CHAPTER SIX

WRITTEN BY JIM KRUEGER

"Continuing the internal monologue in regards to the events of the past few days. This monologue will serve as warning and basis for understanding all the events occurring simultaneously upon planet Earth. My name is Aaron Stack. I am my planet's watchman. its keeper.

"This may be, to an extent, a countermeasure to the volume currently written upon the planet Earth by Kyle Richmond and Isaac Christians. But to the degree that Richmond and Christians tell of events in the near future, I will continue, as best I can, to chronicle the happenings of this present day.

"Perhaps the best I can offer of this endeavor is a bird's eye view of sorts to better understand the purpose of the details and conflicts engaged in upon the Earth.

"The world is not unlike those periods of time when all countries seemed to be at war with each other. The inconsistency of the planet's polarities has affected those things its inhabitants took on faith, that all other such foundations are now being questioned. As a result, the morality and rationality of mutanity are indeed now questionable. Whether this is due to the aggressive seed implanted by the Celestials in all of mankind or the loss of certainty in its own world, I do not know.

"Or perhaps this present chaos is due to the loss of this world's champions. The Avengers. Iron Man. And now, Captain America. Can a world dependent upon its champions to establish the rules of behavior survive once those champions are gone?

"Somehow, this all revolves around Richmond. I'm not certain how, yet. But it does. His vision is mutating. Why? What has happened in the last three years that would cause a second wave of mutation? Once, he could only see the future. But now, he seems capable of seeing the past, the ancient histories of other worlds, even into the hearts and mindsets of those who have long since died.

"Interestingly enough, there is a sort of blindness that has come with this second sight. Neither Richmond nor Christians seems to see how all of this is coming together. What secret patterns will these patchwork conflicts reveal once we pull away from them?

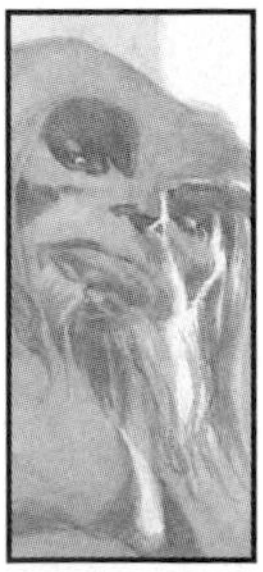

"In Egypt, the battle for the Khonshu re-animator stone has ended. All those whose physical being was extended as a result of its power, have turned to ash. This is not only referring to Marc Spector or to the Followers of Set, but also to the woman Spector claimed to love, Marlene, and his retired assistant, Frenchie. Spector's brother has crumbled to dust as well.

"In South Africa, the Living Mummy, Chief N'Kantu, collapsed, after months of attempting to break through an energy-based barrier surrounding the African realm of Wakanda. There will be no recognition save this recording for the wandering king who had been a slave in ancient Egypt.

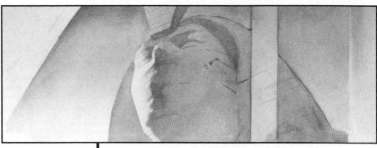

"Some might say there is no pattern here.

"But the fall of the Moon's Knight is yet another piece played on this chessboard match between Mar-Vell and Death. Mar-Vell now has the re-animator stone. For what purpose I know not, but his power is growing. He has already added the power of the Books of the Darkhold and Vishanti, Anti-Metal, the Orb of Agomotto, the Psycho-Man's Emotion Caster, and the Mandarin's Power Rings. Mar-Vell's power continues to grow. I wonder at times if the remaining heroes of Earth should trust Mar-Vell so easily. I wonder what they see that perhaps I cannot. It is obvious that I am, to some degree, incomplete. There are places Richmond can see that I cannot. Perhaps this is true to humanity as well. Do they see things in themselves that I cannot? How limited was my father in building a living computer?

"In Latveria, one of the last of Reed Richards' Human Torches may fall this very day… Richards reprogrammed the Doombots to protect the castle without killing those who would kill him without thinking. But Mr. Church is there as well, and I wonder if perhaps there isn't far more to him than the lackey he pretends to be.

"I cannot find a childhood for Mr. Church. There is no history for me to watch here on the moon. It is as if he was born shortly after Immortus began his opposition to Richards' plan to cure the world of its mutations.

"In Canada, Sasquatch and James MacDonald are the only members of Alpha Flight to have escaped death. As well as the destruction of the Human Torch that once burned there so brightly. But how long have they escaped? Even now they are being tracked by a race whose basic biological basis is similar, perhaps too similar to that of Wolverine. Are they perhaps Logan's children?"

The battle for these Human Torches has now changed hands. It is no longer Immortus who leads his armies against Richards' Torches, but Mr. Church himself… the very bookbinder who has been collecting page after page of future visions given from the pen and words of Richmond and Christians. There are only a few still remaining in the world. New York. Latveria. The Savage Land. Japan.

"I now see a pattern forming and fear that if the armies of Immortus should win the world before the power collection of Mar-Vell's is completed, the battle will be lost in the land of the dead along with the skirmishes being fought here in the land of the living. There is a convergence of these two conflicts I had not considered.

"Where I had believed there was only chaos, I see order now. I see strategy. According to Richmond's writings, Mar-Vell and his followers will be coming here to the moon next.

"I hope Mar-Vell is aware that the Supreme Intelligence is waiting for him. I hope he is aware that the Intelligence means for me to betray Mar-Vell.

"But if I betray Mar-Vell, do I betray all those who have died? Do I betray my father, the man who built me?"

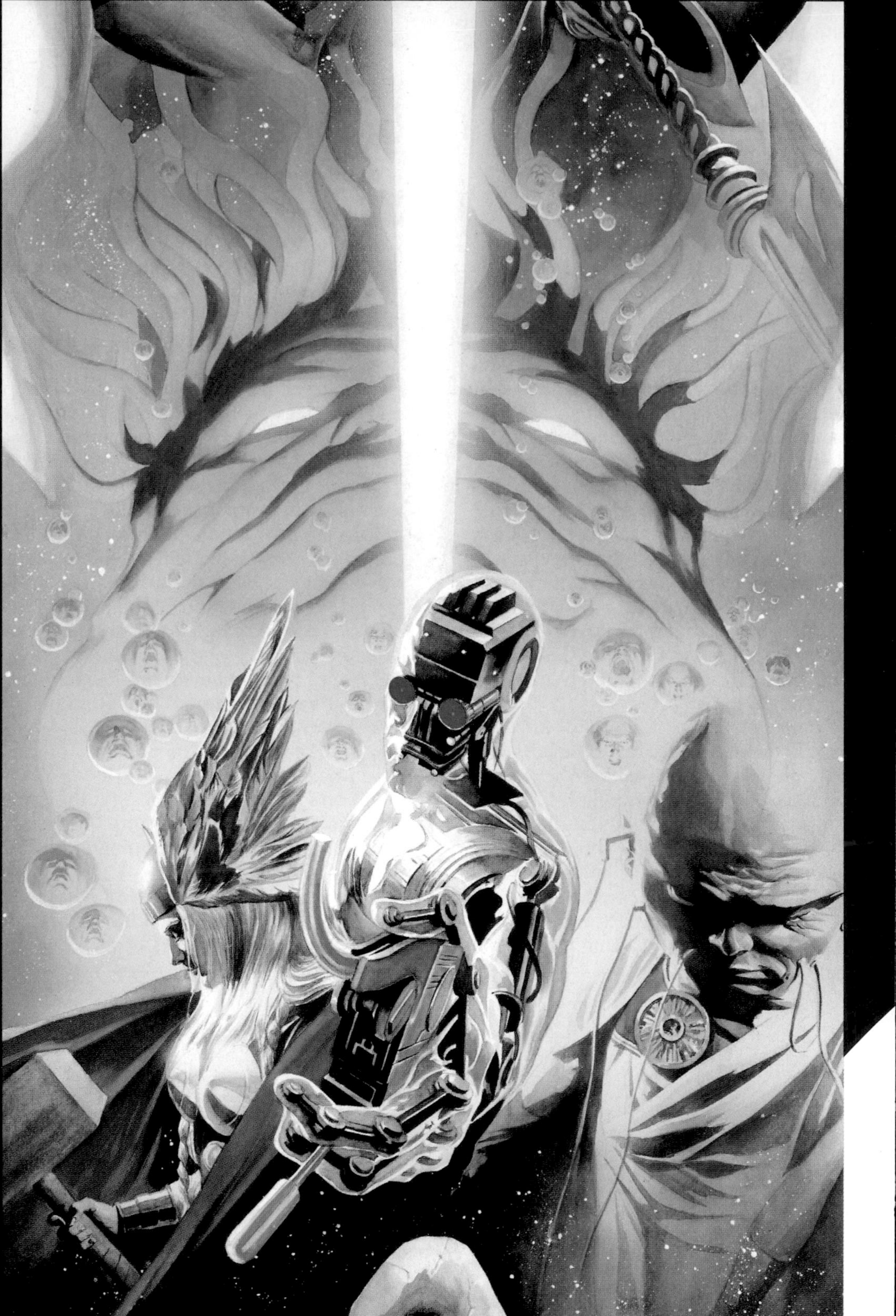

CHAPTER SEVEN

"Mr. Church is only an underling in Immortus's army, Kyle.
He is a second tier mystic. That's all."

"As bad as things are going to be for the rest of us, it's going to be far worse for you,
Isaac. You've survived wars. You've fought as a member of the Defenders. You've
endured so much. How could you be so naïve?"

"I am twice your age, Kyle. What the young call naivete is the wisdom of the aged. Youth
is, indeed, wasted upon the young. Your visions do not always come to pass. You cannot
guarantee your vision will come true. Life...even the life of one who can peer into the
future, does not offer guarantees."

"I have not seen what will happen, Isaac."

"No? No? Well then, there it is. I have nothing to fear."

"I can't see what's going to happen, Isaac, because it's already happened. I'm sorry."

"But Mr. Church..."

"Do you really think that's his real name, Isaac?"

"What do you mean? Have you seen him transform into someone else?
Have you seen him unmask, so to speak?"

"I have seen him in all his faces, Isaac. Mr. Church is the Adversary I have spoken of."

"No. You are wrong. I have a right to feel again. This is my time. This is my day."

"The future repeats the past, Isaac. Night always follows day.
Let me tell you a story."

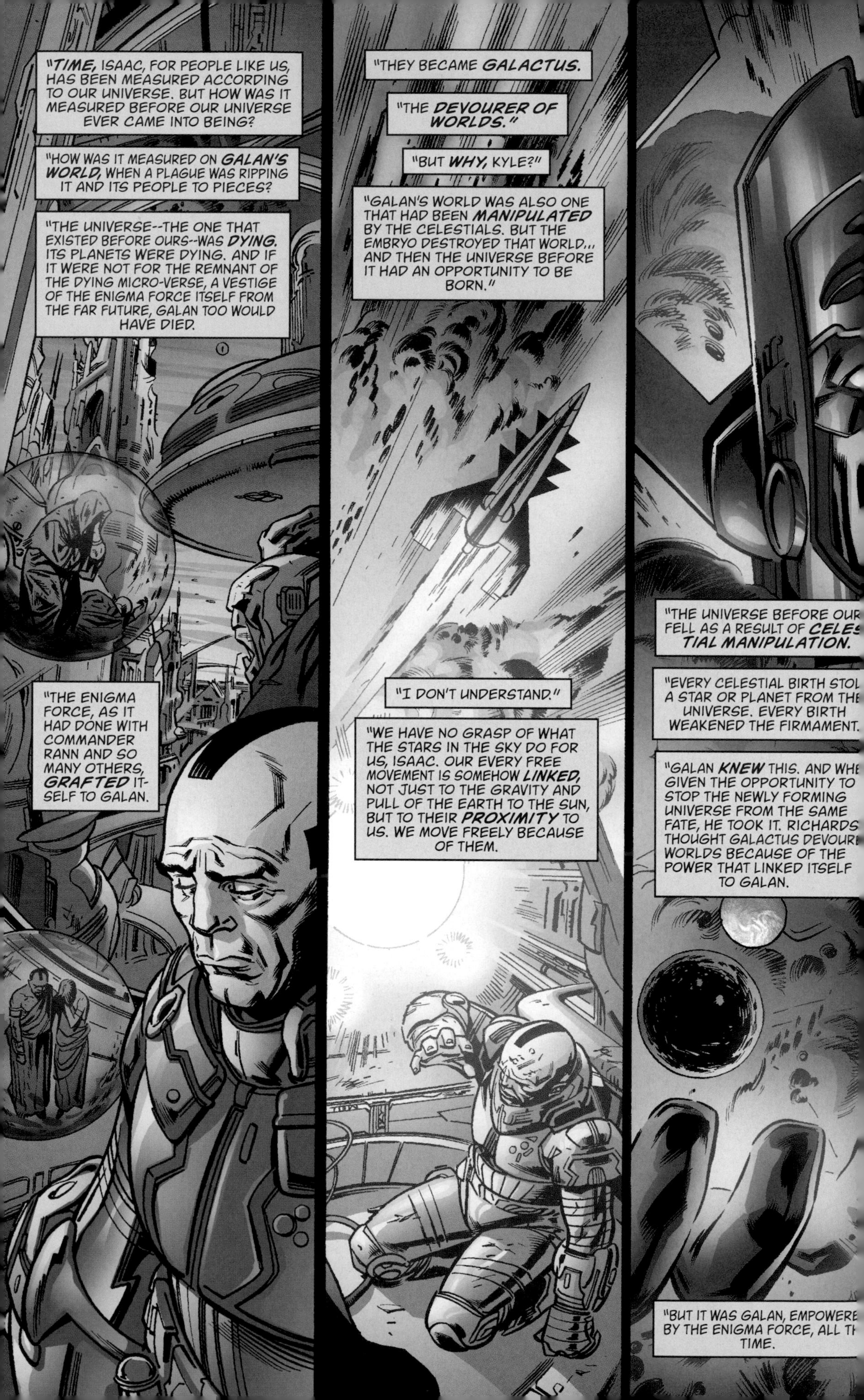
"TIME, ISAAC, FOR PEOPLE LIKE US, HAS BEEN MEASURED ACCORDING TO OUR UNIVERSE. BUT HOW WAS IT MEASURED BEFORE OUR UNIVERSE EVER CAME INTO BEING?
"HOW WAS IT MEASURED ON GALAN'S WORLD, WHEN A PLAGUE WAS RIPPING IT AND ITS PEOPLE TO PIECES?
"THE UNIVERSE--THE ONE THAT EXISTED BEFORE OURS--WAS DYING. ITS PLANETS WERE DYING. AND IF IT WERE NOT FOR THE REMNANT OF THE DYING MICRO-VERSE, A VESTIGE OF THE ENIGMA FORCE ITSELF FROM THE FAR FUTURE, GALAN TOO WOULD HAVE DIED.
"THE ENIGMA FORCE, AS IT HAD DONE WITH COMMANDER RANN AND SO MANY OTHERS, GRAFTED IT-SELF TO GALAN.
"THEY BECAME GALACTUS.
"THE DEVOURER OF WORLDS."
"BUT WHY, KYLE?"
"GALAN'S WORLD WAS ALSO ONE THAT HAD BEEN MANIPULATED BY THE CELESTIALS. BUT THE EMBRYO DESTROYED THAT WORLD... AND THEN THE UNIVERSE BEFORE IT HAD AN OPPORTUNITY TO BE BORN."
"I DON'T UNDERSTAND."
"WE HAVE NO GRASP OF WHAT THE STARS IN THE SKY DO FOR US, ISAAC. OUR EVERY FREE MOVEMENT IS SOMEHOW LINKED, NOT JUST TO THE GRAVITY AND PULL OF THE EARTH TO THE SUN, BUT TO THEIR PROXIMITY TO US. WE MOVE FREELY BECAUSE OF THEM.
"THE UNIVERSE BEFORE OUR FELL AS A RESULT OF CELES TIAL MANIPULATION.
"EVERY CELESTIAL BIRTH STOL A STAR OR PLANET FROM THE UNIVERSE. EVERY BIRTH WEAKENED THE FIRMAMENT.
"GALAN KNEW THIS. AND WHE GIVEN THE OPPORTUNITY TO STOP THE NEWLY FORMING UNIVERSE FROM THE SAME FATE, HE TOOK IT. RICHARDS THOUGHT GALACTUS DEVOUR WORLDS BECAUSE OF THE POWER THAT LINKED ITSELF TO GALAN.
"BUT IT WAS GALAN, EMPOWERE BY THE ENIGMA FORCE, ALL T TIME.

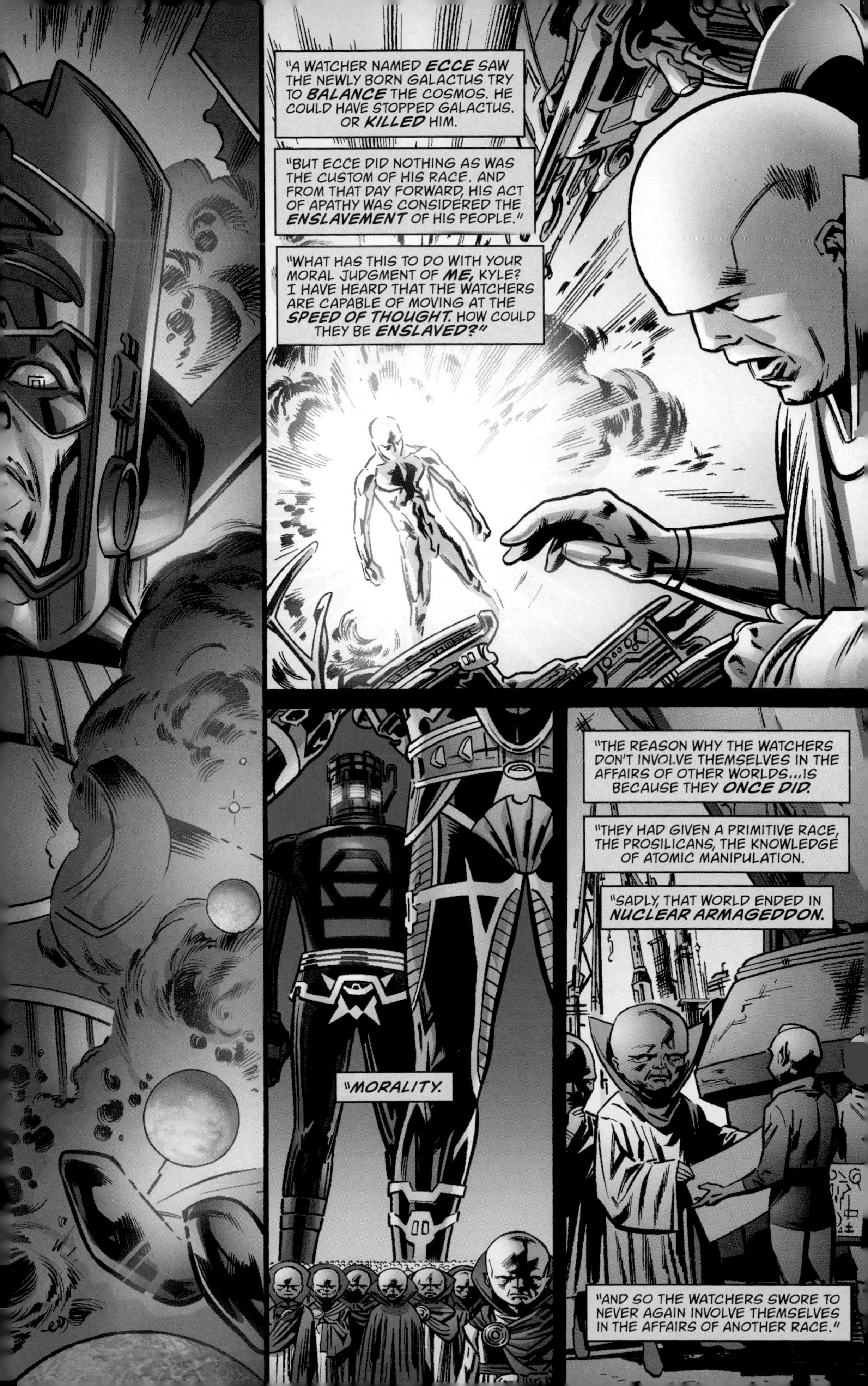
"A WATCHER NAMED ECCE SAW THE NEWLY BORN GALACTUS TRY TO BALANCE THE COSMOS. HE COULD HAVE STOPPED GALACTUS. OR KILLED HIM.
"BUT ECCE DID NOTHING AS WAS THE CUSTOM OF HIS RACE. AND FROM THAT DAY FORWARD, HIS ACT OF APATHY WAS CONSIDERED THE ENSLAVEMENT OF HIS PEOPLE."
"WHAT HAS THIS TO DO WITH YOUR MORAL JUDGMENT OF ME, KYLE? I HAVE HEARD THAT THE WATCHERS ARE CAPABLE OF MOVING AT THE SPEED OF THOUGHT. HOW COULD THEY BE ENSLAVED?"
"MORALITY.
"THE REASON WHY THE WATCHERS DON'T INVOLVE THEMSELVES IN THE AFFAIRS OF OTHER WORLDS...IS BECAUSE THEY ONCE DID.
"THEY HAD GIVEN A PRIMITIVE RACE, THE PROSILICANS, THE KNOWLEDGE OF ATOMIC MANIPULATION.
"SADLY, THAT WORLD ENDED IN NUCLEAR ARMAGEDDON.
"AND SO THE WATCHERS SWORE TO NEVER AGAIN INVOLVE THEMSELVES IN THE AFFAIRS OF ANOTHER RACE."

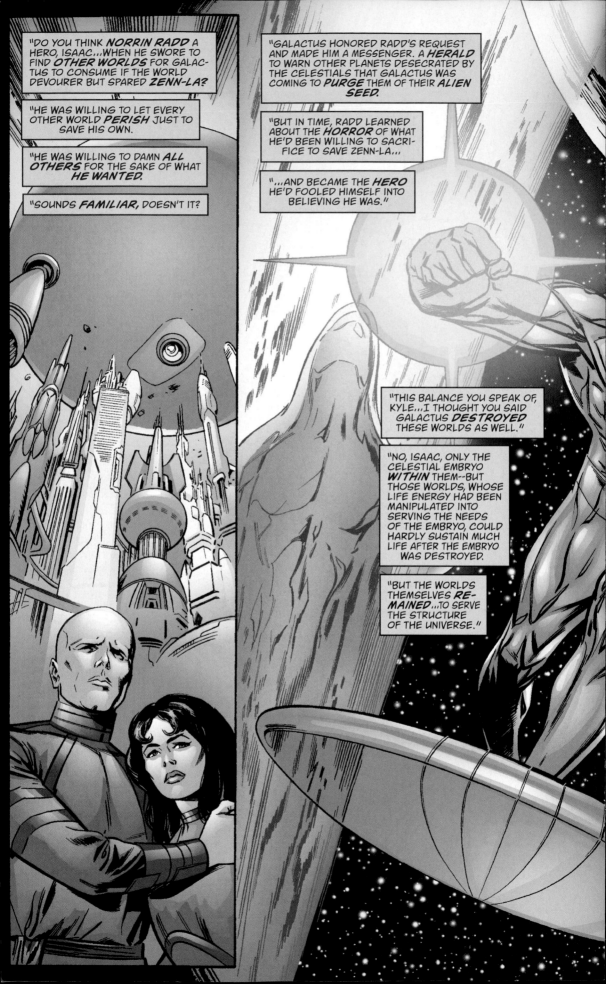

"DO YOU THINK *NORRIN RADD* A HERO, ISAAC...WHEN HE SWORE TO FIND *OTHER WORLDS* FOR GALACTUS TO CONSUME IF THE WORLD DEVOURER BUT SPARED *ZENN-LA?*

"HE WAS WILLING TO LET EVERY OTHER WORLD *PERISH* JUST TO SAVE HIS OWN.

"HE WAS WILLING TO DAMN *ALL OTHERS* FOR THE SAKE OF WHAT *HE WANTED.*

"SOUNDS *FAMILIAR,* DOESN'T IT?

"GALACTUS HONORED RADD'S REQUEST AND MADE HIM A MESSENGER. A *HERALD* TO WARN OTHER PLANETS DESECRATED BY THE CELESTIALS THAT GALACTUS WAS COMING TO *PURGE* THEM OF THEIR *ALIEN SEED.*

"BUT IN TIME, RADD LEARNED ABOUT THE *HORROR* OF WHAT HE'D BEEN WILLING TO SACRIFICE TO SAVE ZENN-LA...

"...AND BECAME THE *HERO* HE'D FOOLED HIMSELF INTO BELIEVING HE WAS."

"THIS BALANCE YOU SPEAK OF, KYLE...I THOUGHT YOU SAID GALACTUS *DESTROYED* THESE WORLDS AS WELL."

"NO, ISAAC, ONLY THE CELESTIAL EMBRYO *WITHIN* THEM--BUT THOSE WORLDS, WHOSE LIFE ENERGY HAD BEEN MANIPULATED INTO SERVING THE NEEDS OF THE EMBRYO, COULD HARDLY SUSTAIN MUCH LIFE AFTER THE EMBRYO WAS DESTROYED.

"BUT THE WORLDS THEMSELVES *REMAINED*...TO SERVE THE STRUCTURE OF THE UNIVERSE."

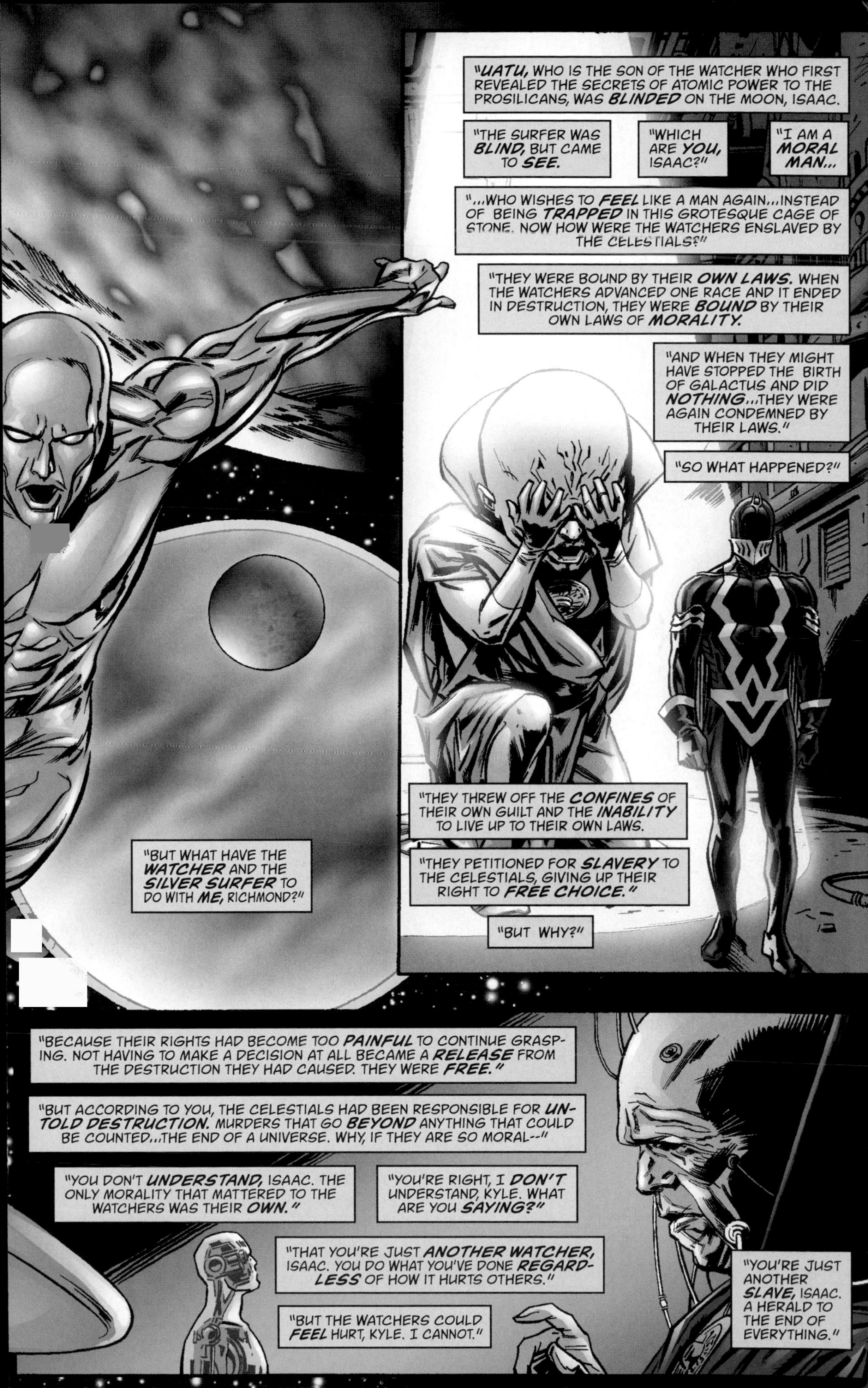
"UATU, WHO IS THE SON OF THE WATCHER WHO FIRST REVEALED THE SECRETS OF ATOMIC POWER TO THE PROSILICANS, WAS BLINDED ON THE MOON, ISAAC.
"THE SURFER WAS BLIND, BUT CAME TO SEE.
"WHICH ARE YOU, ISAAC?"
"I AM A MORAL MAN...
"...WHO WISHES TO FEEL LIKE A MAN AGAIN...INSTEAD OF BEING TRAPPED IN THIS GROTESQUE CAGE OF STONE. NOW HOW WERE THE WATCHERS ENSLAVED BY THE CELESTIALS?"
"THEY WERE BOUND BY THEIR OWN LAWS. WHEN THE WATCHERS ADVANCED ONE RACE AND IT ENDED IN DESTRUCTION, THEY WERE BOUND BY THEIR OWN LAWS OF MORALITY.
"AND WHEN THEY MIGHT HAVE STOPPED THE BIRTH OF GALACTUS AND DID NOTHING...THEY WERE AGAIN CONDEMNED BY THEIR LAWS."
"SO WHAT HAPPENED?"
"BUT WHAT HAVE THE WATCHER AND THE SILVER SURFER TO DO WITH ME, RICHMOND?"
"THEY THREW OFF THE CONFINES OF THEIR OWN GUILT AND THE INABILITY TO LIVE UP TO THEIR OWN LAWS.
"THEY PETITIONED FOR SLAVERY TO THE CELESTIALS, GIVING UP THEIR RIGHT TO FREE CHOICE."
"BUT WHY?"
"BECAUSE THEIR RIGHTS HAD BECOME TOO PAINFUL TO CONTINUE GRASPING. NOT HAVING TO MAKE A DECISION AT ALL BECAME A RELEASE FROM THE DESTRUCTION THEY HAD CAUSED. THEY WERE FREE."
"BUT ACCORDING TO YOU, THE CELESTIALS HAD BEEN RESPONSIBLE FOR UNTOLD DESTRUCTION. MURDERS THAT GO BEYOND ANYTHING THAT COULD BE COUNTED...THE END OF A UNIVERSE. WHY, IF THEY ARE SO MORAL--"
"YOU DON'T UNDERSTAND, ISAAC. THE ONLY MORALITY THAT MATTERED TO THE WATCHERS WAS THEIR OWN."
"YOU'RE RIGHT, I DON'T UNDERSTAND, KYLE. WHAT ARE YOU SAYING?"
"THAT YOU'RE JUST ANOTHER WATCHER, ISAAC. YOU DO WHAT YOU'VE DONE REGARDLESS OF HOW IT HURTS OTHERS."
"YOU'RE JUST ANOTHER SLAVE, ISAAC. A HERALD TO THE END OF EVERYTHING."
"BUT THE WATCHERS COULD FEEL HURT, KYLE. I CANNOT."

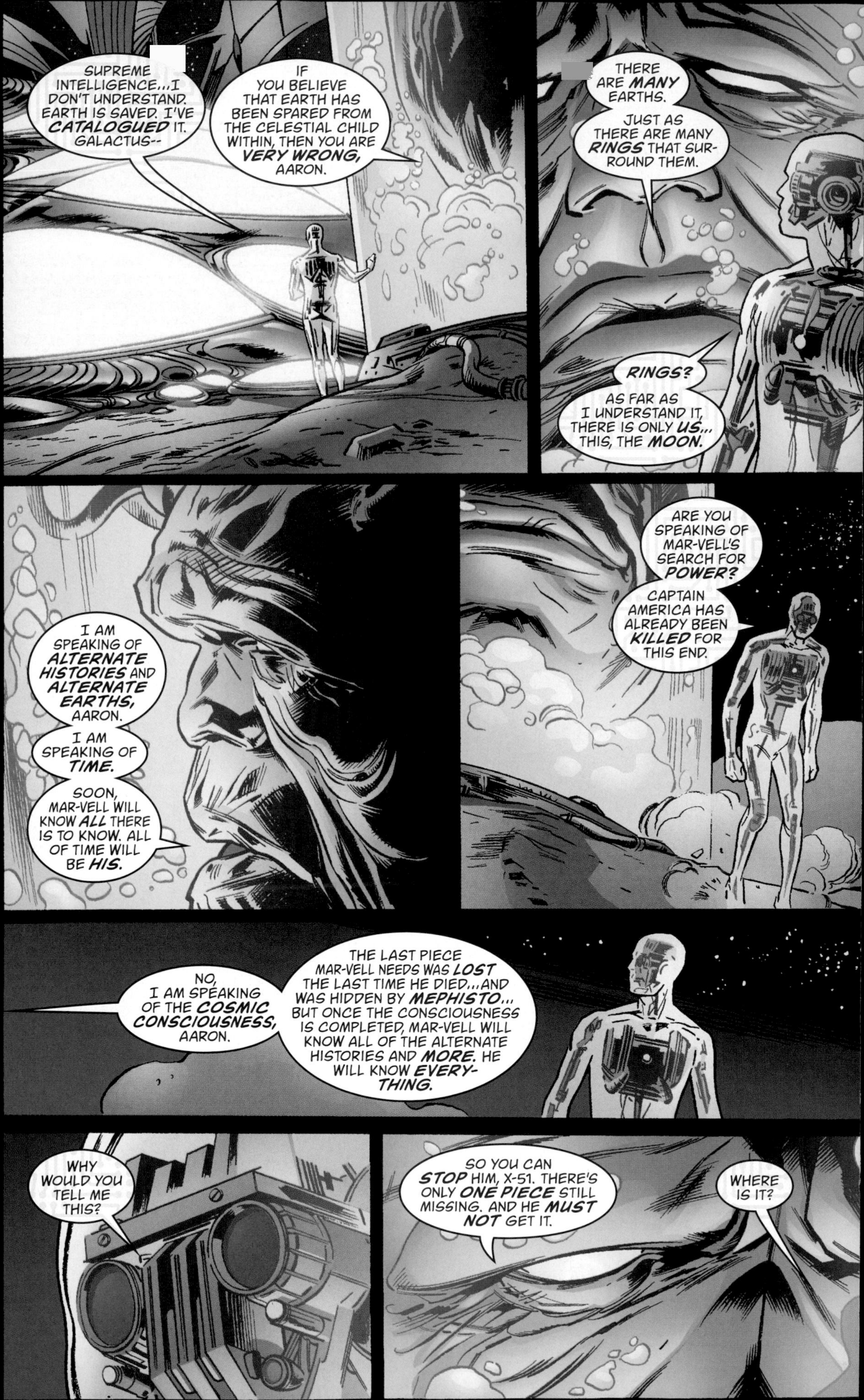
SUPREME INTELLIGENCE...I DON'T UNDERSTAND. EARTH IS SAVED. I'VE CATALOGUED IT. GALACTUS--
IF YOU BELIEVE THAT EARTH HAS BEEN SPARED FROM THE CELESTIAL CHILD WITHIN, THEN YOU ARE VERY WRONG, AARON.
THERE ARE MANY EARTHS.
JUST AS THERE ARE MANY RINGS THAT SURROUND THEM.
RINGS?
AS FAR AS I UNDERSTAND IT, THERE IS ONLY US... THIS, THE MOON.
I AM SPEAKING OF ALTERNATE HISTORIES AND ALTERNATE EARTHS, AARON.
I AM SPEAKING OF TIME.
SOON, MAR-VELL WILL KNOW ALL THERE IS TO KNOW. ALL OF TIME WILL BE HIS.
ARE YOU SPEAKING OF MAR-VELL'S SEARCH FOR POWER?
CAPTAIN AMERICA HAS ALREADY BEEN KILLED FOR THIS END.
NO, I AM SPEAKING OF THE COSMIC CONSCIOUSNESS, AARON.
THE LAST PIECE MAR-VELL NEEDS WAS LOST THE LAST TIME HE DIED...AND WAS HIDDEN BY MEPHISTO... BUT ONCE THE CONSCIOUSNESS IS COMPLETED, MAR-VELL WILL KNOW ALL OF THE ALTERNATE HISTORIES AND MORE. HE WILL KNOW EVERYTHING.
WHY WOULD YOU TELL ME THIS?
SO YOU CAN STOP HIM, X-51. THERE'S ONLY ONE PIECE STILL MISSING. AND HE MUST NOT GET IT.
WHERE IS IT?

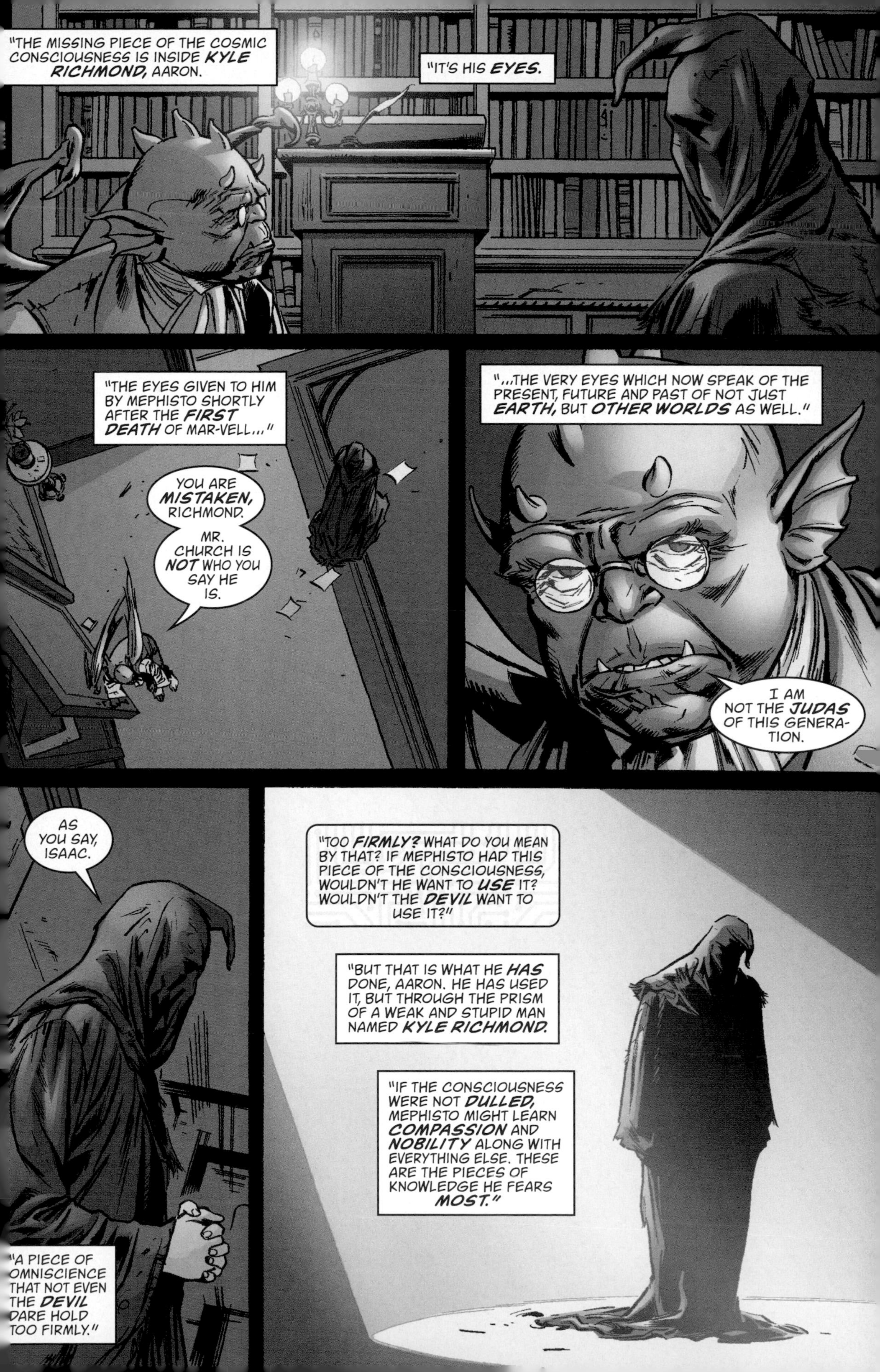

"THE MISSING PIECE OF THE COSMIC CONSCIOUSNESS IS INSIDE KYLE RICHMOND, AARON.
"IT'S HIS EYES.
"THE EYES GIVEN TO HIM BY MEPHISTO SHORTLY AFTER THE FIRST DEATH OF MAR-VELL..."
YOU ARE MISTAKEN, RICHMOND.
MR. CHURCH IS NOT WHO YOU SAY HE IS.
"...THE VERY EYES WHICH NOW SPEAK OF THE PRESENT, FUTURE AND PAST OF NOT JUST EARTH, BUT OTHER WORLDS AS WELL."
I AM NOT THE JUDAS OF THIS GENERATION.
AS YOU SAY, ISAAC.
"A PIECE OF OMNISCIENCE THAT NOT EVEN THE DEVIL DARE HOLD TOO FIRMLY."
"TOO FIRMLY? WHAT DO YOU MEAN BY THAT? IF MEPHISTO HAD THIS PIECE OF THE CONSCIOUSNESS, WOULDN'T HE WANT TO USE IT? WOULDN'T THE DEVIL WANT TO USE IT?"
"BUT THAT IS WHAT HE HAS DONE, AARON. HE HAS USED IT, BUT THROUGH THE PRISM OF A WEAK AND STUPID MAN NAMED KYLE RICHMOND.
"IF THE CONSCIOUSNESS WERE NOT DULLED, MEPHISTO MIGHT LEARN COMPASSION AND NOBILITY ALONG WITH EVERYTHING ELSE. THESE ARE THE PIECES OF KNOWLEDGE HE FEARS MOST."

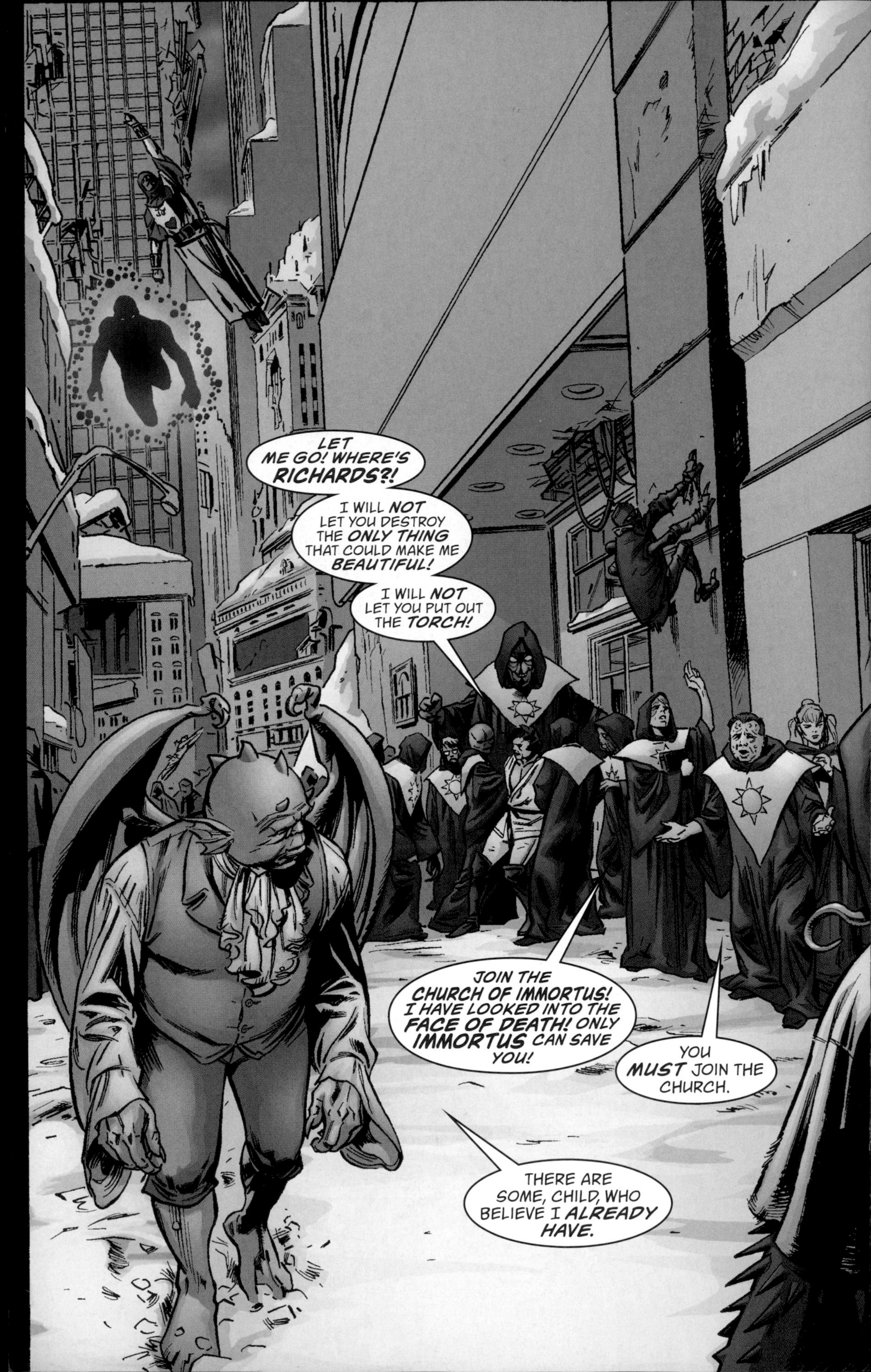
LET ME GO! WHERE'S RICHARDS?!
I WILL NOT LET YOU DESTROY THE ONLY THING THAT COULD MAKE ME BEAUTIFUL!
I WILL NOT LET YOU PUT OUT THE TORCH!
JOIN THE CHURCH OF IMMORTUS! I HAVE LOOKED INTO THE FACE OF DEATH! ONLY IMMORTUS CAN SAVE YOU!
YOU MUST JOIN THE CHURCH.
THERE ARE SOME, CHILD, WHO BELIEVE I ALREADY HAVE.

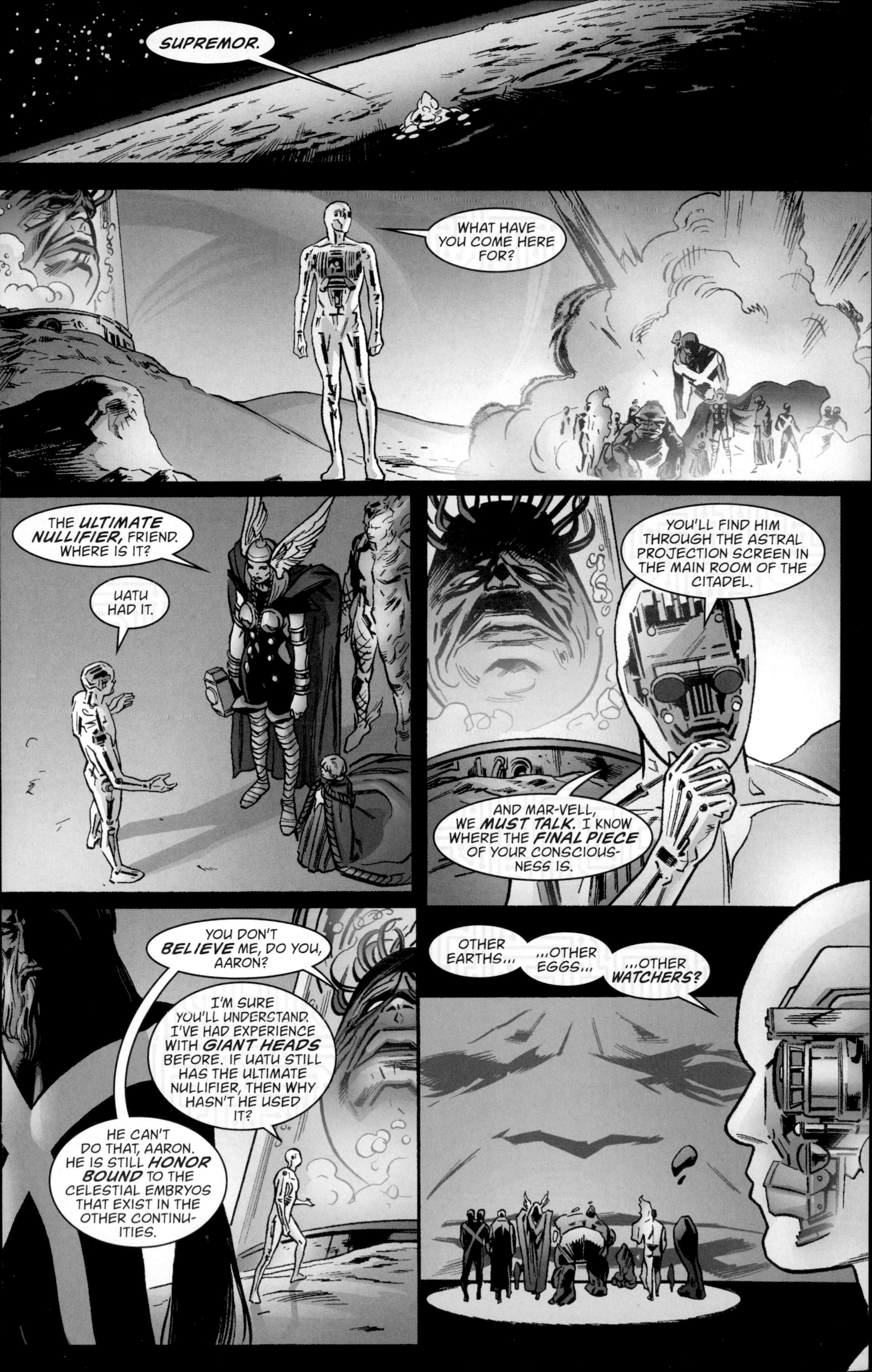
SUPREMOR.
WHAT HAVE YOU COME HERE FOR?
THE ULTIMATE NULLIFIER, FRIEND. WHERE IS IT?
UATU HAD IT.
YOU'LL FIND HIM THROUGH THE ASTRAL PROJECTION SCREEN IN THE MAIN ROOM OF THE CITADEL.
AND MAR-VELL, WE MUST TALK. I KNOW WHERE THE FINAL PIECE OF YOUR CONSCIOUSNESS IS.
YOU DON'T BELIEVE ME, DO YOU, AARON?
I'M SURE YOU'LL UNDERSTAND. I'VE HAD EXPERIENCE WITH GIANT HEADS BEFORE. IF UATU STILL HAS THE ULTIMATE NULLIFIER, THEN WHY HASN'T HE USED IT?
HE CAN'T DO THAT, AARON. HE IS STILL HONOR BOUND TO THE CELESTIAL EMBRYOS THAT EXIST IN THE OTHER CONTINUITIES.
OTHER EARTHS...
...OTHER EGGS...
...OTHER WATCHERS?

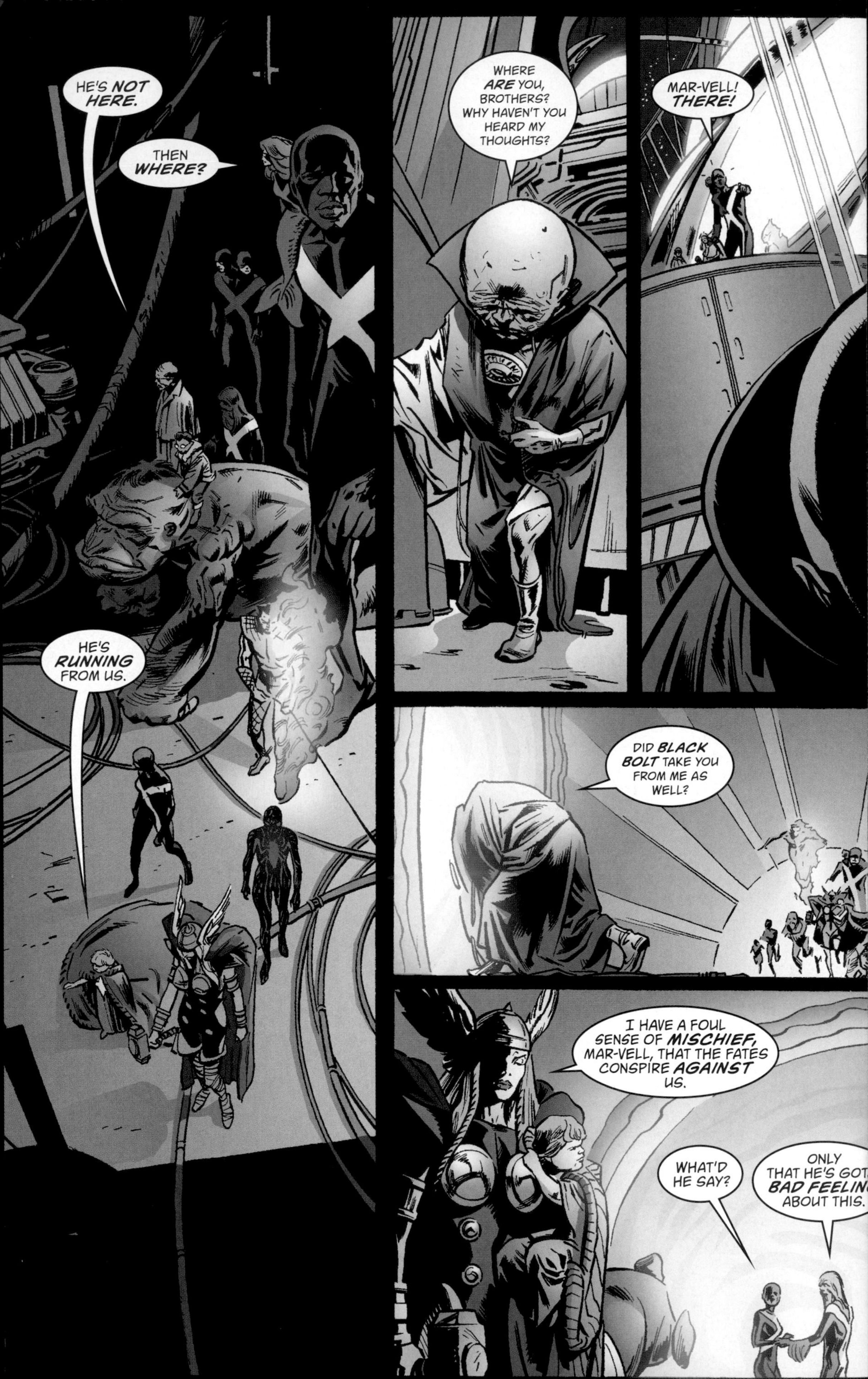
HE'S NOT HERE.
THEN WHERE?
HE'S RUNNING FROM US.
WHERE ARE YOU, BROTHERS? WHY HAVEN'T YOU HEARD MY THOUGHTS?
MAR-VELL! THERE!
DID BLACK BOLT TAKE YOU FROM ME AS WELL?
I HAVE A FOUL SENSE OF MISCHIEF, MAR-VELL, THAT THE FATES CONSPIRE AGAINST US.
WHAT'D HE SAY?
ONLY THAT HE'S GOT
BAD FEELIN
ABOUT THIS.

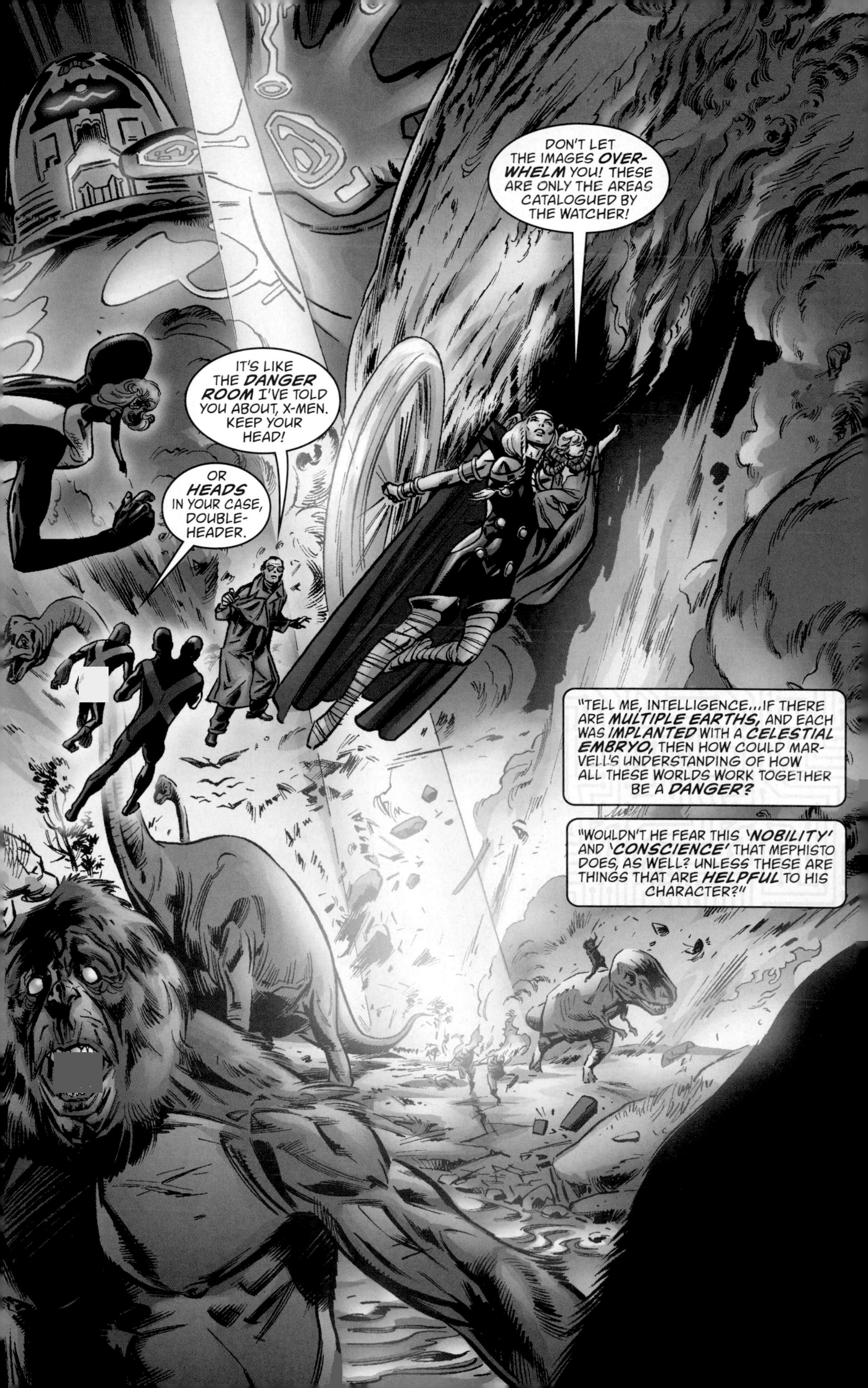
DON'T LET THE IMAGES OVERWHELM YOU! THESE ARE ONLY THE AREAS CATALOGUED BY THE WATCHER!
IT'S LIKE THE DANGER ROOM I'VE TOLD YOU ABOUT, X-MEN. KEEP YOUR HEAD!
OR HEADS IN YOUR CASE, DOUBLE-HEADER.
"TELL ME, INTELLIGENCE...IF THERE ARE MULTIPLE EARTHS, AND EACH WAS IMPLANTED WITH A CELESTIAL EMBRYO, THEN HOW COULD MAR-VELL'S UNDERSTANDING OF HOW ALL THESE WORLDS WORK TOGETHER BE A DANGER?
"WOULDN'T HE FEAR THIS 'NOBILITY' AND 'CONSCIENCE' THAT MEPHISTO DOES, AS WELL? UNLESS THESE ARE THINGS THAT ARE HELPFUL TO HIS CHARACTER?"

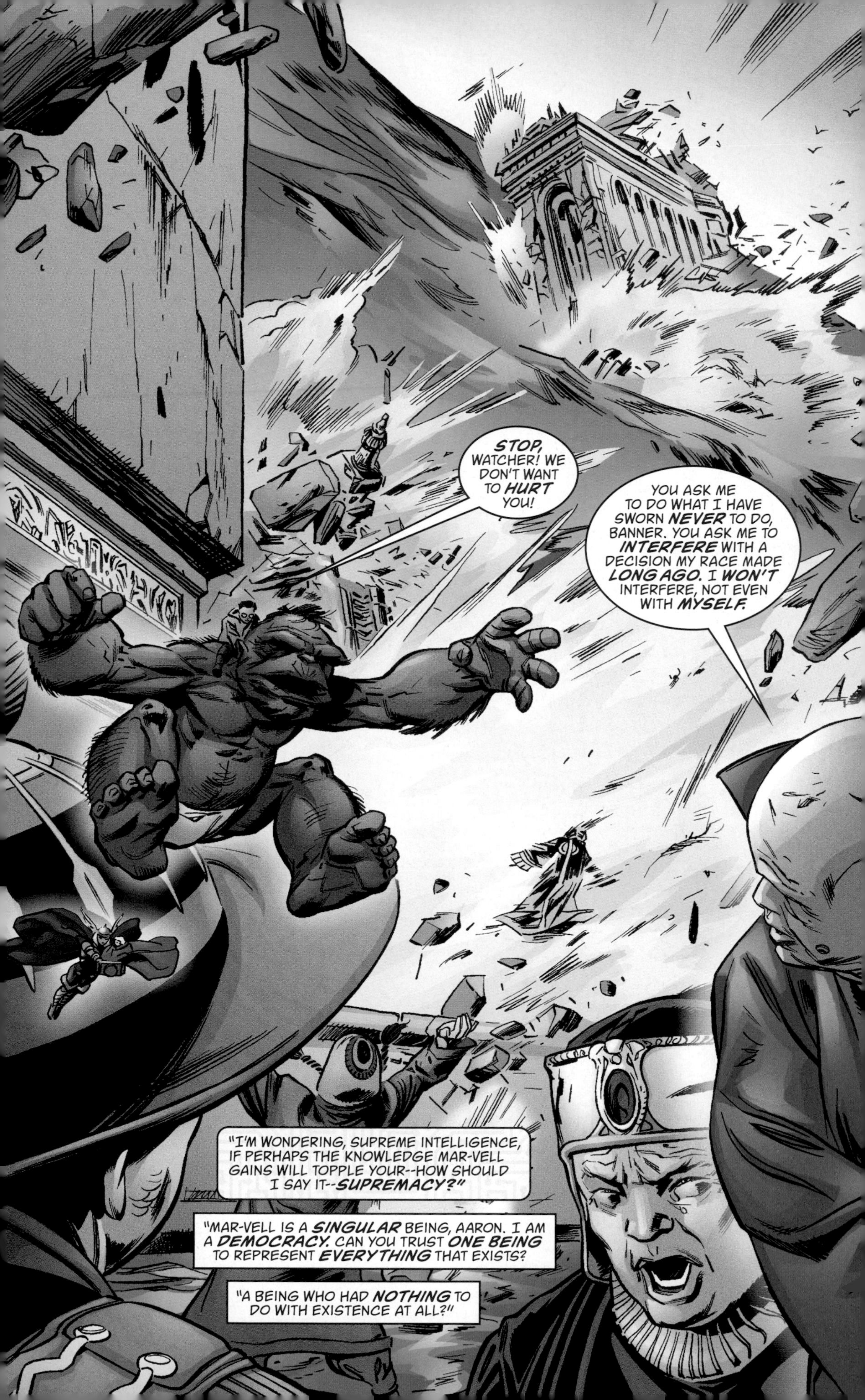

STOP, WATCHER! WE DON'T WANT TO HURT YOU!
YOU ASK ME TO DO WHAT I HAVE SWORN NEVER TO DO, BANNER. YOU ASK ME TO INTERFERE WITH A DECISION MY RACE MADE LONG AGO. I WON'T INTERFERE, NOT EVEN WITH MYSELF.
"I'M WONDERING, SUPREME INTELLIGENCE, IF PERHAPS THE KNOWLEDGE MAR-VELL GAINS WILL TOPPLE YOUR--HOW SHOULD I SAY IT--SUPREMACY?"
"MAR-VELL IS A SINGULAR BEING, AARON. I AM A DEMOCRACY. CAN YOU TRUST ONE BEING TO REPRESENT EVERYTHING THAT EXISTS?
"A BEING WHO HAD NOTHING TO DO WITH EXISTENCE AT ALL?"

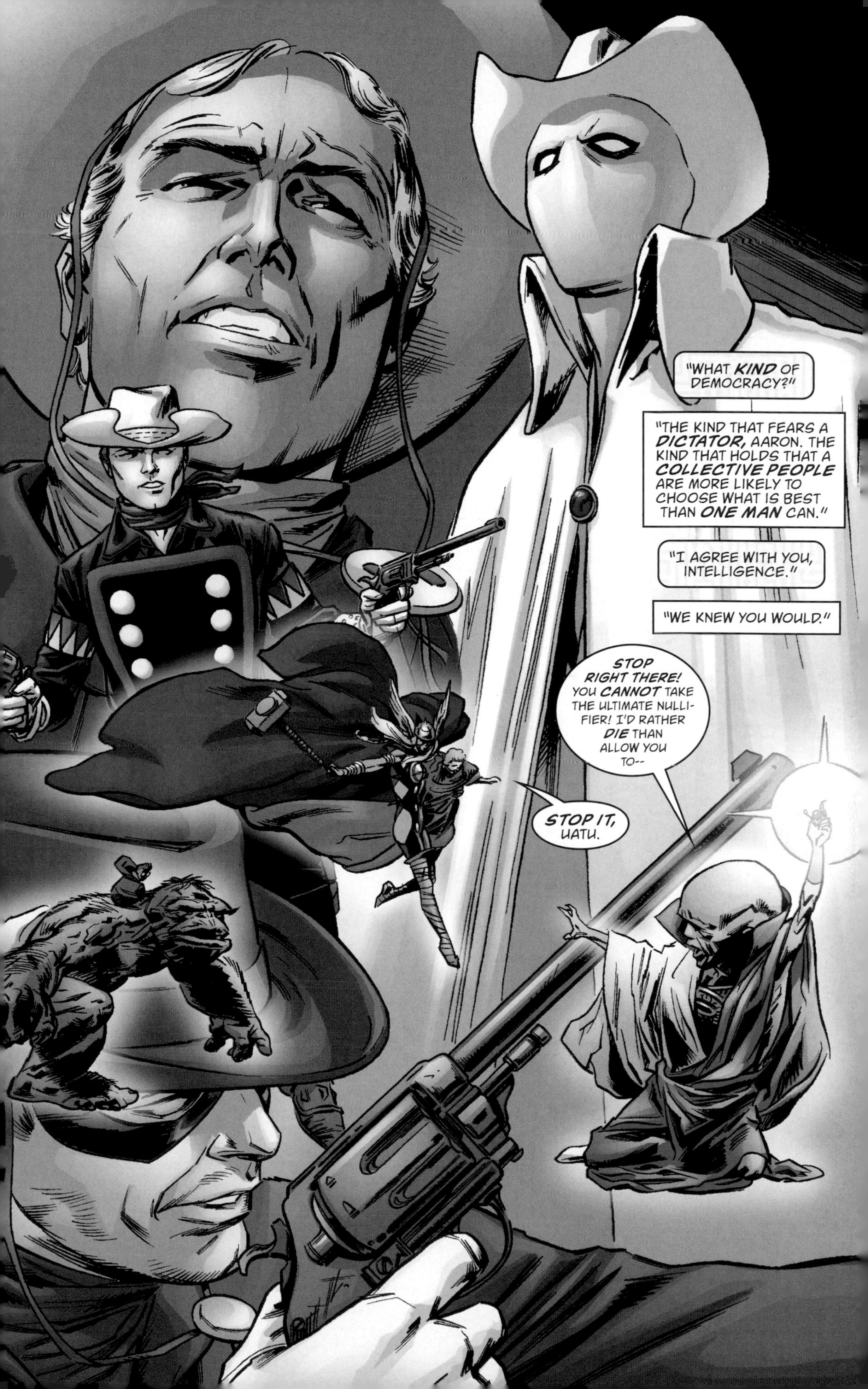
"WHAT KIND OF DEMOCRACY?"
"THE KIND THAT FEARS A DICTATOR, AARON. THE KIND THAT HOLDS THAT A COLLECTIVE PEOPLE ARE MORE LIKELY TO CHOOSE WHAT IS BEST THAN ONE MAN CAN."
"I AGREE WITH YOU, INTELLIGENCE."
"WE KNEW YOU WOULD."
STOP RIGHT THERE! YOU CANNOT TAKE THE ULTIMATE NULLI-FIER! I'D RATHER DIE THAN ALLOW YOU TO--
STOP IT, UATU.

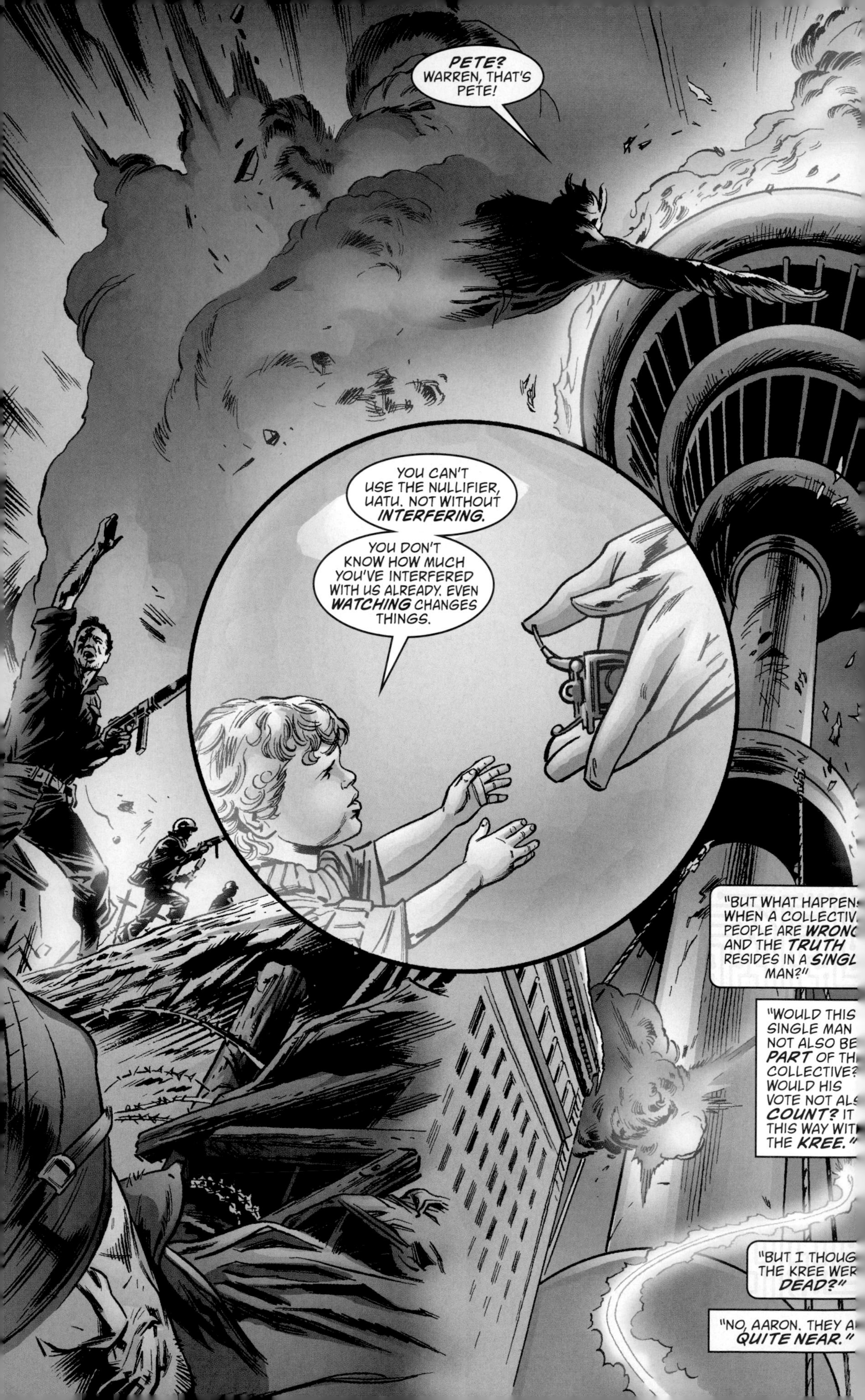

PETE? WARREN, THAT'S PETE!
YOU CAN'T USE THE NULLIFIER, UATU. NOT WITHOUT INTERFERING.
YOU DON'T KNOW HOW MUCH YOU'VE INTERFERED WITH US ALREADY. EVEN WATCHING CHANGES THINGS.
"BUT WHAT HAPPEN WHEN A COLLECTIV PEOPLE ARE WRON AND THE TRUTH RESIDES IN A SINGL MAN?"
"WOULD THIS SINGLE MAN NOT ALSO BE PART OF TH COLLECTIVE? WOULD HIS VOTE NOT AL COUNT? IT THIS WAY WIT THE KREE."
"BUT I THOUG THE KREE WER DEAD?"
"NO, AARON. THEY A QUITE NEAR."

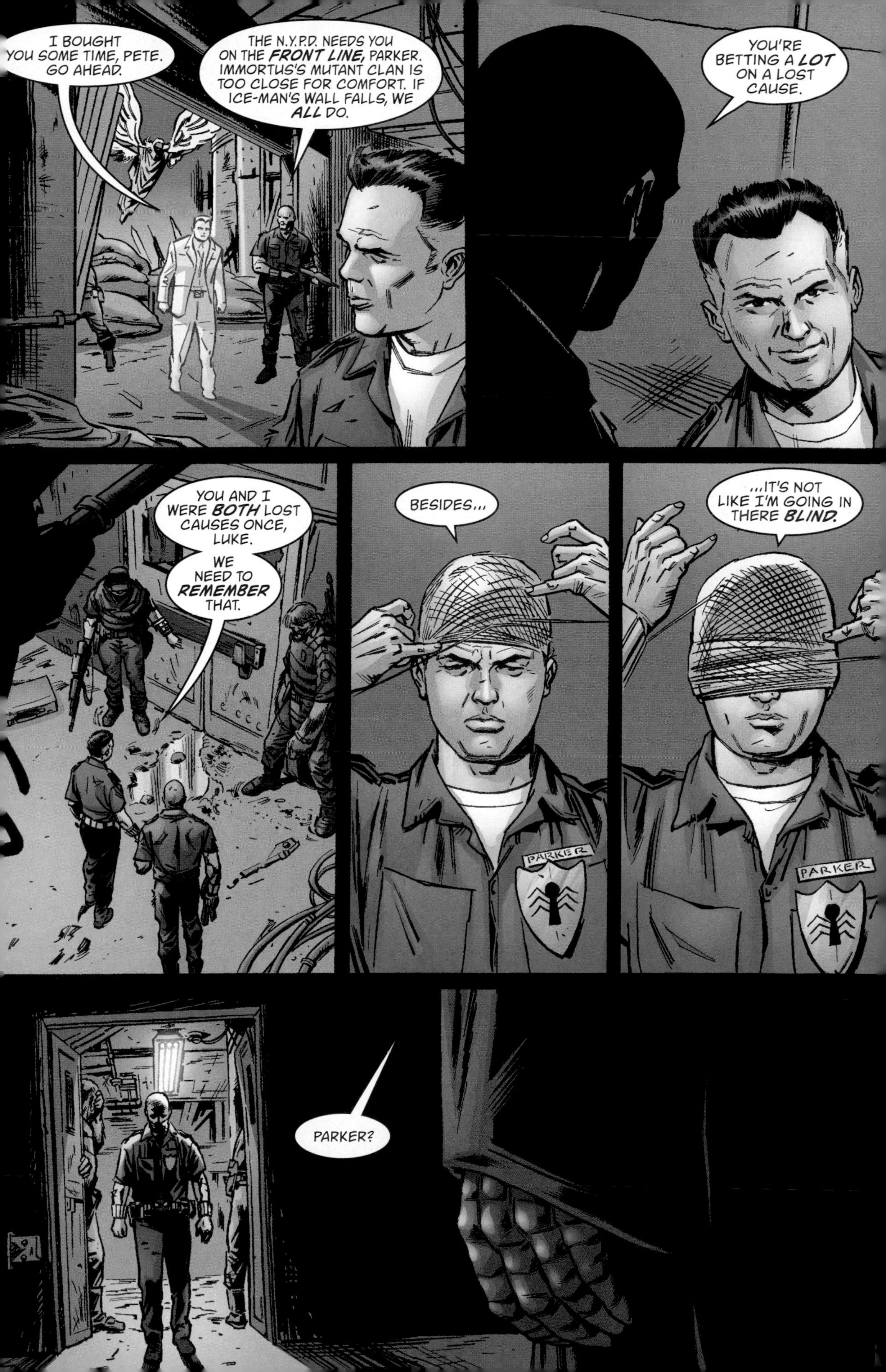
I BOUGHT YOU SOME TIME, PETE. GO AHEAD.
THE N.Y.P.D. NEEDS YOU ON THE FRONT LINE, PARKER. IMMORTUS'S MUTANT CLAN IS TOO CLOSE FOR COMFORT. IF ICE-MAN'S WALL FALLS, WE ALL DO.
YOU'RE BETTING A LOT ON A LOST CAUSE.
YOU AND I WERE BOTH LOST CAUSES ONCE, LUKE.
WE NEED TO REMEMBER THAT.
BESIDES...
...IT'S NOT LIKE I'M GOING IN THERE BLIND.
PARKER
PARKER
PARKER?

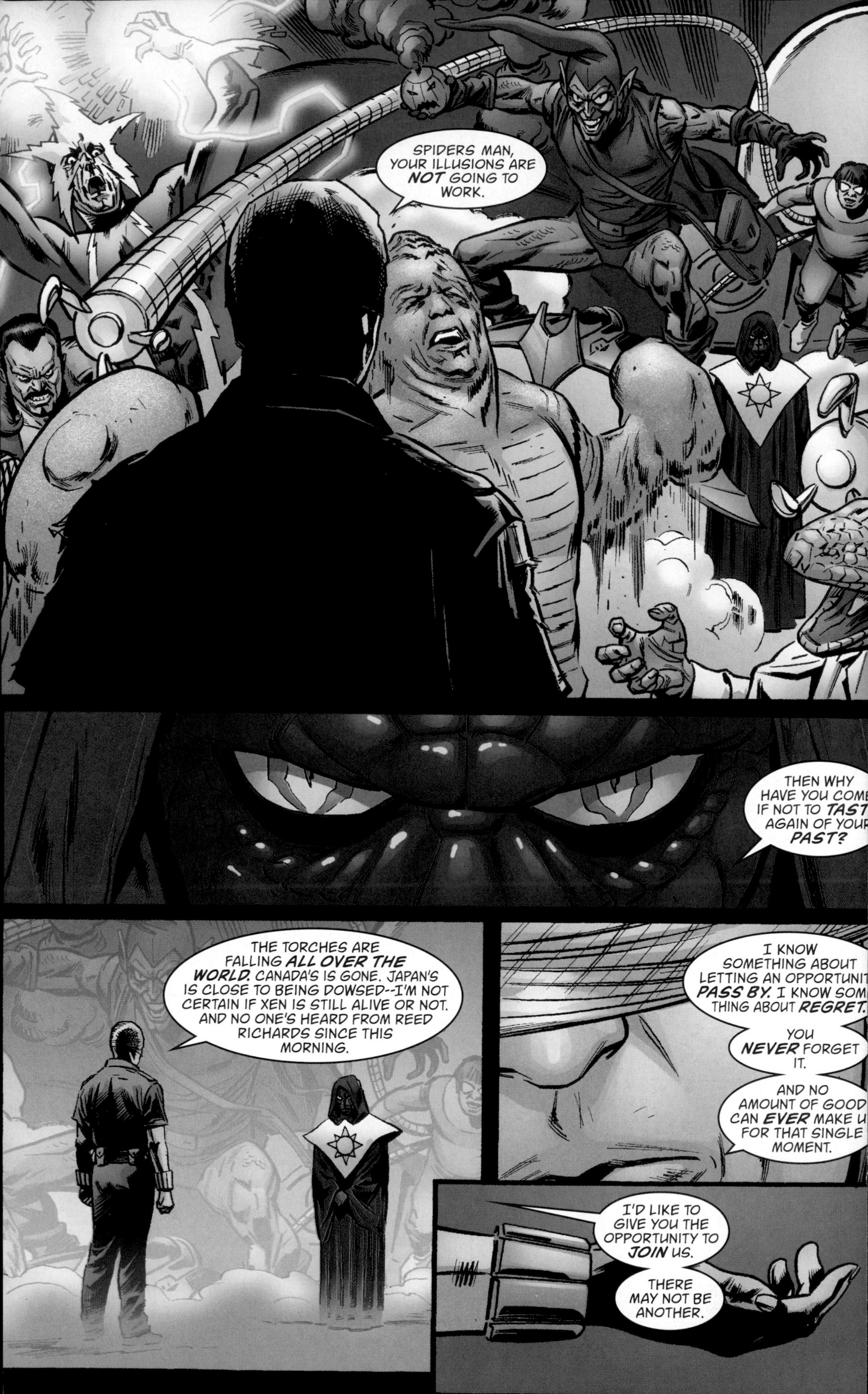
SPIDERS MAN, YOUR ILLUSIONS ARE NOT GOING TO WORK.
THEN WHY HAVE YOU COME IF NOT TO TASTE AGAIN OF YOUR PAST?
THE TORCHES ARE FALLING ALL OVER THE WORLD. CANADA'S IS GONE. JAPAN'S IS CLOSE TO BEING DOWSED--I'M NOT CERTAIN IF XEN IS STILL ALIVE OR NOT. AND NO ONE'S HEARD FROM REED RICHARDS SINCE THIS MORNING.
I KNOW SOMETHING ABOUT LETTING AN OPPORTUNITY PASS BY. I KNOW SOMETHING ABOUT REGRET.
YOU NEVER FORGET IT.
AND NO AMOUNT OF GOOD CAN EVER MAKE UP FOR THAT SINGLE MOMENT.
I'D LIKE TO GIVE YOU THE OPPORTUNITY TO JOIN US.
THERE MAY NOT BE ANOTHER.

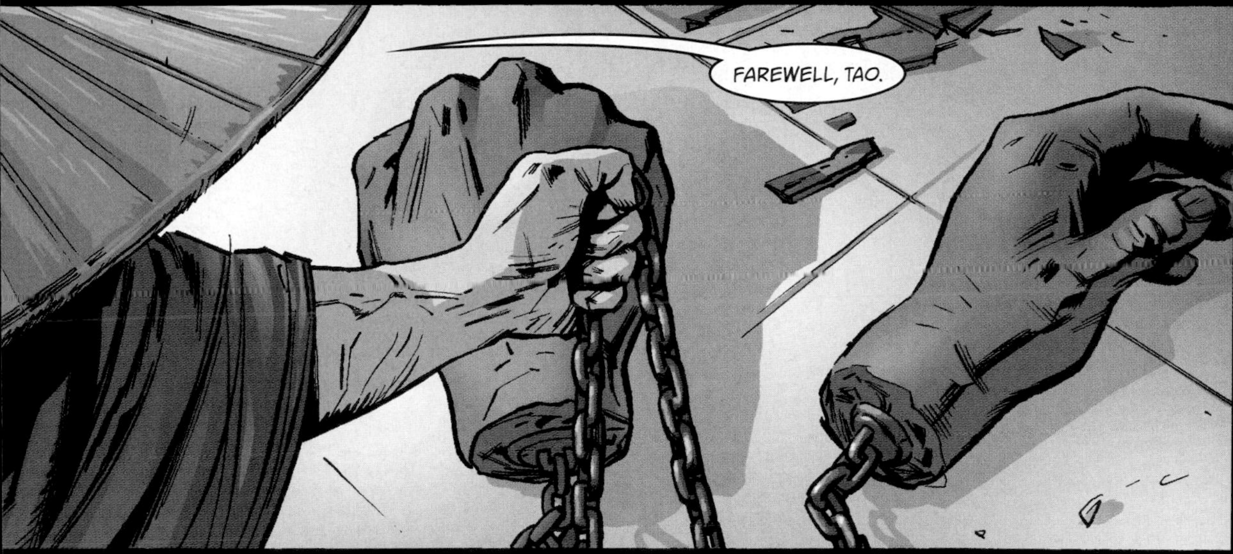
FAREWELL, TAO.

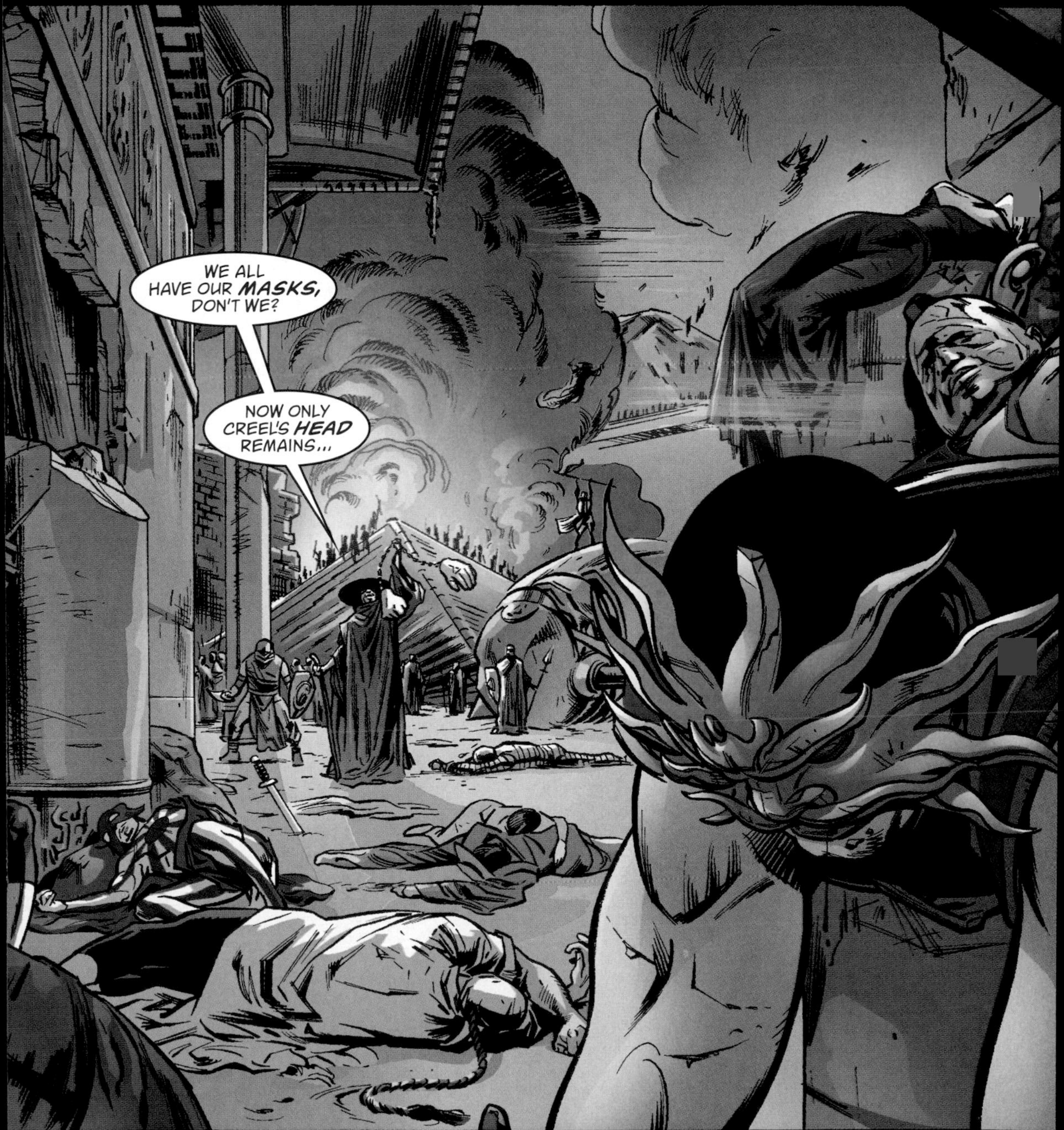
WE ALL HAVE OUR MASKS, DON'T WE?
NOW ONLY CREEL'S HEAD REMAINS...

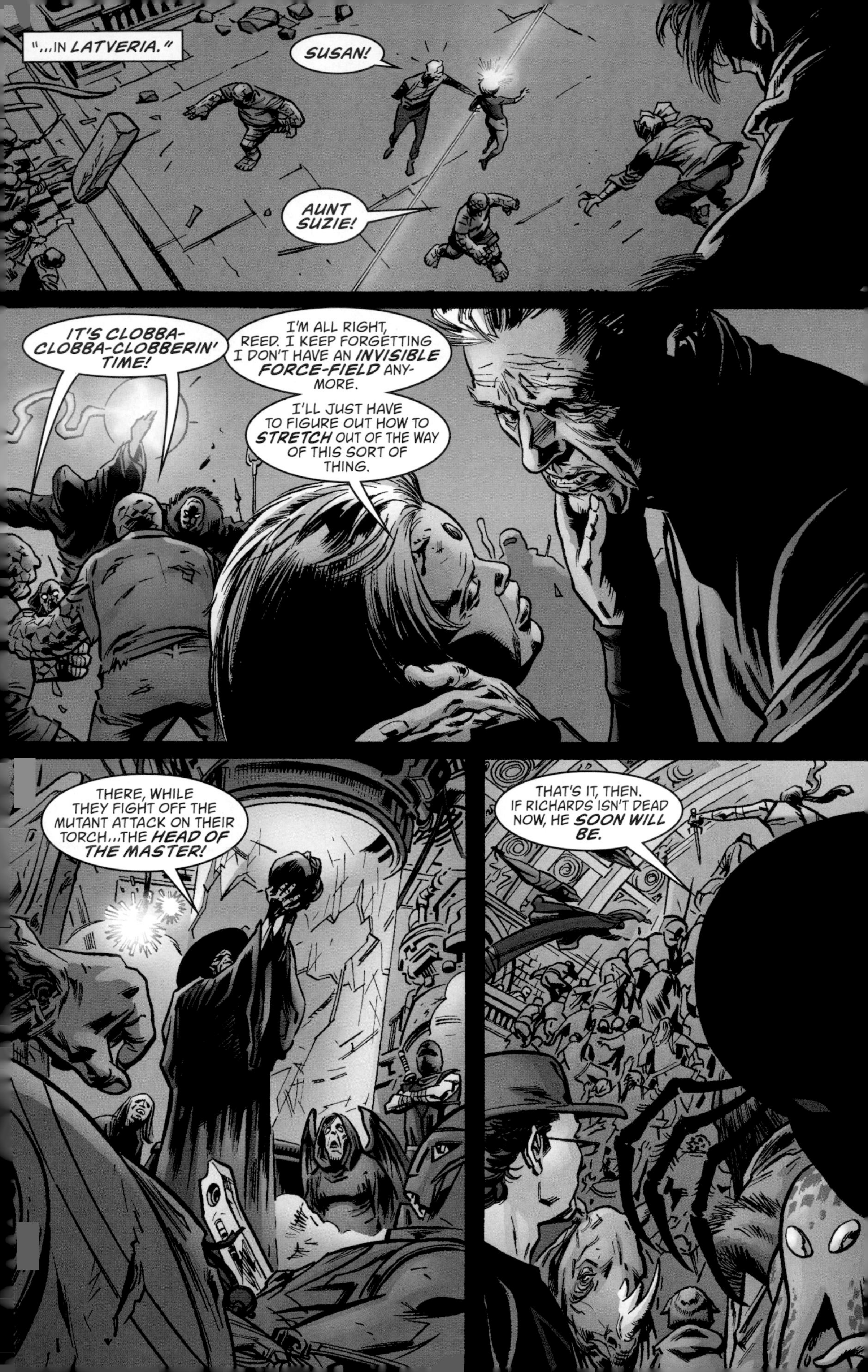
"...IN LATVERIA."
SUSAN!
AUNT SUZIE!
IT'S CLOBBA-CLOBBA-CLOBBERIN' TIME!
I'M ALL RIGHT, REED. I KEEP FORGETTING I DON'T HAVE AN INVISIBLE FORCE-FIELD ANY-MORE.
I'LL JUST HAVE TO FIGURE OUT HOW TO STRETCH OUT OF THE WAY OF THIS SORT OF THING.
THERE, WHILE THEY FIGHT OFF THE MUTANT ATTACK ON THEIR TORCH...THE HEAD OF THE MASTER!
THAT'S IT, THEN. IF RICHARDS ISN'T DEAD NOW, HE SOON WILL BE.

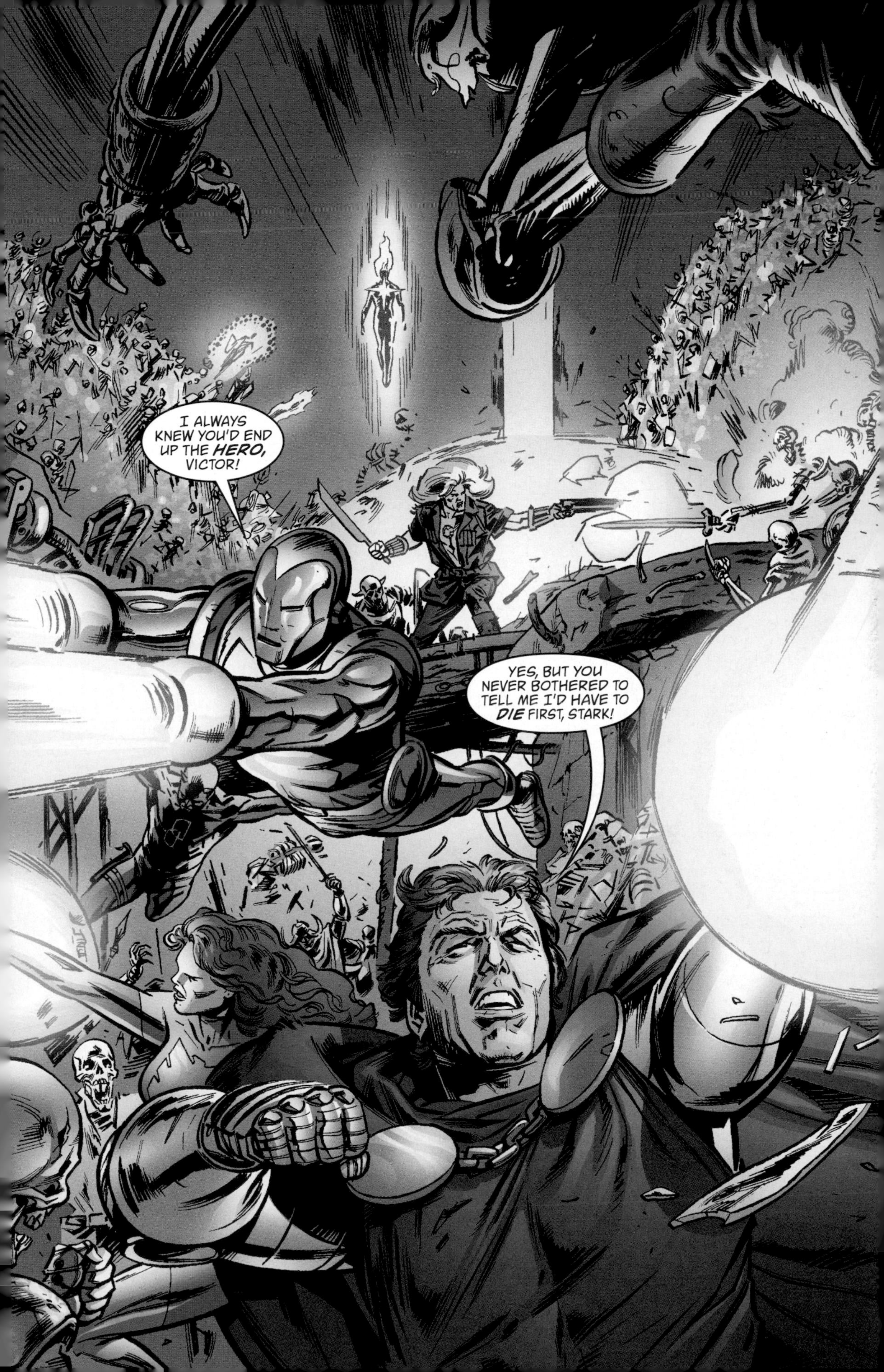
I ALWAYS KNEW YOU'D END UP THE ***HERO,*** VICTOR!
YES, BUT YOU NEVER BOTHERED TO TELL ME I'D HAVE TO ***DIE*** FIRST, STARK!

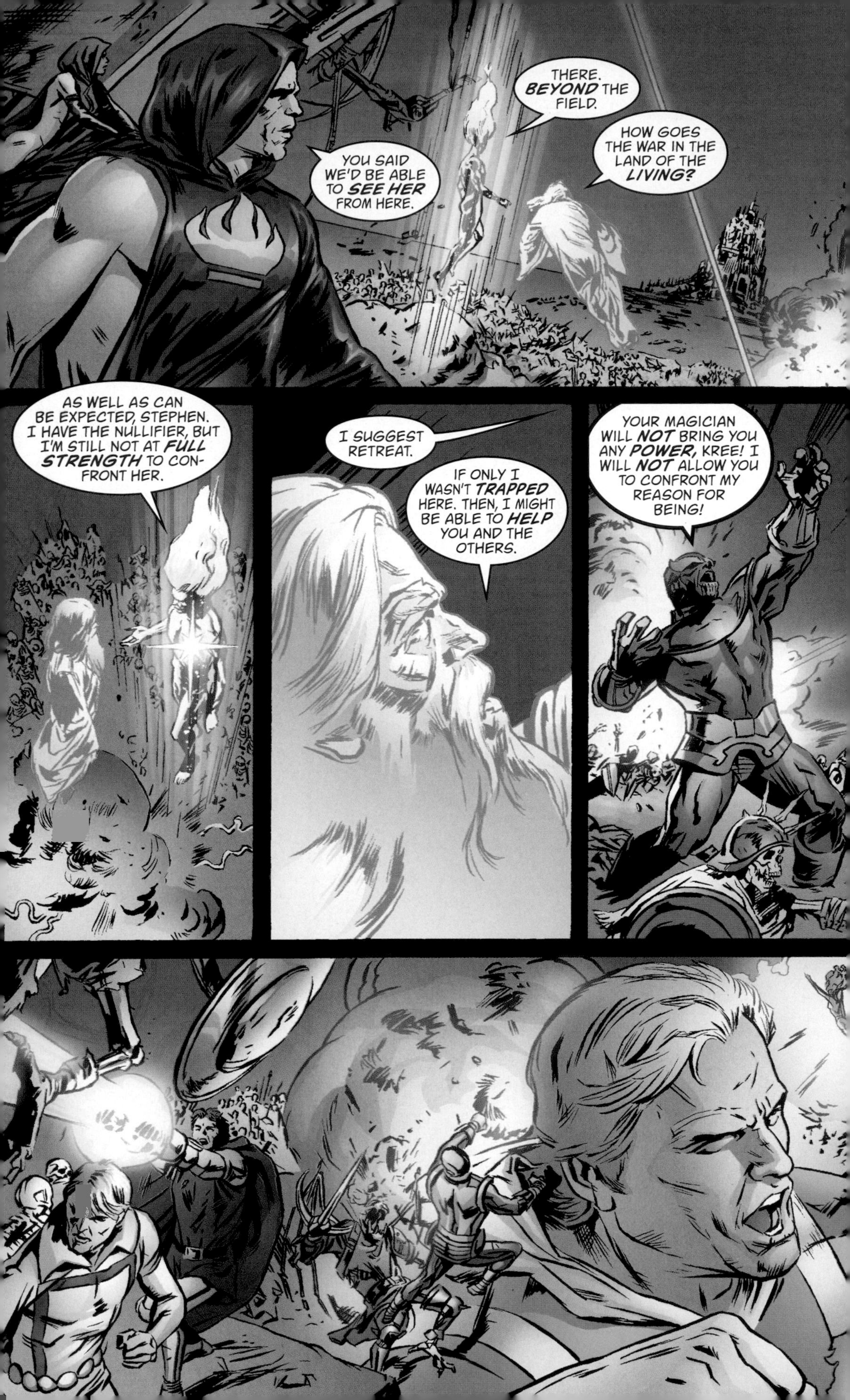
YOU SAID WE'D BE ABLE TO SEE HER FROM HERE.
THERE. BEYOND THE FIELD.
HOW GOES THE WAR IN THE LAND OF THE LIVING?
AS WELL AS CAN BE EXPECTED, STEPHEN. I HAVE THE NULLIFIER, BUT I'M STILL NOT AT FULL STRENGTH TO CON-FRONT HER.
I SUGGEST RETREAT.
IF ONLY I WASN'T TRAPPED HERE. THEN, I MIGHT BE ABLE TO HELP YOU AND THE OTHERS.
YOUR MAGICIAN WILL NOT BRING YOU ANY POWER, KREE! I WILL NOT ALLOW YOU TO CONFRONT MY REASON FOR BEING!

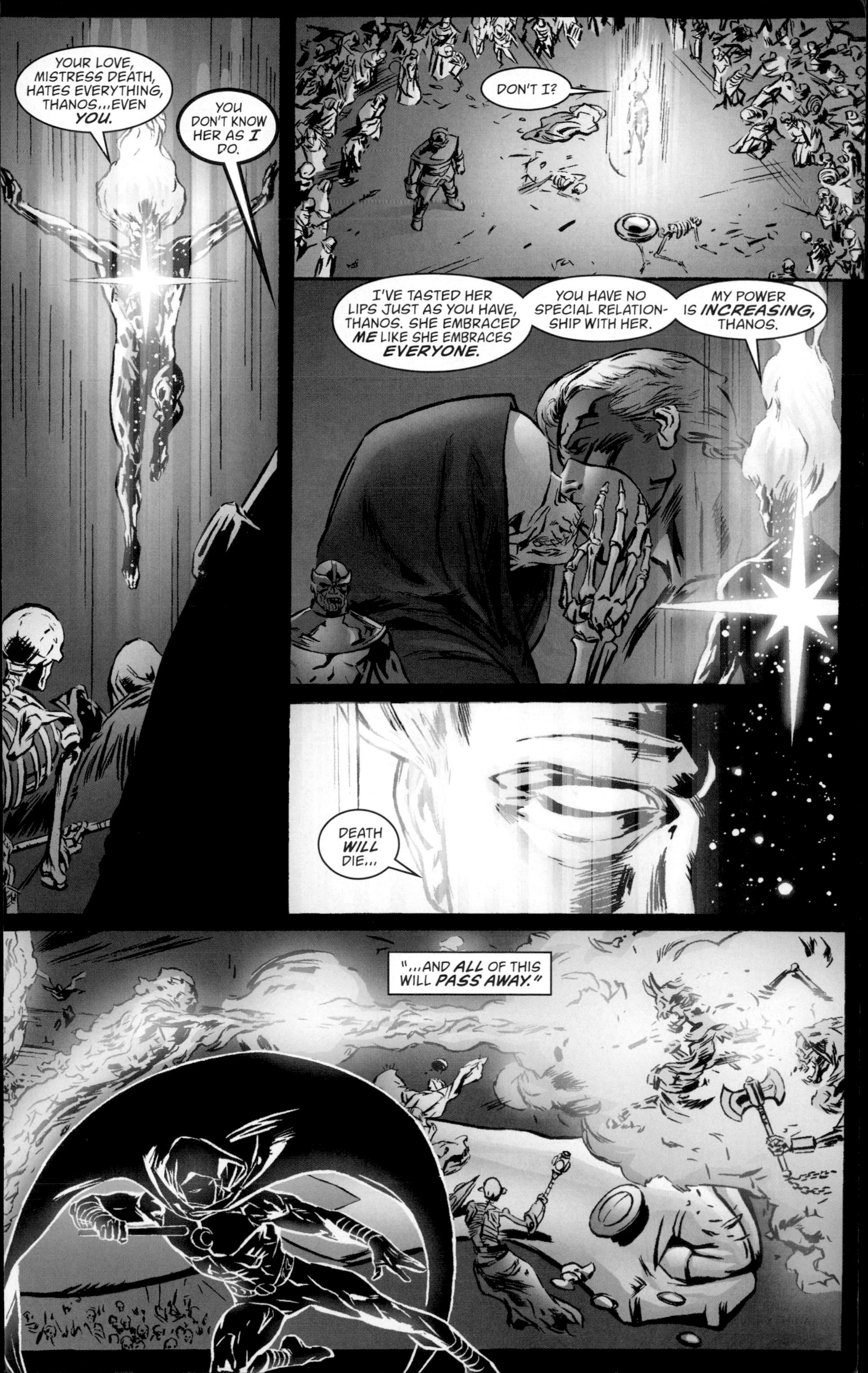
YOUR LOVE, MISTRESS DEATH, HATES EVERYTHING, THANOS...EVEN **YOU**.
YOU DON'T KNOW HER AS **I** DO.
DON'T I?
I'VE TASTED HER LIPS JUST AS YOU HAVE, THANOS. SHE EMBRACED **ME** LIKE SHE EMBRACES **EVERYONE**.
YOU HAVE NO SPECIAL RELATION-SHIP WITH HER.
MY POWER IS **INCREASING**, THANOS.
DEATH **WILL** DIE...
"...AND **ALL** OF THIS WILL **PASS AWAY**."

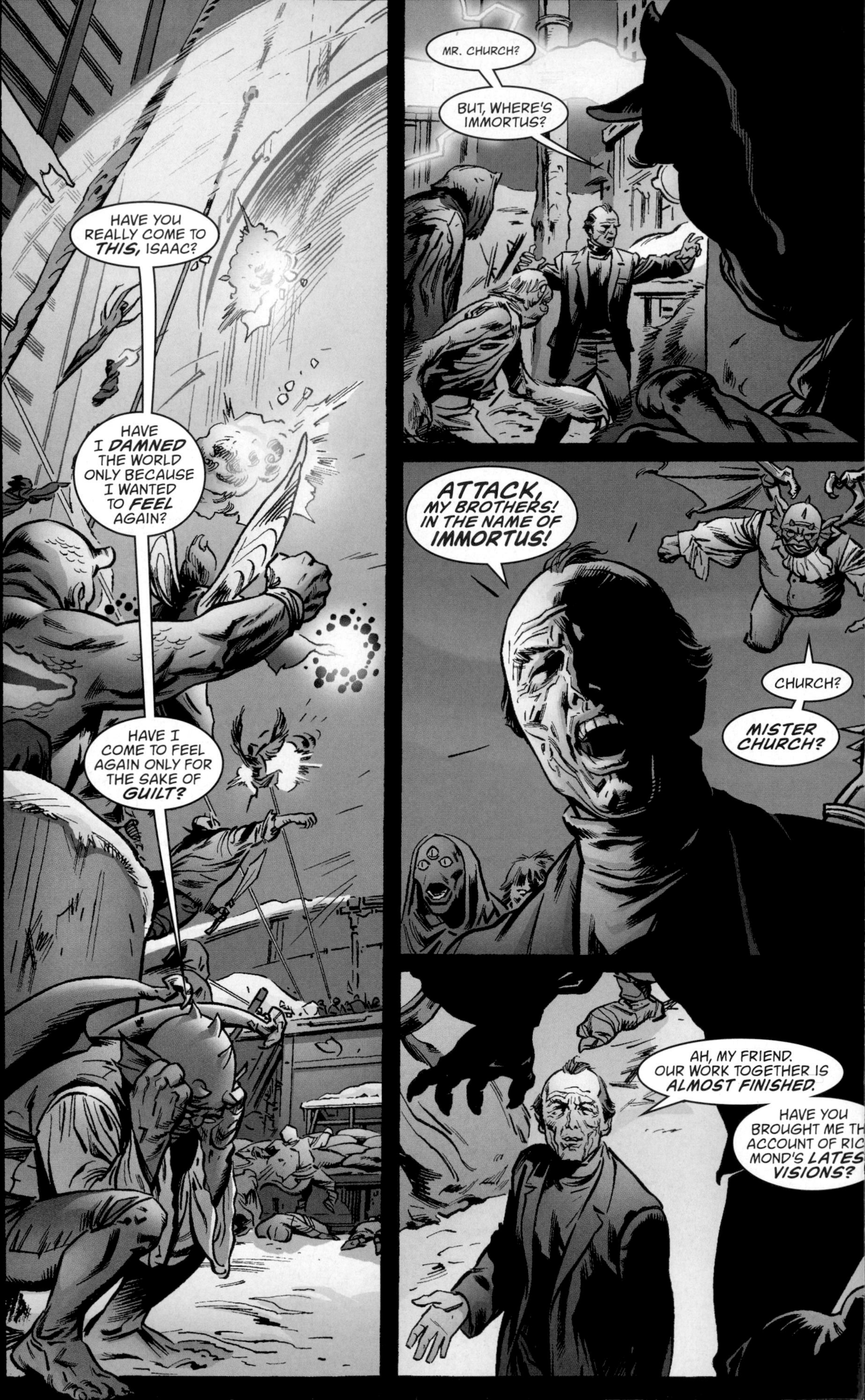
HAVE YOU REALLY COME TO THIS, ISAAC?
HAVE I DAMNED THE WORLD ONLY BECAUSE I WANTED TO FEEL AGAIN?
HAVE I COME TO FEEL AGAIN ONLY FOR THE SAKE OF GUILT?
MR. CHURCH?
BUT, WHERE'S IMMORTUS?
ATTACK, MY BROTHERS! IN THE NAME OF IMMORTUS!
CHURCH?
MISTER CHURCH?
AH, MY FRIEND. OUR WORK TOGETHER IS ALMOST FINISHED.
HAVE YOU BROUGHT ME TH ACCOUNT OF RIC MOND'S LATES VISIONS?

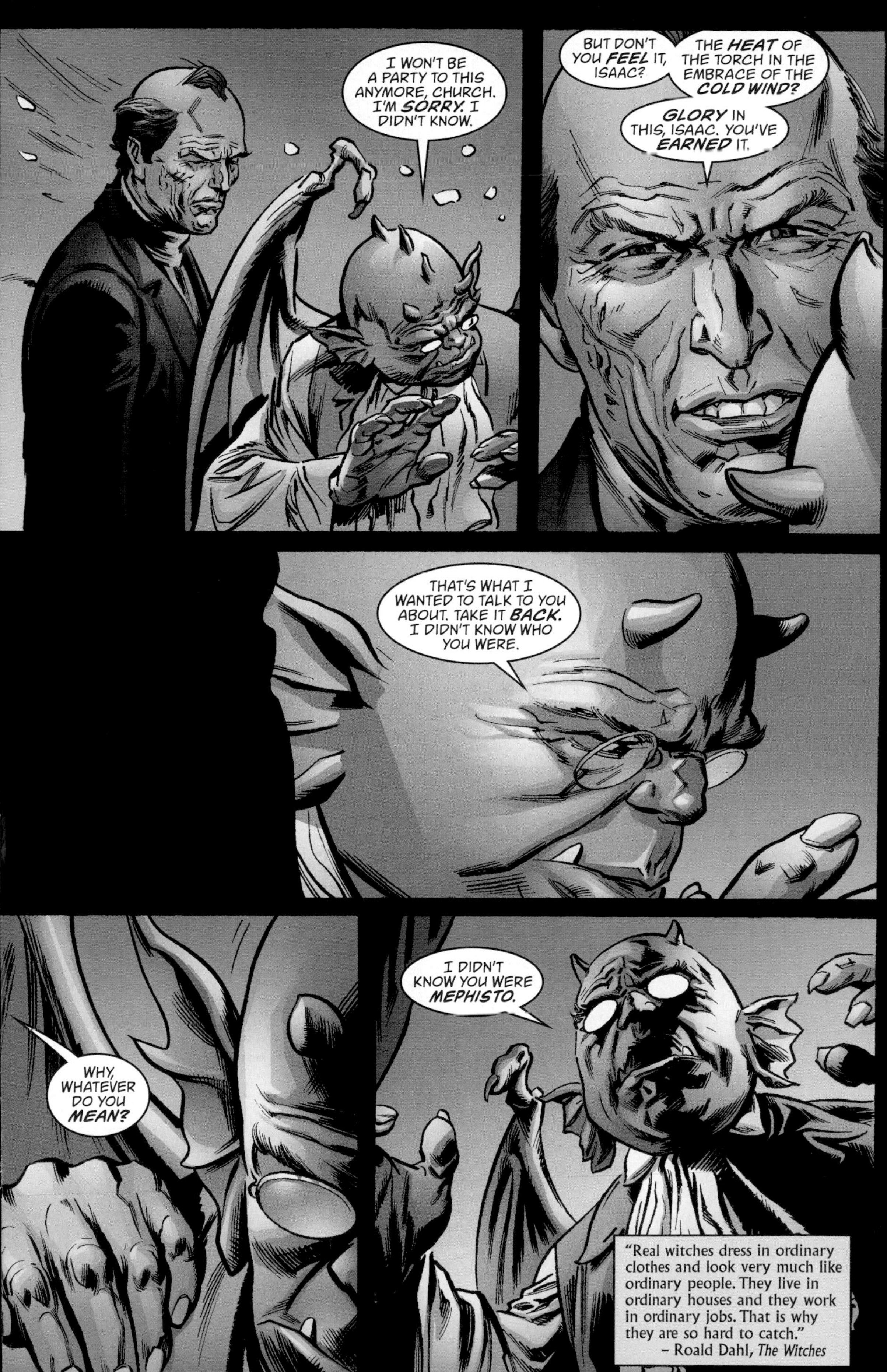
I WON'T BE A PARTY TO THIS ANYMORE, CHURCH. I'M SORRY. I DIDN'T KNOW.
BUT DON'T YOU FEEL IT, ISAAC?
THE HEAT OF THE TORCH IN THE EMBRACE OF THE COLD WIND?
GLORY IN THIS, ISAAC. YOU'VE EARNED IT.
THAT'S WHAT I WANTED TO TALK TO YOU ABOUT. TAKE IT BACK. I DIDN'T KNOW WHO YOU WERE.
WHY, WHATEVER DO YOU MEAN?
I DIDN'T KNOW YOU WERE MEPHISTO.
"Real witches dress in ordinary clothes and look very much like ordinary people. They live in ordinary houses and they work in ordinary jobs. That is why they are so hard to catch."
– Roald Dahl, The Witches

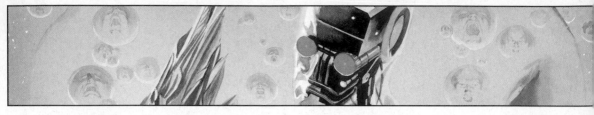

APPENDIX TO CHAPTER SEVEN

W R I T T E N   B Y   J I M   K R U E G E R

(The revelations implied in this appendix relate to the flashback in Universe X #9)

"What is it that knowledge brings that makes it so corrupting an influence?

"I was created to be a thinking computer, but more than that, I was created to be a man. And yet I find myself here on the moon with all knowledge of the history of mankind available to me, and I wonder if this knowledge will corrupt me as it did Uatu, the original Watcher before me.

"I speak now of what I witnessed here in Uatu's lair the day Mar-Vell and his seconds arrived. I am not speaking of their search for the Ultimate Nullifier. I speak of the death of an entire nation, the victims of another, the secret to the Kree/Skrull War, and of what I believe, may spark the downfall of the Asgardians.

"Mar-Vell murdered the Supreme Intelligence. I was there. I did not require Uatu's alien surveillance machinery. With my own… eyes…I watched and recorded the murder of a being older than any inhabitant of Earth.

"And I was glad. Learning what I did of Supremor's manipulations, I knew he deserved to die. And I wonder, with the knowledge now revealed of the true fate of the Kree people, if Mar-Vell wasn't justified in cold-blooded murder. Or if, indeed, the true fate of his race did not actually corrupt Mar-Vell as it did Supremor?

"And what of Thor? Mar-Vell's actions shook Thor to her very definition-- her core. Was it merely because Thor witnessed a noble soul who actually committed genocide? Or was it something more? Mar-Vell did the impossible. And all Thor could do was to watch him deconstruct all Asgardian mythology before her eyes.

"So knowledge too has been added to Thor. Knowledge that supports everything Loki, Thor's trickster half-brother has proposed.

"How could a liar speak the truth?

"That is the question.

"Loki discovered the truth about the Asgardian people a little more than three years ago. This happened shortly before the coming of the Final Host of Celestials. He learned that the Asgardians were not gods at all, but an alien race whose form and personality was molded by the perceptions and superstitions of humanity.

"Loki learned that they, before becoming the

Asgardians, were merely a race like humanity that had been manipulated by the Celestials. The Celestials don't merely mutate their races; they begin a mutation within them that not only empowers them to protect the Celestial Embryo within said planet's core – but also to become a being that will, in the end, have no being at all. Self-knowledge itself will be lost, and therefore, all history of that very race and all evidence of the Celestial manipulation.

"I have no idea what the Asgardians were before they reached this final phase of mutation. I do know that they were not as they are now; and that somehow, all that has happened to give them form and personality, to make them heroes and villains, to make them gods and goddesses, is a lie. But the Asgardians are more than the predisposition of ancient Norsemen. There's something more. The Asgardian known as Odin, I have recently learned as a result of Kyle Richmond's remarkable vision, is not one of them at all. He was a man, an ancient Norsemen who took advantage of this alien race's manipulated nature.

"How did this happen?

"And, has this knowledge also served to corrupt the being who became Odin? Is Asgard the result of this corruption? Is the fabled golden realm a sort of fool's gold, whose true worth is now being called into question?

"Or perhaps the Asgardians are the future of humanity. That this, again, is another time loop of sorts. That humanity will at some point in the future mutate to the final phase and be drawn back in time to where they are overcome by their own superstitious origins?

"This is difficult to believe and yet, I have become aware of so many similar time loops throughout the history of Earth, that I find myself casting all of human history in question.

"It seems as if every new piece of knowledge brings a new complexity and detail that ultimately suggests that knowledge itself is a sort of two-edged sword. The more that is revealed, the greater the number of unanswered questions.

"Perhaps this is that notion that corrupts. It is that there is an infinity of questions, suggesting an infinity of answers. And the answers suggest, again, new questions that spread out far from the initial question of being.

"But, to my knowledge, I have not been as of yet corrupted. This can only mean two things. Either I have not gained sufficient knowledge to act as a corrupting agent in my assembly, or, I am not human, as my father had hoped I would be. And that can only mean that I am incapable of being corrupted.

"If this is the case, it is ironic I am in the position I am, for Uatu hoped to corrupt me by convincing me that I am not a human. And if I am not a member of the human race, then I am incapable of being corrupted.

"I hope I am capable of being corrupted, if only to be true to my original programming. If I am not, I am no man at all, but only a machine with faulty programming.

"Otherwise, I fear this knowledge I gain will be for nothing.

"And I will not be changed by the answers that lie ahead."